TOOLS, TEXTILES AND CONTEXTS

We dedicate this book to Betchen Barber,
the pioneer of the study of Aegean Bronze Age textiles.

TOOLS, TEXTILES AND CONTEXTS

Investigating Textile Production in the Aegean and Eastern Mediterranean Bronze Age

edited by

Eva Andersson Strand and Marie-Louise Nosch

with the editorial and analytical assistance of Joanne Cutler

Oxbow Books
Oxford & Philadelphia

Published in the United Kingdom in 2015 by
OXBOW BOOKS
10 Hythe Bridge Street, Oxford OX1 2EW

and in the United States by
OXBOW BOOKS
908 Darby Road, Havertown, PA 19083

Hardcover Edition: ISBN 978-1-84217-472-2
Digital Edition: ISBN 978-1-78297-051-4

A CIP record for this book is available from the British Library

Library of Congress Cataloging-in-Publication Data

Tools, textiles and contexts : textile production in the Aegean and Eastern Mediterranean Bronze
Age / edited by Eva Andersson Strand and Marie-Louise Nosch.
      pages cm. -- (Ancient textiles series; vol. 21)
  Includes bibliographical references.
  ISBN 978-1-84217-472-2 (hardback)
  1. Bronze age--Middle East. 2. Textile fabrics, Prehistoric--Middle East. 3. Neolithic period--
Middle East. 4. Bronze age--Aegean Islands (Greece and Turkey) 5. Neolithic period--Aegean
Islands (Greece and Turkey) 6. Middle East--Antiquities. 7. Aegean Islands (Greece and Turkey)-
-Antiquities. I. Strand, Eva B. Andersson, editor. II. Nosch, Marie-Louise, editor.
  GN778.32.N4T66 2015
  939.4--dc23
                                    2015027222

Printed in Malta by Melita Press Ltd

For a complete list of Oxbow titles, please contact:

UNITED KINGDOM
Oxbow Books
Telephone (01865) 241249, Fax (01865) 794449
Email: oxbow@oxbowbooks.com
www.oxbowbooks.com

UNITED STATES OF AMERICA
Oxbow Books
Telephone (800) 791-9354, Fax (610) 853-9146
Email: queries@casemateacademic.com
www.casemateacademic.com/oxbow

Oxbow Books is part of the Casemate Group

*Front cover: clockwise: MM II Quartier Mu, Malia, Crete, map (after Poursat 1996, pl. 81),
spindle whorls from Phaistos, Crete (courtesy of P. Militello), Khania, Crete, Late Bronze Age
ribbon, reconstructed loom weights in TTTC experiments.*
Back cover: Splicing (drawing: Annika Jeppsson)

CONTENTS

Introduction vii

Chapter 1 Research history

1.1   An introduction to the investigation of archaeological textile tools 1
Lorenz Rahmstorf

1.2   An introduction to experimental archaeology and textile research 25
Linda Olofsson

Chapter 2 The basics of textile tools and textile technology – from fibre to fabric 39
Eva Andersson Strand

Chapter 3 Survey of archaeological textile remains from the Aegean and Eastern Mediterranean area 61
Irene Skals, Susan Möller-Wiering and Marie-Louise Nosch

Chapter 4 The TTTC experiments

4.1   Experimental testing of Bronze Age textile tools 75
Linda Olofsson, Eva Andersson Strand and Marie-Louise Nosch

4.2   External examination of spinning and weaving samples 101
Susan Möller-Wiering

4.3   Test of loom weights and 2/2 twill weaving 119
Linda Olofsson and Marie-Louise Nosch

4.4   Weaving with crescent shaped loom weights. An investigation of a special kind of loom weight 127
Agnete Wisti Lassen

4.5   From tools to textiles, concluding remarks 139
Eva Andersson Strand

Chapter 5 The TTTC database

5.1   Introduction to the CTR database 145
Eva Andersson Strand and Marie-Louise Nosch

5.2   Mathematical analysis of the spindle whorl and loom weight data in the CTR database 153
Richard Firth

Chapter 6 Textile tools in contexts

6.1   Textile tools and textile production – studies of selected Bronze Age sites: introduction.....................191
      Eva Andersson Strand, Marie-Louise Nosch and Joanne Cutler

6.2   Textile tools from Khania, Crete, Greece...197
      Maria Bruun-Lundgren†, Eva Andersson Strand and Birgitta P. Hallager

6.3   Textile tools from Ayia Triada, Crete, Greece...207
      Pietro Militello, Eva Andersson Strand, Marie-Louise Nosch and Joanne Cutler

6.4   Textile tools from Phaistos, Crete, Greece..215
      Pietro Militello, Eva Andersson Strand, Marie-Louise Nosch and Joanne Cutler

6.5   Textile tools from Quartier Mu, Malia, Crete, Greece...229
      Jean-Claude Poursat, Françoise Rougemont, Joanne Cutler, Eva Andersson Strand and Marie-Louise Nosch

6.6   Textile tools from Akrotiri, Thera, Greece...243
      Iris Tzachili, Stella Spantidaki, Eva Andersson Strand, Marie-Louise Nosch and Joanne Cutler

6.7   Textile tools from Midea, mainland Greece..247
      Katie Demakopoulou, Ioannis Fappas, Eva Andersson Strand, Marie-Louise Nosch and Joanne Cutler

6.8   Textile production at Mycenae, mainland Greece...253
      Iphiyenia Tournavitou, Eva Andersson Strand, Marie-Louise Nosch and Joanne Cutler

6.9   Textile tools from Tiryns, mainland Greece...267
      Lorenz Rahmstorf, Małgorzata Siennicka, Eva Andersson Strand, Marie-Louise Nosch and Joanne Cutler

6.10 Textile tools from Thebes, mainland Greece..279
      *Maria Emanuela Alberti, Vassilis Aravantinos, Ioannis Fappas, Athina Papadaki, Françoise Rougemont,
      Eva Andersson Strand, Marie-Louise Nosch and Joanne Cutler*

6.11 Textile tools from Archontiko, northern Greece...293
      Evi Papadopoulou, Eva Andersson Strand, Marie-Louise Nosch and Joanne Cutler

6.12 Textile tools from Sitagroi, northern Greece...299
      Ernestine S. Elster, Eva Andersson Strand, Marie-Louise Nosch and Joanne Cutler

6.13 Textile tools from Troia, western Anatolia..309
      Marta Guzowska, Ralf Becks, Eva Andersson Strand, Joanne Cutler and Marie-Louise Nosch

6.14 Textile tools from Apliki, Cyprus...329
      Joanna S. Smith, Joanne Cutler, Eva Andersson Strand and Marie-Louise Nosch

6.15 Textile tools from Kition, Cyprus..337
      Joanna S. Smith, Joanne Cutler, Eva Andersson Strand and Marie-Louise Nosch

6.16 Textile tools from Tel Kabri, Israel..347
      Assaf Yasur-Landau, Nurith Goshen, Eva Andersson Strand, Marie-Louise Nosch and Joanne Cutler

Chapter 7 Summary of results and conclusions...351
      Eva Andersson Strand and Marie-Louise Nosch

Appendices

   Appendix A: Textile remains in the Eastern Mediterranean area: Neolithic and Chalcolithic...................385

   Appendix B: Textile remains in the Eastern Mediterranean area: Bronze Age 392

Acknowledgements..402

Introduction

Eva Andersson Strand

The study of tools and textiles – texts and contexts is complex, but important and fascinating; we gain new insights and perspectives on products and a craft that all people in an ancient Bronze Age society were involved in or had a relation to. Via these studies we acquire knowledge not only about everyday life, but also about production, craft specialization, knowledge and skills, and the use of the physical, engendered and economic landscape of textile production.

A textile tool represents a single artefact and can be examined as such, but a tool has also been used in the production of other artefacts, for example a thread or a cloth. Each tool, textile and technology has its own life history which in the widest perspective includes procurement, manufacture, use, maintenance, reuse, recycling, discard and post-depositional formation processes (*e.g.* Leroi-Gourhan 1993; LaMotta and Schiffer 2001, 21; Hollenback and Schiffer 2010, 320). The life-history can help to conceptualize material practice in relation to the study of objects and technology. It is possible to describe the entire sequence of interactions and activities that took place during the life history of an object, emphasizing types of interactions, for example location, archaeological outputs and conjoined elements or associated artefacts, but also decisions, need, desires and tradition (Hollenback and Schiffer 2010, 320). Additionally, tools and textiles can be examined from different approaches, together or separately. The number of methods and theories which can be chosen for investigating textile production are endless and will undoubtedly give various results depending on the questions asked and the material under study. In this publication we have chosen to focus on the specific *function* of the tools and how this information can be interpreted and used in a wider perspective. With this approach it is possible to examine the impact and importance of textiles and textile production in past societies. The aim with this work is, via textile tool studies, experimental archaeology and context analyses, to present new approaches to, and perspectives on, ancient textile production, and to show how new knowledge can be obtained on textile craft and craft production in Bronze Age Aegean and Eastern Mediterranean societies.

This publication is divided into seven chapters that can be read independently of each other, depending on the reader's interest and experience. Each chapter and sub-chapter has its own bibliography and it is inevitable that some information is repeated in more than one chapter or sub-chapter. The authors represent different research fields and include archaeologists, historians, textile conservators, textile specialists and textile technicians. It is important to note that all authors have their own approach and interpretation of the subject under study, depending on their field of expertise. This is intentional, in order to provide a range of perspectives. We are aware that this might seem inconsistent, but it is nevertheless our choice and we hope that our readers will be lenient with this.

The work covers a large area and a long period and it is not possible, or the aim, to write the final history of the development of textiles and textile production in the Bronze Age Aegean and Eastern Mediterranean (Figs. 0.1 and 0.2).

Instead this publication should be read as an introduction to new methods in the field of textile tool studies, the type of new knowledge that can be obtained by analysing tool function, and how this can be applied to archaeological material and contexts.

As demonstrated by Lorenz Ramstorf in chapter 1.1 *An introduction to the investigation of archaeological textile tools,* tools are in general studied as archaeological artefacts with a typological method/approach. Different types of spindle whorls and loom weights are compared and the results are used in different interpretations, especially relating to chronological and regional changes (*e.g.* Carington Smith 1992; 2000; Peyronel 2004; Gleba 2008). The results have been used in the interpretation of the textile production, for example the change in the typology of a tool group or the introduction of a new type has been interpreted as a change in technology (*e.g.* Ramstorf 2005). However, which *types* of textiles were produced and why is rarely discussed. Tools are also used to confirm the presence and scale of textile production, and a general assumption is that many tools represent a large scale production and few tools a small scale production. If there are no finds of tools, either the textile production is not noted at all, or there is a discussion of import and trade of textiles.

Experimental archaeology is another method which has been used in textile research. Linda Olofsson shows in chapter 1.2 *An introduction to experimental archaeology and textile research* how experiments can give important insights and new perspectives. However, it is also clear that experimental archaeology is a method that has been, and is, questioned; whether the results are applicable to archaeological materials and contexts, or should be considered as too subjective, is also a subject of discussion. Another challenge is that only parts of the production process are tested and/or discussed and, furthermore, the results often do not include a consideration of the contexts in which the original tools or textiles are from. Equally problematic are tool tests done with textile tools that have never been found in an archaeological context, or spinning tests conducted with wool not suitable for spindle spinning. The results from these types of test can of course be directly misleading.

The tools are not passive, they are active objects and work together with the producer in a dualistic interrelation. The choice of tools and raw materials depends on what an individual wants to produce, but access, knowledge, skills, ability, need, desire and tradition, as well as a society's expectations and prerequisites, also play a part. There are naturally differences in the production chain depending on time, region and context. In some places it might be the individual craft person who made all the decisions independently, while in others the producer may have received clear instructions of what to produce and how it should be done. It is clear that an object or a group of objects cannot be treated as independent and separated from its/their social or functional contexts. Needless to say, the primary function of the tools when they were used was not, via their appearance, to be compared with other similar or different tool types. The textile tools were produced in order to manufacture textiles and as such they are also our link to the textiles and textile production. The aim of the Tools and Textiles – Texts and Contexts research programme was to further explore this approach, and to demonstrate how knowledge of the tools' function and the *chaine opératoire* of textile production can be integrated into the archaeological interpretation of the production of textiles.[1] This approach will also make it possible to fill the interstices which appear in this research field. It will further allow us to make invisible textile production visible.

In order to understand the textile production *chaine opératoire* it is necessary to have a basic knowledge of the different stages in the production process. Therefore a brief overview is given in chapter 2 *The basics of textile tools and textile technology – from fibre to fabric.*

In chapter 3 *Survey of archaeological textile remains from the Aegean and Eastern Mediterranean area,* the aim is to give an updated overview of the finds of textiles in the area of investigation. It is clear that the number of finds of textiles is rapidly increasing. Today there is an understanding that even a small textile fragment, or an impression of a textile, can give information that is valuable to our understanding of the manufacture of textiles.

The most important link to the textiles are the textile tools. In order to understand the textile tools' primary purpose, as tools to produce textiles, the first step is to become

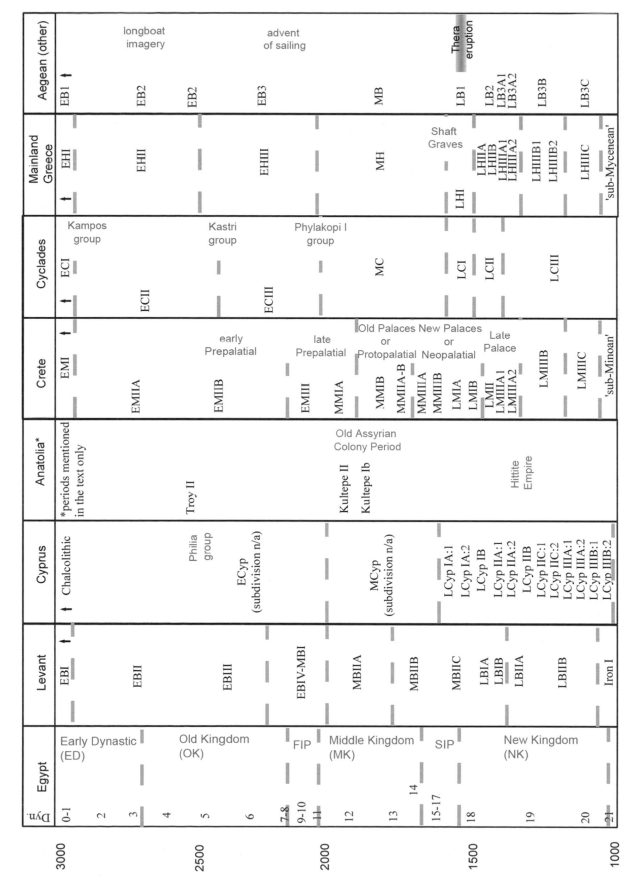

Figure. 0.1. Chronological table by region for eastern Mediterranean Bronze Age. The abbreviations used are as follows: Fip = First Intermediate Period; E, M, L = Early, Middle and Late, respectively, and are found with B= Bronze; Cyp = Cypriot (elsewhere this is usually abbreviated as 'C' but extended here to avoid confusion), M= Minoan, C=Cycladic, H = Helladic (table: courtesy of Andrew Bevan).

*Figure 0.2. Map showing
the location of the sites
included in the tool
database (map: Christian
Schmidt).*

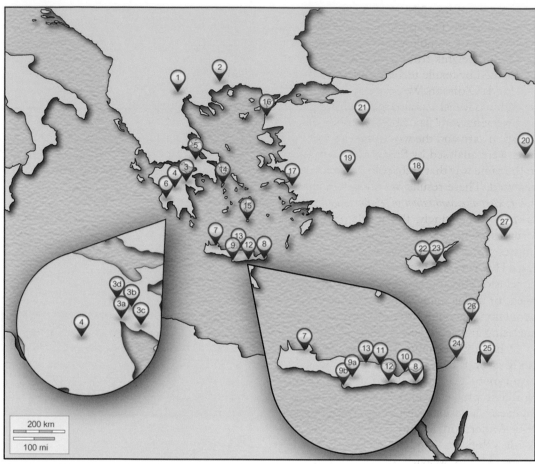

Figure 0.2. Map showing the location of the sites included in the tool database (map: Christian Schmidt).

Northern Greece
1: Sitagroi
2: Archontiko

Mainland Greece
3a: Tiryns
3b: Midea
3c: Asine
3b: Dendra
3d: Mycenae
4: Berbati
5: Thebes

6: Nichoria

Crete
7: Khania
8: Ayia Triada
9a: Phaistos
9b: Kommos
10: Pseira
10: Mochlos
11: Malia
12: Myrtos
13: Knossos

Aegean Islands
14: Ayia Irini
15: Akrotiri

Western Anatolia
16: Troia
17: Miletos

**Central and Eastern
Anatolia**
18: Karahüyük
19: Beycesultan

20: Arslantepe
21: Demircihüyük

Cyprus
22: Apliki
23: Kition

Levant
24: Tell el-Ajjul
25: Abu al-Kharaz
26: Tell Kabri
27: Ebla

conscious of how the tools function, their possibilities and limitations, and what type of production they could have been used for. Through experimental archaeology, informed by knowledge from traditional textile craft and textile techniques, different types of spindle whorls and loom weights were tested, and their functional parameters, i.e. the parameters of the tool that affect the production, identified. In order to ensure reliable results and to make the experimental methods available for a larger audience, one of our first tasks was to

develop guidelines for textile tool experiments. These guidelines were based on previous tests conducted by Eva Andersson Strand and Anne Batzer in the 1990s (Andersson 1999, 2003). All TTTC experiments are conducted on the basis of these guidelines and they are presented and discussed in chapter 4.1 *Experimental testing of Bronze Age textile tools*. In this chapter the TTTC experiments on spinning with different types of spindle whorls are presented. All details and considerations are discussed, from the choice of raw materials and fibre to the thread function and the resulting fabric made on a warp-weighted loom. The spinning tests were made with copies of spindle whorls from Nichoria and loom weights from Troia. All tests were performed by textile technicians Anne Batzer and Linda Olofsson. We primarily worked with wool, but one test was also made with spinning and weaving with flax fibres. Additionally, all the spun yarn and the woven fabrics from the tests were analysed by Susan Möller-Wiering, in the same way that archaeological textiles are analysed. These results are shown in chapter 4.2 *External examination of spinning and weaving samples*. Interestingly, the result of the first analyses contradicted the textile technicians' impression and interpretation of the same tests. However, after several more analyses the conclusions became similar, demonstrating the need for taking many samples; an unexpected deduction that is important for future work on analysing archaeological textiles.

Other experiments have been done at CTR over the years. In 2008, a weaving experiment was carried out as part of the Vorbasse project, which is led by Ulla Lund Hansen.[2] The experiment was designed by Eva Andersson Strand and performed by Linda Olofsson (Andersson Strand *et al.* in press). In this weaving test a 2/2 twill was woven on a warp-weighted loom with four rows of loom weights. This test is of course very relevant for all regions in which the warp-weighted loom has been used, and we kindly thank Ulla Lund Hansen for her permission to include a summary of some of the results from the test in this publication (chapter 4.3 *Test of loom weights and 2/2 twill weaving*). Another experiment on the function of crescent shaped loom weights was designed and performed by Agnete Wisti Lassen. Her tests and results are presented in chapter 4.4 *Weaving with crescent shaped loom weights. An investigation of a special kind of loom weight.*

The results from textile experimental archaeology and the TTTC tests clearly demonstrate how new knowledge can be obtained based on this new method for interpreting a tool's suitability for making different types of textiles. However, it is important to consider the possibilities, and also to take into account the limitations, when interpreting the results from the experiments. The aim with chapter 4.5 *From tools to textiles, concluding remarks* is to combine the new results with previous results and craft knowledge, and to discuss how far these results can be used in our interpretation of the tools' optimal functionality. Furthermore, the aim of this sub-chapter is to determine how studies of textile tools can make textiles and textile production visible.

In order to record all tools in a consistent manner, a common textile tool database was designed within the research programme. In this, 8725 textile tools from 33 sites were recorded. In 24 cases the registration was done together with our collaborators. The remaining nine were recorded from publications. All data were then analysed and the results from 22 of the sites were presented in technical textile tool reports (Andersson *et al.* 2007 a–e; 2008 a–i; Andersson Strand *et al.* 2009 a–b; 2010a–b; Cutler *et al.* 2010 a–b). The brief introduction of this work is presented in chapter 5.1 *Introduction to the CTR database.*

In chapter 5.2 *Mathematical analysis of the spindle whorl and loom weight data in the CTR database* Richard Firth continues the discussion of how all the data recordings can be combined and used, concentrating on the technical aspects, and further presents new mathematical analyses for both spindle whorls and loom weights.

To write the life history of all the 8725 textile tools recorded in the CTR database would of course be interesting, but is not possible. Instead we have, together with our collaborators, chosen different case studies (chapter 6 *Textile tools and textile production – studies of selected Bronze Age sites*) to demonstrate what information and new knowledge one can gain by including textile research. It is our hope that this work will inspire other researchers to study archaeological tools and textiles from these new perspectives, to write their material's life history, which undoubtedly will yield interesting results regarding our knowledge of ancient societies. The methods developed and used in the analyses of textile tools from the case study sites are based on the tools' functionality. The 15 sites presented were chosen with care and we kindly thank all our collaborators for their work and patience. The analysed data from two other sites in our study, Arslantepe, Turkey and Ebla, Syria, have already been published (Frangipani *et al.* 2009; Andersson Strand *et al.* 2010). Different articles based on the technical tools reports have also been co-authored and published in many different publications (see *e.g.* Nosch and Laffineur 2012). The results from the 15 sites presented in this volume, all very different, provide new insights and perspectives and demonstrate the potential of the methods applied.

In the final chapter 7, *Summary of results and conclusions*, we have focused on some of the most significant but more general aspects of the tools. For example, the recorded data allow us to compare and contrast different whorl categories (pierced sherds, conuli, kylix stems and beads) in terms of their suitability for spinning, and to discuss the definition and use of spools as loom weights.

In the second part of chapter 7 we discuss the remaining open issues and unanswered questions. Furthermore, we present our assessment of the extent to which the textile tools enable us to make definite conclusions and we highlight the questions textile tools cannot help us answer. This final chapter completes our work, which we hope will not only be an inspiration for future textile research but also give an understanding of the importance and complexity of textile production in Aegean and Eastern Mediterranean Bronze Age societies.

Notes

1 The textual part of the project was published in Michel, C. and Nosch, M.-L. (2008) *Textile Terminologies in the Ancient Near East and Mediterranean from the Third to the First Millennia BC*. Ancient Textile Series 8. Oxford. Oxbow Books.

2 The Vorbasse textile research project is directed by Professor Ulla Lund Hansen, Copenhagen University. In this project textiles and textile tools from the Late Roman Iron Age site of Vorbasse in Jutland, Denmark, have been analysed (Lund Hansen in press).

Bibliography

Andersson, E. (1999) *The Common Thread: Textile Production During the Late Iron Age – Viking Age*. Lund. Institute of Archaeology, University of Lund.

Andersson, E. (2003) *Tools for Textile Production from Birka and Hedeby: Excavations in the Black Earth 1990–1995*. Stockholm. Birka Project, Riksantikvarieämbetet.

Andersson, E. and Nosch, M.-L. (2007a) *Archontiko, Greece, Technical Textile Tool Report*, Tools and Textiles – Texts and Contexts Research Programme. The Danish National Research Foundation's Centre for Textile Research, University of Copenhagen.

Andersson, E. and Nosch, M.-L. (2007b) *Arslantepe, Turkey, Technical Textile Tool Report*. Tools and Textiles – Texts and Contexts Research Programme. The Danish National Research Foundation's Centre for Textile Research, University of Copenhagen.

Andersson, E., Nosch, M.-L. and Wisti Lassen, A. (2007c) *Ayia Triada, Crete, Technical Textile Tool Report*. Tools and Textiles – Texts and Contexts Research Programme. The Danish National Research Foundation's Centre for Textile Research, University of Copenhagen.

Andersson, E., Nosch, M.-L. and Wisti Lassen, A. (2007d) *Akrotiri, Greece, Technical Textile Tool Report*. Tools and Textiles – Texts and Contexts Research Programme. The Danish National Research Foundation's Centre for Textile Research, University of Copenhagen.

Andersson, E., Nosch, M.-L. and Wisti Lassen, A. (2007e) *Ebla, Syria, Technical Textile Tool Report*. Tools and Textiles – Texts and Contexts Research Programme. The Danish National Research Foundation's Centre for Textile Research, University of Copenhagen.

Andersson, E., Nosch, M.-L. and Wisti Lassen, A. (2008a) *Dendra, Greece, Technical Textile Tool Report*. Tools and Textiles – Texts and Contexts Research Programme. The Danish National Research Foundation's Centre for Textile Research, University of Copenhagen.

Andersson, E., Nosch, M.-L. and Wisti Lassen, A. (2008b) *Berbati, Greece, Technical Textile Tool Report*. Tools and Textiles – Texts and Contexts Research Programme. The Danish National Research Foundation's Centre for Textile Research, University of Copenhagen.

Andersson, E., Nosch, M.-L. and Wisti Lassen, A. (2008c) *Tiryns, Greece, Technical Textile Tool Report*. Tools and Textiles – Texts and Contexts Research Programme. The Danish National Research Foundation's Centre for Textile Research, University of Copenhagen.

Andersson, E., Nosch, M.-L. and Wisti Lassen, A. (2008d) *Midea, Greece, Technical Textile Tool Report*. Tools and Textiles – Texts and Contexts Research Programme. The Danish National Research Foundation's Centre for Textile Research, University of Copenhagen.

Andersson, E., Nosch, M.-L. and Wisti Lassen, A. (2008e) *Asini, Greece, Technical Textile Tool Report*. Tools and Textiles – Texts and Contexts Research Programme. The Danish National Research Foundation's Centre for Textile Research, University of Copenhagen.

Andersson, E., Nosch, M.-L. and Wisti Lassen, A. (2008f) *Phaistos, Crete, Technical Textile Tool Report*. Tools and Textiles – Texts and Contexts Research Programme. The Danish National Research Foundation's Centre for Textile Research, University of Copenhagen.

Andersson, E., Nosch, M.-L., and Wisti Lassen, A. (2008g) *Mochlos, Crete, Technical Textile Tool Report*. Tools and Textiles – Texts and Contexts Research Programme. The Danish National Research Foundation's Centre for Textile Research, University of Copenhagen.

Andersson, E., Nosch, M.-L. and Wisti Lassen, A. (2008h) *Khania, Crete, Technical Textile Tool Report*. Tools and Textiles – Texts and Contexts Research Programme. The Danish National Research Foundation's Centre for Textile Research, University of Copenhagen.

Andersson, E., Nosch, M.-L. and Wisti Lassen, A. (2008i) *Mycenae, Greece, Technical Textile Tool Report*. Tools and Textiles – Texts and Contexts Research Programme. The Danish National Research Foundation's Centre for Textile Research, University of Copenhagen.

Andersson Strand, E., Nosch, M.-L. and Cutler, J. (2009a) *Tel Kabri, Israel, Technical Textile Tool Report*. Tools and Textiles – Texts and Contexts Research Programme. The Danish National Research Foundation's Centre for Textile Research, University of Copenhagen.

Andersson Strand, E., Nosch, M.-L. and Cutler, J.(2009b) *Sitagroi, Greece, Technical Textile Tool Report*. Tools and Textiles – Texts and Contexts Research Programme. The Danish National Research Foundation's Centre for Textile Research, University of Copenhagen.

Andersson Strand, E., Nosch, M.-L. and Cutler, J.(2010a) *Troia, Turkey, Technical Textile Tool Report*. Tools and Textiles – Texts and Contexts Research Programme. The Danish National Research Foundation's Centre for Textile Research, University of Copenhagen.

Andersson Strand, E., Nosch, M.-L. and Cutler, J.(2010b) *Thebes, Greece, Technical Textile Tool Report*. Tools and Textiles – Texts and Contexts Research Programme. The Danish National Research Foundation's Centre for Textile Research, University of Copenhagen.

Andersson Strand, E., Felucca, E., Nosch, M.-L. and Peyronel, L. (2010c) New perspectives on the Bronze Age textile production in the Eastern Mediterranean. The first results with Ebla as a pilot study. In Matthiae, P., Pinnock, F., Nigro, L. and Marchetti, N. (eds), *Proceedings of the 6th International Congress on the Archaeology of the Ancient Near East, Rome 5–10 May 2008*, 159–176. Wiesbaden. Harrassowitz.

Cutler, J., Andersson Strand, E. and Nosch, M.-L. (2010a) *Apliki, Cyprus, Technical Textile Tool Report*. Tools and Textiles – Texts and Contexts Research Programme. The Danish National Research Foundation's Centre for Textile Research, University of Copenhagen.

Cutler, J., Andersson Strand, E. and Nosch, M.-L. (2010b) *Kition, Cyprus, Technical Textile Tool Report*. Tools and Textiles – Texts and Contexts Research Programme. The Danish National Research Foundation's Centre for Textile Research, University of Copenhagen.

Frangipane, M., Andersson Strand, E., Laurito, R., Möller-Wiering, S., Nosch, M.-L., Rast-Eicher, A. and Wisti Lassen, A. (2009) Arslantepe, Malatya (Turkey): textiles, tools and imprints of fabrics from the 4th to the 2nd millennium BC, *Paléorient*, 35 (1), 5–29.

Hollenback L. K. and Schiffer, M. B. (2010) Technology and material life, in Hicks, D. and Beaudry, M. C. (eds), *The Oxford Handbook of Material Cultural Studies*, 313–332. Oxford. Oxford University Press.

LaMotta, V. and Schiffer, M. B. (2001) Behavioral archaeology: toward a new synthesis, in Hodder, I. (ed.), *Archaeological Theory Today*, 14–64. Oxford. Blackwell.

Leroi-Gourhan, A. (1993) *Gesture and Speech* (trans. A. Bostock Berger). Cambridge, MA. MIT Press.

Michel, C. and Nosch, M.-L. 2008 *Textile Terminologies in the Ancient Near East and Mediterranean from the Third to the First Millennia BC*. Ancient Textile Series 8. Oxford. Oxbow Books.

Nosch, M.-L. and Laffineur, R. (eds) (2012) *KOSMOS. Jewellery, Adornment and Textiles in the Aegean Bronze Age*. Liège. Peeters.

CHAPTER 1.1

An introduction to the investigation of archaeological textile tools

Lorenz Rahmstorf

In this introduction the main research approaches applied to textile tools will be outlined. The ways in which the different groups of artefacts have been studied in the past will be investigated, as well as how more innovative approaches came into being in recent decades and, finally, which research potentials have not yet been fully explored. This chapter aims to present the research produced by scholars of textile tools and why and how, if at all, this pool of knowledge has influenced Aegean and Near Eastern archaeological research in general.

First, the chapter will provide an overview of the research approaches and key issues related to textile tools in the Bronze Age Eastern Mediterranean, also in comparison to central and northern Europe. Second, it will discuss the research on various textile tools. Finally, the chapter will conclude by proposing a shared framework to ameliorate the scholarly work on textile tools in the future.

The importance of textiles and textile tools

Textiles have been of tremendous importance since the Neolithic and Bronze Age. As technical matters improved, and as materials such as linen and wool became available and usable, humans understood the wide range of secondary functions of cloth: not only providing protection against various climatic conditions, but also offering a means of displaying and underlining gender issues, personal wealth, rank and status in any given society as well as group affiliation. The production of textiles with such multi-functional potential also required a great amount of time. Unfortunately, only a few Bronze Age textile remains from the Eastern Mediterranean (outside of Egypt) have survived, and this only due to rare cases of exceptional preservation conditions. The tools, however, which were used to produce these textiles are abundant finds in excavations, especially at settlement sites.

From a functional perspective the evidence of tools for textile production is normally based on two types of finds: spindle whorls and loom weights. The loom weight is the only part of the warp-weighted loom which usually remains preserved. In general, no archaeologically traceable remains can be found of other loom types, the horizontal ground loom and the vertical two-beam (tubular) loom (Barber 1991, 79–80, 113–118; Grömer 2010, 140–142; Wild 1970, 69–78), used during the Bronze Age in Europe and the Near East. Besides loom weights, spindle whorls and sewing needles, other more rarely found textile tools are wool combs/hackling boards, whole spindles, distaffs, shuttles, pin beaters, decks for tablet-weaving and spinning bowls. Sewing needles are generally connected to textile production.

It should be emphasised that textile tools have never attracted much attention in the archaeological literature, and this explains why specialised and systematic publications on prehistoric and early historical textile tools on a regional or supra-regional level beyond the evidence of the actual site are very rare. Due to this scarcity, any comparative study has to initiate from primary publications, that is, the final excavation reports. While this implies a thorough handling of the material it also makes it much more difficult to obtain an overview of the data. On the basic level, in the final excavation reports, the intensity of discussing such objects varies considerably. Moreover, the need to publish finds of textile tools in a complete and systematic way is often not understood. In most publications from the 19th and the first half of the 20th century, textile tools were only represented in photographs, if depicted at all. In the case of spindle whorls, the photos are often taken from above and without any further drawing or documentation, thus leaving the scholar with doubts about the exact profile of the whorl. At prehistoric and early historic sites where textiles are preserved, the main focus was obviously put on the textiles themselves, and not the tools which produced them. This was the case regarding textiles from Neolithic Swiss lake dwellings (*e.g.* Vogt 1937; Winiger 1995; Altorfer and Médard 2000) and Bronze Age Danish wooden sarcophagus burials (Hald 1980). In early publications, the tools are mentioned and their possible use explained, but are neither discussed in a detailed way nor associated to the archaeological textiles found on the site (*e.g.* Kimakowicz-Winnicki 1910; Schlabow 1937; von Stokar 1938). Only in more recent decades, much more detailed discussions of the functional and contextual dimensions of textile tools are detectable in scholarly work on central and northern Europe (*e.g.* Médard 2000; Andersson 2003; Huber 2005; Gleba 2008; Grömer 2010).

In contrast to the central and northern European regions, the Eastern Mediterranean, with the exception of Egypt, cannot boast impressive textile remains dating to the Bronze Age. However, there is a considerable stock of data regarding actual textile tools and, to a lesser extent, textual references to textiles, textile exchange and production as well as depictions of textiles on wall paintings, seals and figurines. Despite the abundance of textile tools in the archaeological record, their relevance has largely been neglected so far, with some notable exceptions. For the prehistoric Aegean, the PhD thesis on textile production by J. Carington Smith as well as later studies demonstrated her vast knowledge of textile tools from this region (Carington Smith 1975, 1983, 1992, 2000). The book by L. Crewe is another rare example of a comprehensive study on a specific group of textile tools, the spindle whorls from Early Bronze Age to Middle Bronze Age Cyprus (Crewe 1998). Recently, L. Peyronel has presented a very detailed monograph on textile tools from the important Bronze Age site of Ebla in western Syria (Peyronel 2004). Last, but not least, the massive publication of E. Barber *Prehistoric Textiles. The Development of Cloth in the Neolithic and Bronze Ages with Special Reference to the Aegean* was a ground-breaking contribution to this long neglected field (Barber 1991). While not being the core subject of the work, it does contain good sections on the textile tools. Nevertheless, Barber's overview demonstrates the need for much more detailed information for many periods and regions in order to obtain a more accurate picture of the development and interconnections of textile tools in Europe, the Mediterranean and West Asia. The most recent publication of general interest also for the Eastern Mediterranean is the important study by K. Grömer on prehistoric textile art in central Europe (Grömer 2010). Grömer's main focus rests on textile production, not so much on the textile tools in the archaeological record.

Textile tools in research

Spindles
Specialised studies on spindles are rare due to the fact that there are very few preserved spindles from archaeological excavations in the Bronze Age Mediterranean, as spindles seem to have predominantly been made from wood (Fig. 1.1.1). In rare cases, wooden spindles have been preserved at Neolithic and Bronze Age wetland

sites such as the Alpine region (Arbon-Bleiche at the Bodensee: Leuzinger 2002, fig. 147, 3; Bazzanella *et al.* 2003b, no. 66, 267; Twann, Switzerland: Dunning 1992, 46, fig. 6; Fiavé, Italy: Bazzanella *et al.* 2003b, 137–138), at Early Bronze Age Troia II (Schliemann 1881, 370); in the Iron Age bog find from Hjortspring in Denmark (La Baume 1955, fig. 96, 117) or in the extremely dry climate of Egypt (Petrie 1917, pl. LXVI, 141–147; Granger-Taylor and Quirke 2002). Bronze Age spindles from the Eastern Mediterranean are also known to be made out of bone, ivory (Balfanz 1995b; Barber 1991, fig. 2.27, 2.29, 162–164; Gachet-Bizollon 2007, fig. 36 pl. 19–22, 115–127); and metal (Barber 1991, fig. 2.20–2.22 and 2.24–2.27, 58–62). Clay seems to have never been a material used to make spindles, and it is only known from a clay model from Vounous on Cyprus (Barber 1991; Crewe 1998, fig. 2.29; Webb 2002, fig. 2.2, 8). It remains questionable whether all ivory shafts were really used as spindles and not for other purposes (Charalampos 2003; Gachet-Bizollon 2007). Future scholarship may benefit from comprehensively checking published bone "needles" from the Eastern Mediterranean as possible spindles.

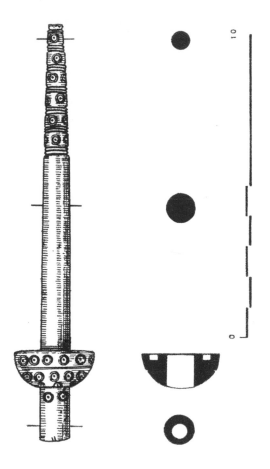

Fig. 1.1.1. Spindle. From Perati, Greece, 12th century BC (drawing: Iakovidis 1969–1971, vol. Γ, fig. 155, D 108).

Spindle whorls

Spindle whorls never had a strong lobby in earlier archaeological research and literature. This is apparent for example, in the following quotation from L. Woolley: "*If I devote a special section of my text to spindle-whorls I do so with apologies [ ]. I suppose that it was Schliemann who first brought the spindle-whorl into prominence – a venial error in his case, but today there is no excuse for wasting space and money on this monotonous and profitless material*" (Woolley 1955, 271). Schliemann, indeed, had a specific interest in spindle whorls after having identified them as such (Hilse 2001) and wrote about them in great detail and illustrated them with drawings in numerous plates in his publications (*e.g.* Schliemann 1881, no. 1801–2000). Schliemann suspected that the decoration or "signs" on the whorls held particular significance (see below). Such almost lavish illustrations also became the standard means of publication of spindle whorls in later publications on the material from Troia (Schmidt 1902, pl. I–IX, 204–224; H. Schmidt in Götze 1902, 424–428). During the 20th century, however, the validity

of such standards of publication became highly questioned within the field of Eastern Mediterranean archaeology as the above quotation of Woolley illustrates. Today, the differences in the quality of documentation of spindle whorls are easily visible when flipping through recent final publications of excavated sites, but a generally accepted standard of publishing textile tools is overdue (see below: *The material-typological approach*).

The materials of spindle whorls

Most of the preserved spindle whorls are made of fired clay ("terracotta"). Nevertheless, in some periods, other materials like stone or wood may have been more commonly used. In the Levant, stone spindle whorls were present since the Pre-Pottery Neolithic (PPN) (*e.g.* Jericho: Wheeler 1982, 626), or in central Europe since the 6th millennium BC. In Anatolia, stone whorls are frequent finds in different periods of the Bronze Age (*e.g.* Alishar Höyük: Schmidt 1932, figs 60–61, 50–52). In the Aegean, stone spindle whorls are typical for the Late Bronze Age, especially on the Mycenaean mainland (LH III), and then they are called *conuli* (see below). In addition to clay and stone, precious material such as ivory, silver, gold, precious stones and even amber (Jovaiša 2001, fig. 7, 154) was used to make spindle whorls in certain periods and regions, probably an indication of a high status of the user (Eibner 2005). It can be assumed that wood was also a significant material used to make spindle whorls, although naturally none are preserved. In ethnographical museums in Greece it can be observed that to the present day wooden spindle whorls appear to have been the most commonly used type of spindle whorl (*Folk Art Museum – Nafplion* 1988, 29). Finally, it is not even necessary to use a spindle whorl for spinning thread (*i.e.* by using only a simple stick – spinning hook: Hald 1980, 135; or thigh spinning: Tiedemann and Jakes 2006, fig. 1, 294–295). To what extent the various possible materials have been used has never been assessed or quantified systematically in the scientific literature.

Typology of spindle whorls

The first attempts of archaeologists to systematically classify textile tools made use of typologies based on shape, *i.e.* profile and the material which the spindle whorl was made from. Typological studies of spindle whorls became increasingly common during the first half of the 20th century. Following the initial interest by Schliemann, the spindle whorls from Troia were classified according to shape, first by H. Schmidt and later by C. W. Blegen (Schmidt 1902, pl. I–IX, 204–224; H. Schmidt in Götze 1902, fig. 455; Blegen *et al.* 1950, fig. 128, 129). The so-called conuli, the stone spindle whorls of Mycenaean Greece, were typologically classified in various schemes by A. W. Persson, A. J. B. Wace, C. W. Blegen and A. Furumark between the 1920s and early 1940s (Frödin and Persson 1924–1925; Wace 1932, 219; Blegen 1937, 313; Furumark 1941, 89, fig. 2; Iakovidis 1977; Andersson and Nosch 2003, 202–203; Rahmstorf 2008, 126–127). Conuli of various shapes were assumed to have existed side by side in the LH III period. Today, it can be demonstrated that the biconical type is only present in the early phase of LH III, *i.e.* LH IIIA (Rahmstorf 2008, 132–133). In general, any typological classification of spindle whorls remains a

difficult task due to the vast possible range of profiles and because definitions of differences between the profile of, for example, a spherical and a biconical whorl is not easily distinguishable (*e.g.* Crewe 1998, 22; Huber 2005, 12). With a detailed typological approach, recent final site reports include a detailed description of the chosen clay, its surface, colour and firing (*e.g.* Obladen-Kauder 1996, 213–214). Comparative typological studies do improve our understanding of the morphological development of spindle whorls, although this type of study has previously been questioned by Banks (Banks 1967, 545). The prerequisites of comparative typological studies are, first, the precise dating of the examples from closed contexts, and secondly, the adequate publishing of the whorls with drawings. With this information readily available, it is possible to ascertain common characteristics of whorls at certain periods, such as was done for the Late Mycenaean whorls from the Peloponnese (*e.g.* Nichoria: Carington Smith 1983; Tiryns: Rahmstorf 2008, 30–34). Yet, much too few studies with a comparative approach have been published thus far.

Decoration on spindle whorls

Spindle whorls can be decorated on the sides, top and bottom. Painted decoration on spindle whorls is rare, but a simple slip or burnishing appears quite often. This may not have been applied only for aesthetic reasons, but may also have had some functional purpose, *i.e.* improving the rotation and handling of the whorl. The most common ornament on spindle whorls made of stone and clay is incision. Indeed, ornamented or incised stone whorls are known from Bronze Age Anatolia (*e.g.* Alishar Höyük: Schmidt 1932, fig. 60, 50), but are much rarer in the Bronze Age Aegean (Rahmstorf 2008, 133–134, pl. 49, no. 88; pl. 91, 9). The application of incisions is easier on clay, and is known from some areas of the Bronze Age Eastern Mediterranean such as the northeast Aegean (*e.g.* Troia: Balfanz 1995a; Anatolia, *e.g.* Demircihöyük: Obladen-Kauder 1996, pl. 90–95, 228–230; Richmond 2006 or on Cyprus: Crewe 1998). In other areas such as the southern Greek mainland or on Crete, decoration occurs only very seldomly (*e.g.* Lerna: Banks 1967, 548–550). In Troia, typical incised motifs include chevrons, bows, circles, crosses and swastikas (Balfanz 1995a). In the 1st millennium BC, spindle whorls can be inscribed in rare cases (*e.g.* Gevirtz 1967; Dinç 1999). Cautiously, it has been suggested that some spindle whorls from Troia might be inscribed with Linear A signs (Sayce 1881, 769–722; Godart 1994; G. Neumann in Balfanz 1995a, n. 133, 135). In this respect it is interesting to note a suggestion that a clay spool from Drama in Bulgaria bears Linear A signs (Fol and Schmitt 2000). However, it is unlikely that the spindle whorls from Troia were inscribed with Linear A signs due to their early dating to the Early Bronze Age (Troia II–III). Thus there is only a superficial visual resemblance of these incisions to script signs (Zurbach 2003, 115). Schliemann believed them to be symbolic signs and not signs of a script (Zurbach 2003, n. 33, 126). M. Gimbutas deduced the symbolism of goddesses from nearly every decoration on pottery, figurines and other decorated finds and so she interpreted the mainly zig-zag incisions on Neolithic/Chalcolithic spindle whorls from southeast Europe as dedications to the patroness of spinning, symbols of the old European goddess Athena/Minerva (Gimbutas 1989, figs 104–105, 67–68). While most archaeologists would not ascribe any significance to the incisions, the question is open to debate as to whether the incisions are decoration or in fact convey any, even the simplest, message. Thus far, any systematic analysis of decoration on spindle whorls is largely lacking. It might be worth trying to study the decoration of spindle whorls from the entire area of the Eastern Mediterranean within a comparative approach.

Functionality of spindle whorls

The main parameter regarding the function of a possible spindle whorl is its weight. Only during recent decades has it become common to include information on weight when publishing spindle whorls. However, many publications still do not provide this particular data. Since the whorl acts as a weight on the spindle, the exact weight of the whorl is of great importance. It has been argued that whorls below a certain mass could not have been used as spindle whorls. For example, a minimum weight of 10–12 g was suggested by Carington Smith (Carington Smith 1992, 685). However, in early Islamic times, whorls weighing less than 1 g were used in the Middle East (Liu 1978,

90–91). Therefore, it appears unwise to argue dogmatically for a certain minimum weight when establishing the functionality of a find. Instead, the interrelation between thread thickness and the weight of the whorl can be suggested (*e.g.* Holm 1996; Andersson 2003; Grömer 2005). It has also been shown that the way the fibres are prepared before spinning is of great importance for the final product (see chapter 4). In publications of excavations of recent years it has become common to provide diagrams of weight distributions and the diameter of spindle whorls, although mostly in central European archaeology (*e.g.* Huber 2005; Andersson 1999) or in studies of Bronze Age material from the Eastern Mediterranean (Obladen-Kauder 1996; Peyronel 2004; Rahmstorf 2008). This information forms the basis of assumptions about the thickness of the fibres used at the site.

Another issue is whether an object with an off-centre hole could have served as a spindle whorl. It has been demonstrated that when attempting to use finds with off-centre holes "the spin does not last and the spindle is unwieldy to use" (Crewe 1998, 9). Nevertheless, quite a few possible spindle whorls have such off-centre perforations. This also applies to another possible type of spindle whorl: the rounded potsherd with central perforation. Finds like these are seemingly common in every prehistoric and ancient culture with pottery production worldwide. Most commonly, they have been interpreted as spindle whorls. However, they can have an off-centre perforation, two or more perforations, or no perforation at all, all of which are factors that make identification as spindle whorls unlikely. For some finds a function as a spindle whorl may be possible, though others may have been used as jar lids (*e.g.* Frankel and Webb 1996, figs 8.7–8.8, 207–209; Rahmstorf 2008, 49–52, pl. 7–9; 89, 7, 9; 90, 1). Thus a systematic, comparative and contextual approach applied to each specific site alongside practical experiments may bring forth new and more decisive knowledge. Finally, it should be remembered that the lack of spindle whorls does not necessarily imply that spinning was not practised. The apparent lack of spindle whorls can be explained by the procedure of thigh spinning (Tiedemann and Jakes 2006, fig. 1, 294–295) or by the use of now decayed wooden tools (Altorfer and Médard 2000, 64).

Quantification of spindle whorls

Due to the lack of regional overviews, an attempt to quantify and compare the number of spindle whorls from one region or period to another has never been undertaken. Occasionally, attempts have been made to compare the number of whorls found at one site to another, taking the sizes of the trenches into account (Carington Smith 1992, 675). However, such calculations should also include the depth of the stratigraphy or better yet, the depth of layers holding artefacts. Such calculations are in fact far more difficult to produce. While at sites of certain periods large numbers of spindle whorls have been found, as in Troia with *c.* 10,000–20,000 finds (Balfanz 1995a, n. 2, 17 and 138; Richmond 2006, 208–209, 234–235; see Troia in chapter 6.13 of this volume), other sites have only a few, such as Late Bronze Age sites on Crete (Carington Smith lists 48 from EM, 15 from MM and 11 from LM sites: Carington Smith 1975; Tzachili 1997, 126; Burke 2003). An example is Minoan Kommos where 163 loom weights have been found but only nine possible spindle whorls (Dabney 1996a; Dabney 1996b, pl. 4.6, 4.8, 18–24). These diversities may be explained by the likelihood that spindle whorls were made of wood and have subsequently not been preserved, or that spindle whorls were not required for spinning (Tzachili 1997, 128–129). It may also be that spinning was done only at some sites whilst weaving was done at others (Carington Smith 1975, 264). However, such explanations are difficult to bring into accordance with excavation results or readings from Linear B texts (Tzachili 1997, 128–129). A possible explanation may also be that all possible spindle whorls, such as the conuli or the rounded potsherds with central perforations have not been considered to be spindle whorls in the archaeological data. To be able to draw conclusions from the archaeological data thorough quantifications are needed which can be differentiated precisely by time period and on a regional level.

Loom weights

While there are several types of looms only the warp-weighted loom provides archaeologists with textile tools that usually survive archaeological deposition: the loom weights (see for example chapter 5.1 for illustrations). Other loom types are the horizontal loom, known to be used in the Bronze Age Near East and Egypt through pictorial sources, and the vertical two-beam loom of the Nordic Bronze Age, which is verified through finds of tube-shaped textiles found in Denmark. The looms themselves were made of wood and no actual parts have survived from the Bronze Age Eastern Mediterranean.

The loom weights are a great source of information to archaeologists working with textiles and textile production of the Bronze Age Mediterranean (Hoffmann 1964, 17). The study of their place of origin by use of distribution of finds as evident from the archaeological record has and continues to be an important and much discussed question. The spread of the technology of the warp-weighted loom during the Neolithic Near East across the Balkans to central Europe has been argued by von Kurzynski (Kurzynski 1996, 11). Barber largely agrees by stating that "*it is clear from mapping Neolithic and Bronze Age loom weights that the warp-weighted loom was born and developed in southeast Europe and perhaps Anatolia in the Neolithic, expanding farther and farther to the north and west in the Late Neolithic, Bronze and Iron Ages, but not generally expanding to the south or east, presumably because the inhabitants of those territories already had a practical loom, the ground loom*" (Barber 1991, 299–300). Finds of possible loom weights have been made for example in Çatal Höyük in Turkey from the late 7th millennium BC and in settlements of the Körös Culture of the early 6th millennium BC, *i.e.* the Early Neolithic in Hungary (*e.g.* Barber 1991; Kurzynski 1996, with further references). Possible loom weights dating to the beginning of the Neolithic have also been found in *Bandkeramik* settlements in central Europe (Schade-Lindig and Schmitt 2003). Nevertheless, the apparent diffusion of the technology of the warp-weighted loom still needs more detailed investigation.

The materials of loom weights

Loom weights in the Bronze Age Mediterranean were usually made of either fired or low baked/unbaked clay. Simple pebbles may also have been used although these are almost impossible to identify in the archaeological record. The difficulty for the ancient weaver would have been to collect pebbles of similar size and weight. Ethnographers observed that in northern Scandinavia stones of similar weight were still in use as loom weights on the loom in the 20th century (Hoffmann 1964, fig. 9, 42; Poursat 2012; Cutler *et al.* 2013; see chapter 6.5, Quartier Mu, Malia). Pierced stone weights or stone rings appear at some sites and periods such as Early Bronze Age Bulgaria (Terzijska-Ignatova 2004) or in Early Bronze Age Jordan (Fischer 2010, 111–113, fig. 3; 5), but were never really common over longer periods of time. A much greater effort was required to produce a stone weight, therefore it is not surprising that they have never played a significant role as loom weights in prehistory.

Typology of loom weights
There is a large variety of loom weight shapes, varying from flat discoid to flat rectangular, from spherical to hemispherical, and conical to pyramidal. There are also cuboid, cylindrical or spool shaped and crescent shaped types. Since the first publications, it has been controversial whether all such shaped artefacts were in fact used as loom weights (see below). This may in part explain the lack of interest in any systematic typological study of these finds. It often happens "that the excavator as a rule lumps them all together and abandons the idea of forming a chronology" (Davidson 1952, 146). As opposed to typological schemes of spindle whorls, typological schemes of loom weights were seldom used. As a consequence, many prehistoric, classical and Near Eastern archaeologists questioned whether any typo-chronological development can be traced from the finds of loom weights. As in the case of all human made artefacts, these objects exhibit variations in shape and manufacture through time and therefore can and should be studied in further detail by the use of typological and chronological surveys. Most important is of course the question how the specific shape might has functioned on a warp-weighted loom and why it was chosen. This can only be investigated with systematic experiments (see chapter 1.2).

Decoration of loom weights
Loom weights are rarely decorated in contrast to spindle whorls. Decoration does not appear to have been important for the functionality of the loom weights. Some loom weights received markings which resemble potters' marks. However, these are rarely discussed (*e.g.* Dabney 1996a, pl. 4.2.42; 4.3.52; 4.5.145,

64–65; Bennet 1996). Loom weights were sometimes stamped with objects whose seal impressions look similar to contemporary seals. Stamped loom weights do appear in contexts of the Bronze Age Eastern Mediterranean, in the Early Bronze Age Aegean (*e.g.* Skarkos: Marthari 2004, no. 169–174 with further references) and Anatolia (*e.g.* Tarsus: Goldman 1956, fig. 395), in the Late Bronze Age Aegean (*e.g.* Palaikastro, Amnisos, Kato Zakros: Burke 1997, pl. CLX c–d, 418; Akrotiri: Tzachili 1990, figs 8, 10, 385) and even the Middle Bronze Age southern Levant (Tell Nami: Artzy and Marcus 1995). Due to the stamped impressions there has been reluctance amongst scholars to classify these finds as loom weights (*e.g.* Weingarten 1990). However, it is noteworthy that it was also common to stamp and mark loom weights in later periods. There are indications that stamping was not only for simple decorative purposes (*e.g.* classical-hellenistic Corinth: Davidson 1952, 146–172), and it has been suggested that these indicate organisation, if not administration, of the textile production, thus indicating that the stamped impressions may indicate owner, product or weight (Burke 1997, 418; Wallrodt 2002, 184–185; Rutschmann 1988). Thus far, the possible function or purpose of stamped impressions on loom weights has only been discussed using the finds from a single site. No attempt has been made to clarify the significance of stamped loom weights by a cross-cultural and diachronic approach (as done *e.g.* by Feugère 2004). Although such a study may not produce definitive answers, it would be worthwhile comparing the context in which stamped loom weights appear, how and with what they are stamped, at which sites *etc.* in order to understand their possible significance over time and space.

Functional identification of finds as loom weights
Even more often than in the case of spindle whorls, the functional identification of loom weights is highly controversial. Four examples shall be presented briefly below:

Net sinkers or loom weights?
It is often thought that simple clay objects with a perforation can also be net sinkers. This is possible, but one should consider that if this was the case, the objects should be well baked

or fired in order not to dissolve in water. This point has already been put forward by Schliemann (Schliemann 1886, 165–166). In fact, typical net sinkers seem to be simple flat and oval pebbles shaped at the middle in order to attach the net to the sinker ("waisted weights") (see Fig. 1.1.2). Similar objects have been found at Late Neolithic lake dwelling sites in southern Germany (*e.g.* Strobel 2000, pl. 5, 159–161; pl. 6, 166–173; pl. 7, 162–163), Switzerland (Leuzinger 2002, 126, fig. 164 – with attached bast binding) or Servia in Greece (Carington Smith 2000, 161–170, fig. 4.19; pl. 4, 9), where these finds date to the late 5th and 4th millennia BC, or at Charavines les Baigneurs in the western Alps in the Early Bronze Age, *c.* 2200–1600 BC (Bazzanella *et al.* 2003b, 282). Similar artefacts are also typical for the western Anatolian Early Bronze Age where they are often described as abstract figurines or 'idols' (Zimmermann 2004). However, as demonstrated by J. Reinhard, the functionality as loom weights of this group of finds should not be excluded (Reinhard 1992, 53–54; Altorfer and Médard 2000, fig. 32.1, 67). In this respect, it should also be noted that typically shaped loom weights are often found at ancient ship wreck sites such as the pre-classical wreck at Campese Bay on the island of Giglio (*e.g.* Bound 1991, fig. 67, 229). These finds may have had a function as net sinkers as similarly shaped finds of pieces of lead found on ship wrecks (Bound 1991, fig. 65–66, 227–228) also dated to the Late Bronze Age (*e.g.* Uluburun: Yalçın *et al.* 2005, cat. no. 185, 629; *e.g.* Cape Gelidonia: Bass 1967, fig. 139, 131) or from cemetery and habitation sites on the Greek mainland, Cyprus and the Levant (Iakovidis 1969–1971, A: 453, 455; B: 355; C: pl. 135b; 2001, 114–115).

Torus weights

The so-called doughnut or torus weights are typical for the Early Iron Age in the southern Levant even if they also appear in various regions of Greece, where most of them weigh more than 1 kg (*e.g.* Tiryns: Rahmstorf 2008, 52–58, pl. 21, nos. 2483–2484, 2486; pl. 90, 3; *e.g.* Lefkandi: Evely 2006, fig. 5.17; pl. 99, 1–4). Their connection to the Levantine examples is not yet proven. There is an ongoing discussion among archaeologists working in the southern Levant regarding the identification of doughnut (or torus) shaped finds as loom weights (Sheffer 1981; Shamir 1996; Friend and Nashef 1998, fig. 10, 11a; Yasur-Landau 2009), bullets (Rabe 1996) or jar/fermentation stoppers (Gal 1989). The recent discovery of such an object in the mouth of a jar puts some credibility to the identification as fermentation stoppers (Homan 2004, 89–91), but it may just have fallen from the floor above. This explanation was given for the doughnut (or torus) weights from Lefkandi, which were often found lying in larger vessels (Popham *et al.* 2006, 32, pl. 7, a–b). On the other hand, doughnut (or torus) weights are the only type of loom weights found in Scandinavia, alongside the pyramidal shaped loom weights (Andersson 1999).

Spool shaped weights

Spool shaped or cylindrical clay objects, which in English publications are referred to as spools, cylinders, reels or bobbins, constitute another controversial loom weight type. Some scholars have termed them loom weights since Schliemann's first identification, whereas others have objected to this term due to their lack of a perforation and their frequent friability (Schliemann 1886, figs no. 70–71, 165–166). Clay spools were present in the Aegean and Thrace since the Early Neolithic (Carington Smith 1983, 290–291; Rahmstorf 2003, 398; Chohadzhiev 2004). It is plausible that clay spools were used as loom weights (Rahmstorf 2003; Rahmstorf 2005) due to contextual reasons: they are sometimes found in sets or rows (Ashkelon: Stager *et al.* 2008, 266), together with (other typical) loom weights or even with fibre (Ashkelon: Lass 2006, 204–205, fig. 12.6), or there are no other possible loom weights from the given site. In addition, there might be practical reasons for their use since spools can hold extra warp thread and finally there exists pictorial evidence for the

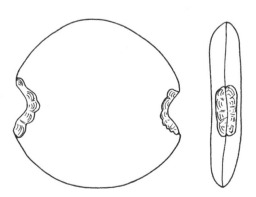

Fig. 1.1.2. Net sinker. From Servia, Greece, 6th millennium BC, scale 1:2 (drawing: Carington Smith 2000, 164, fig. 4.19. SF175).

use of spools as loom weights from the Early Iron Age (Aspiris 1996, fig. 1). Furthermore, it may be that clay spools were used as weights for tablet weaving, at least the lighter examples (Barber 1997, pl. CXCII, c, 516; Gleba 2000; 2008, 140–141, fig. 98). Recent experiments have confirmed the spools' likely function as loom weights in a warp-weighted loom at least for finds weighing over 100 g (see chapter 4 in this volume), while the lighter examples might have indeed been used for tablet weaving.

Crescent shaped weights

The crescent shaped clay loom weights are the final example of the differences in views on the function of a certain group of finds. Crescent shaped clay objects do not only appear in Bronze Age Anatolia and, more rarely, in the Early Bronze Age Aegean (see chapter 6.9, Tiryns; Siennicka 2012, pl. 2h), but are also known from several parts of Europe in the Late Neolithic (Castiglioni 1964; Kreen-Leeb 2001; Baioni *et al.* 2003). The function of crescent shaped clay objects as loom weights has been questioned, and the finds from Bronze Age Anatolia have been alternatively interpreted as a tool used for administrative purposes (Vogelsang-Eastwood 1990; Weingarten 1990). However, there is very good contextual evidence from Demircihüyük that they were in fact used as loom weights as 29 objects were found clustered together at the east wall of a room of the Early Bronze Age A phase E$_1$, and out of those, eight were crescent shaped (Korfmann 1981, fig. 45, 33–34). Thus, their basic function as loom weights cannot be questioned as demonstrated by recent tests (Feldtkeller 2003; Baioni *et al.* 2003, 104–105). In addition, more detailed and rigorous experiments performed recently showed that crescent shaped loom weights have added benefits due to their shape in comparison to "regular" loom weights (see chapter 4.4).

The four examples of interpretations and disagreements about interpretations of various types of loom weight illustrate how important it is to study such objects systematically and contextually and to conduct experiments in order to test how they could have functioned. In the present volume, finds of textile tools are studied by applying exactly these approaches.

Quantification of loom weights

As with spindle whorls, it is difficult to quantify and compare the numbers of loom weights from site to site. Whilst one always has to consider the issue of uneven preservation at various sites, general trends do appear through the amount of material collected. For example, it is apparent that we have far smaller numbers of loom weights at Mycenaean sites than at Minoan centres. It is also difficult to assess the average number of loom weights used on a warp-weighted loom. Unfortunately, there seem to be only a few contexts with preserved, presumed to be more or less complete, sets of looms weights *in situ* from the Eastern Mediterranean (*e.g.* Troia IIg and Aphrodisias, Turkey: Barber 1991, figs 3.14–15, 93–94; Demircihüyük, Turkey: Korfmann 1981, figs 44–45, 33–34; Tell 'Abu al-Kharaz, Jordan: Fischer 2010, 111–113, fig. 3; 5). More systematic collection of data is required for any further assumptions on issues of quantification. Comparisons of the Eastern Mediterranean Bronze Age data with more or less completely preserved sets of loom weights from other regions and periods (*e.g.* Schierer 1987; Berrocal Rangel 2003) might give new insights. Further, it can be shown that statistical analyses of loom weights (as well as of spindle whorls) are of great importance also for their chronological implications, for example ratios of Roman loom weights from Pompeii based among other things on height and weight are indeed chronologically sensitive (Baxter and Cool 2008).

Other textile tools

The following is a short presentation on other relevant textile tools of the Bronze Age Mediterranean which are, however, often not preserved from this period. Recent ethnographic observations and archaeological finds from prehistoric European wetland sites, from the Iron Age and later periods are helpful in this respect.

Wool combs and hackling boards

After rippling, retting, breaking and scutching, the flax plant needs finally to be hackled in order to separate the fibres from each other (Becker 1984; Barber 1991, 13–14; Granger-Taylor 1998). This can be done on hackling boards: a flat wooden board in which teeth are regularly inserted (Fig. 1.1.3). The thorns from the blackthorn (*prunus spinosa*) were often used as teeth, or were later made of iron. Hackling boards with bronze teeth are not known to me. Probably the earliest hackling board is a fragment from the lake-dwelling site of Lüscherz in Switzerland (not Lattringen, according to Winiger 1995, 169, fig. 42, 1; Vogt 1937, Abb. 72, 6–7), later finds are from several Iron Age sites in central Europe (Hallstatt, Austria; Liptovska Mara, Slovakia: Grömer 2010, 77–79, fig. 27; Porz-Lind, Germany: Joachim 2002, 25–27, figs 18–20; pl. 40, 3–4; 41, 1–2; 92, 1–3. 7). Similar objects were also used to comb long staple wool until the present day (Folk Art Museum – Nafplion 1988, 26; Tzachili 1997, 35–37). For this reason it is not really possible to decide whether such objects were used for processing flax or wool (Joachim 2002, 26–27; Grömer 2010, 78), however, from the preserved textile remains it is clear that wool was carefully combed with iron combs leaving the fibres in parallel order only from the Roman period onwards (Rast-Eicher 2008, 161–162, fig. 226–228).

Distaffs

A distaff is "a rod or board onto which prepared fibres are fastened to serve as a source of supply during spinning" (Barber 1991, 69; *Folk Art Museum – Nafplion* 1988, 28–29). It prevents the fibre from tangling with the twisting thread. Such a tool is "useful, although not essential" (Walton Rogers 1997, 1735). This fact might explain to a certain extent that there are few finds of distaffs in the archaeological record until classical times. On the other hand, a simple wooden branch could also be used as a fork-shaped distaff.

Carved distaffs made of wood were used in Greece until recently (Cremer 1996, pl. 25.1, 241; Tzachili 1997, figs 28, 52). In hellenistic and Roman times one end of the distaff was often ring-shaped. In rare cases, distaffs appear in sets together with a spindle and whorl as part of a grave assemblage, as in a hellenistic grave in Ephesos (Trinkl 1994). As in the case of the spindles there is a problem of preservation of distaffs, as they were presumably mainly made of wood, which normally does not survive in archaeological deposits.

Spinning bowls

It is assumed that the fibre was usually held in a basket or bowl. The so-called spinning bowls with internal loops are connected to the production of yarn (Fig. 1.1.4). They were identified by Peet and Woolley at Tell El-Amarna through finds of stone bowls (Peet and Woolley 1923, 61) and in Egyptian wall paintings of the Middle Kingdom at Beni Hasan by G. Crowfoot (Crowfoot 1931, 61). T. Dothan was able to bring together Middle Kingdom spinning bowls from Egypt with Late Bronze Age examples from Palestine (*e.g.* Dothan 1963; Vogelsang-Eastwood 2000, 272–274; Granger-Taylor and Quirke 2002; Hageman 2006, fig. 2). However, there are also examples of bowls with internal loop-handles from the Turkoman steppe in northern Iran (*e.g.* Shah Tepé: Arne 1945, 219, fig. 446a, pl. LVIII, 466a). The problem is that the finds of concave vessels with an internal handle may not be spinning bowls but jar covers. Finds such as these have also been made at Early Bronze Age sites in the Near East, for example at Jemdet Nasr (*e.g.* Arne 1945, 219), or at Habuba Kabira of the late 4th and early 3rd millennium BC (Strommenger

Fig. 1.1.3. Hackling board. Liptovska Mara, Slovakia, 2nd–1st century BC (photo: Grömer 2010, 79, fig. 27).

0   5   10 cm

1970, fig. 24, 66 and 69). Since these objects have never been studied comprehensively or systematically, and since the common ware is often not studied in detail at many Eastern Mediterranean sites, it is too early to conclude that the Egyptians imported the spinning bowl technique from Early Minoan Crete or *vice versa* (Barber 1991, 73–76) simply based on the evidence of spinning bowls from Early Minoan II Myrtos on Crete (Warren 1972, 153, 209, fig. 91, P701, pl. 68, B). The precise function of the spinning bowl remains an object of discussion. According to Barber, the term "spinning bowl" is a misnomer and it could better be referred to as a "fibre-wetting bowl" used in the process of flax spinning (Barber 1991, 72–73). They are known on Crete only from Early Minoan to Middle Minoan sites (Barber 1991, 74). Their seeming absence in the Late Minoan period made Barber suggest that this could reflect the change to wool from flax production (Barber 1991, 76–77). Still, it is hard to imagine "that the creation of linen cloth ceased in Late Minoan times" (Evely 2003, 194). There is also a spinning bowl fragment from the Late Minoan South House at Knossos but it is considered as "stray sherd from an earlier context" (Evely 2003, fig. 7.11, 193).

Shuttles

Shuttles are used to insert the weft yarn during weaving. Shuttles are artefacts that are seldom recognised as such. Shuttles with a terminal hole in order to store yarn during weaving were found at some Greek sites (*e.g.* Kommos: Dabney 1996a, pl. 4.6, 262; Tiryns: Rahmstorf 2008, 197, pl. 73, nos. 1416, 1374, 1366; pl. 97, 5; Lerna: Banks 1967, pl. 13, 427–428). Generally, shuttles were probably made of wood or alternatively bone. A specific tool such as the shuttle may not have been strictly necessary, as the spindle itself, with the spun thread and without the whorl, could be used as a shuttle (Schierer 1987, 81).

Pin and sword beaters

A pin beater is "a multi-purpose weaver's hand tool, used to strum across the warp to even out spacing, to pick out misplaced threads and to push the weft […] into position" (Walton Rogers 1997, 1755). They are made of wood or bone. As with numerous other textile tools, pin beaters are difficult to detect in the archaeological record. Several types of finds may have been used as beaters, but for such simple tools several functions are possible. There are several types of bone awls/points which might have functioned as pin beaters (*e.g.* flat awls made of rib bones mainly of Early Bronze Age date in the Aegean, see Rahmstorf 2008, 200, 202, 204, pl. 78 [type 7]; 98, 1. Compare also Smith 2001; 2012 for LBA Cyprus.). It is likely that pin beaters were usually made of wood, like those found in the Late Neolithic site of Wetzikon-Robenhausen in Switzerland, which is famous for its Late Neolithic textile remains (Altorfer and Médard 2000, fig. 34, 68) and probably also in the Bronze Age site of Fiavé in northern Italy (Bazzanella *et al.* 2003b, 141). From the Late Iron Age site Fellbach-Schmiden in southern Germany or Hallstatt-Dammwiese in Upper Austria there are "wooden swords" which might instead be sword beaters for beating the weft into position, as has been argued (*e.g.* Kurzynski 1996, 14–15; Grömer 2010, 123, fig. 57).

Decks of tablets for tablet-weaving

The origin of the very old technique of tablet-weaving (Schlabow 1965, figs 6–11, 16–21; 1976, figs 49–51, 45–46; 1978; Evely 2000, fig. 197, 492; Grömer 2010, 111, fig. 48–49) is by some thought to be Egypt (Schütte 1956). "The obvious ways of demonstrating the existence of card-weaving would seem to be through ancient pictorial representations or through finds of the tablets" (Barber 1991, 119). No such evidence is known from the Eastern Mediterranean Bronze Age thus far. However, textile finds like the girdle of Ramses III (Barber 1991, fig. 3.34) make it likely that tablet-weaving was known at least in Egypt and possibly also in the Aegean, Anatolia and the Levant. The lack of finds of possible tablets could be due to the decomposition of the material (wood) of which they were made or they may have not yet been identified in the archaeological record. As a rule such objects should be flat with four holes, one in each corner (Fig. 1.1.5). Definite identifications of any such groups of objects are lacking for the 3rd and 2nd millennium BC. Square tablets in clay, stone or bone with a perforation in each corner are known from several different cultures in Eurasia: in the eastern central European Lengyel-culture of the 5th

millennium BC (Neugebauer-Maresch 1995, 103, fig. 48 top centre) or in many Copper Age settlements in Portugal (Spindler and Gallay 1973, 14, pl. 16, 17, 466–469). It is, however, unlikely that they were used for tablet-weaving. These objects are often rather thick and too heavy, and no additional textile evidence can support such claims. With the second half of the second millennium BC there is more convincing evidence for the existence of tablet weaving in central Europe. Textile remains (Schwarza, Germany: Farke 1993, 111) and a possible tablet deck (Abri in Mühltal, Lower Saxony, Germany: Kurzynski 1996, 15, fig. 15; Grömer 2010, 107, fig. 47, 1) may indicate such an interpretation. With the Iron Age there are several pieces of textiles from central Europe (Hochdorf, Hohmichele, Aprement, Hallstatt) and Italy (Sasso di Furbara, Verucchio) which were made through tablet-weaving (Banck-Burgess 1999, 65–82; Grömer 2010, 108). Several pieces of tablet decks were also found in a grave of the 4th century BC in Cigarralejo in Spain (Hundt 1968, 193, fig. 5). But it is only from the 1st millennium AD that we have full archaeological attestations of tablet weaving (Ræder Knudsen 2007): the rich grave from Oseberg in Norway preserved a complete device for tablet weaving with 52 tablets and a partially woven band (Stolte 1990, fig. 5).

Sewing needles

Needles with an eye can normally be identified as sewing needles although an exclusive or additional function as a dress accessory cannot be excluded. The longer the eye of the needle, the less likely the object is to have an exclusive function as a sewing needle. Furthermore, the eye should not be located too far from the end of the needle, in order to enable its use in sewing (*e.g.* Kilian-Dirlmeier 1984b, 59). Again, no systematic investigation of such questions has been applied to the archaeological material thus far.

Approaches to research on textile tools

Research on textile tools originates from six different approaches, some of which are commonly combined. Those mentioned here are the ethnographical and ethnoarchaeological approach, the textual approach, the iconographical approach, the

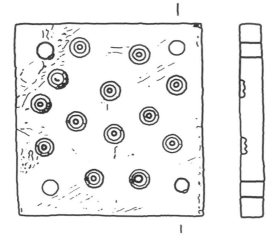

Fig. 1.1.5. Weaving tablet. Abri in Mühltal, Germany, second half of 2nd millennium BC (drawing: Grömer 2010, 108, fig. 47, 1).

material-typological approach, the functional-experimental approach and the contextual approach.

The ethnographical and ethnoarchaeological approach

From the 19th century through the mid 20th century, textile tools were still used in non-industrial textile manufacture in some remote regions of Europe, so it was possible to see similar tools still in use by the local population. Until the 1950s, the traditional warp-weighted loom was still in use in regions of northern Scandinavia, a fact which formed the basis of M. Hoffmann's important work on the warp-weighted loom (Hoffmann 1964). Even within industrialised societies, the identification of loom weights was not difficult. Thus, for example, when in 1860 the Alpine pile dwellings (*Pfahlbauten*) were discovered at Lake Zürich, F. Keller identified finds as loom weights through his discussions with a local textile producer (Keller 1861, 13). A vital problem was to demonstrate that certain objects are in fact loom weights and not weights used for another purpose, or spindle whorls or beads. In the Eastern Mediterranean area, comprehensive studies using ethnographical evidence began rather late (*e.g.* Koster 1976). In the 1990s, I. Tzachili used ethnographical data extensively for her study on the textile production in the 2nd millennium BC Aegean (Tzachili 1997). Ethnoarchaeological approaches have been applied by P. Halstead, using oral history research in order to explore decision making and practices of arable and pastoral farming in the Mediterranean and in particular the Aegean (*e.g.* Halstead 1990, 1998). Similar approaches have yet to be applied to traditional textile production, and it will become increasingly difficult to collect data as any non-industrial textile production disappears. Furthermore, modern ethnologists no longer undertake comparative ethnological studies as was popular in the earlier 20th century AD (*e.g.* Hirschberg and Janata 1980). However, a comparative ethnological study may still be a valid approach today to studies of some regions of the Near and Middle East (*e.g.* Ochsenschlager 1993a, 1993b).

The textual approach

With this approach, descriptions of actual textile production are applied from the ancient textual data. While spinning and weaving are mentioned in the Bronze Age textual data, these are mostly connected to administrative purposes, as in the texts at Early Bronze Age Ebla in Syria (*e.g.* Zaccagnini 1986; Sollberger 1986), in the Sumerian texts of the Ur III period (*e.g.* Waetzoldt 1972) or in the Mycenaean Linear B tablets (*e.g.* Killen 1984, 1988; Nosch 1998, 2003, 2007; Tzachili 2001; Ergin 2007). Detailed descriptions of the actual production processes are lacking. There have also been attempts to explain terms used in the epics of Homer and in later classical literature describing textile production (*e.g.* Onians 1924; Crowfoot 1936–37; Snyder 1981). However, the precise meanings of the words used in these texts remain a matter of debate (*e.g.* Wace 1948; Barber 1991, 260–282; Wagner-Hasel 2000, 147–149). Mentions of spinning and weaving in ancient literature are more often discussed in terms of their implications about society, status and gender (*e.g.* Homer: Pantelia 1993). In the Roman period, sporadic mention of specific textile tools appears more often (*e.g.* Cremer 1996, 241–242; Gottschalk 1996, n. 67, 500). Only rarely have attempts been made to combine the textual evidence with archaeobotanical and archaeological evidence in order to practise historical reconstruction beyond the scope of an analysis of the tools and their functions (*e.g.* hypothetical reconstruction of the development of textile workshops in Mesopotamia, see McCorriston 1997). Essentially, great insight into textile production and tools used in the process can be gained from the study of relevant texts, although these mainly focus on the administrative and economical role of the textiles in the given society as opposed to how the tools were actually used. Thus far, a cross-cultural and diachronic approach with a systematic comparison of the textual data is lacking. An exception is the volume *Textile Terminologies in the Ancient Near East and the Mediterranean Area from the Third to the First Millennia BC* (Michel and Nosch 2010) in which such a research strategy has indeed been explored.

The iconographical approach

A commonly used source for the understanding of ancient textile production has always been the early depictions. We know of depictions and miniature models of looms from Egypt (*e.g.* Barber 1991, figs 3.5–3.6, 84–85; Rooijakkers

2005) and Mesopotamia (*e.g.* Amiet 1961, pl. 16, 273, 275; pl. 19, 319), the Aegean (*e.g.* Barber 1991, fig. 3.12, 92; Burke 1997, pl. CLX, e–f; CLXI, 418–419) and prehistoric Europe (*e.g.* Zimmermann 1988; Bazzanella *et al.* 2003a, figs 11–12). With the beginning of the Iron Age, representations of women spinning become increasingly common. In Neo-Hittite reliefs, women are often depicted spinning (Bonatz 2000, pls. XII, C21–C25; XIII, C27; XIV, C33; XVIII, C50–C51; XX, C59; XXI, C60–C61; XXIII, C68–C69, 79–82). Greek archaic and classical vase painting is one of the best iconographic sources, showing fairly precise representations of vertical looms and spinning women (Keuls 1983; Barber 1991, figs 2.35–2.36; 2.38; 2.45; 3.13; 3.24–3.26; 3.28; Ferrari 2002, 35–60; Bazzanella *et al.* 2003a, no. 70). A study of these depictions is a long-standing tradition, but the limitations due to the simplistic or simplified depictions, especially in regard to the Bronze Age evidence, make interpretations difficult (*e.g.* Johl 1917; Faxon 1932).

The material-typological approach

As textile tools have been found at more or less every archaeological settlement site from the Neolithic period onwards, they do appear in the final site publications. Heinrich Schliemann was probably one of the first scholars of Aegean and Eastern Mediterranean archaeology who discussed possible textile tools in some detail and raised questions, mainly about their function (Schliemann 1878, 21; 1886, 92, 165–166). While not being precise in recording stratigraphical positions or find spots in detail, he had a particular interest in minor objects of daily use. Schliemann's influence explains a number of late 19th and early 20th century excavation reports from the Eastern Mediterranean and beyond describing textile tools in terms of shape and material. A site-specific typology was often provided in the site publications. Other parameters such as shape, weight, diameter and height of the finds were rarely indicated. Today, they are still often missing from final publications. In modern studies, a detailed discussion of the chosen material should always be included, for example in case of objects made of clay a description of their surface, colour, firing, *etc.* should be given (*e.g.* Obladen-Kauder 1996). Thus far, no shared publication standard for

textile tools exists within Eastern Mediterranean archaeology of the Bronze Age. Hopefully, this volume will be a helpful guideline. Standardised information on material-typological data is also a prerequisite for following up the last two approaches presented below. With the material-typological approach, not only the samples from one specific site should be taken into account but also other well published samples from other sites should be compared with each other on a regional or even interregional level.

The functional-experimental approach

From the beginning, the ethnographical approach has been applied in attempts to understand the functionality of the textile tools. The typical question asked was how the spinning or weaving was put into practice with the different objects. The experimental investigation of the order in which complete sets of loom weights might have fallen from the warps when the loom burned down during accidental destruction, might even help to reconstruct the weave produced on the loom as I. Schierer has shown (Schierer 1987). More information and further discussions of this approach can be found in chapter 1.2 of this volume and shall not be presented here in more detail.

The contextual approach

The contextual approach intends to support any functional interpretation of a possible textile tool by analysing in depth and in detail the archaeological context in which it was found. This comprises the description of the find place, its layer, phase, architectural placing *etc.* within the site, which in most cases is a settlement. Despite the fact that Eastern Mediterranean archaeology has brought to light many sites with deep stratigraphies and architectural remains, the detailed three-dimensional extensive recording of the find spot of every object has become common only during recent decades, with a few earlier exceptions. Today, many excavations still clear units or architectural rooms in one sweep. For any reconstruction of the actual placing of looms in a settlement, it is essential to record the exact find spot of every object, even if later disturbances complicate matters in most cases. Thus far, final publications providing detailed phase plans with mapped distributions of the textile tools' find places are few, but are imperative aids to discuss functional and contextual problems of textile tools (*e.g.*

Tiryns/Greek mainland: Kilian 1988, 107, fig. 4; Rahmstorf 2008; Khania/Crete: Hallager and Hallager 2000; Tell Bderi/Syria: Pfälzner 2001; Kamid el-Loz/Libanon: Metzger 1993).

From the six approaches outlined above, archaeologists should present the relevant material with detailed discussions along the lines of the *material-typological* and *contextual approach*. This basic requirement is still too often neglected. A systematic integration of the *functional-experimental approach* into such studies is needed. In addition, a comparative *textual approach* is very important as recently demonstrated (Michel and Nosch 2010). Finally, the *ethnographical and ethnoarchaeological approach* might add important details but its contribution is becoming less important due to the shrinking basis for ethnographical observations in a globalised world with an overwhelmingly industrial textile production. Similarly, the *iconographical approach* will offer only few new insights as it cannot be expected that many new depictions of textile production will turn up in the near future from Neolithic and Bronze Age sites.

Research topics

Certain research topics have been significant in scholarly work on textile tools and textile production in the Bronze Age Mediterranean and can be divided into the following: *craftsmanship and gender* and *trade and migration* as presented below.

Craftsmanship and gender

It is often pointed out that textile production was mainly women's work (Barber 1991, 283–298; 1994). The main reason seems to be that the easily interruptible work of spinning and weaving could be done at home where women could continue to raise children at the same time (Richmond 2006, 218–219 with further references). In the ancient Greek and Roman literature it belongs to the *topos* of the diligence of the housewife (*e.g.* Gottschalk 1996, 494); spinning and weaving is the work of women, war the work of men according to Homer (*Iliad* 6. 490–493; compare Eibner 2005, 31). In Hittite literature, spindle and distaff are the symbols of womanhood (Bonatz 2000, 81; Yakar and Taffet 2007, 783). Similarly, in the Americas "*there is a standard, much quoted portrait of the never idle Andean peasant woman*

spinning endlessly as she stood, sat, and even walked", even if "*in practice, the sexual division of labour was less rigidly defined*" (Murra 1962, 711). Spinning and weaving was a daily activity of women, also women of the 'upper classes', in the Eastern Mediterranean Bronze and Iron Ages as well as in other parts of the world (Nordquist 1997, n. 18, 536). This is underlined by finds of spinning tools made of precious material (gold, silver, amber *etc.*, see above). Traditional scholarship on ancient Greece has always had a different view: that women produced textiles only for their own needs within the *oikos* system, while males were professional weavers or 'artists' who produced high quality textiles for exchange and artistic esteem. According to Reuthner, this modern interpretation is due to the change of perception of the household economy in contrast to the national market economy which emerged as early as the 18th century AD (Reuthner 2006). Due to the loss of significance given to the household economy, the traditional work of women within the household, such as textile production, has been regarded as unproductive and unprofessional. This, however, represents the conceptions constructed by the modern world only, not of the ancient world as Reuthner has clearly illustrated. In classical Greece it was mostly women who produced valuable and artistic textiles and competed in contests, while men were primarily working with raw linen in workshops (Reuthner 2006, chapter 6). This example illustrates modern views on gender and craftsmanship, that there is an often unconscious division into men's work (concrete, important, essential for survival) and women's chores (routine tasks which can be performed on the side) as E. Andersson observed (Andersson 1996, 16).

As in classical Greece, female weavers were the main producers of textiles in the Bronze Age Eastern Mediterranean. In Greece, Egypt and Mesopotamia they laboured in single households or compounds of a royal palace. Male weavers, however, were not unknown within the textile industries of the palatial sector. There are approximately 200 male textile workers mentioned on the Linear B tablets at Knossos (Nixon 1999, 565) and depictions of male weavers come from New Kingdom Egypt (Barber 1991, fig. 13.1, 285–286). Nevertheless, the predominant depictions and textual mentions of textile production from the Bronze and Iron Age focus on women.

Issues of craftsmanship and gender are also interesting in relation to the question of which economic sector the textiles were produced in: a subsistence household economy, a market economy, or a palace economy, or an intermixing of the three. From the Old Akkadian letters from Karum Kanesh in Anatolia we know of women in Ashur who, in addition to their household needs, produced textiles for the market in Karum Kanesh (Veenhof 1972, 104–115; Barber 1991, 287; Michel and Veenhof 2010). While spinning and weaving was the typical work of women, even of higher status, female textile workers mentioned in the Mycenaean Linear B texts are considered by most scholars to have had a dependent or slave status (*e.g.* Nosch 2003, 18–22; Ergin 2007), although some argue that "it is tempting to imagine that at least some of the specialist groups at Pylos were connected with the courts of the elite women" (Nordquist 1997, 536). The women's specialist knowledge of textile production resulted in part-time specialisation, but only a state-like organisation of a given society enabled the existence of full-time specialists. Archaeologists mostly think of metalworkers when imagining early full-time specialists, but in fact scholars should take (female) textile workers into greater consideration in their research. Similarly, the craft of textile production should receive similar attention in archaeological literature as flint working, pottery and metalworking (Andersson 1996).

Trade and migration

It is often assumed that textile production in the Bronze Age Mediterranean was not only a household activity on a subsistence basis but also used in the exchange of goods. Eastern Mediterranean textual evidence clearly demonstrates this for the second millennium BC (*e.g.* Karum Kanesh/Kültepe: Veenhof 1972; Michel and Veenhof 2010) but this use of textiles in trade began much earlier, *i.e.* in the 3rd millennium (*e.g.* Western Asia: Crawford 1973; Good 2004). However, only through quantification of textile tools at various sites might we be able to reconstruct whether textiles were produced only at a household level or for trade and export. Such quantifications have only recently started to be calculated (Richmond 2006; Balfanz 1995a, 137–138); and are of great

importance (see also above: *quantification of spindle whorls*). It is likely that such exchange diffused the textile production technology as well as knowledge of how the exchanged textiles were produced in the first place. Any significant change in the textile tools used or preferred costumes in a given society is often interpreted as evidence of migration where new people, especially women, have brought with them a new technology of textile production. Therefore, new types of loom weights (*e.g.* Bouzek 1997, 440–442; Wagner-Hasel 2001; Rahmstorf 2003, 2005; Yasur-Landau 2010) or costume evident from the archaeological data are occasionally interpreted as evidence of migration, at least of women (Kilian-Dirlmeier 1984a; Hägg 1996). However, tracing migration only through archaeological evidence remains a highly controversial issue (*e.g.* Prien 2005). New groups of finds, such as loom weights, can mark a distinctive break in the stratigraphical assemblage and may thus imply the presence of new people in a certain area. However, this indication should be supported by other data and sources.

Research on textile tools in the past and present – and in the future?

Early scholars of Eastern Mediterranean Bronze Age archaeology tried to identify and classify prehistoric textile tools by a typology based on the morphology of the objects. Functional interpretations of possible textile tools were subsequently put forward, occasionally supported by a still living tradition in these regions of non-modern industrial textile production. The existing ancient depictions of textile production were assembled and analysed. The amount of work invested in these early studies, especially on the typology of spindle whorls, was not always continued in later publications. Detailed studies on typology and chronology of textile tools came to be considered unrewarding, if not meaningless. While it became increasingly common during the second half of the 20th century AD to publish at least a portion of the whole corpus of textile tools in the final publication of a single site, their scientific relevance for reconstructing living conditions of the past remained assumed to be virtually non-existent. Questions beyond typo-chronology were rarely asked. Specific characteristics and basic parameters such as the weight of the spindle whorls and loom weights, their relevance for the actual function of the objects as well as the outcome of the work process were taken into account. However, even today, an acknowledged standard of publication of textile tools is yet to be decided. Detailed information concerning shape, diameter, thickness, weight, dating and context of every textile tool find alongside a thorough evaluation and discussion are not a standard inclusion of a final site publication. Furthermore, there can still be uncertainty as to whether a group of artefacts are textile tools or not.

What is thus lacking is a framework through which an interpretation can be checked and compared systematically by taking into account the location of the site, the period and the typological criteria including all relevant data such as shape, profile, weight, material, height and decoration. A systematic approach can be achieved through the application of a number of carefully undertaken experiments, using replicas of ancient textile tools, and by recording precisely every step taken during these experiments. In current and future studies, scholars will be able to study previous interpretations of textile tools, the resulting textiles, the amount of time and effort the ancient spinners and weavers had to invest, and several other aspects, with the knowledge from these experiments (see also in chapter 1.2 of this volume). Through experiments, scholars are able to provide more definite answers. Therefore, the experimental approach will be the most innovative approach in future studies of textile tools.

Alongside this new approach some fundamental research questions or themes concerning tools and textiles should be tackled systematically in the future:

- *Cross-cultural and diachronic comparison, i.e.* which textile tools are present in which periods? What does this tell us about the state of textile production in a given period?
- *Typo-chronology of textile tools and the fibres, i.e.* how have textile tools changed over the course of time? What is their correlation to the fibres such as bast, nettle, linen and wool as well as the produced textiles and the applied technology?
- *Context, i.e.* where were the majority of textiles produced during the Bronze Age in

the Aegean, Anatolia and the Levant? Was it within specialised compounds of palatial settlements or within the normal households of dependent rural settlements?
- *Quantity, i.e.* what does it tell us when textile tools are abundant, few or absent at one site or period? How can we make quantitative calculations on a local, regional and supra-regional level?
- *Diffusion/independent innovation/migration, i.e.* where lies the origin of certain types of textile tools? Did similar types develop independently? How can textile tools help to trace migration processes?
- *Craftsmanship and gender, i.e.* what was the relationship between gender issues and the textile production processes?
- *Economy, i.e.* how was the textile production organised – on a household or large scale industry level in prehistoric and early historic societies? How can we attempt to quantify the amount of textile production, its administration and appreciation through time?

The careful discussion of the archaeological material along certain standards of publication in combination with results from experiments with textile tools will lead to the most rewarding new insights. The present volume might offer a guide for such an undertaking. Many insights in the archaeology of textile tools are still to be discovered. Hopefully, textile tools will gain greater scientific attention in the general archaeological literature in the near future.

Acknowledgements

For the invitation to the Danish National Research Foundation's Centre of Textile Research during October–December 2006, for the warm welcome, the many fruitful discussions and their general hospitality in Copenhagen I would like to express my gratitude to M.-L. Nosch, E. Andersson Strand, and to the other people of the CTR. I would also like to thank Małgorzata Siennicka for her help.

This text was written in 2006 and revised in 2008. Only a few minor additions were made in 2011. Important new studies are therefore not included in this study.

Bibliography

Altorfer, K. and Médard, F. (2000) Nouvelles découvertes textiles sur le site de Wetzikon-Robenhausen (Zürich, Suisse). Sondages 1999, in Cardon, D. and Feugère, M. (eds), *Archéologie des textiles, des origins au Ve siècle*, 33–75. Montagnac. Editions Monique Mergoil.

Amiet, P. (1961) *La glyptique mésopotamienne archaïque*. Paris. Centre national de la recherche scientifique.

Andersson, E. (1996) Invisible handicrafts. The general picture of textile and skin crafts in Scandinavian surveys, *Lund Archaeological Review*, 7–20.

Andersson, E. (1999) *The Common Thread: Textile Production During the Late Iron Age–Viking Age*. Lund. Institute of Archaeology, University of Lund.

Andersson, E. (2003) *Tools for Textile Production from Birka and Hedeby: Excavations in the Black Earth 1990–1995*. Stockholm. Birka Project, Riksantikvarieämbetet.

Andersson, E. and Nosch, M.-L. (2003) With a little help from my friends: investigating Mycenaean textiles with help from Scandinavian experimental archaeology, in Foster, K. P. and Laffineur, R. (eds), *Metron: Measuring the Aegean Bronze Age*, 197–205. Liège. Université de Liège.

Arne, T. J. (1945) *Excavations at Shah Tepé, Iran*. Stockholm; Göteborg. Elander.

Artzy, M. and Marcus, E. (1995) A loom weight from Tel Nami with a scarab seal impression, *Israel Exploration Journal*, 45, 136–149.

Aspiris, M. (1996) Ein zypriotischer Teller mit der Darstellung eines Webstuhls, *Bonner Jahrbücher*, 196, 1–10.

Baioni, M., Borello, M. A., Feldtkeller, A. and Schlichtherle, H. (2003) I pesi reniformi e le fusaiole piatte decorate della Cultura della Lagozza. Cronologia, distribuzione geografica e sperimentazioni, in Bazzanella, M., Mayr, A., Moser, L. and Rast-Eicher, E. (eds) *Textiles: intrecci e tessuti dalla preistoria europea*, 99–109. Trento. Provincia Autonoma di Trento.

Balfanz, K. (1995a) Bronzezeitliche Spinnwirtel aus Troja, *Studia Troica*, 5, 117–144.

Balfanz, K. (1995b) Eine spätbronzezeitliche Elfenbeinspindel aus Troja VIIA, *Studia Troica*, 5, 107–116.

Banck-Burgess, J. (1999) *Hochdorf IV. Die Textilindustrie aus dem späthallstattzeitlichen Fürstengrab von Eberdingen-Hochdorf (Kreis Ludwigsburg) und weitere Grabtextilien aus hallstatt- und latènezeitlichen Kulturgruppen*. Stuttgart. Konrad Theiss.

Banks, E. (1967) *The Early and Middle Helladic Small Objects from Lerna*. Ph.D. thesis. University of Cincinnati.

Barber, E. J. W. (1991) *Prehistoric Textiles: The Development of Cloth in the Neolithic and Bronze Ages with Special Reference to the Aegean*. Princeton. Princeton University Press.

Barber, E. J. W. (1994) *Women's Work. The First 20,000 Years. Women, Cloth, and Society in Early Times*. New York. W. W. Norton.

Barber, E. J. W. (1997) Minoan women and the challenges of weaving for home, trade and shrine in Laffineur, R. and Betancourt, P. (eds), *TEXNH. Craftsmen, Craftswomen and Craftmanship in the Aegean Bronze Age*, 515–519. Liège. Université de Liège.

Bass, G. F. (1967) *Cape Gelidonya: A Bronze Age Shipwreck* (with the collaboration of Peter Throckmorton). Philadelphia. American Philosophical Society.

Baxter, M. J. and Cool, H. E. M. (2008) Notes on the statistical analysis of some loomweights from Pompeii, *Archeologia e Calcolatori*, 19, 239–256.

Bazzanella, M., Mayr, A. and Rast-Eicher, A. (2003a) I telai preistorici tra Neolitico ed età del Bronzo, in Bazzanella, M., Mayr, A., Moser, L. and Rast-Eicher, E. (eds) *Textiles: intrecci e tessuti dalla preistoria europea*, 87–97. Trento. Provincia Autonoma di Trento.

Bazzanella, M., Mayr, A., Moser, L. and Rast-Eicher, E. (eds) (2003b) *Textiles: intrecci e tessuti dalla preistoria europea*. Trento. Provincia autonoma di Trento.

Becker, D. (1984) *Vom Flachs zum Leinengarn*. Waisenhaus Braunschweig. Braunschweigischen Landesmuseums.

Bennet, J. (1996) Marks on Bronze Age pottery from Kommos, in Shaw, J. W. and Shaw, M. C. (eds), *Kommos I. The Kommos Region and Houses of the Minoan Town. Part 2. The Minoan Hilltop and Hillside Houses*, 313–321. Princeton, Princeton University Press.

Berrocal Rangel, L. (2003) El instrumental textil en Cancho Roano: consideraciones sobre sus fusayolas, pesas y telares, in S. Celestino (ed.), *Cancho Roano IX. Los materiales arqueológicos II*, 213–297. Mérida. Junta de Extremadura.

Blegen, C. W., Caskey, J. L., Rawson, M. and Sperling, J. (1950) *Troy I. General Introduction. The First and Second Settlements*. Princeton. Princeton University Press.

Blegen, C. W. (1937) *Prosymna. The Helladic Settlement Preceeding the Argive Heraeum*. Cambridge. Cambridge University Press.

Bonatz, D. (2000) *Das syro-hethitische Grabdenkmal. Untersuchungen zur Entstehung einer neuen Bildgattung in der Eisenzeit im nordsyrisch-südostanatolischen Raum*. Mainz. Philipp von Zabern.

Bound, M. (1991) The pre-classical wreck at Campese Bay, Island of Giglio. Second interim report, 1983 season, *Studi e Materiali. Scienza dell'antichità in Toscana*, 6, 199–244.

Bouzek, J. (1997) Zwischenehen, in Becker, C., Dunkelmann, M. L., Metzner-Nebelsick, C., Peter-Röcher, H., Roeder, M. and Terzan, B. (eds), *Chronos. Beiträge zur prähistorischen Archäologie zwischen Nord- und Südosteuropa. Festschrift für Bernhard Hänsel*. 437–442. Espelkamp. Leidorf.

Burke, B. (1997) The organization of textile production on Bronze Age Crete, in Laffineur, R. and Betancourt, P. (eds), *TEXNH. Craftsmen, Craftswomen and Craftmanship in the Aegean Bronze Age*, 413–422. Liège. Université de Liège.

Burke, B. (2003) The spherical loomweights, in Mountjoy, P. A. (ed.), *Knossos. The South House*, 195–197. London. The British School at Athens.

Carington Smith, J. (1975) *Spinning, Weaving and Textile Manufacture in Prehistoric Greece from the Beginning of the Neolithic to the End of the Mycaean Ages*. Ph.D. thesis, University of Hobart, Tasmania.

Carington Smith, J. (1983) The evidence for spinning and weaving, in McDonald, W. A., Coulson, W. D. E. and J. Rosser (eds), *Excavations at Nichoria in Southwestern Greece. 3. Dark Age and Byzantine Occupation*, 273–315. Minneapolis. University of Minnesota Press.

Carington Smith, J. (1992) Spinning and weaving equipment, in Macdonald, W. A. and Wilkie, N. C. (eds), *Excavations at Nichoria in Southwestern Greece. 2. The Bronze Age Occupation*, 674–711. Minneapolis. University of Minnesota Press.

Carington Smith, J. (2000) The spinning and weaving implements, in Ridley, C., Wardle, K. A. and C. A. Mould (eds), *Servia I. Anglo-Hellenic Rescue Excavations 1971–73*, 207–263. London. The British School at Athens.

Castiglioni, O. C. (1964) I "reniformi" della Lagozza, *Comum – Miscellanea di scritti in onore di Federico Frigerio*, 129–171. Como Noseda.

Charalampos, P. (2003) Ελεφάντινες ράβδοι στις Σθλλογές του Κυπριακού Μουσείου, *Report of the Department of Antiquies, Cyprus*, 139–144.

Chohadzhiev, A. (2004) Weights and/or spools: distribution and interpretation of the Neolithic "cocoon-like loom-weights" in Noikolov, V., Băčvarov, K. and Kalchev, P. (eds), *Prehistoric Thrace*, 231-238. Sofia; Stara Zagora. Institute of Archaeology with Museum, Sofia; Regional Museum of History, Stara Zagora.

Crawford, H. E. W. (1973) Mesopotamia's invisible exports in the third millenium BC, *World Archaeology*, 5, 232–241.

Cremer, M. (1996) Antike Spinnrocken, *Boreas*, 19, 241–245.

Crewe, L. (1998) *Spindle Whorls: A Study of Form, Function and Decoration in Prehistoric Bronze Age Cyprus*. Jonsered. Paul Åström.

Crowfoot, G. M. (1931) *Methods of Hand Spinning in Egypt and the Sudan*. Halifax. Bankfield Museum.

Crowfoot, G. M. (1936–37) Of the warp-weighted loom, *Annual of the British School at Athens*, 37, 36–47.

Cutler, J., Andersson Strand, E. and Nosch, M.-L., (2013) Textile production in Quartier Mu, in Poursat, J.-Cl. (ed.), *Fouilles exécutées à Malia. Le Quartier Mu V. Vie quotidienne et techniques au Minoen Moyen II*, 95–119. Athens. École Française d'Athènes.

Dabney, M. K. (1996a) Ceramic loomweights and spindle whorls, in Shaw, J. W. and Shaw, M. C. (eds), *Kommos I. The Kommos Region and Houses of the Minoan Town. Part 2. The Minoan Hilltop and Hillside Houses*, 244–262. Princeton. Princeton University Press.

Dabney, M. K. (1996b) Jewellery and seals, in Shaw, J. W. and Shaw, M. C. (eds), *Kommos I. The Kommos Region and Houses of the Minoan Town. Part 2. The Minoan Hilltop and Hillside Houses*, 263–269. Princeton. Princeton University Press.

Davidson, G. R. (1952) *Corinth: Results of Excavations Conducted by the American School of Classical Studies at Athens. XII. The Minor Objects*. Cambridge, Mass. Harvard University Press.

Dinç, R. (1999) Ein Spinnwirtel mit phrygischer Inschrift, *Kadmos*, 38, 65–72.

Dothan, T. (1963) Spinning-bowls, *Israel Exploration Journal*, 13, 97–112.

Dunning, C. (1992) Le filage, *Helvetica Archaeologica*, 23, 43–50.

Eibner, A. (2005) Die Frau mit der Spindel. Zum Aussagewert einer archäologischen Quelle, in Török (ed.), *Hallstatt Kolloquium Verzprém 1984*, 39–48. Budapest.

Ergin, G. (2007) Anatolian women in Linear B texts: A general review of the evidence, in Alparslan, M., Doğan-Alparslan, M. and Peker, H. (eds), *Belkıs Dinçol ve Ali Dinçol'a Armağan Vita/Festschrift in Honor of Belkıs Dinçol and Ali Dinçol*, 269–283. Istanbul. Ege Yayınları.

Evely, D. (2000) *Minoan Crafts: Tools And Techniques. An Introduction*. Göteborg. Paul Åström.

Evely, D. (2006) The small finds, in Evely, D. (ed.), *Lefkandi IV. The Bronze Age. The Late Helladic IIIC Settlement at Xeropolis*, 265–302. London. The British School at Athens.

Evely, D. (2003) The stone, bone, ivory, bronze and clay finds, in Mountjoy, P. A. (ed.), *Knossos. The South House*, 167–194. London. The British School at Athens.

Farke, H. (1993) Textile Reste von Dietzhausen und Schwarza, *Alt Thüringen*, 27, 109–112.

Faxon, H. (1932) A model of an Ancient Greek loom, *Bulletin of the Metropolitan Museum of Art*, 27 (3), 70–71.

Feldtkeller, A. (2003) Nierenförmige Webgewichte – wie funktionieren sie?, *Archaeological Textiles Newsletter*, 37, 16–19.

Ferrari, G. (2002) *Figures of Speech: Men and Maiden in Ancient Greece*. Chicago and London. The University of Chicago Press.

Feugère, M. (2004) L'instrumentum, support d'écrit, *Gallia*, 61, 53–65.

Fischer, P. M. (2010) Textile production at Tell 'Abu al-Kharaz, Jordan Valley. https://openaccess.leidenuniv.nl/bitstream/1887/15866/13/07+ASLU+19+Chapter+7.pdf, accessed 20/05/2011.

Fol, A. and Schmitt, R. (2000) A Linear A text on a clay reel from Drama, south-east Bulgaria?, *Prähistorische Zeitschrift*, 75, 56–61.

Folk Art Museum – Nafplion (1988). Peloponnesian Folklore Foundation.

Frankel, D. and Webb, J. M. (1996) *Marki Alonia: An Early and Middle Bronze Age Town in Cyprus, Excavations 1990–1994*. Göteborg. Paul Åström.

Friend, G. and Nashef, K. (1998) *Tell Taannek 1963–1968. III: 2, The Loom Weights*. Birzeit. Birzeit University.

Frödin, O. and Persson, A. W. (1924–1925) *Rapport préliminaire sur les fouilles d'Asiné, 1922–1924*. Lund. C. W. K. Gleerup.

Furumark, A. (1941) *The Chronology of Mycenaean Pottery*. Stockholm. Kungl. vitterhets historie och antikuitets akademien.

Gachet-Bizollon, J. (2007) *Ras Shamra-Ougarit XVI. Les ivoires d'Ougarit et l'art des ivoiriers du Levant au Bronze Recént*. Paris. Éditions Recherche sur les Civilisations.

Gal, Z. (1989) Loomweights or jar stoppers? *Israel Exploration Journal*, 39, 281–283.

Gevirtz, S. (1967) A spindle whorl with Phoenician inscription, *Journal of Near Eastern Studies*, 26 (1), 13–16.

Gimbutas, M. (1989) *The Language of the Goddess*. London. Thames & Hudson.

Gleba, M. (2000) Textile production at Poggio Civitate (Murlo) in the 7th c. BC, in Cardon, D. and Feugère, M. (eds), *Archéologie des textiles, des origins au Ve siècle*, 77–81. Montpellier. Éditions Monique Mergoil.

Gleba, M. (2008) *Textile Production in Pre-Roman Italy*. Ancient Textiles Series 4. Oxford. Oxbow Books.

Godart, L. (1994) Les écritures crétoises et les basin méditerranéen, *Comptes-rendus de l'Académie des Inscriptions et Belles Lettres*, 138 (3), 707–731.

Goldman, H. (1956) *Excavations at Gozlu Kule, Tarsus. 2. From the Neolithic through the Bronze Age*. Princeton. Princeton University Press.

Good, I. (2004) Textiles as medium of exchange in third millenium BC Western Africa, in Mair, V. H. (ed.), *Contact and Exchange in the Ancient World*, 342–368. Honolulu, University of Hawaii Press.

Gottschalk, R. (1996) Ein spätrömischer Spinnrocken aus Elfenbein, *Archäologisches Korrespondenzblatt*, 26, 483–500.

Granger-Taylor, H. (1998) Evidence for linen yarn preparation in ancient Egypt – the hanks of fibre strips and the balls of prepared rove from Lahun in the Petrie Museum of Egyptian Archaeology, University College London (UC 7421, 7509 and 7510) in Quirke, S. (ed.), *Lahun Studies*, 103–107. Surrey. SIA publishing.

Granger-Taylor, H. and Quirke, S. (2002) *Textile production and clothing*, Digital Egypt for Universities <http://www.digitalegypt.ucl.ac.uk/textil/tools.html>, accessed 06.08.2011.

Grömer, K. (2005) Efficiency and technique – experiments with original spindle whorls, in Bichler, P., Grömer, K., Hofmann-de Keijzer, R, Kern, A. and Reschreiter, H. (eds), *Hallstatt Textiles. Technical Analysis, Scientific Investigation and Experiment on Iron Age Textiles*, 107–116. Oxford. Archaeopress.

Grömer, K. (2010) *Prähistorische Textilkunst in Mitteleuropa. Geschichte des Handwerkes und der Kleidung vor den Römern*. Wien. Wien Naturhistorisches Museum.

Götze, A. (1902) Die Kleingeräte aus Metall, Stein, Knochen, Thon und ähnlichen Stoffen, in Dörpfeld, W. (ed.), *Troja und Ilion. Ergebnisse der Ausgrabungen in den vorgeschichtlichen und historischen Schichten von Ilion 1870–1894*, 320–423. Athens. Beck and Barth.

Hageman, R. K. (2006) A continuous thread: flax spinning in ancient Egypt, *Ostracon*, 17 (1), 14–16.

Hald, M. (1980) *Ancient Danish Textiles from Bogs and Burials*. Copenhagen. The National Museum of Denmark.

Hallager, E. and Hallager, B. P. (2000) *The Greek-Swedish Excavations at the Agia Aikaterini Square, Kastelli, Khania 1970–1987: Results of the Excavations under the Direction of Yannis Tzedakis and Carl-Gustaf Styrenius. II. The Late Minoan IIIC settlement*. Stockholm. Paul Åström.

Halstead, P. (1990) Present to past in the Pindhos: specialisation and diversification in mountain economies, *Rivista di Studi Liguri*, 56, 61–80.

Halstead, P. (1998) Ask the fellows who lop the hay: leaf-fodder in the mountains of northwest Greece, *Rural History*, 9, 211–234.

Hilse, R. (2001) Troianische Spinnwirtel, *Mitteilungen aus dem Heinrich-Schliemann-Museum Ankershagen*, 7, 135–150.

Hirschberg, W. and Janata, A. (1980) *Technologie und Ergologie in der Völkerkunde*. 3rd edition. Berlin. Dietrich Reimer.

Hoffmann, M. (1964) *The Warp-Weighted Loom: Studies in the History and Technology of an Ancient Implement*. Oslo. Universitetsforlaget.

Holm, C. (1996) Experiment med slåndspinning, in Andersson, E. (ed.), *Textilproduktion i arkeologisk kontext. En metodstudie av yngre järnåldersboplatser i Skåne*, 111–116. Lund. Institute of Archaeology.

Homan, M. M. (2004) Beer and its drinkers: an ancient Near Eastern love story, *Near Eastern Archaeology*, 67 (2), 84–95.

Huber, A. (2005) *Zurich-Alpenquai IX. Keramische Kleinfunde und Sonderformen*. Zürich. FO Publishing.

Hundt, H. J. (1968) Die verkohlten Reste von Geweben, Geflechten, Seilen, Schnüren und Holzgeräten aus Grab 200 von El Cigarralejo, *Madrider Mitteilungen*, 8, 187–205.

Hägg, I. (1996) Textil und Tracht als Zeugnis von Bevölkerungsverschiebungen, *Archäologische Informationen*, 19, 135–147.

Iakovidis, S. E. (1969–1971) Περατή. Το νεκροταφείον. Α. Οι τάφοι και τα εθρήματα. Β. Παπατηρήσεις. Γ. Πίνακες. Athens. Archaeological Society of Athens.

Iakovidis, S. E. (1977) On the use of Mycenaean 'buttons', *Annual of the British School at Athens*, 72, 113–119.

Iakovidis, S. E. (2001) *Gla and the Kopais in the 13th Century BC*. Athens. Archaeological Society of Athens.

Joachim, H.-E. (2002) *Porz-Lind. Ein mittel- bis spätlatènezeitlicher Siedlungsplatz im 'Linder Bruch' (Stadt Köln)*. Mainz. Philipp von Zabern.

Johl, F. (1917) *Die Webstühle der Griechen und Römer*. Leipzig. Noske.

Jovaiša, E. (2001) The Balts and amber, in Butrimas, A. (ed.), *Baltic Amber*, 149–156. Vilnius. Vilniaus Dail es Akademijos Leidykla.

Keller, F. (1861) Pfahlbauten, Vierter Bericht, *Mitteilungen der Antiquarischen Gesellschaft in Zürich*, 1 (14), 14–23.

Keuls, E. C. (1983) Attic vase painting and the home textile industry, in Moon, W. G. (ed.), *Ancient Greek Art and Iconography*, 209–30. Madison. University of Wisconsin Press.

Kilian-Dirlmeier, I. (1984a) Der dorische Peplos: ein archäologisches Zeugnis der dorischen Wanderung? *Archäologisches Korrespondenzblatt*, 14, 281–91.

Kilian-Dirlmeier, I. (1984b) *Nadeln der frühhelladischen bis archaischen Zeit von der Peloponnes*. Munich. Beck.

Kilian, K. (1988) Ausgrabungen in Tiryns 1982/1983, *Archäologischer Anzeiger*, 105–151.

Killen, J. T. (1984) The textile industries at Pylos and Knossos, in Shelmerdine, C. W. and Palaima, T. G. (eds), *Pylos Comes Alive. Industry and Administration in a Mycenaean Palace*, 49–63. New York. Fordham University.

Killen, J. T. (1988) Epigraphy and interpretation in Knossos women and cloth records, in Olivier, J. P., Bennett, E. L. and Palaima, T. G. (eds), *Texts, Tablets, and Scribes: Studies in Mycenaean Epigraphy and Economy Offered to Emmett L. Bennett, Jr.*, 166–183. Salamanca. Universidad de Salamanca.

Kimakowicz-Winnicki, M. V. (1910) *Die Spinn- und Webewerkzeuge, Entwicklung und Anwendung in vorgeschichtlicher Zeit Europas*. Würzburg. C. Kabitzsch.

Korfmann, M. O. (1981) *Demircihüyük. Die Ergebnisse der Ausgrabungen 1975–1978. 1. Architektur, Stratigraphie und Befunde*. Mainz. Philipp von Zabern.

Koster, J. B. (1976) From spindle to loom: weaving in the southern Argolid, *Expedition*, 19 (1), 29–39.

Kreen-Leeb, A. (2001) Eine trichterbecherzeitliche Grube mit nierenförmigen Webgewichten von Spielberg bei Melk, Niederösterreich, *Preistoria Alpina*, 37, 118–139.

Kurzynski, K. von (1996) *"... und ihre Hosen nennen sie bracas": Textilfunde und Textiltechnologie der Hallstatt- und Latènezeit und ihr Kontext*. Espelkamp. Leidorf.

La Baume, W. (1955) *Die Entwicklung des Textilhandwerks in Alteuropa*. Bonn. Habelt.

Lass, E. H. E. (2006) Soil flotation and quantitative analysis, in Stager, L. E., Schloen, J. D. and Master, D. M. (eds), *Ashkelon 1. Introduction and Overview (1985–2006)*, 195–206. Winona Lake. Eisenbrauns.

Leuzinger, U. (2002) Textilherstellung, in Capitani, A. de, Deschler-Erb, S., Leuzinger, U., Marti-Grädel, E., Schibler, J. (eds), *Die jungsteinzeitliche Seeufersiedlung*

Arbon-Bleiche 3. Funde, 115–134. Frauenfeld. Amt für Archäologie.

Liu, R. (1978) Spindle whorls. Part I: some comments and speculations, *The Bead Journal*, 3, 87–103.

Marthari, M. (2004) Ios, Archäologisches Museum, in Pini, I. (ed.), *Corpus der minoischen und mykenischen Siegel. 1. Kleinere griechische Sammlungen V*, 281–289. Berlin. Gebr. Mann Verlag.

McCorriston, J. (1997) The fibre revolution. Textile extensification, alienation, and social stratification in ancient Mesopotamia, *Current Anthropology*, 38, 517–549.

Médard, F. (2000) L'artisanat textile au Néolithique. L'exemple de Delley-Portalban II (Suisse) 3272–2462 avant J.C., *Préhistoires*, 4, 113–118.

Metzger, M. (1993) *Kamid el-Loz 8. Die spätbronzezeitlichen Tempelanlagen. Die Kleinfunde*. Bonn. Habelt.

Michel, C. and Nosch, M.-L. (eds) (2010) *Textile Terminologies in the Ancient Near East and Mediterranean from the Third to the First Millennnia BC*. Ancient Textiles Series 8. Oxford. Oxbow Books.

Michel, C. and Veenhof, K. R. (2010) The textiles traded by the Assyrians in Anatolia (19th–18th centuries BC), in Nosch, M.-L. and Michel, C. (eds), *Textile Terminologies in the Ancient Near East and the Mediterranean Area from the 3rd to the 1st Millenium BC*, 210–271. Ancient Textile Series 8. Oxford. Oxbow Books.

Murra, J. V. (1962) Cloth and its functions in the Inca State, *American Anthropologist*, 64, 710–728.

Neugebauer-Maresch, C. (1995) Mittelneolithikum: Die Bemaltkeramik, in Neugebauer, J.-W. (ed.), *Jungsteinzeit im Osten Österreichs*, 57–107. St. Pölten. Niederösterreichisches Pressehaus.

Nixon, L. (1999) Women, children, and weaving, in Betancourt, P., Karageorghis, V., Laffineur, R. and Niemeier, W.-D. (eds), *Meletemata. Studies in Aegean Archaeology Presented to Malcolm H. Wiener as he Enters His 65th Year*, 561–567. Liège. Université de Liège.

Nordquist, G. (1997) Male craft and female industry, in Laffineur, R. and Betancourt, P. (eds), *TEXNH. Craftsmen, Craftswomen and Craftsmanship in the Aegean Bronze Age*, 533–537. Liège. Université de Liège.

Nosch, M.-L. (1998) L'administration des textiles en Crète centrale, hors des séries Lc/Le/Ln, *Bulletin de Correspondance Hellénique*, 122/2, 404–406.

Nosch, M.-L. (2003) The women at work in the Linear B tablets, in Strömberg, A. and Larsson Lovén, L. (eds), *Gender, Cult, and Culture in the Ancient World from Mycenae to Byzantium*, 12–26. Sävedalen. Paul Åström.

Nosch, M.-L. (2007) *The Knossos Od Series*. Vienna. Österreichische Akademie der Wissenschaften.

Obladen-Kauder, J. (1996) Die Kleinfunde aus Ton, Knochen und Metall, in Korfmann, M. (ed.), *Demircihüyük: die Ergebnisse der Ausgrabungen 1975–1978. 4. Die Kleinfunde*, 207–310. Mainz. Philipp von Zabern.

Ochsenschlager, E. L. (1993a) Sheep: ethnoarchaeology at Al-Hiba, *Bulletin on Sumerian Agriculture*, 7, 33–42.

Ochsenschlager, E. L. (1993b) Village weavers: ethnoarchaeology at Al-Hiba, *Bulletin on Sumerian Agriculture*, 7, 43–62.

Onians, R. B. (1924) On the knees of the gods, *The Classical Review*, 38 (1–2), 2–6.

Pantelia, M. C. (1993) Spinning and weaving: ideas of domestic order in Homer, *American Journal of Philology*, 114, 493–501.

Peet, T. E. and Woolley, C. L. (1923) *The City of Akhenaten*. London. Paul Kegan.

Petrie, W. M. F. (1917) *Tools and Weapons Illustrated by the Egyptian Collection in University College, London*. London. British School of Archaeology in Egypt.

Peyronel, L. (2004) *Materiali e Studi Archeologici di Ebla. IV. Gli strumenti di tessitura dall'età del Bronzo al Periodo Persiano*. Rome. Università degli Studi di Roma "La Sapienza".

Pfälzner, P. (2001) *Haus und Haushalt. Wohnformen des dritten Jahrtausends vor Christus in Nordmesopotamien*. Mainz. Philipp von Zabern.

Popham, M., Evely, D. and Sackett, H. (2006) The site and its excavation, in Evely, D. (ed.), *Lefkandi IV. The Bronze Age. The Late Helladic IIIC Settlement at Xeropolis*, 1–136. London. The British School at Athens.

Poursat, J.-C. (2012) Of looms and pebbles. Weaving at Minoan costal settlements, in M.-L., Nosch and Laffineur, R. (eds), *KOSMOS. Jewellery, Adornment and Textiles in the Aegean Bronze Age*, 31–34. Liège. Peeters.

Prien, R. (2005) *Archäologie und Migration. Vergleichende Studien zur archäologischen Nachweisbarkeit von Migrationsbewegungen*. Bonn. Habelt.

Rabe, N. (1996) Perforierte Tonkugeln von Tell el-Oreme, *Zeitschrift des Deutschen Palästinavereins*, 112, 101–121.

Rahmstorf, L. (2003) Clay spools from Tiryns and other contemporary sites. An indication of foreign influence in LH III C?, in Kyparissi-Apostolika, N. and Papakonstantinou, M. (eds), *Η περιφέρεια του μυκηναϊκού κόσμου / The Periphery of the Mycenaean World*, 397–415. Athens. Ministry of Culture.

Rahmstorf, L. (2005) Ethnicity and changes in weaving technology in Cyprus and the eastern Mediterranean in the 12th century BC, in Karageorghis, V. (ed.), *Cyprus: Religion and Society: From the Late Bronze Age to the End of the Archaic Period*, 143–169. Möhnesee-Wamel. Bibliopolis.

Rahmstorf, L. (2008) *Kleinfunde aus Tiryns, Terrakotta, Stein, Bein und Glas/Fayence vornehmlich aus der Spätbronzezeit*. Wiesbaden. Ludwig Reichert.

Rast-Eicher, A. (2008) *Textilien, Wolle, Schafe der Eisenzeit in der Schweiz*. Basel. Archäologie Schweiz.

Reinhard, J. (1992) Etoffes cordées et métiers à pierres, *Helvetia Archaeologica*, 90, 51–55.

Reuthner, R. (2006) *Wer webte Athenes Gewänder? die Arbeit von Frauen im antiken Griechenland*. Frankfurt. Campus.

Richmond, J. (2006) Textile production in prehistoric Anatolia: a study of three Early Bronze Age sites, *Ancient Near Eastern Studies*, 43, 203–238.

Rooijakkers, T. (2005) Unravelling Beni Hasan: textile production in the Beni Hasan tomb paintings, *Archaeological Textiles Newsletter*, 41, 2–13.

Rutschmann, H. (1988) Webgewichte als Bildträger, *Antike Welt*, 19 (2), 46–55.

Ræder Knudsen, L. (2007) "Translating" archaeological textiles, in Gillis, C. and Nosch, M.-L. (eds), *Ancient Textiles. Production, Craft and Society*. Ancient Textiles Series 1. Oxford. Oxbow Books.

Sayce, A. H. (1881) Die Inschriften von Hissarlik, in Schliemann, H. (ed.), *Ilios. Stadt und Land der Trojaner*, 766–781. Leipzig. Brockhaus.

Schade-Lindig, S. and Schmitt, A. (2003) Außergewöhnliche Funde aus der bandkeramischen Siedlung Bad Nauheim – Nieder-Mörlen, "Auf dem Hempler" (Wetteraukreis): Spinnwirtel und Webgewichte, *Germania*, 81 (1), 1–24.

Schierer, I. (1987) Ein Webstuhlbefund aus Gars-Thunau. Rekonstruktionsversuch und Funktionsanalyse, *Archaeologia Austriaca*, 71, 29–87.

Schlabow, K. (1937) *Germanische Tuchmacher der Bronzezeit*. Neumünster. Karl Wachholtz.

Schlabow, K. (1965) *Der Thorsberger Prachtmantel. Schlüssel zum altgermanischen Webstuhl*. Neumünster. K. Wachholtz.

Schlabow, K. (1976) *Textilfunde der Eisenzeit in Norddeutschland*. Neumünster. K. Wachholtz.

Schlabow, K. (1978) Brettchenweberei, *Reallexikon der Germanischen Altertumskunde*, 3, 445–450.

Schliemann, H. (1878) *Mykenae. Bericht über meine Forschungen und Entdeckungen in Mykenae und Tiryns*. Darmstadt. Wissenschaftliche Buchgesellschaft.

Schliemann, H. (1881) *Ilios. Stadt und Land der Trojaner*. Leipzig. Brockhaus.

Schliemann, H. (1886) *Der prähistorische Palast der Könige von Tiryns*. Leipzig. F. A. Brockhaus.

Schmidt, E. F. (1932) *The Alishar Hüyük. Seasons of 1928 and 1929*. The University of Chicago. Oriental Institute Publications.

Schmidt, H. (1902) *Heinrich Schliemann's Sammlung trojanischer Altertümer*. Berlin. Reimer.

Schütte, M. (1956) Brettchenweberei, *CIBA-Rundschau*, 128, 23–34.

Shamir, O. (1996) Loom-weights and whorls, in Ariel, D. T. (ed.) *Excavations at the City of David 1978–1985 Directed by Yigal Shiloh IV*, 135–170. Jerusalem. Hebrew University of Jerusalem.

Sheffer, A. (1981) The use of preforated clay balls on the warp-weighted loom, *Tel Aviv – Journal of the Tel Aviv University, Institute of Archaeology*, 3, 81–83.

Siennicka, M. (2012) Textile production in Early Helladic Tiryns, in Nosch, M.-L. and Laffineur, R. (eds), *KOSMOS. Jewellery, Adornment and Textiles in the Aegean Bronze Age*, 65–75. Liège. Peeters.

Smith, J. S. (2001) Bone weaving tools of the Late Bronze Age, in P. M. Fischer (ed.), *Contributions to the Archaeology and History of the Bronze and Iron Ages in the Eastern Mediterranean. Studies in Honour of Paul Åström*, 83–90. Vienna. Austrian Archaeological Institute.

Smith, J. S. (2012) Tapestries in the Mediterranean Late Bronze Age, in Nosch, M.-L. and R. Laffineur (eds), *KOSMOS: Jewellery, Adornment and Textiles in the Aegean Bronze Age*, 241–250. Liège. Peeters.

Snyder, J. (1981) The web of song: weaving imagery in Homer and the lyric poets, *Classical Journal*, 76 (3), 193–196.

Sollberger, E. (1986) *Archivi reali di Ebla. VIII. Administrative Texts Chiefly Concerning Textiles*. Rome. Missione archeologica italiana in Siria.

Spindler, K. and Gallay, G. (1973) *Kupferzeitliche Siedlung und Begräbnisstätten von Matacães in Portugal*. Mainz. Philipp von Zabern

Stager, L. E., Schloen, J. D. and Master, D. M. (eds) (2008) *Ashkelon 1. Introduction and Overview (1985–2006)*. Winona Lake. Eisenbrauns.

Stolte, H. (1990) Technik des Brettchenwebens, *Experimentelle Archäologie in Deutschland. Archäologische Mitteilungen aus Nordwestdeutschland Beih.*, 4, 434–437.

Strobel, M. (2000) *Die Schussenrieder Siedlung Taubried I (Bad Buchau, Kr. Biberach). Ein Beitrag zu den Siedlungsstrukturen und zur Chronologie des frühen und mittleren Jungneolithikums in Oberschwaben*. Stuttgart. K. Theiss.

Strommenger, E. (1970) Die Grabungen in Habuba Kabira-Süd, *Mitteilungen der Deutschen Orientgesellschaft*, 102, 59–81.

Terzijska-Ignatova, S. (2004) Steingewichte aus der frühen Bronzezeit aus dem Tell Junacite, in Nikolov, V. and Bãčvarov, K. (eds), *Von Domica bis Drama. Gedenkschrift für Jan Lichardus*, 147–153. Sofia. Institute of Archaeology with Museum.

Tiedemann, E. J. and Jakes, K. A. (2006) An exploration of prehistoric spinning technology: spinning efficiency and technology transition, *Archaeometry*, 48 (2), 293–307.

Trinkl, E. (1994) Ein Set aus Spindel, Spinnwirtel und Rocken aus einem Sarkophag in Ephesos, *Jahreshefte des Österreichischen Archäologischen Institutes in Wien*, 63, 81–86.

Tzachili, I. (1990) All important yet elusive: cloth and cloth-making evidence at Akrotiri, in Hardy, D. A., Doumas, C. G., Sakellarakis, J. A. and Warren, P. M. (eds), *Thera and the Aegean World III: 1*, 407–419. London. The Thera Foundation.

Tzachili, I. (1997) Υφαντική και υφάντρες στο προιστορικό Αιγαίο. 2000–1000 π.Χ. *(Yfantike kai Yfantres sto Proistoriki Aigaio)*. Crete. Univeristy Press of Crete.

Tzachili, I. (2001) Counting and recording textiles in the Mycenaean archives of Knossos, in Michailidou, A. (ed.), *Manufacture and Measurement. Counting, Measuring and Recording. Craft Items in Early Aegean Societies*, 176–193. Athens. National Hellenic Research Foundation.

Veenhof, K. R. (1972) *Aspects of Old Assyrian Trade and its Terminology*. Leiden. Brill.

Vogelsang-Eastwood, G. (1990) Crescent loom weights?, *Oriens Antiquus*, 29, 99–113.

Vogelsang-Eastwood, G. (2000) Textiles, in Nicholson, P. T. and Shaw, I. (eds), *Ancient Egyptian Materials and Technology*, 268–298. Cambridge and New York. Cambridge University Press.

Vogt, E. (1937) *Geflechte und Gewebe der Steinzeit*. Basel. E. Birkhäuser & cie.

von Stokar, W. (1938) *Spinnen und Weben bei den Germanen*. Leipzig. Curt Kabitzsch Verlag.

Wace, A. J. B. (1948) Weaving or embroidery, *American Journal of Archaeology*, 52, 51–55.

Wace, A. J. B. (1932) *Chamber Tombs at Mycenae*. Oxford. Society of Antiquaries.

Waetzoldt, H. (1972) *Untersuchungen zur neusumerischen Textilindustrie*. Rome. Istituto per l'Oriente.

Wagner-Hasel, B. (2000) *Der Stoff der Gaben. Kultur und Politik des Schenkens und Tauschens im archaischen Griechenland*. Frankfurt. Campus Verlag.

Wagner-Hasel, B. (2001) Wanderwirtschaft und Migration von Frauen in der Antike. Einige vorläufige Überlegungen, in Krauss, M. and Sonnabend, H. (eds), *Frauen und Migration*, 94–116. Stuttgart. Franz Steiner.

Wallrodt, S. (2002) Ritual activity in Late Classical Ilion: the evidence from a fourth century B.C. deposit of loomweights and spindlewhorls, *Studia Troica*, 12, 179–196.

Walton Rogers, P. (1997) *Textile production at 16–22 Coppergate (The Archaeology of York 17:2)*. York. Council for British Archaeology.

Warren, P. M. (1972) *Myrtos: An Early Bronze Age Settlement in Crete*. London. The British School at Athens.

Webb, J. (2002) New evidence for the origins of textile production in Bronze Age Cyprus, *Antiquity*, 76, 364–371.

Weingarten, J. (1990) The sealing structure of Karahöyük and some administrative links with Phaistos on Crete, *Oriens Antiquus*, 29, 63–95.

Wheeler, M. (1982) Loom weights and spindle whorls, in Kenyon, K. M. and Holland, T. A. (eds), *Excavations at Jericho. 4. The Pottery Type Series and Other Finds*, 622–637. London. British School of Archaeology in Jerusalem.

Wild, J. P. (1970) *Textile Manufacture in the Northern Roman Provinces*. Cambridge. Cambridge University Press.

Winiger, J. (1995) Die Bekleidung des Eismannes und die Anfänge der Weberei nördlich der Alpen, in Spindler, K., Rastbichler-Zissernıg, E., Wilfing, H., Nedden, D. zur and Nothdurfter, H. (eds), *The Man in the Ice 2*, 119–187. Innsbruck. Universität Innsbruck.

Woolley, L. (1955) *Alalakh: An Account of the Excavations at Tell Atchana in the Hatay, 1937–1949*. London. Society of Antiquaries.

Yakar, J. and Taffet, A. (2007) The spiritual connotations of the spindle and spinning: selected cases from ancient Anatolia and neighboring lands, in Alparslan, M., Doğan-Alparslan, M. and Peker, H. (eds), *Belkıs Dinçol ve Ali Dinçol'a Armağan Vita / Festschrift in honor of Belkıs Dinçol and Ali Dinçol*, 781–788. Istanbul. Ege Yayinlari.

Yalçın, Ü., Pulak, C. and Slotta, R. (2005) *Das Schiff von Uluburun. Welthandel vor 3000 Jahren. Katalog der Ausstellung des Deutschen Bergbau-Museums Bochum vom 15. Juli 2005 bis 16. Juli 2006*. Bochum. Deutsches Bergbau-Museum.

Yasur-Landau, A. (2009) Behavioral patterns in transition: eleventh-century B. C. E. innovation in domestic textile production, in Schloen, J. D. (ed.), *Exploring the Longue Durée: Essays in Honor of Lawrence E. Stager*, 507–515. Winona Lake. Eisenbrauns.

Yasur-Landau, A. (2010) *The Philistines and Aegean Migration at the End of the Late Bronze Age*. Cambridge. Cambridge University Press.

Zaccagnini, C. (1986) The terminology of weight measures for wool at Ebla, in Fronzaroli, P. (ed.), *Studies on the Language of Ebla*, 189–204. Firenze. Istituto di linguistica e di lingue orientali, Università di Firenze.

Zimmermann, T. (2004) Abstrakte "Idole" aus Troia, *Archäologisches Korrespondenzblatt*, 34, 31–36.

Zimmermann, W. H. (1988) Frühe Darstellungen vom Gewichtswebstuhl auf Felszeichnungen in der Val Camonica, Lombardei, in Bender Jørgensen, L., Magnus, B. and Munksgaard, E. (eds), *Archaeological Textiles: Report from the 2nd NESAT Symposium*, 26–38. Copenhagen. Copenhagen University.

Zurbach, J. (2003) Schriftähnliche Zeichen und Töpferzeichen in Troia, *Studia Troica*, 13, 113–130.

CHAPTER 1.2

An introduction to experimental archaeology and textile research

Linda Olofsson

Experimental archaeology is a frequently used element in scholarly work within textile research. At the emergence of the field as a discipline, however, only a few scholars from northern Europe played an important role investigating archaeological textiles and reconstructing them. Subsequently, scholars from all over Europe have contributed with experiments and this trend of using experiments within textile archaeology has expanded significantly since the 1980s.

This chapter starts by discussing experimental archaeology, and presents how this field of research has changed and developed from its early beginning until 2007. It then presents the trends and developments specifically of textile experimental archaeology, through a focus on textile tools.

What is understood by *experimental archaeology*?

Experimental archaeology can be seen as a way to gain comparative knowledge that can be used in interpretations of the past. Experimental archaeology achieves its results from practical tests performed today, supplying answers to questions related to archaeological data. Different levels of systematisation and control

over experiments is always an issue. However, it is of vital importance that experiments are well documented if the results are to be applied in current and future research. It is considered that experimental archaeology developed as part of the positivistic research approach applied within the processual archaeology of the 1960s and 1970s (Brattli and Johnsen 1989, 49; Olsen 1997, 53, 59–62). The positivist research paradigm advocates that archaeological material should be interpreted by use of procedures similar to those of the natural sciences, with the aim of reaching objective knowledge free from subjective influences. This approach has been criticised by proponents of the post-processual movement that came into being in the 1980s. The criticism was directed at the suggestion that experimental archaeology was a methodology for conducting objective studies. One of the post-processual arguments was that designs of experiments were influenced by subjective values of the present, which would have affected the outcome of any experiment (Brattli and Johnsen 1989). However, this critique was directed at archaeology in general, suggesting that archaeological interpretations are hardly exempted from influences of cultural, economical and political ideology

(Trigger 2006). Concurrently, and perhaps as a consequence of this criticism, different scholars began to question what actually constituted experimental archaeology (Coles 1983, 79–81; Johansson 1983, 81–83; Malina 1983, 69–78), and the subject of defining and developing experimental archaeology was discussed (Johansson 1987, 2–4). Several attempts were made to define the concept, some trying to divide experimental archaeology into separate areas such as "experiments within archaeology" and "experimental archaeology" (Olausson 1987, 7). Today, experimental archaeology consists of a range of several activities. From these activities, in a simplified form, at least two groups are distinguishable, *i.e.* first, experimental archaeology with a research oriented objective and second, experimental archaeology with an educational objective. In this volume, the research oriented approach will be considered, since it is used here as a methodology within the field of textile research.

Textiles and tools – constructed, reconstructed and tested

The beginning – looms and reconstructions in focus

The interest in constructing prehistoric textiles began before archaeological textiles were brought into scholarly research. For example, in the 19th century, great enthusiasm for the Vikings was expressed in Scandinavia. The so-called "Viking style" was adopted in different types of anachronistic and romanticized social events. Following this trend, people also dressed up as Vikings (Lönnroth 1997, 240–241). The attempts at recreating old costumes were only minimally connected to the archaeological material and not at all to experimental archaeology.

The epoch of archaeological textiles as the focus of textile research developed after World War I. Characteristic of this epoch was an interest in analysing the applied material and technology (Geijer 1979). Technical knowledge based on an analysis of archaeological textiles promoted an early development of reconstruction work and experiments on the subject of textiles. Both the Danish scholar Margrethe Hald and the German scholar Karl Schlabow represent this field of research.

In the first half of the 20th century, Hald and H. C. Broholm published *Costumes of the Bronze Age in Denmark* (Broholm and Hald 1940). This, together with Hald's *Ancient Danish Textiles from Bogs and Burials* (Hald 1980), has served as a standard work within textile archaeology until the present day. In addition to the presentation of exceptional dresses excavated in Denmark, these two publications deal with experiments in several ways. For example, a whole chapter is devoted to weaving tests with an upright loom (Broholm and Hald 1940, 130–134). Several of Hald's own reconstructed textiles are referred to (Broholm and Hald 1940, 139, 154, 155). These copies of dresses were, for example, used on living models to figure out how they were worn (Figs 1.2.1 and 1.2.2). Broholm writes that "consequently it is necessary to try through *experiments* with a dress of the same character and size as the original to clear up the problems" (Broholm and Hald 1940, 155). Their work contains an apparent experimental approach, well founded in the archaeological material, although the aim seems to have been that of producing copies (Broholm and Hald 1940; Hald 1950, 1980). Almost at the same time as Hald, Schlabow studied the Danish archaeological textiles. In 1937, his book *Germanischen Tuchmacher der Bronzezeit* was published, in which he refers to reconstructed Bronze Age textiles (Schlabow 1937). His later work, *Der Thorsberger Prachtmantel* contained reconstruction work and a discussion concerning what loom was used for producing the Thorsberg cloak (Schlabow 1951). Schlabow was also the founder and first director of the Textilmuseum in Neumünster (Harbeck 1982). Both Hald and Schlabow continued working with Bronze Age and Iron Age textiles, with great insight into technological matters. Characteristic of early textile experimental archaeology was the distinct focus on what loom was used, as well as weaving technology and reconstructions.

Ethnography and its importance within experimental archaeology

Experimental archaeology has strong ties to the use of ethnographic parallels in archaeology. Both experimental archaeology and ethno-archaeology are considered to have been developed in the same research tradition related to the use of analogies in archaeology.

Some crafts of interest to archaeology have continued to be practised in the present (Fig. 1.2.3). There is thus information readily available, which, when employed carefully, can be used in scholarly work. For example, in the 1950s, the Norwegian scholar Marta Hoffman started her work on the warp-weighted loom with a focus on the living traditions of its use in the Nordic countries (Hoffmann 1964). Ethnographic knowledge of textile production, such as the use of the warp-weighted loom and other tools, has played an important role in the understanding of ancient spinning and weaving processes to use in attempts to illustrate ancient textile technology in experiments today (Crowfoot 1931; Sylvan 1941, 109–125). In the Eastern Mediterranean area, studies using ethnographical evidence began later (*e.g.* Carington Smith 1975; Barber 1991; Tzachili 1997).

The use of ethnographic parallels has been criticised, however, on the grounds that ethnographic records represent situations far removed in both time and space from the ancient context they set out to illustrate (Coles 1979, 39). This criticism against the use of ethnographic data has not been specifically applied to textile research, but should of course be considered in this field as well. Nonetheless, experiments, such as the use of reconstructed tools, enable adjustments to archaeological interpretations.

Open-air centres and other research institutes

In the period between 1970 and 1990, several open-air centres and museums were founded in Europe.[1] Textile techniques have been practised at a number of these centres. One of the most important is Land of Legends, Centre for Historical and Archaeological

Fig. 1.2.1. (above, left) Copy of the Muldbjerg garment on a live male model. Garment made by Margrethe Hald (photo: Broholm and Hald 1940, 147).

Fig. 1.2.2. (above, right) Copy of the Egtved garment on a live female model. Garment made by Margrethe Hald (photo: Broholm and Hald 1940, 154).

Fig. 1.2.3. Spinning as practised today by Mrs. Sophia Kalogieriolis on Crete (photo: CTR).

with experimental approaches; for example, the project on Tutankhamun's wardrobe (Vogelsang-Eastwood 1999).

Several experiments have been conducted. The list of published reports on different experiments, however, remains short and makes further use of the results difficult.

Textile experimental archaeology of the 1980s onwards

In the 1980s, an increased use of experimental archaeology is evident in textile research. In a paper on weaving techniques presented at the 2nd North European Symposium for Archaeological Textiles (NESAT) in 1984, Egon Hansen stresses the importance of introducing new approaches as well as new methods within the increasing amount of research on archaeological textiles (Hansen 1988). He writes that "among these are reconstruction experiments, where, by producing replicas, the knowledge of basic techniques is improved" (Hansen 1988, 256). It is somewhat debatable if this should be regarded as a new approach. He continues, however: "A profound knowledge of different tools, the use of these, and possible variations within each skill, must be the foundation of any experiment with past techniques, if the experiment is to have any value to research" (Hansen 1988, 256). This quotation can serve as an illustration of early principles of textile experimental archaeology, which required profound knowledge of the tools and their uses. Moreover, not only the knowledge of the tools and their uses, but also the archaeological knowledge of the tools and their context was given far more attention in the scholarly work of the 1980s and 1990s. Previously, most research had been associated with the analysis of specific archaeological textiles. In the 1980s and 1990s, however, questions concerning archaeological tools were also being asked. Whereas different types of looms had already been investigated by textile researchers in the first half of the 20th century, other textile tools came into consideration towards the end of the 20th century. In the late 1980s, Eva Andersson started a range of experiments investigating the functionalities of textile tools in collaboration with skilled craftspeople. These experiments provided the basis on which she interpreted textile production at various sites dated to the Viking Age in Scandinavia (Andersson 1989, 1996,

Research and Communication (CHARC), in Denmark, where a number of experimental archaeology projects relating to textiles have been conducted, some of which have been published (Fig. 1.2.4) (Batzer and Dokkedal 1991; Mannering 1996; Andersson 2003). The majority, however, remain unpublished in-house reports. Abstracts of more recently conducted experiments are available on CHARC's homepage.[2] Another important centre that has practised experimental archaeology is the Institute for Prehistoric Technology in Sweden which helped to initiate a course on ancient techniques and textile production techniques at Bäckedals Folk High School with an aim to preserve old practical knowledge of textile production (Bigrell 2003, 4; Lindblad *et al.* 2007). Furthermore, the University of Borås, Sweden, has been a platform for research on historical and archaeological textiles

Fig. 1.2.4. CHARC, Lejre, Denmark (photo: the author).

2000, 2003; Andersson and Batzer 1999). Experiments with tools and their function will be considered further later in this chapter.

Further approaches to textile experimental archaeology are outlined in an article by Elizabeth E. Peacock (Peacock 2001). She gives several examples of reconstruction work and experiments which investigate techniques and production methods. The described experiments relate to archaeological materials, such as fibres, tools and textiles, most of them conducted in northern Europe. She emphasises that extensive testing has been applied to the investigation of the function of textile tools, primarily relating to the operation of the warp-weighted loom. The main focus of her article, however, is experimental work on the preservation and decay of textiles in different burial environments. Such burial experiments have been conducted since the 1960s and Peacock herself has contributed to this field (Peacock 2001, 182–189). These experiments are closely linked to conservation research on archaeological textiles which can be regarded as a field in its own right. In Peacock's survey there are no indications that textile experimental archaeology is a neglected field, rather the opposite. She underlines the importance of experimental archaeology as a research methodology in ancient textile studies and states that the understanding

of textiles would be far poorer without this input (Peacock 2001). Furthermore, when considering specialist forums and publications relating to archaeological textiles, such as conference publications from NESAT and the *Archaeological Textiles Review (ATR)*, textile experimental archaeology is a common element (NESAT *e.g.* Hansen 1988; Batzer and Dokkedal 1992; Goldmann 1992; Bender Jørgensen 1994; ATN *e.g.* Friedman 1994; Nørgaard and Østergaard 1994; Holm and Olin 1995; Sundström 1995). Consequently, it can be concluded that during the last three decades, at least, experimental archaeology has been a frequently applied approach in textile research.

Elisabeth J. W. Barber and experiments in the Mediterranean

Contributions to textile experimental archaeology within the field of Mediterranean archaeology are limited. This may be due to an overall interest in typology and not function, as demonstrated in chapter 1.1. In 1991, however, Elisabeth J. W. Barber published her monograph, now considered a standard work on Aegean textiles: *Prehistoric Textiles. The Development of Cloth in the Neolithic and Bronze Ages with Special Reference to the Aegean* (Barber 1991). Barber covers a large part of the history and geography in a way that encompasses several approaches to the subject, including experimental archaeology. Experimental archaeology is not a term she explicitly uses in this work, but she does briefly mention experiments in connection with various topics, although no detailed account of how the experiments were conducted is given (Barber 1991). Still, Barber constitutes a good example of how knowledge gained through experiments can bring problems and new questions to light within textile research. She refers not only to her own practical experience from working with textile production, but to the practical experience of other scholars, as well; for example, Avigail Sheffer's experiment using the so-called doughnut shaped loom weights (or torus shaped loom weights) on a warp-weighted loom (Sheffer 1981; Barber 1991, 302; discussed further later in this chapter). Overall, the experiments mentioned are associated with several aspects of textile production, such as fibres, splicing, loom weights and other weaving implements (Barber 1991, 24, 47, 302, 110). In a later article, Barber discusses experimental archaeology and textile research in more detail and, like Peacock, underlines an increasing attention to the subject from the 1990s onwards (Peacock 2001; Barber 2003, 193). She discusses experiments concerning the Mediterranean area such as the collaborative work of Eva Andersson and Marie-Louise Nosch investigating the Mycenaean textile industry (Barber 2003; Andersson and Nosch 2003). Barber states that "the use of *real* materials can provide masses of invaluable information, plugging holes in our knowledge" (Barber 2003, 194).

Other scholars have contributed to experimental work relating to Mediterranean textiles as well (*e.g.* Carington Smith 1992). Since many of these scholars consider the use of archaeological textile tools, their work will be presented in detail in the last part of this chapter, on functional approaches to textile tools.

Textile experimental archaeology today

Through the work of Barber and others, textile research has been made more accessible, which in turn has inspired archaeologists and craftspeople to perform additional experiments. An increased interest in textile experimental archaeology is evident from several articles that have been published in anthologies and journals during the past two decades. Several tests have been made investigating production processes and the functionality of tools in different ways, as well as fibre tests (Mannering 1996; Rast-Eicher and Thijsse 2001), tool tests (see below) and several textile reconstructions (Wardle 1988; Bender Jørgensen 1994; Hedeager Krag 1994; Nørgaard and Østergaard 1994; Ræder Knudsen 1994, 1998, 2002; Sundström 1995; Grömer 2004; Reichert 2006). Furthermore, experimental work relating to the use of textiles as sailcloth and costumes has been conducted (Andersen *et al.* 1989; Lightfoot 1997; Jones 2001, 2003, 2012) as well as attempts to visualise archaeological textiles as they may have originally appeared (*e.g.* Hammarlund 2005). The list of contributors to textile experimental archaeology is too long to discuss in full in this chapter, so only specific examples are referred to here. Furthermore, only works published before 2007 are considered.

Discussions of the use and theoretical framework of experimental archaeology as part of textile research rarely take place. However, Lise Bender Jørgensen has theorised on the epistemology of craftsmanship (Bender Jørgensen 2003a), discussing the use of the craftsperson's knowledge in academic research; a subject which is arguably related to experimental archaeology. Much of the textile experimental archaeology presented in the paragraph above is also based on craft knowledge and is not the result of solely scholarly work conducted without experience of the handicraft itself. A discussion of the use of the craftsperson's knowledge and the influence of this knowledge on textile production processes is thus of the utmost relevance.

Textile experimental archaeology, visible and invisible

It is informative to examine to the extent to which textile experimental archaeology is represented in experimental archaeology and archaeology in general. The *Bibliografie zur experimentellen Archäologie* contains references to publications relating to experimental archaeology until 1991 (Devermann and Fansa 1992). As illustrated in Fig. 1.2.5 textiles are far less represented than for example stone.

From these statistics and other previous examples, it is evident that while textile experimental archaeology is highly visible, it

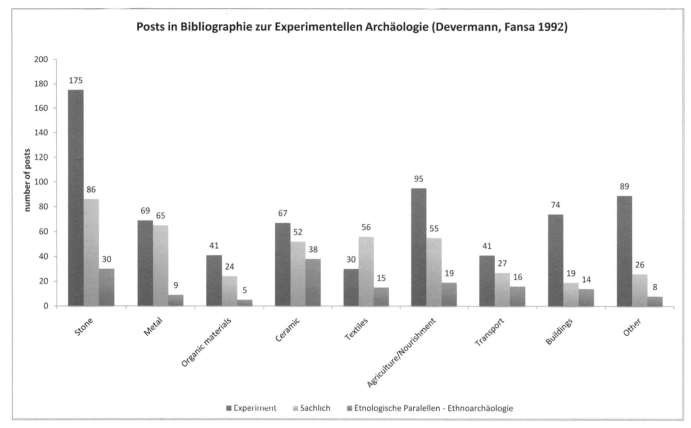

Fig. 1.2.5. Graph showing the representation of textiles in experimental archaeology, compiled from Bibliografie zur experimentellen Archäologie *(Devermann and Fansa 1992). The work includes a useful subject index divided into five themes of various posts, "Einführende literature", "Sachlich", "Experiment", "Ergänzende Literatur" and "Etnologicsche Parallelen-Etnoarchäologie". For example, in the "Experiment" group it is evident that textiles are underrepresented with only 30 posts in contrast to, for example stone with 175 posts.*

appears most commonly in the context of textile research and is not particularly visible in archaeology in general (Devermann and Fansa 1992).

Experimental work on textile production – functional approaches to tools

In the context of the TTTC research project, textile experimental archaeology aims at investigating ancient textile production and the function of tools, *e.g.* the production of yarn and fabrics. Thus neither reconstructions of specific dress nor practice of textile techniques or the so-called "after treatments" or "finishing" of textiles, such as smoothing, fulling, smearing, mending or dyeing is taken into consideration.[3] In any case, published experiments concerning pre-medieval "after treatments" or "finishing treatments" are rare with the exception of the production of dyes and dyeing (*e.g.* Haubrichs 2005; Ruscillo 2006).

Experiments on the production of textiles can be divided into two main groups. One group is concerned with questions arising through analysis of specific archaeological textiles. Experiments conducted by use of this approach often aim to reconstruct the textile, but do sometimes include a consideration of textile tools. The other group, which is the subject of discussion here, is concerned with questions relating to archaeological textile tools. Remains of tools are more common than finds of textiles during the period and area under consideration in this volume, and are thus an important source of information. However, far from all textile tools are preserved since many of them were probably made of wood or bone and have therefore not survived. Ceramic and stone spindle whorls as well as ceramic loom weights are well represented in the archaeological material (chapter 1.1). Thus, studies of tools have mainly focused on spindles and the warp-weighted loom. Experiments on tools used for fibre preparation have not been given much attention. Interest in these tools has recently increased, such as the use of reconstructed flint tools for processing plant fibres which were tested at CHARC, Denmark, during the summers of 2005, 2006 and 2007 (van Gijn and Lammers 2005; Hurcombe 2006, 2007; van Gijn and Verbaas 2006, 2007). Nonetheless, publications on the subject remain rare.

Spindle whorls and loom weights have been given the most attention of all textile tools in experiments and scholarly work. Although detailed reports on how the experiments were conducted are unusual, it is possible to gain insight into different approaches and what questions have been taken into consideration by those performing the experiment. The lack of comprehensive information, however, makes it difficult to get a view of how different results were achieved and thus, how they can be used. In the following, experiments with spinning and weaving will be treated separately.

Spinning

When it comes to producing yarn, spindle whorls have been the primary focus of attention, since the rods are seldom preserved. Because of the many varieties of whorls present in the archaeological material, one of the main questions scholars wished to answer was that of how the whorls function when spinning. Experiments relating to how a spindle works have been divided into three groups, *twist frequency and duration of spin*; *spindle whorl or not?* and *yarn qualities and spindles*.

Twist frequency and duration of spin
Tests of twist frequency and duration of spin were conducted in the 1960s by Alfred Linder (Linder 1967). In this work, the relation between the weight of the spindle and the outcome in metres of yarn per 100 g of raw material was examined (Linder 1967, 50–68). In 1981, the German professor Almut Bohnsack published a history of development in textile techniques and work (Bohnsack 1981). In order to investigate the capacity of the drop spindle, Bohnsack tested spindles of four different sizes and shapes, with a weight of 27 g, 23 g, 15 g and 4 g respectively.

One of these was a reconstructed Stone Age spindle, while the others represented spindles in ethnographic material (Bohnsack 1981, 57–58). Her main interest was to see how long the spindle would rotate, since she assumed that this must be of great importance for the spinner, because it affected how frequently he or she would have to add twist to the spindle (Bohnsack 1981, 57). She concluded that lighter spindles have a higher rotation frequency than heavier ones, but heavier spindles have a longer duration of rotation. She also concluded that the finer the yarn the more time it takes to produce it, that coarser yarns need more material than finer ones and that finer yarns require lighter spindles than coarser yarns. She further deduced that spinning is hard work which required concentration as well as the appropriate tools (Bohnsack 1981, 57–64). Questions concerning twist frequency and duration of spin have also been studied by Karina Grömer. She has tested original whorls from Upper and Lower Austria, dating from the Neolithic to the Roman Period, in order to gain insight into textile production in central European prehistory (Grömer 2005). Both Bohnsack and Grömer work with the assumption that it is of utmost importance to the spinner that the spindle rotates as long as possible after it has been set in motion by hand. Thus, efficiency is understood as high rotation frequency and long duration of spin. In both cases, the results are used in a more general discussion of prehistoric textile production. Similar studies based on textile tools have not been conducted within the Aegean and Near Eastern area.

Spindle whorl or not?
The question of what constitutes a spindle whorl has been another subject of experiment. Light whorls weighing less than 10 g have been tested in relation to finds from both Nichoria in Greece and Demircihüyük in Turkey in order to ascertain whether they could have been used as spindle whorls, as it has also been argued that they could alternatively have been used as beads or buttons. In one case, whorls with an average weight of 10 g were used with a so-called *souvlaki* stick as a rod (Carington Smith 1992, 686–687, 694) and in the other, a whorl weighing 5 g was placed on a wooden rod measuring approximately 30 cm in length (Obladen-Kauder 1996, 233–235). In both

cases, it was concluded that spindles with light whorls are usable, but are too difficult to work with because the spindle continuously required twist from the hand in order to rotate. Both authors consider the results as indicative that light whorls were not used as spindle whorls at the studied sites. However, other experiments have demonstrated that spindle whorls weighing less than 10 g can be used as spindle whorls (Andersson and Batzer 1999; Andersson 2003).

Yarn qualities and spindles

Another approach to yarn production is to investigate what yarn quality it is suitable to produce using different spindles. The topic has been integrated in different experiments with spinning (Linder 1967, 50–68; Bohnsack 1981, 57–64; Holm 1996; Obladen-Kauder 1996, 233–235; Andersson 1999, 2000, 2003, 25–26, 46; Andersson and Batzer 1999; Grömer 2005). A general conclusion is that the heavier the whorl, the thicker or coarser the yarn will be, and the lighter the whorl, the thinner or finer the yarn. Furthermore, results have demonstrated that with heavier whorls (*e.g.* 40 g or more) a large range of qualities of yarn can be produced, according to the spinning technique (Andersson and Batzer 1999, 19; Grömer 2005, 111; Mårtensson 2006). Some of the experiments referred to above stress that it is not only the weight of the whorl that has implications for what yarn can be produced, but that different fibre material and the diameter of the whorl also influence the result (Andersson 1999; 2003, 25). Spindles have also been tested using different spinning techniques; low whorl and high whorl spindles (Holm 1996, 115), supported and suspended spindles (Grömer 2005, 109; Mårtensson 2006), spindles rotating in the hand and spindles without whorls (Mårtensson 2007); spindle spinning and spinning with no tool at all (Tiedemann and Jakes 2006). Spinning tests have mainly been conducted on suspended low whorl spindles. Using this technique, Andersson has devoted several experiments to investigating the relation between different reconstructed spindle whorls and the different yarns that can be produced with them (Andersson 1996, 3; 2000; 2003, 46; Holm 1996; Andersson and Batzer 1999). Characteristic of the research presented by Andersson and the use of experimental archaeology is that interpretations and discussions are closely linked to specific archaeological contexts in

Scandinavia. Andersson's results, however, have been used when interpreting textile tools in the Mediterranean area as well (Andersson and Nosch 2003). The new results, stemming from experimental archaeology from Andersson's earlier experiments and recently conducted by Linda Olofsson (former Mårtensson) and Anne Batzer, are presented in this volume.

Weaving

Different types of looms have been used in connection with reconstruction work throughout the 20th century. However, the focus has mainly been on the textile to be reconstructed and not on the actual tool. When the loom has been the key object of research, it has most commonly been in connection with exhibitions, with the aim of presenting prehistoric tools to a general audience. Although originally with a different purpose, practical handicraft experiences are gained through these reconstructions, which pose new questions relating to weaving and the production of prehistoric textiles as well as generate new possible interpretations (Nørgaard 1999; Stærmose Nielsen 1999, 140–142; Belanová *et al.* 2005; Schierer 2005).

The most visible traces of weaving and looms in the archaeological record, apart from remains of actual textiles, are the loom weights, which are used to tension the warp threads on the warp-weighted loom. Frames of looms are seldom preserved, as they were most likely made of wood. Smaller implements used during weaving are also represented in the archaeological material. Yet experiments with the aim to investigate these tools are rare. However, combs used when weaving have attracted some scholarly attention, such as the use of the narrow bone and antler combs, interpreted as weaving combs, found in north European Iron Age contexts (Bailey 1999). A wooden copy was made based on a find of what was regarded as a typical comb from Danebury, approximately 4 cm in width. The use of the comb was tested for weaving on a warp-weighted loom by Ro Bailey (Bailey 1999). As a result, Bailey concluded that this comb was not the appropriate tool for beating in weft threads or for organising the weft thread before beating, since a pin beater was considered more workable for this purpose. Bailey therefore suggested that the combs may instead have been used for combing wool prior to spinning (Bailey 1999).

The main questions related to weaving have primarily been concerned with what textiles can be produced with the warp-weighted loom and by the use of loom weights. Examples are given in the following paragraph.

Other looms have been the subject of experimentation as well. The Swedish textile historian and hand-weaver Martin Ciszuk investigated the use of a Roman vertical two-beam loom for making taqueté and damask textiles. The loom was made based on pictorial representations of Roman looms. He found the loom to be very usable for this purpose (Ciszuk 2004).

The warp-weighted loom

Weaving can be practised using a large variety of techniques. Questions regarding what textiles it is possible to produce with the warp-weighted loom have been of interest to scholars for decades. As early as 1940, Hald carried out experiments using the warp-weighted loom. Through testing, she concluded, for example, that this type of loom is not suitable to produce cloth with closed loops in the lower end of the warp. The result was used as an indicator for the use of another type of loom during the Bronze Age, which had beams instead of weights (Broholm and Hald 1940, 131, 134). At CHARC, Denmark, separated warp systems have been tested on a warp-weighted loom on several occasions, confirming its many uses as well as the use of multiple notched heddle rods which makes the work easier (Batzer and Dokkedal 1992). Separated systems of warp threads and loom weights facilitate the execution of different weaving techniques, such as various kinds of twills. Another experiment conducted using reconstructed tools had the aim of determining whether textile tools in a defined context at the site of Löddeköping in Sweden could have been used to produce sailcloth (Andersson 2000, 172–176). The experiment involved several stages, from preparing the wool and spinning the yarn, to weaving and fulling. The fabric produced was compatible with the type of fabric suitable for sailcloth. Since the experiment involved several reconstructed textile implements, the results were extremely valuable. The use of supplementary implements, such as bone needles and weft beaters, when weaving was also evaluated. One important result was that a metal sword beater was shown to be more efficient than a wooden sword beater in the production of coarse fabrics made of wool. The results were used for interpreting what types of textile production may have occurred in Löddeköping (Andersson 2000, 172–176).

Loom weights

Loom weights exist in different shapes and weights. Tests have been conducted that demonstrate that different threads need different amounts of tension (Andersson 2003, 28–29). In general, thin and fine warp yarn requires lighter weights than thick and coarse warp yarn. As to the effect that a loom weight's shape has on its use, experimental work is ongoing, but the knowledge base is increasing all the time (*e.g.* Micouin-Cheval 2004). One of the most divergent forms of loom weight is the so-called crescent shaped loom weight. The use of these objects as loom weights has been questioned and has been the subject of extensive testing (*e.g.* Baioni 2003; Feldtkeller 2003; Schlichtherle and Feldtkeller 2003; Grömer 2007; Wisti Lassen 2007). As a result of these tests, it has been concluded that they can function as loom weights (see also chapter 4.4).

The question of whether a find should be interpreted as a loom weight or not has also been tested in Israel as part of the Tel Beer-sheba Expedition (Sheffer 1981). Sun-dried so-called doughnut shaped (or torus shaped) clay balls were tested in order to find out if they would work as loom weights. Reconstructions of so-called doughnut (or torus) weights were made of clay mixed with straw, based on finds from Tel Beer-sheba, and were used on a warp-weighted loom. The yarn used was hand spun and made of wool, arranged on the loom with a density of about five threads per cm. Weaving was considered easy and quick, and most importantly, no damage occurred to the sun-dried loom weights (Sheffer 1981). Loom weights made based on drawings of Bronze Age finds from Nichoria in Greece have also been tested on a warp-weighted loom. The intention of the test was to build and try to operate a warp-weighted loom. Weaving on the loom was considered efficient by the weaver. However, the use of the loom weights was problematic, because they twisted their attached bunch of warp threads and clashed and jangled, making an irritating noise. In an attempt to solve this problem, each row of weights was lashed to a thin rod. The loom weights' top groove fitted against the rod very well and the groove was thus interpreted as having been used this way (Carington Smith 1992, 690).

The future of textile experimental archaeology

Textile experimental archaeology still faces several challenges. First, there is the issue that textile production is seldom treated in its entirety. The fibre, the tools, the yarn, the process of spinning and weaving and the produced fabric are generally discussed as separate elements. Reflections on the entire process of producing textiles and how this process is evident in the archaeological record are desirable regarding the use of experiments in interpretations. Second, the results of textile experimental archaeology are rarely considered in conjunction with archaeological research in general, such as social, economic, and cultural discourses. Most results are used for interpreting matters explicitly concerning textiles and textile tools and do not include a consideration of the context in which they have been found. The approach has been used mostly for typological and functional studies and rarely for contextual studies. Third, it is also difficult for outsiders to relate to the results of experiments, since comprehensive information on the way the experiments were conducted is often lacking or is not easily accessible, for example, what raw material was used and why, how it was prepared and why, who made the tests and what level of skill did they have. Tomas Johansson's discussion of 1983 on the problem of proper descriptions of different processes should still be regarded as relevant today (Johansson 1983, 81–83). A future task for scholars should therefore be to develop a method of disseminating knowledge achieved through experiments in an accessible format which it is possible to analyse. Procedures or guidelines similar to those developed by John Coles as early as in the 1970s and reports of how these were applied and developed have not been employed within the field of textile experimental archaeology (Coles 1973, 15–18; 1979, 46–48). Such guidelines and reporting of the way the experiments were carried out clarify how results were achieved and thus make them far more useful. Since experimental archaeology utilises both known and potential techniques, documentation of the procedures used can rightly be considered of utmost importance in order to demonstrate how experimental archaeology has been conducted and how it can be used as a methodology.

Acknowledgements

I warmly thank Eva Andersson Strand, Marie-Louise Nosch, Margarita Gleba, Henriette Lyngstrøm and Ulla Mannering for their support and advice.

Notes

1 See examples of these museums on www.exarc.net.
2 Sagnlandet Lejre: www.sagnlandet.dk.
3 Reconstructions of textiles are discussed in *e.g.* Nielsen 1979; Barber 2003; Bender Jørgensen 2003b; Jones 2003. The practice of textile techniques are described in *e.g.* Svinicki 1974; Hansen 1978, 1990; Collingwood 1982; Springe and Sydberg 1986; Stærmose Nielsen 1999.

Bibliography

Andersen, E., Milland, J. and Myhre, E. (1989) *Uldsejl i 1000 år.* Roskilde. Vikingeskibshallen.
Andersson, E. (1989) *Grophus som vävstugor.* Lunds Universitet. (unpublished BA dissertation).
Andersson, E. (1996) *Textilproduktion i arkeologisk kontext.* Lund. University of Lund.
Andersson, E. (1999) *The Common Thread: Textile Production During the Late Iron Age–Viking Age.* Lund. Institute of Archaeology, University of Lund.
Andersson, E. (2000) Textilproduktion i Löddeköpinge – endast för husbehov?, in Svanberg, F. and Söderberg, B. (eds), *Porten till Skåne: Löddeköpinge under järnålder och medeltid,* 158–187. Lund. Riksantikvarieämbetet.
Andersson, E. (2003) *Tools for Textile Production from Birka and Hedeby: Excavations in the Black Earth 1990–1995.* Stockholm. Birka Project, Riksantikvarieämbetet.
Andersson, E. and Batzer, A. (1999) Spinning in the Viking Age, in Andersson, E. (ed.), *The Common Thread, Textile Production During the Late Iron Age–Viking Age.* Lund. Institute of Archaeology, University of Lund, 23–25.
Andersson, E. and Nosch, M.-L. (2003) With a little help from my friends: investigating Mycenaean textiles with help from Scandinavian experimental archaeology, in Foster, K. P. and Laffineur, R. (eds), *Metron: Measuring the Aegean Bronze Age,* 197–205. Liège. Université de Liège.
Bailey, R. (1999) Those weaving combs – yet again, *Archaeological Textiles Newsletter,* 28, 5–10.
Baioni, M. (2003) Prova sperimentale di produzione di pesti reniformi e loro applicazione a un telaio verticale, in Bazzanella, M., Mayr, A., Moser, L. and Rast-Eicher, A. (eds), *Textiles: intrecci e tessuti dalla preistoria europea,* 104–105. Trento. Provincia Autonoma di Trento.

Barber, E. J. W. (1991) *Prehistoric Textiles: The Development of Cloth in the Neolithic and Bronze Ages with Special Reference to the Aegean.* Princeton University Press.

Barber, E. J. W. (2003) Archaeology by experiment and reproduction, in Foster, K. and Laffineur, R. (eds) *Metron. Measuring the Aegean Bronze Age*, 193–195. Liege. Universite de Liege.

Batzer, A. and Dokkedal, L. (1991) Opstadvæven – nye forsøgsobservationer, *Eksperimentel arkæologi. Studier i teknologi og kultur* 1, 149–152.

Batzer, A. and Dokkedal, L. (1992) The warp-weighted loom: some new experimental notes, in Bender Jørgensen, L. and Munksgaard, E. (eds), *Archaeological Textiles in Northern Europe: Report from the 4th NESAT Symposium*, 231–234. Copenhagen. Konservatorskolen, Det Kongelige Danske Kunstakademi.

Belanová, T., Harmadyová, K. and Zajonc, J. (2005) Devin: experimentálna rekonstrukcia snovadla a krosien v dobe laténskej, in Kotorová-Jencová, M. (ed.), *Experimentálna archeológia a popularizácia archeologického bádania v múzejnej a skolskej praxi*, 105–122. Hanusovciach nad Toplou. Vlastivedné Museum.

Bender Jørgensen, L. (1994) Ancient costumes reconstructed, in Jaacks, G., and Tidow, K. (eds), *Archäologische Textilfunde (NESAT V)*, 109–113. Neumünster. Textilmuseum Neumünster.

Bender Jørgensen, L. (2003a) The Epistemology of Craftmanship, in Bender Jørgensen, L., Banck-Burgess, J. and Rast-Eicher, A. (eds), *Textilien aus Archäologie und Geschichte: Festschrift für Klaus Tidow*, 30–36. Neumünster. Wachholtz.

Bender Jørgensen, L. (2003b) Krigerdragten i folkevandringstiden, in Rolfsen, P. and Stylegar, F.-A. (eds), *Snartemofunnene i nytt lys*, 53–80. Oslo. Universitetet i Oslo.

Bigrell, E. (2003) Textillinjen 20 år!, *Perga, tidskrift för mnt-kontaktnätet*, 2, 4.

Bohnsack, A. (1981) *Spinnen und Weben: Entwicklung von Technik und Arbeit im Textilgewerbe.* Reinbek bei Hamburg. Deutsches Museum.

Brattli, T. and Johnsen, H. (1989) Noen kritiske kommentarer til den eksperimentelle arkeologien, *Experimentell arkeologi, Kontaktstencil*, 33, 49–52.

Broholm, H. C. and Hald, M. (1940) *Costumes of the Bronze Age in Denmark.* Copenhagen. Nyt nordisk forlag.

Carington Smith, J. (1975) *Spinning, Weaving and Textile Manufacture in Prehistoric Greece from the Beginning of the Neolithic to the End of the Mycaean Ages.* Ph.D. thesis, University of Hobart, Tasmania.

Carington Smith, J. (1992) Spinning and weaving equipment, in Macdonald, W. A. and Wilkie, N. C. (eds), *Excavations at Nichoria in Southwestern Greece. 2. The Bronze Age Occupation*, 674–711. Minneapolis. University of Minnesota Press.

Ciszuk, M. (2004) Taqueté and damask from Mons Claudianus: a discussion of Roman looms for patterned textiles, in Alfaro, C., Wild, J. P. and Costa, B. (eds), *Purpureae vestes I. Textiles y tintes del Mediterráneo en época romana*, 107–113. Valencia. Consell Insular d'Eivissa i Formentera, Universitat de València.

Coles, J. (1973) *Archaeology by Experiment.* London. Hutchinson and Co.

Coles, J. (1979) *Experimental Archaeology.* London. Academic Press.

Coles, J. (1983) Comments on archaeology and experiment, *Norwegian Archaeological Review*, 16 (2), 79–81.

Collingwood, P. (1982) *The Techniques of Tablet Weaving.* London. Faber.

Crowfoot, G. M. (1931) *Methods of Hand Spinning in Egypt and the Sudan.* Halifax. Bankfield Museum.

Devermann, H. and Fansa, M. (1992) *Bibliographie zur experimentellen Archäologie.* Oldenburg. Isensee Verlag.

Feldtkeller, A. (2003) Nierenförmige Webgewichte – wie funktionieren sie?, *Archaeological Textiles Newsletter*, 37, 16–19.

Friedman, T. (1994) Cheveron weave patterns: an experiment in handspinning and weaving, *Archaeological Textiles Newsletter*, 18–19, 19–21.

Geijer, A. (1979) *A History of Textile Art.* London. Pasold Research Fund in association with Southeby.

Goldmann, A. (1992) Experimente am Gewichts-, Rund- und Trittwebstuhl im Mittelalterlichen Museumsdorf Düppel, in Bender Jørgensen, L. and Munksgaard, E. (eds), *Archaeological Textiles in Northern Europe: Report from the 4th NESAT Symposium*, 187–196. Copenhagen. Konservatorskolen, Det Kongelige Danske Kunstakademi.

Grömer, K. (2004) Experimentalarchäologische Rekonstruktion der Brettchenwebereien aus dem Salzbergwerk in Hallstatt, in Endlich, C. (ed.), *Experimentelle Archäologie in Europe. Bilanz 2004*, 145–158. Oldenberg. Isensee.

Grömer, K. (2005) Efficiency and technique – experiments with original spindle whorls, in Bichler, P., Grömer, K., Hofmann-de Keijzer, R., Kern, A. and Reschreiter, H. (eds), *Hallstatt Textiles. Technical Analysis, Scientific Investigation and Experiment on Iron Age Textiles*, 107–116. Oxford. Archaeopress.

Grömer, K. (2007) Experiments with Neolithic weaving tools (lunular or crescent shaped loom-weights). Report. Reference number: HAF 03/07. Sagnlandet Lejre (then Lejre Historical and Archaeological Research Centre). http://www.sagnlandet.dk/DRESSING-AUSTRIA-S-FARMERS.609.0.html

Hald, M. (1950) *Olddanske textilier.* Copenhagen. Nordisk Forlag.

Hald, M. (1980) *Ancient Danish Textiles from Bogs and Burials: a Comparative Study of Costume and Iron Age Textiles.* Copenhagen. The National Museum of Denmark.

Hammarlund, L. (2005) Handicraft knowledge applied to archaeological textiles – visual groups and the pentagon, *Archaeological Textiles Newsletter* 41, 13–19.

Hansen, E. (1988) Technical variations in pre-medieval tablet-weaving, in Bender Jørgensen, L., Magnus, B. and Munksgaard, E. (eds), *Archaeological Textiles: Report from the 2nd NESAT Symposium*, 256–269. Copenhagen. Copenhagen University.

Hansen, E. H. (1978) *Opstadvæv før og nu.* Copenhagen Teamcos.

Hansen, E. H. (1990) *Brikvævning: historie, teknik, farver, mønstre.* Højbjerg. Hovedland.

Harbeck, K.-H. (1982) Vorwort, in Bender Jørgensen, L., and Tidow, K. (eds), *Archäologische Textilfunde* (NESAT 1), 7–8. Neumünster. Textilmuseum Neumünster.

Haubrichs, R. (2005) L'étude de la poupre: histoire d'une couleur, chimie et expérimentations, *Preistoria Alpina*, 40, 133–160.

Hedeager Krag, A. (1994) Reconstruction of a Viking magnate dress, in Jaacks, G., and Tidow, K. (eds),

Archäologische Textilfunde (NESAT V), 114–119. Neumünster. Textilmuseum Neumünster.

Hoffmann, M. (1964) *The Warp-Weighted Loom: Studies in the History and Technology of an Ancient Implement*. Oslo. Universitetsforlaget.

Holm, C. (1996) Experiment med slændspinning, in Andersson, E. (ed.) *Textilproduktion i arkeologisk kontext. En metodstudie av yngre järnåldersboplatser i Skåne*, 111–116. Lund. Institute of Archaeology.

Holm, C. and Olin, P. (1995) The Bronze Age lady from Borum Eshøj, Denmark, *Archaeological Textiles Newsletter*, 20, 21–23.

Hurcombe, L. (2006) A prehistoric functional puzzle: flint serrated edges for plant processing. Report. Reference number: HAF 09/06, http://www.sagnlandet.dk/WAS-NETTLE-CLOTH-ONCE-THE-PREVAILING-FASHION.543.0.html

Hurcombe, L. (2007) Prehistoric cordage and fabric: flint serrated edges, plant processing and the Tybrind Vig fabric. Report. Reference number: HAF 11/07, http://www.sagnlandet.dk/WAS-NETTLE-CLOTH-ONCE-THE-PREVAILING-FASHION.543.0.html

Johansson, T. (1983) Comments on archaeology and experiment technical processes of the past, *Norwegian Archaeological Review*, 16 (2), 81–83.

Johansson, T. (1987) Experimentell arkeologi, *Forntida teknik*, 15. Available from http://www.forntidateknik.z.se/.

Jones, B. (2001) The Minoan "Snake Goddess." New interpretations of her costume and identity, in Laffineur, R., and Hägg, R. (eds), *Potnia: Deities and Religion in the Aegean Bronze Age*, 259–265. Liège. Université de Liège.

Jones, B. (2003) Veils and mantles: an investigation of the construction and function of the costumes of the veiled dancer from Thera and the Camp Stool Banqueter from Knossos, in Foster, K. P. and Laffineur, R. (eds), *Metron: measuring the Aegean Bronze Age*, 441–450. Liège. Universite de Liege.

Jones, B. (2012) The construction and significance of the Minoan side-pleated skirt, in Nosch, M.-L. and Laffineur, R. (eds), *KOSMOS. Jewellery, Adornment and Textiles in the Aegean Bronze Age*, 221–230. Liège. Universite de Liege.

Lassen, A. W. (2007) Et forsøg med bananformede vævevægte. Report. Reference number: HAF 09/07. http://www.sagnlandet.dk/A-BANANA-SHAPED-PIECE-OF-THE-PUZZLE.648.0.html

Lightfoot, A. (1997) Ullseil i tusen år, *Spor – fortidsnytt fra midt-Norge*, 2, 10–15.

Lindblad, K. G., Petterson, A. and Sydberg, E. (2007) The Folk High School of Bäckedal: education in ancient techniques, *EuroREA Journal of (Re)construction and Experiment in Archaeology*, 4, 49–51.

Linder, A. (1967) *Spinnen und Weben einst und jetzt*. Luzern. Bucher.

Lönnroth, L. (1997) The Vikings in history and legend, in Sawyer, P. (ed.), *The Oxford Illustrated History of the Vikings*, 225–249. Oxford. Oxford University Press.

Malina, J. (1983) Archaeology and experiment, *Norwegian Archaeological Review*, 16 (2), 69–78.

Mannering, U. (1996) Oldtidens brændenældeklæde, in Meldgaard, M. and Rasmussen, M. (eds), *Arkæologiske eksperimenter i Lejre*, 73–80. Copenhagen. Rhodos.

Micouin-Cheval, C. (2004) Les textiles gallo-romains de Chartres (Eure-et-Loire). Analyse et expérimentation, in Alfaro, C., Wild, J. P. and Costa, B. (eds), *Purpureae vestes. Textiles y tintes del Mediterráneo en época romana*, 115–120. Valencia. Consell Insular d'Eivissa i Formentera, Universitat de València.

Mårtensson, L. (2006) Multiwhorls? Forsök med tunga sländtrissor. Report. Reference number: HAF 14/06. http://www.sagnlandet.dk/SPINNING-THIN-THREAD-WITH-HEAVY-SPINDLE.540.0.html

Mårtensson, L. (2007) Textilteknologiska studier av sländspinning – träsländan från Hjortspring. Report. Reference number: HAF 05/07. http://www.sagnlandet.dk/THE-SPINNING-STICK.610.0.html

Nielsen, K.-H. (1979) *Kvindedragten fra Skrydstrup: beretning om en ny rekonstruktion af en 3000 år gammel dragt*. Haderslev. Haderslev Museum.

Nørgaard, A. (1999) *Weaving Samples of Sailcloth on a Warp-Weighted Loom*. Viking Ship Museum. Roskilde.

Nørgaard, A. and Østergaard, E. (1994) A reconstruction of a blanket from the Migration Period, *Archaeological Textiles Newsletter*, 18–19, 17–19.

Obladen-Kauder, J. (1996) Die Kleinfunde aus Ton, Knochen und Metall, in Korfmann, M. (ed.), *Demircihüyük: die Ergebnisse der Ausgrabungen 1975–1978. 4. Die Kleinfunde*, 207–310. Mainz. Philipp von Zabern.

Olausson, D. (1987) Experiment på gott och ont, *Forntida teknik: Experimentell arkeologi*, 15, 5–13.

Olsen, Bjørnar (1997) *Fra ting til tekst: teoretiske perspektiv i arkeologisk forskning*. Oslo. Universitetsforlaget.

Peacock, E. E. (2001) The contribution of experimental archaeology to the research of ancient textiles, in Walton Rogers, P., Bender Jørgensen, L., Rast-Eicher, A. and Wild, J. P. (eds), *The Roman Textile Industry and its Influence: A Birthday Tribute to John Peter Wild*, 181–192. Oxford. Oxbow Books.

Rast-Eicher, A. and Thijsse, S. (2001) Anbau und Verarbeitung von Lein: Experiment und archäologisches Material, *Zeitschrift für Schweizerische Archäologie und Kunstgeschichte*, 58 (1), 47–56.

Reichert, A. (2006) Von Kopf bis Fuss – gut behütet und beschuht in der Steinzeit. Rekonstruktion von neolithischer Kopf- und Fussbekleidung und Trageversuche, *Experimentelle Archäologie in Europa. Bilanz 2006*, 7–23. Oldenberg. Isensee.

Ruscillo, D. (2006) Faunal remains and murex dye production, in Shaw, J. W. and Shaw, M. C. (eds), *Kommos V. The Monumental Minoan Buildings at Kommos*, 776–844. Princeton. Princeton University Press.

Ræder Knudsen, L. (1994) Analysis and reconstruction of two tabletwoven bands from the Celtic burial Hochdorf, in Jaacks, G. and Tidow, K. (eds), *Archäologische Textilfunde (NESAT V)*, 53–60. Neumünster. Textilmuseum Neumünster.

Ræder Knudsen, L. (1998) An Iron Age cloak with tablet-woven borders: a new interpretation of the method of production, in Bender Jørgensen, L. and Rinaldo, C. (eds), *Textiles in European Archaeology: Report from the 6th NESAT Symposium*, 79–84. Göteborg. Göteborg University Department of Archaeology.

Ræder Knudsen, L. (2002) La tessitura con le tavolette nella tomba 89, in von Eles Masi, P. and Bendi, C. (eds), *Guerriero e sacerdote: autorità e comunità nell'età del ferro a Verucchio: La tomba del trono*, 230–243. Firenze. All'Insegna del Giglio.

Schierer, I. (2005) Experiments with weaving and weaving tools. Basic considerations after 20 years of work, in Bichler, P., Grömer, K., Hofmann-de Keijzer, R., Kern, A. and Reschreiter, H. (eds), *Hallstatt Textiles. Technical Analysis, Scientific Investigation and Experiment on Iron Age Textiles*, 97–100. Oxford. Archaeopress.

Schlabow, K. (1937) *Germanische Tuchmacher der Bronzezeit.* Neumünster. Wachholtz.

Schlabow, K. (1951) Der Thorsberger Prachtmantel, der Schlüssel zum altgermanischen Webstuhl, in Kersten, K. (ed.), *Festschrift für Gustav Schwantes zum 65. Geburtstag dargebracht von seinen Schülern und Freunden*, 176–201. Neumünster. Wachholtz.

Schlichtherle, H. and Feldtkeller, A. (2003) Sperimentazione per la tessitura di fasce, in Bazzanella, M., Mayr, A., Rast-Eicher, A. and Moser, L. (eds), *Textiles: intrecci e tessuti dalla preistoria europea*, 106. Trento. Provincia Autonoma di Trento.

Sheffer, A. (1981) The use of preforated clay balls on the warp-weighted loom, *Tel Aviv – Journal of the Tel Aviv University, Institute of Archaeology*, 3, 81–83.

Springe, E. and Sydberg, E. (1986) Varptyngd vävstol, *Forntida teknik*, 13, 44.

Stærmose Nielsen, K.-H. (1999) *Kirkes væv: Opstadsvævens historie og nutidige brug.* Lejre. Historisk-Arkæologisk Forsøgscenter.

Sundström, A. (1995) Reproduction of horsehair tablet braid from Scandinavia's migration period, *Archaeological Textiles Newsletter*, 21, 24–26.

Svinicki, E. (1974) *Teinture et filage.* Paris. Dessain et Tolra.

Sylvan, V. (1941) *Woollen Textiles of the Lou-Lan People*, 15. Stockholm. The Sino-Swedish Expedition.

Tiedemann, E. J. and Jakes, K. A. (2006) An exploration of prehistoric spinning technology: spinning efficiency and technology transition, *Archaeometry*, 48 (2), 293–307.

Trigger, B. C. (2006) *A History of Archaeological Thought.* 2nd edition. Cambridge. Cambridge University Press.

Tzachili, I. (1997) Υφαντική και υφάντρες στο προϊστορικό Αιγαίο. 2000–1000 π.Χ. *(Yfantike kai Yfantres sto Proistoriki Aigaio).* Crete. University Press of Crete.

van Gijn, A. and Lammers, Y. (2005) Extracting, processing and using fibres from plants using stone, bone and antler tools. Report. Reference number: HAF 16/05. http://www.english.lejre-center.dk/1000-USES-FOR-PLANT-FIBRE.491.0.html.

van Gijn, A. and Verbaas, A. (2006) Extracting, processing and using fibres from plants using stone, bone and antler tools. Report. Reference number: HAF 16/06. http://www.english.lejre-center.dk/1000-USES-FOR-PLANT-FIBRE.491.0.html.

van Gijn, A. and Verbaas, A. (2007) Extracting, processing and using fibres from common reed and willow bark with unretouched blades and quartier d'orange. Report. Reference number: HAF 13/07. http://www.sagnlandet.dk/1000-USES-FOR-PLANT-FIBRE.491.0.html.

Vogelsang-Eastwood, G. M. (1999) *Tutankhamun's Wardrobe: Garments from the Tomb of Tutankhamun.* Rotterdam. Barjesteh van Waalwijk van Doorn and Co.

Wardle, D. E. H. (1988) Does reconstruction help? A Mycenaean dress and the Dendra suit of armour, in French, E. B. and Wardle, K. A. (eds), *Problems in Greek Prehistory*, 469–477. Bristol. Bristol Classical Press.

CHAPTER 2

The basics of textile tools and textile technology – from fibre to fabric

Eva Andersson Strand

The need for textiles in the Bronze Age Aegean and Eastern Mediterranean would have been substantial. A variety of written and iconographic sources have provided a considerable amount of information on textiles and textile production in certain areas during various periods of the Bronze Age, and have shown that textiles were regarded as being of high value (*e.g.* Waetzoldt 1972; Barber 1991; De Fidio 1998–1999; Killen 2007; Breniquet 2008; Michel and Nosch 2010). People required textiles from the cradle to the grave as protection from the heat and the cold, as well as the rain and the sun. The costumes people wore reflected hierarchy, status and the group(s) to which they did or did not belong. Textiles were needed for sails, and also for tents and for the wrapping of goods. Furnishings such as wall hangings, carpets, pillows and coverings would have been used in many households. All of these textiles were produced by textile craftspeople labouring in various organisational modes.

The production process of a textile from fibre to finished product is complex and includes several stages. The general stages in textile production are fibre procurement, fibre preparation, spinning, weaving and finishing and each stage includes several processes. The focus of this chapter is to briefly explain the different stages and processes in order to provide a better understanding of the complexity of textile production in the Aegean and Eastern Mediterranean region during the Bronze Age.[1] However, the Bronze Age covers a period of *c.* 2000 years, and the nature of textile production of course varied both across space and over time. The Eastern Mediterranean area also encompasses different climatic zones, which provided a range of conditions and possibilities for textile production. Before the production of a textile, several decisions have to be made in order to best achieve the desired result. These choices are influenced by access to fibres and tools, but also craft traditions.

The archaeological finds of textile tools give a good, but by no means complete, representation of textile production in the Eastern Mediterranean region during the Bronze Age. Therefore, in order to provide a better picture of the complexity of textile production and all its possibilities, available craft knowledge from other areas and periods have been included.

Fibres for producing textiles

Several different fibres, both plant and animal, can and have been used to produce textiles. The fibres in use in the Eastern Mediterranean Bronze Age, according to written sources, were primarily sheep wool and flax. However, fibres such as *nettle* and *tree bast,* but also *goat, horse* and *camel wool* could additionally have been used (*e.g.* Helbaek 1959; Ryder 1983; Barber 1991; Völling 2008; Breniquet 2008; Andersson Strand 2012, see also chapter 3).

Silk, sea silk and cotton, as far as it is known, did not come into common use until later periods and will not be discussed in this chapter (*e.g.* Barber 1991; Shishlina *et al.* 2003; Völling 2008).

Plant fibres for textiles

Flax

Flax derives from the annual plant of the *Linacea* species, notably *linum usitatissimum* (Fig. 2.1), and is considered to have always been one of the most important plant fibres used in textile production (*e.g.* Barber 1991, 11). The best quality flax fibre is narrow in diameter (0.002 cm), strong and soft and 45–100 cm in length. It has a silky lustre and varies in colour from a creamy white to a light tan. Linen textiles are cool to wear, since flax fibres conduct heat extremely well. They are able to absorb moisture very easily, but at the same time moisture evaporates from them quickly. Over time, linen can become almost as soft and lustrous as silk, but it creases easily because flax fibres lack elasticity (Kemp and Vogelsang-Eastwood 2001, 26).

The earliest definite evidence of cultivated flax, dating to the 8th millennium BC, is linseed from Tell Aswad in Syria, while one of the earliest known linen textiles, from Nahal Hemar in Israel, is dated to the 7th millennium BC (*e.g.* Bar-Yosef 1985; Schick 1988, 12; see also chapter 3). Other important finds of linen textiles, dated to *c.* 6000 BC, come from Çatal Hüyük in Turkey (*e.g.* Burnham 1965, 169; Barber 1991).

The best conditions for flax cultivation are fertile, well drained loams, while sandy soils should be avoided. Since the roots grow near the surface and are weak, the preparation of the soil has to be done carefully. Flax reduces the nutrients in the soil and a crop rotation

Fig. 2.1. Linum Usitatissimum (drawing: courtesy of Margarita Gleba).

with long gaps between sowing is required. The yield will otherwise be reduced and the flax will become more susceptible to different diseases such as fungi attacks. Flax needs regular access to water during cultivation (*e.g.* Montgomery 1954; Barber 1991, 11; Kemp and Vogelsang-Eastwood 2001, 25–27).

The time of year for sowing and harvesting depends on region and the type of climate. In the Nile Valley sowing takes place in mid-November, while in the northern, colder parts of the Mediterranean sowing takes place during spring. It takes approximately three months for the flax to mature (Vogelsang-Eastwood 1992, 5).

Information on the cultivation and processing of flax in the Bronze Age Eastern Mediterranean comes primarily from archaeological evidence such as macrofossil analyses, but additionally from Egyptian wall paintings and models from Egyptian tombs. For the later periods there are also written sources, for example, Linear B (Late Bronze Age) and the Roman author Pliny (*Natural History* Book 19. 1–3, *e.g.* Barber 1991, 11–15; Vogelsang-Eastwood 1992, 5–15; Kemp and Vogelsang-Eastwood 2001, 34; Gleba 2008, 91–92; Killen 2007; Nosch forthcoming). However, considerable knowledge on linen textiles and the processing of flax fibres has also been obtained from the Neolithic-Bronze Age finds from central Europe (*e.g.* Rast-Eicher 2005). It is interesting to note that the processes in manual flax preparation have changed very little over the millennia and are still used today.

Flax can, depending on what type of fibres are required, be pulled in different stages of ripeness. If the stems are pulled when they are still green, the fibres are very thin and fine textiles woven with thin threads can be produced. If the stems are slightly older and the lower leaves are starting to yellow, the fibres will be slightly coarser and suitable for clothing of a generally good quality. If pulled when the stems are yellow and the seeds are very ripe, the resulting fibres will be coarse, and are more suitable for rope and utilitarian fabrics which require strength (*e.g.* Vogelsang-Eastwood 1992, 6; Kemp and Vogelsang-Eastwood 2001, 27).

Turning the flax stems into processed fibres involves many steps (*e.g.* Barber 1991, 13–15; Vogelsang-Eastwood 1992, 10–12; Völling 2008, 281–282). When flax is ripe it is pulled up by the roots and the seeds are harvested (rippled). In order to separate the fibre bundles from the woody parts of the stems the flax can then be retted. In the retting process the stems can either be placed in water or spread on the ground. The moisture from the water (through the growth of bacteria) or from dew, if spread on the ground (through the growth of fungi), assists in the process of dissolving the pectin between the bundles of fibre in the bark and the stem.

The next step is breaking, in which a wooden club is used to break up the stem and the bark which have to be separated from the fibres (Fig. 2.2). Thereafter, the flax has to be scutched with a broad wooden knife, which scrapes away the remainder of the stem and bark (Fig. 2.3). Finally, the fibres are hackled so that all parts of the stems are removed and the fibres are evenly separated. The stems could also be brushed with a smaller brush to remove the last parts of the stems (Fig. 2.4). After these processes, the fibres are ready to be spun (Fig. 2.5).

The fibres can be processed without retting, but the fibre quality will not be as good as with retted flax and it will be harder to take out the woody parts, *etc.* which have to be removed if the fibres are to be used for clothing or finer textiles.

During processing, for example when scutching the stems, parts of the stems and also the fibres will end up as "waste". This waste can also be processed and spun, but the yarn will be coarser and not suitable for clothing. Some of the waste, containing mostly parts of the stems, but also short broken fibres, can also be used for other purposes such as insulating material in buildings and to careen ships.

The tools used in these production processes are primarily made of wood and it may be surmised that this is why these tools are rarely found in archaeological contexts. However, several wooden mallets that could have been used for beating the flax stem have been found in Middle and New Kingdom sites in Egypt, but unfortunately, according to our knowledge, no scutching boards have been found (Vogelsang-Eastwood 1992, 12). Another exception is the well preserved tools, including scutching tools recovered from the Neolithic-Bronze Age lake dwellings in Italy and Switzerland (*e.g.* Barber 1991, 14).

The manual processing of the flax fibres and other plant fibres such as hemp is dangerous work. *Byssinosis* "brown lung disease" is an occupational lung disease that is still common

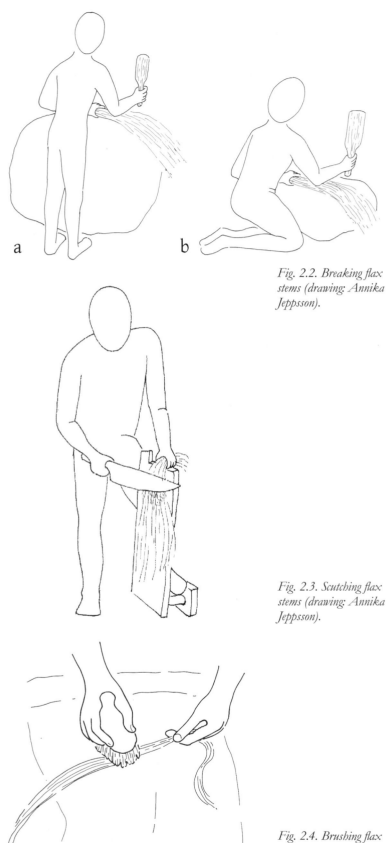

a   b

Fig. 2.2. Breaking flax stems (drawing: Annika Jeppsson).

Fig. 2.3. Scutching flax stems (drawing: Annika Jeppsson).

Fig. 2.4. Brushing flax stems (drawing: Annika Jeppsson).

Fig. 2.5. Flax fibres prepared for spinning (photo: CTR).

among workers who prepare flax manually. The workers who break the stems, and particularly those who scutch the stems, are the most exposed (Noweir *et al.* 1975).[2] The effects are likely to have been recognised in ancient flax producing societies, and it is therefore plausible that this work was well planned and that these processes took place outdoors.

Other plant fibres

Hemp, *Cannabis sativa*, and nettle, *Urtica dioica* are two other textile plant fibres (Barber 1991, 15–20). Since it is difficult to distinguish between hemp, flax and nettle, it has in the past been hard to identify the use of hemp and nettle fibres in textiles. However, new analytical methods have recently made the identification more secure (Bergfjord and Holst 2010; see also chapter 3).

It is thought that hemp was used for the production of textiles by the inhabitants of the Eurasian steppe from the Neolithic period (Shishlina *et al.* 2002 in Gleba 2008, 70), but was not used in the Mediterranean area until the Iron Age (Barber 1991, 18). Hemp is taller than flax and the fibres are generally coarser than flax fibres. Therefore, it has been assumed that hemp was not generally used for clothing, but rather for sails, ropes and nets.

Archaeological finds of textiles made of nettle fibres are also extremely rare, but nettle has been used as a textile fibre in northern and eastern Europe, and is still used today. The nettle fibres are shorter and finer than flax and hemp fibres, but can easily be used to produce textiles not only for clothing, but also for rope as well as other products.

Both hemp and nettle fibres can be processed in similar ways and with the same type of tools as flax fibres (*e.g.* Mannering 1996).

Animal fibres for textiles

Wool and sheep[3]

Wool fibres are flexible and elastic; the fibres also have kinks, producing air pockets between the kinks; these pockets maintain their temperature, which is the reason why a woollen textile, woven or felted, has good insulating qualities (*e.g.* Barber 1991, 20; Völling 2008, 282–284). Moreover, wool is not highly flammable, which makes it excellent to use as a protection against intense heat.

The wool from domesticated sheep was available as a textile fibre throughout the Bronze Age (*e.g.* Barber 1991).[4] It has been suggested that different sheep breeds already existed in the Bronze Age (*e.g.* Waetzoldt 1972). However, the possibility that sheep breeding and variations in wool quality may additionally have developed and changed during the Bronze Age itself also has to be considered (Fig. 2.6).

There is an ongoing discussion regarding the diameter of wool fibres and how this can be related to different sheep breeds and to the development of the woolly sheep (for more information see *e.g.* Barber 1991; Ryder 1992; Rast-Eicher 2008). However, it is important to note that the quality of the wool fibres does not only vary between various breeds, as there is also a difference between individuals within the same breed, and between the wool from a lamb, a ewe, a ram or a wether. Furthermore, there is a great variation in the coarseness of wool fibres depending on which part of the sheep the wool is obtained from. Wool from the thighs, for example, is coarser and longer than the wool from the side and shoulders. Moreover, the wool on each sheep contains three different parts: hair, under wool and kemp (Fig. 2.7) (*e.g.* Ryder 1983; Barber 1991, 20–21). The hair can either be spun on its own into a hard and strong yarn, or can be spun with the under wool. The under wool fibres are thinner, and tend to be shorter than the hair, but can be spun separately from it. Yarn spun partly or entirely from under wool will be softer than a yarn spun with only hair. The kemp fibres are stiff, brittle and break easily; they cannot, therefore, be spun on their own (*e.g.* Barber 1991, 20–21; Rast-Eicher 2008). Textile analyses demonstrate that different types of fibres and yarn have been used for producing different types of textiles. A coarse fibre and a strong yarn would be preferable if producing, for example, a sail, while a soft yarn might have been more suitable for an inner garment.

How much wool one sheep can yield depends on the breed of sheep, but also on whether it is a lamb, ewe, ram or wether. Differences can also be due to the food available to the sheep and also to the type of climate. However, it has been suggested that the annual raw wool yield per mature sheep in a prehistoric society would have been approximately 500 g to 1000 g, with a concentration at just over 750 g (Waetzoldt 1972; Petruso 1986, 30).

During the Bronze Age wool could have been obtained by plucking or cutting. During later periods shears may have been used, but it is likely that knives were the oldest tools utilised. A sheep can be sheared twice a year, but it can only be plucked once a year, when it is moulting. Primitive sheep moult in late spring/early summer, but this of course also depends on which region the sheep are from, since obviously there is not only a difference between the southern and northern areas of the Mediterranean, but also between lowland and highland areas (Barber 1991; Andersson Strand 2012).

The quality of the spun thread partly depends on how carefully the wool is prepared (it also depends on the spinner and spinning tools, see below). After plucking/cutting the different fibre types can be sorted, if desired. The criteria for wool sorting may be colour, fineness, crimp, length, strength and/or structure (Leadbeater 1976, 21–26; Gleba 2008, 98).

The wool can also be washed, either before the wool is plucked/cut or after. However, if the wool is washed before spinning one has to add a little fat, since the lanolin (the natural wool grease) is washed out. The lanolin helps to "glue" the fibres together during the spinning process. If the wool is to be dyed, the fibres have to be washed or the dye stuff will not penetrate the fibres.

The wool can be spun immediately after it has been cut or plucked from the sheep, but usually it is first teased by hand or combed with the aid of wool combs with long teeth. When combed, the long hair is also separated from the under wool (Fig. 2.8). The short wool fibres – the under wool – can also be teased out with the aid of a teasel. Combing and teasing both remove dirt and tangles which makes the spinning process easier and the yarn produced

Fig. 2.6. Different wool types (photos: CTR).

more evenly spun (Fig. 2.9).[5] Another way of preparing the wool is to flog the wool fibres with a whip. One can flog the fibres on a whole fleece, but it is important to do this carefully so that all the fibres become accurately mixed. A lot of wool is wasted during these various processes, but this could have been used for other purposes, such as filling or insulation.

The fact that there was a need for wool fibres of different qualities for various types of textiles, and the fact that the wool can be divided into so many fibre types can also explain why wool is frequently categorised into different categories in the written sources. For example, according to Ur III texts the wool was sorted into no less than five categories or groups: royal quality, next quality (after royal), 3rd quality, 4th quality and poor quality. Only a very small percentage of the wool was of high or poor quality, while 3rd and 4th quality were the largest groups (Waetzoldt 1972).

Pulmonary anthrax, also known as the wool sorter's disease, is a deadly disease for both animals and humans. The earliest known reference to anthrax is in the bible, in the Book of Exodus. This disease is also later well described by the Roman author Virgil (*e.g.* Witkowski and Parish 2002, 336–337). Even if it is clear that this disease may have existed during the Bronze Age, it is of course not possible to say to what extent. Anthrax

was known to be associated with moist soil – rivers, valleys, swampy districts and lake regions (Laforce 1978, 957). The disease can have a devastating effect on a society whose economy is based on wool and textiles. It has been calculated that in the mid 18th century AD, half of all the sheep in Europe died as a result of anthrax. The occupations at risk from anthrax include wool sorters, combers, carders and spinners, as well as cloth and carpet weavers (Witkowski and Parish 2002, 340).

Only sheep wool has been discussed above, but it is clear that the use of goat wool could also have been common in the Bronze Age. However, as is the case with flax, hemp and nettle, it is difficult to distinguish between sheep and goat wool. Goat wool can be processed in the same way as sheep wool.

Spindles and spinning

In textile production, the making of the yarn is one of the most important processes. The yarn can be produced in several different ways and different spinning methods can be identified. A spun yarn can be hard or loosely twisted and the thread can be spun thick or thin. The choices spinners make when producing the yarn depend on what type of yarn is required for producing a certain type of textile and what fibre materials and tools are available. Since few textiles have survived from the area and time under study (see chapter 3), it is difficult to give concrete examples of the types of choices that could have been made by spinners working in the Eastern Mediterranean during the Bronze Age. From other areas and periods where textiles are preserved, textile analyses have, for example, demonstrated that for an inner garment a thin spun thread of either linen or wool was often preferred. For an outer garment that has to be both hard wearing and waterproof, a coarser hard spun wool thread of hair was chosen for the warp and a coarser, but more loosely spun wool thread of under wool was chosen for the weft (*e.g.* Hägg 1984). It is important to take into account that the Eastern Mediterranean Bronze Age covers a large area and a period of more than 2000 years, so the spinners' "choices" are likely to have changed over time and according to region.

One of the simplest methods of spinning, which is probably the oldest, but is also the slowest technique, is "hand spinning". In this

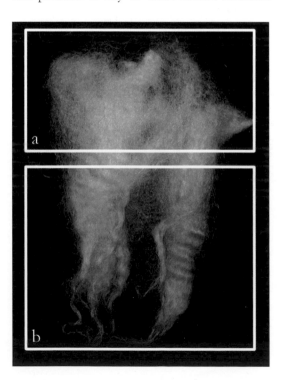

Fig. 2.7. Wool fibres (a) underwool (b) hair (photo: CTR).

method the fibres are drawn out without a tool and the thread is formed by twisting the fibres by hand or by rolling them against the thigh (also known as thigh spinning). A study comparing thigh spinning and spindle spinning has clearly demonstrated that spindle spinning was 2.1 times as fast as the average for the non-spindle technique (Tiedemann and Jakes 2006). Even if the fastest spindle spinner and the slowest thigh spinner were excluded, the spindle spinning was 1.8 times faster (Tiedemann and Jakes 2006, 301).

It is therefore not surprising that spinning tools have probably been used since the Neolithic era, and maybe even earlier, in many areas (*e.g.* Barber 1991, 51). A spindle consists of a spindle shaft, generally made of wood, and often also a spindle whorl. Spindle whorls vary with regards to the material they are made of, for example, fired clay, stone and bone, but they also vary in shape and size (*e.g.* Barber 1991, 52–68; Carington Smith 1992, 675–686; Gleba 2008, 103–109).

Since the shaft is rarely preserved, most of our knowledge about spinning in antiquity is based on finds of spindle whorls. Spindle whorls are known from many areas and different periods of the Bronze Age Eastern Mediterranean. However, it is important to note that spinning cannot be excluded even if no spinning tools are found. Furthermore, there is always a possibility that people at the same place and time could have used different spinning techniques and tools.

After the fibres have been prepared, they are twisted by hand into a short thread which is attached to the shaft. Before spinning, wool can also be prepared in a soft rove or rolag, which is then fastened onto a distaff (Fig. 2.10.a). The spindle shaft is rotated while the spinner simultaneously draws out the fibres, and it is the twisting of the fibres around their own axis that forms the thread. During spinning, the spindle can hang freely (a so-called suspended spindle) (Fig. 2.10.a), or it can be supported, with the shaft resting on the ground or in a bowl, or on the thigh. On a suspended spindle the whorl can be placed at the top (high-whorl), the bottom (low-whorl) or sometimes also in the middle (mid-whorl) of the shaft. On a supported spindle, the whorl is placed at the top of the shaft (Fig. 2.10.b). A third variation is the hand-held spindle, a shaft with or without a whorl that is turned

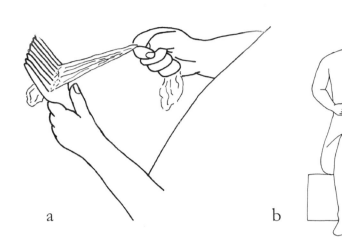

a   b

Fig. 2.8. Wool combing (drawings: Annika Jeppsson).

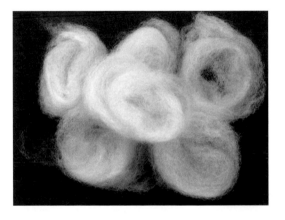

Fig. 2.9. Wool fibres prepared for spinning (photo: CTR).

within the hand (*e.g.* Crowfoot 1931; Barber 1991, 43). Finally, a thread can be spun by using a hooked shaft; in this technique the spinner draws out the fibres and forms the thread by rolling the shaft against the thigh (Fig. 2.10.c) (*e.g.* Crowfoot 1931, 10; Hochberg 1977, 23–24; Barber 1991, 42). The hook helps to control the fibres when they are drawn out.

A slightly different way of producing a thread is splicing, which could also be considered as a variant of the non-spindle technique (Fig. 2.11). This method for producing a linen thread is known from Bronze Age Egypt. When splicing, the ends of the long flax fibres, a few at a time, are joined together by hand in a long string and the result is rolled into a large ball or coil. The spliced threads can be twisted together, probably when wetted, in order to make the thread stronger. With this technique

Fig. 2.10. Different types of spindles and spinning techniques (a) Low whorl spindle/ suspended spinning (b) high whorl spindle/ supported spinning (c) hooked spindle/ supported spinning (drawings: Annika Jeppsson).

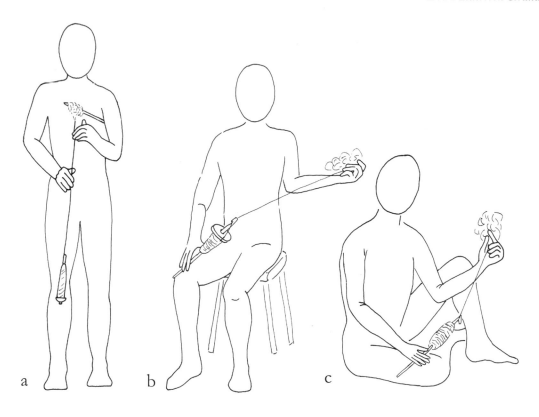

Fig. 2.11. Splicing (drawing: Annika Jeppsson).

it is possible to produce a very thin and delicate linen thread (*e.g.* Barber 1991, 47–50; Vogelsang-Eastwood 1992, 17).

While the choice of spinning tool and technique may be largely dependent on craft traditions, it may also be influenced by the type of fibre used. In early 20th century Trans-Jordan, Crowfoot observed the same spinners using more than one spinning technique (Crowfoot 1931). When they were spinning short clippings of goat hair they used the hand-held spindle, while they used either a supported or a suspended spindle for the long sheep wool (Crowfoot 1931, 14).

The type of fibres used may additionally affect the spinning time. Research has demonstrated that it takes a shorter amount of time to spin hemp and linen thread than it does to spin the same amount of wool thread, and it has been suggested that this is due to the length of the fibres (Tiedemann and Jakes 2006, 301–302).

Spinning time is also dependent not only on the type of tool used, but also on the spinners' experience. In a Finnish study of spinning productivity made in 1956, Vallinheimo compared spindle and spinning wheel techniques (Vallinheimo 1956). A Finnish professional spinner spun no less than 2.4 m of linen thread per minute on a spindle. With a spinning wheel, the winner of a national Finnish spinning competition spun wool yarn at a rate of 7.19 m per minute. In comparison, 21 students with two years' spinning experience (4–5 hours a week), spun linen yarn on a wheel at a rate of 2.3 m per minute (Vallinheimo 1956; Tiedemann and Jakes 2006, 302). This clearly demonstrates that the tool used does not necessarily increase the rate of yarn production and that the spinners' level of experience is of importance when discussing time consumption for textile production.

During spinning the fibres can be twisted to the left, "s", or right, "z" (Fig. 2.12). This choice can be due to tradition, but is also affected by whether the spinner if left or right handed (approximately 90% of the population is right handed). The choice of spinning tool does not, in general, affect if the spinner can spin a s- or z-spun thread, it is always possible to choose direction. However, when spinning on a high-whorl spindle one normally starts to spin by rolling the shaft downwards on the thigh with one's hand and, if right-handed, the thread will automatically be s-spun. On the other hand, when spinning on a low-whorl spindle the spinner starts to flick the spindle by hand. In this case it is more natural for a right-handed spinner to flick the spindle to the right, with a resulting z-spun thread (*e.g.* Crowfoot 1931; Hochberg 1977; Barber 1991, 65–68). For the Bronze Age, low-whorl spindles are known from the northern Mediterranean area, high-whorl spindles from Egypt and middle-whorl spindles from Anatolia. It is therefore interesting to note that textiles from Egypt are generally s-spun while textiles in the northern Mediterranean area are generally z-spun (*e.g.* Barber 1991, 60–61; Gleba 2008, 101).

After a yarn is spun, one thread can be spun together with one or more further threads in order to get a plied yarn; the yarn can be plied both S and Z. A spinning bowl may have been used to apply this technique. A spinning bowl could also have been useful when re-spinning a yarn or, for example, spliced linen (*e.g.* Crowfoot 1931, 27; Barber 1991, 70–76).

It is also interesting to note that yarn with different spin directions can and has been used in the same textile. If the warp in a woollen textile is z-spun and the weft is s-spun, all the fibres will lie in the same direction, which makes the fabric easier to full. It is also known that by combining s- and z-spun yarn in both warp and weft in the same setup one will give the textile a specific lustre; a so-called spin patterned fabric (*e.g.* Bender Jørgensen 1986, 134). It cannot be excluded that s- and z-spun yarn was consciously used for different purposes, for example, for creating a particular pattern.

When spinning with a supported or suspended spindle, it is easier to hold the raw material on a distaff, so that the prepared fibres are not mixed up again. Another advantage is that one can put a lot of spinning material on the distaff, more than can be held in the hand. It has been suggested that long distaffs (held under the arm or in a belt) have been used for longer fibres, while shorter hand-held distaffs have been used when spinning short fibres (Gleba 2008, 109). When one has spun a certain length, depending on whether one stands or sits when spinning, the thread is wound up on the spindle and it is possible

to continue spinning. This is repeated until the spindle shaft has been filled with thread which is then wound up on a reel, onto a weft bobbin or into a ball (Fig. 2.13).

In the case of spun wool, because of the wool fibres' elasticity, especially for warp yarn, it is important to "kill" the thread so that when used it does not roll up or twist together. This is done by winding the yarn very tautly onto a reel and leaving it there for a couple of days. Subsequently the wool yarn can be used as warp yarn on a loom. It is also important that as few as possible of the wool fibres protrude from the thread (Fig. 2.14). The thread has to be as smooth as possible; otherwise, during the weaving process the fibres in threads lying beside each other in the warp will hook into each other. This makes it more difficult to change the shed and in the end the thread will be badly worn, or, in the worst case scenario it will break. This problem can be avoided to a certain extent by adding more twist to the thread when it is spun (Andersson 2003, 24; see chapters 4.1 and 4.2). This is of course also important when spinning flax, but since the wool fibres are shorter the number of fibres protruding is much higher.

The function of the spindle whorls and the functional implications of the spindle whorls' size must also be discussed. Several researchers have suggested that small and light spindle whorls have been used for spinning thin yarn while heavier spindle whorls have been used for spinning thicker yarn (*e.g.* Hochberg 1977; Liu 1978, 99; Barber 1991, 52). In this respect,

Fig. 2.12. An s- and an z-spun thread (drawing: Annika Jeppsson).

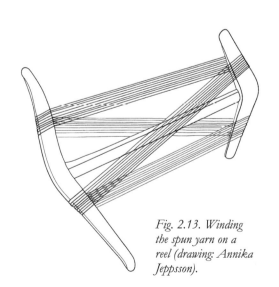

Fig. 2.13. Winding the spun yarn on a reel (drawing: Annika Jeppsson).

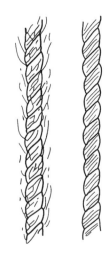

Fig. 2.14. A closed and a non-closed thread (drawing: Tina Borstam†).

Carington Smith has suggested, in her work with textile tools, that whorls weighing less than 10 g are not suitable for spinning and that their identification as whorls is therefore suspect (Carington Smith 1992, 674). However, in a wide ranging study of spindle whorls, Liu has demonstrated that it is often difficult to distinguish between beads and whorls and furthermore that many beads have functioned as spindle whorls and spindle whorls have also been re-used as beads (Liu 1978). The smallest spindle whorl examined by Liu weighed 1 g and had a diameter of 8 mm (Liu 1978, 90). This whorl, dating to the Islamic period, was from Afghanistan and was used for spinning cotton (*i.e.* very short fibres).

Experiments with the suspended spindle using spindle whorls of various sizes (weighing 5 g, 10 g, 20 g, 27 g, 30 g, 40 g, 70 g and 74 g) and different types of wool have previously been undertaken. The test results demonstrated that it is primarily the weight of the spindle, the fibre material and how well the fibre material is prepared that affects the outcome. It is clear that the lightest spindle whorl could be used for spinning, but only for producing a very thin thread. With the heavier spindle whorls, weighing 40 g and above, one could only spin a thicker thread (Holm 1996, 111–116; Andersson 1999, 23–25; 2003, 25–26). The tests also demonstrated that it is easier to vary the thickness of the spun yarn when spinning with a 15–30 g spindle whorl than when spinning with a lighter spindle whorl or with a heavier spindle whorl. When spinning different fibres (under wool, hair and mixed wool) with the same spindle, the tests showed that the choice of fibres affected the spun thread, and different yarns were produced by use of the same spindle.

Another important result was the degree to which the length of the spindle shaft affected the spinning. When spinning with the lightest 5 g spindle whorl, only a short shaft (< 12 cm) could be used; when using a longer shaft the spindle became unbalanced which negatively affected the spinning process (see chapter 4.1). Finally, the spinning test was primarily made with wool fibres, but the spinners also tested the spinning of flax fibres with the 5 g spindle whorl. The spinners concluded that it was not a problem to spin the flax fibres with this small spindle whorl. The resulting thread was very thin. To conclude, the tests demonstrated

that it was possible to spin both short and long fibres with a whorl weighing 5 g. Furthermore, the tests supported the earlier suggestions that a small spindle whorl can be used for spinning thinner yarn and a heavier spindle whorl for spinning thicker yarn (Andersson 1999, 23–25; 2003, 25–26; Andersson *et al.* 2008).

The difference can be explained by the fact that the lighter the spindle whorl, the less fibre is used per metre; in general, the lighter the spindle, the lighter and thinner the thread; the heavier the spindle whorl, the heavier and thicker the thread.

In the study of textiles from prehistoric central Europe, the terms thread, cord and rope have been defined according to their thread diameter. A thread is up to 2 mm in diameter, a cord is between 2 and 8 mm in diameter and a rope is more than 8 mm (Rast-Eicher 1997, 305, 313). It is important to note that what is a thin and thick yarn is highly subjective even if based on archaeological material. However, it is clear that various types of yarn, from thin to thick, as well as thin cords have been used to produce different types of fabrics in the Eastern Mediterranean.

When spinning with a supported spindle or a handheld spindle and when using the hand/thigh spinning technique one can also spin thinner and thicker threads, but in this case it is only the spinner that controls the outcome, *i.e.* the thickness of the thread.

However, it is important to note that no thread, not even a machine spun thread, is 100 percent evenly spun and a thread can vary in thickness even if spun with the same spindle, the same type of wool and the same spinner (see also chapter 4.1, 4.2, 4.5).

Looms, weaving and weaving techniques

Weaving techniques
A fabric is created by weaving together two thread systems. One of these systems, the warp, runs parallel to the side of the loom and is kept stretched during weaving. The other system, the weft, lies at right angles to the warp and runs alternately over and under the warp threads (Fig. 2.15.a).

A loom can be used to produce a variety of weaves. Tabby weave is the simplest weaving technique. In a tabby the warp threads are divided into two layers, so that the weft runs alternately over one warp thread and under the next (Fig. 2.15.a). A variation of tabby is basket weave, where the warp and weft yarns are used in parallel pairs (Fig. 2.15.b) (*e.g.* Barber 1991, 127; Kemp and Vogelsang-Eastwood 2001, 92).

These techniques are considered to be the oldest known techniques. Tabby is thought to be the technique that was most commonly used in the Eastern Mediterranean during the Bronze Age. However, very few textile fragments dating to this period have been preserved, and the existence of other weaving techniques therefore cannot be excluded (Barber 1991, 167; Spantidaki and Moulhérat 2012; see also chapter 3).

Another technique is twill weaving, which entails the use of more than two layers of warp threads. There are many variations of twill. In a 2/2 twill there are four layers of warp threads and the weft runs alternately over two warp threads, under two warp threads, *etc.* (Fig.

2.16.a). An alternative twill technique is 2/1 twill which uses three layers of warp threads, with the weft thread passing over two warp threads and under one, over two and under one, and so on (Fig. 2.16.b). Other twill weaving techniques are made by operating with different numbers of warp thread layers and by changing how many warp threads the weft goes over and under. Examples of this are diamond twill and chevron twill. Finally, other weaving techniques with non-continuous patterns include brocade, tapestry and pile (for more information see *e.g.* Broudy 1979; Barber 1991).

A textile can be open, with a few threads per centimetre, or the threads can be packed closely together. In a balanced fabric there are an approximately equal number of weft and warp threads of the same type per square centimetre (cm^2). Alternatively, the number of warp and weft threads in a cm^2 may differ. For example, a fabric may be weft faced (with a greater number of weft threads than warp threads

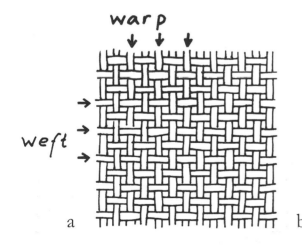

a

b

a

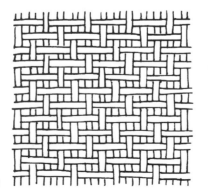

b

Fig. 2.15. Different types of plain weaves (a) tabby (b) basket weave (drawings: Annika Jeppsson after Stærmose Nielsen 1999).

Fig. 2.16. Different types of twill (a) 2/2 twill (b) 2/1 twill (drawings: Annika Jeppsson after Stærmose Nielsen 1999).

and/or thicker weft threads), or warp faced (with a greater number of warp threads than weft threads and/or thicker warp threads). Different types of yarn may also be used in the warp and weft respectively. Both single spun and plied yarn can be used in both warp and weft. The thread count refers to the number of warp and weft threads per cm² and is often used when describing an archaeological textile. Even a small difference in thread diameter, sometimes not even visible to the eye, will affect the finished fabric.

Looms

There is evidence for the use of different types of looms in the Eastern Mediterranean region during the Bronze Age. The presence of loom weights in the archaeological record indicates that the warp-weighted loom was used in some areas of the Eastern Mediterranean at certain periods during the Bronze Age. However, depictions and models also attest that the vertical two-beam loom and the horizontal ground loom were used in other areas (*e.g.* Barber 1991, 81–115; Vogelsang-Eastwood 1992, 28–30). The looms themselves were made of perishable material and are therefore rarely preserved.

Fig. 2.17. Different warping techniques (a) wall warping (b) ground warping frame (c) Sami warping frame (drawings: Annika Jeppsson).

Warping and heddling: the setup of the loom

Before weaving, the warp threads have to be pre-arranged in a more or less fixed set. The setup is done in slightly different ways depending on which loom type is used, but the principles for these three loom types are generally the same. The first step is to warp the warp threads (Fig. 2.17). Depending on the length of the fabric and the desired number of threads per centimetre, the number of metres of yarn required has to be calculated. For example, a fabric that is 1 m wide and 4 m long, with 20 threads per centimetre, requires approximately 8000 m of warp yarn. Each warp thread has to be the length of the decided length of the fabric plus approximately 2–5% needed for thrums.[6] In order to make the warping easier, one can warp several threads together. One warping method known from Middle Bronze Age Egypt as well as from ethnographic sources, is to wind the yarn between pegs fastened on a wall (Fig. 2.17.a) (Kemp and Vogelsang-Eastwood 2001, 314 ff.). Another method also known from the Bronze Age Mediterranean is to wind the warp yarn on supported uprights (Fig. 2.17.b) (Vogelsang-Eastwood 1992, 23). The length between the first and the last peg/upright is the length of the warp threads, including thrums. A third warping method for the horizontal ground loom is to warp and heddle at the same time. This method is still today used by the Beduins in for example Jordan. The process of warping the warp-weighted loom can be slightly different; in this case, the warp threads are woven into a band known as a starting border band. This method is well-known from ethnographic studies in northern Scandinavia, which have documented the use of slightly different warping frames associated with this technique; for example, the warping frame with three uprights as used by the Sami (Fig. 2.17.c) (*e.g.* Hoffmann 1964, 65).

The prepared warp is then stretched between two beams (horizontal and vertical two-beam looms) or, in the case of the warp-weighted loom, the starting border is tied to the starting border rod and the warp threads are fastened to loom weights (Fig. 2.18.a and c). It is important that the warp threads are held taut; if the threads are too loose it will not be possible to change the shed (the space through which the weft is passed) when weaving (Fig. 2.18.d), and if they are too taut they will break. Another

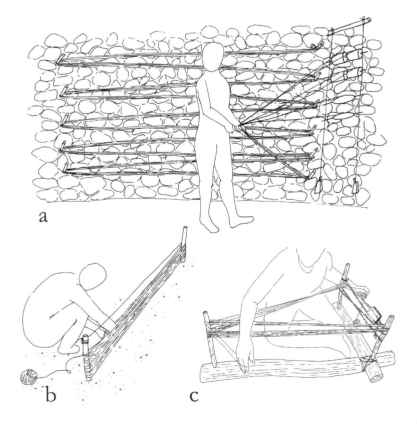

a

b   c

important factor is that the warp threads should point straight or slightly outwards. This is generally demonstrated on depictions of looms, independently of which type of loom is represented (*e.g.* Hoffmann 1964; Barber 1991, 81–115; Gleba 2008, 29–33).

In the process of weaving, the weft is inserted between the warp threads. To facilitate this, the warp threads are first divided into different layers so that sheds can be created. The next step is to heddle the warp threads to heddle rods (Fig. 2.18.b). The heddles, usually made of string, are used to attach each individual warp thread to the heddle rods. When weaving tabby on a vertical two-

beam loom or a horizontal ground loom, warp threads number 1, 3, 5, 7, 9, *etc.* are attached to a heddle rod. The heddle bar can then be used to lift all these alternate warp threads at the same time, thus creating a shed. The heddling on a warp-weighted loom is slightly different (see below).

Once the setup is completed, one can start to weave. In a tabby weave, the heddle rod is lifted and the weft thread is inserted between the two layers of warp threads. In the next step, the first layer of threads goes back into its original position and the weft thread is again inserted between the two layers. The heddle rod is then lifted again, and so on. When

Fig. 2.18. Warp-weighted loom with a tabby setup (with all details) (a) tying the starting border (b) heddling (c) fastening the loom weights (d) changing shed (drawings: Annika Jeppsson).

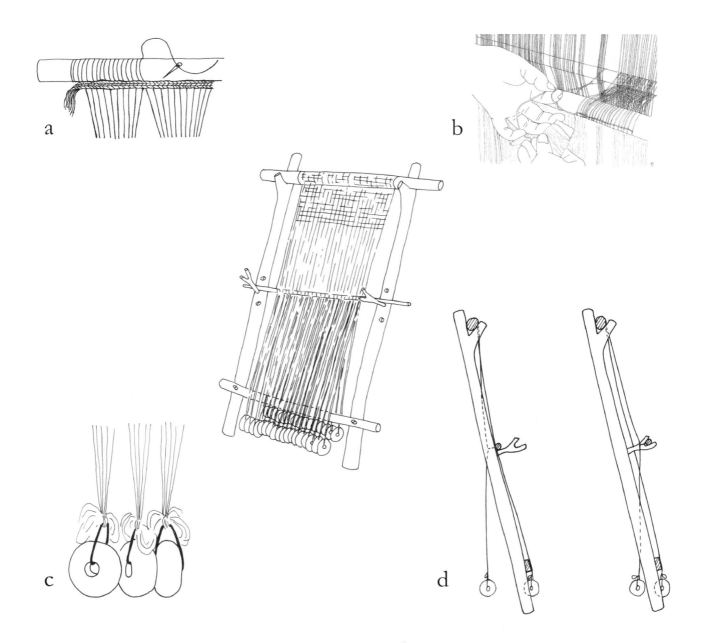

a

b

c

d

weaving twill, which requires more than two sheds and more than one rod, the weaving depends on how many layers of threads need to be lifted at the same time; for example, in a 2/2 twill two of the four layers are always lifted at the same time.

Before inserting a new weft thread, the first weft has to be packed with a tool such as a wooden knife (Fig. 2.19.a). The weft can be kept on a shuttle, which could be a wooden stick or a bone pine on which the weft yarn is wound (Fig. 2.19.b). A multifunctional weaving tool is the single ended or double ended pin-beater, a wooden or bone stick with one or two pointed ends (Fig. 2.19.c). The pin-beater can be used to separate the threads in the weave. A pin-beater is also useful when producing a tapestry weave, to help lift the warp threads (*e.g.* Smith 2001). Finally, another weaving tool is a weaving comb, especially used for weaves with non-continuous patterns (Fig. 2.19.d).

Horizontal ground loom

The idea of stretching the warp threads between two beams appears in different variations in many different cultures and time periods all over the world. The horizontal ground loom is considered to be the oldest loom type, but the earliest depiction is dated to the Late Neolithic and comes from Badari, Egypt (Broudy 1979, 38; Barber 1991, 83). There are different types of the horizontal ground loom, which operate in slightly different ways. For the Bronze Age Eastern Mediterranean, information on how this loom functioned comes principally

from Egypt. Iconographic representations and models show the warp threads stretched over two beams that have been fastened with four corner-pegs (Fig. 2.20). In general, two weavers are depicted, sitting on either side of the loom, changing the shed, entering and beating the weft. The heddle rod is supported with heddle jacks (Barber 1991, 84). The available evidence indicates that this loom type was mainly used for weaving tabby and basket weaves (*e.g.* Vogelsang-Eastwood 1992, 28–29).

Warp-weighted loom

Based on finds of loom weights it has been suggested by Elisabeth Barber that the warp weighted loom was used in central Europe, for example Hungary and perhaps Anatolia already in 6th and maybe 7th millennium, the early Neolithic period. The use expanded into Greece and Northern Italy, further to the west for example Switzerland and to Scandinavia and UK in the Bronze age (Broudy 1979, 26; Barber 1991, 91). A warp-weighted loom (Figs 2.18 and 21) is upright and can be placed leaning against a wall or a beam in the roof. When weaving, one stands in front of it and weaves from the top down. The weft is beaten upwards. The length of the warp can be quite substantial, for example as much as 12.5 m according to Icelandic sources (Geijer 1965, 118).

The vertically hanging warp threads are kept taut by the weight of the attached loom weights. Loom weights can be made of either clay or stone; in the Eastern Mediterranean region during the Bronze Age, the majority of

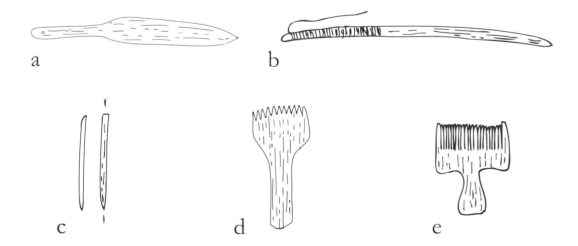

Fig. 2.19. (a) weft beater (length c. 50 cm) (b) shuttle (length c. 42 cm) (c) pin-beater (length c. 10 cm) (d) weaving comb (e) weaving comb (drawings: Annika Jeppsson after Broudy 1979 (a and b) and Shishlina, Orfinskaya and Golikov 2000 (c, d and e).

a

b

c

d

e

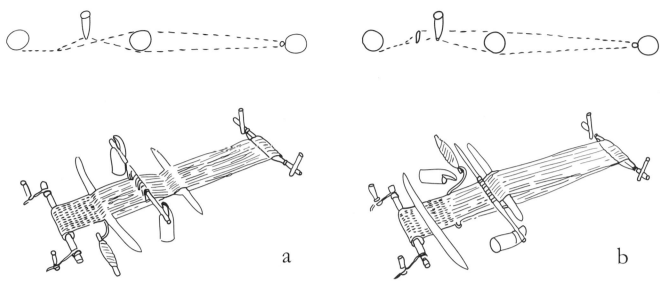

Fig. 2.20. Horizontal ground loom (a) and (b) illustrating the two sheds (drawings: Annika Jeppsson after Broudy 1979).

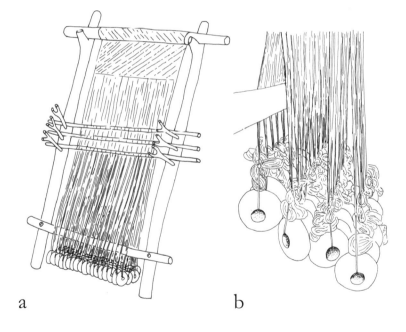

the loom weights are made of clay (chapters 5, 6 and 7). Loom weights vary in size, and clay weights can also vary considerably in shape. However, it is interesting to note that in depictions of warp-weighted looms from various time periods and areas, the loom weights on any given loom are generally shown as being of the same size (*e.g.* Hoffmann 1964; Barber 1991, 81–115; Gleba 2008, 29–33).

The size of the loom weights affects the type of fabric that they are best suited to produce. Thin threads needs less warp tension, while thicker threads require more warp tension; it has been suggested that small, light loom weights have been used for producing fabrics with thinner threads, and larger, heavier loom weights have been used when producing coarser fabrics. It has also been suggested that because linen yarn lacks elasticity, a linen thread requires more tension than a wool thread (Andersson 2003, 28–29).

In order to attach the warp threads to a loom weight, a loop is tied through the loom weight hole and the warp threads are attached to the loop. When using stone or clay weights without a hole, a loop is tied around the weight.

To weave a tabby on a warp-weighted loom, alternate warp threads are placed in front of or behind a rod or shed bar on the loom. Two rows of loom weights are generally used (Fig. 2.18). One row of loom weights lies in front of the shed bar, while the other lies behind it. The

first warp thread is fastened to a loom weight in the front layer, the second to a loom weight in the back layer, the third to the front layer and so on. Depending on the size of the loom weight, a certain number of threads is attached to each individual weight (*e.g.* Andersson 2003, 34). The warp threads lying behind the shed bar are then, via individual strings for each warp thread, attached to a heddle rod. Because the loom leans at an angle, a natural shed is created between the front and back layer of

Fig. 2.21. (a) warp-weighted loom with a twill setup (b) the four rows of loom weights in the setup (drawings: Annika Jeppsson).

warp threads. Once the weft has been passed through this shed, an 'artificial' shed, the so-called counter shed, is created by pulling the heddle rod backwards. This means that the warp threads in the back layer are brought to the front, and the weft thread can be passed through this second shed. This process is then repeated. It is also possible to weave a tabby with the two layers of warp threads attached to just a single row of loom weights, but the warp threads are still separated into one back and one front layer (Hoffmann 1964; see also chapter 4.1).

In a 2/2 twill the first four warp threads lie in four different warp layers, and this pattern is repeated for every following set of four warp threads (Fig. 2. 21). The four layers can be attached to two or four rows of loom weights (Haynes 1975). Experimental work has shown that it is preferable to weave a 2/2 twill with four rows of loom weights (Batzer and Dokkedal 1992), but the alternative method of using just two rows of loom weights is recorded in Icelandic ethnographic sources (Hoffmann 1964). In a 2/1 twill the three different warp thread layers are attached to two or three rows of loom weights. If weaving a twill, two or more heddle rods are used.

Vertical loom with two beams

It has been suggested that the vertical two-beam loom originated in Syria or Mesopotamia, but the earliest representation occurs in Egypt during the last part of the second millennium BC. It has also been suggested that this loom could have been developed in connection with the introduction of wool. Wool is quite easy to dye and this could have inspired tapestry weaving; the two-beam loom is considered to be the most convenient loom for this weaving technique (Broudy 1979, 44; Barber 1991, 113). However, tabby and twill fabrics can also be produced on this loom (Fig. 2.22) (*e.g.* Barber 1991, 116; Gleba and Mannering 2012).

Like the warp-weighted loom, the two-beam loom stands upright. The length of the warp is limited to the size of the loom, since the warp threads are stretched by being attached to the loom. On this loom the weft is packed from the bottom and up, the opposite to the warp-weighted loom. The warp threads are placed side by side and not in layers. It is of course possible to also weave twill and in this case use more heddle rods. However, there are few depictions of this type of loom and they only show one heddle rod (Barber 1991, 113).

Summary

These three loom types all have their advantages and disadvantages. The advantage of the horizontal ground loom is that the warp can be very long. "The length of the cloth woven on a ground loom is limited only to the amount of thread spun..." (Vogelsang-Eastwood 1992, 29). There is ethnographic evidence for fabrics that are over 9 m long, but the warp could probably be much longer (Hilden 1999). According to textile analyses, the width could be substantially more than 2.8 m, but the average width of cloth known from Bronze Age Egypt is 0.9–1.2 m (Barber 1991, 85).

The advantage of the warp-weighted loom is also that the warp can be long; at least 12.5 m, as mentioned above and it can also be more than 1.2 metres wide (Andersson 2003). Furthermore, this loom is also very suitable for weaving dense fabrics and twills. This is because on a warp-weighted loom the warp threads can be separated into layers that lie one behind the other, while on a vertical two-beam and a horizontal ground loom all the warp threads lie side by side in one layer.

The advantage of the two-beam loom is that a very wide fabric can be woven and it is excellent for tapestry weaving. How many weavers work on each type of loom depends on how wide the looms are.

Fig. 2.22. Vertical loom with two-beams, tabby setup (drawing: Annika Jeppsson).

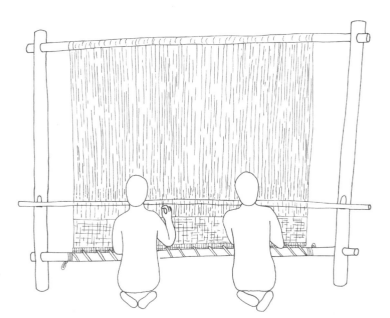

Threads made of all types of fibres can be woven on any of these three loom types, but it is clear that linen is related to the horizontal ground loom while wool is above all related to the warp-weighted and two-beam loom.

As discussed in the previous sections, in order to get the best yield and the most desired result, several decisions have to be made when producing a fabric. The access to fibres and yarn, different types of loom, the need for different types of textiles and last but not least craft traditions, have influenced these choices. Finally the studies on loom types in Egypt demonstrate that in the same period and society, different looms can be used for producing different types of textiles (*e.g.* Barber 1991; Vogelsang-Eastwood 1992).

Dyeing

As mentioned above, it has been suggested that the introduction of wool as a textile fibre also contributed to the introduction of more elaborately coloured textiles. Plant fibres, such as flax and hemp, are more difficult to dye than wool. However, if the waxes and the pectins are removed from the fibres by boiling them, it is possible to dye them, and it should be noted that dyed plant fibre fabrics have occasionally been found (Broudy 1979, 44; Cardon 2007, 11; Gleba 2008, 155). Plant fibres are generally shades of creamy white to light tan. Flax fibres can be bleached by various methods. The simplest method is to expose the linen fabric to the sun (or snow). Another method is to use different types of treatments, for example sulphur. How common these methods were during the Bronze Age is uncertain, however (*e.g.* Barber 1991; Cardon 2007; Gleba 2008).

Wool, on the other hand, comes in a variety of natural colours; brown, black, white, grey, *etc.* It should also be noted that an individual sheep or goat can have several natural shades and this can be utilised in textile production. The different colours can be sorted and spun separately, taking advantage of the shades in the weave.

According to iconography and written sources, it is clear that some textiles were dyed in the Bronze Age Eastern Mediterranean (*e.g.* Barber 1991). It has been suggested that traces of a red colour found in the string holes of a group of beads from Çatal Hüyük, dated

to the very end of the 7th millennium BC, indicate that the beads were originally strung on a red thread (Mellaart 1967, 219; Barber 1991, 223). The earliest finds of dyed textiles are of a later date, however. Fragments of dyed cloth dating to the 4th millennium BC are known from the Levant (Nahal Mishmar, Israel); in Egypt, dyed linen mummy wrappings appear in the 1st Dynasty (*c.* 3100–2890 BC), while in Mesopotamia the earliest evidence is dated to the mid 3rd millennium BC (Barber 1991, 224). In the Aegean, the multi-coloured costumes depicted in frescoes, together with recent evidence for the use of embroidery on fragments of textiles from Akrotiri (Spantidaki and Moulhérat 2012), suggest that fabrics were already being dyed by at least the mid–2nd millennium BC. Dyes are well attested in the Late Bronze Age Aegean Linear B records (Nosch 2004; Nosch forthcoming).

In this respect, it is important to bear in mind that the few finds of dyed textiles from certain areas of the Eastern Mediterranean are likely to reflect the lack of archaeological textiles in general. It is also important to note that textile dye analyses have clearly demonstrated that even if a textile has been dyed, the colour can disappear as a result of the preservation conditions.

The stage at which dyeing takes place varies according to the type of textile fibre used and the effects desired, but in general the dyer can choose to dye the fibre, the yarn or the woven fabric.

Different dyeing techniques can be used. One method is *direct dyeing*, in which dye plants are boiled, or sometimes soaked, in water to prepare a dye bath. In general, the remains of the plants are removed before the textile or yarn is put in the bath. How long the plants are boiled and how long the material has to stay in the bath depends on the plant. One bath can be used several times, but each time the colour of the dyed yarn or textile will be a weaker shade of the original (since there will be less and less dye stuff left in the bath).

However, the majority of the dyeing molecules extracted from plants do not bind strongly with the textile fibres. In order to make them colourfast, the extracts can be combined with various metallic salts and this is known as *mordant dyeing*. Mordants include alum, urine, and salts of copper and tin (Cardon 2007, 20–49). Since it is difficult to detect the use of mordants in dye analyses, it is not clear when dyers started to use mordants and it is therefore uncertain whether they were used during the Bronze Age (*e.g.* Barber 1991, 225–226, 236–237; Cardon 2007). New analyses may change this perception, however.

Numerous plants can be used for dyeing; for example, a blue colour can be obtained from woad (*Isatis tinctoria L.*) (Fig. 2.23.a), a red colour from dyer's madder (*Rubia tinctorum L.*) (Fig. 2.23.b) and a yellow colour from dyer's weed (*Reseda luteola L.*) and saffron (*Crocus sativus L.*) (Cardon 2007). However, very few plants give a red or blue colour, while colours such as yellow, brown, and green can be obtained from several plants. The colour obtained can additionally depend on when the plant is collected; for example, birch leaf should be collected as soon as the leaves have opened up in order to give the strongest colour. The obtained colour can also depend on where the plant is growing; for example, if the plants are growing in earth that naturally contains a significant amount of alum, this will affect the final result, since alum is a mordant. An endless number of combinations can be used to obtain different nuances of colours. If, for example, a grey yarn is dyed in a yellow dye bath, the yarn will become greenish; if one dyes an indigo coloured yarn in a red dye bath, the yarn will be purple.

Another dyeing technique is *vat dyeing*. This is the technique used to dye with indigo plants (blue colours) and with molluscs such as murex (with different types of mollusc giving different colours, including red, blue and purple). Indigotin and shellfish purple are insoluble and it is necessary to submit them to a reduction process in alkaline conditions before they can be absorbed by the textile fibres (Cardon 2007, 4). Cardon writes that "the fibres absorb the dyes in their soluble reduced forms that are barely coloured, being a greenish-yellow. When the fibres are taken out of the vat and exposed to oxygen in the air, indigo and purple precipitate again both inside the textile fibres and at the surface of the textile, which gradually take on blue or violet shades respectively" (Cardon 2007, 4).

Other archaeological evidence for dyeing is scarce, but it is nevertheless important to study contexts and tools that may be related to dyeing. Before dyeing, the fibres, yarn or textiles have to be washed and water is also needed for the different dye baths, and to rinse the fibres, yarn or textiles after dyeing. Different water installations can indicate an area for dyeing and big pots or vats may also have been used in these processes. In order to prepare the dye material and/or mordants, different tools may have been used, such as grinders, pestles and mortars. Finally, raw material debris such as pollen from dye plants and murex shells can indicate dyeing (Cardon 2007; Gleba 2008, 155).

Finishing and felting

After a textile has been woven it can be treated in different ways, depending on its intended future use.

On a wool textile a smooth, napped surface can be produced by brushing and then cutting the fibres on the surface (*e.g.* Gleba 2008, 41–42). Another finishing technique is fulling, which is used in order to make a wool cloth more waterproof. The fabric is then kneaded, stomped and pounded in wet and preferably warm conditions until the surface is matted to the degree desired (Barber 1991, 216). The time it takes depends on how hard fulled one wants the textile to be. This method is important when the textile is going to be used as an outer garment or maybe as a sail.

Felting is a similar method to fulling (although it is not a finishing technique). When felting, only cleaned, loose wool fibres are handled and not a complete woven textile. Layers of the fibres that can be dyed are placed into the finished shape desired; for example, into the shape of a glove or rectangle for a bed covering (Barber 1991, 216). Depending on what type of textile is to be produced, the layers can be thin or thick. Furthermore, the wool fibres will shrink at least 25% and it is therefore important to make the shape much larger than the resulting textile. Finally, the layers are rolled and re-rolled and treated the same way as when fulling a woven textile. Felted textiles can be used as tent cloth, for example, while smaller and thinner pieces can be used as applications on bigger felted or woven textiles. The first well-documented felted textile is from Beycesultan in Turkey and is dated to the Early Bronze Age (Barber 1991, 216).

Smoothing (the old method of ironing) can be done in order to give the fabrics, especially linen, a shiny and smooth surface. Hard materials such as stone or glass can be used as smoothing stones in this process.

Fig. 2.23. Dye plants (a) woad (b) madder (drawings: courtesy of Margarita Gleba).

Other textile techniques

It is not only the types of fabric discussed above that may have been produced. From iconography and written sources it is clear that the Bronze Age textile craftspeople had knowledge of other techniques, such as making different types of bands, using different braiding techniques and probably many other textile production techniques that are not evident from the archaeological record (*e.g.* Barber 1991, 311–382; Breniquet 2008; Völling 2008). Knowledge of other textile techniques is scarce, which is partly due to the fact that these techniques either do not require any tools at all, or the tools are made of perishable material.

Band weaving and plaiting

Although there is evidence to suggest that different types of bands were produced, the earliest finds of band looms date to the middle of the 1st millennium BC. On the other hand, a band can be woven on any loom, for example, a backstrap loom, which is a type of horizontal ground loom (*e.g.* Barber 1991, 116–117).

Tablet weaving is another band weaving technique in which thin tablets made of bone, hardened leather or wood and with two or more holes are used. The warp threads are threaded in the same direction through the holes in the tablets and several tablets are packed together. One method is for the warp threads to hang vertically, with the warp threads held taut by small loom weights, for example small spools (Gleba 2008, 139–140). Another method is to stretch the warp horizontally by tying one end of the warp to a hook and attaching the other end to a belt worn around the waist. Instead of weights, the warp is stretched by the weaver's own body. To weave the simplest band, all the tablets are turned a quarter-turn to create a shed and after inserting the weft, the tablets are turned another quarter-turn and a new shed is created through which the weft is inserted. This process is then repeated. If creating patterns, each tablet can be individually turned (Fig. 2.24). The finished result can vary from a simple band woven with just a few threads to elaborate bands with many warp threads and complex thread patterns. Tablet weaving is often associated with weaving on a warp-weighted loom, as these bands have been used both as starting borders and edge borders (see above). This technique is known from northern and western Europe from the 1st millennium BC, but although the warp-weighted loom was used in parts of the Eastern Mediterranean area during the Bronze Age, it is uncertain whether tablet woven borders were common (Barber 1991, 119; Collingwood 1996, 13).

Plaiting (or braiding) is a technique that does not require any tools. What differentiates plaiting from weaving is that one works with a single thread system and no weft threads are inserted. There are many different variations of plaiting, and elaborate and long bands can be made with threads in different colours and different patterns (Fig. 2.25). Fringes used as decorations or finishing on woven fabrics can also be plaited.

Sprang is one of the more complicated plaiting techniques and for this method a frame is used (Fig. 2.26). Sprang textiles have been

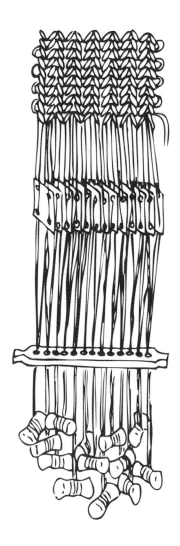

Fig. 2.24. Tablet weaving (drawing: Annika Jeppsson after Ræder Knudsen in Gleba 2008).

used for producing very elastic textiles such as hairnets and stockings, for example. The technique is known from a Neolithic imprint on a potsherd from northern Germany, but it is uncertain whether sprang was used in the Eastern Mediterranean region during the Bronze Age (Barber 1991, 122–123).

Sewing

Needles are known from the Late Palaeolithic (Barber 1991, 39). However, there is little available information on sewing techniques or different types of stitches and furthermore, the finds of Bronze Age sewing needles from the Eastern Mediterranean region are few. Nevertheless, it is very likely that at least some textiles were sewn together, as suggested, for example, by the elaborate patterns depicted in iconographic representations and the impression that some textiles may also have been embroidered and/or that applications may have been sewn on to the fabric (Barber 1991; Spantidaki and Moulhérat 2012). When sewing a fine fabric it is best to use a thin needle, while it is easier to sew coarser and fulled fabrics with a larger bone needle.

The lack of needles from the archaeological material of the Bronze Age Eastern Mediterranean can of course be explained by the fact that they were made of perishable material, but tests made on linen fabrics have demonstrated that it is possible and also quite efficient to sew with the use of an awl and a hard fibre such as horsehair or a bristle used as a needle. In this technique a small hole is made in the fabric with the awl and the thread, attached to the bristle, is pulled through the hole. Different types of stitches can be used. This is a technique well-known from sewing in skin.

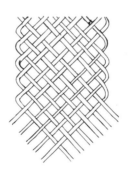

Fig. 2.25. Diagonal plaiting (drawing: Tina Borstam†).

Fig. 2.26. Sprang (drawings: Tina Borstam†).

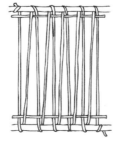 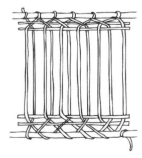 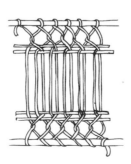

Concluding remarks

In this chapter, different textile techniques and tools have been presented in order to give an overview of different possibilities and to demonstrate the complexity of textile production. Some techniques and tools were used in several regions and over long periods of time, but it is clearly not possible to give an exact picture of the textile production. Even if the 'possibilities' are known, it is not possible to judge which of these the craftspeople would have chosen; only suggestions can be given. Craft traditions and access to raw material, but also regulations and fashion trends, could to a large extent affect the textile craftspeoples' choices and possibilities. In some regions and some periods, the spinner may have had access to many different raw materials, in others not. Additionally, some areas might have had very strong craft traditions that were not easily influenced by new ones. The organisation of the textile production would also have affected the finished results, since there is a difference in a production for household needs and, for example, production within a textile industry. However, it is clear that the production of textiles was hugely important, and would have affected people at all levels of the different Aegean and Eastern Mediterranean Bronze Age societies.

Notes

1 In the following, the Aegean is included when referring to the Eastern Mediterranean.
2 In Noweir *et al.* 1975, certain processes have been named differently. By hackling the authors actually refer to scutching and by combing they refer to hackling (the final process).
3 Wool = all variations of wool fibres on a sheep, hair = the long wool fibres, under wool = the short wool fibres, kemp = stiff and brittle hair.
4 For the discussion concerning the introduction of wool for textiles, see for example Barber 1991; Ryder 1983, 2005; Rast-Eicher 2007; Breniquet 2008; Levy and Gilead 2012.
5 The preparation of the fibres must also be taken into consideration when discussing the development and presence of different sheep breeds. A test was made during the spring of 2009, in which six wool samples (two mixed, two combed and two carded) were taken from two ewes. The samples were sent for fibre analyses, without any information on how many sheep were involved, and the result demonstrated

clearly that according to the wool classification system none of the wool would have come from the same sheep.

6 In weaving, thrums are the extra yarn needed in the setup, which is left over when the fabric is finished. On the horizontal and two-beam loom, unwoven yarn is left at the either end of the warp, where the cloth has been attached to the beams. In the case of the warp-weighted loom, the extra yarn is the result of needing to attach the loom weights. It is possible to use the thrums to make fringes at the end(s) of the cloth, if desired.

Bibliography

Andersson, E. (1999) *The Common Thread: Textile Production During the Late Iron Age–Viking Age*. Lund. Institute of Archaeology, University of Lund.

Andersson, E. (2003) *Tools for Textile Production from Birka and Hedeby: Excavations in the Black Earth 1990–1995*. Stockholm. Birka Project, Riksantikvarieämbetet.

Andersson Strand, E. (2012) The textile *chaîne opératoire*. Using a multidisciplinary approach to textile archaeology with a focus on the ancient Near East, *Paléorient*, 38 (1), 21–40.

Andersson Strand, E., Mårtensson, L., Nosch, M.-L. and Rahmstorf, L. (2008) New Research on Bronze Age Textile Production, *Bulletin of the Institute of Classical Studies* 51, 171–174

Bar-Yosef, O. (1985) *A Cave in the Desert: Nahal Hemar*. Jerusalem. Israel Museum.

Barber, E. J. W. (1991) *Prehistoric Textiles: The Development of Cloth in the Neolithic and Bronze Ages with Special Reference to the Aegean*. Princeton. Princeton University Press.

Batzer, A. and Dokkedal, L. (1992) The warp-weighted loom: some new experimental notes, in Bender Jørgensen, L. and Munksgaard, E. (eds) *Archaeological Textiles in Northern Europe; Report from the 4th NESAT Symposium*, 231–234. Copenhagen. Konservatorskolen, Det Kongelige Danske Kunstakademi.

Bender Jørgensen, L. (1986) *Prehistoric Scandinavian Textiles*. Copenhagen. Det kongelige nordiske oldskriftselskab.

Bergfjord, C. and Holst, B. (2010) A procedure for identifying textile bast fibres using microscopy: flax, nettle/ramie, hemp and jute, *Ultramicroscopy*, 110 (9), 1192–1197.

Breniquet, C. (2008) *Essai sur le tissage en Mésopotamie; des premières communautés sédentaires au milieu du IIIe millénaire avant J.-C*. Paris. De Boccard.

Broudy, E. (1979) *The Book of Looms: A History of the Handloom from Ancient Times to the Present*. London. Studio Vista.

Burnham, B. H. (1965) Çatal Hüyük, the textiles and twined fabrics, *Anatolian Studies*, 15, 169–174.

Cardon, D. (2007) *Natural Dyes: Sources, Tradition, Technology and Science*. London. Archetype.

Carington Smith, J. (1992) Spinning and weaving equipment, in Macdonald, W. A. and Wilkie, N. C. (eds), *Excavations at Nichoria in Southwestern Greece. 2. The Bronze Age Occupation*, 674–711. Minneapolis. University of Minnesota Press.

Collingwood, P. (1996) *The Techniques of Tablet Weaving*. McMinnville. Robin and Russ Handweavers.

Crowfoot, G. M. (1931) *Methods of Hand Spinning in Egypt and the Sudan*. Halifax. Bankfield Museum.

De Fidio, P. (1998–1999) On the routes of Aegean Bronze Age wool and weights, *Minos*, 33–34, 39–63.

Geijer, A. (1965) Var järnålders "frisiska" kläde tilverkat i Syrien? Reflektioner i anslutning till ett arbete om tyngdvävstolen, *Fornvännen*, 60, 112–132.

Gleba, M. (2008) *Textile Production in Pre-Roman Italy*. Ancient Textiles Series 4. Oxford. Oxbow Books.

Gleba, M. and Mannering, U. (2012) *Textiles and Textile Production in Europe from Prehistory to AD 400*. Ancient Textiles Series 11. Oxford. Oxbow Books.

Haynes, A. E. (1975) Twill weaving on the warp-weighted loom: some technical considerations, *Textile History*, 6, 156–164.

Helbaek, H. (1959) Notes on the evolution and history of linum, *KUML*, 103–129.

Hilden, J. M. (1999) Beduin weaving looms. http://www.beduinweaving.com/webarchive/loom/loom01.htm, accessed February 12, 2010.

Hochberg, B. (1977) *Handspindles*. Santa Cruz. Bette and Bernard Hochberg.

Hoffmann, M. (1964) *The Warp-Weighted Loom: Studies in the History and Technology of an Ancient Implement*. Oslo. Universitetsforlaget.

Holm, C. (1996) Experiment med sländspinning, in Andersson, E. (ed.), *Textilproduktion i arkeologisk kontext. En metodstudie av yngre järnåldersboplatser i Skåne*, 111–116. Lund. Institute of Archaeology, University of Lund.

Hägg, I. (mit Beiträgen von Grenander Nyberg, G. and Schweppe, H.) (1984) *Die Textilfunde aus dem Hafen von Haithabu*. Neumünster. K. Wachholtz.

Kemp, B. J. and Vogelsang-Eastwood, G. (2001) *The Ancient Textile Industry at Armana*. London. Egypt Exploration Society.

Killen, J. T. (2007) Cloth production in Late Bronze Age Greece: the documentary evidence, in Gillis, C. and Nosch, M.-L. (eds), *Ancient Textiles. Production, Craft and Society*, 50–58. Ancient Textiles Series 1. Oxford. Oxbow Books.

Laforce, F. M. (1978) Woolsorters' disease in England, *Bulletin of the New York Academy of Medicine*, 54 (10), 956–963.

Leadbeater, E. (1976) *Handspinning*. Bradford. Charles T. Brandford Company.

Levy, J. and Gilead, I. (2012) The emergence of the Ghassulian textile industry in the southern Levant, Chalcolithic period (*c*. 4500–4000 B.C.E.), in Koefoed, H., Nosch, M.-L. and Andersson Strand, E. (eds), *Textile Production and Consumption in the Ancient Near East Archaeology, Epigraphy, Iconography*, 26–44. Ancient Textiles Series 12. Oxford. Oxbow Books.

Liu, R. (1978) Spindle whorls. Part I: some comments and speculations, *The Bead Journal*, 3, 87–103.

Mannering, U. (1996) Oldtidens brændenældeklæde, in Meldgaard, M. and Rasmussen, M. (eds), *Arkæologiske eksperimenter i Lejre*, 73–80. Copenhagen. Rhodos.

Mellaart, J. (1967) *Çatal Hüyük: A Neolithic Town in Anatolia*. London. Thames & Hudson.

Michel, C and Nosch, M.-L. (2010) *Textile Terminologies in the Ancient Near East and Mediterranean from the Third to the First Millennnia BC*. Ancient Textiles Series 8. Oxford. Oxbow Books.

Montgomery, B. (1954) The bast fibers, in Mauersberger, H. R. and Matthews, J. M. (eds), *Matthew's Textile Fibers; Their Physical, Microscopic and Chemical Properties* (6th edition), 257–359. New York. J. Wiley & Sons.

Nosch, M.-L. (2004) Red Coloured Textiles in the Linear B Inscriptions, in Cleland, L. and Staers, K. (eds), *Colour in the Ancient Mediterranean World*, 32–39. Oxford.

Nosch, M.-L. (forthcoming) Textile crops and textile labour in Mycenaean Greece, in C. Varias Garcia (ed.) *Land, Territory and Population in Ancient Greece: Institutional and Mythical Aspects*. Barcelona. University of Barcelona.

Noweir, H. M., El-Sadik, M. Y., El-Dakhakhny, A.-A., and Osman, A. H. (1975) Dust exposure in manual flax processing in Egypt, *British Journal of Industrial Medicine*, 32, 147–154.

Petruso, M. K. (1986) Wool-evaluation at Knossos and Nuzi, *Kadmos* 25, 26–37.

Rast-Eicher, A. (1997) Tessuti dell'età del bronzo in Europa, in Barnabó Brea, M., Cardarelli, A. and Cremaschi, M. (eds), *Le Terremare. La più antica civilatà padana*, 545–553. Milan. Electa.

Rast-Eicher, A. (2005) Bast before wool: the first textiles, in Bichler, P., Grömer, K., Hofmann-de Keijzer, R, Kern, A. and Reschreiter, H. (eds), *Hallstatt Textiles: Technical Analysis, Scientific Investigation and Experiment on Iron Age Textiles*, 117–131. Oxford. Archaeopress.

Rast-Eicher, A. (2008) *Textilien, Wolle, Schafe der Eisenzeit in der Schweiz*. Basel. Archäologie Schweiz.

Ryder, M. (1983) *Sheep and Man*. London. Duckworth.

Ryder, M. (1992) The interaction between biological and technological change during the development of different fleece types in sheep, *Antropozoologica*, 16, 131–140.

Ryder, M. (2005) The human development of different fleece-types in sheep and its association with development of textile crafts, in Pritchard, F. and Wild, J. P. (eds), *Northern Archaeological Textiles, NESAT VII*, 122–128. Oxford. Oxbow Books.

Schick, T. (1988) Nahal Hemar Cave: cordage, basketry and fabrics, *Atiqot,* 18, 31–43.

Shishlina, N., Orfinskaya, O. and Golikov, V. (2003) Bronze Age textiles from the North Caucasus: new evidence of fourth millennium BC fibres and fabrics, *Oxford Journal of Archaeology*, 22 (4), 331–334.

Shishlina, N., Orfinskaya, O. and Golikov, V. (2002) Textile from the Bronze Age North Caucasus, in Piotrovsky, Y. Y. (ed.), *Eurasian Steppe in the Bronze Age and the Middle Ages*, 253–257. St Petersburg. The Hermitage.

Smith, J. (2001) Bone weaving tools of the Late Bronze Age, in Fischer, P. M. (ed.), *Contributions to the Archaeology and History of the Bronze and Iron Ages in the Eastern Mediterranean. Studies in Honour of Paul Åström*, 83–90. Vienna. Austrian Archaeological Institute.

Spantidaki, Y. and Moulhérat, C. (2012) Textiles from the Bronze Age to the Roman period preserved in Greece, in Gleba, M. and Mannering, U. (eds), *Textiles and Textile Production in Europe from Prehistory to AD 400*, 189-200. Ancient Textile Series 11. Oxford. Oxbow Books.

Stærmose Nielsen, K.-H. (1999) *Kirkes væv: Opstadsvævens historie og nutidige brug*. Lejre. Historisk-Arkæologisk Forsøgscenter.

Tiedemann, E. J. and Jakes, K. A. (2006) An exploration of prehistoric spinning technology: spinning efficiency and technology transition, *Archaeometry*, 48 (2), 293–307.

Vallinheimo, V. (1956) *Das Spinnen in Finnland*. Helsinki. Helsinki Suomen Muinaismuistoyhdistys.

Vogelsang-Eastwood, G. (1992) *The Production of Linen in Pharaonic Egypt*. Leiden. Textile Research Centre.

Völling, E. (2008) *Textiltechnik im Alten Orient*. Wurzburg. Ergon.

Waetzoldt, H. (1972) *Untersuchungen zur neusumerischen Textilindustrie*. Rome. Istituto per l'Oriente.

Witkowski, A. J. and Parish, L. C. (2002) The story of anthrax from antiquity to present: a biological weapon of nature and humans, *Clinics in Dermatology,* 20 (4), 336–342.

CHAPTER 3

Survey of archaeological textile remains from the Aegean and Eastern Mediterranean area

Irene Skals, Susan Möller-Wiering and Marie-Louise Nosch

Remains of textiles from the Aegean, the Near East and Egypt in the Neolithic, Chalcolithic and Bronze Ages are mostly small fragments that are mostly fragile, often mineralised or charred, and are sometimes just impressions in the surface of clay, or imprints in the soil surrounding objects. They are like flashes of what once was. They originate from burial contexts in which they served as garments or other types of burial textiles from ritual offerings, or from shelters and settlements, where they can have had a variety of either decorative or functional uses. Due to the poor preservation of the finds, the information they can yield is limited, but an increased interest in textiles in recent years, aided by improved scientific methods of analyses, have inspired new studies of old finds which have resulted in new information. Additionally, a growing awareness of the possibility of finding textiles and improved excavation methods on the archaeological sites have resulted in new finds which help to increase the knowledge of prehistoric textile technology.

This technology is visualised through many factors, such as the identification of the fibres, the methods of spinning, splicing and the plying of the threads, the regularity and thickness of the threads, the kind of weave

and the uniformity and number of threads per centimetre. From these analyses it is possible to draw conclusions regarding the tools and the technological stages of textile production and its developments over time as well as to gain an idea of the use of different types of textiles for different purposes.

Background and framework of the present survey

Defining the geographical boundaries for this survey of textile finds from the Mediterranean area has been somewhat difficult. It is based on Elizabeth Barber's work *Prehistoric Textiles. The Development of Cloth in the Neolithic and Bronze Ages with Special Reference to the Aegean* which contains references to almost all the relevant archaeological material until 1988 (Barber 1991). Barber includes Egyptian textiles as comparative material in her publication and it was decided to also include them in the present survey, as they constitute a natural part of the collected material. New Egyptian finds as well as analyses of old finds have since been published and are also listed (Vogelsang-Eastwood 1999; Kemp and Vogelsang-Eastwood 2001; Jones 2002b, 2–8). Additionally, Elisabeth Völling's publication *Textiltechnik im Alten Orient* from 2008 is used (Völling 2008). Elisabeth Völling lists all textile finds from the earliest spun thread dated *c.* 18000 BC to finds from about 500 BC in present day Iran, Iraq, Syria, Israel, Jordan, Lebanon and Turkey, and has a comprehensive list of references regarding each find. Furthermore, information from Catherine Breniquet's *Essay sur le tissage en Mésopotamie* from 2008 is incorporated (Breniquet 2008). The work has a summary of the textile finds from the area of the Tigris-Euphrates rivers from the Neolithic until *c.* 3000 BC.

The most recent information regarding textile finds from the Aegean and Eastern Mediterranean area was obtained by the research team working in the research programme *Tools and Textiles – Texts and Contexts* whose data is also included in this survey. We are most grateful to all colleagues who have shared their published and unpublished data with us, in particular Nicole Reifarth, Ulrike Rothenhäusler, Jana Jones and Orit Shamir. Based on the information from these different sources, this survey covers the Aegean, the neighbouring areas around the Eastern Mediterranean and the Near East.

Chronologically, this survey concludes with the end of the Bronze Age and the beginning of the Iron Age around 1000 BC. Finds from the Neolithic have been included since they are few and can help to give some suggestions regarding the development of textile production. The finds are listed according to their dating and the location of the sites (see Appendix A and B).

It has been attempted to provide a comprehensive list of all textiles and textile impressions mentioned in the relevant literature. This was possible to some extent although, in some cases, a different approach has been necessary. Regarding textile finds from Egypt, the Neolithic sites have yielded few textile finds, but from the time of the Old Kingdom the preserved material, especially from burial contexts, is so abundant that it is rather the types of textiles than each textile find that are listed. The textile material from the well-known Neolithic finds from Çatal Hüyük and Nahal Hemar are also so abundant that it is not possible to give information about each textile find and thus we list the types of attested techniques. Therefore, the reader is recommended to seek further information

from the available literature for more detailed information about the textile finds.

The manner of annotating the different aspects of the technical analyses varies somewhat in the literature and can cause misunderstandings. This is particularly evident from descriptions of the plying of threads, the thread diameter and the thread count. When it was possible to interpret the data, the following method of describing thread count is used: the number of threads in one system x the number of threads in the other system per centimetre (in the cases where warp and weft can be distinguished this is mentioned). In cases where the data are not easily interpreted, thread counts are listed as found in the literature.

Regarding the spinning and plying of threads, the following annotations are used:

s- or z- spun.
S2z – for threads that are plied S of 2 z-spun threads.
Z2s – for threads that are plied Z of 2 s-spun threads.
S2s – for threads that are plied S of 2 s-spun threads.

This method of listing the data is used when possible.

The thread diameter is listed as found in the literature (see Appendix A and B).

The fibres

The preserved material could not be studied in any uniform manner and the obtainable information is, occasionally, very scant and, in other cases, quite detailed. The types of fibre are often unidentified, but when identification has been possible, it is mainly plant fibres of the bast type which has been preserved, specifically flax. Other types of bast fibres have also been found. Fibres of hemp and jute have been identified in textiles from Shahr-i Sokhta (Good 2007, 179–184) and nettle has been identified in a ribbon from Khania (Moulhérat and Spantidaki 2009). Cotton as a possibility is only mentioned once from the Neolithic site Dhuweila (Breniquet 2008, 57). Reed and grass fibres are listed, which are the most likely fibres to have been used in basketry (Völling 2008, 208–209; Frangipane *et al.* 2009, 19). Tree bark fibres have been identified in a necklace (Médard *et al.* 2004, 19–25) and palm fibres are mentioned as a possible fibre in a find from Jordan (Völling 2008, 227–228).

Wool is extremely rare in these early textile finds. Wool is mentioned as a possibility in a mineralised fragment on a silver figurine from Susa (Barber 1991, 164) and as the fibre used in the textile impression from Telul eth Thalathat (the information is questioned by Völling 2008, 206). Scholarly work on the textile impressions from Abu Hamid mentions wool as a possible fibre (Breniquet 2008, 56) and it is claimed to have been preserved from an unnamed location in Egypt (Burlington Fine Arts Club Catalogue, 23). But no evidence for wool in the Neolithic and Chalcolithic is conclusive; and wool is also rare in Bronze Age archaeological textiles.

The number of finds of textiles made of wool seems to increase throughout the Bronze Age, and can be an indication of an increasing use of wool during that period. According to Shamir 2014, wool appears only from the Middle Bronze Age in the southern Levant. In some cases, it has been possible to distinguish the type of wool, such as sheep wool, camel wool or goat hair, which is found in textiles from Shahr-i Sokhta (Good 2007, 179–184; Völling 2008, 203). From Ur, sheep wool and goat hair have been identified in strings and ropes (Waetzoldt 2007, 112–121) and goat hair has been identified in textiles from Timna (Shamir and Baginski 1993, 9–10), in a ribbon from Khania (Moulhérat and Spantidaki 2009) and in a textile from Arslantepe (Frangipane *et al.* 2009, 19).

Unspecified wool fibres or the possibility/probability of such fibres is mentioned in textiles from the entire area:

- Tell el-Armana (Kemp and Vogelsang-Eastwood 2001).
- Timna (Sheffer 1986, 8; Shamir and Baginski 1993, 9–10; Rothenhäusler forthcoming-a).
- Tel Masos (Barber 1991, 166; Rothenhäusler forthcoming-a).
- Qatna/Tell Mishrife (James *et al.* 2009, 1109–1118).
- Arslantepe (Frangipane *et al.* 2009)
- Tell Mozan (Rothenhäusler forthcoming-a).
- Tepe Hissar (Völling 2008, 203).
- Ur (Barber 1991, 164; Völling 2008, 208; Breniquet 2008, 58).
- Santorini (Spantidaki and Moulherat 2012).
- Lefkandi (Spantidaki and Moulherat 2012).
- The Caucasian sites of Martkopi (Barber 1991, 168), Eastern Manych River, Kalmykia/Russia (Orfinskaya *et al.* 1999) and Shakhaevskaya, Manych River (Shishlina *et al.* 2005, 6–9).

Thread thickness

Measuring the thread diameter or the thickness of the threads is a parameter which has become standard procedure in textile research during recent years and most often data in this regard only exist from the finds which have been found and analysed recently. It is a parameter which has to be understood as a range, because it is impossible to spin completely evenly. There is a lack of systematic recording of measurements, and sometimes the obtainable data are not altogether clear, but the collected data show that the thread diameters, to a large extent, range between 0.1 mm to 1 mm. Coarser weavings with threads measuring between 1–2 mm are also found in several cases, but in only three cases are threads thinner than 0.1 mm found. In a fragment from Tell Brak the threads measure *c.* 0.07 mm (Völling 2008, 216) and from Arslantepe fragments of a funerary sheet have thread diameters around 0.08 mm (Frangipane *et al.* 2009, 18). Threads that are thicker than 2 mm are equally rare in weavings. In fact only one of the four cases where it is found, is a weaving. It is a fragment from Bronze Age Tepe Hissar with both s and z spun threads perhaps made from wool (Völling 2008, 203). Of the three remaining examples, two are cords (Laurito 2007, 380–394) and one is simply a loose thread (Möller-Wiering 2006).

Neolithic and Chalcolithic fibres, yarn and textiles

Spinning, splicing and plying in the Neolithic and Chalcolithic

In the Neolithic and Chalcolithic, there is only evidence for plant fibre textiles and plant fibre thread. The Chalcolithic textiles from Nahal Mishmar previously considered as wool are now identified as flax (Shamir 2014). Likewise, the debated textiles at Çatal Hüyük are identified as being entirely of plant fibre (Vogelsang-Eastwood 1987a).

Thread can be made by either spinning or splicing, and is often subsequently plied. There seems to be a wide mix of both z and s spinning traditions. Threads which are spun or spliced, but not plied, are also widely attested and mostly with an s-spin (Deb Luran, Nahal Hemar, Judean Caves III/3, III/7, V/49, VI/46, VIII/9, Nahal Lehat, Christmas Cave, Naga-el-Der, Abydos, Hierakonpolis), and a few with an z-spin (Nahal Hemar, Dhuweila, Çatal Hüyük).

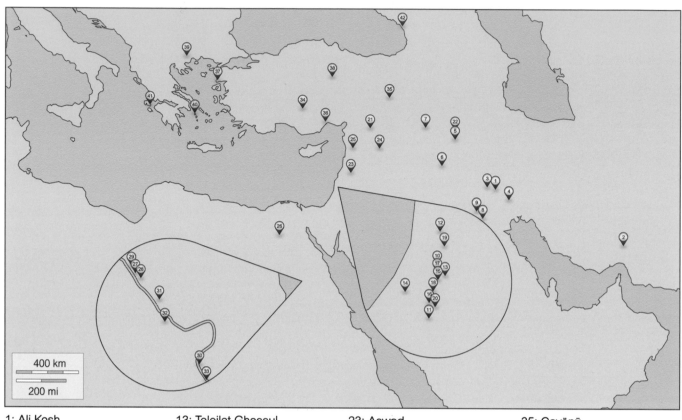

1: Ali Kosh
2: Tepe Yahya
3: Deb Luran
4: Susa
5: Jarmo
6: Sawwan
7: Telul eth Thalathat
8: Eridu
9: Oueili
10: Netiv Hagdud
11: Nahal Hemar
12: Beit She'an

13: Teleilat Ghassul
14: Tel Lachish
15: Judean Desert Caves
16: Nahal Mishmar
17: Wadi Makkukh. Cave of
the Warrior
18: Wadi Murabba'at
19: Abu Hamid
20: Nahal Zeelim
21: Jerf el-Ahmar
21: Tell Halula
22: Shimshara

23: Aswad
24: El Kowm 2
25: Hama
26: Fayum
27: Badari
28: Qau
29: Mostagedda
30: Naga-el-Gherira
31: Naga-ed-Dêr
32: Abydos
33: Hierakonpolis
34: Çatalhöyük

35: Cayönü
36: Mersin
37: Gülpınar Köyü (Khryse)
38: Alisar Höyük
39: Sitagroi
40: Keos
41: Kephalonia. Drakaina
Cave
42: Ochamchire

Fig. 3.1. Neolithic and Chalcolithic sites with textiles. See Appendix A for more information.

There are, generally, more sites with s-spinning than with z-spinning but the amount of material is too small to draw any definite conclusions on spin directions. In the southern Levant, however, which has a high concentration of finds, Shamir (2014, 145) notes that the threads are primarily s-spun coinciding with the natural spin direction of flax fibres. She also observes that Chalcolithic warps and weft are similar in textiles in the southern Levant (2014). A very small piece of fibre with a slight z-twist from Neolithic Greece (Nosch *et al.* 2011) may not be secure evidence for z-spinning.

Regarding plying, there are more sites with attestations of S2z plying (Susa, Judean Desert

Cave V/49, Nahal Lehat, Nahal Mishmar, Cave of the Warrior, Wadi Muranna'at, Dhuweila, Ghassul, Tell Halula, Fayum, Abydos, Hierakonpolis, Cayönü) than of sites with Z2s plying (Netiv Hagdud, Nahal Hemar, Çatal Hüyük) or S2s plying (Cave of Warrior, Christmas Cave, Naga-ed-Der, Hierakonpolis), but again, the numbers are too small to draw conclusions.

Israel and Egypt are the only two areas with abundant Neolithic and Chalcolithic textile and yarn evidence. In the southern Levant sites, both S2z plying and Z2s plying, and even S2s plying are encountered. In the Egyptian sites, there is s-spinning and there is also both S2z and S2s plying, but no evidence of Z2s plying, nor of

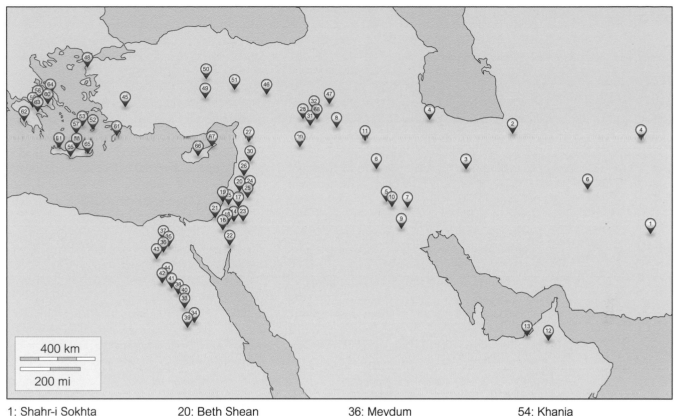

1: Shahr-i Sokhta
2: Tepe Hissar
3: Tepe Sialk
4: Marlik Tepe
5: Tell Abu Salabikh
6: Hafagi
7: Tello
8: Karrana 3
9: Ur
10: Nippur
11: Nuzi
12: Hili
13: Umm an-Nar
14: Arad
15: Bareqet
16: Ramon I
17: Jericho
18: Tel Masos
19: Tell Qasileh

20: Beth Shean
21: Deir el-Balah
22: Timna
23: Bâb edh-Dhrâ
24: Tell Abu al-Kharaz
25: Tell es-Sa'idyeh
26: Kamid el-Loz
27: Tell Mardikh, Ebla
28: Tell Beydar
29: Terqa
30: Tell Mishrife
31: Tall Bderi
32: Tall Mozan
33: Umm el-Qaab
34: Tomb of Dier
34: Deir el-Bahari
34: Tomb of Thutmoses IV
34: Ramses III
35: Tarkhan

36: Meydum
37: Saqqara
38: Qau
39: Gebelein
40: Naga ed-Dêr
40: El-Hawawish
41: Asyût
42: Meir
43: Kahum
44: Tell el Amarnah
45: Afrodisias
46: Arslantepe
47: Tekeköy
48: Troia
49: Acemhüyük
50: Kaman-Kalehöyük
51: Kültepe-Kanish
52: Agia Kyriaki
53: Amorgós

54: Khania
55: Kommos
56: Knossos
57: Akrotiri, Santorini
58: Thebes
59: Mycenae
60: Athens
61: Pylona, Rhodes
62: Kazarma
63: Dendra
64: Lefkandi
65: Azoria
66: Idalion
67: Paleoskoutella
68: Tell Brak

z-spinning that is not subsequently S-plied. This may be the result of the random preservation situation. Jones (2002b), however, concludes that from 3500 BC there is no evidence of z-spun yarns in Egypt, and only s-spinning appears to have been practised. Jones (2002a, 326) notes that the earliest samples from Fayum (5000 BC) and Abydos (3600 BC) are z-spun, but subsequently, the majority of yarns in pharaonic Egypt are s-spun.

Neolithic and Chalcolithic textiles
Neolithic and Chalcolithic textiles are overwhelmingly tabbies, either balanced or slightly faced tabbies. Most evidence comes from Egypt and Israel. Generally, the Neolithic and Chalcolithic textiles are of a high quality and weaving mistakes are rare (Shamir 2014, 148). There is one possible example of twill (Alişar Höyük dated to the Chalcolithic by excavator, but probably Early Bronze Age).

Fig. 3.2. Bronze Age sites with textiles. See Appendix B for more information.

The earliest archaeological textiles are from Çatal Hüyük and Cayönü in Turkey, but even earlier imprints from Jarmo illustrate the use of textiles and the loom.

Examples of high thread counts are 40 × 40 (Tepe Lungar, dated 4000 BC), 30 × 36 in Chalcolithic Desert Cave VI/46 and 44 × 45 in Nahal Mishmar, Israel, 21 × 25 in Hierakonpolis, Egypt dated 3500 BC. Low thread counts are 7 × 5 in Cayönü of the 8th–6th millennia, 6 × 14 in Abydos in Egypt dated 3250 BC, 8 × 8 in El Kowm 2, Syria dated 7100–6000 BC. The average thread count seems to be *c.* 10–15 threads per centimetre in the Neolithic and Chalcolithic textiles. Shamir (2014, 148) observes a slightly higher number of warp threads than weft threads in the southern Levant. There are examples of other textile techniques, particularly from the earliest sites, especially twining (Chalcolithic Wadi Murabba'at), weft-twining (PPNB Halula, Syria, PPNB Çatal Hüyük, Cayönü of the 8th–6th millennia, and Nahal Hemar, dated *c.* 7000 BC) and tablet weaving (Neolithic Dhuweila, Jordan). Nahal Hemar is also the find place of many other textile techniques: looping, knotted netting and interlinking. Finally, there is evidence for a Neolithic 3/3 basket weave from Mersin, Turkey. None of these techniques are attested in the Egyptian textile material.

In predynastic Egypt, Jones concludes that fabrics are mostly balanced (2002a, 329) but unbalanced fabrics also seem quite common, especially for the fine qualities.

The Weaving

It can be very difficult to analyse weavings from mineralised or charred textiles or from impressions. It is often only possible to see one side of the weaving and the threads and the structure can be deformed and fossilised in their positions. The remains are so fragile that the slightest touch will destroy them.

Some weaving techniques employed will appear similar on both sides of the textile so it does not matter if only one side is visible. A tabby weave has no front or back side, and 2/2 twill weavings will look the same on both sides. Other types of twill, such as a 2/1 twill have distinct back sides, which can be mistaken for tabby weaves.

By far the majority of the textiles throughout the period are registered as tabby weaves. There are variations, such as either warp- or weft faced tabby or basket and half basket weaves. Twill was previously believed not to have appeared until the Iron Age. From the Bronze Age, twills are documented in fragments from Timna (Rothenhäusler forthcoming-a), Bâb edh-Dhrâ (Ballard and Skals 1996, 6–10), Tell Bderi (Rothenhäusler forthcoming-b), Alişar Höyük (Barber 1991, 167) and Martkopi (Barber 1991, 168) and two questionable twills are found in Marlik Tepe (Völling 2008, 204) and Tell Beydar (Breniquet 2008, 58).

Other techniques, such as twining, looping and knotted netting are listed for several textiles at a very early date, whereas a technique such as tapestry is not seen before *c.* 1500 BC in Egypt and in Shahr-i Sokhta (Barber 1991, 159; Good 2007, 179–184) and from Kaman-Kalehöyük (Völling 2008, 240).

The textile impression from Dhuweila dated to the Neolithic is believed to have been made by tablet weaving (Breniquet 2008, 57), a technique which is not attested again until the Late Bronze Age (Barber 1991, 156).

Bronze Age fibres, yarn and textiles

Flax is still by far the most commonly preserved textile fibre in the Bronze Age. However, in the 3rd millennium, wool thread and wool textiles start to appear in Iran and Iraq at Shahr-i Sokhta, Tepe Hissar, Ur, and in the Caucasian sites. In the southern Levant and the Aegean, the earliest evidence for the use of wool in textiles is from the Middle Bronze Age (Jericho, Akrotiri). Only in Late Bronze Age sites do wool finds begin to appear more frequently (Timna, Tall Mozan). However, this distribution may also be due to conservation, and in any case, the material is too small for definite conclusions about the spread of animal fibres. Currently, the oldest animal fibre textile of the Eastern Mediterranean area is from Arslantepe dated 3000–2900 BC (Frangipane *et al.* 2009). They are followed by Tall Mozan with two wool textile pieces, a coarse tabby dated 2700/2600–2500/2400, and a fine tabby dated 2500/2400–2100 (Rothenhaüsler forthcoming a). It is worth noting that the early wool fibre textiles are of a very fine quality.

The Bronze Age wool is generally identified as from sheep and, in a few cases, also from goat (Arslantepe, Ur, Khania, Tell el-Armana, Timna) or camel (Shahr-i Sokhta).

Spinning in the Bronze Age is both z and s. There are fabrics woven of two s-spun threads (s/s at Arslantepe, Timna, Tall Mozan, Mochlos) or of two z-spun threads (z/z at Tell Abu al-Kharaz, Lefkandi and Caucasian sites), or of a mixture (s/z) which suggests that the spin direction is used to obtain a visual effect on the fabric's surface. At Tall Bderi, all three combinations are attested. At Tall Mozan, Rothenhaüsler observes that most yarn is s-spun and if z-spun yarns are used, these are interwoven with s-spun yarn, and she suggests that this is a design choice. "Egyptian textiles are distinguished by the s-direction of the spin", notes Jones (2002a, 326).

In the Bronze Age, plying is still in use, both Z2s and S2z. It seems that as the thread counts increase, plying becomes less used.

Weaves in the Bronze Age are overwhelmingly tabbies. Outside Egypt there are a few attestations of other technologies, primarily for decorative purposes, such as tablet weave (Shahr-i Sokhta), knotless netting (Karrana), twill bands (Ur), twill (Bâb edh-Dhrâ), and tapestry (Shahr-i Sokhta, Qatna, Kaman-Kalehöyük).

Most Bronze Age textiles have thread counts of 10–12 threads per centimetre (tpc) and are balanced. A few have lower thread counts (Timna, Tall Bderi, Akrotiri). Thread counts over 20 tpc are very rare outside Egypt but do exist at Qatna (16 × 70–80), Bâb edh-Dhrâ (11 × 30 and 16 × 39), Tell Abu al-Kharaz (25 × 13), Tell es-Sa'idyeh (24 × 14), Kamid el-Loz (24 × 14), Arslantepe (38 × 18) and Tall Mozan (10 pieces have 51 × 100 tpc). Moreover, most Egyptian dynastic textiles are unbalanced, according to Jones (2002a, 329), with an average ratio of 2:1.

Faced fabrics with a remarkable difference in thread counts between the two thread systems are attested at Bareqet (15 × 8), Timna (3–5 × 8–20), Bâb edh-Dhrâ (11 × 30 and 9 × 22 and 16 × 39), Tell Abu al-Kharaz (25 × 13), Tell es-Sa'idyeh (24 × 14), Kamid el-Loz (24 × 14), Qatna (16 × 70–80), Tall Mozan (26–96 × 3–17) and Arslantepe (38 × 18). It should thus be noted that outside Egypt, fabrics with high thread counts are mostly strongly faced, with a high thread count in only one system.

The textiles and garments from Egypt are very well preserved, and real costume studies are possible. Again, the linen fabrics dominate, with the special pleating technique as a prominent feature (Jones 2014).

Conclusion

The data collected for this survey only provide a little insight into the textile production of the past. Although a large geographic area is covered, the information remains limited. What has been passed on to us is only a small fraction of a large production through thousands of years. Looking at these snippets of information, it is important to keep in mind that the textiles were created through conscious choices made by the people working with the material. Choices made in order to obtain the desired qualities of their finished textiles. The textiles are not only the result of the limitations of a primitive technology.

The relatively limited number of textiles preserved and the randomness of the finds raises a wide range of questions, and although a somewhat surprising number of fine qualities with high thread counts and small thread diameters have come to light, emphasising the technical skills of the people of the past, a critical reflection should also be made here: we tend to excavate palaces and elite funerary contexts, and this may explain the large amount of fine archaeological textiles. The selection of textile qualities is thus precisely as random as the excavation activities themselves.

The finds from the southern Levant differ in techniques and are generally less uniform in their manufacture. This conclusion must, however, also be contextualised: these finds are primarily from caves where they have been used, disposed, or lost, while many of the other textile finds in this present survey are from urban environments or burials where they were intentionally deposited.

The obvious need for standard procedures in the manner of analysing and describing the textiles has revealed itself in the course of the results presented here. In several cases, the annotation of the data is not immediately understood and the information risks being lost or misunderstood. It could easily be avoided if a few agreed, shared guidelines were followed. Short forms, which can be understood universally, are recommended. This way making notes whilst working is facilitated and long descriptive explanations can be avoided.

Spinning and plying:

The standard for describing spinning and plying used in this survey is recommended. For single spun threads lower case *s* or *z* is used to describe the direction of the spinning. Capital *S* or *Z* is used to annotate the plying of threads followed by the number of *s*- or *z*-spun threads (*i.e.* S2z or Z2s).

Thread diameter:

For the thread diameter measurements are given in millimetres. The measurements should be understood as a range and as the numbers are quite small – often less than 1 millimetre, 1 or 2 digits are adequate (*i.e.* 0.1–0.3 mm; 0.05–0.1 mm).

Thread count:

Thread count is easily understood if it is listed as the number of threads from one system × the number of threads from the other system per centimetre. If warp and weft can be distinguished, warp should be listed before weft. It is also a range and can never be completely the same throughout one textile (*i.e.* 10–12 × 14–15 threads per centimetre).

The data which yield the most thought-provoking information in this chapter seems to be the spinning of the threads. Tradition can be one answer but is perhaps only a partial answer. Why is it that the common Neolithic use of plied yarns decreases through the Bronze Age? Is it the contact with new people and new materials, better technology, and improved skills? Or the introduction of wool?

The span of thread counts is also illuminating. It reveals a very large variety in the otherwise very simple technique of the tabby weave.

With the technological development and improved scientific methods of analysis it also seems that the concept of a 'primitive' textile technology of the past is being pushed further back into the Neolithic. The more we learn, the more advanced the past technology seems. In this respect finding more textiles and studying old finds again appear crucial to any scholarly progress and will hopefully be inspired by the results of the studies presented in this volume.

Bibliography

Adovasio, J. (1975–1977) The Textiles and Basketry Impressions from Jarmo, *Paléorient* 3, 223–230.

Adovasio, J. and Andrews, R. (1981) Textile Remains and Basketry Impressions from Bâb Edh-Dhrâ and a Weaving Implement from Numeira, *Annual of ASOR* 46, 181–185.

Adovasio, J. and Lamberg-Karlovsky, C. C. (1986) Note: Textile Impression from Tepe Langa, in Lamberg-Karlovsky, C. C. and Beale, T. W. (eds), *Excavations in Tepe Yahya, Iran 1967–1975*, American School of Prehistoric Research. Cambridge, Massachusetts. Harvard University Press, 206.

Adovasio, J. and Yedlowski, L. (1989) Textiles, in Schaub, T. and Rast, W. E. (eds), *Bâb Edh-Dhrâ, Excavations in the Cemetery 1965–67*. Winona Lake, Indiana. Eisenbrauns, 523–528.

Adovasio, J. and Andrews, R. (1982) Some Perishable Artifacts from Bâb edh-Dhrâ, *The Bulletin of the American Schools of Oriental Research*, 247, 59–69.

Aharoni, Y. (1961) Expedition B, *Israel Exploration Journal* 11, 15.

Bar-Yosef Mayer, D. E. and Porat, N. (2010) Glazed Steatite Paste Beads in the Chalcolithic of the Levant: Long Distance Trade and Manufacturing Processes, in Rosen, S. A. and Roux, V. (eds), *Techniques and People: anthropological perspectives on technology in the archaeology of the proto-historic and early historic periods in the Southern Levant*. Paris. De Boccard, 111–123.

Alfaro, C. (2012) Textiles from the Pre-Pottery Neolithic Site of Tell Halula (Euphrates Valley, Syria), *Paléorient* 38, 1–2.

Allgrove McDowell, J. (1986) Kahun: Textile Material from Twelfth Dynasty Egypt, *Archaeological Textiles Newsletter* 3, 9–10.

Amiet, P. (1986) L'usage des sceaux à l'époque initiale de l'histoire de Suse, in de Meyer, L., Gasche, H. and Vallat, F. (eds), *Fragmenta Historiae Elamicae. Mélanges offerts à M. J. Stève*. Paris. Editions Recherche sur les Civilisations, 17–24.

Amiran, R. (1978) *Early Arad I. The Chalcolithic Settlement and Early Bronze City: First-fifth Seasons of Excavations, 1962–1966*. Jerusalem. Israel Exploratory Society.

Andersson, E., Felluca, E., Nosch, M.-L., and Peyronel, L. (2010) New Perspectives on Bronze Age Textile Production in the Eastern Mediterranean. The First Results with Ebla as a Pilot Study, in Matthiae, P., Pinnock, F., Nigro, L. and Marchetti, N. (eds), *Proceedings of the 6th International Congress on the Archaeology of the Ancient Near East*, Wiesbaden, Harrassowitz, 1, 159–176.

Ballard, M. and Skals, I. (1996) Masking and Misinterpreting Cotton Fibers: Dangers Associated with the Fibre Analysis of Archaeological Textiles, in Roy, A. and Smith, P. (eds), *Archaeological Conservation and its Consequences. Preprints of the Contributions to the Copenhagen Congress, 26–30 August 1996*, The International Institute for Conservation of Historic and Artistic Works, 6–10.

Balpinar, B. (1989) *The Goddess from Anatolia. IV. Anatolian Kilims Past and Present*. Milano. Eskenazi.

Bar-Yosef, O. (1985) *A Cave in the Desert: Nahal Hemar*. Jerusalem. Israel Museum.

Barber, E. J. W. (1991) *Prehistoric Textiles: The Development of Cloth in the Neolithic and Bronze Ages with Special Reference to the Aegean*. Princeton University Press.

Barber, E. J. W. (2007) Weaving the Social Fabric, in Gillis, C. and Nosch, M.-L. B. (eds), *Ancient Textiles. Production, Craft and Society, Proceeding of the First International Conference on Ancient Textiles, held at Lund, Sweden, and Copenhagen, Denmark on March 19–23, 2003*, Ancient Textiles Series 1. Oxford. Oxbow Books, 173–178.

Bender Jørgensen, L. (1988) Appendix A. An 8-thousand-year old Textile Impression from Hama, in Thuesen, I. (ed.), *Hama, Fouilles et Recherches de la Fondation Carlsberg 1931–1938. The Pre- and Protohistoric Periods*, Copenhagen. Nationalmuseet, 1, 188.

Betancourt, P., Berkowitz, L. and Zaslow, R. L. (1990) Evidence for a Minoan Basket from Kommos, Crete, *Cretan Studies* 2, 73–77.

Betts, A., Van der Borg, K. and De Jong, K. (1994) Early Cotton in North Arabia, *Journal of Archaeological Science* 21, 489–499.

Biggs, R. D. (1974) *Inscriptions from Tell Abu Salabikh*. Oriental Institute Publications 99. Chicago. University of Chicago Press.

Blegen, C. W., Caskey, J. L., Rawson, M. and Sperling, J. (1950) *Troy I. General Introduction: The First and Second Settlements*. Princeton. Princeton University Press.

Born, H. (1997) Troianische Silbergefässe. Forschungsprojekt zu Material und Herstellung und Möglichkeiten der Restaurierung, *Acta Prähist.* 29, 110–121.

Breniquet, C. (1987) Les petits objets de la fouille de Tell el'Oueili 1983, in Huot, J. L. (ed.), *Larsa (10e campagne, 1983) et í Oueili (4e campagne, 1983): rapport préliminaire*. Paris. Editions Recherche sur les Civilisations. 141–157.

Breniquet, C. (2008) *Essai sur le tissage en Mésopotamie; des premières communautés sédentaires au milieu du IIIe millénaire avant J.-C.* Paris. De Boccard.

Brunton, G. (1937) *Mostagedda and the Tasian Culture*. London. B. Quaritch.

Brunton, G. (1940) Objects from Fifth Dynasty Burials at Gebelein, *Annales du Service des antiquités de l'Égypte* 40, 521–527.

Brunton, G. and Caton Thompson, G. (1928) *The Badarian Civilisation and Predynastic Remains near Badari*. London. British School of Archaeology in Egypt.

Burlington Fine Arts Club (1922) *Catalogue of an Exhibition of Ancient Egyptian Art (1922)*. Egyptian Textiles Museum Catalogue, Egyptian Textiles Museum.

Burnham, B. H. (1965) Çatal Hüyük – The Textiles and Twined Fabrics, *Anatolian Studies* 15, 169–174.

Carington Smith, J. (1977) Cloth and Mat Impressions, in Coleman, J. E. (ed.), *Keos I: Kephala, a Late Neolithic Settlement and Cemetery*. Princeton. American School of Classical Studies, 114–125.

Carter, H. and Newberry, P. E. (1904) *Catalogue général des antiquités égyptiennes: The Tomb of Thoutmosis IV*. Westminster. Constable and Co.

Çatal Hüyük Archive Report (2008), 146–147. http://www.catalhoyuk.com/downloads/Archive_Report_2008.pdf

Caton Thompson, G. and Gardner, E. W. (1934) *The Desert Fayum*. London. Royal Anthropological Institute of Great Britain and Ireland.

Chassinat, E. and C. Palanque (1911) *Une campagne de fouilles dans la nécropole d'Assiout*. Cairo. L'Institut français d'archéologie orientale du Caire.

Cindorf, E., Horowitz, S. and Blum, R. (1980) Textile Remains from the Cave of Nahal Mishmar, in Bar-Adon, P. (ed.), *The Cave of the Treasure; App. C 229–234*. Jerusalem. Israel Exploration Society, 153–185.

Costantini, L., Delle Donne, M. and Mansour Scyycd Sajjadi, S. (2012) Textile remains from Shahr-i Sokhta (Excavations 1999–2006), Sistan, Iran, in Matthews, R. and Curtis, J. (eds), *Proceedings of the 7th International Congress on the Archaeology of the Ancient Near East*. Wiesbaden. Harrassowitz.

Crowfoot, E. (1960) Textiles, Matting and Basketry, in Kenyon, K., *Excavations at Jericho 1*. London. British School of Archaeology in Jerusalem, 519–526.

Crowfoot, E. (1965) Appendix G. Textiles, Matting and Basketry, in Kenyon, K. *Excavations at Jericho 2*. London. British School of Archaeology in Jerusalem, 662–663, plate iv–vi.

Crowfoot, E. (1982) Textiles, Matting and Basketry, in Kenyon and Holland (eds), *Excavations at Jericho 4*. London. British School of Archaeology in Jerusalem, 546–550, plates 42, 150, 158, 161.

Crowfoot, G. M. and De Garis Davies, N. (1941) The Tunic of Tutankhamun, *Journal of Egyptian Archaeology* 27, 113–130.

Crowfoot, G. M. (1955) The Linen Textiles, in Barthélemy, D. and Milik, J. T. (eds), *Qumran Cave I*, Discoveries in the Judean Desert 1. Oxford. The Clarendon Press, 18–38.

Crowfoot, G. M. (1961) The Textiles and Basketry, in Benoit, P., Milik, J. T. and de Vaux, R. (eds), *Les Grottes de Murabba'ât*, Discoveries in the Judean Desert 2. Oxford. Clarendon Press, 51–63.

De Genoulliac, H. (1934) *Fouilles de Telloh*, 1. Paris. P. Geuthner.

De Wild, D. (2001) Textile Remains on Vases from Tomb 1 and Tomb 2C, *BAR International Series: The Mycenaean Cemetery at Pylona on Rhodes*. Oxford. Archeopress, 988, 116–119.

Delougaz, D. (1940) *The Temple Oval in Khafajah*. OIP 53. Chicago.

Dollfuss, G. (2001) Abu Hamid (Jordanie) et les communautés de 5e et 4e millénaires au Levant Sud, in Guilaine, J. (ed.), *Communautés villageoises du Proche-Orient à l'Atlantique (8000–2000 avant notre ère)*. Errance. Seminaire du Collège de France, 65–82.

Dothan, T. (1979) *Excavations at the Cemetery of Deir el-Balah*, Qedem 10. Jerusalem. Institute of Archaeology.

Dörpfeld, W. (1902) *Troja und Ilion*. Athens. Beck and Barth.

Egami, N. (1970) *Telul eth Thalathat. The Excavation of Tell II, 1956–1957*. Tokyo. Yamakawa Publications.

Ellis, T. (1989) Note on a Textile Sample from the Main Mound at Tappeh Hesar, 1976, in Dyson, R. H. and Howard, S. M. (eds), *Tappeh Hesar*. Firenze Casa Editrice le Lettere, 287–289.

Elster, E. S. (2003) Tools and the Spinner, Weaver and Mat Maker, in Elster, E. S. and Renfrew, C. (eds), *Prehistoric Sitagroi: Excavations in Northeast Greece, 1968–1970. 2. The Final Report*, 229–251, 258–282. Los Angeles. Institute of Archaeology, UCLA.

Evans, A. J. (1935) *The Palace of Minos*, 4. London. Macmillan.

Fairbairn, A. (2004) Archaeobotany at Kaman-Kalehöyük 2003, *Anatolian Archaeological Studies* 13, 107–120.

Fedorova-Davidova, E. A. and Forbenko, A. A. (1974) Excavation of the Shakhaevskaya Burial Ground in 1971, in Moshkova, M. G. and Shelov, D. B. (eds), *Archaeological Sites of the Lower Don Region*. Moscow, 83–137.

Fogelberg, J. M. and Kendall, A. I. (1937) Chalcolithic Textile Fragments, in von der Osten, H. H., Wilson, J. A. and Allen, T. G. (eds), *The Alishar Hüyük III, 1930–32*. Chicago. Oriental Institute Publications 30, University of Chicago Press, 234–235.

Frangipane, M., Andersson Strand, E., Laurito, R., Möller-Wiering, S., Nosch, M.-L., Rast-Eicher, A. and Wisti Lassen, A. (2009) Arslantepe, Malatya (Turkey): Textiles, Tools and Imprints of Fabrics from the 4th to the 2nd Millennium BC, *Paléorient* 35 (1), 5–29.

Frangipane, M. (2001) New Symbols of a New Power in a 'Royal' Tomb from 3000 BC, Arslantepe, Malatya (Turkey), *Paléorient* 27 (2), 105–139.

Frifelt, K. (1991) *The Island of Umm an-Nar. Volume 1: Third Millennium Graves*. Jutland Archaeology Society. Aarhus.

Frölich, B. and Ortner, D. J. (1982) Excavations at the Early Bronze Age Cemetery at Bab edh-Dhra, Jordan, *Annual of the Department of Antiquities, Amman, Jordan* 26, 249–268.

Garcia-Ventura, A. (2009) Neo-Sumerian Textile Wrappings. Revisiting some Foundation Figurines from Nippur. Paper presented at the ESF International Exploratory Workshop: "Textile Terminologies in the Ancient Near East and the Mediterranean basin during the 3rd and 2nd millenia BCE" (Copenhagen, Denmark. Unpublished).

Garstang, J. (1953) *Prehistoric Mersin. Yümük Tepe in Southern Turkey*. Oxford. Clarendon Press.

Gillet, B. (1981) Botanical Samples, in Safar, F., Mustafa, A. M. and Lloyd, S. (eds), *Eridu*, 318.

Girshman, R. (1938) *Fouilles de Sialk I*. Paris. P. Geuthner.

Girshman, R. (1939) *Fouilles de Sialk II*. Paris. P. Geuthner.

Good, I. (2007) Invisible Exports in Aratta: Enmerkar and the Three Tasks, in Gillis, C. and Nosch, M.-L. B. (eds), *Ancient Textiles. Production, Craft and Society, Proceeding of the First International Conference on Ancient Textiles, held at Lund, Sweden, and Copenhagen, Denmark on March 19–23, 2003*. Ancient Textiles Series 1. Oxford. Oxbow Books, 179–184.

Hachmann, R. and Kuschke, A. (1966) *Kamid El-Loz 1963–64*. Bonn. Habelt.

Haines, R. C. (1956) Where a Goddess of Love and War Was Worshipped 4000 Years Ago, *Illustrated London News* 229, 266–269.

Hall, R. (1981a) Fishing-net Dresses in the Petrie Museum, *Göttinger Miszellen* 42, 51–58.

Hall, R. (1981b) Two Linen Dresses from the Fifth Dynasty Site of Deshasheh now in the Petrie Museum of Egyptian Archaeology, University College London, *Journal of Egyptian Archaeology* 67, 168–171.

Hall, R. (1982) Garments in the Petrie Museum of Egyptian archaeology, *Textile History* 13:1, 27–45.

Hall, R. and Pedrini, L. (1984) A Pleated Linen Dress from a Sixth Dynasty Tomb at Gebelein now in the Museo Egizio, Turin, *Journal of Egyptian Archaeology* 70, 136–139.

Hansen, D. P. (1970) A Proto-Elamite Silver Figurine in the Metropolitan Museum of Art, *Metropolitan Museum Journal* 3, 5–26.

Helbaek, H. (1963) Textiles from Çatal Hüyuk, *Archaeology* 16, 39–46.

Hirsch, U. (1989a) *The Goddess from Anatolia. III. Environment, Economy, Cult and Culture*. Milano. Eskenazi.

Hirsch, U. (1989b) *The Goddess from Anatolia. I. Plates/text*. Milan. Eskenazi.

Hoffmann, H. (1972) *Early Cretan Armorers*. Mainz. Philipp von Zabern.

Hole, F. and v. Flannery, K. (1962) Excavations at Ali Kosh, Iran, 1961, *Iranica Antiqua* 2, 97–148.

Hole, F., v. Flannery, K., and Neely, J. A. (1969) *Prehistory and Human Ecology of the Deh-Luran Plain*. Ann Arbor, Michigan. University of Michigan.

Hägg, I. (1993) The Textile Fragment from Burial 14, in Wilhelm, G. and Zaccagnini, C. (eds), *Tell Karrana*. Mainz, 207–214.

Istanbul, Catalogue. The Anatolian Civilisations. Volume 1. Prehistoric/Hittite/Early Iron Age (1983). Turkish Ministry of Culture and Tourism. Istanbul.

James, M. A., Reifarth, N., Mukherjee, A. J., Crump, M. P., Gates, P. J., Sandor, P., Robertson, F., Pfälzner, P. and Evershed, R. P. (2009) High prestige Royal Purple dyed textiles from the Bronze Age royal tomb at Qatna, Syria, *Antiquity* 83, 1109–1118.

Jones, B. (2001) The Minoan "Snake Goddess." New interpretations of her costume and identity, in Laffineur, R. and Hägg, R. (eds), *Potnia: deities and religion in the Aegean Bronze Age*, Aegaeum 22, 259–265. Liège. Université de Liège.

Jones, J. (2002a) The Textiles from Abydos: New Evidence, *Mitteilungen des Deutschen Archäologischen Instituts, Abteilung Kairo* 58, 323–340.

Jones, J. (2002b) Predynastic Textiles from Egypt: A Reassessment, *Archaeological Textiles Newsletter* 34, 2–8.

Jones, J. and Oldfield, R. (2006) Egypt's Earliest Linen, *Egyptian Archaeology* 29, 33–35.

Jones, J. (2014) The enigma of the pleated dress: New insights from Early Dynastic Helwan reliefs, *JEA* 100, 209–231.

Kadish, B. (1969) Excavations of Prehistoric Remains at Aphrodisias, 1967, *AJA* 73, 49–65.

Kamal, A. B. (1914) Rapport sur les fouilles de *Said Bey Khachaba* au Déir-el-Gabraoui, *Annales du Service des antiquités de l'Égypte* 13, 161–178.

Karaulašvili, T. (1979) Peasant Methods of Preparation of Cloth at Kakheti (Georgian), *Vestnik Gosudar-stvennogo Muzeja Gruzii* 34B, 32.

Kelly-Buccellati, M. (1978) Terqua, *Syro-Mesopotamian Studies* 2 (6), 13–14.

Kemp, B. J. and Vogelsang-Eastwood, G. (2001) *The Ancient Textile Industry at Armana*. Egypt Exploration Society, Excavations Memoirs 68. London.

Kipling, M. A. (2004) Preventive Conservation at Kaman-Kalehöyük, *Kaman-Kalehöyük* 13, 175–178.

Kuftin, B. A. (1950) *Arkheologicheskije izyskanija v Rionskoj Nizmenosti*. Tbilisi.

Kökten, K., Özgüç, N. and Özgüç, T. (1945) Türk Tarih Kurumu Adma Yapilan Samsun Bölgesi Kazilari Hakkinda Ilk Kisa Rapor, *Türk Tarih Kurumu: Belleten* 9 (35), 361–400.

Landi, S. and Hall, R. M. (1979) The Discovery and Conservation of an Ancient Egyptian Linen Tunic, *Studies in Conservation* 24, 141–151.

Lansing, A. and Hayes, W. C. (1937) The Egyptian Expedition 1935–1936: The Museum's Excavations at Thebes, *Bulletin of the Metropolitian Museum of Art* 32 (2), 4–39.

Laurito, R. (2007) Ropes and Textiles, in Frangipane, M. (ed.), *Arslantepe V. Cretulae: An Early Centralised Administrative System Before Writing*, 380–394. Rome: Università degli studi di Roma "La Sapienza".

Lecaisne, M. Z. (1912) Note sur les tissus recouvrant des haches en cuivre, in Pottier, E., Morgan, J. and de Mequenem, R. (eds), *Recherches Archéologiques. Mémoire de la Délégation en Perse* 13, 163–164. Paris.

Luffman-Yedlowski, N. and Adovasio, J. M. (1989) Perishable Artifacts from Bâb edh-Dhrâ, in Schaub, R. T. and Rast, W. E. (eds), *Bâb edh-Dhrâ: Excavations in the Cemetary Directed by Paul W. Lapp (1965–67)*. Winona Lake, Indiana. Eisenbrauns, 521–543.

Lythgoe, A. M. and D. Dunham (eds) (1965) *The Early Dynastic Cemeteries of Naga-ed-Dêr. Part 4. The Predynastic Cemetery N 7000*. University of California Publications. Egyptian Archaeology vol. 7. Berkeley. University of California Press.

Maréchal, C. (1989) Vannerie et tissage du site Néolithique d'El Kown, in APDCA (ed.), *Tissage, corderie, vannerie: Approches archéologiques, ethnographiques, technologiques. IXe Rencontres Internationales d'Archéologie et d'Histoire d'Antibes, 20–22 Octobre 1988*, 53–68.

Martin, L. (1993) *La vannerie et le textile du VIIe au IIIe millénaire avant J.-C., mémoire de maîtrise*. Paris. Picard/ERC.

Matsutani, T. (ed.) (1991) *Tell Kashkashok. The Excavations at Tell No. II*. Tokyo. University of Tokyo Press.

McFarlane, A. (1991) A pleated linen dress from El-Hawawish, *Bulletin of the Australian Centre for Egyptology* 2, 75–80.

Médard, F., Moulhérat, C. and Méry, S. (2004) Discovery of Charred Yarn in a Bronze Age Burial at Hili (Abu Dhabi Region, United Arab Emirates), in Maik, J. (ed.), *Priceless Invention of Humanity – Textiles, Report from the 8th North European Symposium for Archaeological Textiles, 8–10 May 2002 in Łódź, Poland*, Acta Archaeologica Lodziensia 50 (1), 19–25.

Mellaart, J. (1962) Excavation at Çatal Hüyük, *Anatolian Studies* 12, 41–56.

Mellaart, J. (1963) Excavation at Çatal Hüyük, *Anatolian Studies* 13, 99–101.

Mellaart, J. (1964) Excavation at Çatal Hüyük, *Anatolian Studies* 14, 86–92.

Mellaart, J. (1967) *Çatal Hüyük*. London. Southampton.

Mellaart, J. (1989) *Çatal Hüyük and Anatolian Kilims. The Goddess from Anatolia II*. Milano. Adenau.

Midgley, T. (1928) The Textiles and Matting, in Brunton, G. and Caton Thompson, G. (eds), *The Badarian Civilisation and Predynastic Remains near Badari*. London, 64–67.

Midgley, T. (1937) Notes on the Badarian Cloth and Matting, in Brunton, G. (ed.), *Mostagedda and the Tasian Culture*. London, 145.

Midgley, W. W. (1911) Linen of the IIIrd Dynasty, in Knobel, E. B., Midgley, W. W., Milne, J. B., Murrey, M. A. and Petrie, W. M. F. (eds), *Historical Studies. British School of Archaeology in Egypt 19*. London, 37–39.

Midgley, W. W. (1912) Textiles, in Petrie, W. M. F., Wainwright, G. A. and Mackay, E. (eds), *The Labyrinth, Gerzeh and Mazghuneh*, 6. London.

Midgley, W. W. (1915) Reports on Early Linen, in Petrie, W. M. F. and Mackay, E. (eds), *Heliopolis kafr Ammar and Shurafa*. London, 48–51.

Molist Montana, M. (2001) Halula, village néolithique en Syrie du Nord, in Guilaine, J. (ed.), *Communautés villageoises du Proche-Orient à l'Atlantique (8000–2000 avant notre ère)*. Errance. Séminaire du Collège de France, 35–50.

Mortensen, P. (1970) *Tell Shimshara. The Hassuna Period*. København. Kongelige Danske videnskabernes selskab.

Moulhérat, C., Spantidaki, Y. and Tzachili, I. (2004) Υφάσματα, δίχτυα, σπάγκοι, κλωστές από το Ακρωτήρι Θήρας, (Textiles, nets, strings and threads from Akrotiri Thera), *Arachne* 2, 15–19.

Moulhérat, C. and Spantidaki, Y. (2007) Preliminary results from the textiles discovered in Santorini, in Rast-Eicher, A. and Windler, R. (eds), *Archaeological Textiles, NESAT IX Braunwald, 18–21 Mai 2005*, 49–52. Ennenda. ArcheoTex.

Moulhérat, C. and Spantidaki, Y. (2008) Première attestation de la laine sur le site protohistorique d'Akrotiri à Théra, in Alfaro, C. and Karali, L. (eds), *Purpureae Vestes II. Actas del II symposium Internacional sobre textiles Y Tintes del Mediterraneo en el mundo antiguo (Atenas, 24 al 26 noviembre 2005)*. Universitat de València, 37–42.

Moulhérat, C. and Spantidaki, Y. (2009) Cloth from Kastelli Chania, *Arachne* 3, 8–15.

Mylonas, G. (1973) *Ho Taphikos Kyklos B' ton Mykenon*. Athens.

Möller-Wiering, S. (2006) Tools and Textiles – Texts and Contexts. Bronze Age textiles found in Crete, 1–6. http://ctr.hum.ku.dk/tools/Bronze_Age_textiles_found_in_Crete.PDF/.

Möller-Wiering, S. (2008) A textile impression from Tell Abu al-Kharaz, in Fischer, P. M. (ed.), *Tell Abu al-Kharaz in the Jordan Valley, Vol. I: The Early Bronze Age*, Österreichische Akademie der Wissenschaften, Denkschriften der Gesamtakademie XLVIII, Contributions to the Chronology of the Eastern Mediterranean XVI. Wien, 399–400.

Möller-Wiering, S. (2011) *War and Worship: Textiles from 3rd to 4th-century AD Weapon Deposits in Denmark and Northern Germany*, Ancient Textiles Series 9. Oxford. Oxbow Books.

Munro, P. (1983) *Der Unas-Friedhof Nord-West 4./5*, 81–109. Mainz. Philipp von Zabern.

Naville, E., Hall, H. R. and Ayrton, E. R. (1907) *The XIth Dynasty Temple at Deir el-Bahari*. London. William Clowks and sons, Limited.

Negahban, E. O. (1996) *Marlik. The Complete Excavation Report, The University Museum Monograph 87*, Philadelphia. University of Pennsylvania Museum of Archaeology and Anthropology.

Nosch, M.-L., Murphy, B., Holst, B., Skals, I., Stratouli, G. and Sarpaki, A. (2011) A rare find from the Greek Neolithic: A fibre from Drakaina Cave, Kephalonia, Ionian Islands http://www.drakainacave.gr/index.php?option=com_content&view=article&id=83&Itemid=73&lang=en.

Orfinskaya, O. V., Golikov, V. P. and Shishlina, N. I. (1999) Complex Experimental Research of Textile Goods from the Bronze Age Eurasian Steppe, in Shishlina, N. I. (ed.), Текстиль Эпохи Бронзы Евразийских Степей (*Textiles of the Bronze Age Eurasian Steppe*), 58–184 (English summary of the Russian article, pp. 240–245). Papers of the State Historical Museum 109. Moscow. Poltex.

Panagiotakopulu, E., Buckland, P. C., Doumas, C., Sarpaki, A. and Skidmore, P. (1997) A Lepidopterous cocoon from Thera and evidence for silk in the Aegean Bronze Age, *Antiquity* 71, 420–429.

Persson, A. W. (1931) *The Royal Tombs at Dendra near Midea.* Lund.

Petrie, W. M. F. (1898) *Deshasheh 1897.* London. Egypt Exploration Society.

Petrie, W. M. F. (1910) *The Arts and Crafts of Ancient Egypt.* London.

Petrie, W. M. F. (1914) *Tarkhan II.* London.

Petrie, W. M. F. and Mackay, E. (1915) *Heliopolis, Kafr Ammar, and Shurafa.* London. Egypt Exploration Society.

Pfister, R. (1937) Les Textiles du tombeau de Toutankhamon, *Revue des arts asiatiques* 11, 207–218.

Popham, M. R. (1984) *The Minoan Unexplored Mansion at Knossos*, Annual of the British School at Athens Suppl. 17. London.

Pritchard, J. B. (1985) *Tell Es-Sa'Idyeh, Excavations on the Tell 1964–1966*, University Museum Monographs 60. University Museum, University of Philadelphia.

Pritchard, J. B. (1980) *The Cemetary at Tell Es-Sa'Idiyeh, Jordan.* Philadelphia. The University Museum.

Protonotariou-Deilaki, E. (1969) Tholotos Taphos Kazarmas, *Athens Annals of Archaeology (Arkhaiologika Analekta ex Athenon)*, 2, 3–6.

Rast-Eicher, A. (2008) *Textilien, Wolle, Schafe der Eisenzeit in der Schweiz*, Antiqua 44. Basel. Archäologie Schweiz.

Reade, W. J. and Potts, D. T. (1993) New evidence for late third millennium linen from Tell Abraq, Umm al-Qaiwain, UEA, *Paléorient* 19 (2), 99–106.

Reisner, G. A. (1932) *A Provincial Cemetery of the Pyramid Age, Naga-ed-Der, Part 3.* Berkeley. University of California Press.

Renfrew, C. (1972) *The Emergence of Civilisation: The Cyclades and the Aegean in the 3rd millennium BC.* London. Methuen and Co Ltd.

Riefstahl, E. (1944) *Patterned Textiles in Pharaonic Egypt.* Brooklyn. Brooklyn Museum, Brooklyn Institute of Arts and Sciences.

Riefstahl, E. (1970) A Note on ancient fashions: Four early Egyptian dresses in the Museum of Fine Arts, Boston, *Boston Museum Bulletin* 354, 244–259.

Rothenhäusler, U. (forthcoming-a) Textilabdrücke von Tall Mozan.

Rothenhäusler, U. (forthcoming-b) Textilabdrücke an Gipsgefäßen – textiltechnologische Auswertung, *Ausgrabungen in Tall Bderi, Kleinfunde.*

Ryder, M. (1965) Report of Textiles from Çatal Hüyuk, *Anatolian Studies* 15, 175–176.

Ryder, M. (1991) Weaving Combs, *Archaeological Textiles Newsletter* 13, 11–12.

Scamuzzi, E. (1965) *Egyptian Art in the Egyptian Museum of Turin.* New York.

Schiaparelli, E. (1927) *Relazione sui lavori della Missione archeologica italiana in Egitto. 2. La Tomba intatta dell'Architetto Cha.* Turin.

Schick, T. (1986a) Arad, *Archaeological Textiles Newsletter* 2, 5.

Schick, T. (1986b) Nahal Lahat Cave, *Archaeological Textiles Newsletter* 2, 8.

Schick, T. (1986c) Nahal Hemar Cave, *Archaeological Textiles Newsletter* 2, 5–8.

Schick, T. (1988a) Nahal Hemar Cave: Cordage, Basketry and Fabrics, *'Atiqot* 18, 31–43.

Schick, T. (1988b) A Neolithic Cult Headdress from the Nahal Hemar Cave, *The Israel Museum Journal* 7, 25–33.

Schick, T. (1989) Early Neolithic Twined Basketry and Fabrics from the Nahal Hemar Cave, Israel, in Association pour la Promotion et la Diffusion des Connaissances Archéologiques (APDCA) (ed.), *Tissage, corderie, vannerie: Approches archéologiques, ethnographiques, technologiques. IXe Rencontres Internationales d'Archéologie et d'Histoire d'Antibes. 20–22 Octobre 1988.* Juan-les-Pins, 41–52.

Schick, T. (1992) A Weaving(?) Comb From Wadi Murabba'at, Judean Desert, *Archaeological Textiles Newsletter* 14, 4–6.

Schick, T. (1995) A 10,000 Year Old Comb from Wādī Murabba'ât in the Judean Desert, *'Atiqot* 27, 199–206.

Schick, T. (1997) Miscellaneous Finds: A Note on the Perishable Finds from Netīv Hagdūd, in Bar-Josef, O. and Gopher, A. (eds), *An Early Neolithic Village in the Jordan Valley, Part I: The Archaeology of Netiv Hagdud*, 197–200. Cambridge, MA. Peabody Museum of Archaeology and Ethnology, Harvard University.

Schick, T. (1999) 6000 Year Old Textiles from the Cave of the Warrior, Judean Desert, *Archaeological Textiles Newsletter* 29, 2–9.

Schick, T. (2000) The Cave of the Warrior-A Fourth Millennium Burial in the Judean Desert, in Cardon, D. and Feugère, M. (eds), *Archéologie des textiles des origines au Ve siècle. Actes du colloque international de Lattes. October 1999.* Monograph Instrumentum 14. Montagnac, 15–21.

Schick, T. (2002) The Early Basketry and Textiles from Caves in the Northern Judean Desert, *'Atiqot* 41, 223–239.

Schliemann, H. (1880) *Ilios: The City and the Country of the Trojans.* London.

Shamir, O. (1992) A Twelfth-century BCE Linen Textile Fragment from Beth Shean, *Archaeological Textiles Newsletter* 14, 4.

Shamir, O. (1992a) Re-examination of the Blue Dye from the Qasile Temple, *Archaeological Textiles Newsletter* 15, 7.

Shamir, O. (2002) Textile production in Eretz – Israel, *Michmanin* 16, 19–32.

Shamir, O. (2005) Textile Remains on Metal from Bareqet, Israel, *Archaeological Textiles Newsletter* 40, 20.

Shamir, O. (2014) Textiles, Basketry, and Other Artifacts of the Chalcolithic Period in the Southern Levant, in Sebbane, M., Misch-Brandl, O. and Master, D. M. (eds) *Masters of Fire: Copper Age Art from Israel.* Princeton University Press, 138–152.

Shamir, O. (forthcoming) Textiles from the Chalcolithic Period, Early Bronze Age and Middle Bronze Age in the Southern Levant, in Siennicke, M., Ulanowska, A. and Rahmstorf, L. (eds) *First textiles. The beginnings of textile manufacture in Europe and the Mediterranean.* Ancient Textiles Series. Oxford. Oxbow Books.

Shamir, O. and Baginski, A. (1993) Textiles from the Mining Camps at Timna, *Archaeological Textiles Newsletter* 16, 9–10.

Shamir, O. and Rozen, S. A. (2014) Early Bronze Age Textiles from the Ramon I Rock Shelter in the Central Negev. *Israel Exploration Journal.*

Shamir, O. and Schick, T. (forthcoming) Textiles of the Chalcolithic Period from Judean Desert caves: Lower Wadi el-Makkukh and adjacent area, in Patrich, J. (ed.), *Survey and Excavations in the Judean Desert.* Haifa.

Shamir, O. and Sukenik, N. (2010) The Christmas Cave Textiles Compared to Qumran Textiles, *Archaeological Textiles Newsletter* 51, 26–30.

Shamir, O. and Sukenik, N. (2011) Qumran Textiles and the Garments of Qumran's Inhabitants. *Dead Sea Discoveries* 18. Brill, 206–225.

Sheffer, A. (1986) Timna, *Archaeological Textiles Newsletter* 2, 8.

Sheffer, A. (1976) Comparative Analysis of a 'Negev Ware' Textile Impression from Tel Masos, *Tel Aviv - Journal of the Tel Aviv University, Institute of Archaeology* 3, 81–88.

Sheffer, A. and Tidhar, A. (1988) Textiles and Textile Impressions on Pottery, in Rothenberg, B. (ed.), *The Egyptian Mining Temple at Timna*. London. Thames and Hudson, 224–231.

Shimony, C. and Rivka, J. (1988) Nahal Hemar Cave, The Fibres and Yarn Measurements, *Atiqot* 18, 44.

Shishlina, N., Orfinskaya, O. and Golikov, V. (2005) Headdress from the Catacomb Culture Grave of Shakhaevskaya Burial Ground in the Rostov Region, *Archaeological Textiles Newsletter* 40, 6–9.

Solovjev, L. N. (1950) Selitsy s tekstil'noj keramikoj iz poberezh'ja Zapadnoj Gruzii, *Sovjetskaja Arkheologija* 14, 265–305.

Spantidaki, Y. and Moulhérat, C. (2012) Textiles from the Bronze Age to the Roman Period Preserved in Greece, in Gleba, M. and Mannering, U. (eds), *Textiles & Textile Production in Europe from Prehistory to AD 400*. Ancient Textiles Series 11, Oxford. Oxbow Books, 185–200.

Starr, R. S. (1939) *Nuzi I*. Massachusets. Cambridge.

Staudigel, O. (1975) Tablet-weaving and the Technique of the Rameses-girdle, *Bulletin de liaison du CIETA* 41–42, 71–100.

Stevenson Smith, W. (1935) The Old Kingdom Linen-List, *ZÄS* 71, 34–49.

Stordeur, D. (2002) Reprise des fouilles à Tell Aswad de Damascène. Résultats préliminaires, in Margueron, J.-C., de Miroschedji, P. and Thalmann, J.-P. (eds), *Proceedings of the Third International Congress on the Archaeology of the Ancient Near East, Paris, 14–19 April 2002*. Eisenbrauns (in press).

Stordeur, D. and Jammous, B. (1997) D'énigmatiques plaquettes gravées néolithiques, *Archéologia* 332, 37–41.

Stratouli, G. *Drakaina Cave, Kephalonia Island, Greece. An Archaeological Project*, <http://www.drakainacave.gr/>, accessed 22 June 2011.

Takaoğlu, T. (2006) The Late Neolithic in the Eastern Aegean: Excavations at Gülpinar in the Troad, *Hesperia* 75, 289–315.

Teissier, N. (1997) The Glyptic (Season 1994), *Subartu* 3, 155–168.

Tosi, M. (ed.) (1983) *Prehistoric Sistan*. IsMEO Reports and Memoirs Volume 19, 1, Rome.

Tsori, N. (1967) On two Pithoi from the Beth-Shean Region and the Jordan Valley, *PEQ* 99, 101–103.

Tufnell, O., Charles, I. and Lankester, H. (1958) *Lachish IV. (Tell ed-Duweir), The Bronze Age*. Oxford. Oxford University Press.

Tuohy, T. (1990) Weaving Combs – Curved or Straight?, *Archaeological Textiles Newsletter* 11, 6–8.

Tuohy, T. (1992) Long Handled 'Weaving Combs', *The Netherland. ProcPrehistSoc* 58, 385–388.

Tzachili, I. (2007) Weaving at Akrotiri, Thera. Defining Cloth-making Activities as a Social Process in a Late Bronze Age Aegean Town, in Gillis, C. and Nosch, M-L. (eds), *Ancient Textiles. Production, Craft and Society, Proceeding of the First International Conference on Ancient Textiles. Lund, Sweden, and Copenhagen, Denmark 19–23 March 2003*. Ancient Textiles Series 1. Oxbow Books, 190–196.

Unruh, J. (2007) Ancient Textile Evidence in Soil Structures at the Agora Excavations in Athens, Greece, in Gillis, C. and Nosch, M.-L. B. (eds), *Ancient Textiles. Production, Craft and Society, Proceeding of the First International Conference on Ancient Textiles. Lund, Sweden, and Copenhagen, Denmark March 19–23 2003*, Ancient Textiles Series 1. Oxford. Oxbow Books, 167–172.

Veselovskij, N. I. (1898) Kubanskaja oblast: Raskopki, *Russkaja Arkheologicheskaja Kommissija: Otchët*, 29–39.

Vogelsang-Eastwood, G. M. (1985) The Workmen's Village, Tell el-'Amarna, *Archaeological Textiles Newsletter* 1, 8.

Vogelsang-Eastwood, G. (1987a) A Re-examination of the Fibres from the Çatal Hüyük Textiles, *Oriental Carpet and Textile Studies* 3, 1, 15–19.

Vogelsang-Eastwood, G. M. (1987b) Tell el-'Amarna, *Archaeological Textiles Newsletter* 4, 4.

Vogelsang-Eastwood, G. M. (1993) The Çayönü textile, *Archaeological Textiles Newsletter* 16, 4–7.

Vogelsang-Eastwood, G. M. (1999) *Tutankhamun's Wardrobe. Garments from the tomb of Tutankhamun*. Rotterdam. Barjesteh van Waalwijk van Doorn.

Völling, E. (2008) *Textiltechnik im Alten Orient*. Würzburg. Ergon.

Vogelsang-Eastwood, G. M. (2000) Textiles, in Nicholson, P. T. and Shaw, I. (eds) *Ancient Egyptian Materials and Technology*. Cambridge University Press, 268–298.

Wace, A. J. B. (1921–23) Excavations at Mycenae: 2, The Granary, *Annual of the British School at Athens* 25, 38–61.

Waetzoldt, H. (2007) The use of Wool for the Production of Strings, Ropes, Braided Mats, and Similar Fabrics, in Gillis, C. and Nosch, M.-L. B. (eds), *Ancient Textiles. Production, Craft and Society, Proceedings of the First International Conference on Ancient Textiles. Lund, Sweden, and Copenhagen, Denmark 19–23 March 2003*. Ancient Textiles Series 1. Oxford. Oxbow Books, 112–121.

Wattrall, E. (2000) Excavations at Locality HK11, *Nekhen News* 12, 11–12.

Webb, J. (2002) New evidence for the origins of textile production in Bronze Age Cyprus, *Antiquity* 76, 364–371.

Wendrich, W. Z. (2000) Basketry, in Nicholson, P. T. and Shaw, I. (eds), *Ancient Egyptian Materials and Technology*. Cambridge University Press, 254–267.

Whitley, J. (2005) *Archaeology in Greece 2004–2005*. Archaeological Reports, 51, 1–118.

Winlock, H. E. (1942) *Excavations at Deir el-Bahri, 1911–1931*. New York. Macmillan Co.

Winlock, H. E. (1945) *The Slain Soldiers of Neb-hepēt-Rē'Mentūhotpe*. New York. Metropolitan Museum of Art

Wolley, L. (1934) *The Royal Cemetery*, Ur Excavations, 2. London. Society of Antiquaries.

Zisis, V. G. (1955) Cotton, Linen, and Hempen Textiles from the Fifth century B.C., *Praktika tes Akademeias Athenon* 29, 587–593.

Özdoğan, A. (1999) Çayönü, in Özdoğan, M. and Bašgelen, N. (eds), *Neolithic in Turkey. The Cradle of Civilization. New Discoveries*, Ancient Anatolian Civilizations Series. Istanbul. Arkeoloji ve Sanat Yayinlari, 35–63.

Özgüç, N. (1966) Excavations at Acemhöyük, *Anatolia-Anadolu* 10, 29–52.

Özgüç, N. and Tunca, O. (2001) *Kültepe-Kaniš, Sealed and Inscribed Clay Bullae*, Türk Tarih Kurumu yayınlarından. Ankara. Türk Tarih Kurumu Basımevi.

Åström, P. (1964) Remains of Ancient Cloth from Cyprus, *Opuscula Atheniensia* 5, 111–114.

CHAPTER 4.1

Experimental testing of Bronze Age textile tools

Linda Olofsson, Eva Andersson Strand and Marie-Louise Nosch

Introduction

Experimental archaeology with textile tools has an important role to play regarding the understanding of the technological parameters for textile production in ancient societies. For archaeologists working with ancient textiles and textile techniques, there is the advantage that many of the techniques that were used during antiquity are still in use today. Through ethnographical sources, knowledge is readily available of tool functions and different processes, such as fibre preparation, spinning and weaving. However, one of the challenges is that craftspeople today may not use exactly the same type of tools or techniques, or even the same type of fibre material. Therefore, an important component in this research is the testing of the function and efficiency of archaeological textile tools. In the following, the experimental tests on archaeological textile tools carried out in 2005–2010 within the *Tools, Textiles, Texts and Contexts* (TTTC) research programme will be presented. The results from the experiments, supplemented with results from earlier experiments, have formed the basis for interpreting the function of different tools and for the evaluation of what textiles may have been produced at different sites represented in

the TTTC tool database. This inter-disciplinary approach involving archaeologists, craftspeople and historians was presented already in 2002 at the 9th International Aegean Conference (Andersson and Nosch 2003). At the conference, experimental archaeology conducted on the basis of Scandinavian Viking Age textile tools was applied to illustrate the Mycenaean textile production. In this chapter, however, Scandinavian tools have been replaced by tools from the Bronze Age Aegean and Eastern Mediterranean. The methods in use in these tests are developed from the experience gained from the Scandinavian experiments which were directed by Eva Andersson Strand (Andersson 1999; 2003).

Since the majority of excavated textile tools consist of spindle whorls and loom weights, the priority in the research presented in the following was to investigate these tools, their definition and function. The experiments are thus principally divided in two parts, one concerning the function of spindle whorls and the other concerning loom weights. The two parts were subdivided into different stages with different questions and aims.

Specific principles developed for experimental investigations on the function of textile tools will be presented, and by applying these to experimental testing the aim is to give new insight into textile production through textile experimental archaeology. Furthermore, this chapter presents an investigation of the extent to which the individual spinner or the tool affects the yarn produced and the issue of whether light whorls can be used as spindle whorls will be discussed. Since earlier experiments with light whorls yielded contradictory results, it was necessary to carry out new tests, using the new proposed principles as described below to elucidate the functionality of light whorls for spinning yarn.

Finally, the results of the experimental testing of the function of loom weights are discussed. Different shapes of loom weights were tested. Most shapes seem useful as weights on a warp-weighted loom. What is interesting, however, is which textiles different loom weights are optimal to produce. It has earlier been demonstrated that the weight of a loom weight influences the number of threads that can be attached to each loom weight in order to obtain a suitable warp tension (Mårtensson *et al.* 2009).[1] However, loom weights have not been investigated with the aim of understanding if other parameters influence the types of textiles which different loom weights are most suitable to produce. Via the TTTC experiments these have now been identified and will be presented below.

Our working hypothesis is that textile manufacturing in the Aegean and Eastern Mediterranean during the Bronze Age was well-planned, and that this was essential to the production. Planning and preparing as well as selection of equipment was done with great care. Furthermore, the people making textiles were experienced and knew what decisions should be taken in order to facilitate optimal production of textiles and to attain the desired result. Of course, it cannot be excluded that beginners' and children's work form part of the archaeological record (see discussion in chapter 2). However, in the TTTC programme it is assumed that textile production was primarily conducted systematically and by a large part of the population with long and extensive experience in textile techniques.

Principles for utilising experimental archaeology as a method

The majority of the tests were performed by two craftspeople. The aim of working with two craftspeople with different textile backgrounds, both experienced in the processes involved in making textiles, was to ascertain whether these different backgrounds might also affect the individual outcome, such as the type of spun yarn. Anne Batzer (spinner/weaver 1), is a professional weaver at Sagnlandet Lejre (Land of Legends), Centre for Historical and Archaeological Research and Communication (CHARC), (previously Lejre Historical and Archaeological Research Centre) in Denmark. Linda Olofsson, formerly Mårtensson (spinner/weaver 2), trained in prehistoric technology at Bäckedal Residential College for adult education and Umeå University in Sweden.[2]

It could be argued that interpretations of archaeological finds are often based on experiments performed only in our minds. With experimental archaeology, these questions are tested in practice. The results can be used to improve our understanding of the archaeological record. However, the results from experiments can only provide a basis for interpretations. Thus every step of the experimental process as well as the results must be interpreted individually and critically. For this reason, every experiment should be designed based on principles or guidelines of importance for the specific test. It is also of importance to explain the motivation behind every decision taken during an experiment. To be able to use experimental archaeology and its results in research, it is fundamental that these principles and considerations are described, and that the experiments are carefully documented. Through a detailed and published documentation, the aim is to enable other scholars to use the results. Secondly, this will also enable future scholars to repeat the experiments and possibly obtain the same results. The development and use of principles is considered a way of developing experimental archaeology as a method within the field of textile experimental archaeology. In its most optimal design, experimental archaeology with textile tools should be based on the following eight principles:

- The primary parameter to be investigated is *function* and the purpose is not to make reconstructions of ancient textiles.
- Tools must be reconstructed as precise copies of archaeological artefacts.
- Raw materials, such as wool and flax, must be selected according to our knowledge of the time and area under investigation.
- All processes must be performed by at least two skilled craftspeople.
- Every new test should be preceded by some practice time.
- All processes must be documented and described in writing, photographed and some filmed.
- All processes must be studied individually.
- All products must be submitted to external experts on textile analysis.

The last principle, *all products must be submitted to external experts on textile analysis,* is a new parameter within textile experimental archaeology. In addition to internal evaluations of the results made by us, within the research programme, samples from spinning and weaving with the spun yarn were submitted to an external expert for archaeological textile analysis (see chapter 4.2). The aim was to gain further knowledge, beyond the primary evaluations of the experiments. Furthermore, the introduction of external analysis would allow us to evaluate the methodology used in textile analyses: would analysis of yarn and textiles made by the craftspeople within the experimental process shed new light on technical analysis of archaeological textiles? Would an external expert be able to see all the documented processes carried out by the craftspeople? How far would differences in tools, fibres, skills and training be reflected in the fabrics? These were some of the methodological questions addressed during the investigation. Samples from both spinning and weaving with spun yarn were sent to external textile expert Susan Möller-Wiering (see chapter 4.2). Finally, even if a craftsperson is experienced, as soon as the textile making process is altered, or new tools or fibres are introduced, the learning process starts again. Every test was therefore preceded by some practice time before the actual test began. When testing the function of loom weights it was neither possible nor necessary to apply all principles, depending on the specific experiment. Some of the principles will

therefore be presented again in connection to the tests of loom weights, which are described below.

Function of textile tools: spinning and TTTC spindle whorl tests

Previous spinning tests have yielded different results. The experiments performed by Carington Smith led to the conclusion that whorls weighing less than 10 g are too light to be used as spindle whorls (Carington Smith 1992, 674, 694; Obladen-Kauder 1996, 233–235). On the other hand, the spinning tests performed by Andersson established that there are differences in spinning with different weights of whorls, weighing from 5 g to 30 g, and that the resulting yarn is generally thinner and lighter, the lighter the spindle is, because there are fewer fibres per metre (Andersson 1999; 2003). Among the excavated whorls in the area under investigation, one group stands out in the discussion of what is an adequate spindle whorl, *i.e.* the whorls that weigh less than 10 g, the so-called beads, buttons or conuli.[3] As a consequence of the tests done by Carington Smith and Andersson, the need to reconsider the interpretation of the whorls weighing less than 10 g found in the Mediterranean area is clearly demonstrated (Carington Smith 1992; Andersson 1999; 2003; Grömer 2010). Furthermore, it has not been established to what extent the spinner or the whorl primarily defines the outcome.

In order to further investigate these issues, the TTTC tests were conducted on different weight classes of whorls, using identical fibres and two spinners working in parallel. The functionality of three different weights of whorls, weighing 4 g, 8 g and 18 g, were tested using wool fibres, in order to examine if the results obtained by the two spinners were similar or not. The same 8 g whorl was also tested using flax fibres, in order to investigate if this light whorl's functionality was influenced by a change in the type of fibre used.

Tools: reconstructing spindle whorls
When the function of tools, in this case spindles with whorls, is to be investigated, it is of great importance that the tools are precise reconstructions of the originals. All spindle whorls used in the experiments were reconstructed copies of biconical and conical ceramic whorls from Nichoria in Greece dated

Fig. 4.1.1. Reconstructed spindle whorls based on finds from Nichoria, Greece (photo: CTR).

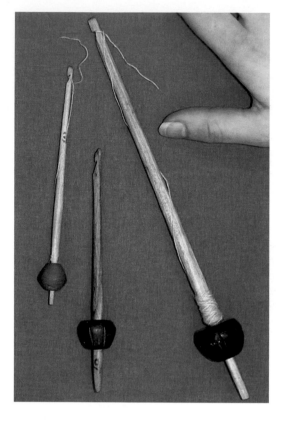

```
☐ 1 cm
```

Fig. 4.1.2. Reconstructed low-whorl spindle used in experiments, 18 g whorl (photo: CTR).

to the Bronze Age (Fig. 4.1.1) (Carington Smith 1992, no. 2605, 2656, 2647). Ceramist Inger Hildebrandt, CHARC, produced all the whorl reconstructions. The reconstructions were made of local Lejre clay but their weight and dimensions were identical to those of three specific whorls from Nichoria.

It was only possible to construct, not reconstruct the rods of the whorls, since no rods from the same site have been preserved. Since spinning in present times suggests that rods were made of wood, wooden rods were used in the experiments (Fig. 4.1.1). The rod diameter was based on the size of the whorl hole. In a previous experiment, a whorl weighing 5 g was put on a wooden rod measuring about 30 cm in length (Obladen-Kauder 1996, 235). In another case, whorls with an average weight of 10 g were used with a so-called *souvlaki* stick as a rod (Carington Smith 1992, 694). In both cases, the spinning tests were regarded as unsuccessful, with the conclusion that the spindle was too difficult to work with. It must be noted that a conventional *souvlaki* stick is far too long to use as a rod for a small spindle whorl, as it would not provide adequate balance or regularity in the rotation. The experiments by

Andersson clearly demonstrated that lighter whorls require a smaller and lighter rod than heavier whorls (Andersson 1999). If the sizes of the rod and the whorl are not in balance, the spindle will wobble and feel uncomfortable to use. Therefore, in the TTTC experiment the 18 g whorl was put on a rod with a length of *c.* 24 cm and a weight of 3.5 g (Fig. 4.1.2). The 8 and 4 g whorls were used on smaller rods with a length of *c.* 14 cm and a weight of 2 g (Fig. 4.1.3) and 1 g (Fig. 4.1.4) respectively. Each whorl was fixed on the lower end of the rod as a low-whorl spindle. This arrangement is the most common in European traditions since antiquity, as opposed to the high-whorl spindle (Barber 1991, 53. See also discussion in chapter 2 of this volume).

Raw materials: searching for Bronze Age fibres

The selection of fibre material for the TTTC tests was based on Linear B inscriptions mentioning sheep, wool and linen (Ventris and Chadwick 1973, 313–323). At the time of the experiments, to our knowledge, no results from fibre analyses of Bronze Age textiles were available. The quality of fibres varies significantly between different sheep, within each breed, and even in a single fleece. Wool with low uniformity in its fleece was used in the tests as there is a discussion regarding the breed of sheep that may have provided the wool in the Bronze Age Aegean and Eastern Mediterranean (*e.g.* Waetzoldt 1972; Ryder 1992; see chapter 2). According to wool specialist and archaeologist Carol Christiansen from the Shetland Islands, this heterogeneous mix of fibres in one fleece is considered as a characteristic feature of primitive sheep, in contrast to most modern sheep, which have a high uniformity of fibres (Christiansen, personal communication). For the experiments, wool from Shetland sheep was used, since this breed of sheep, among other breeds, has this characteristic feature. From several fleeces provided by Christiansen for the experiments, a white fleece was selected, weighing 2.7 kg, which had a staple length of 19–22 cm. This choice was made based on information concerning coloured textiles from the Bronze Age (Ventris and Chadwick 1973, 313–323; Carington Smith 1992, 691–692). White wool has good dyeing possibilities.

No information on what type of flax was used in the Bronze Age and how it might have been prepared was available. Due to the lack of information, pre-prepared flax fibres were used. Flax fibres were provided for the experiments by CHARC, weighing about 100 g and measuring approximately 50–100 cm in length (Fig. 4.1.5). The fibres had been stored for many years at CHARC, they were water retted and they were traditionally prepared (see chapter 2). The use of wool from the same sheep and the same kind of flax in every test made it possible to repeat the tests and compare the results from spinning with different tools.

Fibre preparation

Before the wool can be used it is usually processed (see chapter 2). The wool used in the experiments was prepared as follows: Felted parts, dirt and the most irregular parts, such as the back and belly were first removed. After sorting the 2.7 kg fleece, 1.1 kg of rather homogeneous wool remained to be used in the experiments. The discarded wool should not, however, be regarded as waste material as it could have been used for other purposes. Tufts of wool from three different places on the fleece were then mixed and teased by hand. Earlier experiments have demonstrated that too much underwool in thin yarn will make it open and irregular and it will break easily (Andersson 1999; 2003). Using wool combs can reduce the underwool (Fig. 4.1.6). Linear B inscriptions describe "wool carders" (Ventris and Chadwick 1973, 570, *pe-ki-ti-ra₂*), but it is not known what the associated tools may have looked like or how they may have been applied. Since there is no evidence for the carding of wool until later times (Barber 1991, 261), the choice of using wool combs in this experiment was considered more appropriate. In order to hold as the warp on a loom, the yarn needed to be strong and sturdy. To obtain the best results, a wooden comb was used (Fig. 4.1.7), even if to our knowledge, none have been found in the Bronze Age Mediterranean area. It is likely that they were made of perishable materials. The comb used in the experiments took its inspiration from the combs made of bone and wood found in the Caspian Sea area, some of them dated to the Bronze Age (Shishlina *et al.* 2000).

By using the comb primarily on the ends of the wool fibres, the wool could better

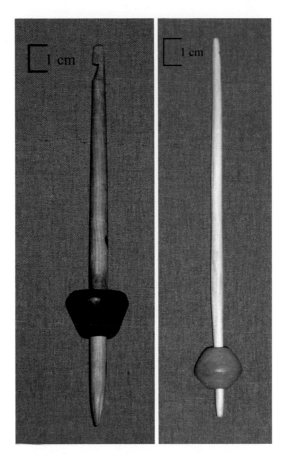

Fig. 4.1.3. (left) Reconstructed low-whorl spindle used in experiments, 8 g whorl (photo: CTR).

Fig. 4.1.4. (right) Reconstructed low-whorl spindle used in experiments, 4 g whorl (photo: CTR).

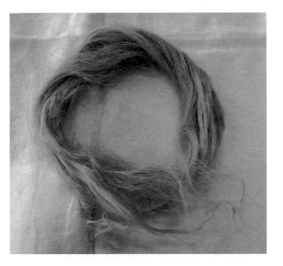

Fig. 4.1.5. Flax fibres used in the experiment (photo: CTR).

be cleaned from defects such as wrong cuts, felted parts and exceptionally fuzzy and short underwool. In this way, the wool was not truly combed, but rather hackled at the ends; 22% of the wool was discarded in this process. Finally, the wool was fastened in the comb and pulled out of the comb with one hand into a band of fibres (Fig. 4.1.7). The wool was now ready for spinning.

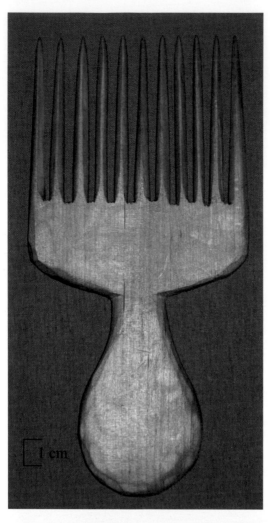

Fig. 4.1.6. Wooden wool comb, used in the experiments (photo: CTR).

1 cm

Further preparation before 4 g whorl spinning

By conducting some initial test spinning with the 4 g whorl it was noticed that the process of providing wool fibres with the hand while spinning took more time than reasonable. Even though the wool was specially prepared, the spinners still experienced difficulties in spinning with this light spindle whorl. Therefore, in order to test whether the 4 g spindle whorl was a suitable spinning tool at all, both spinners conducted a small reference test, spinning with another type of wool. This test was made with rather fine and homogenous wool that had been machine carded and washed. It appeared to be much easier to spin with these fibres and the yarn produced was strong. Based on this experience, the wool for the primary experiments was washed, in order to obtain a fibre material more suitable for the 4 g whorl. It should be noted that it is known from other periods that wool was washed before spinning (Waetzoldt 1972, 109–119). The wool was thus washed in 40–60 centigrade water to reduce dirt and some of the lanolin. Afterwards, the wool was combed as in the previous test.

Spinning wool and flax – two different processes

As one research question was how two individual spinners affect the spun thread, the

Fig. 4.1.7. Pulling out wool from the comb into a band of fibres (photo: CTR).

detailed technology of spinning or the final wool yarn was not compared between the two spinners during the experiments. This was only done afterwards when the results were evaluated.

There were some restrictions, however, for example, to sit on chairs when spinning (Fig. 4.1.8). Furthermore, the yarn was spun in a z direction (Fig. 4.1.9), because this is considered to be the usual method in the area under study (Barber 1991, 66). All spindles were used with the suspended spinning technique, which is a common technique when spinning with a spindle and a whorl (Fig. 4.1.8; see chapter 2 for alternative techniques). The spinners commonly gave the spindle three twists by hand and then two final twists after approximately 1–1.5 m of spun thread. By doing so, the spinners felt that the thread would thus hold as warp. The spinning continued until the spindle was filled, meaning that the weight of the threads affected the rotation of the spindle negatively.

Spinning flax, however, involved several additional procedures, such as the use of a distaff for keeping the long fibres organised and water for moistening the yarn during spinning. Flax fibres need to be moistened during spinning to make them flexible. This can be done by putting saliva or water on the thread while spinning. Using saliva was not considered in the experiment because this is rather unpleasant when one is spinning a large amount of yarn. Instead, water was used and some linseed oil was also added to the water. One tablespoon of linseed oil was mixed with 12 centilitres of water. Because of the pectin, linseed oil is assumed to have a gluing effect on the yarn, making it sufficiently strong to function as warp. This procedure may also prevent fibres sticking out of the yarn. The arrangement of these items, distaff and water cups (Fig. 4.1.10), and the use of them were to some extent discussed between the spinners beforehand. The equipment was arranged and prepared together by the spinners and both the technique of spinning and the yarn were compared during the spinning. Therefore, the opportunity was taken to check if it was possible to deliberately spin similarly by only watching each other spin. It was assumed that this would make the yarn more similar. According to the external evaluation, however, this did not turn out to be the case (see chapter 4.2).

Fig. 4.1.8. Working position. Anne Batzer (spinner 1) is spinning wool fibres. The spindle is hanging freely, i.e. a suspended spindle (photo: CTR).

Fig. 4.1.9. Depending on whether the yarn is spun clockwise or anti-clockwise, the yarn will be twisted in different directions called s or z. Depending on how much the yarn is twisted, the twist angle will be high or low (drawing: Annika Jeppsson).

Internal and external evaluation of spinning and yarn

In order to assess the results of the experiments, two evaluations took place. One was done by the spinners themselves, the other by the external textile expert Susan Möller-Wiering (for the external evaluation see chapter 4.2). The aim of the evaluations was to assess if there are any differences between the two

Fig. 4.1.10. Linda Olofsson (spinner 2) is spinning flax fibres. The fibres are organised on a stand (distaff) which is fixed on a table (a reel was used for this purpose). Please note the small glass with water on the table (photo: CTR).

As part of this the weight and length of the yarn was measured and documented by the spinners, as was the time it took to spin a full spindle. Finally, the thread was tested for weaving on a warp-weighted loom.

Spinning with 4 g, 8 g and 18 g whorls using wool fibres

In the conducted tests, 350 m to 800 m of yarn was spun, depending on what whorl was used. The results from spinning wool fibres with the 4 g, 8 g and 18 g spindle whorls confirmed previous results. When spinning with a suspended spindle and similar type of wool, the lighter the spindle whorl, the lighter and in general the thinner the thread will be. The new results from the TTTC experiments are that the output quantities of yarn became similar for both spinners when using identical spinning tools and fibre material. The main differences are not seen between the spinners but between the three different whorl weight classes (Fig. 4.1.11). These results indicate that it is the tool and fibre rather than the spinner that defines the outcome yarn. If one tries to spin thin yarn with few fibres per metre with a heavy suspended spindle, the thread will break, because of the weight of the spindle. On the other hand, if spinning thick yarn on a light spindle, the spindle will only rotate with much effort, and the yarn will not be strong enough to be used in a weave. Furthermore, it should also be noted that it was of great importance how the fibres were prepared before spinning. Although the 4 g whorl worked for spinning yarn, both spinners reported that further wool preparation or another type of wool, which is finer and more homogenous, would be preferable in order to produce strong yarn when using the 4 g spindle.

While spinning, further important observations were made. It was for example observed that spinning was greatly affected by whether the spindle whorl hole was centred or not. One of the 8 g whorls had a hole that was only slightly off-centre. This spindle whorl required more force from the hand to rotate properly. The resulting yarn from spinning with the whorl with the slightly off-centre hole did not appear significantly different from yarn spun by the other 8 g whorls, but the measurements later showed a slightly lower output for the unbalanced whorl (see chapter 4.2).[4] However, it was reported that the spinner's hands ached

spinners, yarn, or between the yarns spun using different whorls. The following questions were discussed in the evaluation:

- How many metres are spun per 100 g spun fibres compared between the two spinners and the different tools?
- Did the spinning require the same amount of time for the two spinners or were there major differences in time consumption?
- Was the spun thread suitable as warp?
- Were the threads spun by the different spinners suitable to use in the same weave?

after working with this specific whorl. On this basis, it was concluded that it is possible to spin with an unbalanced spindle whorl. This should not, however, be regarded as the spinner's first choice.

Spinning with an 8 g whorl using flax fibres
Overall, the result demonstrates that an 8 g whorl works well as a spindle whorl for spinning flax fibres. It was reported, however, that it was hard to spin homogenous linen yarn that was highly similar within all spinning tests. This could be due to the fact that the spinners had less experience in spinning flax as opposed to wool. The difference between the spinners appears clearly if one calculates how many metres of yarn were spun per 100 g flax fibre (Fig. 4.1.12). This result is interesting, since both spinners in this case were trying to spin similarly. The matter may be clarified by some observations made while spinning. One important factor that might have affected the differences in the two spinners' yarn was the application of water mixed with linseed oil, but this was not discussed in detail during the spinning experiment. It was reported later that one spinner used much more linseed water whilst spinning than did the other. The water and linseed mix may have helped to connect more

fibres and thus made some threads thicker, *i.e.* the more watery spun thread was shorter than the other (Fig. 4.1.12). In this case, the difference between the spinners was probably caused by the habits of the spinner rather than the spindle in use.

It should be noted that yarn made of wool and yarn made of flax have a different appearance and feel different irrespective of whether the yarn contains a similar amount of fibres in grams. A comparison of the experience of spinning flax and wool fibres with the same whorl indicates two main differences according to the tool's function while spinning. Firstly, when the spindle was almost full of yarn, it started to wobble in a more extreme way while spinning with flax than it did with wool. The spindle changed quite abruptly to being hard to twist, it stopped and rotated in the opposite direction. It could be that the whorl may have managed to twist the flax fibres in a more balanced way if the rod had been thinner in width, to expand the whorl's diameter in relation to the rod.[5] Secondly, the linen yarn also easily slipped off the spindle while spinning, which was a rather distracting interruption. Perhaps the spindle would be more suitable in its function for spinning linen yarn if the whorl had a larger diameter. This, however, was not tested.

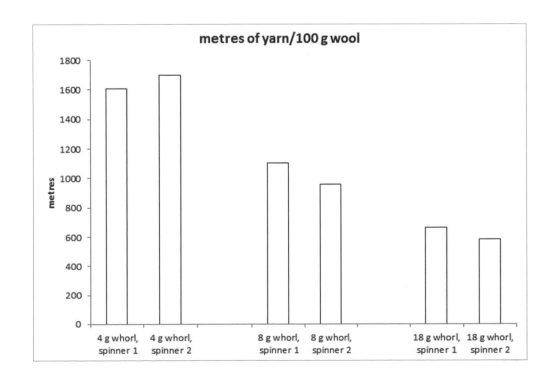

Fig. 4.1.11. Calculation of metres of yarn per 100 g wool, 4 g, 8 g and 18 g whorls, and comparing the metres of yarn spun by the two spinners.

Spinning yarn takes time

The time consumption of prehistoric textile production is considerable. Almost endless hours must have been spent on producing textiles, even if it was only for one piece of cloth. In order to emphasise this almost infinite work, some conclusions drawn from the results from the TTTC spinning experiment will be outlined in the following. By making time studies of these processes today it is possible to get an idea of how time consuming this work can be. Owing to the design of the experiments, it is also possible to compare the spinning time when using different spindles and between different spinners. The results of these comparisons made it clear that there is a difference in time consumption when spinning with different whorls, though the differences must be seen as marginal (Fig. 4.1.13). It is more time consuming to spin yarn with a light whorl than it is with a heavier one. The reason is probably that it requires a lot of concentration to spin with the 8 g and 4 g whorls. The need for concentration, according to our experience, makes it doubtful that other household duties could be performed while spinning with these light whorls. Spinning flax fibres with an 8 g whorl took longer than spinning wool fibres using the same whorl. This contradicts other experiences and experiments where flax typically has taken less time to spin than wool (see chapter 2). A slight difference in time consumption can be identified between the two spinners as well. This is probably due to the individual habits of the spinners and the strength in the spinners' hands.

In the experiments, it took about 12 hours to prepare 133 g of wool for spinning. 1138 m yarn was spun from the 133 g of wool using the 8 g and 18 g whorls. This work took approximately 25 hours. Altogether, the spinners on average spun 27 m of yarn before the spindle was considered full (that is, when the weight of the threads wound on the spindle affected the rotation of the spindle negatively). This meant that in order to spin 1138 m of yarn, the spindle had to be filled *c.* 42 times. Furthermore, time must be added for the winding of the yarn on the spindle, which is estimated at three hours for 1138 m of yarn. Based on these calculations, it would take approximately 40 hours for one person, including wool preparation, to produce 1138 m of yarn. This illustrates the considerable amount of time needed for spinning, particularly when noting that even the 1138 m of yarn would only be sufficient for half a square m of fabric with *c.* ten warp threads per centimetre.

Useful threads?

In order to understand the quality of a yarn, its use and function in a textile must be taken into consideration. A further component of the experiment was thus to examine the function of the spun yarn in a textile. Yarn can be spun for different purposes, for making bands, nets,

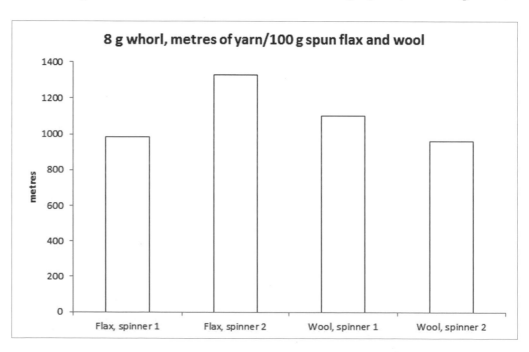

Fig. 4.1.12. Calculation of metres of yarn per 100 g flax fibres and 100 g wool fibres, 8 g whorl, and comparing the metres of yarn spun by the two spinners.

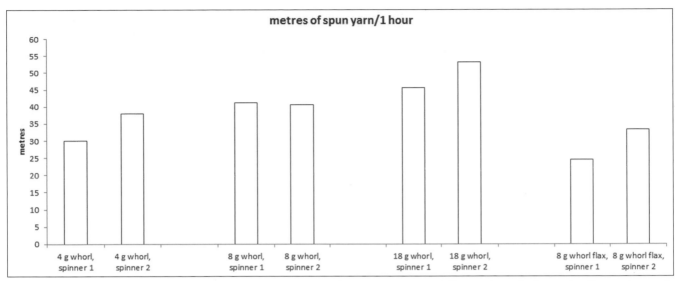

Fig. 4.1.13. Calculation of metres of yarn spun per hour with 4 g, 8 g and 18 g whorls using wool fibres, and 8 g whorl using flax fibres, and comparing the metres of yarn spun by the two spinners.

clothes and sails for example. Since the aim was to test the function of whorls and not to make reconstructions of textiles, no specific textile was targeted while spinning. As tabby weaving is considered the most common weaving technique during the Bronze Age, weaving samples were made in this technique.[6] Yarn from both wool and flax fibres spun with the 8 g whorl and wool fibres spun with the 4 g whorl were tested in warp-weighted loom setups. The loom weights used were reconstructions made based on a ceramic loom weight from Troia (Becks and Guzowska 2004, cat. no. 2). The reconstructions consisted of a set of discoid, grooved loom weights weighing 183–187 g each and with a thickness of 2 cm. This accurately reflects the shape, thickness and weight of the original Troia loom weights.

Before weaving, one has to set up the warp. One half of the warp consisted of only Batzer's yarn and one half only Olofsson's (Fig. 4.1.14). Different types of yarn require different weight tension when the yarn is used as the warp on a warp-weighted loom. In order to find out what tension these specific threads needed, small tests were made tensioning the different yarns spun with 4 g and 8 g whorls. The wool and linen threads spun with the same 8 g whorl required similar weight tension in the warp *i.e.* approximately 19 g per warp thread. The thin wool yarn spun with the 4 g whorl required *c.* 13 g per warp thread. It is notable that the yarn spun by using spindle

Fig. 4.1.14. Weaving sample on a loom. This is the setup for the linen thread spun with the 8 g whorl. The two spinners' warp threads were marked with sewing thread (photo: CTR).

whorls with different weights was not suitable to be used in the same weave. The number of warp threads attached to each loom weight was thus regulated according to the weight tension needed per warp thread, *e.g.* 14 threads per loom weight used for yarn spun with the 4 g whorl. All three loom setups were arranged in order to get an even distribution of loom weights in relationship to the width of the starting border, *i.e.* the total width of loom weights in a row was similar to the total width of the starting border (Fig. 4.1.15).

Both wool and linen yarn spun with the 8 g whorl worked well when weaving. The wool yarn spun with the 4 g whorl worked, but was very sensitive to work with due to the wear on the threads caused by changing shed. However, this problem must be seen as natural when weaving tabby fabrics with a close warp on a warp weighted loom. The threads would probably work better if they were arranged in a more open tabby with more space between the warp threads, or if they were treated with a type of glue that would ensure the fibres stuck together.

Generally, the different spinners' wool threads appeared similar in the weaving

samples. The linen threads, on the other hand, appeared different, since one of the spinners had spun thinner thread than the other. There was an obvious imbalance between the two halves of the linen weave, as one half tended to be more tightly packed than the other, resulting in an asymmetrical effect on the textile (Fig. 4.1.14). It took about 50 minutes to weave 4 cm linen textile.

No weaving test was made on yarn spun with the 18 g whorl since the main aim of the TTTC experiments was to test whorls lighter than 10 g.

To conclude, the weaving tests demonstrated that it is possible to produce yarn with whorls weighing less than 10 g which is strong enough for weaving. How the two spinners' yarns appeared in the weaving samples is reported in the external analysis (see chapter 4.2).

Other spinning tests

The experiments could of course have included several spindle whorl weight classes. The spinners from the TTTC programme tested heavier spindle whorls in a project performed by Linda Olofsson at CHARC in 2006.[7] The whorls were reconstructed based on finds from Nichoria with a weight of 30 g and 50 g. The tests were designed similarly to the TTTC tests. However, the aim was also to investigate different spinning techniques. It was concluded that heavier spindle whorls are suitable to produce a wider range of yarns than lighter whorls. This is valid if the spindle is worked with either supported or suspended spinning techniques (Mårtensson 2006). It was not possible within the framework of the TTTC programme to further test heavier whorls (for other tests on Scandinavian spindle whorls weighing up to 44 g see Andersson 1999; 2003).[8]

Results of the TTTC tests of spindle whorls

The tests confirmed that whorls weighing less than 10 g are suitable for spinning fine and thin threads. Consequently, whorls lighter than 10 g should be regarded as possible spindle whorls. This result does not, however, exclude the whorls' possible function as beads or buttons. The problem of having a spindle rod with a length that does not fit with the whorl may have been the reason why whorls with a weight under 10 g have been regarded as problematic in their use as spindle whorls in earlier experiments.

Furthermore, it is also of great importance what fibres are used and how the fibres are

Fig. 4.1.15. Warp-weighted loom. The width of the starting boarder is adjusted to the width of the row of loom weights. This is the setup for the wool thread spun with the 8 g whorl. The loom weights are reconstructed based on finds of discoid loom weights from Troia (photo: CTR).

prepared prior to spinning. To use thin fibres is preferable when producing thread with a light whorl. When it comes to what is the lower weight limit of a suitable spindle whorl, conclusions can only be drawn from what has been tested, *i.e.* that a 4 g whorl is well suited for spinning. It is not unlikely, however, that even lighter whorls can be used as spindle whorls, on the condition that correct fibre preparation has taken place. If this were the case, the whorl would need a very small rod made of a light material in order to achieve a balanced tool. Such spindles would probably be useful for spinning extremely thin yarn.

One important aim was to determine to what extent it is the spinner or the spindle that affects the outcome, that is, the type of yarn produced. The spinning experiments with suspended spindles confirmed that it is primarily the quality of fibres and the weight of the spindle whorl that affect the finished product, *i.e.* the spun yarn. The height of the spindle whorl is of minor importance for the finished product. The diameter of the spindle whorl may affect the yarn to some extent, such as the twist angle. A large diameter might also prevent linen yarn slipping off the spindle while spinning. Thus, spindle whorls with a large diameter would be preferable when spinning flax.

To conclude, the weight of whorls is found to be the key to understanding archaeological whorls. In general, different weights of whorls suggest production of different types of yarn. Whorls of similar weight, particularly with respect to lighter whorls, may suggest production of similar types of yarn. The weight of a whorl is thus of importance when interpreting archaeological whorls and what yarn may have been produced with them. Furthermore, the context the whorls are recovered from may provide additional information.

However, it is not the object that dictated what fibres, tools and techniques should be used. It is of course the given society's desire, choices and needs that is reflected in the archaeological record, in this case the spindle whorls. It is thus a human being and the society surrounding them who primarily decided what yarn was spun. The assumption is that these decisions were taken with an awareness of the influence of the tools and fibres. With comprehensive data on archaeological whorls it becomes possible to interpret what whorls were preferred at a given site and in a particular context. This information, combined with results from experiments, can thus indicate what types of yarn were once spun. With no information on what fibres were used and what spinning technique was employed, however, the whorls can only be interpreted in terms of suggestions of what it was possible to produce with them. Our suggestion is that the lighter the whorl, the lighter and in general thinner the produced yarn is.

Based on results from textile experimental archaeology in the TTTC research programme, the following conclusions can be made concerning whorls and spinning:

- Two spinners will never be able to produce identical threads, although some degree of uniformity can be achieved by using the same fibre and tool.
- Apart from the spinner, it is primarily the quality of fibres and the weight of the spindle whorl that affect the finished product, *i.e.* the spun yarn.
- Whorls lighter than 10 g should be regarded as possible spindle whorls.
- In general, the lighter the whorl, the lighter and thinner is the yarn produced.
- Wool yarn spun with the same spindle whorl but by different spinners could be used in the same weave, whilst yarn spun with different spindles was not optimal for use in the same weave, since the thread needed different amounts of tension.

Function of textile tools: loom weights and TTTC weaving tests

There are several shapes and weights represented among the loom weights in the archaeological material. The diversity in shape and weight has been explained in terms of cultural, geographical or chronological factors. In the following, however, investigations exploring whether the diversity in shape and weight instead reflects the loom weights' function will be considered. By such investigations our aim is to further identify important factors in the weaver's choice of loom weights. It will be investigated if it is possible to elucidate what textiles different loom weights are suitable to produce. Comprehensive knowledge of these factors is of importance when recording and interpreting loom weights as archaeological material.

Weaving on the warp-weighted loom

The warp-weighted loom can be operated in several ways, depending on, for example, what weaving technique is employed, such as tabby or twill. Since tabby weaving is considered the most common weaving technique during the Bronze Age (see chapter 3), we have used only this technique in the TTTC experiments and based calculations on this type of fabric. The technical expressions and techniques mentioned below only demonstrate tabbies of relevance for this chapter (see also chapter 2). A balanced tabby has the same number of threads and the same type of yarn in both warp and weft. A weft faced tabby is when the weft is covering the warp threads. In a warp faced tabby the two thread systems work the opposite way. A fabric can also be open or closed. When producing a tabby weave, the loom weights hang from two thread layers (front and back). The loom weights in each row are positioned side by side. Every other warp thread is attached to a loom weight in the front layer, and every other warp thread to a loom weight in the back layer. One *can* use different sizes and weights of loom weights if one spends much time on calculating and distributing them evenly among the warp threads. Our approach, based on archaeological finds of loom weights *in situ*, iconography and ethnographic knowledge, is that similar loom weights were used in a loom setup consisting of homogenous warp threads (*e.g.* Hoffmann 1964; Barber 1991; Mannering and Andersson Strand 2009).

The following list demonstrates features we consider required for optimal weaving on a warp-weighted loom. Obvious features such as good light and comfortable working position are not included. This list provided the criteria for optimal weaving when evaluating the weaving tests.

- Loom in stable position.
- Appropriate weight tension per warp thread.
- Even distribution of weight per warp thread in the whole loom setup.
- Loom weights positioned at the same level.
- Loom weights positioned side by side.
- Loom weights stable, *i.e.* not whirling or tangling.
- Warp threads hanging vertically and evenly distributed.
- Warp threads do not tangle.
- Warp threads do not break.
- Shed easy to change.
- Weft easy to insert evenly.
- Identical width of fabric throughout the weaving.
- Edges of the weave are straight.
- Even and regular feeling when weaving.

Simple weights, but complex components in the warp-weighted loom

Previously, craftspeople and different scholars have established that the weight of loom weights influences weaving on a warp-weighted loom.[9] Different types of yarn need different tension and this limits how many warp threads can be attached to one loom weight. If the yarn needs 20 g tension per warp thread, and the loom weight weighs 500 g, one can attach approximately 25 warp threads to this loom weight. If, however, one uses a yarn that requires 50 g tension, one can only attach ten warp threads to the loom weight. Likewise, if one uses a loom weight with a weight of 300 g, and a yarn that needs a tension of 20 g per warp thread, one can attach only 15 warp threads to each loom weight, but if the required tension is 10 g per warp thread, then the weaver can attach 30 warp threads. The setup is therefore strongly related to the type of yarn; and the choice of loom weights is connected to the desired fabric and the type of yarn.

In order to obtain an arrangement where the loom weights are hanging side by side at the same level and with an optimal warp tension per thread, the loom weight maximum thickness must play an important role. The loom weight thickness defines how closely they can hang side by side. The height of the loom weight as well as its diameter partly defines its weight. However, these two parameters are of minor importance during weaving since neither the height nor the diameter of the loom weights affect the weaving process. The distribution of warp threads should thus depend on the weight and the thickness of loom weights (Fig. 4.1.15). Furthermore, there is no advantage to attaching more than 30 threads to one loom weight. If more threads are attached, it will create problems during the setup and weaving, thereby affecting the final product. On the other hand, if just a couple of threads are attached to one loom weight, considerably more loom weights will be required, thus also creating problems. At least ten or more threads should be attached to each loom weight. If the fabric to be produced has an extremely open warp system, however, it might be relevant to have fewer warp threads attached to each loom weight.

In order to obtain a better knowledge of the function of loom weights and their arrangement on the loom, extensive experimental testing was undertaken within the TTTC research programme focusing on the thickness of loom weights. The thickness does not appear to have been a subject of discussion when interpreting loom weights in the archaeological scholarly works. Nor has the influence of the thickness of loom weights on weaving been an object of systematic studies in experimental archaeology.

Two stages of tests on loom weights in tabby weaving were made within the TTTC research programme with different aims (Mårtensson *et al.* 2009). The aim of the first stage was to establish which parameters were to be included in tests of the function of loom weights. These parameters were established in order to establish a methodology applicable to experiments using reconstructions in later investigations. In the second stage, the aim was to demonstrate optimal weaving based on the results from the first stage and was developed by making case studies using reconstructed spool shaped loom weights.

Principles for investigating loom weights
The principles for utilising experimental archaeology, which was applied in the experiments with spinning (see above), were not strictly followed through the entire procedure of testing loom weights. The principles which were diverged from are explained in the following:

- *Raw materials, such as wool and flax, must be selected according to our knowledge of Bronze Age fibres and work processes.* The yarns used in the TTTC experiments were machine spun; they were thus not made with work processes or fibre qualities known from the Bronze Age. The yarns were, however, selected in accordance with what it is possible to spin with Bronze Age whorls.
- *Tools must be reconstructed as precise copies of archaeological artefacts.* In the first stage of the loom weight tests, in order to fulfil our requirements of specific thicknesses and weights, constructed loom weights were

used, *i.e.* not reconstructions. However, in the second stage, loom weights reconstructed from the archaeological record were used.

- *All processes must be performed by at least two skilled craftspeople.* Two weavers were working in parallel in the first stage in order to get two people's opinions of the weaving and what the most optimal setup is regarding loom weights' thickness. For the second stage, only one weaver was weaving. The arrangement of the loom and weaving, however, were made based on both weavers' opinions.
- *All products must be submitted to external experts for textile analysis.* The resulting fabric was not submitted to external experts for analysis. Instead, samples from weaving with the hand spun yarn from the TTTC tests were given priority, since more information could be obtained from these samples in the external analysis, *e.g.* warp and weft could be traced back to who had spun it and with what tool (see chapter 4.2).

From loom weights to loom setups
When weaving, it is usually the textile to be produced that defines how the loom is set up and what loom weights are used. In this test, however, the work procedure was reversed, since the aim was not to produce a specific textile, but to test the loom weights' influence on weaving. The working procedure went from loom weights to loom setups and finally the weaving of the textile. The tests were carried out by weaver 1, Anne Batzer and weaver 2, Linda Olofsson working in parallel. For the test, two different sets of constructed ceramic loom weights made by ceramist Inger Hildebrandt, CHARC, were used on two warp-weighted looms. One set was composed of 22 loom weights with a thickness of 4 cm each (Fig. 4.1.16), and the other set was composed of 22 loom weights with a thickness of 2 cm each (Fig. 4.1.17). All loom weights had an identical weight (*c.* 275 g each) regardless of their thickness. In this experiment, they were not replicas of archaeological textile tools *i.e.* the loom weights were specially designed for these tests, having identical weights, but divided into two sets of loom weights with a thickness of 2 cm and 4 cm respectively. The loom weights were positioned side by side, close to each other, at the same level. This position of the loom weights has a practical function. If the loom weights hang in a zigzag line at various

Fig. 4.1.16. Loom weight, thickness 4 cm, weight c. *275 g: 22 loom weights, 11 in each row. Total width* c. *50 cm (photo: CTR).*

Fig. 4.1.17. (below) Loom weight, thickness 2 cm, weight c. *275 g: 22 loom weights, 11 in each row. Total width* c. *28 cm (photo: CTR).*

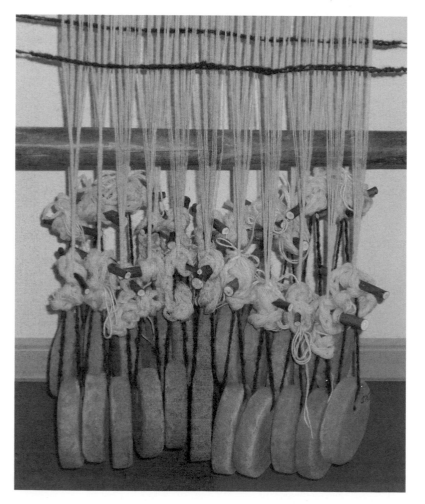

levels, the upper loom weights may cause wear damage on the warp threads. If they are not hanging side by side, they might cause a wavy appearance of the warp threads resulting in disturbance while weaving, and they might also tangle and twist the warp threads attached to them. Problems of tangling and jangling loom weights have been experienced and described elsewhere (Carington Smith 1992, 690). Having the loom weights positioned side by side, closely and at the same level, affects the total width of the row of loom weights. A narrow row of loom weights can be regulated with a chain spacing cord. Spreading out the loom weights, however, forms gaps between warp threads attached to different loom weights. These gaps can be hard to eliminate with a spacing cord and are often visible and undesired elements in the textile (Fig. 4.1.18). Spreading out loom weights is thus not regarded as optimal. Therefore, in optimal weaving, the loom weight thickness defines the width of the row of loom weights.

In order to test how the total width of loom weights affects the weaving and the woven fabric, two identical warps with starting borders measuring 34 cm in width were arranged on the two looms. They were placed in identical setups, but using different thicknesses of loom weights. On one loom, one row of loom weights had a total width of 50 cm, and in the other loom the total width of one row of loom weights was 28 cm. There was thus a difference of 22 cm in the total width of loom weights between the two different loom setups.[10] The number of warp threads was chosen in accordance with the number of loom weights and their weight. The yarn used was machine spun and made of wool. It was as similar as possible to the wool yarn spun with the 8 g whorl: *c.* 1,000 m per 100 g yarn. This yarn required a warp tension of approximately 20 g per thread, resulting in groups of 14 threads per loom weight of 275 g in both setups. Identical numbers of warp threads attached to each loom weight were used throughout all weaving tests.

Thickness of loom weights and its importance

In the two loom setups, the influence of the loom weights was clearly demonstrated. On the loom with the wide row of loom weights, the warp threads were hanging outwards (Fig. 4.1.19) and on the loom with the narrower row of loom weights they were hanging slightly inwards (Fig. 4.1.20). In order to clarify how these arrangements influenced the weaving, both of them were compared to the list of features in optimal weaving, which was presented above. Both setups had negative features, some of which were shared by both setups. In both setups, the warp threads were not hanging vertically and were not evenly distributed and the weaving was neither even nor regular. Both setups could thus be regarded as not being optimal for weaving. The resulting fabric from the setup with the widest total width of loom weights, however, was a quite regular fabric in comparison to the fabric woven with the narrower row of loom weights. Thus, it was concluded that it is preferable to use loom weights with a total width that is identical or slightly larger than the width of the fabric to be produced. In order to verify the result, the two looms, re-using the same loom weights, were set up again with new warps. Now, the warp threads were distributed evenly according to both the weight and thickness of the loom weights. Using the same yarn as before, the setup with two narrow rows of loom weights, 28 cm, was suitable for producing a warp faced fabric (Fig. 4.1.21). The setup with two wider

rows of loom weights, instead, was suitable for producing an open and balanced or weft faced tabby (Fig. 4.1.22).

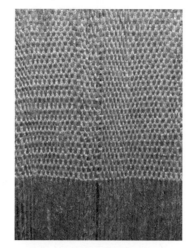

Fig. 4.1.18. Gaps between warp threads caused by the warp threads slanting outwards (photo: CTR).

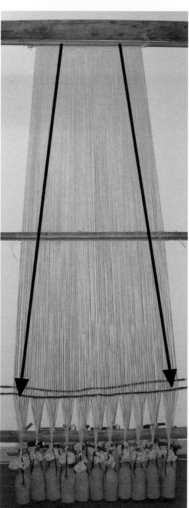

Fig. 4.1.19. The arrows indicate the direction of the warp threads, which are slanting outwards (photo: CTR).

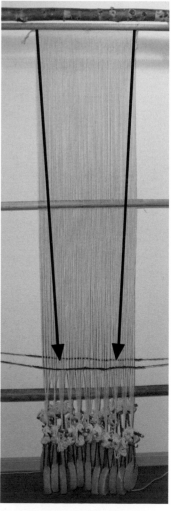

Fig. 4.1.20. The arrows indicate the direction of the warp threads, which are slanting slightly inwards (photo: CTR).

To conclude, by weaving samples of fabrics with different thicknesses of loom weights, it was clearly demonstrated that the thickness does play an important role when weaving and hence influences the choice of loom weights. If this would not have been the case, the weaving samples would have appeared more similar. We have concluded that in order to obtain a setup on the warp-weighted loom regarded as optimal for weaving, the thickness and the weight of loom weights play an important role. Furthermore, we have concluded that it is preferable to use loom weights with a total width, when hanging in a row, which is identical or slightly larger than the width of the fabric to be produced. It is thus vital to record both the weight and maximum thickness of loom weights in archaeological assemblages. These factors form the key to the understanding of the textiles produced with these tools. Based on this information we find it possible to outline what kind of tabby textiles could have been produced with a given yarn quality. Such estimates will be presented in the following.

Spool shaped loom weights from Khania – a case study

By using the spool shaped loom weights from Khania, we wanted to investigate further how different loom weight shapes function on a warp-weighted loom. This case study was carried out by Linda Olofsson.

The so-called spools have been a subject of discussion. It has been questioned if they could be used as loom weights at all (Rahmstorf 2003; 2005, 156; Gleba 2009). It was therefore of interest to reconstruct such spools for a case study (Figs 4.1.23 and 4.1.24). Spools are often found in sets of similar shape and weight (Rahmstorf 2003, 402). Such sets could thus represent weights for one loom setup.

Different groupings of spool shaped loom weights of similar weight and thickness have been found in Khania on Crete. To represent two different weight and thickness types of loom weights, two unfired clay spools with different thickness and weight were selected from a pit deposit in Building 1, Room I, in Khania dated to LM IIIC (Hallager and Hallager 2000, 40–41).

Fig. 4.1.21. (left) The warp threads are hanging vertically and are evenly distributed as a warp faced tabby (photo: CTR).

Fig. 4.1.22. (right) The warp threads are hanging vertically and are evenly distributed as a balanced tabby (photo: CTR).

Fig. 4.1.23. Reconstructed "small" spool (photo: CTR).

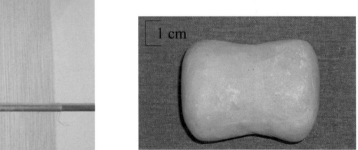

Fig. 4.1.24. Reconstructed "large" spool (photo: CTR).

Based on these finds, two sets of unfired clay spools were reconstructed by ceramicists Inger Hildebrandt and Marianne Gedsø Smith, CHARC. One set of 24 spools, each with a thickness of *c.* 4 cm and a weight of *c.* 105 g, here called small spools (Fig. 4.1.23), and another set of 16 spools, each with a thickness of *c.* 5.5 cm and a weight of *c.* 280 g, here called large spools (Fig. 4.1.24), were reconstructed.[11] Two loom setups were made on warp-weighted looms: one loom was set up with only large spools, and the other with only small spools. In accordance with our previous results, the warp threads were arranged according to the thickness and weight of the spools. The weft thread, however, is less influenced by the loom weights and can be inserted as desired. If a fabric is made as an open tabby, it would thus be possible to make a weft faced tabby in the same loom setup.

Large spools

In accordance with the TTTC test results, the thickness and weight of the spools were taken into account when selecting a suitable yarn for this setup. With two rows of loom weights for tabby weaving, the 16 large spools were divided into two layers, with eight spools in each. The total width of each row of spools was 46 cm. Since we wanted the starting border to be of identical width or slightly narrower than the row of loom weights, this meant that the warp threads needed to be distributed over a length of about 40–46 cm.

A wool yarn was selected to use in the TTTC tests. Similar yarn could have been spun using a spindle with a whorl weighing *c.* 8 g.[12]

This estimate was based on the results from the experimental research reported above. Such yarn requires a tension of *c.* 18–20 g per warp thread on the warp-weighted loom, and consequently 16 threads were attached to each spool. With two rows of loom weights for tabby weaving, this meant 32 warp threads per 5.5 cm, and therefore only about six warp threads per centimetre, thus resulting in an open or weft faced fabric. One sample, sample 1, (Fig. 4.1.25) with this yarn as warp was woven, providing a suggestion as to a suitable textile to produce with these spools. In sample 1, the same yarn was used in weft as warp. On average the sample consisted of 6.1 warp threads per centimetre and 7.4 weft threads per centimetre, *i.e.* an open and rather balanced fabric, giving a transparent impression.

Small spools

With two rows of loom weights for tabby weaving, the 24 reconstructed small spools had to be divided into two layers with 12 spools in each. The total width of each row of spools was thus 48 cm. Taking into account the light weight of the spools, this meant that the spools would be suitable to produce an open fabric where the warp threads were distributed over the entire width of 48 cm.

The spools in this setup had a lighter weight and narrower thickness than the large ones. Therefore it was necessary to use another type of yarn. An extremely thin yarn was more suitable. With thin yarn requiring *c.* 10 g tension, the distribution would be *c.* 5 warp threads per centimetre, thus giving a very open fabric.

Fig. 4.1.25. Sample 1 made using large spools, producing an open and rather balanced fabric, giving a transparent impression (photo: CTR).

With a slightly thicker yarn requiring *c.* 15 g tension, the distribution would be only *c.* 3.5 warp threads per centimetre and would thus result in an open fabric as well. With a yet thicker yarn requiring *c.* 25 g tension, these small spools would be suitable in a setup with only about two warp threads per centimetre; in this case, it would however be much easier to choose heavier and thicker loom weights. The first mentioned setup with the highest number of warp threads per centimetre (five warp threads), was tested on a warp-weighted loom.

The thinnest machine spun wool yarn available requiring *c.* 10 g tension was used and consequently 10 threads were attached to each spool. Similar yarn could have been spun using a spindle whorl weighing *c.* 4 g, if very fine wool was used. This estimate is based on the results from the TTTC experiments as presented above. With this yarn as warp, two samples were woven, thus giving two possible suggestions regarding what fabric it is most suitable to produce using these small spools (see Figs 4.1.26.a and 4.1.26.b): In sample 2a, the same yarn was used in weft as warp. On average, the sample consisted of 5 warp threads per centimetre and 8 weft threads per centimetre, *i.e.* a very open fabric, giving a transparent impression (Fig. 4.1.26.a). The hard spun yarn and the very open setup gave a lively and flexible appearance to the fabric. After washing the fabric, it shrank and the flexible and crepe-like appearance became more apparent (Fig. 4.1.27). This suggests a production of a rather transparent fabric.

Sample 2b was produced by using a thicker machine made wool yarn as weft, corresponding to thread spun with an 8 g whorl. The weft was beaten harder with the wooden sword beater in order to produce a weft faced fabric. On average the sample consisted of 5.8 warp threads per centimetre and 14.8 weft threads per centimetre, *i.e.* a very weft faced fabric (Fig. 4.1.26.b). This suggests a densely woven and yet thin fabric.

On the functionality of spool shaped loom weights

The spools functioned perfectly as loom weights on a warp-weighted loom. Weaving was accomplished without any problems. Furthermore, there were no problems with the spools being unfired in their use as loom weights. Used as loom weights in a loom setup with thin warp threads, we actually found the spools to be superior to other shapes of loom weights, such as discoid and torus shapes. The spool shape was especially efficient when warping and when regulating the length of the warp on the loom.

Warping was made with a ribbon as starting border. By pulling out the weft of the ribbon while weaving it, the weft becomes the warp. When enough weft threads are pulled out, equivalent to the number of warp threads attached to two loom weights, the threads are divided and usually tied to a bobbin or laced together in order to keep control of the threads (Fig. 4.1.28). In the present test, however, every bunch of warp threads was attached to a spool during warping (Fig. 4.1.29). The spools functioned perfectly as bobbins storing the warp as long as they were resting on the floor and did not pull down the starting border with their weight (Fig. 4.1.30). In this way the thin and lively yarn could be treated

Fig. 4.1.26. (a) Sample 2a: sample made using small spools. A very open fabric, giving a transparent impression. (b) Sample 2b: sample made using small spools and a thicker weft thread, i.e. weft faced (photo: CTR).

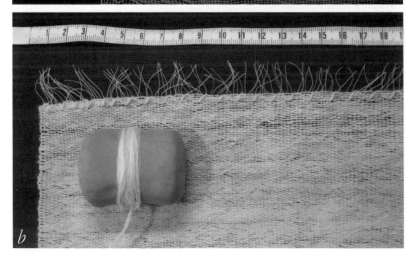

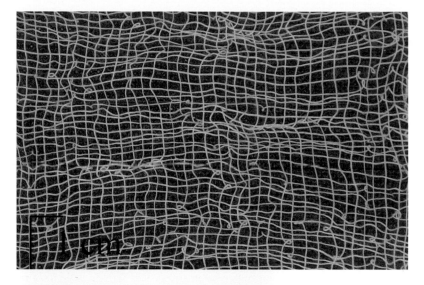

in a very controlled and gentle way. Since the warp threads were already tied to the spools with a loop around them when the warp was arranged on the loom, they could simply be pulled down and the length of the warp could easily be corrected if needed (Fig. 4.1.31). The process of tying and arranging the loom weights on the warp threads in the loom was therefore not necessary. In this sense, setting up the warp on the loom was easier with the spools than if using, for example, discoid loom weights, which need to be tied to the warp. Furthermore, it was possible to work with several metres of warp without having the extra metres wound onto separate implements tied to the loom weights or hanging freely by the side of the loom weights (Fig. 4.1.31).

To conclude, the shape of spools does have a practical function whilst warping and weaving. It facilitates the work when setting up the warp on the loom and keeps extra warp organised while weaving. Spool shaped loom weights might thus signify a well-planned and efficient production of textiles. The weight and the thickness of loom weights, however, we conclude to be the most important parameters influencing what types of textiles that are produced.

Fig. 4.1.27. (above) Washed sample 2a made using small spools. The threads curled in a three dimensional way after washing, giving the piece a flexible and crêpe-like appearance (photo: CTR).

From loom weight research to interpretations of fabrics

The weaving tests have confirmed that in order to produce an open fabric or weft faced fabric using thick yarn, it would be optimal to choose heavy and thick loom weights; in order to weave a dense fabric using thick yarn, it would be optimal to choose heavier but thinner loom weights. On the other hand, in order to make a dense fabric using thin yarn with many threads per centimetre, it would be preferable to use light and thin loom weights. Finally, if an open fabric or a weft faced fabric using thin yarn is desired, lighter and thicker loom weights would be the best choice.

By recording weight and maximum thickness of loom weights and combining these data with the results of experimental weaving, it becomes possible to suggest the kind of textiles that could have been produced with a given yarn quality.

The TTTC experiments and the associated interpretation of loom weights resulted in a suggestion of the TTTC choice of tools for a

Fig. 4.1.28. Laced warp threads: the warp threads are laced together in bunches corresponding to what will be attached to one loom weight (photo: CTR).

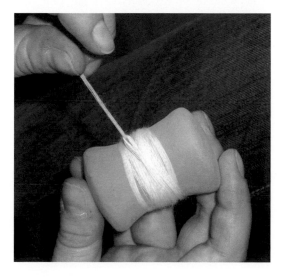

Fig. 4.1.29. Warp on a spool: attaching the warp threads to a spool by tying them with a loop around them (photo: CTR).

Fig. 4.1.30. Spools resting on the floor during warping (photo: CTR).

Fig. 4.1.31. Arranging small spools on the loom. The warp is already attached to them (photo: CTR).

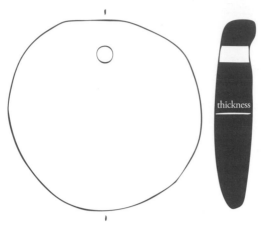

Fig. 4.1.32. Loom weight, weight 150 g, thickness 2 cm (drawing: CTR).

fabric, *i.e.* what is optimal. The TTTC choice of tools is presented below. Furthermore, several loom weights could be used for various types of fabrics and consequently there can be more than just one TTTC choice. The example below is not based on any archaeological loom weights, but demonstrates how a calculation can be made. There is also an estimate of how many loom weights and how many metres of yarn would be required for various loom setups.

The following is a suggestion of fabrics that could be made using a set of loom weights each with a weight of 150 g and a thickness of 2 cm (Fig. 4.1.32). The example demonstrates how such loom weights function with various types of warp yarn. The weight of the 150 g loom weight defines how many warp threads can be attached to it. If a warp yarn requires 10 g warp tension (A), the weaver must attach 15 threads to each loom weight. If a yarn requires 20 g tension (B), 7.5 warp threads can be attached to each loom weight. On the other hand, if a warp thread requires 30 g tension (C), the weaver can only attach 5 warp threads to each loom weight. Finally, if a warp thread requires 40 g tension (D), the weaver can only attach 3.75 warp threads to each loom weight (see Fig. 4.1.33).

The loom weight has a thickness of 2 cm. In case (A), 15 warp threads from the loom weight in the front layer and 15 warp threads from the back layer must be packed in the space of 2 cm. The result is a fabric with 15 warp threads per centimetre. In case (B), the result is a fabric with 7.5 warp threads per centimetre and in case (C), the result is a weave with 5 warp threads per centimetre. Finally, if the weaver chooses yarn requiring 40 g (D) warp tension,

Loom weight; weight 150 g, thickness 2 cm				
Setups	A	B	C	D
Warp threads requiring	10 g warp tension	20 g warp tension	30 g warp tension	40 g warp tension
Numbers of warp threads per loom weight*	15	7.5	5	3.75
Numbers of warp threads per two loom weight (one in front layer, one in back layer)**	30	15	10	7.5
Warp threads per cm***	15	7.5	5	3.75
TTTC's evaluation of suitability of the tool	TTTC choice	Not optimal	Not optimal	Not optimal

*Fig. 4.1.33. Loom weight, weight 150 g, thickness 2 cm. * Loom weight 150 g divided by 10 (warp tension). ** result above multiplied by number of rows of loom weights. *** Results above divided by loom weight thickness in centimetres (2 cm).*

the weaver could only attach 3.75 threads per loom weight, thus there would be 3.75 warp threads per centimetre.

In cases (B), (C) and (D) it would have been sensible to choose a heavier loom weight instead. We therefore suggest that this type of loom weight is suitable when weaving with thin yarn requiring little tension. We consider (A) to be the best choice, the TTTC choice, since the loom weights were used in an optimal setting (*i.e.* 10 or more threads per loom weight).

With focus on the best choice (A), we can hypothesise the following loom setup (Fig. 4.1.34).

It is possible to calculate the necessary yarn for producing specific fabrics. The required amount of yarn depends on the number of threads per square centimetre. The calculations are all based on a fabric with a length of two metres and a width of one metre. If the fabric contains 15 warp threads and 15 weft threads per centimetre, 3000 m of warp threads and 3000 m of weft threads are needed, so a total of 6000 m of yarn is required. However, if the fabric is weft faced, a larger amount of weft thread is required; if double the amount of weft thread is needed, the total amount of thread is 9000 m. A tabby is the result of interlacing two thread systems crossing each other at right angles. Even if both the warp and weft threads are taut, the threads will never be fully stretched or lie completely straight since they cross over and under each other. Furthermore, it is not technically possible to weave the last part of the warp, meaning that there will always be some waste warp yarn. For these reasons, one has to add approximately 2–5% more yarn when calculating the amount of yarn

Loom setup A (calculated on 10 g warp tension)
Starting border (width of the fabric): 100 cm
Number of loom weights needed: 100 (50 in front layer and 50 in back layer)
Number of warp threads: 1500 threads, 2 m each = 3000 m
Weft in a balanced tabby = 3000 m
Total amount of yarn with weft (+ 2%) = 6120 m

required for one setup. In this calculation, we have chosen to add 2% more yarn for the calculated setup.

Fig. 4.1.34. Calculation of a setup based on the TTTC best choice (A).

Producing textiles takes time

In the following, an estimate of how long it would take to make a textile using setup (A) will be presented. The example above demonstrates the substantial requirement of yarn. The time needed to spin a specific amount of yarn is difficult to estimate and it depends on a variety of parameters such as the spinner's skill, the quality of the fibres, as well as the tool. According to the spinning experiments, the production of the 6120 m yarn for a balanced tabby in this setup would take approximately 175 hours to spin with a 4 g whorl (spinning rate 35 m/h). It would thus take approximately 22 days (eight hours per day of uninterrupted spinning) to produce the yarn. It would take approximately 262 hours, *e.g.* approximately 33 days of eight hours, to spin the 9180 m yarn for a weft faced tabby with double the amount of weft yarn. To this the time for sorting wool and preparation of fibres must be added.

When the yarn is spun, time for warping and setting up the loom must be added as well as possible treatment of the yarn, such as gluing. According to results from weaving in the TTTC experiments, one can weave *c.* 40–80 cm in eight hours, including preparation of yarn and adjustments made while weaving. The time consumption when weaving depends on how many weft threads are inserted per cm and how thin the yarn is. Thick yarn with few weft threads per centimetre will of course be quicker to weave than thin yarn with several weft threads per centimetre. It would thus take approximately five days to weave 2 m with thin yarn corresponding to the yarn spun with a 4 g whorl. To this, even more time must be added for cutting down the fabric and for finishing. The calculations presented above are based on specific examples and are thus not valid in all cases. It is important, however, to understand that producing textiles takes a lot of time. In the example above, it would take at least 27 days to make only two metres of fabric, working a constant eight hours a day. Note that spinning the yarn corresponds to 22 of these days.

Conclusion: from experimental archaeology to interpretations of archaeological textile tools

The fundamental principle in all the experiments was to investigate and test the *function* of tools according to the eight principles outlined in the introductory section.

In Aegean archaeology, it has been debated what is an adequate spindle whorl in terms of size and weight, and a terminological confusion exists around the terms beads, buttons or conuli (Lakovidis 1977; Carington Smith 1992; Obladen-Kauder 1996; Becker 2005).

When spinning with a suspended spindle and a similar type of wool, the lighter the spindle whorl, the lighter and, in general, thinner the thread. The new results yielded from the TTTC tests are that the output quantities of yarn became similar for both spinners when using identical spinning tools. The main differences are not seen between the spinners, but between the three weight classes of whorls. These results indicate that it is the tool rather than the spinner that defines the yarn produced. Even though the 4 g whorl worked for spinning yarn, both spinners reported that further wool preparation or another type of

wool, which is finer and more homogenous, would be preferable in order to produce strong yarn. In this study it is thus demonstrated that light spindle whorls, even weighing only 4 g, function well as spindle whorls.

The experiments in spinning demonstrated that a substantial part of the raw wool was discarded during cleaning, fibre preparation and spinning. After sorting the 2.7 kg fleece, 1.1 kg of rather homogeneous wool remained to be used in the experiments. It took about six hours for two people to prepare 133 g of wool for spinning. Approximately 133 g prepared wool was the amount of wool used in the experiment for spinning with the 8 g and 18 g whorls. About 1138 m yarn was spun using these whorls. This work took about 25 hours. Based on these calculations, it would take about 40 hours for one person, including wool preparation, to produce 1138 m yarn. This would not be enough for even the warp when producing a one metre wide and two metre long fabric with 10 warp threads per centimetre.

Weaving is not as time consuming as spinning the yarn, but weaving has also occupied hours and hours of labour. The most significant, and often only, archaeological remains from weaving, however, are loom weights. Despite the importance of this tool group, loom weights have not been investigated extensively from a functional perspective until now. Experiments were conducted with weaving on warp-weighted looms, focusing primarily on the loom weights' function. Two parameters, the weight and the maximum thickness, were identified. Based on this information it is possible to outline what type of tabby textiles could have been produced with a given yarn quality. In order to obtain an optimal setup on the warp-weighted loom, the thickness and the weight of loom weights play an important role. It is preferable to use loom weights with a total width, when hanging in a row, which is identical or slightly larger than the width of the fabric to be produced. The warp threads should thus be distributed evenly according to both the loom weight thickness and the warp tension needed, as was demonstrated by the TTTC experiments. The shape of loom weights also has a practical function while weaving. Flat sides of loom weights are easy to handle when hanging in a row. Spool shaped loom weights appeared to be excellent when setting up the loom and weaving, due to their spool shape, which enables the warp to be easily fastened to the spool. Spool shaped loom weights might thus signify a well-planned production of textiles. The specific usefulness of other loom weight shapes than spools and crescents (chapter 4.4) was not investigated within the TTTC research programme. No matter the shape, however, it is above all the weight and the thickness of loom weights that are the most important factors influencing what types of textiles are most optimal to produce. Comprehensive data on weight and thickness are thus of importance when recording and interpreting archaeological loom weights.

Based on results from textile experimental archaeology in the TTTC research programme, the following conclusions can be drawn concerning loom weights:

1. The weight and the maximum thickness of loom weights are the most important parameters for the understanding of textile production.
2. Loom weights should have a total width, when hanging in a row, which is identical or slightly larger than the width of the fabric to be produced. At the same time, the loom weights must give a suitable tension per warp thread.
3. With data on the weight and maximum thickness of loom weights it is possible to outline what kind of tabby textiles could have been produced.

Acknowledgements

Our sincerest gratitude to Marianne Rasmussen and CHARC, who have provided raw material, tools and expertise. We warmly thank Anne Batzer for her contribution to the experiments. We also thank Margarita Gleba, Henriette Lyngstrøm, Ulla Mannering, Marta Guzowska, Costas Paschalidis, Carole Christiansen and all our collaborators for their advice.

Notes

1 In general, thin yarn requires less warp tension and thick yarn needs more warp tension. By warp tension we mean the weight per warp thread needed for optimal weaving. Different fibre material in the yarn and variations in the yarn quality might also influence what warp tension is suitable (*e.g.* Andersson 2003, 27–29; Gleba 2009, note 11).

2 Anne Batzer has more than 40 years, experience of working with prehistoric textile technology. Linda Olofsson has more than ten years, experience of working with prehistoric textile technology.
3 For further discussion see Andersson and Nosch 2003, 202–203.
4 The average of the total amount of metres of yarn from five full spindles was: unbalanced whorl (IId) spinner 1, Batzer: 946.6 m/100 g yarn; balanced whorl (IIb) spinner 1, Batzer: 1110.4 m/100 g yarn; unbalanced whorl (IId) spinner 2, Olofsson: 906.6 m/100 g yarn; balanced whorl (IIb) spinner 2, Olofsson: 971.5 m/100 g yarn.
5 It should also be remembered that the wooden spindle rod and the yarn absorbed some of the linseed water, which may have affected the spindle's weight above the whorl to a greater extent.
6 For Bronze Age textiles see chapter 3.
7 We are grateful to the Lejre Historical-Archaeological Experimental Centre in Denmark for making the project on heavy spindles possible. The experiment was conducted at CHARC on reconstructions of heavier whorls from Nichoria, weighing *c.* 30 and 50 g (Mårtensson *et al.* 2006). Depending on what spinning technique was employed, suspended or supported, as well as what kind of fibre material was used, the spindles were suitable for producing different types of both thick and thin yarn. By supporting a heavy spindle, even a 50 g whorl is suitable to produce thin yarn corresponding to yarn spun with a whorl weighing less than 10 g. Thick yarn, on the other hand, cannot be spun with a suspended light spindle.
8 Previous tests with much heavier suspended spindles have also demonstrated that the heavier the spindle, the thicker the thread will be (*e.g.* Holm 1996; Andersson 1999; 2003; Mårtensson *et al.* 2006). In the latter of these tests, however, the spindles were used with both suspended and supported spinning methods.
9 Regarding warp tension when weaving with the spun yarn mentioned above, it was established that wool yarn spun with a 4 g whorl needed *c.* 13 g tension per thread, wool yarn spun with a 8 g whorl needed *c.* 19 g tension per thread and linen yarn spun with the same 8 g whorl needed similar weight tension per thread as the yarn made of wool, *c.* 19 g per thread.
10 Please note that in a tabby weave two rows of loom weights are used, one in the front and one behind. The total width in one row of loom weights was identical for both rows in all weaving tests.
11 Smaller spools have also been found in the same context in Khania but were not taken into consideration in this test. These may have been

appropriate to use as supplementary weights or when weaving bands, as was demonstrated by Lise Ræder Knudsen. She used spools, typical of Italian Iron Age contexts weighing maximum 50 g as warp tension in tablet weaving, for making borders on a mantle (Gleba 2009; Ræder Knudsen 2002).

12 We warmly thank hand weaver Anna Nørgård for providing the yarn. Perinnelanka (Nm 12/1) 100 g = n. 1150 m 100% wool, Z twist.

Bibliography

Andersson, E. (1999) *The Common Thread, Textile Production During the Late Iron Age – Viking Age.* Lund. Institute of Archaeology, University of Lund.

Andersson, E. (2003) *Tools for Textile Production from Birka and Hedeby: Excavations in the Black Earth 1990–1995.* Stockholm. Birka Project, Riksantikvarieämbetet.

Andersson, E., Mårtensson, L., Nosch, M.-L. and Rahmstorf, L. (2008) New research on Bronze Age textile production, *Bulletin of the Institute of Classical Studies,* 51, 171–174.

Andersson, E. and Nosch, M.-L. (2003) With a little help from my friends: investigating Mycenaean textiles with help from Scandinavian experimental archaeology, in Foster, K. P. and Laffineur, R. (eds), *Metron: Measuring the Aegean Bronze Age*, 197–205. Liège. Université de Liège.

Barber, E. J. W. (1991) *Prehistoric Textiles: The Development of Cloth in the Neolithic and Bronze Ages with Special Reference to the Aegean.* Princeton. Princeton University Press.

Becker, C. (2005) Spindle whorls or buttons? Ambiguous bone artefacts from a Bronze Age *castelliere* on Istria, in Luik, H., Choyke, A., Batey, C. and Lougas, L. (eds), *From Hooves to Horns, from Mollusc to Mammoth,* 157–174. Tallinn. Tartu Ülikool.

Becks, R. and Guzowska, R. (2004) On the Aegean-type weaving at Troia, *Studia Troica,* 14, 101–115.

Carington Smith, J. (1992) Spinning and weaving equipment, in Macdonald, W. A. and Wilkie, N. C. (eds), *Excavations at Nichoria in Southwestern Greece. 2. The Bronze Age Occupation,* 674–711. Minneapolis. University of Minnesota Press.

Gleba, M. (2009) Textile tools and specialisation in Early Iron Age female burials, in Herring, E. and Lomas, K. (eds), *Gender Identities in Italy in the 1st Millennium BC,* 69–78. Oxford. Archaeopress.

Grömer, K. (2010) *Prähistorische Textilkunst in Mitteleuropa, Geschichte des Handwerkes und der Kleidung vor den Römern.* Wien. Verlag des Naturhistorischen Museums in Wien.

Hallager, E. and Hallager, B. P. (2000) *The Greek-Swedish Excavations at the Agia Aikaterini Square, Kastelli, Khania 1970–1987: Results of the Excavations Under the Direction of Yannis Tzedakis and Carl-Gustaf Styrenius. II. The Late Minoan IIIC Settlement.* Stockholm. Paul Åström.

Hoffmann, M. (1964) *The Warp-Weighted Loom: Studies in the History and Technology of an Ancient Implement.* Oslo. Universitetsforlaget.

Holm, C. (1996) Experiment med slåndspinning, in Andersson, E. (ed.), *Textilproduktion i arkeologisk kontext. En metodstudie av yngre järnåldersboplatser i Skåne,* 111–116. Lund. Institute of Archaeology, University of Lund.

Iakovidis, S. E. (1977) On the use of Mycenaean `buttons´, *Annual of the British School at Athens* 72, 113–119.

Lassen, A. W. (2007) Et forsøg med bananformede vævevægte Report. Reference number: HAF 09/07. http://www.sagnlandet.dk/A-BANANA-SHAPED-PIECE-OF-THE-PUZZLE.648.0.html

Lund Hansen, U. (ed.), (Forthcoming) *Late Roman Grave Fields of the Vorbasse Settlement. Grave Fields, Settlement, Environment and Textile Production. Late Roman Jutland Reconsidered* (Det Kongelige Nordiske Oldskriftselskab).

Mannering, U. and Andersson Strand, E. (2009) Dress images on gold-foil figures, in Adamsen, C., Lund Hansen, U., Nielsen, F. O. and Watt, M. (eds), *Sorte Muld, Wealth, Power and Religion at an Iron Age Central Settlement on Bornholm,* 54–61. Bornholm. Bornholm Museum.

Mårtensson, L. (2006) Multiwhorls? Forsök med tunga sländtrissor. Report. Reference number: HAF 14/06. Lejre. http://www.sagnlandet.dk/SPINNING-THIN-THREAD-WITH-HEAVY-SPINDLE.540.0.html.

Mårtensson, L., Nosch, M.-L. and Andersson, E. (2009) Shape of things: understanding a loom weight, *Oxford Journal of Archaeology,* 28 (4), 373–398.

Mårtensson, L., Andersson, E., Nosch, M.-L. and Batzer, A. (2006) Technical Report, Experimental Archaeology, Part 2:2. Whorl or Bead? Tools and Textiles – Texts and Contexts Research Program. http://ctr.hum.ku.dk/tools/Technical_report_2-2__experimental_arcaheology.PDF.

Obladen-Kauder, J. (1996) Die Kleinfunde aus Ton, Knochen und Metall, in Korfmann, M. (ed.), *Demircihüyük: die Ergebnisse der Ausgrabungen 1975–1978. 4. Die Kleinfunde,* 207–310. Mainz. Philipp von Zabern.

Rahmstorf, L. (2003) Clay spools from Tiryns and other contemporary sites. An indication of foreign influence in LH III C?, in Kyparissi-Apostolika, N. and Papakonstantinou, M. (eds), *Η περιφέρεια του μυκηναϊκού κόσμου,* 397–415. Athens. Ministry of Culture.

Rahmstorf, L. (2005) Ethnicity and changes in weaving technology in Cyprus and the eastern Mediterranean in the 12th century BC, in Karageorghis, V. (ed.), *Cyprus: Religion and Society: from the Late Bronze Age to the End of the Archaic Period,* 143–169. Möhnesee-Wamel. Bibliopolis.

Ryder, M. (1992) The interaction between biological and technological change during the development of different fleece types in sheep, *Antropozoologica,* 16, 131–140.

Ræder Knudsen, L. (2002) La tessitura con le tavolette nella tomba 89, in von Eles (ed.), *Guerriero e sacerdote: autorità e communità nell'età del ferro a Verucchio: La tomba del trono,* 230–243. Firenze. All'Insegna del Giglio.

Shishlina, N. I., Orfinskaya, O. V. and Golikov, V. P. (2000) Bronze Age textiles of the Caspian Sea maritime steppes, in Davis-Kimball, J., Murphy, E. M., Koryakova, L. and Yablonksy, L. T. (eds), *Kurgans, Ritual Sites, and Settlements: Eurasian Age and Iron Age,* 109–117. Oxford. Archaeopress.

Ventris, M. and Chadwick, J. (1973) *Documents in Mycenaean Greek.* Cambridge. Cambridge University Press.

Waetzoldt, H. (1972) *Untersuchungen zur neusumerischen Textilindustrie.* Rome. Istituto per l'Oriente.

CHAPTER 4.2

External examination of spinning and weaving samples

Susan Möller-Wiering

Introduction and methodology

The experimental archaeological programme *Tools, Textiles, Texts and Contexts* (TTTC) included external analyses of various spinning samples and woven fabrics produced by the expert textile technicians Anne Batzer (spinner/weaver 1) and Linda Olofsson (spinner/weaver 2).

The main questions of the external investigation by the present author were: What do the products, (*i.e.* the yarn and fabric samples) say about the tools? Would it be possible to detect individual traits of the spinners/weavers? Can the threads and weaves tell something about textile production in ancient times? What information can they provide for interpreting archaeological textiles?

The material to be examined consisted of three groups:

- Wool yarn spun with 8 g and 18 g whorls and a sample of fabric
- Wool yarn spun with 4 g whorls and a sample of fabric
- Flax yarn spun with 8 g whorls and a sample of fabric.

All threads are z-spun. The first aim within each group was to describe the products and, in particular, the differences between the spinning samples, both within the woven fabric and between spinning samples and weave. This was carried out without access to any information concerning the craftspeople, *i.e.* which sample had been made by whom or the type of tools they had used. The results of the external analyses were only to be related to the information about spinners, spinning tools and loom at a later stage.

The most important criteria to analyse were the thread diameter and the spinning angle of the threads. Additionally, the fuzziness was assessed. Furthermore, in the woven pieces, thread count, cover factor and thickness were measured.

Before starting any measurements, a visual description of the samples was made. In doing so, the samples were investigated only with the naked eye and with 10 × magnification. The examination of the fuzziness is restricted to general impressions, because there is no method for quantifying it. To examine the diameter and the spinning angle, 40 × magnification was used.

Another three criteria had to be established and followed: firstly, a procedure for choosing where to make the measurements; secondly, what constituted a sufficient number of measure points for suitable sets of data, and lastly, what was the least number of measure points that could be taken.

In principle, these criteria remained the same throughout the project. In detail, however, the procedures had to be adjusted as new questions arose. Particularly, the necessary number of points to be measured per sample was difficult to determine.

The spinning samples were wound on pieces of cardboard (Fig. 4.2.1). The measurements were taken along two lines in the middle of each sample, *i.e.* halfway between both edges and crossing 10 threads, one line on the front side (see Fig. 4.2.2 with marked spots for measuring along that line, although only every third thread was chosen there), one on the back, resulting in 20 measurements per sample.

On the weaving samples, areas of 10 × 10 threads were marked off (Figs 4.2.3 and 4.2.4) and examined in detail. All spinning and weaving samples were documented by scanning. For measuring the spinning angle, close-ups of the scans were used. It should be kept in mind, however, that the angle may change within very few mm, and even from fibre to fibre. Therefore, the decision concerning where to fix the mark for measuring the angle is always, to some extent, subject to

interpretation and therefore the results are not always as exact as they pretend to be.

The thread count of a weave is usually determined by counting the number of threads per centimetre. Here, however, it was measured, as a first step, in terms of how wide a row of ten threads was. Differences in the shape of marked off rectangles of 10 × 10 threads could regularly be seen with the naked eye (Figs 4.2.3 and 4.2.4). The data were then transformed to the usual version of threads per centimetre.

The density of a fabric may be expressed by the 'cover factor' (Hammarlund 2004, 8–9). It is calculated according to the formula:

$$WA + WE - (WA \times WE)$$

WA is the thread count in cm × yarn diameter in cm for the warp, WE is the equivalent for the weft. Theoretically, the maximum cover factor is =1.[1] According to hand weaver Lena Hammarlund, a factor between 0.75 and 0.94 might be regarded as medium dense while a figure below 0.75 represents an open weave. Furthermore, Hammarlund calculates the thickness of a woven woollen textile by counting the mean diameters of warp and weft yarns (in mm) (Hammarlund 2004, 10). She then

Fig. 4.2.1. Cardboard with three wool yarn spinning samples (photo: Susan Möller-Wiering).

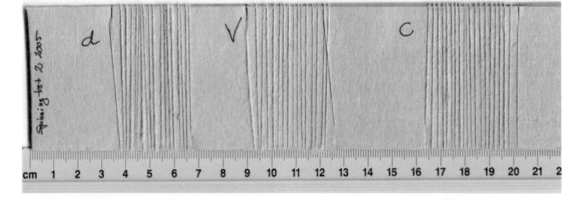

Fig. 4.2.2. (left) Wool yarn sample "B", spun with a 4 g whorl, with fine dots marking every third thread section for measurements along a middle line. The dots were added after the woollen wool sample (photo: Susan Möller-Wiering).

Fig. 4.2.3. (right) Marked off areas of 10 × 10 threads on the weaving sample produced with 8 g whorls (photo: Susan Möller-Wiering).

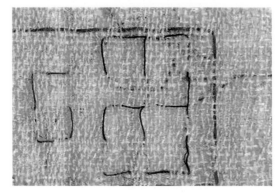

establishes seven thickness groups ranging from very thin (≤ 0.6) to very coarse (≥ 2.4).

Wool yarn produced with 8 g and 18 g whorls

The material consisted of four pieces of cardboard with three spinning samples each (Fig. 4.2.1) and one weaving sample (Fig. 4.2.5). All the threads are considerably fuzzy, *i.e.*, many fibres stick out of the threads (see for comparison Fig. 4.2.2). This is due to the structure of the fibres (their curliness) and the extent to which they were – or could be – aligned. As might be expected, the fuzziness is generally higher in thicker and more loosely spun sections than it is in finer, harder spun threads. At first, ten measurements of diameter and spinning angle respectively were taken on each spinning sample, *i.e.*, only on the front. The results turned out to be unexpected and inconsistent with the measurements taken during the experimental work. Since the most probable explanation was an insufficient number of measured spots, another ten measurements each were taken on the reverse side. Thus, the distance between every two measured spots was approximately 12 cm.

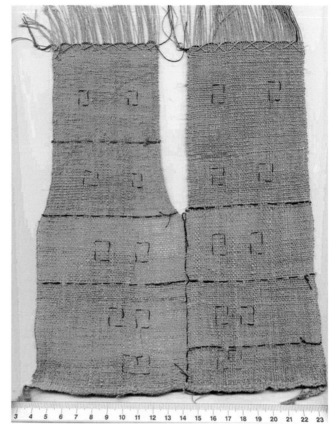

Fig. 4.2.4. Weaving sample made of linen yarn with areas marked for measurements (photo: Susan Möller-Wiering).

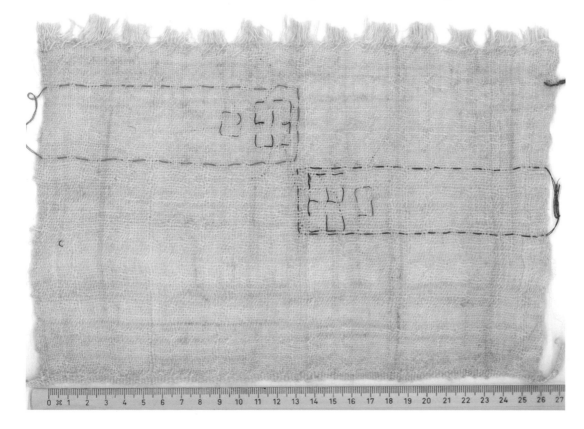

Fig. 4.2.5. Wool weaving sample produced with 8 g whorls (photo: Susan Möller-Wiering).

Diameter of spinning samples

Based on the experience with archaeological textiles, the general impression of the diameters is that of fine and mostly evenly spun wool threads with some sections of clearly lower quality. Such sections appear in all samples. The diameter depends on several factors such as the tools used (spindle whorls), the fibres (preparation, length, smoothness, curliness), the skill of the spinner, and perhaps other factors as well.

The measurements for each sample are compiled in Figure 4.2.6, including the mean and the range. Based on the raw data of 240 measurements, the diameters vary between 0.2 and 0.75 mm, while the mean diameters of the 24 samples differ between 0.29 and 0.515 mm. The quality in terms of evenness is indicated by the range, which is the difference between the highest and the lowest value per sample; the smaller the range, the greater the evenness. According to this, the most evenly spun threads are those with a range of only 0.2 mm. Including a small diameter as a possible criterion for quality, samples "4b" and "13b" would be the best.

Figure 4.2.7 presents the diameters of the front line in a cumulative graph. An important question was whether it is possible to identify any groups of samples clearly distinguishable from the rest and possibly related to individual spinners or certain tools. A relation between the weight of the whorl and the thickness of thread might be expected and has been demonstrated in earlier experiments (Andersson and Nosch 2003, 198). Yet, the distribution of all measurements of the front line turned out to be quite even, allowing no clear grouping. A corresponding graph for the back line gave a similar picture, including the slight depression at 0.35 mm.

This situation changed when basic information about spinners and whorls was included. The samples of the upper half of Figure 4.2.6 (samples 4a, 4b, 8a, 8b, 13a and 13b) were spun with whorls weighing 8 g, those of the lower half (samples a, b, c, d, v, and x) with whorls of 18 g. Thus, the overall mean diameter for the lighter whorls is 0.363 mm, for the heavier ones 0.434 mm. The difference, however, is still not more than 0.071 mm.

Sample		Diameter in mm										Mean	Range
4a	front	0.45	0.45	0.4	0.3	0.4	0.55	0.3	0.25	0.35	0.35	0.38	0.3
	back	0.25	0.3	0.25	0.3	0.5	0.35	0.35	0.4	0.4	0.3	0.34	0.25
4b	front	0.25	0.3	0.3	0.35	0.4	0.3	0.25	0.2	0.4	0.25	0.3	0.2
	back	0.25	0.35	0.3	0.25	0.25	0.3	0.2	0.4	0.3	0.3	0.29	0.2
8a	front	0.35	0.35	0.3	0.4	0.3	0.25	0.25	0.25	0.55	0.35	0.335	0.3
	back	0.3	0.5	0.2	0.3	0.25	0.2	0.3	0.4	0.4	0.3	0.315	0.3
8b	front	0.6	0.45	0.4	0.65	0.45	0.35	0.4	0.35	0.45	0.4	0.45	0.3
	back	0.45	0.55	0.45	0.35	0.55	0.4	0.6	0.4	0.6	0.3	0.465	0.3
13a	front	0.4	0.3	0.5	0.45	0.4	0.45	0.45	0.4	0.35	0.4	0.41	0.2
	back	0.25	0.25	0.6	0.35	0.35	0.6	0.35	0.6	0.3	0.4	4.405	0.35
13b	front	0.03	0.3	0.4	0.3	0.3	0.35	0.3	0.2	0.3	0.25	0.3	0.2
	back	0.25	0.35	0.4	0.25	0.2	0.3	0.35	0.3	0.3	0.3	0.3	0.2
a	front	0.5	0.4	0.55	0.45	0.5	0.6	0.5	0.5	0.5	0.55	0.202	0.2
	back	0.45	0.5	0.55	0.5	0.45	0.45	0.7	0.55	0.4	0.6	0.515	0.3
b	front	0.65	0.45	0.5	0.45	0.45	0.5	0.6	0.35	0.4	0.3	0.465	0.35
	back	0.55	0.35	0.5	0.45	0.45	0.75	0.4	0.5	0.4	0.4	0.475	0.4
c	front	0.35	0.45	0.6	0.3	0.3	0.35	0.4	0.25	0.45	0.35	0.38	0.35
	back	0.4	0.3	0.3	0.45	0.4	0.35	0.45	0.5	0.6	0.4	0.415	0.3
d	front	0.25	0.3	0.5	0.25	0.4	0.45	0.4	0.35	0.45	0.5	0.385	0.25
	back	0.4	0.45	0.35	0.4	0.55	0.4	0.35	0.3	0.35	0.4	0.395	0.25
v	front	0.4	0.55	0.4	0.4	0.5	0.3	0.3	0.35	0.35	0.3	0.985	0.25
	back	0.35	0.3	0.3	0.4	0.4	0.35	0.5	0.3	0.4	0.45	0.385	0.2
x	front	0.5	0.75	0.45	0.4	0.45	0.5	0.35	0.4	0.55	0.04	0.475	0.4
	back	0.5	0.45	0.4	0.4	0.65	0.4	0.45	0.6	0.5	0.5	0.485	0.25

Fig. 4.2.6. Diameters of wool single threads, spun with 8 g / 18 g whorls, their mean and range.

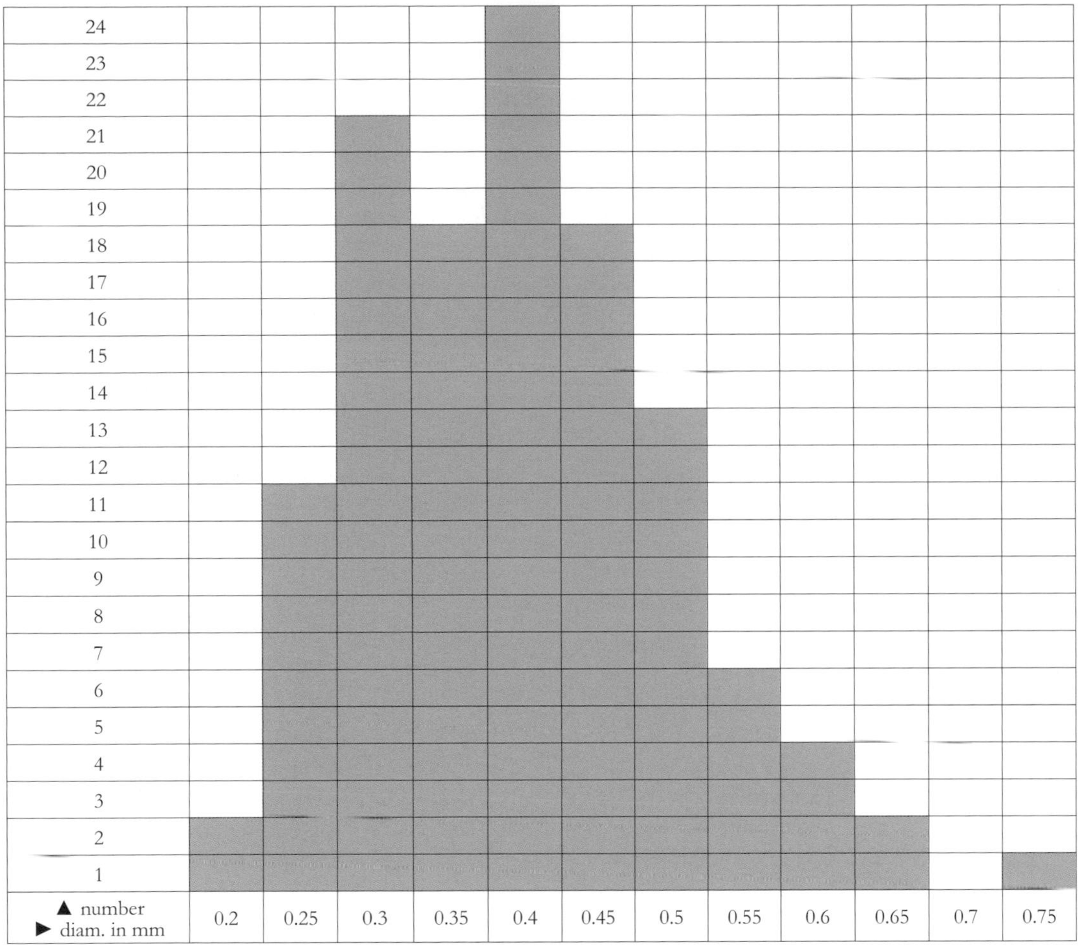

Fig. 4.2.7. Diameters of wool single threads, spun with 8 g/18 g whorls, measured along the front lines.

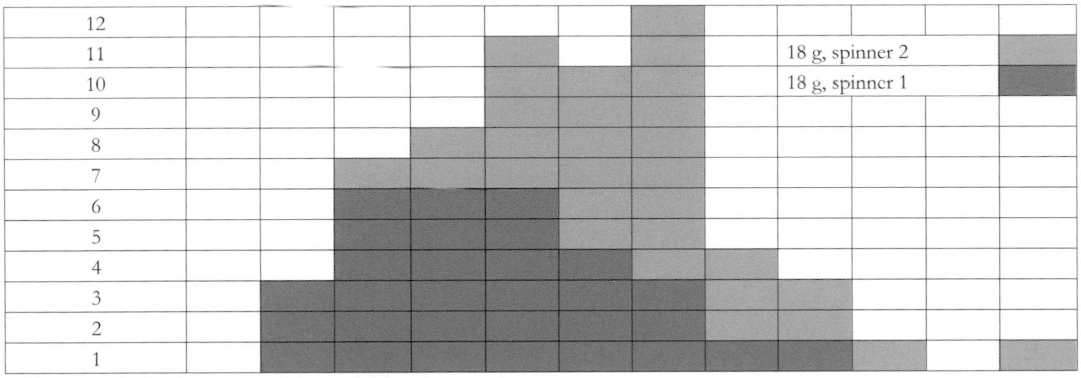

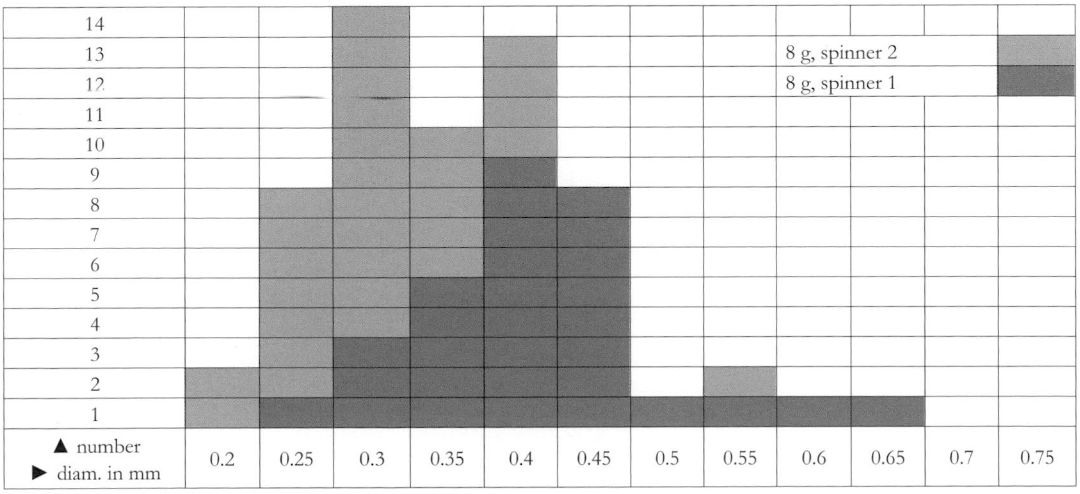

Fig. 4.2.8. Diameters of wool single threads, spun with 8 g/18 g whorls, according to weight of whorls and spinners (front lines).

The data were then related to the spinners.[2] Relating this information to Figure 4.2.6, it turned out that the yarns of spinner 1 are a little more homogeneous, as can also be seen in Figure 4.2.8, where the measurements are plotted according to weight of whorls plus spinner. Spinner 2 clearly spun different threads depending on the weight of the whorl, with a mean diameter of 0.31 mm and 0.48 mm respectively. The depression at 0.35 mm is solely due to spinner 2, where it indeed provides the clue for differentiating the figures for both categories of spindle whorls. Quite unexpectedly, however, the figures for spinner 1 are not only quite similar for both weight classes of whorls, but the mean yarn diameter for the 8 g whorl is even slightly larger than that for the 18 g whorl, the figures being 0.41 mm and 0.38 mm respectively. The analysis of the back line gave the same results.

To verify how far these results are representative, four additional spinning samples were tested on which the distance between every two measured points was considerably larger, *c.* 64 cm compared to *c.* 12 cm previously. The distribution in the resulting cumulative graph was rather regular, with one clear peak at 0.4 mm (10 out of 40 measurements), without any depression. It was now spinner 2 whose figures for the 8 g and the 18 g whorl were very much alike, whereas spinner 1 produced yarns with a discernible difference. However, this difference only became visible after including the appropriate background information. When all figures of the first set of samples are combined with those of the additional sets, the mean thread diameters for 8 g whorls are 0.3667 mm for spinner 1 and 0.3759 mm for spinner 2, while for 18 g whorls, the means are

0.4421 mm and 0.4734 mm respectively. Thus, the previously registered difference in the work of the two spinners is not an individual trait which can be followed throughout, but must be related to the fact that the number and/or selection of the first set of samples was not representative for their entire work – the difference disappeared when more samples with more distance between the measured points were investigated. This is in accordance with the spinners' own recordings indicating no major differences in their work.

Additional information was provided concerning the tools: one of the light spindle whorls was slightly unbalanced. Both spinners stated that this whorl did work, but that it took longer to spin with it and that it was very uncomfortable to handle. When the figures for the corresponding samples (4a, 8a, 13a) are compared to those of the other more balanced samples from an 8 g whorl, the threads spun with the better whorl are indeed slightly thinner (0.35 mm compared to 0.375 mm), but the variations are comparable. In other words, though it was harder to spin with the slightly unbalanced whorl, the quality of the threads is as good as if they had been spun with a perfect whorl.

Spinning angle of spinning samples

At first impression, the spinning angles were mostly considered medium and might be described as even. The measured data for the front line are presented in Figure 4.2.9. Again, it is the range which may tell something about the quality, in this case reflected in the evenness of the spinning angle. A cumulative graph of the data is much more diverse than the corresponding figure of the diameters, showing three peaks at 31, 38 and 45°.

Once more the question was whether the samples could be grouped in any way based on the information about spinning angles. However, the cumulative graph did not allow this until introducing additional information about the weight of the whorls and the spinners: then it became clear that the yarns spun with 8 g whorls (spinner 1: 31.03°, spinner 2: 37.27°) tend to be more loosely spun than those spun with 18 g whorls (spinner 1: 36.83°, spinner 2: 40.5°). Most of the hardest spun yarns derive from the heavier whorls. Furthermore, the spinning angles in the threads of spinner 2 are somewhat larger, *i.e.*, her yarns are spun a little harder on average. However, the differences are not discernible without this additional background information.

Fig. 4.2.9. Spinning angles of wool single threads, spun with 8 g/18 g whorls, their mean and range (front lines).

Sample	Spinning angles in °										Mean	Range
4a	36	30	31	35	31	26	27	31	32	27	30.6	10
4b	44	26	33	25	36	30	44	45	45	39	36.7	20
8a	38	30	39	32	38	37	37	45	34	26	35.6	19
8b	31	28	28	23	28	37	31	31	22	25	28.4	15
13a	38	46	38	28	32	32	30	31	33	33	34.1	18
13b	34	45	31	37	31	44	45	45	45	39	39.5	14
a	38	46	45	46	31	40	37	32	47	37	41.9	16
b	41	49	48	47	39	39	48	41	40	36	42.8	13
c	36	30	23	36	46	46	34	44	36	35	36.6	23
d	30	45	34	38	40	37	45	38	31	31	36.9	15
v	23	29	35	38	37	44	45	38	37	44	37.0	22
x	32	30	30	27	38	41	47	39	39	45	36.8	20

Relation between diameter and spinning angle in the spinning samples

According to Cooke and Christiansen, the angle or "twist distribution is highly geared to yarn diameter" (Cooke and Christiansen 2005, 72). Also apparent from experience, it often seems that the thinner threads within a fabric are spun harder than are the thicker ones. The data presented above offer the opportunity to test this hypothesis by combining Figs 4.2.6 and 4.2.9. If the correlation was strong, the figures in a resulting graph should cluster around a diagonal line. Here, a slight trend towards this was discernible, but many thin, but loose threads as well as thick, hard spun yarns blurred the overall picture.

Fibre consumption

Some information gathered during the experiment about the consumption of wool and the weight of the final product may be evaluated here. As expected, both spinners needed much more wool for the work with the heavier whorl than with the lighter one (see chapter 4.1; Andersson and Nosch 2003, 200). Theoretically, the wool consumption should be related to the yarn diameter as well as to the spinning angle. Given a certain diameter, the thread should contain more wool the harder it is spun, which is indeed the case (Fig. 4.2.10).[3]

From Figure 4.2.10 it is evident that the mean weight is 0.0976 g/m for the 8 g group and 0.1606 g/m for the 18 g group, the former weighing about two-thirds of the latter, which seems quite a large difference. The figures for the mean diameters, on the other hand, are 0.3713 mm and 0.4582 mm respectively, here the former being about four-fifths of the latter, a considerably smaller difference at first sight. Yet, the figures for the diameter reflect only one dimension. When the second dimension

(πr^2) is calculated, *i.e.* taking the yarn as an approximately cylindrical feature, the results are 0.1083 mm² and 0.1649 mm², respectively. Thus the cross section of the average yarn spun with an 8 g whorl is only two-thirds of the size of the yarn produced with an 18 g whorl. This relation is consistent in the yarn weight and the wool consumption.

Weaving sample

The weaving sample is 18 cm long and 27 cm wide, and gives the impression of a light, open weave. The yarn had been spun with 8 g whorls. The warp is less evenly spaced than the weft and there are weaving faults such as doubled or floating warp ends. Two areas are outlined in green and red, respectively (Fig. 4.2.5). A cover factor of 0.62 and 0.64 for the red and the green rectangle respectively confirms the "open" character. The fabric thickness, following Hammarlund's proposals (Hammarlund 2004, 10), is calculated to 0.84 and 0.825 for the red and green rectangles, respectively, thus falling into the "thin" category and again confirming the visual impression of a light and open weave.

Furthermore, based on an examination of wool tabbies from Mons Claudianus in Egypt, Hammarlund has proposed a pentagon model, *i.e.* five features describing a fabric (Hammarlund 2005). Besides the regularly given characteristics of binding, yarn and thread count, she includes "weaving" (*i.e.* loom type, tools for weaving, weaver's work) and "finishing". Using these five criteria, Hammarlund is able to explain the differences between the seven groups of tabbies into which she had initially grouped the material based on visually distinguishable qualities. Being a wool tabby, the present weaving sample can be compared to Hammarlund's results and thus be related to the group called "movable tabby", which "has a curving or undulating movement in the yarn in one or both thread systems [...]". Twist

Fig. 4.2.10. Mean thread diameter of wool single threads, spun with 8 g/18 g (front lines, back lines + supplement samples), spinning angle (front lines) and weight of yarn according to spinning whorls and spinners.

	8 g			18 g		
	Spinner 1	Spinner 2	Mean	Spinner 1	Spinner 2	Mean
Diameter in mm	0.3667	0.3759	0.3713	0.4421	0.4734	0.4582
Spinning angle in °	31.03	37.26	34.15	36.86	40.50	38.68
Weight in g/m	0.0898	0.1054	0.0976	0.1489	0.1722	0.1606

Fig. 4.2.11. Diameters of the threads in the weaving sample produced with 8 g whorls, their mean and range.

	Sample	Yarn diameter in mm										Mean	Range
Warp	red rectangle	0.4	0.6	0.2	0.5	0.55	0.5	0.45	0.4	0.3	0.3	0.42	0.4
	green rectangle	0.2	0.5	0.35	0.4	0.9	0.3	0.4	0.4	0.3	0.5	0.425	0.7
Weft	red rectangle	0.45	0.6	0.45	0.3	0.4	0.4	0.35	0.25	0.3	0.7	0.42	0.45
	green rectangle	0.3	0.35	0.4	0.35	0.45	0.35	0.5	0.6	0.3	0.3	0.39	0.3

Fig. 4.2.12. Spinning angles of the threads in the weaving sample produced with 8 g whorls, their mean and range.

Sample		Angles in °										Mean	Range
Warp	red rectangle	48	40	52	42	34	44	38	41	45	33	41.7	19
	green rectangle	52	35	39	37	40	27	38	32	45	31	37.6	25
Weft	red rectangle	32	38	45	37	22	31	40	38	30	34	34.7	23
	green rectangle	33	38	31	37	35	45	35	30	32	33	34.9	15

Sample		Diameter in mm										Mean per marked line	Mean per sample	Range
B	front	0.3	0.3	0.2	0.35	0.25	0.35	0.2	0.3	0.3	0.3	0.285	0.2925	0.2
	back	0.3	0.3	0.35	0.4	0.3	0.3	0.2	0.35	0.25	0.25	0.3		
D	front	0.25	0.35	0.2	0.3	0.3	0.3	0.3	0.15	0.3	0.3	0.275	0.265	0.2
	back	0.3	0.25	0.2	0.2	0.35	0.25	0.3	0.25	0.25	0.2	0.255		
E	front	0.3	0.35	0.35	0.35	0.35	0.4	0.3	0.25	0.4	0.25	0.33	0.2975	0.2
	back	0.3	0.3	0.2	0.3	0.3	0.3	0.25	0.25	0.25	0.2	0.265		
I	front	0.3	0.2	0.25	0.35	0.3	0.4	0.25	0.3	0.35	0.25	0.295	0.29	0.2
	back	0.3	0.35	0.25	0.25	0.25	0.3	0.3	0.3	0.3	0.25	0.285		
N	front	0.35	0.25	0.3	0.3	0.3	0.4	0.35	0.3	0.45	0.3	0.33	0.3275	0.3
	back	0.2	0.35	0.35	0.35	0.25	0.3	0.35	0.3	0.3	0.5	0.325		
S	front	0.25	0.45	0.4	0.3	0.4	0.3	0.35	0.25	0.2	0.35	0.325	0.3225	0.4
	back	0.3	0.2	0.3	0.4	0.3	0.35	0.3	0.2	0.6	0.25	0.32 (0.26)*	(0.3079)*	(0.25)*
T	front	0.3	0.25	0.25	0.25	0.3	0.3	0.35	0.25	0.15	0.2	0.26	0.26	0.2
	back	0.2	0.2	0.25	0.3	0.3	0.3	0.25	0.25	0.25	0.3	0.26		
U	front	0.2	0.25	0.3	0.3	0.3	0.2	0.3	0.2	0.25	0.2	0.25	0.2625	0.15
	back	0.3	0.3	0.25	0.2	0.3	0.3	0.2	0.35	0.25	0.3	0.275		

Fig. 4.2.13. Diameters of single wool threads, spun with 4 g whorls, their mean and range. In sample S: measurements, excluding the very thick point of 0.6 mm.

in the yarn, combined with sufficient spacing between threads, allows for movement" (Hammarlund 2005, 108).[4]

Thread diameter, spinning angle and thread count in the weaving sample

Within the red and green rectangles, respectively, one spinner/weaver produced the warp and weft yarn and did the weaving as well. Five areas of 10 × 10 threads were outlined in both rectangles by the present author (Fig. 4.2.3), arranged symmetrically.[5] Figure 4.2.11 reveals that the diameters in warp and weft are practically the same. When compared to the threads of the spinning tests (Fig. 4.2.6), the mean diameters of the threads in the woven fabric lie within approximately the same spectrum. However, in three of four cases, the range of diameters in the fabric is higher than in all spinning samples. This indicates a lower yarn quality in the woven piece. Similarly, the range of spinning angles (Fig. 4.2.12) is wider in the fabric sample than in the analysed single threads (Fig. 4.2.9).

As might be expected in comparison to many archaeological textiles, the spinning angles are slightly higher in the warp than in the weft, assuming that the spin decreases a little during weaving. Yet, the difference to the loose material spun with 8 g whorls seems noteworthy. Given the fact that the green rectangle was spun and woven by spinner/weaver 1 and the red one by her colleague spinner/weaver 2, it appears that the mean angles in spinner 1's work are 31° for the spinning samples but 37.6° in her warp and 34.9° in her weft in the fabric sample. For spinner 2, the corresponding figures are 37.2, 41.7 and 34.7° respectively. Seemingly, the spinning angles are higher in the warp than in the loose material. A possible explanation could be that the spinning samples were stretched considerably when wound on the pieces of cardboard.

The mean thread counts for the warp are 11.15 threads per centimetre (red) and 10.95 threads per centimetre (green) respectively. For the weft, the figures are 6.675 threads per centimetre in the red and 8.325 threads per centimetre in the green rectangle or 7.5 threads per centimetre on average. While the smaller variation in the warp is predicted by the arrangement of the loom, the larger differences in the weft depend on the weavers, *i.e.*, weaver 1 beats the weft in a little harder.

Wool yarn produced with 4 g whorls

In the case of this experiment, the material comprised four pieces of cardboard with two spinning samples each (samples B, D, E, I, N, S, T and U) and one woven piece. The only information given in the beginning was that the material was spun with whorls weighing only 4 g. The overall appearance of the samples is clearly fuzzy due to many fibres sticking out (Fig. 4.2.2). Yet, along the yarns, rather smooth, very thin sections of several cm length alternate with thicker, more fuzzy parts. The fibres are fine and homogeneous. The pieces of cardboard are about 10.5 cm wide and every two measured points, alternating front and back, were *c.* 31.5 cm distant from each other.

Diameter of spinning samples

In general, the threads look fine to very fine, while some variability is clearly visible already to the naked eye. It is not surprising that the yarns are knotted once in a while, although the knots do not necessarily occur in the thinnest parts. For the analyses, 160 measurements were taken, 20 on each sample. The thinnest points measure only 0.15 mm, whilst the thickest point measures 0.6 mm (Fig. 4.2.13). In most cases, the mean values for the front and the back line of each sample are similar, with deviations from zero to 0.02 mm, indicating evenness. Two samples, however, show a difference of 0.065 mm. This relatively large difference surely emphasises the need of many measurements in order to obtain a sound basis of values.

When plotted as a cumulative graph, 146 measurements (*c.* 91%) fall into the narrow span from 0.2 to 0.35 mm with one striking peak at 0.3 mm (62 measurements). This emphasises the homogeneity of this material. It differs from the graphs discussed above, which are broader and lower. Related to the individual spinners, the data show that spinner 1's threads have a mean diameter of 0.278 mm, compared to 0.301 mm for spinner 2's yarns.[6]

Spinning angle of spinning samples

In general, the spinning angles are medium and sometimes low. Their means mainly vary between only 28.1 and 31.8° (Fig. 4.2.14). Only sample I with a mean angle of 37.4° differs from the others with its considerably harder spin. This hard spin is combined with the lowest range, 13°, indicating an evenness which was also observed in the diameter. This sample belongs to spinner 2's output whose mean spinning angle is 34.97°, compared to 32.55° for spinner 1.

Relation between diameter and spinning angle

As pointed out above, a small diameter should be related to a light whorl and to a hard spin. When the figures for diameters and angles measured along the front lines were combined in a graph, they would be expected to cluster to a diagonal line. This correlation turned out not to be very strong, but nevertheless more obvious than in the material spun with 8 g and 18 g whorls. Taking the weight of whorls into account, an unexpected result is that the figures rather point to a combination of lighter whorls with looser spin.

Weaving sample

The weaving sample made from this yarn is rather small, 23–24 cm wide and 7.5 cm long. The surface of the tabby is a bit wavy. In the weave, not in the starting border, the warp is spaced irregularly, resulting in a sometimes balanced and open, sometimes warp-faced structure (Fig. 4.2.15). There are a few faults along the starting border and some doubled warp ends. Only a limited number of measurements were taken, based on two marked off areas of 10 × 10 threads; thus, the

Sample	Angles in °										Mean	Range
B	34	31	28	16	20	20	36	35	30	31	28.1	20
D	24	27	46	17	27	21	16	46	36	36	29.6	30
E	22	27	35	32	28	28	34	37	27	38	30.8	16
I	41	46	33	36	36	40	34	41	34	33	37.4	13
N	28	32	28	38	36	28	32	36	24	36	31.8	14
S	32	16	28	34	24	45	29	41	39	25	31.3	29
T	23	27	35	21	23	40	27	27	38	40	30.1	19
U	33	19	25	27	29	29	26	45	39	40	31.2	26

Fig. 4.2.14. Spinning angles of single wool threads, spun with 4 g whorls, their mean and range (front lines).

results as given in Figure 4.2.16 must be taken with caution regarding their representativeness.[7] This becomes obvious when they are compared to the results found in the individual thread samples: the mean diameter of spinner 2's yarns in the thread samples is 0.301 mm, but 0.27 mm in area A with her warp ends in the fabric sample. For spinner 1, the figures are 0.278 mm compared to 0.32 mm in area B, which includes her threads as warp. Similar observations were made and discussed when dealing with the material produced with 8 g and 18 g whorls. The weft is clearly larger in diameter than the warp. The mean thread count of 18.35 × 8 threads per centimetre is closer to the figures of the Bronze Age finds than in the sample woven with yarn from 8 g whorls. The cover factor categorises both areas as "open" and regarding the thickness, they may be called "thin".

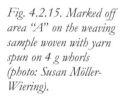

Fig. 4.2.15. Marked off area "A" on the weaving sample woven with yarn spun on 4 g whorls (photo: Susan Möller-Wiering).

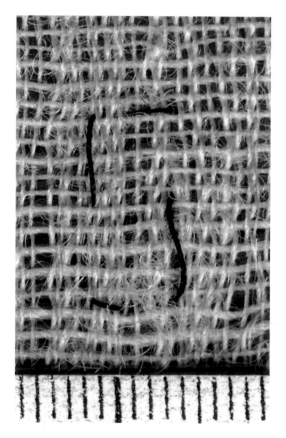

Linen yarn produced with 8 g whorls

The linen material consisted of six spinning samples (a, d, g, c, f, and e) and one woven piece (Fig. 4.2.4). The raw material was not always split up into ultimate fibres. These bundles of non-separated fibres become most obvious within some fuzzy spots which interrupt the otherwise even and smooth threads in all samples. The general fuzziness of the linen threads is, as might be expected, much less than within the wool material. Some broken threads were repaired by making knots. They occur on thinner as well as on thicker yarns. The distance between every two measured points on the spinning samples was *c*. 31.5 cm, with 20 measurements per sample and a total of 120 measurements.

Diameter of spinning samples

Within the 120 measurements, the diameter varies between 0.1 mm and, at a fuzzy spot, 0.6 mm, while the mean figures for the six samples lie between 0.205 mm and 0.357 mm (Fig. 4.2.17). The mean of all measurements is 0.299 mm. The finest thread (F) can easily be recognised by the naked eye, being more than 0.06 mm thinner than the second finest yarn.

The evenness as a criterion for the yarns' quality is evaluated in two ways. The first one is again to look at the range (Fig. 4.2.17). Mostly, it varies between 0.2 mm and 0.25 mm, which is comparable to the fine wool yarns spun with 4 g whorls. The second way is to follow the diameters along the threads as reflected in the 20 measurements per sample. While the graphs for most samples oscillate considerably, sample E reveals a rather smooth course, thus strengthening the impression of evenness as is indicated in the identical mean diameters of front and back line, but in contrast to the visual impression, which is fuzzy. In other words, the visual impression of fuzziness is not well reflected in the measured diameters.

The cumulative graph (Fig. 4.2.18) emphasises the overall evenness of this material, with 90% of all figures (108 measurements) within the span from 0.2 mm to 0.4 mm. The main peak

Fig. 4.2.16. Measurements in marked off areas in the weaving sample woven with yarns spun on 4 g whorls.

Area		Mean yarn diameter in mm	Width of the area in cm	Length of the area in cm	tpc	Cover factor	Thickness
A	warp	0.27	0.5	1.2	20 × 8.3	0.687	0.655
	weft	0.385					
B	warp	0.32	0.6	1.3	16.7 × 7.7	0.674	0.71
	weft	0.39					

Linen sample		Diameter in mm										Mean per marked line	Mean per sample	Range
A	front	0.3	0.25	0.2	0.3	0.25	0.4	0.35	0.2	0.45	0.35	0.305	0.275	0.25
	back	0.25	0.2	0.2	0.25	0.3	0.3	0.2	0.3	0.25	0.2	0.245		
D	front	0.35	0.2	0.2	0.4	0.35	0.25	0.2	0.4	0.3	0.3	0.285	0.3575	0.3
	back	0.4	0.45	0.4	0.35	0.3	0.4	0.4	0.35	0.3	0.5	0.43		
G	front	0.4	0.4	0.3	0.3	0.35	0.5	0.4	0.3	0.4	0.5	0.385	0.355	0.25
	back	0.4	0.35	0.3	0.3	0.3	0.35	0.4	0.3	0.3	0.25	0.325		
C	front	0.35	0.35	0.2	0.4	0.3	0.2	0.25	0.25	0.3	0.25	0.285	0.2825 (0.266)*	0.4 (0.2)*
	back	0.2	0.2	0.3	0.2	0.25	0.3	0.6	0.25	0.2	0.3	0.28 (0.244)*		
F	front	0.15	0.15	0.2	0.15	0.3	0.25	0.25	0.15	0.2	0.2	0.2	0.205	0.2
	back	0.25	0.2	0.25	0.3	0.25	0.15	0.2	0.2	0.2	0.1	0.21		
E	front	0.3	0.35	0.2	0.35	0.4	0.3	0.35	0.3	0.3	0.35	0.32	0.32	0.2
	back	0.25	0.3	0.3	0.25	0.4	0.4	0.35	0.4	0.25	0.3	0.32		

*Fig. 4.2.17. Diameters of single linen threads, spun with 8 g whorls, their mean and range. * Figures excluding the measurement of 0.6 mm.*

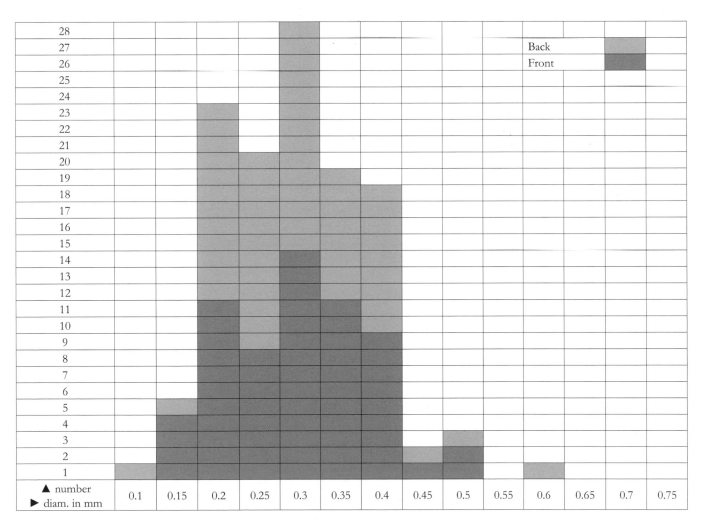

Fig. 4.2.18. Diameters of single linen threads spun with 8 g whorls.

Sample	Angles in °										Mean	Range
A	21	23	33	13	11	24	27	17	37	40	24.6	29
D	33	17	13	36	28	25	23	30	41	18	26.4	28
G	22	17	24	27	14	25	29	32	23	19	23.2	18
C	32	40	27	37	41	32	30	45	23	22	32.9	23
F	27	41	41	19	22	35	28	36	31	27	30.7	22
E	27	26	31	30	25	27	19	27	25	24	26.1	11

Fig. 4.2.19. Spinning angles of single linen threads, spun with 8 g whorls, their mean and range (front line).

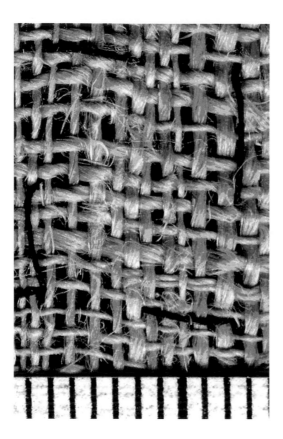

Fig. 4.2.20. Marked off area IIb of the linen weave with doubled weft and a twine-like spot within the pick right above the doubled one (to the right) (photo: Susan Möller-Wiering).

at 0.3 mm reflects very well the overall mean diameter of 0.299 mm. The few diameters lower than 0.2 mm are restricted to the finest sample F. The slight depression at 0.25 mm resembles the graph for the wool spun with 8 g and 18 g whorls (Fig. 4.2.6). When the figures are related to the individual spinners, the depression marks the difference between spinner 2's yarns with a mean diameter of 0.269 mm and spinner 1's material with a mean diameter of 0.329 mm.[8] This difference will be discussed below.

Spinning angle of spinning samples
The general impression of the spinning angles is medium to low and clearly softer than in the wool samples. Very hard spun and therefore crimping sections are rare. The overall mean spinning angle is 27.3° (Fig. 4.2.19). The lowest angle is only 11° and 20% are below the lowest measured angle in the woollen samples (22°). Not surprisingly, the long flax fibres give the possibility to spin with considerably less twist. When looking at the range as a reflection of evenness, sample E, which was mentioned above because of its evenness in diameter, is clearly the one with the most even angle as well. Related to the spinners, the mean spinning angle of spinner 1's yarns is 24.7°, while for spinner 2's threads it is 29.9°.

Relation between diameter, spinning angle and fibre consumption
When the figures for diameter and spinning angle are combined in a graph, the expected correlation between low diameter and hard spin would be expressed in diagonally clustering dots. In this case, clustering indeed appears more clearly than in the wool samples.

When the cumulative graph for the diameters was discussed, a depression was mentioned representing the difference between the spinners' work. A similar feature in the first graph for wool samples could later be explained as due to non-representative data material. Therefore, the same explanation might be assumed here, where the depression is only present in the measurements along the front line. Yet, it may be a real difference in this case. An argument for this is the calculation of the length of yarn per 100 g spun fibres. Spinner 1 spun 984 m yarn of 100 g fibres and her mean thread diameter is 0.329 mm. In comparison, spinner 2 spun 1328 m, with a mean diameter of 0.269 mm. While these figures match very well, they seem to be contradictory to the spinning angles. Since spinner 2's yarns possess a higher spinning angle, one might expect a higher fibre consumption, resulting in less yarn per 100 g as was the case in the wool experiment. Perhaps the difference in diameter is sufficiently large to compensate for the influence of the higher angle.

Weaving sample
The linen weaving sample is 22.5 to 22.9 cm long and 19.7 cm wide at the start and 16.6 cm wide at the end (Fig. 4.2.4). About 11.5 cm from the start, the weft is divided, thus creating two broad bands. The material is stiff and the surface not fuzzy to the naked eye. Weaving faults are rare, except for some irregularities

along the transition from the starting border to the weave. Already at first sight, the warp in the left half looks coarser than that in the right half. The upper half of the sample is a quite open weave and the warp tends to build groups with different spacing between the yarns, sometimes resulting in a rep-like, warp-faced structure. Within the bands, the weave is denser and the warp more evenly spaced, particularly in the left half. In many places, the threads fall a little apart, thus giving the impression of twined yarn (Fig. 4.2.20). This might be due to the spinning process, taking and combining groups of parallel, non-separated fibres. Under the microscope, it can easily be seen that the threads are often flattened, as if the fabric had been ironed.

On the sample, ten sections were delineated, partly by coloured threads inserted by the weavers, partly by prolonging these threads virtually, which was done by the present author.[9] For the measurements, a series of small areas were marked off, again each being 10 × 10 threads wide. The size and shape of these areas do vary to a great extent, as can be seen with the naked eye (Fig. 4.2.4). The calculated cover factor closely corresponds to the visual impression, *i.e.*, that the upper half is rather open where eleven out of twelve marked off areas have a cover factor belonging to the "open" group. Within the visibly more

densely woven lower half, seven areas out of eight are "medium dense". Furthermore, the cloth thickness was determined according to Hammarlund's proposals (Hammarlund 2004, 10).[10] The majority of the 13 areas may be called "thin". The other seven areas belong to the group called "thin-medium".

Thread diameter in the weaving sample

The measurements of the threads (Fig. 4.2.21) reveal a mean diameter of 0.42 mm in the warp and 0.45 mm in the weft.[11] These are much higher figures compared to the loose threads with their overall mean diameter of 0.299 mm. However, they do correspond to the above mentioned observation that the yarns are often flattened. Thus, the term "diameter" is far from being precise here. Analysing the fabric as if it was an archaeological find, these figures emphasise possible effects of any finishing process.

Naturally, the higher thread diameters compared to the loose samples are also visible in a cumulative graph for the warp. Yet, the main peak occurs at 0.3 mm which is practically the same figure as the mean diameter of the loose threads, 0.299 mm. Nonetheless, other peaks are to be found at 0.4 mm and 0.7 mm, resulting in a more heterogeneous picture compared to the loose material. And in this case, it does not become more illuminating when

Area	Diameter in mm										Mean	Range
Ia	0.45	0.4	0.35	0.3	0.7	0.75	0.55	0.85	0.3	0.3	0.495	0.55
Ib	0.45	0.35	0.55	0.5	0.7	0.5	0.3	0.2	0.7	0.45	0.47	0.5
IIa	0.3	0.3	0.7	0.4	0.2	0.35	0.3	0.3	0.3	0.4	0.355	0.5
IIb	0.25	0.4	0.6	0.45	0.6	0.45	0.4	0.25	0.65	0.8	0.485	0.55
IIIa	0.45	0.65	0.3	0.4	0.3	0.25	0.45	0.45	0.45	0.35	0.405	0.4
IIIb	0.25	0.3	0.45	0.5	0.5	0.7	0.3	0.2	0.7	0.5	0.44	0.45
Iva	0.25	0.25	0.3	0.2	0.15	0.3	0.4	0.25	0.3	0.35	0.275	0.25
IVb	0.5	0.7	0.35	0.5	0.3	0.4	0.4	0.4	0.3	0.25	0.41	0.45
Va	0.3	0.4	0.3	0.35	0.25	0.35	0.45	0.7	0.35	0.65	0.41	0.45
Vb	0.4	0.35	0.35	0.4	0.7	0.7	0.5	0.4	0.65	0.45	0.49	0.35
Via	0.3	0.3	0.35	0.35	0.2	0.35	0.3	0.3	0.4	0.35	0.32	0.2
VIb	0.8	0.3	0.3	0.3	0.45	0.8	0.6	0.3	0.25	0.3	0.44	0.55
VIIa	0.9	0.5	0.7	0.5	0.55	0.55	0.4	0.6	0.45	0.4	0.555	0.5
VIIb	0.5	0.25	0.5	0.3	0.6	0.55	0.45	0.4	0.55	0.4	0.45	0.35
VIIIa	0.45	0.4	0.4	0.45	0.35	0.4	0.5	0.3	0.4	0.4	0.405	0.15
VIIIb	0.4	0.45	0.5	0.7	0.4	0.4	0.45	0.45	0.35	1.0	0.51	0.65
IXa	0.5	0.5	0.35	0.45	0.3	0.35	0.45	0.3	0.5	0.45	0.415	0.15
IXb	0.3	0.25	0.3	0.45	0.6	0.55	0.4	0.4	0.5	0.5	0.425	0.35
Xa	0.3	0.25	0.35	0.2	0.3	0.3	0.35	0.3	0.5	0.3	0.315	0.3
Xb	0.35	0.25	0.3	0.35	0.25	0.4	0.4	0.3	0.25	0.35	0.32	0.15

Fig. 4.2.21. Diameters of warp threads in marked off areas on linen weave.

split up according to the spinners/weavers, the warp of the left half being spun by spinner 1, that of the right half by spinner 2. This shows again that homogeneity and thus one aspect of quality is lost during weaving and/or finishing. A corresponding graph for the weft looks similar, apart from the somewhat higher mean diameter in the weft. The mean diameter of the warp threads in spinner 1's half is 0.4555 mm and thus 0.072 mm larger than in spinner 2's half, 0.3835 mm. This corresponds well to the difference of 0.06 mm between spinner 2's and spinner 1's spinning samples of threads.

Spinning angles and thread count in the weaving sample

The angles in four marked off areas were measured, from left to right and from top to bottom (Fig. 4.2.22). The mean angle of the 40 warp measurements is 22.5°, hard spun points are missing. In the weft, the mean is 27.8°. This result is different from many archaeological textiles, where the spinning angle of the weft is often lower than in the warp. When these figures are compared to 27.3° within the spinning samples of threads described above (Fig. 4.2.19), it seems as if the warp had been stretched while the weft corresponds to the spinning samples of yarns.

The mean thread count in spinner 1's weave is 13.0 × 8.43 threads per centimetre, while it is 13.13 × 9.69 threads per centimetre on spinner 2's part. Generally, it varies within 10.0–17.2 × 7.7–11.8 threads per centimetre with a mean of 13.065 × 9.06 threads per centimetre.

Some comparative results

The data and results presented above allow for some comparisons between the different sets of samples.

Comparison between spinning angles of both spinners

Within the linen spinning samples, the mean spinning angle of spinner 1's yarns was 24.7°, while for spinner 2's threads it was 29.9°, which is 5.2° more. Apart from the fact that flax does not require as much spin as wool does, these figures are directly comparable to the spinning samples of woollen yarns. In the case of the 8 g whorls, the mean angle of spinner 1's threads was 31.03°, that of spinner 2's threads 37.26°, a difference of 6.23°. For the 18 g whorls, the figures were 36.86° for spinner 1 and 40.5° for spinner 2, with a difference of 3.64°. In the case of the 4 g whorls, spinner 1's yarns have a mean angle of 32.55°, while spinner 2's have a mean angle of 34.97°, *i.e.* 2.42° more. Seemingly, the lower spin is a individual trait in spinner 1's work. Yet, the similarities within both spinners' output predominate, concealing the differences and making it impossible to distinguish between their work without background information.

Relation between diameter, spinning angle and spindle whorl

As described above, the correlation between a low diameter of threads and a high spinning angle was discernible as a tendency, but not as strongly as might be expected. Indeed, it became apparent that many very thin woollen threads had remarkably low spinning angles, pointing to another parameter influencing that correlation. In Figure 4.2.23, the diameters of the wool threads produced by spinner 1 are plotted against their spinning angles. The stronger the above mentioned correlation, the more obvious the cluster along a line from top left to bottom right should be. Although the overall distribution does not seem to support this at first sight, it is easy to distinguish

Fig. 4.2.22. Spinning angles in warp and weft of selected marked off areas on linen weave.

Area	Angles in °, warp										Mean
IIIb	30	34	29	21	11	22	20	24	15	16	22.2
Via	19	14	17	25	27	27	19	23	18	29	21.8
VIIa	17	10	10	23	22	26	27	26	17	30	20.8
Xb	30	28	26	30	27	28	17	23	20	23	25.2

Area	Angles in °, weft										Mean
IIIb	26	27	32	29	37	36	31	43	29	33	32.3
Via	25	13	18	21	38	25	19	41	41	28	26.9
VIIa	43	30	27	29	25	31	35	39	26	29	31.4
Xb	12	20	19	24	21	27	17	17	19	32	20.8

between the whorls of different weight. The measures related to the 4 g whorl concentrate to the bottom and to the left while those deriving from the 8 g whorl are to be found further to the right and to the top, followed by those for the 18 g whorl still further right and top. Thus, Figure 4.2.23 reveals at least two results. Firstly, the figures for each type of whorl do show the expected correlation, although only within broad margins. Secondly, the weight of a whorl possesses a decisive influence. It is these measurable parameters that make up the basis for the final result, besides the selection of the raw material and the spinner's individual skill or habit. The latter is also visible within the data obtained during these experiments, since the threads spun by spinner 1 do clearly meet the expectations better than those produced by spinner 2. Spinner 2's work, which is not included in Figure 4.2.23, is more unconventional, with generally higher spin. This shows that there can also be a considerable individual component in the work.

The knowledge of this correlation may have had consequences for the textile production, especially mass production. To give an example: a quality with threads of 0.3–0.35 mm diameter is desired. Threads of that thickness can easily be spun with whorls at least from 4–18 g, as the experiments have shown. The warp must be strong and is therefore made with hard spin. Taking a raw material similar to the wool used in this experiment, a whorl of at least 8 g and probably more than 10 g may be most suitable for these yarns.[12] On the other hand, the weft may be a little looser, thus saving an enormous amount of wool (see above). For spinning such threads – same diameter but less material – a whorl of less than 8 g may be chosen in the case of this example. In fact, within archaeological material, the weft is often a little bit looser spun than the warp is. The common explanation for this is that the weft untwists a little during work. However, according to the results of these experiments and analyses, it must be taken into account that warp and weft may have been produced specifically, although they appear very much alike.

Comparisons between warp and weft

Hypothetically, when using similar yarn material for warp and weft, the diameter in the weft may be a little larger while the spinning angle may

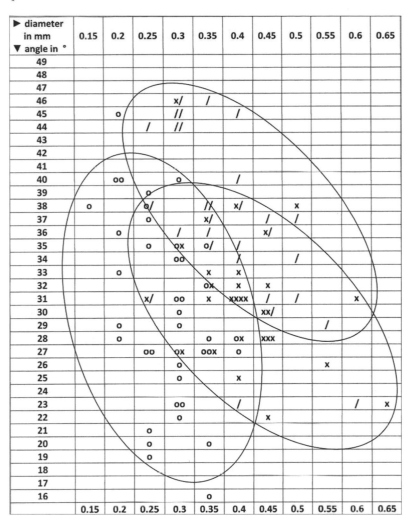

▶ diameter in mm ▼ angle in °	0.15	0.2	0.25	0.3	0.35	0.4	0.45	0.5	0.55	0.6	0.65
49											
48											
47											
46				x/	/						
45		o			//		/				
44				/	//						
43											
42											
41											
40		oo		o		/					
39			o								
38	o			o/		//	x/		x		
37				o		x/		/	/		
36		o		/		/		x/			
35			o	ox		o/	/				
34				oo		x		/			
33		o			x	x					
32					ox	x	x				
31				x/	oo	x	xxxx	/	/	x	
30					o			xx/			
29			o		o				/		
28			o			o	ox	xxx			
27				oo	ox	oox	o				
26					o					x	
25					o		x				
24											
23					oo					/	x
22					o			x			
21				o							
20				o		o					
19				o							
18											
17											
16						o					
	0.15	0.2	0.25	0.3	0.35	0.4	0.45	0.5	0.55	0.6	0.65

be somewhat lower, possibly due to untwisting during weaving. The weaving samples may be used for checking this.

Within the wool weave sample made with yarn spun on 8 g whorls, there is only a small difference in the diameter between warp and weft. Within the rectangle produced by weaver 1, the mean diameter in the warp was 0.425 mm, in the weft it was 0.39 mm, *i.e.*, the weft is even a little thinner (0.035 mm) than the warp measurments. The corresponding figures for spinner 2's weave were 0.42 mm both in warp and weft. Regarding the spinning angles, the expectations are met with mean angles in the warp of 37.6° (spinner 1) and 41.7° (spinner 2) and in the weft of 34.9° and 37.6°, respectively. It should be kept in mind that these means are based on only ten measurements each.

The data from the wool fabric sample woven with yarn spun with 4 g whorls is similarly based on a low number of measurements. Here, the

Fig. 4.2.23. Relation between diameter and spinning angle, wool thread samples, spinner 1 (front lines). The three circles mark the three clusters.
o: 4 g, x: 8 g, /: 18 g.

weft (0.3875 mm) is 0.0925 mm wider than the overall mean of the warp (0.295 mm). This might be the result of some problems that the weavers experienced during their work, *i.e.*, that the yarn was not optimal for the setup.

Within the linen weaving sample, the overall difference between warp and weft is 0.03 mm, the warp (0.42 mm) being a little thinner than the weft. Yet, it is possible to take a closer look, concentrating on those four marked off areas in which warp, weft and weave were made by the same person. This includes 40 measurements per person, per warp and weft, respectively. As a result, both spinners/weavers had one area with the weft being thicker than the warp and one the other way round, with differences of 0.017 and 0.14 mm. Turning to the spinning angles, it was described above that, unexpectedly, in three out of four examined areas, the angles were lower in the warp than in the weft. Two of these areas have warp and weft produced by the same person, in one case with lower, in the other case with higher angle in the warp than in the weft. The corresponding figures are 20.8° (warp) and 31.4° (weft) for spinner 1 compared to 25.2° and 20.8° for spinner 2.

The picture gained so far reveals mostly only small differences between warp and weft and the results do not all point in the same direction. The only example with an obvious difference is the wool piece woven from very thin yarn in which case the weaving set turned out not be optimal for the yarn. Since possible changes in the thread material during weaving are not restricted to hand spun yarn, three weaving samples produced with machine spun threads – same type in warp and weft –

Fig. 4.2.24: Diameters of threads in marked off areas on samples woven with machine spun yarns.

and made for testing different loom weights were included in order to further examine this point.[13] The measurements are given in Figure 4.2.24. It turns out that in five marked off areas, the weft is a little thicker than the warp while in one case, they are the same. However, the maximum difference is only 0.05 mm, in the samples woven with discoid weights, area A, and with spools of 280 g, area B. This means that some untwisting may have happened, but it is hardly visible.

To conclude: when using similar hand spun material for warp and weft, the weft does not necessarily end up with larger diameters. The weft may even be thinner. Neither will the spinning angle necessarily decrease. The tests on samples woven with machine spun yarn indicate some untwisting. But in most cases presented here, the differences are so small that they would not be recognised when examining archaeological material – warp and weft would appear to be identical. Consequently – and assuming a well-planned loom setup – a discernible difference between warp and weft in an archaeological textile will probably point to different material used. However, there may be further parameters influencing the picture, such as the type of loom.

Conclusions

The material analysed consisted mainly of a series of spinning samples and three pieces of woven fabric made from these yarns. Generally, the visual impression of the woven samples regarding their structure is in good accordance with the results gained by applying Lena Hammarlund's proposals for the density

Weaving sample and area			Diameter in mm										Mean	Range
Woven with discoid weights (2 cm thick)	A	warp	0.5	0.6	0.6	0.6	0.4	0.7	0.5	0.5	0.6	0.6	0.56	0.3
		weft	0.6	0.6	0.6	0.7	0.6	0.6	0.6	0.7	0.6	0.5	0.61	0.2
	B	warp	0.6	0.7	0.6	0.5	0.7	0.5	0.5	0.6	0.5	0.5	0.57	0.2
		weft	0.8	0.5	0.4	0.7	0.6	0.8	0.5	0.6	0.5	0.7	0.61	0.4
Woven with spools of 100 g, optimal set up	A	warp	0.25	0.25	0.25	0.25	0.3	0.2	0.25	0.3	0.25	0.3	0.26	0.1
		weft	0.3	0.3	0.25	0.35	0.25	0.25	0.25	0.3	0.3	0.3	0.275	0.1
	B	warp	0.3	0.25	0.3	0.2	0.25	0.25	0.25	0.25	0.25	0.25	0.255	0.1
		weft	0.3	0.3	0.3	0.25	0.25	0.3	0.25	0.25	0.3	0.3	0.28	0.05
Woven with spools of 280 g, optimal set up	A	warp	0.5	0.4	0.6	0.5	0.6	0.4	0.5	0.6	0.6	0.7	0.54	0.3
		weft	0.6	0.6	0.5	0.5	0.5	0.6	0.5	0.5	0.7	0.4	0.54	0.3
	B	warp	0.5	0.5	0.4	0.5	0.7	0.4	0.4	0.5	0.6	0.5	0.5	0.3
		weft	0.5	0.5	0.5	0.7	0.7	0.6	0.5	0.4	0.5	0.6	0.55	0.3

etc. The main measured features were thread diameters and spinning angles. The external analyses were carried out and the results – at first – were interpreted without any knowledge about the tools or the two spinners/weavers, *i.e.*, which sample was done by whom. This information was included at a later stage, allowing for more detailed interpretations and explanations.

The measurements on the woollen spinning samples spun with 8 g and 18 g whorls resulted in a bulk of data which did not allow a distinction between tools and/or spinners. Given the corresponding background information, some individual traits regarding the thread diameters seemed to appear, but disappeared again when more material was taken into account. Concerning the two types of whorls, the threads spun with the lighter whorls are thinner, as expected. Yet the difference in the mean thread diameter is only 0.071 mm, which is too small to be recognisable without further information, or in an archaeological fabric. Furthermore, the quality of some yarns made with a slightly unbalanced whorl was as good as if the whorl had been perfect.

Regarding the spinning angles, again little could be said based only on the thread and fabric samples, without information about the tools and spinners. It appeared that the threads spun by spinner 1 are generally looser spun than those of her colleague and that the yarn produced with the lighter whorls has a looser spun spin than that spun with 18 g weight. However, even if the differences in thread diameter and/or spinning angle are small, they result in remarkably different wool consumption. It is reasonable to assume that the weavers and spinners of the past were aware of this.

The yarns in the light, open tabby woven from the 8 g material have lost some of their evenness and thus quality compared to the threads in the spinning samples also spun on an 8 g whorl.

The results gained from the woollen material spun with 4 g whorls, as well as from the linen samples, are similar to the just described fabrics in several respects. While the thread diameter does not say anything specific about the spinners, the mean spinning angle of spinner 1 is again generally a little lower than that of spinner 2. The thread diameters in the linen weave are considerably higher than in linen thread spinning samples, thus revealing some influence of finishing.

When comparing some features of the three groups of samples, one notable observation is the above mentioned fact that the thread material of spinner 1 is generally produced with lower spin angle than that of spinner 2. This is the only individual trait that can be stated here.

The material offers a good opportunity to prove any correlation between hard spin and low diameter. The first result is that this correlation exists, but that it is not as strong as might be expected and to some extent dependent on individual habits of the spinner. Perhaps even more important is the fact that a third, measurable component plays an important role, *i.e.*, the weight of the whorl. The lower the weight, the lower the overall spin. Since the spin influences the fibre consumption to a remarkable degree, this correlation may have been used for saving raw material.

Within the woven pieces, warp and weft appear very similar. Sometimes the warp is a little thinner than the weft, sometimes it is thicker. In some examined areas the spin angle in the warp is harder, in other areas it is looser spun. With the exception of one piece deriving from a non-optimal loom setup, the differences are so small that they were undetectable in archaeological fabrics. Similar small variations can be found in the weaving samples made from machine spun yarn. This result probably indicates that any recognisable difference between warp and weft in a prehistoric piece is not just due to the process of weaving, but to selection of material. Further investigations would be useful regarding this point, including other possible parameters such as the type of loom.

Finally, the main factors predicting the quality of a cloth are the preparation of the raw fibre, the thickness and quality of the yarn, the chosen type of weave, the skill of the weaver and the finishing. The experiments and the external analysis have confirmed that lighter spindle whorls are suitable for spinning thinner threads. The finer and thinner the final cloth should be, the lighter the spindle whorls should be. For weaving standard cloth, the use of whorls of similar weight appears to be logical. Furthermore, the influence of their weight on the wool consumption is immense, as is the spinning angle. Probably, these correlations were also known and made use of in prehistoric times.

The microscopic analyses of the material have shown, however, that the range of yarn diameter and quality produced with a specific weight can be considerable. Many threads were alike, no matter which whorl they had been spun with. The use of different tools could be traced only when a large amount of material was taken into account and some background information was provided. The consequence for future experiments should be that the various steps are planned – as was done in this case – with the aim of making them extensive enough to ensure a larger data set and thus to avoid wrong conclusions based on too few data. In other words, the results have confirmed how misleading far-reaching calculations for reconstructing the past may be when they are based on very limited material. The same applies to the interpretation of archaeological textile finds. Quite often there are only a few threads that are suitable for detailed measurements (*e.g.* Möller-Wiering 2010). The results are very valuable, but one should be aware that they represent only a very small section of the whole product.

Notes

1 In practice, the cover factor can also be >1: "This can occur because the formula is based on the assumption that yarns are compact cylinders in the shape of a circle, but in reality, a yarn may be more or less elliptical." (Hammarlund 2004, 9).

2 Spinner 1, Anne Batzer, spun the samples 4a, 8b, 13a, c, d and v. Spinner 2, Linda Olofsson, spun the others.

3 However, this confirmation was not gained when only the first sets of samples were analysed. The expected results were achieved only when the additional sets were included, thus increasing the amount of data and representativeness.

4 Confirmation of this grouping by Hammarlund and Möller-Wiering June, 2006, personal communication.

5 Those marked in black were used to measure the thread count while the red ones were chosen for examining the threads. The measurements were taken from left to right and from top to bottom, respectively.

6 Wool samples B, E, T and U were made by spinner 1, Anne Batzer; S, I, N and D were produced by spinner 2, Linda Olofsson.

7 The position of area A is 2.5 cm off the starting border and 5 cm away from the right selvedge, area B is marked off 2.5 cm above the finishing line and 5 cm away from the left selvedge. The measurements were taken on magnified scans.

8 Linen samples A, D and G were made by spinner 1, Anne Batzer, while samples C, F and E were spun by spinner 2, Linda Olofsson.

9 Sections I, III, V, VII and IX from top to bottom on the left half, sections II, IV, VI, VIII and X from top to bottom on the right half.

10 This was done in order to allow for comparisons with others pieces, although the threads in this weave are clearly not round and the resulting figures do not represent the real thickness of the fabric.

11 They are taken in the middle of each area, from left to right and from top to bottom, respectively.

12 Of course, the figures of this example do not imply that in general, whorls for spinning warp material have to weigh at least *c.* 10 g. On the contrary, earlier experiments with other wool types showed that it is very possible to spin a warp thread with a whorl of less than 10 g (Andersson Strand 2003).

13 Again, areas of 10 × 10 threads were marked off for this purpose, two on each weaving sample. In each case, one area (A) was marked 5 cm off the starting border and 5 cm away from the right selvedge while the other one (B) was located in the bottom left corner, with 5 cm distance to the left selvedge and the finishing line. The marked off areas were scanned and the measurements then taken on magnified prints. The angles were not measured.

Bibliography

Andersson, E. and Nosch, M.-L. (2003) With a little help from my friends: investigating Mycenaean textiles with help from Scandinavian experimental archaeology, in Foster, K. P. and Laffineur, R. (eds), *Metron: Measuring the Aegean Bronze Age*, 197–205. Liège. Université de Liège.

Andersson Strand, E. (2003) *Tools for Textile Production– from Birka and Hedeby: Excavations in the Black Earth 1990–1995.* Stockholm. Birka Project for Riksantikvarieämbetet.

Cooke, B. and Christiansen, C. (2005) What makes a Viking sail?, in Pritchard, F. and Wild, J. P. (eds), *Northern Archaeological Textiles, NESAT VII*, 70–74. Oxford. Oxbow Books.

Hammarlund, L. (2004) Handicraft knowledge applied to archaeological textiles – fabric thickness and density: a method of grouping textiles, *Archaeological Textiles Newsletter,* 39, 7–11.

Hammarlund, L. (2005) Handicraft knowledge applied to archaeological textiles, *The Nordic Textile Journal,* 87–119.

Möller-Wiering, S. (2010) *War and Worship: Textiles from 3rd to 4th-century AD Weapon Deposits in Denmark and Northern Germany.* Ancient Textiles Series 9. Oxford. Oxbow Books.

CHAPTER 4.3

Test of loom weights and 2/2 twill weaving

Linda Olofsson and Marie-Louise Nosch

Introduction

In the experiments described in chapter 4.1, all weaving tests were tabbies. Experimental testing of textile tools and weaving techniques was also conducted for twill weaving. These tests were conducted at CTR in 2008 as a collaboration between the TTTC research programme and a research project on the textile production at the Danish Iron Age site of Vorbasse.[1] The site of Vorbasse contains both a settlement with textile tools and a cemetery with partly preserved textiles, in particular twills. Since both textile tools (torus shaped loom weights) and textiles were recovered, Vorbasse provides an extraordinary opportunity to test the textile tools, and to base the Vorbasse tests on knowledge about the yarn types and weaving techniques attested in the archaeological textiles at the site, which is not possible with the Mediterranean material. This chapter therefore aims to examine how well the finds of loom weights from Vorbasse correlate to the finds of textiles at the same site. The test was conducted by Linda Olofsson (née Mårtensson).[2]

Twill has long been considered an Iron Age weaving technique. This is due to exceptional twill textile finds from the Iron Age, for example in central Europe (Barber 1991; Grömer 2010). However, in recent years, Bronze Age twill has also come to light (see chapter 3). Secondly, measurements and recordings of Bronze Age textile tools, for example the analyses of textile tools from Malia, Crete, suggest that the tools would be highly suitable for twill weaving (Breniquet 2008; Cutler *et al.* 2013).

Even though several twill setups have been tested in the past, it is highly relevant to test whether loom weights can be used indiscriminatingly for tabbies and/or twills; whether loom weights have characteristic features facilitating the weaving of twill or of tabbies; and if such functional features can be identified. In this chapter, the results of twill weaving relevant for the purpose of Bronze Age textile technology and textile tools are summarised.

Weaving at Vorbasse in the Roman Iron Age

During the Iron Age, twill fabrics became more common and the 2/2 twill is a common technique in the Vorbasse textile fragments. Since previous investigations focused on tabby weaving, it is important to investigate if loom weights, in this particular case the torus shaped loom weights attested at Vorbasse, are suitable for making the type of twill textiles that have been found at the site.

The twill weaving case study

A warp-weighted loom can be operated in several ways, depending on for example what weaving technique is employed, such as tabby or twill. Yarn types and choice of equipment also affect the weaving and there can be a difference in different weavers' habits. Different sizes and weights of loom weights can be used for all types of weaving techniques.

The twill weaving tests followed the guidelines for experimental textile archaeology outlined above for weaving in chapter 4.1. Obvious features such as good light and a comfortable working position could be added. Furthermore, the conclusions from previous weaving tests in chapter 4.1 should be included, *i.e.* that the total width of loom weights hanging in a row should be similar or slightly wider than the fabric to be produced. Also, each warp thread should be given a suitable tension (see also Mårtensson *et al.* 2009).

Reconstructed loom weights

The model for the loom weight reconstructions for the test was a torus shaped loom weight (Fig. 4.3.1) with a weight of 280 g and a thickness of 3.9 cm (Fig. 4.3.2).

Based on this find, several identical loom weights were reconstructed by ceramists Inger Hildebrandt and Marianne Smith at CHARC (Andersson Strand and Olofsson in Lund Hansen forthcoming) (Figs 4.3.3 and 4.3.4). The ceramists mixed clay and crushed stone in order to match the right features of the original item, particularly regarding weight and thickness. The loom weights were lightly baked.

The use of similar loom weights in one loom setup facilitates the loom setup and a homogenous and equal warp tension.

Other tools for weaving

Apart from the essential loom and loom weights, there are additional textile tools of vital importance for the weaving process. Some kind of shuttle is needed to insert the weft properly. For the warp-weighted loom,

a simple wooden yarn holder is sufficient. In this weaving test, a thin and smooth twig was used (Fig. 4.3.5). Second, a smooth pin beater is very useful when inserting and positioning the weft and for separating the warp threads. With a pin beater, the weft can be positioned in a controlled manner and the warp threads can be adjusted individually if needed. The weft thread can be beaten or pressed up between the warp threads with a sword beater. In the twill weaving test, a wooden sword was used as a weft beater (Fig. 4.3.6) and a bone needle as a pin beater (Fig. 4.3.7).

Yarn

In this case study, only machine spun yarn was used because of time constraints.[3] It is not possible to buy a yarn that matches the fairly hard spun and single spun archaeological yarn represented at Vorbasse. Since a single spun yarn was required, a loosely spun yarn close to the archaeological finds was bought.[4] This yarn was thus woollier and more loosely spun than would normally have been preferred as warp. The yarn required a warp tension of approximately 18 g per warp thread. The same yarn was used in both warp and weft.

Loom setup for 2/2 twill weaving

Two-row and four-row system

A loom setup made for twill weaving is done differently than for tabby weaving. In tabby weaving, every other warp thread is tied to the heddle rod. These threads are attached to a row of loom weights, and the other warp threads are attached to a second row (see chapter 2).

For 2/2 twill weaving, the warp threads are grouped in a four-shed system. For every change of shed, the system is moved one warp thread to the side thus producing the diagonal appearance that is the characteristic feature of twill weaving. The diagonal direction can be changed according to the desired pattern. In a 2/2 twill weave, the warp threads must be tied to three heddle rods.

Two main methods to set up and weave 2/2 twill on a warp-weighted loom exist: one method has the warp threads attached to two rows of loom weights, the so-called *Icelandic system* (Hoffman 1964); the other method has the warp threads attached to four rows of loom weights, the so-called *four separate weight*

Fig. 4.3.1. Original torus shaped loom weight (photo: CTR).

system or *four-row system* (Haynes 1975).[5] In the Icelandic system, it is difficult to control the distribution of weight on the warp threads. Furthermore, loose threads might interfere negatively with taut warp threads. On the other hand, the Icelandic system does not require that many loom weights.

An important benefit of the four-row system is that uniform warp tension is constantly maintained (Haynes 1975, 163–164). On the other hand, a large number of loom weights are required. A variant of the four-row system was also tested in combination with the so-called crescent shaped loom weights as discussed in chapter 4.4 (see also Lassen 2007).

Loom setup for 2/2 twill weaving

Before setting up the loom, the weaver decides what fabric to produce and with what thread density. These decisions then define the setup of the loom and are thus directly related to the loom weights' weight and thickness.

As previously mentioned, the loom weights employed were *c.* 4 cm thick and weighed *c.* 280 g. The yarn chosen required about 18 g tension per warp thread. Therefore there are two possible setups: 15 warp threads per centimetre in the four-row system and 7.5 warp threads per centimetre in the two-row system.

As shown in Fig. 4.3.8, in the two setups with identical loom weights, identical thread type, identical warp tension and thus identical

Fig. 4.3.2. (top right) Loom weight: 280 g, Thickness: 3.9 cm, Diameter: 8.5 cm, Hole diameter: 1.8 cm (photo: CTR).

Fig. 4.3.3. (bottom left) Reconstructed loom weights by Inger Hildebrandt and Marianne Schmidt at CHARC (photo: CTR).

Fig. 4.3.4. (bottom right) Reconstructed loom weights by Inger Hildebrandt and Marianne Schmidt at CHARC (photo: CTR).

*Fig. 4.3.5. The shuttle
used in the TTTC
experiment, made from
a thin and smooth twig
(photo: CTR).*

*Fig. 4.3.6. (right)
Wooden sword used as a
weft beater (photo: CTR).*

*Fig. 4.3.7. Bone needle
used as a pin beater
(photo: CTR).*

number of warp threads per loom weight, with
four rows of loom weights, a denser fabric with
higher thread count is achieved.

In contrast, using two rows of loom weights
would only be suitable for producing weft-faced
twills. The first suggestion, 15 threads per
centimetre, corresponds well with the textile
finds from Vorbasse and was thus chosen.

Weaving test

The warp was made on a so-called Sami warping
frame (Fig. 4.3.9). The starting border was made
using tablet weaving. The weft of the tablet
woven band was pulled out like a loop while
weaving the starting border (see chapters 2 and
4.1). In this way, the weft threads were inserted
two by two. These threads were to become
the 3 m long warp which was to be set up in
the loom (Fig. 4.3.10). When a group of warp
threads had been produced, they were taken
off the pegs of the warping frame and rolled
onto small spools. Since the loom weights with
this type of yarn could provide optimal tension
for 15 warp threads each, the group had to
contain 60 warp threads which were divided
into four layers.

The starting border was made 60 cm wide,
consisting of 15 warp threads per centimetre
and thus resulting in a total of 900 warp threads.
There were 15 warp threads per loom weight
and a total of 60 loom weights, 15 in each of
the four rows. When the starting border had
been fixed onto the upper beam of the loom,

Four Rows of loom weights: Loom weight; weight 280 g, thickness 4 cm	
Warp requirement (warp tension)	**18 g**
Number of warp threads per loom weight	15 threads
Number of warp threads per four loom weights	60 threads
Warp threads per cm in loom setup	15 threads

Two Rows of loom weights: Loom weight; weight 280 g, thickness 4 cm	
Warp requirement (warp tension)	**18 g**
Number of warp threads per loom weight	15 threads
Number of warp threads per four loom weights	30 threads
Warp threads per cm in loom setup	7.5 threads

*Fig. 4.3.8. Calculations of the number of warp threads per loom weight and thread density
in the two types of setup, the four-row and two-row systems. The number of warp threads
per loom weight is calculated by dividing the weight of the loom weight (280 g), by the warp
tension needed per thread (18 g). The number of warp threads per centimetre is calculated
by multiplying the number of threads per loom weight by the number of rows, and dividing
it by the thickness of the loom weight (4 cm).*

Fig 4.3.9. Sami warping frame (photo: CTR).

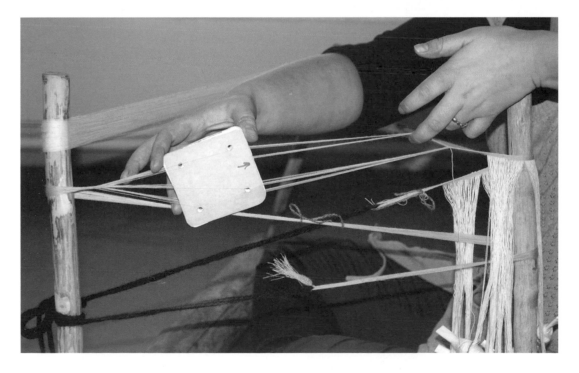

Fig 4.3.10. Tablet weaving of the starting border (photo: CTR).

the warp was rolled down and loom weights were attached to the four layers (Fig. 4.3.11). The warp threads in the three back layers were then attached to heddle rods, one rod for each layer (Fig. 4.3.12). The warp threads in the front layer were simply left hanging over the shed rod on the loom. Since the loom was leant at an angle against the wall, in this way, a natural

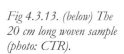

shed was produced, making a fourth heddle rod unnecessary. A sample of 20 cm fabric was woven (Fig. 4.3.13).

Measurements taken on the sample fabric indicated an even distribution of warp threads per centimetre, but the warp threads appeared more open at regular intervals all over the sample. Fourteen quite indistinct stripes are detectable in the fabric (Fig. 4.3.13). These open parts are directly related to where the warp threads are divided and attached to different loom weights. The use of four rows of 15 loom weights is thus slightly visible in the fabric. It can be concluded that the appearance of open warp threads at regular intervals is directly related to the use of loom weights and thus a characteristic for this technology and for fabrics made on the warp-weighted loom.

Other irregularities in the warp thread spacing could also be detected. There are several reasons that might cause such irregularities. Among these are irregularities in the warp yarn. Only a small variation in the thread thickness will affect the formation of warp and weft and the appearance of a fabric. There is no reed to ensure a consistent warp thread count in the warp-weighted loom. However, by selecting loom weights with an accurate weight and thickness and arranging the loom weights side by side and in straight lines, a more regular warp thread count can be achieved, in both tabbies and twills.

Clearing the shed

Before inserting the weft, the sheds always had to be cleared by hand (Fig. 4.3.14). In this setup, four sheds were used. Three of the sheds were easy to shift, whereas one was a struggle. Combining warp threads from the very back layer and the very front layer made this shed difficult to clear (shed 0+III according to Batzer and Dokkedal 1992, 232; see Fig. 4.3.15).[6] Taking into account the quite woolly yarn, which easily tangles together, the difficulty was accepted as a normal part of weaving as long as it did not cause too much wear and tear on the warp threads. The problem would probably have been worse in a dense tabby.

Comments on the loom weights

The four rows of loom weights were placed sloping so that the front rows were placed higher than the back rows. The aim was to avoid loom weights from the back layers slipping up on top of the front layers when the shed

Fig 4.3.14. Clearing the shed (photo: CTR).

I + 0

0 + III

III + II

I + II

Fig 4.3.15. Four different sheds. A 2/2 twill requires a 4 shed system. A shed is where the weft is inserted. In this system the warp threads are moved forward in pairs. Every fourth warp thread is attached to one row of loom weights and is tied to one heddle rod, except for the front layer. By moving the heddle rods it is decided what pairs of warp threads should be in the front and what pairs should be in the back. The shed made by combining warp threads from the very back layer and the very front layer, shed 0+III, was most difficult to clear (photos: CTR).

was changed. This initiative was successful. The four rows of loom weights had stable positions, were not whirling and tangling, and did not slip on top of each other. Furthermore, the loom weights were hanging level side by side (Fig. 4.3.11).

Conclusions

The test demonstrated that the loom weights were suitable for producing the type of twill fabrics recovered from the site, using four rows of loom weights. They could of course, also be used in other types of weaves. If used to produce a tabby with two rows of loom weights, using the same type of warp thread, the warp thread count would be 7.5 threads per cm, so the fabric would be very open or weft-faced.

The warp-weighted loom is excellent for weaving dense twills, especially if using thin loom weights, although in general all types of loom weights could be used in a twill setup. Although very few Bronze Age textile fragments have been preserved in the Eastern Mediterranean and twills fabrics are extremely rare, the use of loom weights and thereby the warp-weighted loom clearly indicates the possibility of twill weaving during this period.

Notes

1 Our sincere gratitude to professor Ulla Lund Hansen for the possibility to discuss the results of the Vorbasse weaving experiment here.
2 The Vorbasse weaving experiment was designed by Eva Andersson Strand, and was conducted and reported by archaeologist Linda Olofsson (formerly Mårtensson) in consultation with the Vorbasse textile project team. A more comprehensive description of the experiment, in relation to the site of Vorbasse can be found in Linda Olofsson's contribution in the publication of the Vorbasse textile analysis: Lund Hansen forthcoming.
3 It would have taken too long to spin the yarn by hand, see chapter 4.1 for spinning results and time consumption. For the weaving, on average, it took 20 minutes to weave 8 wefts. This means that it would take about eight days (*c.* eight hours a day) of intensive weaving to produce a 1 m

sample. Weaving would have been faster if it was done with less woolly yarn; the different steps in the process would also have been quicker as more routine was achieved.
4 *Perinnelanka* 100% wool, (Nm 12/1) 100 g = n. 1150 m of wool from New Zealand.
5 Thanks to hand weavers Ellinor Sydberg and Anne Batzer for interesting discussions on different loom setups.
6 This shed, as well as the shed made when the two back layers are moved up in front of the two front layers (shed III+II according to Batzer and Dokkedal 1992, 232), was also difficult to clear in the weaving experiment discussed in chapter 4.4 (see also Lassen 2007, 20).

Bibliography

Barber, E. J. W. (1991) *Prehistoric Textiles: The Development of Cloth in the Neolithic and Bronze Ages with Special Reference to the Aegean.* Princeton. Princeton University Press.

Batzer, A. and Dokkedal, L. (1992) The warp-weighted loom: some new experimental notes, in Bender Jørgensen, L. and Munksgaard, E. (eds), *Archaeological Textiles in Northern Europe: Report from the 4th NESAT Symposium*, 231–234. Copenhagen. Konservatorskolen, Det Kongelige Danske Kunstakadem.

Breniquet, C. (2008) *Essai sur le tissage en Mésopotamie; des premières communautés sédentaires au milieu du IIIe millénaire avant J.-C.* Paris. De Boccard.

Cutler, J., Andersson Strand, E. and Nosch, M.-L. (2013) Textile production in Quartier Mu, in Poursat, J.-Cl. (ed.), *Fouilles exécutées à Malia. Le Quartier Mu V. Vie quotidienne et techniques au Minoen Moyen II*, 95–119. Athens. École Française d'Athènes.

Grömer, K. (2010) *Prähistorische Textilkunst in Mitteleuropa. Geschichte des Handwerkes und der Kleidung vor den Römern.* Wien. Wien Naturhistorisches Museum.

Haynes, A. E. (1975) Twill weaving on the warp-weighted loom: some technical considerations, *Textile History*, 6, 156–164.

Hoffmann, M. (1964) *The Warp-Weighted Loom. Studies in the History and Technology of an Ancient Implement.* Oslo. Universitetsforlaget.

Lassen, A. (2007) Weaving with crescent shaped loom weights. Unpublished report. Reference number: HAF 09/07. Lejre Forsøgscenters Forskningslegater til kulturhistoriske eksperimenter.

Lund Hansen, U. (ed.) (forthcoming) *Late Roman Grave Fields of the Vorbasse Settlement. Grave Fields, Settlement, Environment and Textile Production. Late Roman Jutland Reconsidered* (Det Kongelige Nordiske Oldskriftselskab).

Mårtensson, L., Nosch, M.-L. and Andersson, E. (2009) Shape of things: understanding a loom weight, *Oxford Journal of Archaeology*, 28 (4), 373-398.

Springe, E. and Sydberg, E. (1986) Varptyngd vävstol, *Forntida teknik*, 13, 44.

CHAPTER 4.4

Weaving with crescent shaped loom weights. An investigation of a special kind of loom weight

Agnete Wisti Lassen

Loom weights can take on many different shapes and dimensions, but essentially they all perform the same task: they keep the warp threads taut on the warp-weighted loom. Due to their specific purpose, loom weights are usually a lump of clay or stone with a perforation. The particular shape of the weight, be that a carefully crafted pyramid or simply a crude sphere, usually does not influence the fabric woven on the loom, whereas the weight and size of the loom weights to some degree determine the type and density of the cloth. However, the loom weight treated in this chapter, namely the crescent shaped loom weight, seems to prove an exception to the rule that shape is less important for the weave (see Fig. 4.4.1).

Crescent shaped loom weights appear in excavations in central and southern Europe in contexts dating from the Neolithic period onwards. In the Mediterranean area, they have been recovered in Italy and Greece, and functionally similar loom weights have been found in Spain (Batzer and Dokkedal 1992, 231–234). Most notably, however, they appear quite frequently in Early and Middle Bronze Age layers in central Anatolia (see Fig. 4.4.2).

When found *in situ*, crescent shaped loom weights appear in all types of contexts:

palaces, temples, domestic areas and graves. They are found in larger or smaller groups as well as individually. This rather ambiguous find pattern does not immediately reveal any connection to textile production, although it does *not* exclude the crescent shaped objects from being loom weights (for a view that the crescent shaped loom weights are not loom weights, see Vogelsang-Eastwood 1990, 103–104).

An interpretation of them as loom weights is underpinned by the context in which they were found in the Early Bronze Age village of Demircihüyük. At this site, crescent and pyramid shaped weights were found lying close together, in a manner indicating that they were used together on the same loom (Baykal-Seeher and Obladen-Kauder 1996, 239). To test the functionality of the crescent shaped loom weights, I conducted an archaeological experiment using reconstructed tools and

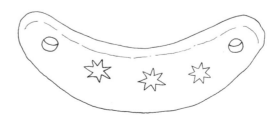

Fig. 4.4.1. Crescent shaped loom weight from Karahöyük Konya (drawing: Annika Jeppsson, after Alp 1968, 187 no. 574).

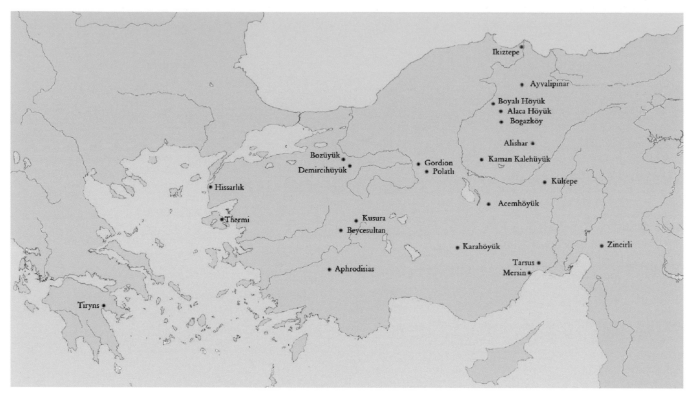

Fig. 4.4.2. Find spots for crescent shaped loom weights in the Bronze Age. Please note that the list of sites is not exhaustive (map: Agnete W. Lassen).

Fig. 4.4.3. (right) O. C. Castiglioni's reconstruction of crescent shaped loom weights in which the weights were attached to the warp in a single row and used for a tabby (drawing: Annika Jeppsson, after Castiglioni 1964).

thread. This experiment, and the research history of the crescent shaped loom weight, will be outlined below.

Previous research

Previous attempts have been made to explain the possible function of these crescent shaped objects.[1] In 1964, O. C. Castiglioni published a study on crescent shaped loom weights (Italian *'pesi reniformi'*) and suggested a reconstruction in which the weights were attached to the warp in a single row as indicated in Figure 4.4.3 (Castiglioni 1964). Groups of warp threads from the front thread layer were attached to one of the holes in the weight, and groups of threads from the thread layer at the back were attached to the other hole. In this way only one row of loom weights was used on the loom. The reconstruction was not tested in real life until recently, but Castiglioni's idea for a reconstruction seems to have been generally accepted among archaeologists working in the Eastern Mediterranean, and was adopted by B. Kull in her work from 1988 which included a description of the crescent shaped loom weights from Demircihöyük (Kull 1988).

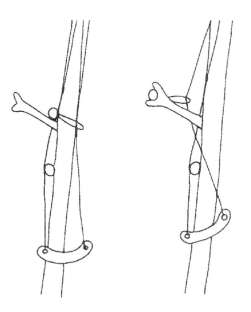

An experiment to test Castiglioni's *one row* reconstruction was recently conducted by M. Baioni (see Fig. 4.4.3) (Baioni 2003, 104–109). The published photographs indicate that only three crescent shaped loom weights were made and attached to the loom, which, in my opinion, makes the results of the experiment less convincing. The loom was provided with heddle bars, but not with a lacing cord above the weights, which caused a great deal of friction between the threads during shedding. Baioni concluded that although the crescent shaped weights could be used for weaving, there are a number of drawbacks. For example, the weights swing back and forth during weaving, causing them to collide and create an unevenness in the fabric. Baioni suggested that a cord or a stick connecting all the loom weights might alleviate this problem. However, had a lacing cord been crocheted to the warp threads (which is virtually what Baioni suggests), and had more weights been attached to the loom to make a proper row, this swinging would probably not have occurred. Further testing was necessary.

An experiment on crescent shaped loom weights (*Nierenförmige Webgewichte*) from central Europe was published in 2003 by A. Feldtkeller (Feldtkeller 2003, 16–19). She suggests a completely different reconstruction in which the weights are not used on a warp-weighted loom but instead on a band loom (see Fig. 4.4.4). Here, the warp threads are divided into two layers for a tabby, but each of the thread layers is *also* divided in two groups, with one group being attached to one hole in the loom weight and the other group being fastened to the other hole. According to Feldtkeller, the advantage of this setup is that the warp threads are pulled apart, which does not only prevent the band from eventually tapering, but also facilitates the shedding process. In 2007, Karina Grömer tested Feldtkeller's reconstruction of the Neolithic crescents on the band loom, but she found that the weave was unbalanced with a tendency to create a gap in the middle of the band and denser parts at the edges (Grömer 2007, 5). Grömer also tested the crescents in a *one row* setup for tabby on a warp-weighted loom and concluded that they functioned well, provided that the loom was equipped with a shed rod (Grömer 2007, 6).

Hypotheses and technical considerations

In the following, I suggest and test a new reconstruction in which *two* rows of loom weights are attached to the loom. The reconstruction is possible with two different setups: 1) the crescents are used as 'regular' loom weights in a tabby where the warp is

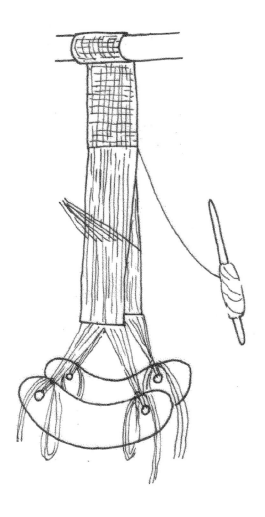

Fig. 4.4.4. A. Feldtkeller's reconstruction of crescent shaped loom weights on a band loom (drawing: Annika Jeppsson, after Feldtkeller 2003).

divided into two layers which are fixed to the crescents with a string that is fastened to each of the crescent's holes (see Fig. 4.4.5) and 2) the warp is divided into four layers for a twill and each thread layer is attached to a hole in the crescents (see Fig. 4.4.6).

Both setups were tested in an experiment, and it was shown that crescent shaped weights can be used as 'regular' loom weights, *i.e.* with each shed fastened to a row of weights. Although this type of setup does make the weaving process both stable and easy, it takes advantage neither of the particular shape of the weights, nor of the unusual double perforation with which they have been fashioned. In setup 2), each hole may be viewed as a 'fastening point' that can be attached to a layer of warp threads, and thus, two rows of crescent shaped loom weights can support *four* natural thread layers (see Fig. 4.4.7). This setup takes full advantage of the shape of the cresent loom weights.

A setup with four separate thread layers was actually suggested in 1975 by A. E. Haynes,

Fig. 4.4.5. (left) The first setup of the experiment with two rows of crescent shaped loom weights attached to the loom. The warp was divided into two layers, each with a row of loom weights (photo: Agnete W. Lassen).

Fig. 4.4.6. (right) The second setup of the experiment. The warp was divided into four thread layers and each layer attached to a hole in the crescents (photo: Agnete W. Lassen).

who proposed a setup in which four thread layers were attached to four rows of 'regular' loom weights (see Fig. 4.4.8) (Haynes 1975). One layer was placed in front of the shed bar and the remaining three were placed behind it. Each of the thread layers behind the shed bar was heddled individually and thus had its own heddle bar. This setup has been dubbed

the *separate weights system*. The advantages of the separate weights system is that it offers the possibility to weave and shift between tabby, panama, 2/2 twill, 3/1 twill and certain patterned weaves, without the time consuming task of having to change the setup. Furthermore, because the warp threads are separated in four layers, less friction occurs between them during shedding, thus making it possible to weave fabrics with a high thread density. It also avoids some of the problems inherent to the other known method of twill weaving (the Icelandic) on the warp-weighted loom (Haynes 1975, 156).

In spite of these advantages Haynes also points to some problems with his system. When the sheds 0+III and III+II (dubbed sheds B and D by Haynes) are created, layer III with its loom weights is pulled forward, causing interference with the other rows of loom weights. The loom weights of layer III collide with the weights of layers II and I, thereby pulling all the layers forwards. This causes the shed to diminish and makes it difficult to insert the weft (see Fig. 4.4.9).

To deal with this problem Haynes suggested that the loom should be equipped with the so-called 'double notched heddle brackets.' These special heddle brackets make it possible to pull out the thread layers both half way and all the way. In a 2/2 twill woven in this setup, two thread layers together create the shed. When layer 0 (the stationary thread layer in front of the shed bar)

Fig. 4.4.7. (left) In the second setup, each hole may be viewed as a 'fastening point' that can be attached to a layer of warp threads, whereby two rows of crescent shaped loom weights can provide tension for four thread layers (drawing: Agnete W. Lassen).

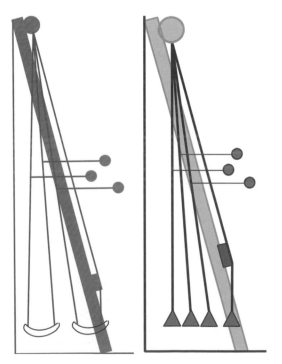

Fig 4.4.8.(right) The setup suggested by Haynes in which four thread layers were attached to four rows of regular loom weights (drawing: Agnete W. Lassen, after Haynes 1975).

forms part of the shed, the other thread layer only needs to be pulled out enough to align itself with layer 0 – which is only half way (see Figs 4.4.10a and 4.4.10b): I+0 and 0+III). It is only when a shed is created with two layers that are both behind the shed bar (III+II and II+I) that the heddle bars need to be pulled forward all the way. Using the double notched heddle brackets would thus solve the problem with interference in sheds I+0 and 0+III (Haynes 1975, 161).[2]

I suggest that the crescent shaped loom weights can function in a way similar to the separate weights system and have all the inherent advantages. In addition, the crescent shape of the loom weights adds certain benefits to the setup. To test this suggestion I conducted an experiment at Sagnlandet Lejre (Land of Legends) Centre for Historical and Archaeological Research and Communication (CHARC), in 2007 employing the guidelines for experimental archaeology devised by the TTTC research programme (see chapter 4.1).

An experiment with crescent shaped loom weights: materials and tools

Both thread and loom weights for the experiment were chosen on the basis of tools discovered in Middle Bronze Age layers in Karahöyük Konya and Demircihöyük in Turkey.

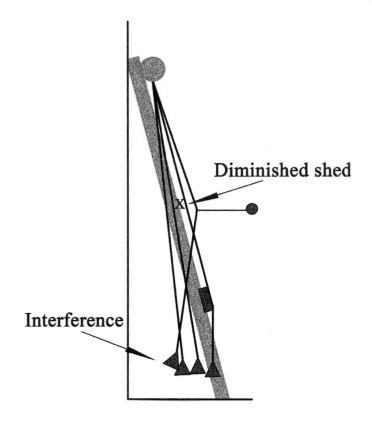

Fig. 4.4.9. Haynes' identified issues: when the sheds 0+III and III+II (dubbed sheds B and D by Haynes) are created, layer III and its loom weights are pulled forward, causing interference with the other rows of loom weights. The loom weights of layer III collide with the weights of layers II and I, thereby pulling all the layers forwards. This causes the shed to diminish and makes it difficult to insert the weft (drawing: Agnete W. Lassen, after Haynes 1975).

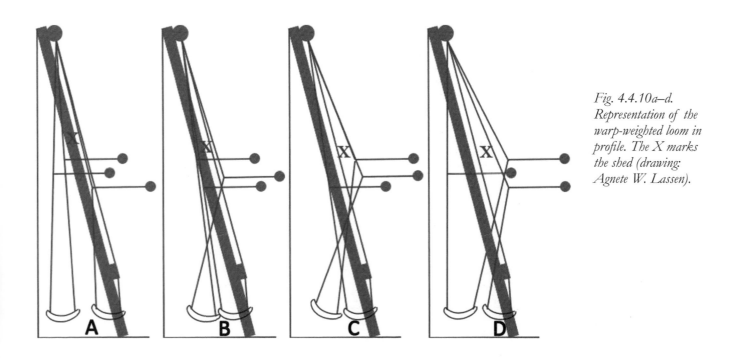

Fig. 4.4.10a–d. Representation of the warp-weighted loom in profile. The X marks the shed (drawing: Agnete W. Lassen).

	Thickness (cm)	Weight (g)	Distance between holes (cm)
Front layer	3.2	250	9.5
	3.2	245	9
	3.1	253	10
Back layer	3.0	247	9
	3.2	257	9.5
	3.1	255	9

Fig. 4.4.12. Measurements of six randomly chosen reconstructed loom weights.

On the basis of the analysis of the spindle whorls from these sites I decided to use a machine spun thread similar to one hand-spun with a 14–18 g spindle whorl (Lassen 2007, 10). The thread used in the experiment was suited to endure a vertical pull of *c.* 25 g. For a discussion of Bronze Age fibres and experimental archaeology, see chapter 4.1.

The loom weights were crafted by the potter's workshop in Lejre on the basis of the archaeological loom weights from Middle Bronze Age layers in Karahöyük Konya published by Sedat Alp in 1968 (Alp 1968) (see Fig. 4.4.11).

The potters made a total of 42 crescents with an average thickness of 3.2 cm and a weight of 250 g. Measurements were taken on six randomly chosen reconstructed loom weights (Fig. 4.4.12).

The thread density per cm for the fabric woven on the loom can be calculated according to the following formula:

Thread density = (Weight of LW/Warp tension) × 2/Thickness of LW.

The number of warp threads per loom weight can be calculated according to this formula:

Weight of LW/Warp tension (chapter 5.2).[3]

Figure 4.4.13 shows possible loom setups with a crescent shaped loom weight with a thickness of 3.2 cm and a weight of 250 g.

According to the guidelines outlined by the TTTC programme for the calculation of loom setups, it is not considered practical to attach fewer than 10 or more than 30 threads to a loom weight. Thus, this particular loom weight would not be optimal for use with 30 g tension thread. Furthermore, the warp threads would be very widely spaced in a one row reconstruction, and the textiles produced would therefore be very open, unless they were weft faced.

The weight distribution of the spindle whorls from Karahöyük Konya indicates that threads that could carry between 15 g and 25 g tension were most common. Such threads used with a batch of Karahöyük Konya loom weights would result in a fabric with a thread density between 10–11 and 6–7 threads per centimetre in the two row reconstruction (see Fig. 4.4.13).

The TTTC experiment

The thread used in the experiment was suited to endure a vertical pull, *i.e.* warp tension, of some 25 g, meaning that each loom weight weighing

Warp tension	15 g	20 g	25 g	30 g
Warp threads per loom weight (two holes)	16–17	12–13	10	8–9
Thread density per cm (one row reconstruction)	5	4	3	2–3
Warp threads per two loom weights (four holes)	33	25	20	16–17
Thread density per cm (two row reconstruction)	10–11	7–8	6–7	5–6

Fig. 4.4.13. Possible loom setups with a crescent shaped loom weight with a thickness of 3.2 cm and a weight of 250 g.

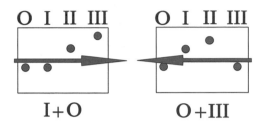
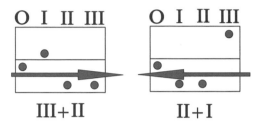

Fig. 4.4.14. Schematic representation of the 2/2 twill shedding sequence (drawing: Agnete W. Lassen).

250 g would require 10 threads to hold its weights, five in each hole. With 42 loom weights this resulted in a total of 420 warp threads. The row of loom weights was 67.2 cm wide (21 × 3.2 cm) but we decided to make the textile 70 cm wide, making the thread count 6 threads per centimetre (420 threads/70 cm).

The warping was done on a so-called 'Sami warping frame', which makes it easy to produce long warp threads of equal length, and which divides the warp into the two thread layers before the warp has been attached to the loom. The 6 m long warp was initially arranged on the loom with only two thread layers for a tabby weave, which meant that extensive modification had to be done when the setup was later changed to four thread layers for twill weaving. A lacing cord was crocheted across each of the thread layers, with each warp thread in its own loop. After weaving some centimetres of tabby, the loom setup was changed to twill weaving and each of the three thread layers behind the shed bar were heddled. The heddle bars were placed in two double notched heddle brackets. Heddle bar no. II was placed in the upper heddle bracket and heddle bars I and III were placed in the lower heddle bracket.

2/2 twill

Weaving was done by inserting the weft between the four thread layers, always with two layers in front, and two behind the weft. One of the two warp threads the weft passed behind shifted either to the left or to the right with

Fig. 4.4.15. Interference (photo: Agnete W. Lassen).

each shedding (see Figs 4.4.14 and 4.4.10a–d) and this movement created the diagonal lines characteristic of twill.

Figure 4.4.14 shows a schematic representation of the 2/2 twill shedding sequence. The line in the centre of the figures marks the shed bar, the arrow signifies the weft direction and each dot represents a warp thread, or warp thread layer. In the first figure (I+O) thread layer I is pulled halfway forwards, aligning itself with layer O, thus creating the shed I+O. The weft is inserted behind layer I and O, and in

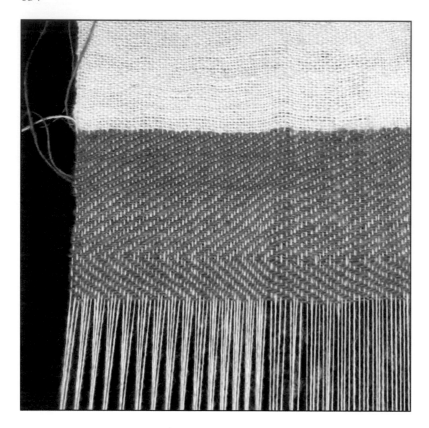

Fig. 4.4.16. 2/2 twill. The image also illustrates the groups of four warp threads that are created by the four rows of loom weights (photo: Agnete W. Lassen).

front of II and III. One thread layer is changed in each motion. The second figure (O+III) shows a shed in which layer O is retained, and layer I exchanged with III.

In the sheds O+III and III+II some interference between the two weight systems did occur (Fig. 4.4.15). The degree of friction did not hinder the weaving, but the shed was slightly diminished. The problem encountered in Haynes' separate weight system, where weights slipped on top of each other, was not encountered here. The crescents would simply tip, and the ends of the loom weights would lift up. As layers III and II were attached to the same loom weight they, of course, could not in any way interfere with each other. I wove 11.5 cm of 2/2 twill with a thread density of 12 weft threads per centimetre. After the first half was woven, I reversed the shedding sequence, causing the diagonal lines to change direction (Fig. 4.4.16).

3/1 twill

A change of weft colour and a simple change in shedding procedure marked the transition from 2/2 to 3/1 twill (see Figs 4.4.17, 4.4.18 and 4.4.19). 3/1 twill is an asymmetrical weave, and the weft passes over three warp

threads and below one, unlike the 2/2 twill, in which the weft passes over two and below two. This causes the textiles woven in 3/1 twill to have uneven faces, making the weft threads dominant on the front of the textile and the warp threads dominant on the back (Figs 4.4.19a and 4.4.19b).

I wove 9 cm of the 3/1 twill with 11 weft threads per centimetre.

Patterned weave

Two different types of patterned weave were created with red and white weft thread. The first test was done with a type of floating weft. The second test involved an attempt to explore the possibilities of the four thread layers: one thread layer was pulled forwards and the other three left in resting position. Working only with these three layers, every second group of threes was pulled out on a bar for patterned weaving (see Fig. 4.4.20). The red weft was inserted, and the bar was removed. It was then inserted again, this time with the groups of three that had not been pulled out on the bar before. Then a white weft was inserted. The bar was removed, the heddle bar released and another heddle bar pulled forward. The heddle bars were pulled forward in the same sequence as in a regular 3/1 twill, and the pattern created by the process was much like the pattern of a regular 3/1 twill, except for the fact that every other of the diagonal lines was done in red and every other in white (see Figs 4.4.20 and 4.4.21).

Had the threads not been divided and heddled in four layers, the pattern would still be possible to produce, but each thread would have to be counted in order to determine which threads to use in each motion, making it a very time consuming task. By using the crescents and the separate weights system, the shift between the thread groups that cause the diagonal lines was carried out automatically with the heddle bars. The threads would naturally be clustered in groups of three, and so the bar could be inserted simply by moving it over and under the groups without the need for the time consuming counting. This advantage in a systematisation and mechanisation of the process applies to all patterns and weaves with four threads as the basic unit.

A setup with three thread layers is also possible. One thread layer with regular one-hole loom weights would be placed in front of the

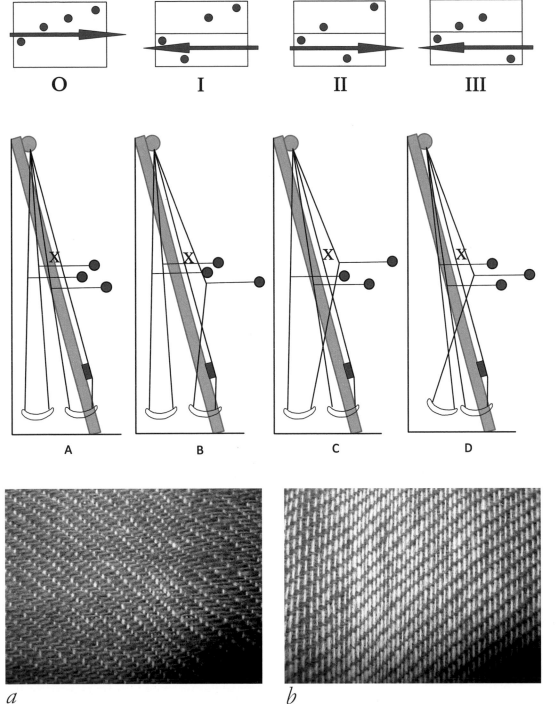

Fig. 4.4.17. Schematic representation of the 3/1 twill shedding sequence (drawing: Agnete W. Lassen).

Fig. 4.4.18. A) shed 0 B) shed I C) shed II D) shed III (drawing: Agnete W. Lassen).

Fig. 4.4.19. 3/1 twill (a) front and (b) back (photo: Agnete W. Lassen).

shed bar, and two thread layers attached to crescent shaped loom weights would be placed behind the shed bar. This setup would be able to produce 2/1 twill and pattern weaves with three threads as its basic unit. Such a setup may have been discovered in Early Bronze Age Demircihüyük, as mentioned above.[4]

Wear marks

The experiment lasted 15 days, and this rather limited time of weaving did not produce any wear marks on the loom weights. It does, however, seem possible to predict where such marks would occur. The weaving movement was quite uniform and regular, and it produced

Fig. 4.4.20. Groups of warp threads are pulled forward and placed in front of a flat bar, thus creating the additional shed (photo: Agnete W. Lassen).

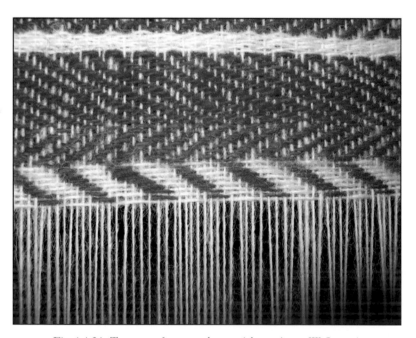

Fig. 4.4.21. Two types of patterned weave (photo: Agnete W. Lassen).

a consistent stress on two areas on the loom weights. Pulling forward thread layer III (and to a lesser degree also layer II) made the tips of the two rows of weights bump into each other, which might cause some chipping although this was not observed during the experiment.

Also, the string that tied the warp threads to the loom weights rubbed against the upper part of the fastening hole and around it in an approximately 90 degree angle. Wear marks of this nature have been noted on the crescent shaped loom weights of Demircihöyük (Kull 1988, 201, Abb. 195). One might also have expected wear marks on the sides of the loom weights caused by friction as they hung closely side by side. However, in using the loom it became clear that the weights all moved in unison during shedding, causing no, or only very limited, friction on the sides of the loom weights.

Conclusions

The present experiment proves beyond any doubt that the crescent shaped loom weights *can* be used as loom weights on the warp-weighted loom; it even proves that they function well, both in a tabby and a twill setup. They can be employed in much the same way as Haynes' separate weights system, and draw on the same advantage of flexibility. Furthermore, as a result of their particular shape, a setup with crescent shaped loom weights avoids the problems of interference. The thread layers are automatically kept apart and in place by the crescents. In his article on the crescent shaped loom weights from Italy, Baioni (2003) writes that the main advantage of the crescents was that they had two holes so that their weight could be distributed on two thread layers instead of just one. Thus, in effect, they would halve the weight the threads would carry. According to Baioni, this was desirable, because the Italian potters of the time supposedly were unable to produce lightweight loom weights that would not break in use. The same reasoning cannot apply for the crescents from Turkey, as the potters of the Middle Bronze Age showed considerable skill, and did in fact also produce functional light-weight loom weights. The present experiment rather suggests alternative advantages over other types of loom weight. Plainly, the two holes make it possible to create four thread layers with only two rows of loom weights. The crescent shape facilitates a steady, smooth movement when the thread layers are pulled forwards and one end of the loom weights is lifted. To exploit this advantage, the loom weights must be used in a loom setup with three heddle rods. This makes a very flexible setup that can change instantly between 2/2 and 3/1 twill, tabby, panama, as well as pattern weaves with four threads as the basic unit. Furthermore, if a row of regular loom weights were attached to one thread layer in front of the shed bar, and two thread layers tied to the two holes in a row of crescent shaped loom weights behind the shed bar, it would also be possible to weave 2/1 twill and pattern weaves with three threads as the basic unit.

Notes

1 The earliest archaeological experiment on such objects was done by Danish and Spanish scholars in Lorca in Spain in 1991. In this area a number of so-called '*heart-shaped loom weights*' have been unearthed in excavations, and terracotta reconstructions of such objects were used in the experiment. Although the shape of the heart-shaped loom weights does not correspond exactly to the crescents from Anatolia, the two types appear to be functionally very similar. See Batzer and Dokkedal 1992, 231–234.

2 In 1975, when Haynes suggested the separate weights system, the existence of double notched heddle brackets was only a technical assumption. Yet, during the later excavations in Trondheim in Norway in the late 1970s and 1980s, six medieval heddle brackets of this type were uncovered, thus providing archaeological evidence for a hitherto hypothetical tool (Stærmose Nielsen 1999, 93). On behalf of Trondheim Museum, Land of Legends Lejre (then Lejre Historical and Archaeological Research Centre) carried out an experiment with the separate weights system and the double notched heddle brackets (Batzer and Dokkedal 1992, 231–234). Their assessment of the functionality was generally positive, although they did encounter slightly diminished sheds as a result of interference between the weight systems. They also noticed that when thread layer III (and to some degree also II) was pulled forwards, and the attached weights were lifted, these weights had a tendency to slip over the other lower hanging loom weights (Batzer personal communication). The lacing cords (and a string through the holes in the loom weights) ensured that the weight systems did not get entangled, but a lot of extra tension was put on the threads attached to loom weights that were weighted down.

3 Note that the crescent shaped loom weight has *two* holes per loom weight and so to calculate the number of warp threads per hole the number of warp threads per loom weight must be divided by two.

4 2/1 twills are particularly suited for sacking, and clay impressions of this twill type have in fact been found in Turkey (see Kt. 90/499 (rev) from Kültepe, identified by Anne Batzer). Note also the extant textile fragments from Alishar (see chapter 3).

Bibliography

Alp, S. (1968) *Konya civarinda Karahöyük kazilarinda bulunan silindir mühürleri*, Türk Tarih Yayinlarindan V. Ankara. Türk Tarih Kurumu Basimevi.

Baioni, M. (2003) Prova sperimentale di produzione di pesi reniformi e loro applicazione a un telaio verticale, in Bazzanella, M., Mayr, A., Moser, L. and Rast-Eicher, A. (eds), *Textiles: intrecci e tessuti dalla preistoria europea*, 104–105. Trento. Provincia Autonoma di Trento.

Batzer, A. and Dokkedal, L. (1992) The warp-weighted loom: some new experimental notes, in Bender Jørgensen, L. and Munksgaard, E. (eds), *Archaeological Textiles in Northern Europe: Report from the 4th NESAT Symposium*, 231–234. Copenhagen. Konservatorskolen det Kongelige Danske Kunstakademi.

Baykal-Seeher, A. and Obladen-Kauder, J. (1996), *Demircihüyük, die Ergebnisse der Ausgrabungen 1975–1978. IV. Die Kleinfunde*. Mainz. Philipp von Zabern.

Castiglioni, O. C. (1964) I "reniformi" della Lagozza, in Calderini, A. *et al.*, *Comum – Miscellanea di scritti in onore di Federico Frigerio*, 129–171. Como. Noseda.

Feldtkeller, A. (2003) Nierenförmige Webgewichte – wie funktionieren sie?, *Archaeological Textiles Newsletter*, 37, 16–19.

Grömer, K. (2007) Experiments with Neolithic weaving tools (lunular or crescent shaped loom-weights). Report. Reference number: HAF 03/07. Land of Legends Lejre(then Lejre Historical and Archaeological Research Centre). http://www.sagnlandet.dk/DRESSING-AUSTRIA-S-FARMERS.609.0.html

Haynes, A. E. (1975) Twill weaving on the warp-weighted loom: some technical considerations, *Textile History*, 6, 156–164.

Kull, B. (1988) *Demircihüyük. Die Ergebnisse der Ausgrabungen 1975–1978. V. Die mittelbronzezeitliche Siedlung*. Mainz. Phillip von Zabern.

Lassen, A. W. (2007) Weaving with crescent shaped loom weights. Unpublished report. Reference number: HAF 09/07', (Lejre Forsøgscenters Forskningslegater til kulturhistoriske eksperimenter).

Stærmose Nielsen, K.-H. (1999) *Kirkes væv: Opstadsvævens historie og nutidige brug*. Lejre. Historisk-Arkæologisk Forsøgscenter.

Vogelsang-Eastwood, G. (1990) Crescent loom weights?, *Oriens Antiquus* 29, 99–113.

von der Osten, H. H. (1937) The Alishar Hüyük, seasons of 1930–32, *Oriental Institute Publications*, 28–30.

Chapter 4.5

From tools to textiles, concluding remarks

Eva Andersson Strand

The TTTC experiments combined with results from earlier experiments and textile craft knowledge clearly demonstrate that new knowledge has been obtained with the TTTC tests, as well as confirm previous suggestions on textile tool suitability (*e.g.* Barber 1991; Andersson 2003). The aim in this section is to combine the new results with previous results and craft knowledge, to conclude and summarise what the limitations and the possibilities are, and to determine how far these results can be used in our interpretation of the tools' suitability. Furthermore, the aim of this section is to determine how studies of textile tools can make textiles and textile production become visible, and finally, what further information could be useful in order to develop and expand on these results.

From registrations of tools to interpretation of function

Testing spindle whorls of different sizes confirms earlier results that it is preferable to spin a thin thread with a light spindle and a thick thread using a heavier spindle. Furthermore, testing spindle whorls confirms that when the spinners use the same type of fibre they get a similar result if using the same type of tool. The spinning tests with reconstructed spindles demonstrate that the most important technical parameter to record on a spindle whorl is the weight. Via the registration of the weight of spindle whorls it is possible to get a good indication of what could have been produced in a certain site, region and period. However, the analyses of the spinning tests also showed that, even if using the same spindle and the same prepared fibre material, there is a small but significant difference in the resulting yarn between the spinners. Furthermore, it is also important to note that the choice of fibres and the preparation of fibres will undoubtedly affect the result. Earlier tests with spinning wool have demonstrated that there is a difference when spinning wool from different sheep breeds and also according to whether hair, mixed wool or underwool is being spun (Andersson 2003, 25–26). The methods used to prepare flax fibres will also affect the result (see chapter 2).

When comparing the measurements of the thread diameter, there is a small but significant difference between the two spinners and the different spindles (Fig. 4.5.1) (see also chapter 4.2). When spinning with the same spindle, the biggest difference between the two spinners

Spinning tests	Spinner 1	Spinner 2	Difference in thread diameter between spinner 1 and 2	Difference in thread diameter between spinner 1 and 2 (percentage)	Average spinner 1 and 2
Wool 4 g spindle whorl	0.2780 mm	0.3010 mm	0.0230 mm	7.64%	0.2895 mm
Wool 8 g spindle whorl	0.3667 mm	0.3759 mm	0.0092 mm	2.5%	0.3713 mm
Wool 18 g spindle whorl	0.4421 mm	0.4734 mm	0.0313 mm	6.6%	0.4582 mm
Flax 8 g spindle whorl	0.3290 mm	0.2690 mm	0.0600 mm	18.0%	0.2990 mm
The difference in thread diameter between 4 g and 8 g	0.0887 mm	0.0749 mm			
The difference in thread diameter between 8 g and 18 g	0.0754 mm	0.0975 mm			

Fig. 4.5.1. The results of the spinning tests: thread diameter of the spun yarn.

	Weight in g/1000 m (TEX)		Difference in TEX between spinners 1 and 2	Difference in TEX between spinners 1 and 2 (percentage)	Average
Spinning tests	Spinner 1	Spinner 2			Spinners 1 + 2
Wool 4 g spindle whorl	62.14	58.96	3.18	5%	60.55
Difference in TEX between 4 g and 8 g spindle	27.76	46.44			
Difference in TEX between 4 g and 8 g spindle (percentage)	30.9%	44%			*c.* 38%
Wool 8 g spindle whorl	89.90	105.40	15.50	14.7%	97.65
Difference in TEX between 8 g and 18 g spindle	59	66.8			
Difference in TEX between 8 g and 18 g spindle (percentage)	39.5%	38.7%			*c.* 39.1%
Wool 18 g spindle whorl	148.90	172.20	23.30	13.5%	160.55
Flax 8 g spindle whorl	75.27	101.59	26.32	26%	88.43

Fig. 4.5.2. The results of the spinning tests: weight of the spun yarn.

can be seen in the flax spinning test, while the difference in the wool spinning varies between 0.0092 and 0.0313 mm.

Moreover, the analysis of the spun thread demonstrated that the diameter on the same thread can vary greatly (see chapter 4.2), and showed a high degree of overlap between the threads spun with the different spindles. However, there is a very clear and interesting difference in yarn weight. In modern times textile fibres and yarn are weighed, and wool was also weighed in both classical and Mycenaean Greece (Barber 1991). Today, different types and qualities of yarn are defined according to different "yarn numbers" and thread diameter is never used as a means of classification of yarn type. Basic Tex Unit

(TEX) is one common international system of classification: in this system the yarn number[1] is based on the weight of yarn per 1000 m; in general, the finer the yarn, the lower the number. When applying the TEX system to the TTTC spinning tests it is clear that the wool yarn spun with the different spindles would be given different yarn numbers. Although there is a difference in weight between the yarn spun by the two spinners on the same spindle, the difference in weight between yarn spun with the different spindles is much greater (Fig. 4.5.2). For example, the difference between the two spinners in the weight of the wool yarns spun with the same spindle varies between 5% and 14.7%. However, the difference in the weight of the spun thread between the 4 g and 8 g spindle, and between the 8 g and 18 g spindle, is 30.9–44% and 38.7–39.5% respectively.

On the other hand, the flax yarn varied by as much as 26% when comparing the yarn spun by the two spinners with the same spindle. This greater difference compared to spinning with wool is interesting and should be considered, but can be explained by the different spinning methods the two spinners used (see chapter 4.2).

To conclude, by registering a spindle whorl's weight (together with its diameter) one will get an indication of this whorl's suitability for spinning certain types of yarn. Even if the same spindle can be used for producing slightly different types of yarn depending on the chosen fibre and the fibre preparation, the tests demonstrate that by using the same spindle, the same prepared raw material and the same technique, it is likely that the spinners would produce a similar type of yarn that could be used in the same loom setup. This would be of highest importance in an organised and standardised production.

These results also demonstrate why it was hard to use average diameter to analyse the yarn produced in the experiments. It additionally explains why the result changed when more diameter measurements were taken. When analysing yarn or textiles there is a practical limitation to how many measurements one can take. By weighing a textile or a yarn the results will be more reliable and accurate and will give a better indication of the yarn type. Obviously, archaeological textiles are mostly very fragmentary and it is therefore not possible to do this, but when analysing larger preserved textiles weighing would be a good complementary method of analysis.

The results of the combined spinning and weaving tests are summarised in Fig. 4.5.3.

The wool yarn spun by the two spinners with a whorl of a particular weight could be used in the same loom setup and with the same tension. This demonstrates that

although there was a difference of up to 13% in the weight of the yarn spun by the two spinners when using the same spindles, the yarn spun with the same spindle required the same tension on the loom. In contrast, the wool yarn spun with different spindles required different tension on the loom, which demonstrates that a weight difference of more than 31.5% requires another tension.

It is also important to note that the yarn diameter was larger in the weaving test than in the spinning tests. This indicates that the wool thread opened up (*i.e.* became slightly thicker) after spinning; for example, the thread spun with the 8 g spindle had an average diameter of 0.3713 mm (Fig. 4.5.1), while the same thread on the loom had an average of 0.42 mm (weaving test 1a) (Fig. 4.5.4). It further demonstrates that it is difficult to estimate the original thread diameter, and thereby the exact size of spindle whorl used, when analysing a textile. Finally, it clearly demonstrates that using thread diameter when calculating the tension required by a yarn in a loom setup is not reliable, since it is the weight of the thread and not the diameter that determines the tension needed. Furthermore, when calculating the cover factor on the basis of the number of threads per centimetre and the thread diameter, it is important to note that this is the minimum cover factor; *i.e.* the calculations are based on the average diameter of the yarn when it is removed from the spindle, and do not take into account any subsequent opening up of the thread, *etc.*[2]

Spinning flax with an 8 g spindle whorl, spinner 1 produced a thread with an average diameter of 0.329 mm and spinner 2 produced a thread with an average diameter of 0.269 mm (Fig. 4.5.3). These threads were set up with 18 g warp tension per thread. This tension is the same as was needed for the wool thread spun with the 8 g spindle whorl. During the weaving of the linen fabric, the difference in the

Fig. 4.5.3. Yarn weight/ yarn diameter/thread tension for yarn spun by the two spinners with the different spindles.

Spinning test	Thread diameter on average		Yarn weight (TEX)		Thread tension required	
	Spinner 1	Spinner 2	Spinner 1	Spinner 2	Spinner 1	Spinner 2
Wool 4 g spindle whorl	0.2780 mm	0.3010 mm	62.14	58.96	13 g	13 g
Wool 8 g spindle whorl	0.3667 mm	0.3759 mm	89.90	105.40	18 g	18 g
Wool 18 g spindle whorl	0.4421 mm	0.4734 mm	148.90	172.20	*c.* 25–30 g	*c.* 25–30 g
Flax 8 g spindle whorl	0.3290 mm	0.2690 mm	75.27	101.59	> 18 g	< 18 g

	Weaving tests	Thread diameter	Threads/cm	Cover factor
Wool fabric woven with thread spun with 8 g spindle whorl	Weaving sample 1a	Warp 0.42 mm	Warp 11.500	0.62
		Weft 0.42 mm	Weft 6.675	

Fig. 4.5.4. An example of the thread diameter and cover factor in weaving test 1a after the weave was removed from the loom.

warp threads per centimetre became visible and therefore produced two rather different fabrics (see chapter 4.2). This can partly be explained by the difference in the yarn spun by the two spinners. When the thread tension was calculated the overall average was used, but when comparing the difference in the weight, which is 26%, it is clear that this difference affected the fabric produced. If the yarn spun by the two spinners had been used in separate loom setups it is likely that the weavers would have chosen different tensions. The yarn spun by spinner 1 would probably require more than 18 g tension, and spinner 2's yarn less than 18 g tension (Fig. 4.5.3). The comparison with the weight tension needed for the wool yarn spun with the same (8 g) spindle is also interesting, since it has been assumed that linen thread in relation to wool yarn needs more tension on a loom, because the linen thread is less elastic than the wool yarn (Batzer, personal communication). It was therefore surprising when the thread tension needed for the linen setup was calculated to be the same as for the setup with the wool thread. When comparing the average of the TEX weight between the wool and the linen yarn spun with the 8 g spindle there is a difference of only 9%. However, when comparing the TEX weight between the linen threads spun by the two spinners, spinner 1's linen thread was 23% lighter than the average of the wool yarn, while the linen thread spun by spinner 2 was 3% heavier than the average of the TEX weight of the wool yarn. To conclude, the experiments demonstrated that the linen yarn needed more tension.

The weaving experiments (see chapters 4.1, 4.3; Mårtensson *et al.* 2009) demonstrate and confirm that different types of yarn need different amounts of tension when they are used in the warp on a loom. Furthermore, it is the weight and not the diameter of the thread that dictates how many threads can be attached to a loom weight, although in general a thicker yarn would need more tension than a thinner thread. The experiments and the results of the analyses of the textiles produced have demonstrated that it is not reliable to use thread diameter as a parameter of analyses. While it is possible to give a certain range, these calculations can never be exact and it is not possible to use a specific thread diameter to determine a specific required tension.

Since different types of yarn need different tensions, this dictates how many warp threads can be attached to an individual loom weight (see also chapter 4.1). Therefore, in estimating the type(s) of fabric(s) that a particular loom weight would be suitable for producing, the first step is to calculate how many threads can be attached to it. One can calculate with different tensions but since only a range can be estimated it is easiest to calculate with 5 g, 10 g, 15 g, 20 g, 25 g, 30 g *etc.* Furthermore, the experiments have demonstrated that attaching very few or very many warp threads to a single loom weight is not advantageous. Weavers have suggested that a range of ≥ 10 warp threads and ≤ 30 warp threads on one loom weight are the limits of what could be considered practical. However, 30 warp threads on one loom weight is, according to weaving experience, a lot and one might consider that a maximum of 20 to 25 threads on one weight would be more likely. If the resulting number of threads per loom weight is less than 10 or more than 30, then this loom weight would not be optimal for this thread tension. As can clearly be seen in Figure 4.5.5, lighter loom weights are more suitable for threads needing little tension (in general, thinner threads) while heavier loom weight are more suitable for threads needing more tension (in general, thicker threads). For example, a loom weight weighing 100 g can be used with threads needing tension between 5 g and 10 g while a loom weight weighing 700 g is more suitable for threads needing 25 to 70 g warp tension (Fig. 4.5.5).

The weaving experiments have demonstrated that it is optimal that the loom weights in a setup hang closely together or slightly spaced. The width of the finished cloth is determined by both the width of the starting borders and the total width of the loom weights in each

Calculated warp thread tension required per thread (g)	5 g	10 g	15 g	20 g	25 g	30 g	35 g	40 g	45 g	50 g	55 g	60 g	65 g	70 g
Loom weight 100 g	20	10	<10	<10	<10	<10	<10	<10	<10	<10	<10	<10	<10	<10
Loom weight 300 g	>30	30	20	15	12	10	<10	<10	<10	<10	<10	<10	<10	<10
Loom weight 500 g	>30	>30	>30	25	20	16.6	14.28	12.5	11.11	10	<10	<10	<10	<10
Loom weight 700 g	>30	>30	>30	>30	28	23.33	20	17.5	15.5	14	12.72	11.66	10.76	10

Fig. 4.5.5. Example of loom weights with different weights and the number of threads, needing different tensions, that is suitable to attach to them.

row. If these widths differ, the width of the fabric will vary and/or the weaving process will become unnecessarily complicated. The total width of the fabric produced would therefore be equal to or slightly less than the total thickness of the loom weights in a row.

The thickness of the loom weights, in combination with the number of warp threads attached to an individual weight and the number of rows of loom weights needed according to the type of weave can therefore be used to calculate the maximum thread count per centimetre in the finished textile (Figs 4.5.6.a and 4.5.6.b).

Thus, both the weight and the thickness of a loom weight govern the suitability of its use in the manufacture of different types of cloth. For example, heavy, thick loom weights would be optimal for the production of a coarse open fabric using thick yarn; in contrast, light, thin loom weights would be preferable when weaving a dense fabric using fine yarn, with many threads per centimetre (see chapter 4.1; Mårtensson *et al.* 2009).

From tool to textile

The experiments clearly demonstrate that by testing different textile tools it is possible to gain information regarding what type of thread could have been produced with a specific spindle whorl and what types of fabrics a loom weight would have been suitable for making.

However, when visualising the finished textiles it is important to take into account that a thread changes when it is wound up from the spindle; as described, a spindle spun wool thread is elastic and to function as a warp thread it has to "set" so that it loses its elasticity. A woven fabric also changes after it is cut down from the loom. During weaving the warp threads are held taut, but when the fabric

Loom weight, weight 100 g, thickness 2 cm		
Warp threads requiring	5 g warp tension	10 g warp tension
Numbers of threads per loom weight	20	10
Numbers of threads per two loom weights (one in front layer one in back layer)	40	20
Warp threads per cm (the total no. per two loom weights divided by the thickness)	20	10

a

Loom weight, weight 500 g, thickness 5 cm		
Warp threads requiring	25 g warp tension	50 g warp tension
Numbers of threads per loom weight	20	10
Numbers of threads per two loom weights (one in front layer one in back layer)	40	20
Warp threads per cm (the total no. per two loom weights divided by the thickness)	8	4

b

is cut down the threads are not stretched any more, with the consequence that the fabric's texture will change. For example, the threads can move a little bit, especially if it is an open fabric (Fig. 4.5.7) and/or the fabric can shrink, especially when washed or fulled (Fig. 4.5.8).

How much the texture can change depends on several different variables. Because of the structure of the wool fibres, a woollen textile will change more than a textile produced with plant fibres. The density (how many threads per centimetre) and weaving technique are other factors that have to be considered when estimating how much the textile will change.

Fig. 4.5.6. Number of threads per cm calculated from a loom weight's weight and thickness (a) loom weight weight 100 g and loom weight thickness 2 cm (b) loom weight weight 500 g and loom weight thickness 5 cm. The calculations are made on a tabby weave with two rows of loom weights.

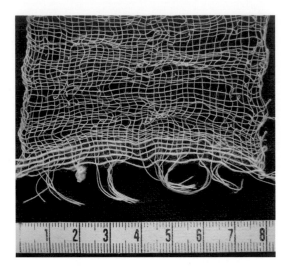

Fig. 4.5.7. An open fabric where the threads have become moveable (photo: CTR).

Fig. 4.5.8. A nettle fabric before and after washing (photo: CTR).

After washing

Before washing

Further perspectives

By analysing more textiles, new knowledge will be obtained on fibres, yarn types, *etc.* This information will provide new data that can be used together with the results of tool analyses.

Furthermore, more experiments with textile tools and different types of fibres and different textile techniques can also contribute to a better understanding of textile production.

However, the results from the TTTC testing clearly demonstrate that it is already possible to interpret the textile production in a given site, region and period if the functional parameters of the spindle whorls and the loom weights are recorded. With these registrations it is possible to give an estimation of the range of textiles manufactured and to discuss the likely nature and scale of textile production in the past.

Acknowledgements

The author kindly thanks Elizabeth Barber and Joanne Cutler for constructive comments and useful advice. The discussion took place in London, April 2010, when we were all stranded because of the Icelandic volcanic eruption.

Notes

1   For wool, linen and cotton.
2   "The definition of cover factor is the ratio of the area covered by the yarn, to the total area covered by the fabric" (Hammarlund 2005, 115).

Bibliography

Andersson, E. (2003) *Tools for Textile Production from Birka and Hedeby: Excavations in the Black Earth 1990–1995.* Stockholm. Birka Project, Riksantikvarieämbetet.

Barber, E. J. W. (1991) *Prehistoric Textiles: The Development of Cloth in the Neolithic and Bronze Ages with Special Reference to the Aegean.* Princeton. Princeton University Press.

Hammarlund, L. (2005) Handicraft knowledge applied to archaeological textiles, *The Nordic Textile Journal,* 87–119.

Mårtensson, L., Nosch, M.-L. and Andersson, E. (2009) Shape of things: understanding a loom weight, *Oxford Journal of Archaeology,* 28 (4), 373–398.

CHAPTER 5.1

Introduction to the CTR database

Eva Andersson Strand and Marie-Louise Nosch

One of the main objectives of the TTTC research programme has been to record textile tools from several types of sites within our target area and date: the Aegean and the Eastern Mediterranean area in the Bronze Age. It has also been important to be able to compare tools in and between different contexts, sites and areas.

The challenge in this research programme has been that the recording of tools and contexts were done by not one person, but by a number of collaborators. In the past, the manner in which textile tools have been recorded has often been specific to a given archaeological site, making comparisons between sites difficult. It has also often been the case that just one or two of a tool's measurable dimensions have been documented; for example, only the height and diameter of loom weights, or only the diameter of spindle whorls, etc. To avoid the problem of different methods of recording, a textile tool database was designed in Microsoft Access 2003, based on earlier textile tool databases (*e.g.* Andersson 1999; Andersson 2003).[1] Forms were created for different types of tools: *loom weights, spindle whorls, needles* (Fig. 5.1.1), *spinning bowls* and *shuttles* (Fig. 5.1.2). In order to record tools of uncertain use that might be textile tools, a form for *other textile tools* was included. Each

form contains data fields that are specific to the function and morphology of a particular tool class, which makes it possible to record each tool type's dimensions; for example, weight and diameter on the spindle whorls and weight and thickness on the loom weights. Data fields such as *site, context, absolute date, relative date etc.* are the same in all forms (Fig. 5.1.3). Finally, a database manual was written in order to facilitate the work of our collaborators.

The original weight of incomplete loom weights, spindle whorls and 'other' textile tools was calculated where possible. In general, it is the *maximum* diameter, height, width and thickness that is recorded.

Textile tools are commonly recorded by type (see chapter 1). In the TTTC research programme it was important that all textile tools were recorded according to the same typology. To achieve this, we chose to use a typology principally based on only basic types of textile tools, and tables of illustrations of these different tool types were included in the database manual (Figs. 5.1.4 and 5.1.5). It should additionally be noted that, even when working with only basic textile tool shapes, some degree of subjectivity will always remain in the classification of textile tool assemblages. There is therefore inevitably some overlap between

Individual data fields for loom weights	Individual data fields for spindle whorls	Individual data fields for needles
Type	Type	Maximum length (mm)
Weight (g)	Weight (g)	Maximum thickness (mm)
Weight if not complete (g)	Weight if not complete (g)	Thickness at mid-shaft (mm)
Calculated weight (g)	Calculated weight (g)	Shape of head
Maximum height/diameter (mm)	Maximum diameter (mm)	Eye size (mm)
Maximum thickness (mm)	Maximum height (mm)	
Maximum width (mm)	Maximum hole diameter (mm)	
Number of holes	Hole shape	
Position of hole(s)	Surface treatment	
Maximum hole diameter range (mm)		
Groove		
Surface treatment		
Use wear		
Use wear description		

Fig. 5.1.1. Individual data fields for loom weights, spindle whorls and needles, used for recording the textile tools for all the sites.

Individual data fields for other textile tools	Individual data fields for spinning bowls	Individual data fields for shuttles
Weight (g)	Material	Maximum length (mm)
Weight if not complete (g)	Rim diameter (mm)	Minimum length (mm)
Calculated weight (g)	Base diameter (mm)	Maximum width
Maximum length (mm)	Maximum thickness (mm)	Minimum width
Minimum length (mm)	Maximum height (mm)	Maximum thickness (mm)
Maximum thickness (mm)	Number of handles	Opening
Minimum thickness (mm)	Thickness of handles	
Maximum diameter (mm)		
Minimum diameter (mm)		
Maximum height (mm)		
Minimum height (mm)		

Fig. 5.1.2. Individual data fields for "other" textile tools, spinning bowls and shuttles, used for recording the textile tools for all the sites.

Common data fields in all forms		
Find ID		Find category
Context ID		Number
Photo ID		Preservation status
Pictures		Material
Site		Material analysis
Region		Material description
Site type	settlement, farmhouse, villa, palace, citadel, necropolis, other	Object description
Context type	workshop, household, tomb, other	Production quality
Context description		Remarks
Context date: absolute		Comments
Context date: relative		Bibliography
Object date		Storage place

Fig. 5.1.3. Common data fields in all forms in the database.

	discoid rounded (width and height similar)		hemispherical		crescent
	discoid elliptical (height considerably larger than width)		cylindrical: standard (axis length similar to width)		biconical
	discoid tabulated		long (axis length considerably larger than width)		pyramidal
	semi-discoid		short (axis length considerably shorter than width)		pyramidal truncated
	flat trapezoidal		conical		torus
	flat rectangular		conical truncated		cube
	spool				spherical rounded (regular sphere) spherical ovoid (axis length larger than width)

Fig. 5.1.4. Loom weight types (drawings after Evely 2000; Dabney 1996; Stærmose Nielsen 1999; Barber 1991).

certain shape categories; for example, between torus and cylindrical short loom weights. However, the accompanying description in the database and photograph/drawing of a given tool generally make it possible to identify such discrepancies.

Once the textile tools from the sites included in the programme had been recorded, the individual databases were sent to CTR and all the data were processed as part of the TTTC research programme. Material from 24 sites was recorded by the collaborators (Fig. 5.1.6). In order to assess how published textile tools could be included in the overall discussion, material from another nine sites was recorded in the database from publications.

A total of 8725 textile tools, that is, 3896 loom weights, 3994 spindle whorls, 124 needles, 21 shuttles, 17 spinning bowls and 673 'other' textile tools (Fig. 5.1.7) were registered in the database. The loom weights and the

spindle whorls constitute the two major classes of objects.

Of the 3896 loom weights, 1643 are complete, 624 have small fragments missing, while the remaining 1629 are incomplete. In the spindle whorl category, 2353 of the total 3994 spindle whorls are completely preserved, 692 whorls have small fragments missing and the remaining 949 are incomplete (Fig. 5.1.8).

Altogether, 2263 of the total number of loom weights have a complete/estimated weight recorded. Of these, 2031 also have a recorded preserved thickness (Fig. 5.1.9).

For the calculations of how a given loom weight would function in various loom setups, it is only possible to work with the loom weights that have both a weight and thickness recorded. In the majority of cases, these make up only a small proportion of the total number of tools from a context, site or region (Fig. 5.1.10). It has been important to take this into account

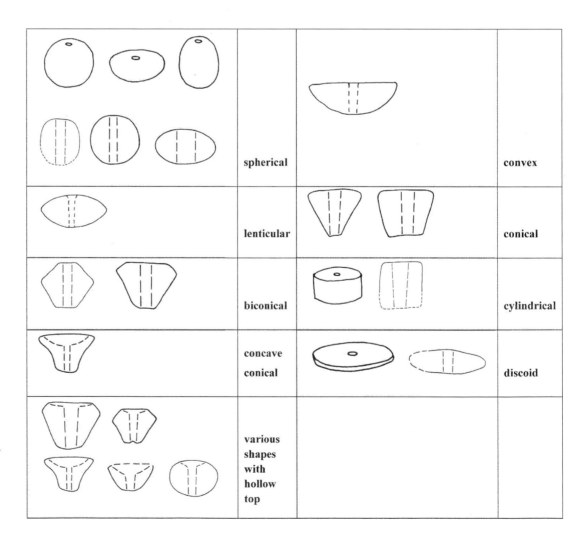

Fig. 5.1.5. Spindle whorl types (drawings after Beck 1928; Carington Smith 1992 and Gleba 2008).

Northern Greece	Mainland Greece	Crete	Aegean Islands	Western Anatolia	Central and Eastern Anatolia	Cyprus
Sitagroi	Tiryns	Khania	**Ayia Irini**	Troia	**Karahüyük**	Apliki
Archontiko	Midea	Ayia Triada	Akrotiri	Miletos	Arslantepe	Kition
	Asine	Phaistos			Beycesultan	
	Berbati	**Pseira**			Demircihüyük	
	Dendra	**Kommos**				
	Thebes	Mochlos				
	Mycenae	Malia				
	Nichoria	**Myrtos**				
		Knossos				

Fig. 5.1.6. The sites included in the research programme. The sites from which published materials were recorded are in boldface.

when calculating the weight range of the loom weights from each site/context. The weight range of the incomplete tools has therefore also been assessed in order to identify any object with a partial weight that indicates that its weight, if complete, would fall outside the weight range of the tools with complete/estimated weights.

For the calculations of what types of thread a given spindle whorl would be suitable for spinning, it is necessary to work with the spindle whorls which have a recorded weight and diameter. Of the 3994 spindle whorls registered in the database, 2819 spindle whorls (71%) have both weight and diameter recorded (Fig. 5.1.11). It should be noted that the reason that there are no spindle whorls with recorded weight and diameter from, for example, the Aegean islands, is not the lack of whorls, but a lack of recorded necessary data (Fig. 5.1.12).

For sites recorded by the collaborators, a technical textile tool report was written based solely on the information gathered from the textile tools, and giving the results of the analyses of the tools' dimensions, material and find contexts. In the processing of the data, all functional parameters were assessed, *i.e.* the parameters that affect textile production (based on the results of the experiments and on existing knowledge). The results for different periods and for different contexts within the site were also compared. Finally, a short summary was included on the interpretation of the textile production at the specific site based on the recordings, on the analyses of the material in the database, and on the site contexts.

Although tools from a large number of Bronze Age sites in the Aegean and Eastern

Textile Tools	Number
Loom weights	3896
Spindle whorls	3994
Needles	124
Other textile tools	673
Shuttles	21
Spinning bowls	17
Total	**8725**

Fig. 5.1.7. Number and type of textile tools. NB the number and type of tools are the tools recorded in the database. In the processing of the data, some tools were excluded as textile tools and some spindle whorls were reclassified as loom weights and vice versa.

Mediterranean have been included in the TTTC programme, it has of course not been possible to include data for every site from which textile tools have been recovered in this area. The sites analysed cover a wide time span and geographical area, with some areas/periods within the Bronze Age being much better represented in the database than others. Therefore, the results of the analyses cannot provide a wholly representative insight into textile production in this region during the Bronze Age.

Furthermore, in many cases it has not been possible to record all the tools from a site. For example, not all tools from Tiryns and Troia are included in the database. This makes it impossible to assess how representative the tools are from a given site, since the tools not recorded could change the overall conclusions.

Many of the tools have been recovered from mixed contexts or do not have a secure date. This has considerably reduced the number of tools which it has been possible to work with in terms of assessing textile production during a particular period or within a particular building at a specific site.

Fig. 5.1.8. Number of tools and preservation status.

	Loom weights	Spindle whorls
Complete	1643	2353
Small fragments missing	624	692
Rest	1629	949
Total	**3896**	**3994**

Fig. 5.1.9. Number of loom weights with a complete or estimated weight, and the number that also has a preserved thickness.

	Weight	Weight and thickness
Loom weights	2263	2031

Fig. 5.1.10. Loom weights with recorded weights and thicknesses, by region.

	Loom weights
Mainland Greece	107
Northern Greece	44
Aegean Islands	23
Crete	1136
Cyprus	97
Western Anatolia	404
Central and Eastern Anatolia	177
Levant	43
Total	**2031**

Fig. 5.1.11. Number of spindle whorls with a complete or estimated weight, and the number that also has a preserved diameter.

	Weight	Weight and diameter
Spindle whorls	2849	2819

Fig. 5.1.12. Spindle whorls with recorded weight and diameter, by region.

	Spindle whorls
Mainland Greece	578
Northern Greece	101
Aegean Islands	0
Crete	419
Cyprus	10
Western Anatolia	1548
Central and Eastern Anatolia	73
Levant	90
Total	**2819**

However, these problems are not related to the database, they are rather related to the nature of the material itself. The database greatly facilitates the sorting of the information it contains; for example, to pick out a particular tool type, context and time period within a given site. It also makes it easy to compare different time periods within a particular

building or given site as a whole. Even if the material cannot be taken as representative for the Aegean and Eastern Mediterranean Bronze Age, the tools recorded have provided a lot of new information on textile production. The strength of this research is that one can give an interpretation of how every single tool (with all functional dimensions recorded) could have functioned, and what type of production it was best suited for. Furthermore, in those cases where the tools are from good contexts, it is possible to discuss the textile production in this given context.

Therefore, in this publication we have focused on the evidence for the nature of textile production at given sites. The potential in this is that, as new material becomes available, it will be possible to integrate this with the existing results in order to build a much broader picture of Bronze Age textile production in the Aegean and Eastern Mediterranean. Whilst we cannot exclude the possibility that other types of textiles were also produced, the detailed information that the individual tools from the various sites can provide on textile production opens up new perspectives on what types of textiles *were* produced in this region during this period. This new information now makes it possible to include textile production in wider discussions concerning Bronze Age societies.

Note

1 We thank Birgitta Piltz Williams, Margarita Gleba, Marta Guzowska, Anne Batzer, Joanne Cutler and Linda Olofsson (former Mårtensson) for the collaborative work in the creation of the CTR database.

Bibliography

Andersson, E. (1999) *The Common Thread: Textile Production During the Late Iron Age–Viking Age.* Lund. Institute of Archaeology, University of Lund.

Andersson, E. (2003) *Tools for Textile Production from Birka and Hedeby: Excavations in the Black Earth 1990–1995*, Stockholm. Birka Project for Riksantikvarieämbetet.

Barber, E. J. W. (1991) *Prehistoric Textiles: The Development of Cloth in the Neolithic and Bronze Ages with Special Reference to the Aegean.* Princeton. Princeton University Press.

Beck, H. (1928) *Classification and Nomenclature of Beads and Pendants, Communicated to the Society of Antiquaries.* Oxford. John Johnson.

Carington Smith, J. (1992) Spinning and weaving equipment, in Macdonald, W. A. and Wilkie, N. C. (eds), *Excavations at Nichoriain in Southwestern Greece.*

2. The Bronze Age Occupation, 674–711. Minneapolis. University of Minnesota Press.

Dabney, M. K. (1996) Ceramic loomweights and spindle whorls, in Shaw, J. W. and Shaw, M. C. (eds), *Kommos I. The Kommos Region and Houses of the Minoan Town. Part 2. The Minoan Hilltop and Hilside Houses*, 244–262. Princeton. Princeton University Press.

Evely, D. (2000) *Minoan Crafts: Tools and Techniques. An Introduction*. Göteborg. Paul Åström.

Gleba, M. (2008) *Textile Production in Pre-Roman Italy*. Ancient Textiles Series 4. Oxford. Oxbow Books.

Stærmose Nielsen, K.-H. (1999) *Kirkes væv: opstadsvævens historie og nutidige brug*. Lejre. Historisk-Arkæologisk Forsøgscenter.

CHAPTER 5.2

Mathematical analysis of the spindle whorl and loom weight data in the CTR database

Richard Firth

Chapter 5.1 presented an introduction to the CTR database of textile tools and included some preliminary discussion about how the data can be used. The aim of this chapter is to develop that discussion further, concentrating primarily on the technical aspects of the textile tools.

Since the database includes all of the textile tool data from particular, specified areas of archaeological sites, it enables scholars to use these to make conventional archaeological analyses. These bring together a description of all the textile tool data from a part of an archaeological site and then make an attempt to describe what sort of fabrics these tools could have been used to manufacture and how those tools fit into the broader archaeological context. Good examples of this are Carington Smith's discussion of the textile tools from Nichoria (Carington Smith 1992) and Friend's discussion of the loom weights of Tell Taannek (Friend 1998).

However, in this work it is possible to take this a step further by using the results of the experiments described in chapter 4 and the type of methods outlined by Mårtensson *et al.* (Mårtensson *et al.* 2009). Thus, the analysis is not reliant on qualitative statements, that light whorls and loom weights imply light fabrics and heavy whorls and weights imply heavy fabrics. Instead it is possible to give a quantitative analysis that is specific to the textile tools found at each site. Chapter 6 gives presentations of the Bronze Age textile tools found at the sites of Malia, Sitagroi, Thebes, Tiryns and Troia amongst others.

It is important to re-emphasise the point made in the last section on the representivity of the data. It is not being claimed that the data are representative of the regions under discussion or even, necessarily of the individual sites. Nevertheless, it would be a missed opportunity if the large amount of data in the CTR database were brought together but only analysed on a site-by-site basis. The objective of this chapter is to use the data in the CTR database to present a study of the technological aspects of the textile tools. This includes a presentation of the development of a set of mathematical methods together with the results of analyses of the recorded tools in the database. This is rendered possible because care was taken to ensure that the data from different archaeological sites were recorded in the same way within the CTR database wherever possible. Thus it is possible to pool the data and consider large groups of textile tools of the same type even though these are from different sites.

It is the hope, that by presenting these mathematical analyses, it is possible to draw conclusions that would otherwise be obscured within smaller data samples and also that these methods of analysis are useful and could be adopted within future studies.

In the following sections, mathematical analyses for both spindle whorls and loom weights will be presented. It is convenient to begin by considering spindle whorls. As might be expected, the functional analysis of spindle whorls is more straightforward than that for loom weights since the whorl is simply used to store angular momentum in the spindle whereas the loom weight is a part of the more technologically complex warp-weighted loom.

Spindle whorls

This section has two objectives. The first is to discuss briefly some issues arising from consideration of the physics of spindle whorls[1] and to give some guidance to eliminate items that would probably not have acted as spindle whorls. The second objective is to provide an overall description of the contents of the CTR database of spindle whorls.

Physics of spindle whorls
Moments of inertia
Essentially spindle whorls are mini flywheels that are set on a spindle shaft to form a spindle, therefore, scientists have sometimes chosen to characterise them according to their moments of inertia.[2]

As examples, the moments of inertia of a few solid bodies can be quoted:

sphere and ellipsoid	$0.1 \, mD^2$
cylinder	$0.125 \, mD^2$
cone	$0.075 \, mD^2$

where m is the mass (which is usually referred to as weight) and D is diameter of the body.[3]

However, it is clear, even from these formulae, that two bodies of the same type of shape could have the same moment of inertia but very different weights and diameters. This is particularly true for cones, cylinders and ellipsoids since the moment of inertia is independent of the height of a solid body. Thus, by judicious choice of diameters and material densities, it would be possible to find a flywheel with the same moment of inertia as a one-metre long cylinder but, whereas the flywheel might be an excellent spindle whorl, the 1 metre long cylinder would be useless. For this reason, it is not sufficient to describe spindle whorls in terms of moment of inertia alone.[4]

It could be suggested that spindle whorls should be described in terms of, say, moment of inertia and weight. However, since the concept of moment of inertia is not generally familiar to all, it is simpler to describe spindle whorls in terms of weight and diameter.

It is worth considering briefly whether cylindrical spindle whorls perform better than conical, ellipsoidal or spherical spindle whorls because they have a higher moment of inertia for the same weight and diameter. In practical terms, these differences are minor and a spinner would readily be able to apply a slightly larger rotational velocity to those spindles with the lower moments of inertia to compensate and, in this way, achieve the same level of rotational energy. It should not be forgotten that the moment of inertia of a spindle arises not only from the whorl and its shaft but also from the spun yarn that is wound around the spindle. Clearly the amount of spun yarn varies as the spinning process proceeds and the weight of this yarn can become comparable with the weight of the spindle whorl. Therefore, the moment of inertia is a variable during the spinning process and the spinner has to compensate for this. Thus, although this is a discussion about the physics of spindle whorls, the skill of the spinner should not be underestimated.

Calculating weight from density
In cases where measurements of dimensions are available but not of weight, it is has been suggested that it is possible to give a reasonably accurate estimate of the weight using a density, ρ, obtained from reference tables (Verhecken 2010). Thus, for example, for a solid sphere,

$$weight = \rho \, \pi \, D^3 / 6$$

However, there are three sources of error in this calculation and the final result would generally be too unreliable to be useful.

- The first source of error is the measurements themselves. The weight of sphere is a function of the third power of diameter and so any error in the measurement of diameter is approximately magnified threefold.

- The second source of error is in the shape. Although an excavated spindle whorl might approximate to a simple geometrical shape, it is unlikely to be a perfect mathematical shape and any discrepancy will generate an error in the estimate of a weight calculated from a density.

- The third source of error is in the density obtained from reference tables. For example, if the spindle whorl is made from clay, the density of clay can vary over a range depending on its composition and the extent that it has been fired.

For these reasons, the present study relies on the measured weights of spindle whorls and does not use calculated values based on densities.

It is worth adding that the calculation of moments of inertia based on densities is even more prone to error because, for example, the moment of inertia of a sphere is proportional to the fifth power of its diameter and so any error in the diameter is approximately magnified fivefold. In addition, there remain the latter two sources of error listed above.[5]

Spindle shafts
Spindle whorls were each set on a shaft to form a spindle, however, the spindle shafts are rarely preserved.

The spindle shaft would have contributed to the moment of inertia of the spindle, although for the practical operation of the spindle, the contribution of the shaft would have been much smaller than that of the spindle whorl.[6] However, although the spindle shafts are not preserved, it can be argued, in general terms, that a light spindle whorl would have had a shorter lighter shaft and a heavier whorl would have required a longer heavier shaft.[7]

It is clear that the operation of the spindle requires that the spindle whorl does not wobble on the shaft because that would cause irregularity in the spinning of the spindle. This simple statement has three consequences. First, the hole in a spindle whorl should have a uniform diameter or be cone-shaped. Holes that have been roughly drilled are often double

cone-shaped (if drilled from two sides) and items with double cone-shaped holes are unlikely to have been used as spindle whorls.[8] Second, the hole in a spindle whorl should be approximately coincident with the axis of symmetry of the whorl. It follows that items with holes that are "off-centre" are unlikely to have been spindle whorls. Third, the diameter of the spindle shaft would have been equal to the diameter of the hole in the spindle whorl. It is worth extending the latter point by noting that, from a practical view point, the most convenient type of spindle shaft would have a taper so that the spindle whorl could be fitted onto the shaft at precisely the position where its diameter was equal to the diameter of the shaft.

In practice, numerous items that have holes that are double conical or off-centre or oblique are categorised by archaeologists as spindle whorls. However, since they would not function well as spindle whorls, such items will not be considered further in this section.[9]

In particular, it is demonstrated in chapter 7, that many of the pierced sherds that were recorded as possible spindle whorls could not have not have efficiently been used in that way. The discussion below includes consideration about whether these items could have been loom weights.

The size of hole in a spindle whorl
The diameters of the holes of the whorls listed in the CTR database vary from 1–18 mm. However, Barber states that "one would need excellent reason to assign an object to the category of [spindle] whorl rather than bead if its hole size fell outside the range of 3 to 10 mm in diameter" (Barber 1991, 52). This obviously leads to the question whether the 40 items in the database with hole diameters of <3 mm and the 80 items with hole diameters of 11–18 mm are actually spindle whorls. The whorls with a hole size of <3 mm have diameters ranging from 18–30 mm. These whorls could conceivably be large beads and will be excluded on this basis. The whorls with hole diameters of 11–18 mm are at the heavier end of the range and the larger hole size does not seem disproportionate and therefore these have been retained within the analysis that follows.[10]

CTR database of spindle whorls

The contents of the CTR database can now be examined in more detail. This process begins by considering a standard plot of 948 clay spindle whorls, plotting diameter *vs.* weight (Fig. 5.2.1).[11]

There are a number of points that are immediately evident from Fig. 5.2.1. The distribution of spindle whorls on this scatter plot shows a clear pattern. The majority of clay spindle whorls weigh less than 60 g and have a maximum diameter less than 50 mm. Furthermore, there is a concentration of whorls that are less than 30–40 g with a maximum diameter less than 35 mm. There are 473 stone spindle whorls in the database. These predominantly weigh less than 30 g with a maximum diameter less than 35 g and their distribution coincides with that for clay whorls.

These points become clearer in Figure 5.2.2, which is a plot of the number of whorls grouped

Fig. 5.2.1. Scatter plot of clay spindle whorl data (maximum diameter vs. weight).

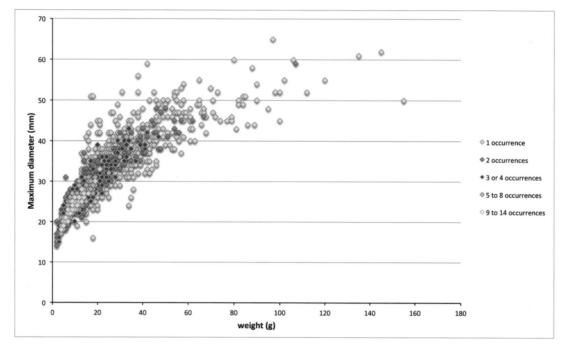

Fig. 5.2.2. Distribution of spindle whorls by weight.

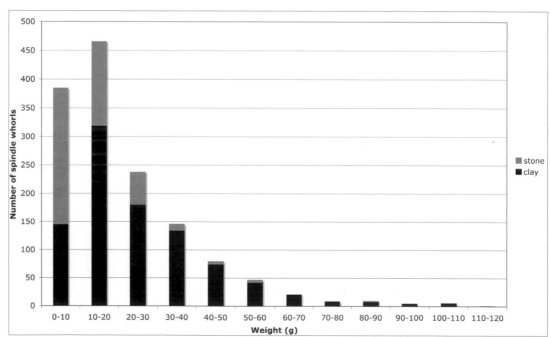

together in bins according to their weight. The distribution shown in these figures clearly reflects the usage of these spindle whorls.[12]

From spindle whorl to thread
In principle, these spindle whorl data could be used to estimate the relative production of threads of different characteristics, whether categorised by thickness or weight per unit length. However, there are difficulties that prevent this being done. These are considered in some detail in chapter 4.5. In essence, firstly, there is a marked variability in the characteristics of the thread produced by a spinner within the same length of yarn and, secondly, the spinner can influence these characteristics. In principle, it should be possible to determine the statistical variations of these characteristics and that would allow a determination of the most likely thread that could be produced from the spindle whorls. However, this would require a great deal of experimentation and is beyond the scope of the current work.

Shape of spindle whorls
In the CTR database, of 947 complete (or almost complete) clay spindle whorls, the three most frequent shapes are biconical (39%), cylindrical (16%) and conical (13%). However, 36% of these spindle whorls are from Troia, and, considering spindle whorls from this location alone gives a different pattern of results: biconical (61%), cylindrical (<1%) and conical (6%). So that the results for the sites in the database excluding Troia are: biconical (27%), cylindrical (25%) and conical (17%). Thus, the evidence shows that there can be marked variations in the frequency of shapes from site to site. However, since clay whorls can readily be manufactured in a range of shapes, it is not surprising that the preferred shape can vary with location.

The corresponding analysis of the 470 stone spindle whorls shows a marked preference for conical whorls (63%), with only 10 of these from Troia.

As already noted in the discussion on moments of inertia, the shape of a whorl has minimal implications for its performance in the hands of an experienced spinner. Therefore, within the range given above, the shape would seem to be mainly a matter of convenience in manufacture and convention rather than something that was specified by practical considerations of the textile worker.

Other parameters
Figs. 5.2.3 and 5.2.4 show the distribution of spindle whorl diameters and hole diameters for the complete (or almost complete) spindle whorls.

Each of these distributions shows conformity to a simple pattern. Thus, although the analysis began with many hundreds of spindle whorls

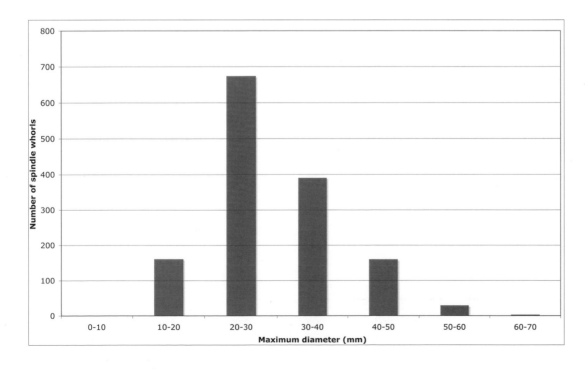

Fig. 5.2.3. Distribution of spindle whorl diameters (1417 data points).

Fig. 5.2.4. Distribution of hole diameters of spindle whorls (1417 data points).

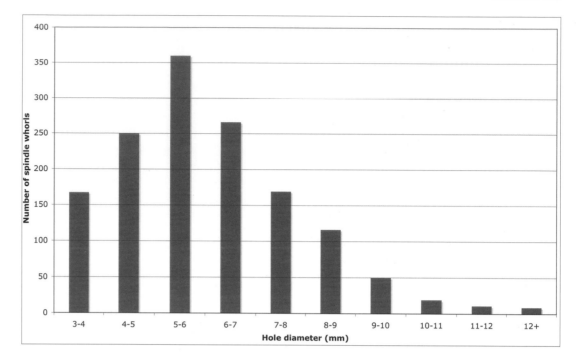

of numerous types from over thirty different sites, there is an underlying broad specification that almost certainly arises primarily from the functional requirements of spindle whorls.

The archaeologists participating in the TTTC programme were asked to assess the production quality of the whorls. Of the 1114 whorls that were categorized in this way, the production quality of 10% were judged to be excellent, 50% good, 33% medium and 7% poor.

There may be some variability here in the way that whorls were classified, for example, as "excellent" or "good". However, the general point is that, in the majority of cases, the production quality is better than average.

Loom weights

It has already been noted that the process of weaving on a warp-weighted loom is technologically more complex than the process of spinning. Thus it is inevitable that, if a full treatment of loom weights is given, their description will be longer and more detailed than was given for spindle whorls. Therefore, the next paragraph sets out the structure of the sections that follow.

On the basis of the CTR experiments, described in chapter 4, it is possible to derive a mathematical approach to the analysis of loom weights. Rather than spread them

through the text, it is convenient to bring most of these mathematical methods together into one section. Then, armed with these analytical methods, the sections that follow consider, firstly, the database of loom weights as a whole, and secondly give an analysis of the data for each type of loom weight separately. Finally, there is consideration of the analysis techniques that could be used for groups of weights found together in good contexts.

Mathematics of weaving
Warp thread tension
The primary purpose of the loom weights in a warp-weighted loom is to provide tension to the warp threads. The principles determining the required warp thread tension can be simply stated. The tension has to be sufficiently great that the threads are taut but not so great that the threads become stretched and start to break.

The actual tension that should be used for the most efficient weaving of textiles is essentially an empirical observation arising from the experience of weavers (see chapter 4.5). Clearly different tensions are needed for different thread qualities. For example, a woollen thread with a thickness of 0.1 mm might need a tension of, say, 5 g, whilst a woollen thread that is 1.4 mm thick might need a tension of 70 g. However, it is not possible to assert, for example, that all 0.1 mm threads required a tension of 5 g.

There are two reasons for this. Firstly, some threads are harder spun than others and so could withstand more tension. Secondly, there is a marked variability in the thickness of hand-spun thread, and the maximum tension that the thread can withstand is determined by its minimum thickness and not the average. There are further points to note. In general, woollen threads have a "fuzziness" which enhances their diameter, but does not contribute to their strength, whereas linen threads do not have this intrinsic "fuzziness". It would be expected that plying two woollen threads would not double the thickness of a single thread because of this "fuzziness". For these reasons, it is not possible to draw a simple correspondence between the thickness of a hand-spun thread and the amount of tension that it would require in a weaving loom.

Openness of textiles

An analogous point can be made when calculating how much space is needed between the warp threads to allow for the weft threads.

In theory, the maximum number of warp threads per centimetre for threads of different thickness can be estimated for a tabby weave. Thus, if the average thickness of the warp thread is 0.1 mm, the maximum number of threads per centimetre is 100, and so on. However, this makes no allowance for the weft threads and the amount of space these require varies according to weaving techniques. In a balanced tabby, every second thread is a weft thread; therefore, at first sight, if the same type of thread is used for the warp and weft, it follows that 50% of the space should be needed for the weft. Therefore, in a 1 cm wide sample, the combined width of the warp threads is 0.5 cm. However, amongst the specimens identified by Spantidaki and Moulhérat (2012),[13] there are a number of examples where the diameter of the thread multiplied by the number of threads per centimetre exceeds 0.5 cm. The most likely explanation for this is that the threads are compressed and their diameters reduced at the points of contact between the warp and weft threads so that the space required for weft threads is less than 50% and, therefore, thread counts can be higher than implied by the initial estimate suggested above.

Calculating the openness of fabrics is more straightforward. Here, it is necessary to be specific about the nature of both the warp and the weft threads and the number of warp and weft threads per centimetre. Let the warp thread have an average thickness of t_1 mm and with n_1 warp threads per centimetre; let the weft thread have an average thickness of t_2 mm with n_2 weft threads per centimetre. Then the percentage openness is given by,[14]

$$\{1 - [(n_1 \times t_1)/10 + (n_2 \times t_2)/10 - (n_1 \times n_2) \times (t_1 \times t_2)/100]\} \times 100$$

where $(n_1 \times t_1)/10 + (n_2 \times t_2)/10 \leq 1$ for tabby; and $(n_1 \times t_1)/10 \leq 1$ and $(n_2 \times t_2)/10 \leq 1$ for 2/2 twill (following the above discussion on the upper limit for the possible number of threads per centimetre).

The next stage is to show what percentage openness means in practical terms.

Figure 5.2.5A shows a sample made in a CTR experiment. It has five warp threads per centimetre and eight weft threads per centimetre. It was woven with 10 g tension and so the thread diameter is ~0.2 mm. Thus the calculated percentage openness is ~76%.

The sample shown in Fig. 5.2.5B has 6.1 warp threads per centimetre and 7.4 weft threads per centimetre. It was woven with 18 g tension and

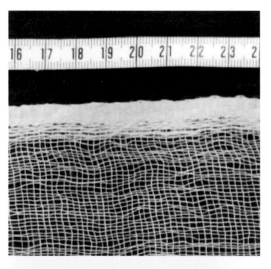

Fig. 5.2.5A Sample 1 from CTR weaving experiments.

5 cm warp

Fig. 5.2.5B Sample 2 from CTR weaving experiments

so the thread diameter is ~0.36 mm. Thus the calculated percentage openness is ~57%.

A third sample is shown in Fig. 5.2.6. It has 5.8 warp threads per centimetre and 14.8 weft threads per centimetre. It was woven with 10 g tension and so the warp thread diameter is ~0.2 mm. The weft thread diameter is larger and has been estimated as ~0.35 mm. Thus the calculated percentage openness is ~43%.

Although there may be some uses for very open fabrics, primarily as luxury items, it is evident that, in practical terms, textiles are most useful if they have a low level of openness.

It is possible for the weaver to reduce the openness by packing more threads into the weft or by using thicker weft threads. Spantidaki and Moulhérat (2012) survey the evidence for textile remains found in Greece. For the Bronze Age, the number of samples is limited but they usually show balanced tabbies. However, there is an example of a weft-faced tabby from Akrotiri with a weft thread count up to three times greater than the warp thread count. There is also an example of a "sack" from Akrotiri where the warp and weft thread counts were similar but the weft thread diameter was several times greater than the warp thread diameter.

Finally in this section, it should be noted that the fulling of woven woollen fabrics deliberately shrinks the cloth to reduce the level of openness.

The number of loom weights in a set
The next point to consider is the practical number of loom weights in a set. It is readily

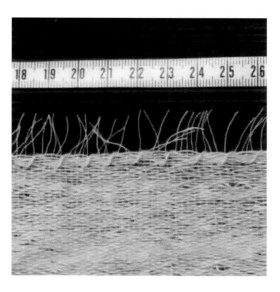

Fig. 5.2.6. Sample 3 from CTR weaving experiments.

possible to do calculations assuming that there were several hundred loom weights used for a loom weight setup. However, common sense dictates that this would be impractical.

In modern times, for Scandinavian warp-weighted looms, Hoffman found a range of 13 to 59 loom weights in a set, with most falling in the range 20 to 30 (Hoffmann 1974, 24, 57). Barber (1991, 104) notes that, on the basis of archaeological evidence from looms set up at the time of destruction, the sets of loom weights range from 6 to 30, with occasional numbers that are higher (Barber 1991, 104, *i.e.* 44 at Troia and 80 at Hradčany).[15] However, in experiments at CTR it has been shown that it is readily possible to operate a warp-weighted loom with 60 loom weights to weave a 2/2 twill using four rows of loom weights (see chapter 4.3).

The number of loom weights required for a loom setup can be calculated as follows:

No. of LWs =
$$\frac{(\text{width of textile}) \times (\text{no. of rows of LWs})}{(\text{thickness of LW})}$$
(where LW is an abbreviation for loom weight).

Thus, when weaving a metre width of textile using a given type of loom weight, then the number of loom weights is proportional to the number of rows of weights required.

If the thickness of the loom weights are relatively small compared to the width of the textile, then this can lead to a requirement for a very large number of loom weights, particularly for 3 or 4 row twill weaves. In these circumstances, it might be judged that an expert weaver would choose a different kind of loom weight rather than try to proceed with an excessive number of thin weights. Whilst, theoretically, there is no limit to the number of loom weights in a loom setup, it may be considered that a number of 100 or 150 seems unreasonably large because it would make the setting up of the loom impractical.

Fig. 5.2.7 illustrates this question, showing the numbers of weights required to weave a textile one metre wide using loom weights with a range of different thicknesses.

Loom setups for 1-row tabby or 2-row twills
In chapter 4.4, it was suggested that in some loom setups, weights would have been used to provide tension to the warp threads from two rows. In this way, it would have been possible to weave 1-row tabby or 2-row twills. The

advantage of this is that it would have reduced the number of loom weights. However, it would not have reduced the number of sets of threads to be tied to weights and would have involved the added complexity of attaching threads from both rows to the same weight, so it is not immediately obvious that this type of arrangement would be very beneficial. Nevertheless, since this type of loom setup was evidently used, it will be considered further.

A good example of a loom weight designed to provide tension to two rows of threads is the crescent-shaped loom weight (see chapter 4.4). If a group of threads from the front row is tied to one vertex of the crescent and similarly threads from the back row are tied to the other vertex, then the loom weight is clearly giving tension to threads from both rows. When the sheds are changed, the movement of warp threads is significant, however, for the crescent-shaped loom weight this movement is less than the *separation of the suspension points* on the weight. Thus, the crescent-shaped loom weight continues to give tension to both sets of threads throughout shed changes and the effect of the shed change is simply to cause the loom weight to have a rocking motion.

This latter point is very important. If the movement of the warp threads during shed changes were greater than the separation of suspension points then the weight of the loom weight would only be supported by one set of threads, with no tension in the other set of threads, so this arrangement simply would not work. In order to ensure that this does not happen then the separation of suspension points should be several centimetres for tabbies, with a greater allowance for twills where the movement of threads during shed changes would be larger.

It is tempting to suggest that 2-holed loom weights were intended to be used to weave 1-row tabby (or 2-row twills) but, in many cases, the separation between the two holes is too small, compared to the movement required for the warp threads during shed change, and so could not be used in this way.

The mathematics of weaving on a warp-weighted loom
In chapter 4.1, it was shown that the width of the cloth was determined both by the width of the heading band and the total width of the loom weights in each row (or shed). If these

Thickness	Number of rows of weights			
	1 row	2 rows	3 rows	4 rows
80 mm	~12	25	~37	50
40 mm	25	50	75	100
20 mm	50	100	150	200
10 mm	100	200	300	400

Fig. 5.2.7. Numbers of loom weights required to weave a 1 m wide textile.

widths differ then the width of the cloth will vary along its length, which is generally not desirable. Therefore, it is reasonable to assume that the sum of the thicknesses of the loom weights in each row is approximately equal to the width of the cloth.[16]

The weight of the loom weight is naturally also important because the tension that it applies to the thread must be sufficient to cause the thread to be taut but not so great that the threads become stretched and start to break.

Thus the key parameters of a loom weight are its thickness and weight. Later in this chapter, practical examples will be considered where there are significant variations between loom weights in the same set. However, in the first instance, the optimal performance of the warp weighted loom will be considered, where the loom weights in a set are effectively identical.

It is often possible for a wide range of different types of textile to be woven using any particular set of such loom weights. In principle these can range from

- Textiles made from thin threads or thick threads;
- Textiles that are open with a relatively small number of threads per centimetre to textiles where the threads are densely packed;
- Textiles that are plain with an equal number of warp and weft threads or textiles that are weft-faced (with a greater number of weft threads than warp threads) or perhaps less likely, textiles that are warp-faced (with a greater number of warp threads than weft threads);
- Tabby textiles made with a setup using two rows of loom weights or twills using three or four rows of loom weights.

At first sight, this can seem to be an overwhelming range. However, it is possible to describe the range of textiles that can be produced using each type of loom weight more precisely by considering the mathematics of weaving using a warp-weighted loom.

There are two basic equations. Firstly,

$$\text{warp thread tension} = \frac{(\text{weight of LW})}{(\text{no. of warp threads per LW})} \quad (1)$$

i.e. if more threads are attached to a loom weight then the tension on each thread is reduced.

It is easier to demonstrate the second equation if it is derived by using two intervening steps.

$$\text{warp threads per cm in each row of weights} = \frac{(\text{no. of warp threads per row})}{(\text{width of textile})}$$

(where the width of the textile is measured in centimetres).

If the loom weights are identical, then the number of warp threads in each row is equal to the number of warp threads on each loom weight, multiplied by the number of loom weights in each row. Further, as already noted, the width of the cloth is equal to the width of a loom weight multiplied by the number of loom weights in each row. If these are substituted into the equation and the numerator and denominator are divided by the number of loom weights in each row then,

$$\text{warp threads per cm in each row of wts} = \frac{(\text{no. of warp threads per LW})}{(\text{thickness of LW})}$$

Now, considering the number of warp threads per centimetre in the loom as a whole (rather than just one particular row),

$$\text{warp threads per cm} = \frac{(\text{no. of threads per LW}) \times (\text{no. of rows of LWs})}{(\text{thickness of LW})} \quad (2)$$

The next stage is to consider the limitations of what is practical. For example, it is not practical to have an extremely small or an extremely large number of threads attached to each loom weight because these would make the process of weaving more difficult. For the present, these limits will be expressed as n_{min} and n_{max}, *i.e.*

$$n_{min} \leq (\text{no. of warp threads per LW}) \leq n_{max} \quad (3)$$

There are also practical limits on the number of threads per centimetre. If the number of threads is too few then the textile will be too open and if the number is too great then the textile is too dense. There is an additional problem associated with weaving with wool because if the threads are too close they catch on each other and make weaving more difficult. These limits will be expressed as N_{min} and N_{max}.

$$N_{min} \leq (\text{warp threads per centimetre}) \leq N_{max} \quad (4)$$

Thus now there are two equations (Eqns. 1 and 2) and a set of constraints (Eqns. 3 and 4) on the permitted range of two of the parameters. The most straightforward way to proceed is to determine how these constraints limit the range of loom weights that can be used to produce textiles requiring the same warp thread tension. In order to do this, the constraints in Eqns. (3) and (4) will be expressed in terms of warp thread tension, as follows:

$$\frac{(\text{weight of LW})}{n_{max}} \leq (\text{warp thread tension})$$
$$\leq \frac{(\text{weight of LW})}{n_{min}} \quad (5)$$

$$\frac{1}{N_{max}} \frac{(\text{wt. of LW}) \times (\text{no. of rows})}{(\text{thickness of LW})}$$
$$\leq (\text{warp thread tension})$$
$$\leq \frac{1}{N_{min}} \frac{(\text{wt. of LW}) \times (\text{no. of rows})}{(\text{thickness of LW})} \quad (6)$$

[These have been derived by substituting Eqn. (1) into Eqn. (3) and rearranging and by substituting Eqns. (1) and (2) into Eqn. (4) and rearranging.]

Fig. 5.2.8 then shows the area on the thickness *vs.* weight graph within which the constraints given in Eqns. (5) and (6) are satisfied for a particular warp thread tension.

For convenience, in Fig. 5.2.8 the following abbreviations have been introduced: R = no. of rows of loom weights and th = thickness of each loom weight. The values of thickness given in Fig. 5.2.8 correspond to the values at the four nodes of the quadrilateral. The vertical limits are provided by the constraints given in Eqn. (5) and define the maximum and minimum weights permitted in order to achieve the required warp thread tension:

$$w_1 = n_{min} \times (\text{warp thread tension})$$
$$w_2 = n_{max} \times (\text{warp thread tension})$$

The oblique lines are derived from Eqn. (6). These are straight lines, which if extended, would pass through the origin.

If the loom weight has a weight and thickness that lies within the solution space for a particular tension then a set of such loom weights could operate at that tension.

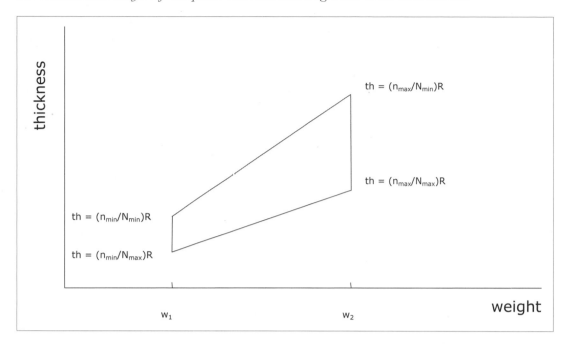

Fig. 5.2.8. Solution area for Eqns (5) and (6) for a given warp thread tension.

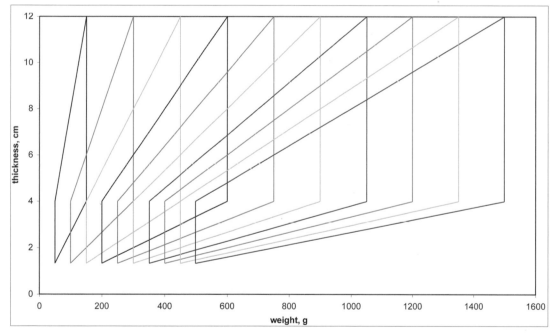

Fig. 5.2.9. Solution areas for Eqns (5) and (6) for a range of warp thread tensions (5–70 g).

Furthermore, this can be used to give rough estimates for the number of threads per loom weight and the number of warp threads per centimetre for operating at this tension simply by gauging the position of a loom weight relative to the boundaries of the solution space. It could even be made more precise by drawing a grid within the solution space, where the gridlines correspond to intermediate values of the number of threads per loom weight and the number of warp threads per centimetre.

It is now possible to repeat the above analysis for a range of warp thread tensions and the results of this are presented in Fig. 5.2.9.

In Fig. 5.2.9, in order to make the presentation less abstract, particular ranges have been used where,

$$10 \leq (\text{no. of warp threads per LW}) \leq 30$$
$$5 \leq (\text{warp threads per centimetre}) \leq 15$$

In addition, the number of rows of loom weights has been set to two. These values roughly correspond to a wool tabby weave. However, it should be emphasised that these ranges are only included here as an example and should not be regarded as recommendations. The subject of the appropriate values for these ranges will be considered in some detail later in this chapter.

The important points to note from Fig. 5.2.9 are that there are frequent overlaps between the solution areas for different tensions and thus a loom weight within an area of overlap would serve in loom setups for the corresponding range of tensions. Secondly, the combination of all of the solution areas effectively covers most of the space on the graph.

As noted, Fig. 5.2.9 broadly corresponds to a wool tabby weave. It is possible to draw analogous figures for wool twill and for linen tabby and, similarly, the combined solution space on each of these figures should cover most of the space on those graphs.

If the data for complete loom weights for a large region (and for a suitable time span) are plotted onto Fig. 5.2.9, it may reasonably be expected that most (if not all) of the data would be within the combined solution space area. If any complete 'loom weights' were found with parameters that could not be plotted within the solution space for Fig. 5.2.9 or for analogous graphs for twill and linen, then it would be worthwhile questioning whether these items were actually loom weights.

If all of the complete loom weight data fall within the solution space for wool tabby textiles and there is no additional evidence for twill, then it would be worth considering the possibility that weavers at that time did not make twill textiles.

Let us now take a step further and presume that all of the complete loom weight data for a sufficiently large region and time period fall within the solution space on the wool tabby graph. Then, it would be possible to get a better impression of the limitations of the ranges of threads per loom weight and the number of warp threads per centimetre actually used by considering reducing the permitted ranges so that there was a reasonable match between the solution area and the area covered by thickness *vs.* weight data points from complete loom weights. This approach will be developed further later in this chapter.

Considering the range of loom weights

The aim of this section is to provide a general overall discussion of the physical properties of the loom weights in the CTR database and determine what these general considerations imply about loom setups and the tensions of the warp threads.

It is emphasized again that all the discussion in this chapter is based on the loom weights in the CTR database. Although this represents thousands of loom weights, it is not being claimed that these are strictly representative of any particular chronological period or geographical region. Nevertheless, the loom weights in this database do form a large body of data and are worth considering on that basis alone.

Weight of loom weights

It is appropriate to begin by considering the weight of the loom weights. Fig. 5.2.10 is a plot of all of the loom weights in the CTR database that are more than half preserved and for which measurements (or estimates) are available for their weight when complete (or almost complete). The data are plotted in bins of 50 g.

Fig. 5.2.10 shows a predominance of weights in the range 0–400 g, with relatively small numbers of weights above 400 g. It also seems to imply that there is a tendency to have large numbers of lighter weights with a decreasing profile in the numbers of weights greater than 150 g. However, this is due to the use of a linear scale on the x-axis, which exaggerates the impression that there were relatively few heavy loom weights. A 50 g difference can be very significant for lighter weights but much less significant for heavier weights; therefore it is more appropriate to use a logarithmic scale along the x-axis (see Fig. 5.2.11). The resulting graph is almost symmetrical, with a form roughly approximating to a normal distribution. It also demonstrates that there are more weights in the range 100–400 g than those lighter or heavier than this range.

It is the experience of modern weavers that the practical range of the number of warp threads per loom weight is 10 to 30.[17] If that number were less than ten for each loom weight, then it would result in an excessive number of loom weights and increase the time required for setting up the loom, whereas if it were more than 30, then there would be difficulty

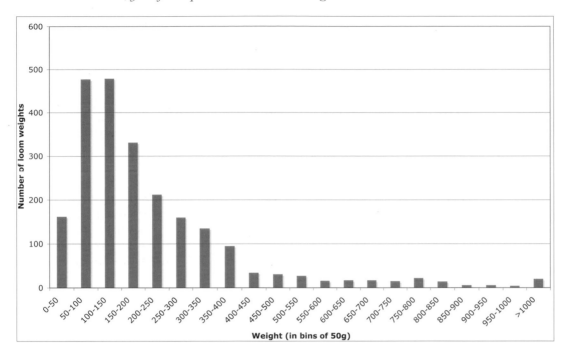

Fig. 5.2.10. Distribution of the weight of loom weights (2280 data points).

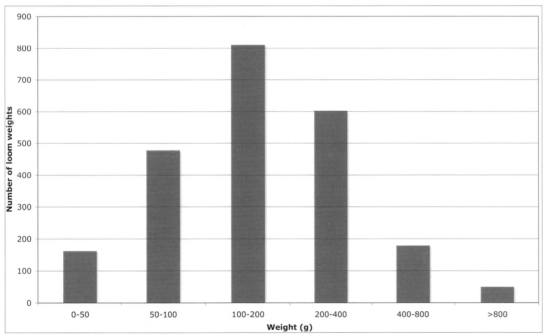

Fig. 5.2.11. Distribution of the weight of loom weights in the CTR database using a logarithmic scale (2280 data points).

managing such a large number of warp threads and ensuring that they all have equal tension. It would follow that the minimum weight of a loom weight should be ~10 times the minimum tension required for warp threads. On the basis of the limited number of samples of textiles found from the Greek Bronze Age, the minimum thread diameter is 0.25–0.3 mm (Spantidaki and Moulhérat 2012). However, there are a small number of examples of thin threads within the range 0.05–0.1 mm described

in chapter 3. Such thin threads would have required lighter loom weights and it is evident, from Figures 5.2.10 and 5.2.11, that there are a large number of weights below 100 g. In order to investigate this further, Fig. 5.2.12 presents data from the lower end of the weight range, plotted in bins of 10 g.

The first thing to note is that a significant number of spools were listed within the loom weight part of the CTR database on the basis that they could potentially have been used as loom weights. It is evident from Fig. 5.2.12 that these spools are predominantly lighter than loom weights and show a very different weight profile. Thus, the impression is that spools were designed for a different purpose to loom weights and whilst it is technically possible to use some of the spools as loom weights, it seems much more likely that, for the most part, they served a different purpose. Therefore, it seems reasonable to suggest that spools should only be categorised as loom weights if there is some positive indication from the archaeology that a set of spools were actually being used on a loom or if a suitably large number of spools of similar dimensions were found stored together.

If the spools are discounted and the focus is concentrated on the loom weights in Fig. 5.2.12, there is clear evidence of a decline of numbers in the lower weight bins, but there is not a definite cut-off. This would imply that these weights were being used with very thin threads.[18]

It is now appropriate to consider the heavier loom weights (see Fig. 5.2.13). In this case, bins of 200 g have been used to show the distribution of these weights.

It is immediately evident from Fig. 5.2.13 that the majority of weights are less than 400 g. There are only seven weights over 1200 g (three from Troia, and one each from Ayia Triada, Khania, Sitagroi and Ayia Irini; the

latter is described as a spool). Within the group of 13 loom weights in the range 1000–1200 g, six of these are from Troia (indeed, five are from the same trench, although these are not all from the same set), three are from Archontiko, two from Malia, one from each of Khania and Sitagroi.

An obvious comparison can be made between textiles for clothing (which in the geographical area considered would tend to require lighter weight materials) and textiles for blankets, tents, sacks, rugs and sails (which would necessarily be heavier and stronger). The above data and discussion would seem to imply that the main focus of textile manufacture was on the lighter weight textiles for the textile tools listed in the CTR database.

Loom weights with more than one hole
For completeness, some statistics on loom weights with more than one hole will be included here (see Fig. 5.2.14). In this part of the study, only complete loom weights or those with just small fragments missing will be considered so it is possible to be confident about the hole count. Spools will be excluded, for the reasons described above. Of the remaining weights in the CTR database, eight are listed with no holes. It is possible that these represent omissions on data entry in the database or that they genuinely have no holes, however, for the purpose of this study this small number of weights will be discounted.[19]

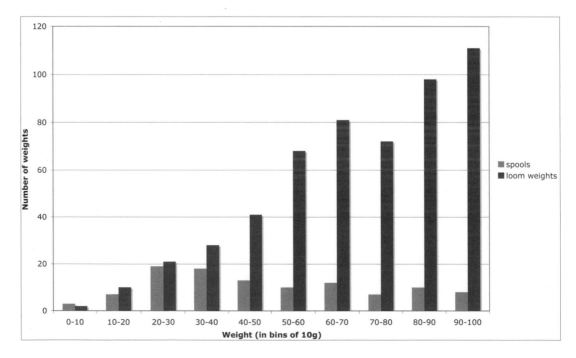

Fig. 5.2.12. Distribution of the weights of lighter loom weights (639 data points).

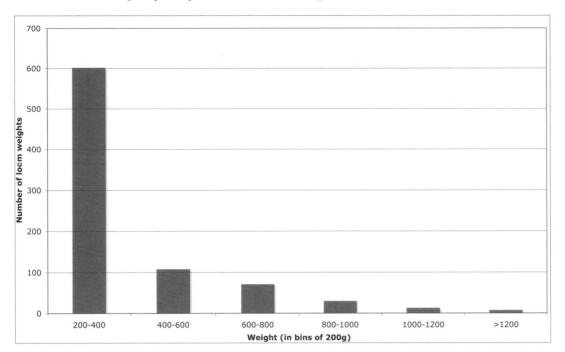

Fig. 5.2.13. Distribution of the weights of heavier loom weights (831 data points).

Of the 284 loom weights with two holes, 126 are crescent-shaped and 135 are discoid. All but two of the crescent-shaped weights were found in Anatolia (the remaining two were found at Tiryns). Of the 135 two-holed discoid weights, 65 were found at Malia and 24 were found both at Miletus and Kommos. For the reasons outlined above, it is possible that the crescent-shaped weights may have been used to weave 1-row tabby or 2-row twills. It is much less likely that the 2-holed discoid weights were used in this way because of the proximity of the holes.

The two 3-holed weights were found at Miletus and Phaistos. The 4-holed weights are all cuboid and were found at Malia. This latter type of weight is also found at other sites in Eastern Crete although these are not included in the CTR database (see Evely 2000, 498).

Other features

Before going on to consider in detail the shape of loom weights, it is worth briefly summarising other features of the loom weights that are listed in the CTR database.[20]

Only 16% of the loom weights are indicated as showing signs of wear (based on a sample size of 1933 weights). The work done by the loom weight is simply to provide tension, and no significant frictional wearing of the loom weight by the threads would

No. of holes	No. of loom weights	Percentage of total
1	1469	83.5%
2	284	16.1%
3	2	0.1%
4	4	0.2%
Total	1759	

Fig. 5.2.14. Distribution of the number of holes in loom weights.

be expected. On the other hand, it would be expected that wear would be caused by adjacent loom weights rubbing against each other. However, the contributors were not specifically asked to look for this latter kind of wear and so it might not be fully recorded within the CTR database.

16% of weights have a groove(s) (based on a sample size of 1933 weights). The presence of grooves has frequently been of interest to archaeologists in their attempts to categorise loom weights (see, for example, Evely 1984, 247–248). However, in terms of the actual function of the loom weight it is not clear if the grooves served any useful purpose.

The production quality of 47% of the weights was described as good (or, in a very small number of cases, excellent). For 40% of weights it was described as medium and for 13% of weights it was described as poor (based on a sample size of 790 weights).

Shape of loom weights

At first sight, it would seem that the shape of loom weights is simply a matter choice and that loom weights of one shape would have served as well as those of another. However, it can be shown that the physical shape of the loom weight can govern its usage to some extent. Therefore, the aim of this section and the sections that follow is to consider the importance of the shape of loom weights.

Figure 5.2.15 is a scatter plot of loom weights on a weight *vs.* thickness chart.[21]

Although this seems complex, with the cataloguing of many different loom weight shapes, there has already been some simplification of the numbers of types of loom weights. For example, the term spherical loom weights here includes not only weights that are 'strictly' spherical but also those described as spherical rounded, spherical flattened, spherical lenticular, spherical ovoid and spherical bowl shaped; discoid includes discoid rounded, discoid elliptical, spherical discoid [sic] and discoid tabulated; flat includes flat rectangular and flat trapezoidal; cylindrical includes standard and short cylinders. In these cases it is immediately evident that, for

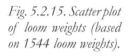

Fig. 5.2.15. Scatter plot of loom weights (based on 1544 loom weights).

example, the small distinction between discoid elliptical and discoid rounded has no effect on the function of the loom weights. Furthermore, there is often inconsistency in the way that these are described from site to site (so that some 'rounded' discoid weights can be more elliptical than some 'elliptical' discoid weights and *vice versa*) and in this case it is more straightforward to simplify the description to discoid rather than resolve these inconsistencies which are not important for the function of the loom weight.

These loom weights come from a wide range of sources, over a relatively wide geographical area and over a lengthy chronological period. Nevertheless, even within a plot as coarse as that shown in Fig. 5.2.15, it is possible to see that the loom weights of the same shape tend to be grouped together. These groupings are primarily a result of the geometry of the loom weights and the fact that they are mostly made from clay or stone.

The next section is a detailed study of the functional analysis of loom weights based on their shape as well as their weight and thickness and this will show the importance of these groupings in defining the function of each type of loom weight.

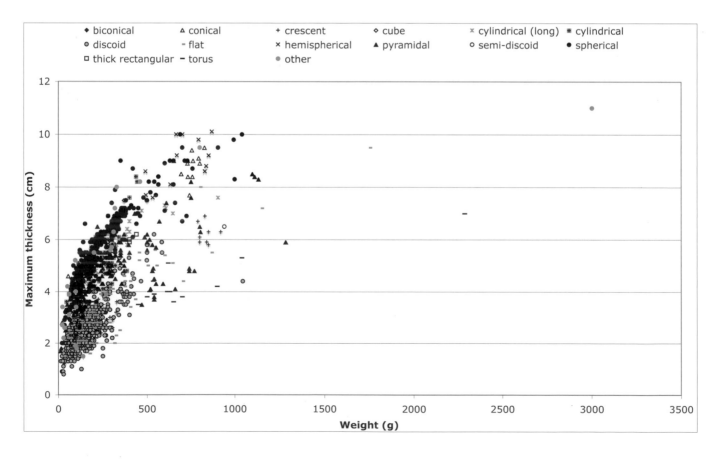

Functional analysis of the loom weights

The aim of this lengthy section is to consider the functional analysis of the loom weights in the CTR database, to determine the range of textiles that could have been manufactured by these different types of loom weights and to show the extent of functional differences between different types.[22] Thus, if the warp weighted loom is regarded as an early example of textile engineering, the aim of this section is to examine in detail an important component of this technology. It is not the aim of this section to consider the chronological or geographical distribution of the loom weights as these will be considered elsewhere.

The first step is to consider in detail the functional analysis of spherical, discoid and pyramidal loom weights. It will become apparent that the spherical and discoid loom weights are not only physically very distinct but also have markedly different functional properties, whereas pyramidal loom weights have functional properties that are intermediate between those two extremes. Therefore, the aim here is to describe these three different types of loom weights with their distinct functional properties and then let these form a basis for the discussion of the many other different types of loom weight.

Spherical loom weights

This discussion of spherical loom weights includes all of the different types of spherical loom weight listed in the CTR database, *i.e.* spherical bowl, flattened, lenticular, ovoid, rounded.

To a reasonable approximation, the weights of spherical loom weights are simply a function of their diameter (or thickness) and the density of the material from which they were made. Therefore, on the thickness *vs.* weight plot, they form a particularly well-defined group (see Fig. 5.2.16).[23]

Fig. 5.2.17 shows the distribution of warp thread tensions that could have been used with these loom weights on the basis that each loom weight would have been attached to 10 to 30 warp threads.

Fig. 5.2.18 shows the numbers of spherical loom weights that would be required to weave a one-metre wide textile with 1, 2, 3 or 4 rows of spherical loom weights. The numbers of loom weights shown in this figure are broadly sensible

Fig. 5.2.16. Scatter plot of spherical loom weights (based on 380 loom weights).

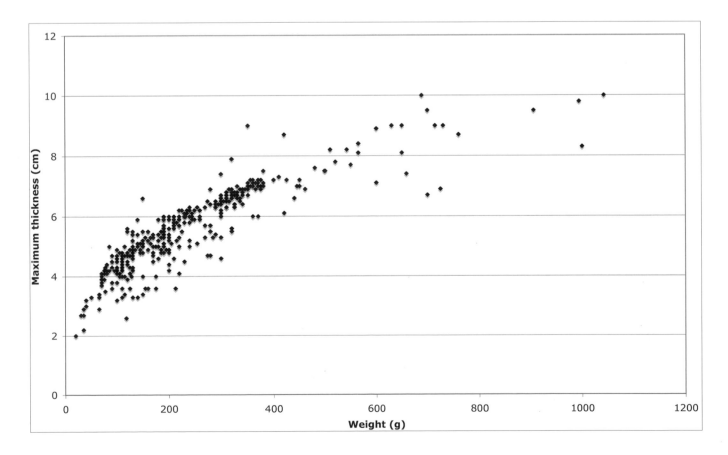

with only one example requiring more than 200 loom weights for weaving a 4-row twill.

Using the methods described earlier in this chapter, it is possible to calculate the (weighted) average of the number of threads for different warp thread tensions. Fig. 5.2.19 shows the results of a calculation for a 2-row tabby.[24]

It is worth briefly noting that the spherical loom weights in the CTR database would not be appropriate for use with a 1-row tabby loom setup unless very open fabrics were required.

Discoid loom weights
The discoid-shaped loom weights will now be considered. This discussion will include all of the different types of discoid loom weights, including the semi-discoid weights. It will also include the weights that are described as flat rectangular, flat trapezoidal *etc.,* since the

Fig. 5.2.17. Distribution of warp thread tensions for spherical loom weights (based on 380 loom weights).

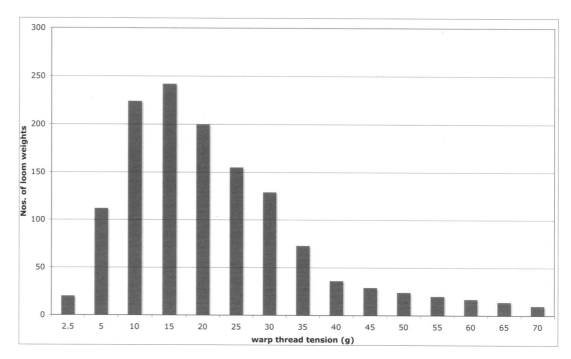

Fig. 5.2.18. Numbers of spherical loom weights required to weave a 1 metre wide textile (based on 380 loom weights).

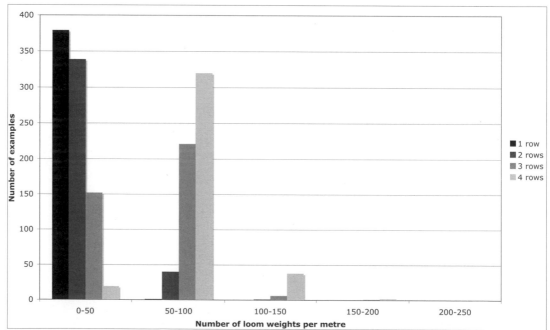

Warp thread tension per thread (g)	2.5	5	10	15	20	25	30	40	50	60	70
Average no. of warp threads/cm	13	10	7	6	5	4	3.5	3.5	3	3	3

Fig. 5.2.19. Average thread count per cm as a function of warp thread tension for spherical loom weights (2-row tabby).

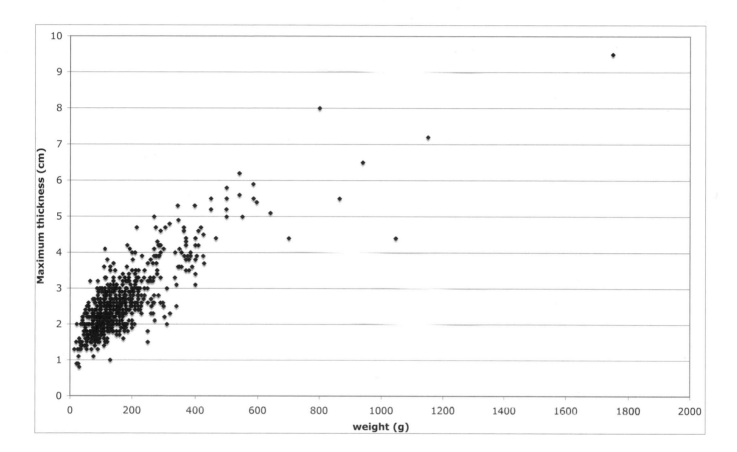

Fig. 5.2.20. Scatter plot of discoid loom weights (660 loom weights).

function of the loom weight is not dependent on the shape of this cross-section. However, the stone discoid weights will be excluded as they are denser and these will be considered together with the torus weights below.

By the nature of their geometry, discoid loom weights are heavier than spherical loom weights of the same thickness. Therefore, it is expected that the characteristics of these weights are markedly different from those described in the previous section.

Fig. 5.2.20 is a plot of the discoid weights on a thickness *vs.* weight chart.

The scatter on Fig. 5.2.20 for discoid weights is much greater than that on Fig. 5.2.16 for spherical weights. This is due to the fact that the thickness of a spherical weight is equal to its diameter and therefore this single dimension defines its shape and, to some extent, its weight. However, this is not the case for discoid weights.

Fig. 5.2.21 shows the distribution of warp thread tensions that could have been used with these weights.

It is possible to contrast Fig. 5.2.21 with Fig. 5.2.17. Figure 5.2.21 shows a clear preference for low warp thread tensions, implying very thin threads needing very little tension (5–10 g), whereas the distribution for spherical loom weights (shown in Fig. 5.2.17) indicates that the warp thread tension distribution favours thin to medium threads.

Fig. 5.2.22 shows the numbers of loom weights that would be required to weave a one-metre wide textile with 1, 2, 3 or 4 rows of discoid loom weights.

Again, there is a marked contrast between Fig. 5.2.22 based on discoid loom weights and Fig. 5.2.18 that used data from spherical loom weights. In the latter case, with the exception of a single example, all the spherical loom weights

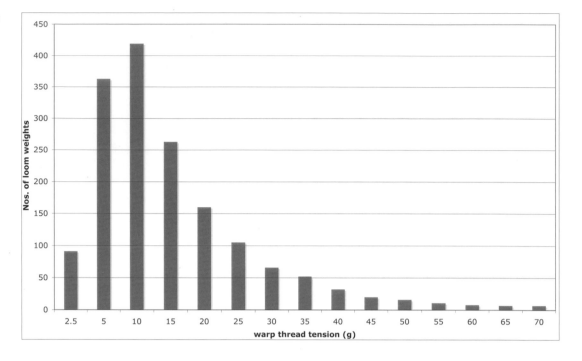

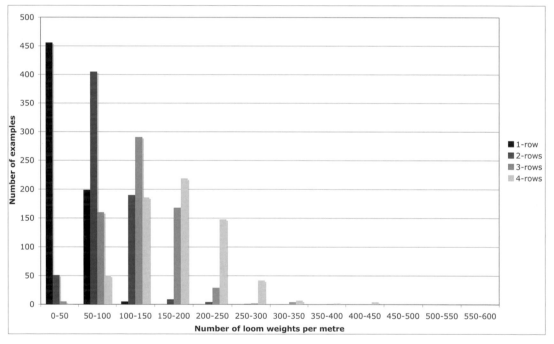

could be used for all of the weaves with less than 200 loom weights per metre width of textile. However, because the discoid loom weights are generally thinner than spherical loom weights, it requires more discoid loom weights to traverse a metre. In consequence, for many of the thinner discoid weights, it could require over 200 of these loom weights for loom setups for weaving a one metre width of 3 or 4-row twill. Fig. 5.2.22 shows that 30% of

these weights would have required a set of more than 200 to weave this width of 4-row twill. In practice, it would have been very laborious to set up a loom with so many weights and it seems most likely that weavers would have taken a more pragmatic approach and chosen a more suitable set of loom weights for this purpose.

It is now possible to calculate the (weighted) average and range of the number of threads for different warp thread tensions. The results for

2-row tabby are presented in Fig. 5.2.23, as a comparison between the (weighted) averages and range of thread counts for spherical and discoid weights. The thread counts for 4-row 2/2 twill would be approximately double those given in Fig. 5.2.23.[25]

It is evident that the average thread count for discoid loom weights is roughly double that for spherical loom weights. This is a simple consequence of the geometry of the loom weights. As can be seen in Fig. 5.2.15, for a given weight, a spherical loom weight has a greater thickness than a discoid loom weight and this generally results in lower thread counts in tabby textiles woven using spherical loom weights compared to those woven using discoid weights. A similar statement could equally be made for weaving 3-row twill or 4-row twills.

Pyramidal loom weights
On average, pyramidal loom weights in the CTR database have a height that is 73% greater than their thickness.[26] So, in general terms, if comparing weights of the same thickness and density, then the pyramidal loom weight has a greater height than a spherical weight and so is heavier. But, compared to a discoid weight, it has a smaller cross-section and so is lighter. Therefore, the properties of pyramidal loom weights would be expected to be intermediate between those of spherical and discoid loom weights.

In principle, pyramidal loom weights could show a lot of scatter on a thickness *vs.* weight plot because the weight is determined by both the height of the loom weight, its thickness and the clay density. However, Fig. 5.2.24 shows that, in practice, the data are reasonably well-behaved.

Fig. 5.2.25 shows the distribution of warp thread tensions that could have been used with these weights.

This distribution is reminiscent of that shown for the spherical weights in Fig. 5.2.17.

Fig. 5.2.26 shows the numbers of loom weights that would be required to weave a one-metre wide textile with 1, 2, 3 or 4 rows of discoid loom weights.

Warp thread tension per thread (g)	2.5	5	10	15	20	25	30	35	40	45	50	60	70
Spherical loom weights	13	10	7	6	5	4	3.5	3.5	3.5	3.5	3	3	3
Discoid loom weights	25	20	13	11	9	8	7	6	5.5	5	5	5	4.5

Fig. 5.2.23. Average thread count per cm as a function of warp thread tension for discoid and spherical loom weights (2-row tabby).

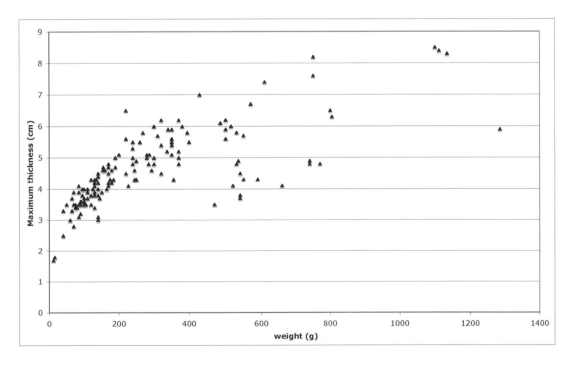

Fig. 5.2.24. Scatter plot of pyramidal loom weights (148 data points).

This again is more similar to that for spherical weights than for discoid loom weights.

It is now possible to calculate the (weighted) average and range of the number of threads for different warp thread tensions. Fig. 5.2.27 presents the results by comparing the (weighted) averages and range of thread counts between pyramidal, spherical and discoid weights.[27]

Thus, this analysis has demonstrated the expected result, that the pyramidal loom weights have characteristics that are intermediate between spherical and discoid loom weights.

At this stage, three different types of loom weight have been considered in some detail (*i.e.* spherical, discoid and pyramidal). In the following sections the other types of loom weight are briefly considered (in alphabetical

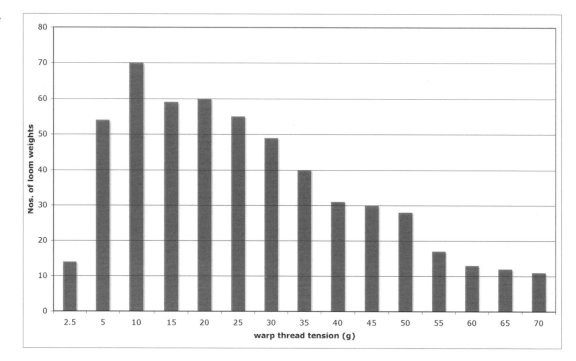

Fig. 5.2.25. Distribution of warp thread tensions for pyramidal loom weights (based on 148 loom weights).

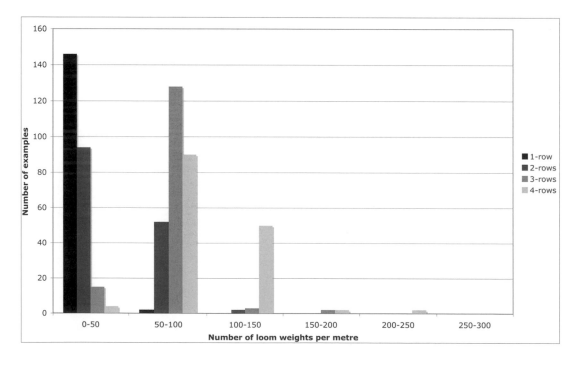

Fig. 5.2.26. Numbers of pyramidal loom weights required to weave a 1 metre wide textile (based on 148 loom weights).

order). It is shown that, for the most part, they can be put into the same category as one of these three types of loom weight.

Biconical loom weights
There are 20 biconical loom weights listed in the CTR database, out of a total of nearly 4000 weights. Seventeen of these weights were found at Tell el-Ajjul and the remaining three were from Malia, Phaistos and Sitagroi. Unfortunately the database does not include data for the weights and dimensions for most of these items.

Conical loom weights
The difference between a conical and pyramidal shape is its horizontal cross-section, which is circular instead of square. However, since this cross-section has no effect on the weaving characteristics of loom weights, then, in principle, their characteristics would be expected to be similar for conical and pyramidal loom weights.

Fig. 5.2.28 compares these two types of weights on a thickness *vs.* weight graph. It shows that the two types of loom weights sit in a similar position on the graph, especially if allowance is made for the differing height to width ratios.[28]

Crescent-shaped loom weights
There are 405 crescent-shaped loom weights in the database. Almost all of these are from Anatolian sites, with 76% from Karahöyük, 20% from Demircihüyük, 3% from Beycesultan and 0.5% from Troia. (The remaining two weights in the database are from Tiryns.) There has already been some discussion of this type of loom weight earlier in this chapter in connection with the same weight being used to provide tension to threads from each of two rows (as for 1-row tabby or 2-row 2/2 twill). The finding that 115 of the 121 complete crescent-shaped weights have two holes supports this suggestion further.

Fig. 5.2.29 shows the distribution of those crescent-shaped weights that have measured

Warp thread tension per thread (g)	2.5	5	10	15	20	25	30	35	40	45	50	60	70
Spherical loom weights	13	10	7	6	5	4	3.5	3.5	3.5	3.5	3	3	3
Pyramidal loom weights	15	11	8	7	7	6.5	6	5.5	5.5	5.5	5	4.5	4
Discoid loom weights	25	20	13	11	9	8	7	6	5.5	5	5	5	4.5

Fig. 5.2.27. Average thread count per cm as a function of warp thread tension for spherical, pyramidal and discoid loom weights (2-row tabby).

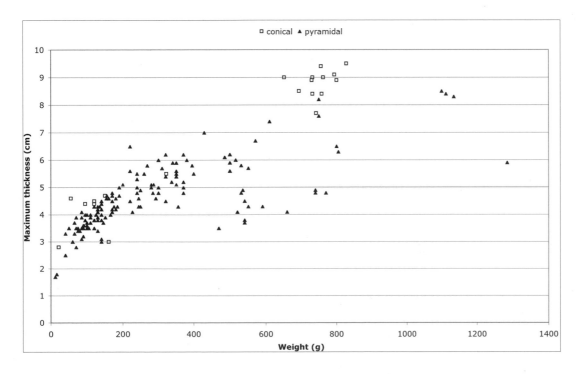

Fig. 5.2.28. Scatter plot of conical and pyramidal loom weights (20 conical weights and 148 pyramidal weights).

(or estimated) weights for their original undamaged state.

The crescent-shaped loom weights are within the same range on the thickness *vs.* weight chart as the discoid loom weights and so will have the same characteristics for 2-row tabby or 4-row twill weaving.

It is interesting to note that Fig. 5.2.29 shows a cluster of points that are separated from the remainder. These are a group of 2-holed weights from Demircihüyük, which were found together with pyramidal and other shaped loom weights in a group totalling 29 weights. These will be investigated in detail in the discussion on groups of weights later in this chapter.

Cuboid loom weights
There are 17 cuboid loom weights in the CTR database. Six are from Malia, three from Kition, two each from Demircihüyük, Khania and Phaistos, and one each from Aghia Irini and Tell el-Ajjul.

The six cuboid weights from Malia each have four vertical holes, positioned one at each vertex. This presents a particularly interesting problem. Using the naïve formula of one hole giving tension to threads from one row, two holes to two rows, then four well-spaced holes might potentially give tension to four rows of loom weights. However, the possibility that a single loom weight could give tension to warp threads from all four rows throughout all of the shed changes stretches credibility, whatever arrangement of loops might be used. Furthermore, Evely suggests that this style of loom weight is "perhaps an inheritance from Neolithic habits" (Evely 2000, 498). This would tend to imply that that they are more likely to be based on an early style of weight rather than being a later technological development for weaving 1-row tabby or 2-row twills. They could undoubtedly be used in loom setups for 2-row tabby or 3 or 4-row twills and, despite the somewhat elaborate arrangement of holes, this was probably their intended use.

As might be expected, from their shape, the cuboid loom weights are within the scatter range of spherical loom weights on the thickness *vs.* weight graph and will therefore have the same functional characteristics as spherical weights.

Cylindrical loom weights
The cylindrical loom weights are variously described as cylindrical short, standard or long.

This discussion will begin by considering loom weights that have been classified as 'cylindrical long', which have an axis that is considerably longer than their width (*i.e.* their diameter). The first point to consider is whether their 'thickness' (as loom weights) is equal to their axial length or to their diameter. There are two reasons for suggesting that their 'thickness' was not equal to their axial length. Firstly, if this were the case, then, for a given weight, the

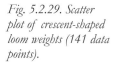

Fig. 5.2.29. Scatter plot of crescent-shaped loom weights (141 data points).

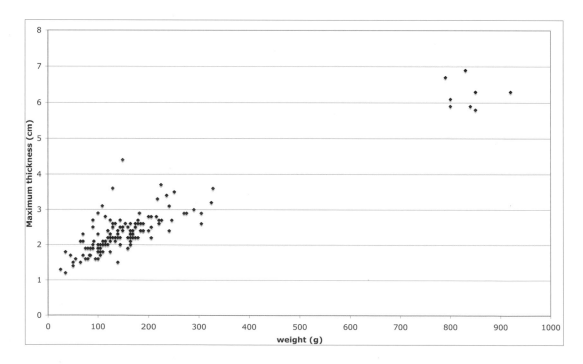

thickness of the long cylindrical loom weight would be greater than that of a spherical loom weight and so the textile it produced would be more open. Since the textiles produced by spherical loom weights are already more open than the discoid or pyramidal loom weights, this would seem undesirable. Secondly, there would be an inherent instability in the loom setup because it would assume that the loom weights were only touching at their ends and so if the weights became slightly displaced they would have the freedom to move out of line. For these reasons, it is suggested that the thickness of the long cylindrical loom weights is equal to their diameters.

Once this step has been taken, then it would seem that the long cylindrical loom weights are in principle similar to the pyramidal weights. It can be demonstrated that this is the case by plotting the two types of weights together (see Fig. 5.2.30).

In practice, the short and standard cylindrical loom weights fall within the same scatter band as the long cylindrical weights. It follows that all cylindrical loom weights will have similar functional characteristics to pyramidal loom weights.

'Hemispherical' loom weights
There are 21 loom weights described as 'hemispherical' in the CTR database. Of these, 20 are from Arslantepe and the remaining

one is from Midea. From the dimensions given, these weights are clearly not literally hemispherical since that would require that their dimensions in one direction would be half of their dimensions in the other two directions, whereas these weights are recorded as having similar dimensions in all three directions. It might be more useful to regard them as misshapen spheres. It can be shown that these so-called 'hemispherical' weights sit within the scatter band of spherical loom weights and they will therefore have the same functional characteristics.

Thick rectangular loom weights
There are 11 thick rectangular loom weights in the CTR database and these are all from Malia. On the thickness *vs.* weight chart, these sit within the scatter band of spherical loom weights and will therefore have the same functional characteristics.

Torus loom weights
There are 95 torus-shaped loom weights listed in the CTR database, of which 31 are from Apliki, 25 are from Malia, and 14 from Ayia Triada.

It is interesting to compare the torus-shaped loom weights from the Bronze Age with those from the Viking sites at Birka and Hedeby (see Fig. 5.2.31).[29]

Fig. 5.2.31 shows that, despite the ~2000 years and ~2000 kilometres separating these

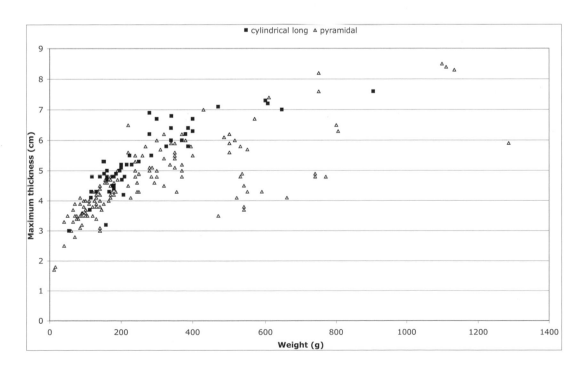

Fig. 5.2.30. Scatter plot for long cylindrical and pyramidal loom weights (50 long cylindrical weights and 148 pyramidal weights).

two sets of torus-shaped loom weights, there is a high level of overlap between the data as presented on a thickness *vs.* weight plot. This essentially demonstrates that the characteristics of torus-shaped loom weights are intrinsic to the shape of the loom weight and to a large extent independent of chronology and geography.

Intuitively, it might be expected that the torus-shaped loom weights in the CTR database most closely resemble discoid loom weights. In practice, on a thickness *vs.* weight graph, the torus data form a band that has a slightly flatter gradient to that for discoid weights. However, there is an insufficient number of torus-shaped weights in the CTR database to permit the type of full analysis that has been given above for spherical, discoid and pyramidal weights.

Pierced sherds

Before completing this section, the pierced sherds that have been categorised as loom weights should be considered.

In fact, pierced sherds have been variously categorised in the CTR database by archaeologists as loom weights, spindle whorls or other textile tools. The 58 sherds that were listed as spindle whorls have already been considered and it was concluded that sherds should not be categorised as spindle whorls unless there is good evidence that the sherd

has been skilfully adapted to function as a spindle whorl. In the discussion that follows, the hypothesis will be considered that these items could have been loom weights.

Fig. 5.2.32 is a plot of all of the pierced sherds that are more than half preserved and that have a measured or estimated weight for the original complete item. The solution areas shown are based on the overall maxima and minima in Fig. 5.2.9 for 2-row tabby.

There are 116 sherds shown on Fig. 5.2.32 and it is clear that a large majority of these sherds sit outside the solution areas. It is possible that some of the lighter sherds could have been used for weaving very thin threads with thread counts in the range of 35–60 per cm, as this would extend the lowest solution area and, thus, encompass more data points. However, there is no evidence that fabrics with thread counts as high as this were made in Bronze Age Greece (Spantidaki and Moulhérat 2012) although there is some evidence given in chapter 3 of higher thread counts in the Near East and Egypt. Thus, in principle, it is possible that some pierced sherds could have been used as loom weights but it seems likely that that the majority of the pierced sherds would not have served this function.

Summary of the discussion on the functional analysis of loom weights

It has been shown that it is possible to divide the loom weights of the CTR database into three

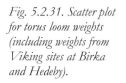

Fig. 5.2.31. Scatter plot for torus loom weights (including weights from Viking sites at Birka and Hedeby).

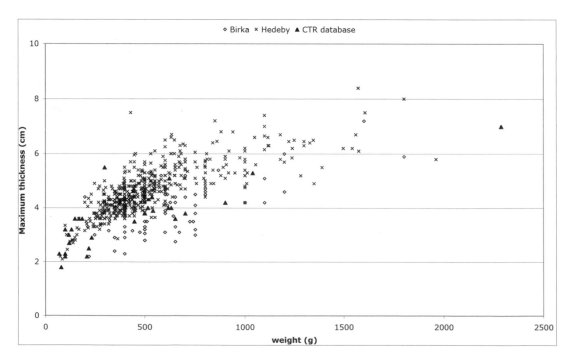

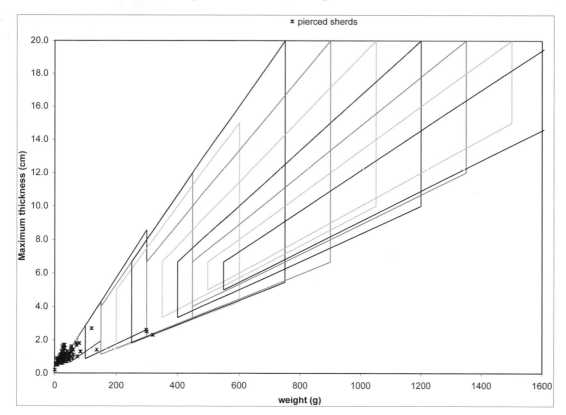

Fig. 5.2.32. Scatter plot of sherds (116 sherds).

broad groups for the purposes of functional analysis (Fig. 5.2.33).

Considering groups of loom weights

The previous section described the functional analysis of loom weights based on the individual analyses of several thousand weights. In this section, consideration will be given to the analysis of groups of loom weights that were found together. In particular, a method of analysis will be derived that is appropriate to considering a large group of weights. The aim is to determine whether the weights in these groups actually formed part of a functional set and, if so, what sort of fabric could be woven by such a set of loom weights on a warp-weighted loom.

Before continuing, it is worthwhile defining the terms, 'set', 'group' and 'cache', which are used in this section for a collection of loom weights. The term 'set' is being used to specify the complete number of loom weights that would have been used to set up a loom. The terms 'group' or 'cache' are used to specify those weights that were found together in good contexts. It is possible that a 'group' of weights is an assemblage of loom weights from

Group 1	Group 2	Group 3
spherical	pyramidal	discoid
cuboid	cylindrical	crescent
hemispherical	conical	flat
thick rectangular		torus

Fig. 5.2.33. Groups of loom weight shapes based on functional analysis.

different 'sets'. It is also possible that all of the weights in a 'group' could be from the same 'set'. However, in general, not all the weights in a set would be preserved and so it will not be assumed that the preserved 'group' of weights constitutes the entire 'set'.

Ideally all of the loom weights in a set would be identical and indeed this is generally the case in modern experiments that aim to reconstruct the workings of a warp-weighted loom (for example, see chapter 4.1). However, almost as soon as one begins to investigate sets of archaeological loom weights, one is confronted with the fact that there are significant variations of loom weights within sets, both in the archaeological examples discussed below and even in the more recent ethnographic descriptions.[30] These differences encompass not only weight and thickness but also type.

It naturally follows that if the loom weights in a set are not identical, it was not necessary that there are the same number of loom weights in each row of the corresponding loom setup. Thus, for example, if there are an odd number of loom weights in a set, it cannot automatically be assumed that the set was not used to weave 2-row tabby or that one of the loom weights is missing.

Since the weights in a set varied, then it follows that, in general, there would not have been the same number of warp threads attached to each loom weight. It would have been part of the skill of the weaver to set up a loom with varying weights and accommodate these variations by tying different numbers of warp threads to each loom weight whilst retaining approximately the same tension in each warp thread and approximately the same number of warp threads per centimetre.

From the point of view of the textile archaeologist, the analyses are obviously made more complex by the variations of weights within a set. However, there is a distinct advantage that the types of fabric that could be woven by all of the weights in a set are more restricted than the types that would be obtained by the extrapolation from a single weight. Therefore, by analysing groups of weights, it is possible to identify more precisely the types of fabric that they were used to weave.

In this section, attention will be restricted to those groups of loom weights that were found in good contexts since it is much more likely that these weights were intended to be used within the same set. This will include consideration of, not only weights that were in use as part of a loom setup but also weights that were found together in storage.[31]

Method of analysis
The aim here is to set out a method for the analysis of group of loom weights of varying weights, thicknesses and types.

Clearly, one could analyse each of the weights separately and determine the range of textiles that is common to all loom weights individually. However, a simpler and more satisfactory approach is to consider the weights as a group.

The first step of this analysis is to show whether the weights are suitably compatible so that they could have been used with the same set. In order to do this it is necessary to show that the number of warp threads per centimetre and the warp thread tensions would be within an acceptable range across the textile and therefore across the thickness of each loom weight. In an earlier section of this chapter, the following equations were derived:

$$\text{warp thread tension} = \frac{\text{(weight of LW)}}{\text{(no. of warp threads per LW)}} \quad (1)$$

$$\text{warp threads per cm} = \frac{\text{(no. of threads per LW)} \times \text{(no. of rows of LWs)}}{\text{(thickness of LW)}} \quad (2)$$

Combining these it can be shown that,

$$\text{(warp threads per cm)} \times \text{(warp thread tension)} = \frac{\text{(wt. of LW)} \times \text{(no. of rows of LWs)}}{\text{(thickness of LW)}}$$

Thus, to have the number of warp threads per centimetre and the warp thread tensions within an acceptable range, then it follows that the ratio of weight to thickness of each loom weight within a set should fall within an acceptable range. This, of course, begs the question about what is an acceptable range but that will become clearer as the archaeological evidence is investigated.

It should be emphasised that when the weights were manufactured, the specification would have been that the weights should have similar weights and thicknesses rather than that they should have similar weight to thickness ratios. Therefore, it is frequently found that the variation in weight to thickness ratio is greater than the variation in thickness. In addition, the weight to thickness ratio often tends to increase as the weight increases. For a fixed warp thread tension, this often gives rise to a variation in the numbers of warp threads per centimetre. In practice, the weaver could have reduced this variation by having a slightly lower tension for the lighter loom weights and a slightly higher tension for the heavier loom weights.

For the second step of the analysis, the set of loom weights will be replaced by a single *average loom weight*, with a weight equal to the average of the set and a weight to thickness ratio equal to the average of set, but using the definition,

average thickness =
(ave. wt.) / (ave. wt. to thickness ratio)

The third step is to analyse the *average loom weight* in the manner described by Mårtensson *et al.* (Mårtensson *et al.* 2009).

Whilst the characteristics of the fabric as a whole will be determined by the *average loom weight*, the extent of local variations of the thread count will be determined by the individual weights. Therefore, it is important to consider a small number of extreme examples from the set of weights to demonstrate the range of warp threads per centimetre that would have been present within the woven fabric (*i.e.* lightest and heaviest loom weight and the weights with the lowest and highest weight to thickness ratios).

For convenience, it is usual to begin by doing the analysis for 2-row tabby, but it is straightforward to use the information provided to assess the thread counts for weaving 3 or 4-row twills. Thus, if the same weights were used to weave 3 or 4-row twills, then the number of warp threads per loom weight would remain the same but the thread counts per centimetre would increase by 50% for the 3-row twills and by a factor of two for the 4-row twills.

If the combined width of all of the loom weights in a set is known, it can readily be divided by two to calculate the width of tabby fabric that could be woven using this set. However, a group of loom weights may not necessarily comprise the entire set. If clay loom weights in a set were made from high quality ceramic clay that had already been fired then it is possible that there are at least some remains from each of the loom weights. However, if clay loom weights were made from poorer quality clay and were unfired or poorly fired, then it is possible that some of the loom weights would not have been preserved.[32] In the discussion that follows, an estimate of the width of the fabric based on the group of loom weights that have been preserved will be included. However, for the reasons given above, this should be regarded as the minimum width that might have been woven with a complete set.[33]

There is not sufficient space here to present an analysis of all of the groups of weights listed within the CTR database. However, it is possible to include examples from two sites, one from the Acropolis House at Knossos and the other from Demircihüyük.

Acropolis House, Knossos (LM IA, 1725–1625 BC)

55 loom weights appear to have been stored in a large, decorated, clay tub, which was found lying on its side on the floor of Room I (Catling, Catling and Smyth 1979, Catling 1974–1976). At the edge of the group of loom weights were found a small bronze implement, a rod of squarish section with spatulate terminals. Inside the group were six conical cups, all of which had a hole knocked in their bases.[34] The loom weight data are shown in Fig. 5.2.34.

It is immediately clear that the range of the weight to thickness ratios is too great for all the weights to be used on the same loom setup for weaving 2-row tabby or 3 or 4-row twills. Furthermore, it seems highly unlikely that spherical loom weights would be used for weaving 1-row tabby or 2-row twills. Therefore, it seems most likely that these weights represent two or more groups that were stored together. For the purpose of providing an illustration, it will be assumed that the 30 lightest loom weights formed one group and that the remaining 25 were in the other group (*i.e.* dividing the group of weights on the basis of being less than or greater than 260 g).

For the group weighing less than 260 g, the total combined width is 1.6 m and the *average loom weight* weighs 184.1 g, with a thickness of 54.4 mm. The analysis for 2-row tabby is given in Fig. 5.2.35.

For the group weighing more than 260 g, the total combined width is 1.8 m and the *average loom weight* weighs 421.7 g with a thickness of 71.9 mm. The analysis for 2-row tabby is given in Fig. 5.2.36.

Whilst this is a viable division into two groups, clearly it would have been possible to divide the group in other ways, however, the above analyses can be regarded as representative.

Groups of weights found together at Demircihüyük
Cache of 29 weights found in Room 6 (Phase E1, EBA)
The weights with sufficient data are shown in Fig. 5.2.37.

At first sight, the combination of two-holed weights (crescent-shaped and semi-discoid) and single holed weights (pyramidal and flat rectangular) suggest that this might be a group of weights for weaving a 2-row 2:1 twill.[35] However, if that were the case, then the weights would fall into two separate groups with one group having double the weight (and double the weight to thickness ratio) of the other. In practice, this is a simple spread of weights

Fig. 5.2.34. Group of loom weights from Acropolis House, Knossos.

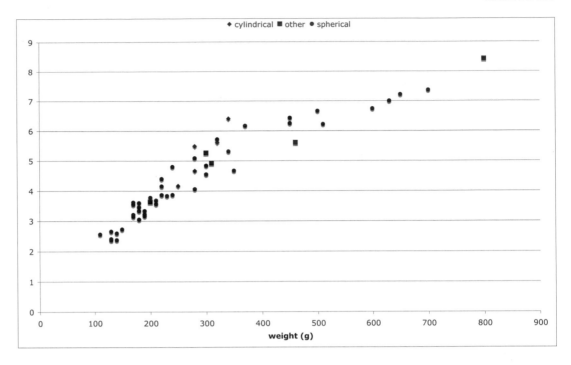

Fig. 5.2.35. Parameters of a tabby fabric based on loom weights weighing <260 g from Acropolis House, Knossos.

	10 g tension	
	threads per l.w	threads per cm
average l.w.	18	7
lightest l.w.	11	5
lowest wt./th.	13	5
heaviest l.w.	25	8
highest wt./th.	24	10

Fig. 5.2.36. Parameters of a tabby fabric based on loom weights weighing >260 g from Acropolis House, Knossos.

	25 g tension		30 g tension		35 g tension	
	threads/l.w.	threads/cm	threads/l.w.	threads/cm	threads/l.w.	threads/cm
average l.w.	17	5	14	4	12	3
lowest wt.	11	3	9	3	8	2
highest wt.	32	7	27	6	23	5

as seen in previous examples. Thus, this is a group of assorted but compatible loom weights, where each weight was probably used to provide tension from threads in the same row. Therefore, it is possible to analyse them in the same way as for the previous groups of weights.

The total combined width of the 27 weights shown in Fig. 5.2.37 is 1.5 m, which would become 1.6 m if allowance were made for the two other weights. The average weight is 699 g and the average weight to thickness ratio is 12.95. Therefore the *average loom weight*

has a weight of 699 g and a thickness of (699.3/12.95) = 54 mm.

The results of the analysis are given in Fig. 5.2.38 for 2-row tabby.

It can be seen that this group of loom weights could be used to weave a wide range of fabrics. However, some of these would have variable thread counts across the fabric, which would increase even further if the weights were used to weave twills. These variations could be reduced to some extent by having slight variations on the warp tensions as described above. These weights allow a more consistent thread count for higher tensions. Therefore, it is perhaps more likely that they were used for the weaving of heavy tabby fabrics with warp tensions greater than ~40 g (corresponding to thread diameters greater than ~0.8 mm).

It is interesting to note that nine of the weights have had a lump of clay added to the bottom to increase their weights (including weights of each of the four different types). This would also have served to reduce the variation in thread count across the fabric and is another example of the ingenuity of the weaver.[36]

Cache of 33 weights found in Room 999 (Phase H, EBA)

These 33 loom weights were found in a hollow lying partially in a row in room 999 (phase H, Early Bronze Age). The weights with sufficient data are shown in Fig. 5.2.39.

The total combined width of the 28 loom weights shown in Fig. 5.2.39 is 1.5 m. If this is extrapolated to allow for the five weights with insufficient data then it becomes 1.8 m. The *average loom weight* is 295 g, with a thickness of 54.3 mm.

The results of the analysis are given in Fig. 5.2.40 for 0.9 m width of 2-row tabby.

The fabrics that could be woven using this group of weights are more restricted in scope than the previous group from Demircihüyük because the physical properties of the loom weights are spread over a wider range. This would also result in variable thread counts across the fabric and this variation would increase even further if the weights were used to weave twills. The variations in thread count could be reduced to some extent by having slight variations on the warp tensions as described above. They would also be reduced if they were used for the higher tension shown in Fig. 5.2.40.

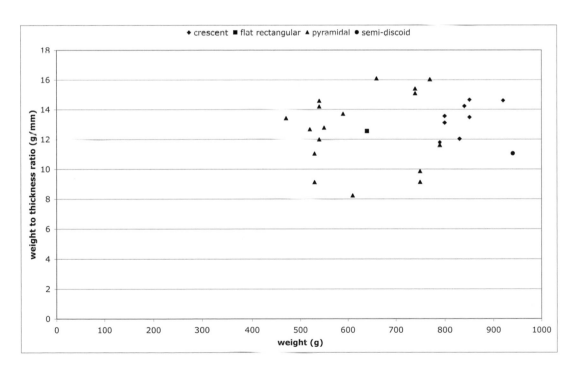

Fig. 5.2.37. Group of loomweights from Room 6, Demircihüyük (based on 27 weights).

Fig. 5.2.38. Parameters of a tabby fabric based on loom weights from Room 6, Demircihüyük.

	30 g tension		40 g tension		50 g tension		60 g tension	
	threads/l.w.	threads/cm	threads/l.w.	threads/cm	threads/l.w.	threads/cm	threads/l.w.	threads/cm
ave. l.w.	23	9	17	6	14	5	12	4
low wt.	16	9	12	7	9	5	8	5
low wt./th.	20	5	15	4	12	3	10	3
high wt.	31	10	24	7	19	6	16	5
high wt/th	22	11	17	8	13	6	11	5

Cache of 12 crescent-shaped loom weights in the 'Apsidenhaus' (MBA)

The third group of loom weights from Demircihüyük are 12 crescent-shaped weights found near a wall in the 'Apsidenhaus' in GH10 (layer 2, Middle Bronze Age), see Fig. 5.2.41.

The *average loom weight* weighs 188.8 g and has a thickness of 25.5 mm. The combined total thickness of the eight weights with sufficient data is 0.2 m, even if this is extrapolated up to 12 weights, then it only becomes 0.3 m. As this is a relatively low value, and since all of the complete weights have two holes, then it seems reasonable to assume that these weights were intended to weave 1-row tabby. Fig. 5.2.42 gives the results of this analysis.

As already noted, the variation in thread count could be reduced by some judicious variation in warp thread tension during the loom setup.

It is interesting to note that in these latter two examples from Demircihüyük, the weavers'

task is made more difficult because the weight to thickness ratio increases as the weight increases. In other words, the loom weights have been manufactured with varying weights but without the same variation in the thickness to compensate. This clearly suggests that the person who made the loom weights was unlikely to have been the weaver who had an expert understanding of the way in which the weights were going to be used.[37]

Discussion

There are numerous important points arising from the analysis of groups of loom weights in the CTR database.

Mixed types of weights in the same set

The most surprising finding is the number of instances where the groups of loom weights contain examples with very different shapes. Analyses have shown that a number of such groups in the CTR database could function

Fig. 5.2.39. Group of loom weights from Room 999, Demircihüyük.

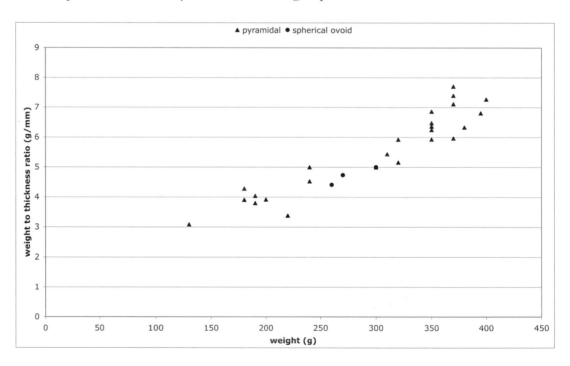

Fig. 5.2.40. Parameters of a tabby fabric based on loom weights from Room 999, Demircihüyük.

	15 g tension		20 g tension	
	threads/l.w.	threads/cm	threads/l.w.	threads/cm
average l.w.	20	7	15	6
lowest wt.	9	4	7	3
next lowest wt.	12	5	9	4
high wt.	27	10	20	7
high wt./th.	25	10	19	8

in an acceptable way as part of a set of loom weights. However, since loom weights are often simple clay items that could be manufactured quickly and easily by a potter, there would not seem to have been an obvious necessity to have a small number of odd loom weights in the set. Furthermore, the exclusion of a few odd loom weights from a set would often only decrease the width of the fabric by a small amount and so they would not seem to be essential. Since there appears to be no functional need to have mixed types within the same set, perhaps it is necessary to look wider for a possible explanation.

This discussion can be extended to consider imported loom weights (see also Cutler 2012). A recent study of the loom weights from Malia particularly highlighted two MM II discoid loom weights that are made from the same fabric (fabric E) as contemporary ceramic imports from the Mirabello region (Cutler *et al.* 2013). Within the CTR database entries from Quartier Mu, there are a total of five weights

that are indicated either as being made from fabric E or from the Mirabello region and these were not found together. Similarly, one of the Pseira weights is said to have Mirabello fabric and three of the weights from Ayia Irini were probably imported. In addition, ten of the weights from Miletos were probably imported, five from Mesara on Crete. Two of the weights found at Mochlos had inclusions that were typical of objects found at Gournia. Finally, three of the weights found at Akrotiri appear to be from Miletos and one from Naxos. Thus, there is widespread evidence of weights being imported onto sites.

Barber notes that simple clay loom weights had no intrinsic value and had value only to the craftswoman and so they had no reason to travel except with her (Barber 1991, 299). In a discussion of the loom weights from Mochlos, Soles drew attention to the two loom weights that had been produced at Gournia but placed a different emphasis on the reason for them having been taken to Mochlos: "These

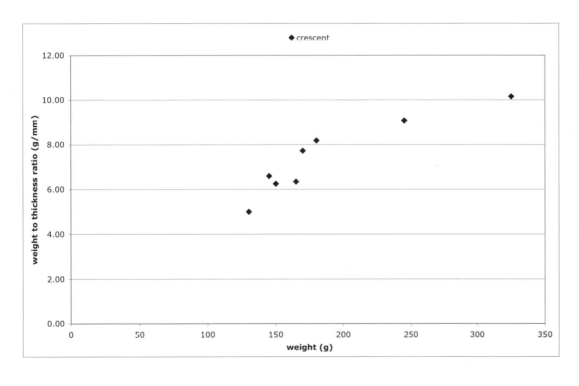

Fig. 5.2.41. Group of loom weights from 'Apsidenhaus', Demircihüyük.

	10 g tension		15 g tension	
	threads per l.w	threads per cm	threads per l.w	threads per cm
average l.w.	19	7	13	5
lightest l.w.	13	5	9	3
heaviest l.w.	25	9	16	6

Fig. 5.2.42. Parameters of a tabby fabric based on loom weights from 'Apsidenhaus', Demircihüyük.

exceptions probably were not imports because simple clay weights had no intrinsic value. Nevertheless, such weights were of great value to a craftswoman making her cloth, and they were probably transported with her upon her "marriage" or in a short-distance migration" (Soles 2004, 28–29).

Whilst loom weights might have been carried during short-distance migration, this is less plausible for travel from Crete to Miletos. Furthermore, there is the finding that most of the weights in the Akrotiri group were made locally but one appears to be from Naxos and three from Miletos. Taken together, these give the impression that isolated weights were travelling rather than whole sets. Perhaps a parallel should be drawn here with the weights of odd shapes being incorporated into sets.

It is tentatively suggested that, sets of loom weights incorporating weights of mixed types and mixed provenance might be due to craftswomen incorporating 'odd' weights into their set of loom weights for personal rather than wholly practical reasons. The most obvious personal reasons for a craftswoman to use odd weights would be because they were heirlooms or had a connection with her mother or place of birth.

Variations of weight and thickness within sets
Fig. 5.2.43 sets out the variation of weights and thicknesses of loom weights of the same type within the same set.[38] There are a number of points arising from this table.

The greatest variations in both weight and thickness arise from the pebbles of Malia. Clearly these differ from all of the other sets listed because they were not manufactured. Since the amount of skill demanded from the weaver in setting up a loom increases with the variation of the loom weights, it follows that the weavers at Malia who used these weights were particularly skilled.[39]

The next greatest variation in thickness is in the pyramidal weights from the group of 29 weights from Demircihüyük. As already noted, this group had been modified by adding lumps of clay to the bottom of nine of the loom weights to increase their weights. It seems reasonable to assume that the group is actually an assemblage of weights from different sets that had to be modified to make them compatible.

For the remaining groups, the maximum to minimum ratio of the thicknesses varies from 1.2 up to 1.8, and the maximum to minimum ratio of weights varies from 1.3 up to 3.4. The general finding is that the variation of weights within a group is usually greater than that of thicknesses. However, as can be noted from the figures in the above analyses, the resulting variations in the weight to thickness ratio tend to be large. This shows that the makers of the loom weights either were not aware that it was important to keep this ratio constant in order to achieve a uniform thread count or were not concerned about variability in warp thread count.

In modern experiments and in craft weaving, it is usually taken for granted that all the loom weights are identical and that there should be the same number of weights in each row. It may reasonably be expected that there would be some variation between weights in a set manufactured in ancient times because they did not have access to modern instrumentation. However, it seems certain that the extent of variation in ancient sets of loom extends well beyond measurement uncertainties. This is because there were balance weights weighing as little as 5 g from Knossos and weighing 12 g or less found at Ayia Irini, Akrotiri, Palaikastro, Tylisos and Mavro Spelio (Petruso 1992). It can only be concluded that the makers of loom weights did not consider it to be important that loom weights each weighed the same and so they worked on judgement rather than taking the trouble to measure the weight of the clay being used for each weight. Furthermore, it is evident from some of the higher weight ratios that the amount of judgement used in these cases was minimal.

Considering the fabric
In modern weaving, a key aim is to get a uniform thread count across the fabric. It is apparent from the analyses of groups of loom weights that, for these groups, the thread count would often be variable as a consequence of the variability of the loom weights. It is worth stressing that, if uniformity of thread count was important, it could readily have been achieved by an insistence on using a uniform set of weights. The fact that there is such a variability of weights within a set appears to demonstrate that the uniformity of warp thread

Group	Type	Weight (g)			Thickness (mm)		
		min.	max.	ratio	min.	max.	ratio
Akrotiri	discoid	130	270	2.1	18	28	1.6
Apliki	torus	50	140	2.8	23	40	1.7
Arslantepe 24	discoid	279	584	2.1	35	62	1.8
Arslantepe 12	conical	652	828	1.3	77	95	1.2
Arslantepe 22	hemispherical	492	870	1.8	76	101	1.3
Demircihüyük 29	pyramidal	470	790	1.7	35	82	2.3
Demircihüyük 33	pyramidal	130	400	3.1	42	65	1.5
Demircihüyük 12	crescent	130	325	2.5	22	32	1.5
Khania 33	spherical	425	1042	2.5	66	100	1.5
Khania 13	spherical	200	500	2.5	54	73	1.4
Kommos	discoid	47	160	3.4	14	24	1.7
Malia 41	spherical	175	380	2.2	50	72	1.4
Malia 30	spherical	105	185	1.8	40	55	1.4
Malia 34	pebbles	40	220	5.5	18	65	3.6
Malia 62	spherical rounded	290	380	1.3	61	72	1.2

Fig. 5.2.43. Variation of weights and thicknesses of loom weights of the same type within the same set.

count was not considered to be of primary importance.[40] One possible reason for this is that many textiles were probably weft-faced and so the warp threads would not have been dominant in the final fabrics. Another possible reason is that woollen fabrics might have been fulled, creating a thin layer of felted fibres on the fabric surface that would have covered the irregularities of the woven threads.

Concluding remarks

In chapter 5.2, the aim has been to present a series of mathematical analyses of the spindle whorls and loom weights listed within the CTR database. The mathematical methods presented here have been developed specifically for this application. They have been presented in some detail as it is hoped that they will be applied more widely in future to other databases of textile tools.

It cannot be claimed that the results of the analyses presented are generally applicable to any particular chronological period or geographical area. Nevertheless, they are clearly representative of the large number of textile tools within the CTR database. Furthermore, initial comparisons of torus loom weights from Aegean and Viking sites

have shown that, although such data are from very diverse archaeological settings, they can readily be plotted together on the same graph. It remains to be shown the extent to which the results presented here have a validity that extends beyond the textile tools in the CTR database.

Finally, it is worth noting that it would have been possible to extend these analyses much further if there had been more experimental information available on the relationship between thread diameter and the tension required in a warp-weighted loom. At first sight, there should be a simple relationship between the thread diameter and the required tension. However, this is complicated by the variability of thread diameters of hand-spun threads and also the fact that the maximum tension is determined by the weakest point of the thread, rather than the average diameter. With more experimentation it may be possible to overcome these difficulties by characterizing more fully hand-spun threads and relating these threads to the tension required in a loom. However, there would still remain the limitations that are implicit in this area of experimental archaeology, in particular, the challenge of reproducing the type and quality of fibre.

Notes

1 A number of these points have already been considered by Verhecken (Verhecken 2010).

2 Moment of inertia is the inertia of a rotating body. It can be understood as the rotational analogue of mass for linear motion. It is a measure of an object's resistance to change in its rate of rotation. Thus, a flywheel, which is a device used for storing rotational energy has a relatively high moment of inertia. If we consider the abstract concept of a 'point mass' (an object with all of its mass concentrated at a point), then its moment of inertia is its mass multiplied by the square of its distance from the axis of rotation. Mathematically, moments of inertia of real objects can be calculated by assuming that the real object is made up 'point masses' and integrating over the volume of the object. However, for practical applications, the moments of inertia for many shapes have been calculated and tabulated in engineering handbooks and on the internet.

3 For the convenience of readers, the commonly used term 'weight' will be used in this discussion rather than 'mass'. [Strictly, weight is a force equal to mass multiplied by the acceleration of gravity.]

4 This discussion runs counter to the proposal of Verhecken (Verhecken 2010).

5 Verhecken suggests an error estimate of 20% or more for moments of inertia calculated in this way, however, it would seem to be over optimistic to expect errors as low as this, particularly for clay spindle whorls where the material density is poorly defined (Verhecken 2010).

6 Verhecken makes the reasonable suggestion that the contribution of the shaft would generally be less than the error in the calculation of moment of inertia. Note that in his calculation of moments of inertia of spindles from the estimated density of the spindle whorl, Verhecken chooses to take account of the hole in the whorl but neglects the shaft (Verhecken 2010). However, if the moment of inertia of the shaft is neglected, then it is more accurate also to neglect the hole in the whorl since the 'fictitious' material in the hole compensates to some extent for the neglect of the shaft.

7 See Andersson 2003. It is for this reason that Verhecken's estimate that shaft lengths were 30 centimetres is misleading (Verhecken 2010).

8 See Crewe, who demonstrated that it was not efficient to use spindle whorls with holes that were double cone-shaped (Crewe 1998).

9 Of the ~4000 items listed as spindle whorls, 68 have double cone-shaped holes (including 37 pierced sherds); 138 of the holes are described as off-centre and these were also excluded from the analysis. However, those with holes that are slightly off-centre were not excluded on that basis since a slight irregularity would seem to be acceptable.

10 The lighter whorls with large holes are frequently made from bones that have very probably suffered a loss of bone density during the millennia since the object was used.

11 This plot excludes those items specified above. It is also restricted to those spindle whorls that were weighed and are complete or have only small fragments missing (because weights that are estimated tend to have weights rounded to the nearest multiple of ten grams and this introduces additional inaccuracy).

12 The 54 bone whorls sit on a higher trajectory than shown in Figure 5.2.1, with whorls of the same weight having a larger diameter. For these objects, their weights today are less than they would have been when they were originally manufactured because of loss of bone density during the millennia whilst the object was buried. Since it is not possible to give an accurate estimate of the original weight of these objects, it has been decided to exclude them from further consideration in this section.

13 See for example, the Spantidaki and Moulhérat (2012) samples identified as Akrotiri pillar pit no. 52, Pylona jar 16495, Korfu bronze basin 26636, Merenda bronze urn, Falère iron pin.

14 Within the square brackets, the first two terms are the areas of the warp and weft threads respectively and the third term is subtracting the overlap area of the warp and weft threads (to avoid this area being double accounted). These calculations do not take into account changes due to fulling.

15 Grömer (2012, 54) gives an example of the archaeological remains of an extraordinarily wide loom (*c.* 3 m) at Kleinklein, Austria with 125 loom weights of different shapes, sizes and weights.

16 Because ancient loom weights were not perfectly manufactured, it is likely that the actual width of a row of loom weights is slightly larger than the sum of the measured thicknesses of each loom weight. However, as already noted, this is acceptable and does not usually cause problems.

17 See chapter 4.1. It should be emphasized that it is not being suggested that 10 is an absolute minimum of the number of threads per loom weight and 8 or 9 are totally unacceptable. It will be shown that the weights of loom weights within a set can be very variable. Therefore, it is quite possible that, within the same set of loom weights, some weights were used with 10 threads but others were used, for example, with 8, 9, 11 or 12 threads, depending on size and weight variations.

18 It is interesting to note that, of the eight loom weights that weigh less than 20 g, five were from Tell el-Ajjul, two were from Demircihüyük and one from Miletus. However, it will also be suggested in chapter 6.5 that some of the lighter items from Malia that were categorised as loom weights are more probably spindle whorls.

19 It is possible to use loom weights with no holes by binding the weights and then attaching the warp threads to the bindings (see, for example, Hoffmann 1964, 66–67).

20 These assessments are for weights that are either complete or have only small fragments missing (excluding spools).

21 These loom weights are whole, have small fragments missing or are partial but with more than half the loom weight remaining. In the latter case, data are only included if an estimate has been made of the weight of the complete loom weights. Spools have been excluded. The numbers of loom weights in this figure are as follows: biconical 1; conical 20; crescent 141; cube 7; cylindrical (long) 50; cylindrical 65; discoid 561; flat 89; hemispherical 13; pyramidal 148; semi-discoid 10; spherical 380; thick rectangular; 8; torus 28; other 23; total 1544.

22 All of the loom weights considered in this chapter are whole, have small fragments missing or are partial but with more than half the loom weight remaining. In the latter case, data are only used if an estimate has been made of the weight of the complete loom weights.

23 For completeness, we should note that the variations from a perfect line occur: because the "spherical" loom weights are not literally spherical; because the density of clay is variable; because some of these loom weights were fired and others are made from unfired clay; because the size of the hole through the loom weight varies. In addition, there are three stone spherical loom weights included in this plot, although their presence does not increase the scatter on the plot.

24 These calculations assume that each loom weight is attached to 10 to 30 threads and there are no more than 200 loom weights per metre width of fabric. The thread counts for 2/2 twills would be approximately double those shown in Fig. 5.2.19.

25 The ranges of threads/cm shown in these tables exclude values based on only one or two instances since these can be regarded as atypical of the general mass of data. They also exclude the examples requiring more than 200 loom weights to weave a one metre width of textile.

26 For loom weights where more than half is preserved.

27 As before, the ranges of threads/cm shown in these tables exclude values based on only one or two instances since these can be regarded as atypical of the general mass of data. They also

exclude the small number of examples requiring more than 200 loom weights to weave a one metre width of textile.

28 There are 20 conical weights and 148 pyramidal loom weights shown in Fig. 5.2.28. The height to thickness ratio for the conical weights is 1.28 (cf. 1.73 for the pyramidal weights).

29 On Fig. 5.2.31, there are 69 data points from Birka, 514 from Hedeby and 28 from the CTR database.

30 See Hoffmann (for example 1964, 42). It could be objected that such examples are based on people who were not actively involved in weaving but were trying to recall the techniques that they had seen many years previously using the weaving equipment that they had inherited. However, the main text refers to the sets of loom weights they were using rather than the detailed weaving techniques and so we are not relying here on fading memories. Nevertheless, we should also note that the loom weights shown in the drawings of an Icelandic loom, dating from a period when the warp-weighted loom was actively being used (*c.* 1778–80; Hoffmann 1964, 116–117), appear to be more uniform than those shown in the example quoted (Hoffmann 1964, 42).

31 Many loom weights that were in use would have fallen from upper floors (where there was more daylight for weaving). In these cases, there is some ambiguity about whether or not the weights belong to the same set. Therefore, these are excluded from the analysis in this section.

32 We can see this from the remains of a loom at the Iron Age settlement on Bornholm (Mannering and Andersson Strand 2009, 60). In this case, there are clearly the remains of two rows of loom weights but many of the loom weights in one of rows are completely absent.

33 For this reason, all references will be to groups of loom weights rather than to sets because the latter term would tend to imply that the set was complete.

34 In principle, conical cups might have been used as loom-weights, however, that seems most unlikely in view of the discussion on sherds and loom weights given in the previous section.

35 Baykal-Seeher and Obladen-Kauder (Baykal-Seeher and Obladen-Kauder 1996, 239) make an alternative suggestion (that these weights were used to weave tabby using a hybrid combination, with the 2-holed weights giving tension to threads from both front and back rows, but one-holed weights only giving tension to one row of threads) but the same objection applies.

36 There are three other weights in the CTR database with lumps of clay attached and these were found at Troia.

37 A fuller discussion of the textile tools of Demircihüyük is given by Firth (2012).

38 Note that Fig. 5.2.43 does not compare the weights and thicknesses of weights of different types since these would generally be quite large and it would not provide information about the repeatability of manufactured loom weights. Similarly, it does not include the weights from Akrotiri that might have been imported. Fig. 5.2.43 also excludes the large storage groups of loom weights from Malia and Knossos in cases where there is insufficient confidence that the weights were from the same set. Finally, it excludes the group from Troia because of the small numbers.

39 Strictly, it is also possible that the people of Malia were particularly poor weavers. However, this seems unlikely in view of the large number of loom weights found at this site and, hence, the importance of weaving in that community.

40 It is also possible that the variability of weights within a cache occurs because each cache is made up of small numbers of loom weights from numerous different sets. However, whilst this is technically feasible, it is judged to be unlikely.

Bibliography

Andersson, E. (2003) *Tools for Textile Production from Birka and Hedeby: Excavations in the Black Earth 1990–1995*. Stockholm. Birka Project, Riksantikvarieämbetet.

Barber, E. J. W. (1991) *Prehistoric Textiles: The Development of Cloth in the Neolithic and Bronze Ages with Special Reference to the Aegean*. Princeton. Princeton University Press.

Carington Smith, J. (1992) Spinning and weaving equipment, in Macdonald, W. A. and Wilkie, N. C. (eds), *Excavations at Nichoria in Southwestern Greece. 2. The Bronze Age Occupation*, 674–711. Minneapolis. University of Minnesota Press.

Catling, E. A., Catling, H. W. and Smyth, D. (1979) Knossos 1975: Middle Minoan III and Late Minoan I Houses by the Acropolis, *Annual of the British School at Athens* 74, 1–80, sp. 61–65.

Catling, H. W. (1976–1977) The Knossos Area, 1974–1976, *Archaeological Reports* 23, 3–23, sp. 7–8.

Crewe, L. (1998) *Spindle Whorls: A Study of Form, Function and Decoration in Prehistoric Bronze Age Cyprus*. Jonsered. Paul Åström.

Cutler, J. (2012) Ariadne's thread: the adoption of Cretan weaving technology in the wider southern Aegean in the mid-second millennium BC, in Nosch, M.-L. and Laffineur, R. (eds), *KOSMOS. Jewellery, Adornment and Textiles in the Aegean Bronze Age*, 145–154 . Liège. Peeters.

Cutler, J., Andersson Strand, E., Nosch, M.-L. (2013) Textile production in Quartier Mu, in Poursat J.-Cl. (ed.), *Fouilles exécutées à Malia. Le Quartier Mu V. Vie quotidienne et techniques au Minoen Moyen II*, 95–118. Athens. École Française d'Athènes.

Evely, D. (2000) *Minoan Crafts: Tools and Techniques: An Introduction*. Göteborg. Paul Åström.

Evely, R. D. G. (1984) The other finds of stone, clay, ivory, faience, lead etc., in Popham, M. (ed.), *The Minoan Unexplored Mansion at Knossos*, 223–259. Oxford. Thames and Hudson.

Firth, R. (2012) The textile tools of Demircihüyük in Nosch, M.-L. and Laffineur, R. (eds), *KOSMOS. Jewellery, Adornment and Textiles in the Aegean Bronze Age*, 131–138. Liège. Peeters.

Frangipane, M., Andersson Strand, E., Laurito, R., Möller-Wiering, S., Nosch, M.-L., Rast-Eicher, A. and Wisti Lassen, A. (2009) Arslantepe, Malatya (Turkey): textiles, tools and imprints of fabrics from the 4th to the 2nd millennium BC, *Paléorient*, 35 (1), 5–29.

Friend, G. (1998) *Tell Taannek 1963–1968*. III: 2. *The Loom Weights*. Birzeit. Birzeit University.

Grömer, K. (2012) Austria: Bronze and Iron Ages, in Gleba M. and Mannering U. (eds), *Textiles and Textile Production in Europe from Prehistory to AD 400*, 27–64. Ancient Textiles Series 11. Oxford. Oxbow Books.

Hammarlund, L. (2005) Handicraft knowledge applied to archaeological textiles, *The Nordic Textile Journal*, 87–119.

Hoffmann, M. (1964) *The Warp-Weighted Loom: Studies in the History and Technology of an Ancient Implement*. Oslo. Universitetsforlaget.

Mårtensson, L., Nosch, M.-L., and Andersson, E. (2009) Shape of things: understanding a loom weight, *Oxford Journal of Archaeology*, 28 (4), 373–398.

Petruso, K. M. (1992) *Keos VIII. Ayia Irini: The Balance Weights. An Analysis of Weight Measurement in Prehistoric Crete and the Cycladic Islands*. Mainz. Philipp von Zabern.

Soles, J. S. (2004) *Mochlos IC: Period III: Neopalatial Settlement on the Coast: The Artisans' Quarter and the Farmhouse at Chalinomouri. The Small Finds*. Philadelphia. INSTAP Academic Press.

Spantidaki, Y. and Moulhérat, C. (2012) Greece, in Gleba, M. and Mannering, U. (eds), *Textiles and Textile Production in Europe from Prehistory to AD 400*, 185–200. Ancient Textiles Series 11. Oxford. Oxbow Books.

Verhecken, A. (2010) The moment of inertia: a parameter for functional classification of worldwide spindle whorls from all periods, in Andersson Strand, E., Gleba, M., Mannering, U., Munkholt, C. and Ringgaard, M. (eds), *North European Symposium for Archaeological Textiles (NESAT) X*, 257–270. Ancient Textiles Series 5. Oxford. Oxbow Books.

CHAPTER 6.1

Textile tools and textile production – studies of selected Bronze Age sites: introduction

Eva Andersson Strand, Marie-Louise Nosch and Joanne Cutler

This chapter will focus on the evidence for the nature of textile production at 15 selected Bronze Age sites (Fig. 6.1.1). As written in the introduction to the database (chapter 5.1), many of the tools have been recovered from mixed contexts or do not have a secure date. In other cases the tools have been dated very widely; for example, to the Early, Middle or Late Bronze Age. Furthermore, in several cases a period or a context is only represented by a few tools. The case studies discussed in this chapter are sites with one or more securely dated contexts represented by several tools.[1]

The aim is to give good examples of how textile tools can be used to discuss textile production during a particular period or within a particular building at a specific site. In each case the chronological system adopted by the collaborators has been used (for a general chronological chart please see the introduction). Each case study is based on the technical textile tools report (chapter 5.1) and incorporates the results of the analyses of the textile tool assemblage from the individual site, together with a context description, in collaboration with the collaborators for the site.

In order to provide a wide range of examples, the various studies presented have various perspectives and slightly different approaches, all relating to the site in question. The results of the tool analyses are presented in a similar way in each case, however. The different textile tools from a particular site are presented in tables (chapter 5.1). The weight and diameter of spindle whorls with a recordable weight and diameter (that is, with both a complete or estimated original weight and a preserved diameter) and the weight and thickness of loom weights with a recordable weight and thickness (that is, with both a complete or estimated original weight and a preserved thickness) are presented in graphs. In some cases, the markers in a graph can represent more than one spindle whorl or loom weight, if two or more spindle whorls or loom weights have the same weight and diameter/thickness. Where this is the case, it has been noted in the caption. The fact that some markers represent more than a single tool does not alter the visible clusters, since the extra tools lie within the visible groupings.

The spinning experiments with suspended spindles conducted in the TTTC research programme have confirmed that the quality of fibres, the spinner and the weight of the spindle whorl affect the finished product, *i.e.* the spun yarn, with the weight of the whorl having a significant effect (chapter 4.1). However, as it is not possible to determine exactly what types of yarn were produced with a specific spindle whorl, the thread range will only be referred to in general categories: 'very thin', 'thin', 'medium', 'thick' or 'very thick' (Fig. 6.1.2). Furthermore,

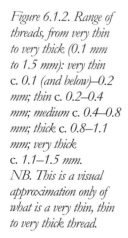

Figure 6.1.1. Map showing the location of the sites discussed in the case studies (map: Christian Schmidt).

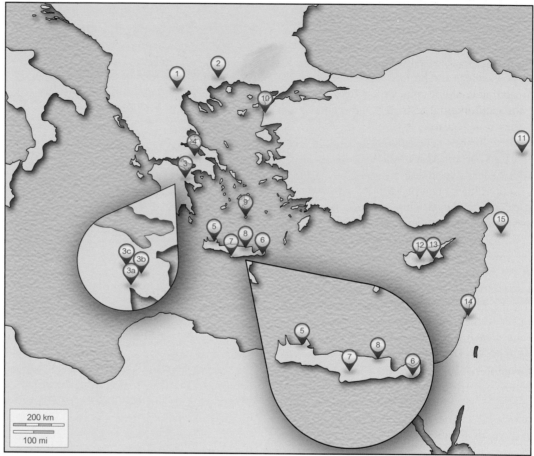

Northern Greece
1: Sitagroi
2: Archontiko

Mainland Greece
3a: Tiryns
3b: Midea
3d: Mycenae
4: Thebes

Crete
5: Khania
6: Ayia Triada
7: Phaistos
8: Malia

Aegean Islands
9: Akrotiri

Western Anatolia
10: Troia

Central and Eastern Anatolia
11: Arslantepe

Cyprus
12: Apliki
13: Kition

Levant
14: Tell Kabri
15: Ebla

Figure 6.1.2. Range of threads, from very thin to very thick (0.1 mm to 1.5 mm): very thin c. 0.1 (and below)–0.2 mm; thin c. 0.2–0.4 mm; medium c. 0.4–0.8 mm; thick c. 0.8–1.1 mm; very thick c. 1.1–1.5 mm. NB. This is a visual approximation only of what is a very thin, thin to very thick thread.

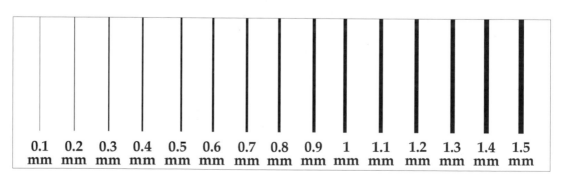

when discussing yarn produced with a specific spindle whorl it is important to bear in mind that there will always be a range and that it is not possible to suggest a particular thread diameter (chapter 4.5). Since so few textiles have been preserved in the area under study, the categories of thread thickness used are largely based on wider analyses of ancient textiles from other regions and time periods (for example, the preserved textiles from Egypt; see Barber 1991; Kemp and Vogelsang-Eastwood 2001) and on the possibilities and limitations of the range of thread that could be spun with different whorls in the experimental tests. If a large corpus of textiles was available, it would be possible to establish firmer categories regarding what a 'very thin', or 'very thick', *etc.* thread looked like.

In order to visualise the range of fabrics that could have been produced with a specific loom weight and/or cluster of loom weights, calculations have been made based on the TTTC loom weight tests (chapter 4). However, it should be noted that while it is possible to estimate the number of warp threads, the number of weft threads can only be guessed at (chapter 4.5). Evidence of tabby weaving exists from the area and period under study and since tabby weaving is considered to be the most common weaving technique during the Bronze Age (chapter 3), the analyses were carried out for this type of fabric. Twill weaving cannot be excluded (see chapters 3 and 4) and the loom weights could also be used to make twill fabric.

The calculations are based on the weight and the thickness of the loom weights and the different parameters, such as there being no less than 10 threads and no more than 30 threads on a loom weight, defined in the loom weight tests (chapters 4.1 and 4.5). It is also important to note that what is presented will always be a range of possible fabrics, since all loom weights can be used with different types of thread

needing different tension. For example, if a loom weight weighs 300 g the weaver can attach 10 threads needing 30 g tension or 30 threads needing 10 g tension (chapter 4.5).

Thread tensions of 5 g, 10 g, 15 g and further 5 g intervals up to 70 g tension, were used when evaluating an individual loom weight's suitability for use with threads needing different tensions. Occasionally, 7.5 g and 12.5 g thread tensions have also been included in order to demonstrate the functional range of a particular loom weight group. It is important to note that these tensions have been chosen in order to give a general spread, since the tension needed could also be 6 g, 11 g, 16 g, *etc.* In general, a thicker thread needs more tension than a thinner thread; however, the tension required is also related to the weight of the thread (see chapter 4.5).

Thread needing *c.* 10 g tension or below is in this chapter described as 'very thin'; *c.* 15 g to *c.* 20 g tension thread is described as 'thin'; *c.* 25 g to *c.* 35 g tension thread is 'medium'; *c.* 40 g to *c.* 50 g tension thread is 'thick; *c.* 55 g to *c.* 70 g tension thread is 'very thick'. However, harder spun thread will also need more tension than thread that is not so hard spun (see chapter 4.5).

As concluded in the TTTC experiments, thread that needs slightly different tension can be used in the same loom setup; for example, thread needing 40 g tension could be used together with thread that requires 45 g tension. Furthermore, the exact number of warp threads per centimetre can of course vary within the same fabric. If a fabric is dense, *i.e.* the warp threads are close together, whether they are thin or thick threads, there is not much room for the threads to move, meaning that the number of threads per centimetre will be more consistent. However, if the fabric is more open, there is a greater possibility that the threads can move, and the warp thread count

Figure 6.1.3. Different types of tabby fabrics illustrated with different numbers of threads per centimetre. The thread thickness is based on the average of the wool thread spun with spindle whorls of different weights in the TTTC experiments (chapter 4), (left) 4 g spindle (needing 13 g tension per warp thread), (middle) 8 g spindle (needing 18 g tension per warp thread), (right) 18 g spindle (needing 25–30 g tension per warp thread).

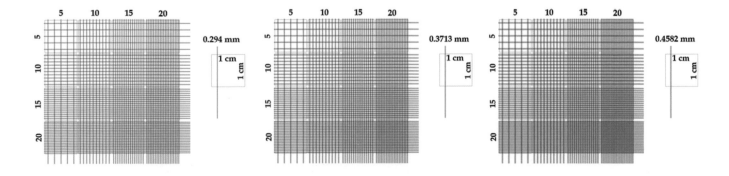

can therefore vary more (see also chapter 4.5). For example, at one point in the fabric there could be 5 threads per centimetre, but 7 threads per centimetre at another point. In general, the warp threads in a tabby are more moveable than in a twill fabric. According to analyses of archaeological textiles, tabby fabrics often vary by 1–3 threads in a centimetre, and sometimes more. Moreover, the thread count in a textile when it is on the loom can alter when it is cut down, and when it has been finished (see chapter 4.5). The visual appearance of a fabric will vary according to the thickness of the thread and the number of threads in the warp and the weft (Fig. 6.1.3). A fabric can be balanced, with approximately the same number and type of threads in both the warp and the weft (Figs. 6.1.4–5). A fabric can also be unbalanced; in a weft faced fabric there are more and/or thicker weft threads than warp threads per centimetre[2] (Fig. 6.1.6), while in a warp faced fabric there are more and/or thicker warp threads than weft threads per centimetre[2]. For a 2/1 twill using three rows of loom weights the thread count would be approximately 1.5 times the estimated thread count given for tabby fabrics, while for a

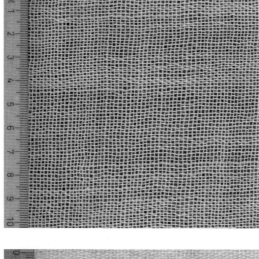

Figure 6.1.4. Balanced open tabby, with an average of 6.1 warp threads and 7.4 weft threads per cm (wool fabric) (photo: CTR).

Figure 6.1.5. (left) Balanced tabby, 14 warp and 14 weft threads per cm (linen fabric) (photo: CTR).

Figure 6.1.6. (right) Weft faced tabby, with an average of 5.8 warp threads and 14.8 weft threads per cm (wool fabric) (photo: CTR).

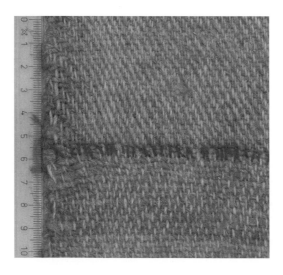
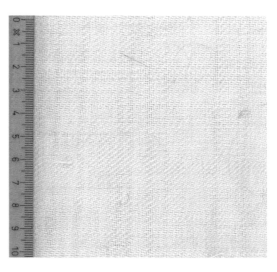

Figure 6.1.7. (left) 2/1 twill, with an average of 6 warp threads and 4 weft threads per cm. The top half shows the twill structure, while the lower half shows the reverse side with the tabby structure (photo: CTR).

Figure 6.1.8. (right) 2/2 twill, with an average of 14.6 warp threads and 14.6 weft threads per cm (photo: CTR).

Warp thr/cm	5 g, N=0	7.5 g, N=0	10 g, N=0	12.5 g, N=13	15 g, N=35	20 g, N=35	25 g, N=35	30 g, N=35	35 g, N=35	40 g, N=22	45 g, N=0	50 g, N=0	55 g, N=0	60 g, N=0	65 g, N=0	70 g, N=0
1 thr																
2 thr																
3 thr																
4 thr																
5 thr									3	9						
6 thr								3	21	6						
7 thr							3	21	11	7						
8 thr							15	4								
9 thr						3	10	7								
10 thr						15	7									
11 thr						6										
12 thr					3	4										
13 thr					6	7										
14 thr				3	9											
15 thr					10											
16 thr				6												
17 thr																
18 thr					7											
19 thr				4												
20 thr																

2/2 twill using four rows of loom weights the thread count would be approximately double (Figs. 6.1.7–8).

The N number (used in the figures throughout chapter 6 that show the number of warp threads per centimetre in relation to thread tension) refers to the number of loom weights from the specific group that could be used with thread needing the given tension; for example, 30 g, N=35 indicates that 35 of the loom weights from this specific group would function well with a thread needing 30 g tension (see Fig. 6.1.9). With these loom weights and 30 g warp tension, it would be possible to weave fabrics with 6–9 warp threads per cm. Most of them (21) would be suitable for producing a fabric with 7 warp threads per cm.

The sites analysed cover a wide time span and geographical area, with some areas and periods within the Bronze Age being much better represented in the database than others (see chapter 5.1). Therefore, of course, the results of the analyses cannot provide a wholly representative picture of textile production in this region during the Bronze Age. Instead, the different sites will give information on how textile production can be visualised in different contexts, periods and regions and how it is possible to combine the recording of textile tools, textile technology, experimental archaeology and context description in order to obtain a better understanding of textile production in the past.

Note

1 Please note that the analyses of textiles and textile production at the two sites, Arslantepe, Turkey and Ebla, Syria have already been published (Frangipane *et al.* 2009; Andersson *et al.* 2010).

Bibliography

Andersson, E., Felluca, E., Nosch, M.-L. and Peyronel, L. (2010) New perspectives on Bronze Age textile production in the Eastern Mediterranean. The first results with Ebla as a pilot study, in Matthiae, P., Pinnock, F., Nigro, L. and Marchetti, N. (eds), *Proceedings of the 6th International Congress on the Archaeology of the Ancient Near East,* 1, 159–176. Wiesbaden. Harrassowitz Verlag.

Barber, E. J. W. (1991) *Prehistoric Textiles: The Development of Cloth in the Neolithic and Bronze Ages with Special Reference to the Aegean.* Princeton. Princeton University Press.

Frangipane, M., Andersson Strand, E., Laurito, R., Möller-Wiering, S., Nosch, M. –L., Rast-Eicher, A. and Wisti Lassen, A. (2009) Arslantepe, Malatya (Turkey): textiles, tools and imprints of fabrics from the 4th to the 2nd Millennium BC, *Paléorient,* 35 (1), 5–29.

Kemp, B. J. and Vogelsang-Eastwood, G. (2001) *The Ancient Textile Industry at Armana.* London. Egypt Exploration Society.

Figure 6.1.9. The number of warp threads per cm in relation to thread tension. N= the number of loom weights from the specific group (in this case 35 loom weights) that could be used with thread needing the given tension.

CHAPTER 6.2

Textile tools from Khania, Crete, Greece

Maria Bruun-Lundgren†, Eva Andersson Strand and Birgitta P. Hallager

The Greek-Swedish Excavations at Khania, west Crete, are situated on the Kastelli hill, which lies in the middle of the old town of Khania. Systematic excavations started in 1970 and are still ongoing (Fig. 6.2.1). Five thousand years of the history of the town have been uncovered in a depth of 2.5 metres. The site was first inhabited in the Early Minoan period (around 3000 BC) and, with a small gap between *c.* 1150–750 BC, it has had a continuous history until the present day. A significant amount of material dating to the Late Minoan period (1550–1150 BC) was recovered during the course of the excavations, including the textile tools presented here. Seven Late Bronze Age settlements, one on top of the other, have been unearthed and so far no other excavations in Crete have presented a comparable stratigraphy for the final 400 years of the Bronze Age. Visible at the site today is one complete, large building and parts of another three which were destroyed in a violent conflagration around 1450 BC. Linear A documents found in these, as well as in other Greek excavations in the town, reveal the importance of the site, and it is thought likely that a Minoan palace is situated somewhere in the vicinity of these houses. After the destruction the inhabitants re-settled in the ruins, but shortly after 1375 BC a profoundly changed settlement emerged. This, however, was still one of the most important centres of the island, as witnessed by the discovery of large transport stirrup jars inscribed with Mycenaean Linear B signs, as well as Linear B tablets which elsewhere on Crete have to date only been recovered from the palace at Knossos. When this settlement was destroyed it was rebuilt several times, before it was finally abandoned by its inhabitants sometime in the middle of the 12th century BC.[1]

Textile production at the Late Minoan settlement is evidenced by a carbonised fragment of cloth,[2] and is also well attested by the presence of textile tools. The large amount of bones from sheep and goat, as well as quantities of murex shells found at the site, suggests that the raw material for the textiles included goat's hair (as evidenced in the preserved textile fragment) and wool, and that textiles of a better quality may have been brightly coloured. Needles of bone and bronze provide additional evidence for textile production. Even implements that are not obviously associated with textile production, such as percussion stones, pestles and grinders, might have been used for extracting and preparing pigments from herbs or murex shells used in the dying process of textiles,

THE GREEK-SWEDISH EXCAVATIONS, Kastelli, Khania, 1970–1987

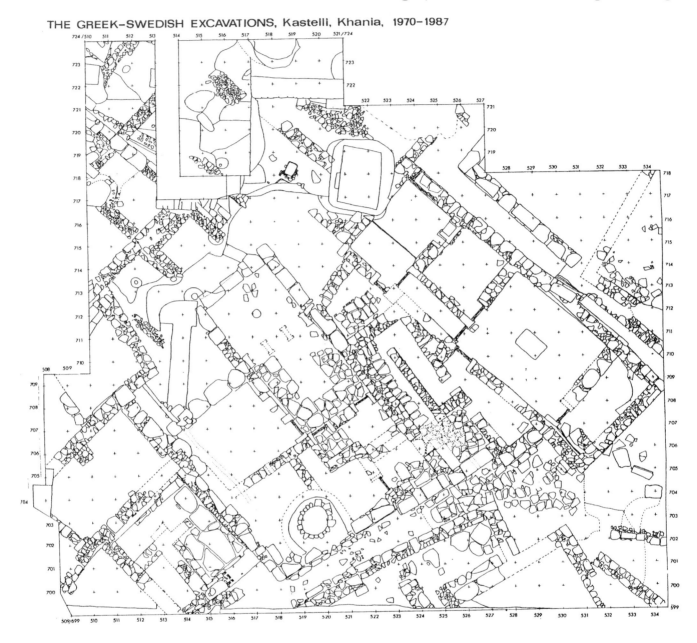

Fig. 6.2.1. Plan of all levels, the Greek-Swedish Excavations, Kastelli, Khania, 1970–1987 (drawing: courtesy of E. Hallager).

and polishers might have been useful for smoothing out cloth.

In general, objects associated with various craft activities were found scattered over most of the settlement during the different periods, thus not indicating any significant degree of concentration or specialisation in the different craft activities. In most cases, textile implements were found together with objects related to the manufacture of bronze, stone or bone artifacts. Weaving, alongside other handicraft and domestic activities, seems at least sometimes to have taken place in rooms

with an oven or a fireplace. In three cases, spool-shaped loom weights were found near an oven in LM III contexts. In Room M in the LM I House I, spherical loom weights that are likely to have fallen from a loom (see below) were found beside a hearth. Further spherical loom weights were stored in the adjacent Room E.

There is a general difference between the quality of the spindle whorls and the loom weights of terracotta. The spindle whorls are made of better quality clay, properly fired, covered with a slip and/or paint and occasionally decorated (those that are cut out of kylix stems

	Spindle whorl	Kylix stem whorl	Spindle whorl/bead	Loom weight	Spool	Pin/pinbeater	Needle	Total
LM I			1	52		1		54
LM IIIA2		1	3	6	1			11
LM IIIB1	3	11	2	17		1	1	35
LM IIIB2	5	9	8	13	4	6	1	46
LM IIIC	8	11	3	7	18			47
Total	16	32	17	95	23	8	2	193

Fig. 6.2.2. Textile tools from securely dated contexts, by type and date.

	Spherical	Discoid	Cylindrical	Spool	Torus	Other	Unspecified	Total
LM I	40	6	6					52
LM IIIA2		6		1				7
LM IIIB1	1	9	3			2	2	17
LM IIIB2		11		4			2	17
LM IIIC		5		18	2			25
Total	41	37	9	23	2	2	4	118

Fig. 6.2.3. Loom weights, by type and date.

are *a priori* of a good quality). The explanation is probably that since a spindle whorl was carried around in both indoor and outdoor activities (when its owner combined spinning with different activities such as looking after children, guarding cattle, *etc.*), it was probably considered as part of an individual's personal equipment, in contrast to a loom weight which was more a part of the domestic household equipment and was kept inside the house.

A total number of 452 objects from the buildings on Kastelli hill excavated up to 2001 are recorded in the database. Of these, 193 are from securely dated Bronze Age contexts (Fig. 6.2.2).

Loom weights and weaving

A number of loom weight shapes are represented among the 118 loom weights from dated contexts, with spherical, discoid and spool types being the most frequent (Fig. 6.2.3). The discoid loom weights are present in each period, while the majority of the spherical loom weights date to LM I (Neopalatial period) and the spools are primarily from LM IIIB2 and LM IIIC deposits.

Most of the 52 loom weights from LM I contexts are found within the houses. Forty-eight of these were recovered from House I, with the majority deriving from two floor deposits, one in Room M and the other in Room E (Fig. 6.2.4).

Fig. 6.2.4. LM IB House I, Room M. Details of loom weights on floor. Carbonised remains in the upper part are probably remains of the loom (photo: courtesy of E. Hallager 1982).

The majority of the LM I loom weights are spherical, but six discoid and six cylindrical weights are also present (Fig. 6.2.3). Thirty-seven of the loom weights had a recordable weight and thickness (Fig. 6.2.5).

In Room M, one loom weight was found in the north part of the room and 13 loom weights (11 spherical and two cylindrical) were found together with carbonised wood in the south-eastern part. This group of loom weights has been interpreted as the possible remains of a warp-weighted loom (Hallager and Hallager forthcoming-b). Nine of the loom weights had a recordable weight and thickness (Fig. 6.2.5). All of these weights would function well with thread requiring *c.* 15 g tension; in a tabby weave, the resulting warp thread range would be *c.* 4–7 threads per centimetre (Fig. 6.2.6). In a twill weave, the thread count would be approximately double. Eight of the loom weights would also be suitable for use with thread requiring *c.* 20 g tension, and would give a warp thread count of *c.* 4–6 threads per centimetre in a tabby. In a balanced tabby, the resulting fabric would be very open, however, so it is likely that the textiles were weft faced.

The thirteen loom weights side by side in a row have a thickness of approximately

89.5 cm. Since a loom setup requires an even number of loom weights, it is likely that 14 loom weights were used. The thickness of the loom weights side by side would thus have been approximately 100 cm. On the loom, the loom weights would have hung in two rows, therefore the fabric would have had a width of a minimum of 50 cm. It has been posited that the loom was standing at an angle to the north wall, *c.* 1 m away from the east wall, where a window may have been placed (Hallager and Hallager forthcoming-b). If so, the light would have been excellent for weaving. Interestingly, there is no indication of the loom leaning against a wall; if the loom was standing upright, the natural shed provided by leaning the loom at an angle could not have been used, unless the loom was lent against a roof beam or some other form of support.

Thirty-two loom weights (29 spherical, two cylindrical and one discoid) were found

Fig. 6.2.5. Loom weights, LM I: context and weight/thickness. Please note that some markers represent more than one loom weight.

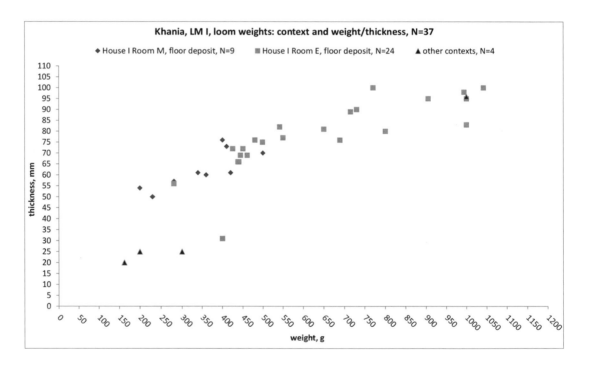

Fig. 6.2.6. Loom weights, LM I, House I Room M: weight tension/ number of threads per cm in a tabby. The total number of analysed loom weights is nine.

Warp thr/cm	10 g, N=5	15 g, N=9	20 g, N=8	25 g, N=6	30 g, N=6	35 g, N=4	40 g, N=1	45 g, N=1
3 thr					1	4	2	1	1
4 thr		1	3	3	2	2		
5 thr		3	3	2				
6 thr	1	3	2					
7 thr	1	2						
8 thr	1							
9 thr	1							
10 thr	1							

in Room E, which functioned as a store room (Hallager and Hallager forthcoming-b). Twenty-four of the weights had a recordable weight and thickness, the weight varying from 280 g to 1042 g and the thickness from 3.1 cm to 10 cm (Fig. 6.2.5). Twenty-three of these loom weights would be suitable for use with thick thread requiring *c.* 35–40 g tension; in a tabby weave, the fabric produced would have a thread count of *c.* 3–6/7 warp threads per centimetre (Fig. 6.2.7). If the weave was balanced, this would produce an open fabric, and it is likely that the textiles made with these loom weights would have been weft faced. A number of the weights would also be suitable for use with thread requiring *c.* 15–30 g and *c.* 45–70 g tension, but only one would be suitable for use with very thin thread, needing less than 15 g tension. The loom weights in Room E could therefore have been used to produce a wider range of fabrics than the loom weights in Room M, and the majority of them would have been best suited for use with thicker thread. Since the loom weights were in storage, it is possible that the various loom weights were used in different combinations with other loom weights found in the building, in various loom setups.

Fig. 6.2.7. Loom weights, LM I, House I Room E: weight tension/ number of threads per cm in a tabby. The total number of analysed loom weights is 24.

Warp thr/cm	10 g, N=1	15 g, N=7	20 g, N=12	25 g, N=16	30 g, N=18	35 g, N=23	40 g, N=23	45 g, N=21	50 g, N=16	55 g, N=13	60 g, N=12	65 g, N=8	70 g, N=8
3 thr						1	9	11	8	7	9	6	8
4 thr					1	6	11	6	5	6	6	3	2
5 thr			1	9	8	4	5	5	2				
6 thr			4	3	2	4	3						
7 thr		1		6	2	1	3						
8 thr		2			1								
9 thr		3											
10 thr	1				1								
11 thr													
12 thr													
13 thr				1									
14 thr													
15 thr													
16 thr													
17 thr		1											

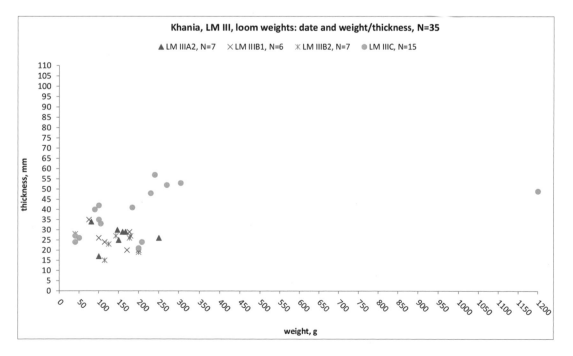

Fig. 6.2.8. Loom weights, LM III: date and weight/thickness. Please note that some markers represent more than one loom weight.

Fig. 6.2.9. Discoid loom weight 74-TC 004 (photo: courtesy of E. Hallager).

Fig. 6.2.10. Spool 71-TC 107 (photo: courtesy of E. Hallager).

Fig. 6.2.11. Loom weights, LM III: type and weight/thickness.

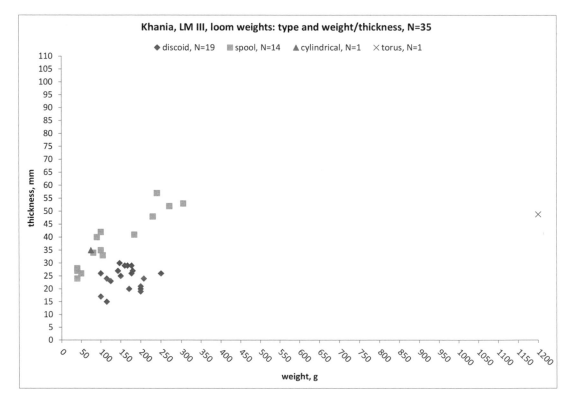

Khania, LM III, loom weights: type and weight/thickness, N=35

◆ discoid, N=19   ■ spool, N=14   ▲ cylindrical, N=1   ✕ torus, N=1

The six discoid loom weights found in LM I contexts (three from House I and three from House IV) would be suitable for producing denser textiles, with a higher number of warp threads per centimetre.

More than half of the 66 loom weights from LM III contexts are from the LM III Building 1; the remainder are mostly from areas external to the excavated buildings. Only eight were recovered from floor deposits (seven from

Building 1 and one from Building 2). Thirty-five of the LM III loom weights had a recordable weight and thickness (Fig. 6.2.8). In contrast to the loom weights from LM I deposits, the majority of the loom weights dating to LM III weigh less than 300 g and would therefore be best suited for use with thread requiring less than 30 g tension. Furthermore, there is a concentration of loom weights weighing less than 150 g, which would have been suitable for use with very thin thread needing less than 15 g tension.

The majority of the LM III loom weights are discoid or spool types (Figs. 6.2.3, 6.2.9 and 6.2.10). The discoid loom weights and the spools form two distinct weight/thickness groups (Fig. 6.2.11). There is a large degree of overlap between the weights of the two loom weight types, indicating that they would be suitable for use with thread needing a similar range of tensions. However, the resulting fabrics would be visually different, since the thinner discoid loom weights would produce a denser textile, with more warp threads per centimetre, than the thicker spools. If the spools were used to weave a balanced tabby, the finished fabric would be very open, and they would therefore be more suitable for producing weft faced textiles. The spools

weighing less than 50 g, if used as loom weights, would only be suitable for use with thread requiring less than 5 g tension, or with thread requiring *c.* 5 g tension, but with fewer than ten threads attached to them.

Eight spools were found in an LM IIIC pit deposit in Building 1, Room I. Of these, five weigh 40–100 g, while three weigh 230–305 g (Fig. 6.2.12). The spools weighing 100 g or less would function with thread needing *c.* 5 g tension. However, the resulting warp thread count in a tabby weave would be quite large: *c.* 6–11 threads per centimetre. The heavier spools would all function with thread needing *c.* 15–25 g tension; with thread requiring *c.* 15 g tension they could produce a textile with *c.* 6–8 warp threads per centimetre, and with thread needing *c.* 20 g or 25 g tension the thread count would be *c.* 5–6 and 4–6 threads per centimetre respectively. The lighter and the heavier spools would not work well together in the same setup.

In addition to the loom weights, 11 stones of almost equal size were found in an LM IIIB1 floor deposit (Space G); they lay close to a wall, in an almost straight row *c.* 0.75 m in length. It is possible that these stones may have been used as loom weights on a loom that leant against the wall (Hallager and Hallager

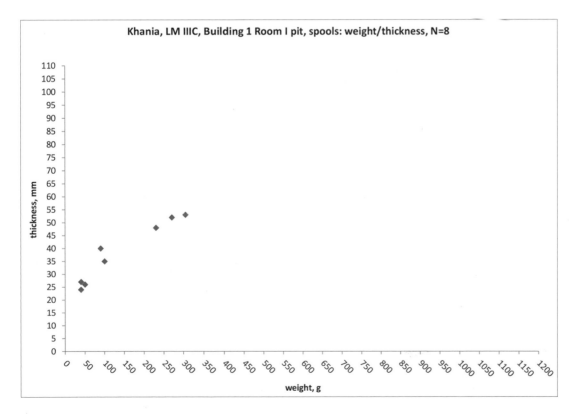

Fig. 6.2.12. Spools, LM IIIC, Building 1, Room I pit: weight/thickness.

Fig. 6.2.13. (left) Spindle whorl, biconical 76-TC 006 (photo: courtesy of E. Hallager).

Fig. 6.2.14. (right) Spindle whorl, KS whorl 80-TC 010 (photo: courtesy of E. Hallager).

Fig. 6.2.15. Bead/ Button/Spindle whorl 72-S 094 (photo: courtesy of E. Hallager).

2011). Four discoid loom weights and a kylix stem whorl were recovered from LM IIIB1 contexts in the same area.

Spindle whorls and spinning

Of the 65 whorls from dated contexts, 16 are recorded as spindle whorls, 32 as kylix stem whorls and 17 as beads (Figs. 6.2.13, 6.2.14 and 6.2.15) (for the discussion on the interpretation of different categories of spindle whorls please see chapter 7). The majority are made of clay, but eight whorls recorded as beads are made of stone and one is made of bone. The majority of the spindle whorls and the beads have a conical shape, while the kylix stem whorls are cylindrical or discoid.

Only one whorl (from a floor deposit in House I Room D), recorded as a bead, is

dated to the Neopalatial period. The shape (cylindrical), weight and diameter indicates that it could have been used as a spindle whorl.

Only four whorls (one kylix stem whorl and three beads) were recovered from LM IIIA2 deposits. Of the 60 whorls deriving from LM IIIB1, LM IIIB2 and LM IIIC contexts, 41 were from Building 1 (13 of these are from LM IIIB1 deposits, 10 are from LM IIIB2 contexts and 18 are from LM IIIC deposits). Most of the remainder were recovered from areas external to the excavated buildings.

All except one of the LM IIIB-C whorls had a recordable weight and diameter. The whorls from LM IIIB1 contexts vary in weight from 1 g to 15 g and in diameter from 1.3 cm to 2.9 cm (Fig. 6.2.16). The yarn that could have been spun with these tools would be very thin or thin. The whorls from LM IIIB2 and LM IIIC contexts weigh 1–39 g and 4–27 g respectively. The wider range of whorl weights present in both these periods suggests a slightly more varied production than during LM IIIB1, with the heavier whorls being suitable for spinning thicker thread than could be produced using the lighter whorls found in LM IIIB1 contexts. However, there appears to have been an emphasis on the production of thinner yarn: some threads might have been as thin as 0.1–0.3 mm. This type of yarn would demand very well prepared raw materials, and the fabrics produced with these threads would have taken a considerable time to make.

Summary

Only one spindle whorl is dated to the LM I period and it is therefore not possible to reach any conclusions regarding the nature of textile production during this period on the basis of the spindle whorl data. The analysis of the

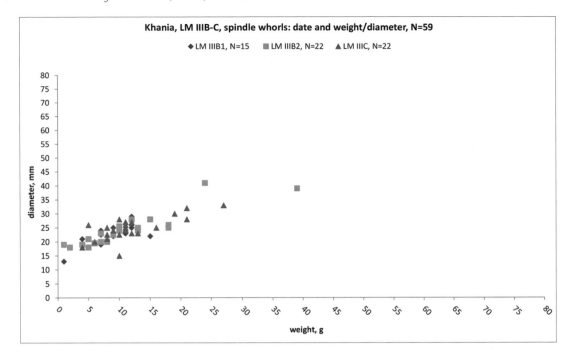

Fig. 6.2.16. Spindle whorls, LM IIIB-C: date and weight/diameter. Please note that some markers represent more than one spindle whorl.

loom weights deriving from LM I, however, suggests a varied production of different fabric types. A number of spherical loom weights that could have been used to produce a wide range of fabric qualities date to this period. A few discoid loom weights also dating to this period would have been suitable for the production of denser fabrics. Thus, the tools deriving from LM I do not suggest a specialised production, but rather the manufacture of a broad range of textiles, perhaps with an emphasis on open or weft faced weaves.

The analysis of the loom weights from LM III contexts suggests a focus on the production of finer fabrics. The spindle whorls from this period support this conclusion. There would also have been a need for coarser textiles, however. It is possible that these may have been produced using thread spun on other types of spindles (for example, using spindle whorls made of wood) and woven on a different type of loom. Alternatively, since the majority of the loom weights and spindle whorls from excavated contexts within the buildings are from Building 1, it may be the case that production in this building was focused on the manufacture of textiles made with thinner thread, and that coarser fabrics were produced elsewhere in the settlement.

Acknowledgements

We thank Maria Vlasaki, Erik Hallager, Carl-Gustaf Styrenius and Yannis Tzedakis for access to the material and Marie-Louise Nosch and Joanne Cutler for their collaboration on the textile tool analyses.

Notes

1 The LM IIIA2, LM IIIB1, LM IIIB2 and LM IIIC strata at the site have been published (Hallager and Hallager 2000, 2003 and 2011). The LM IIIA1, LM II, Neopalatial and Middle Minoan/Early Minoan strata are forthcoming (Hallager and Hallager forthcoming-a, forthcoming-b and forthcoming-c).
2 Chapter 3.1 of this publication.

Bibliography

Hallager, E. and Hallager, B. P. (2000) *The Greek-Swedish Excavations at the Agia Aikaterini Square, Kastelli, Khania 1970–1987: Results of the Excavations Under the Direction of Yannis Tzedakis and Carl-Gustaf Styrenius. II: The Late Minoan IIIC Settlement.* Stockholm. Paul Åström.

Hallager, E. and Hallager, B. P. (2003) *The Greek-Swedish Excavations at the Agia Aikaterini Square, Kastelli, Khania 1970–1987 and 2001: Results of the Excavations Under the Direction of Yannis Tzedakis and Carl-Gustaf Styrenius. III: The Late Minoan IIIB2 Settlement.* Stockholm. Paul Åström.

Hallager, E. and Hallager, B. P. (2011) *The Greek-Swedish Excavations at the Agia Aikaterini Square, Kastelli, Khania 1970–1987 and 2001: Results of the Excavations Under the Direction of Yannis Tzedakis and Carl-Gustaf Styrenius. IV: The Late Minoan IIIB1 and IIIA2 Settlements.* Stockholm. eddy.se AB.

Hallager, E. and Hallager, B. P. (forthcoming-a) *The Greek-Swedish Excavations at the Agia Aikaterini Square, Kastelli, Khania 1970–1987, 2001, 2005 and 2008: Results of the Excavations Under the Direction of Yannis Tzedakis and Carl-Gustaf Styrenius. V: The Late Minoan IIIA1 and Late Minoan II Settlements.*

Hallager, E. and Hallager, B. P. (forthcoming-b) *The Greek-Swedish Excavations at the Agia Aikaterini Square, Kastelli, Khania 1970–1987, 2001, 2005 and 2008: Results of the Excavations Under the Direction of Yannis Tzedakis and Carl-Gustaf Styrenius. VI: The Neopalatial Settlement.*

Hallager, E. and Hallager, B. P. (forthcoming-c) *The Greek-Swedish Excavations at the Agia Aikaterini Square, Kastelli, Khania 1970–1987, 2001, 2005 and 2008: Results of the Excavations Under the Direction of Yannis Tzedakis and Carl-Gustaf Styrenius. VII: The Middle Minoan and Early Minoan Settlements.*

CHAPTER 6.3

Textile tools from Ayia Triada, Crete, Greece

Pietro Militello, Eva Andersson Strand, Marie-Louise Nosch and Joanne Cutler

---

Ayia Triada is located in the westernmost part of the hill system of Phaistos, in the Mesara plain, southern Crete. The site has been excavated by Federico Halbherr (1902–1914), Luisa Banti (1939, 1950) and Vincenzo La Rosa (1977–2012). The site (Fig. 6.3.1) was first settled, perhaps by people from Phaistos, at the very beginning of EM I. EM IIA houses have been brought to light in the so-called *Quartiere Laviosa* (Todaro 2003). EM IIB-MM I are represented by Tholos A and some structures nearby, while MM IB-II and MM IIIA-B are represented by Tholos B and scattered remains of houses, plastered floors and large dumps of material (Carinci 2003).

At the end of MM IIIB the first great period of Ayia Triada began, with the construction of the villa complex to the south, with courts and one monumental entrance from the north (Militello 2006), a granary (*Bastione*), a kiln and the urban reorganisation of the *Villaggio*, divided into two parts by a huge wall (*Muraglione a denti*) (Puglisi 2007). Administration is represented by Linear A documents (Militello 1988). To the north a second architectural complex was built, comprising the *Casa della Mazza di Breccia* and the so-called *Tomba degli Ori*, perhaps linked with the (ritual) managing of the nearby necropolis (La Rosa 2000). One

(or more) destructions at the end of LM IB brought about the collapse of this system (Puglisi 2003).

Only scanty traces can be attributed to LM II, but during LM IIIA the site was still a centre with monumental buildings: to the south of the settlement the large Megaron ABCD, the Stoa FG and Shrine H were built, the *Bastione* (second phase) was remodelled and reused. In the northern part of the settlement, three periods of intense building activity have been identified, spanning from LM IIIA1 to LM IIIA2 culminating with the construction of a monumental area made up of a large open area (the *Piazzale*) surrounded by the *Stoà dell'Agorà* (to the east), the *Edificio Nord-Ovest/P*, the *Edificio Ovest* and *Casa VAP* (La Rosa 1997; Cucuzza 2003). According to Linear B documents the site was under Knossian control, and is to be identified with *da-wo* or, according to some scholars, with the area of *pa-i-to* (Cucuzza 2003, 244–247). The uncertainty about the date of the final destruction of Knossos leaves open the possibility that LM IIIA2 Ayia Triada (second half of the 14th century) was the capital of an independent kingdom (the 'ville capitale': La Rosa 1997) or still part of the wider Mycenaean authority.

Fig. 6.3.1. Site plan (plan: courtesy of P. Militello).

Ayia Triada was deserted during LM IIIB without any sign of destruction. People perhaps moved to the nearby site of Phaistos. An open air shrine was established in the *Piazzale dei Sacelli*, and was the focus of a regional cult activity (D'Agata 1999).

During the Neopalatial period the settlement was small, comprising only the villa and a few houses, but the villa was the managing centre of an agricultural area of *c.* 15–30 km² (Militello 1988; Schoep 2002). The villa was also the centre of agricultural production (mainly grain, barley, olives, grapes), craft production (bronze tools, textile tools, kiln) and conspicuous and prestige consumption (fine painted pottery, relief stone vases, bronze figurines, feasting activities) especially linked with ritual activity. During the Final Palatial period (LM IIIA) Ayia Triada continued to be the managing centre of a large area with a still strong political and ritual character (Cucuzza 2003; Militello 2007). Agricultural and industrial activities were surely under its control, but they were not performed within the limits of the town. Decline characterizes the LM IIIB phase, with the silent disappearance of the settlement.

Textile activity in the Prepalatial and Protopalatial periods is likely to have been largely devoted to local consumption, mainly for clothing and furnishings. The iconography of seals and paintings reveals, however, the possibility of a special production of elaborate clothes to be used in rituals during the two "palatial" phases (LM I and LM IIIA) (Militello 2007). Export oriented production is not attested, but in LM IIIA according to the Linear B tablets of Knossos, Ayia Triada (*da-wo*? The area of *pa-i-to*?) was part of the larger Mycenaean system of textile production, with a huge numbers of sheep and with the *da-wi-ja* and *pa-i-ti-ja* women working within the *ta-ra-si-ja* system of production (Nosch 2001).

No pollen analysis is at the moment available. The only fibre recorded in Linear A texts is wool, while both wool and flax are recorded in Linear B. Sheep bones from the site indicate that sheep were butchered at a mean age of three years, representing more of a meat oriented than a wool oriented breeding, but this may be the results of the selective archaeological data.

Most of the evidence for textile production dates to the Neopalatial period. Very few spindle whorls have been recovered from the site. Five spinning bowls were found in well defined LM IB contexts, together with loom weights, in the workshop annex of the *Casa della Mazza di Breccia*. In general, it seems that spinning and weaving belonged to different spheres of action. Spindle whorls are often abandoned in secondary contexts, suggesting they belonged to the realm of private activities, requiring nothing else but the skill of the spinners. On the other hand, loom weights are often associated with other working tools, both in storage areas and in working areas, demonstrating that they belonged to specialised craft activities.

At least three different contexts revealed a large concentration of such tools. In the Neopalatial villa two main groups were found in Room 27 and in the northwestern quarter (80 items) (Militello 2006). Both of them come from the older excavations and are no longer preserved. In the first case, many sphcrical ovoid loom weights were stored in a room that seemed to be a clearing area, where conical cups, bronze working tools and pithoi were also stored. A special concern with the redistribution of wool, probably for weaving, is attested by 45 *noduli* lying on the sill of the window from Room 27 to Corridor 9 and by one important Linear A tablet, tablet HT 24, found nearby (Hallager 2002). On the sill two needles lay together with the noduli (Halbherr *et al.* 1977, 41). It therefore seems likely that working tools and raw material were distributed to workers for manufacture.

The exact context of the second group of 80 spherical loom weights from the north western quarter of the villa is unfortunately not known, since it was found during the very early days of excavation.

Fig. 6.3.2. Textile tools from dated Bronze Age contexts, by type and date.

	Spindle whorl	Kylix stem whorl	Loom weight	Spool	Total
EM I			8		8
EM II-MM IA			1		1
EM III-MM IA			1		1
Prepalatial			1		1
MM II			1		1
MM III			1		1
LM I	1		57	1	59
LM IIIA			10	1	11
LM III	3	1			4
LM I-III			3		3
Total	4	1	83	2	90

Fig. 6.3.4. LM I discoid loom weights (photo: courtesy of P. Militello).

and textile activity is curious, unless in the final Neopalatial phase this room had a change in function.

Two further groups of loom weights were recovered from two major houses, the *Casa delle Sfere Fittili* and the *Casa del Lebete*. These were elite dwellings, the latter of the two linked with Linear A administration. As such they had their own craft activity, and it is probable that weaving, together with food processing, served the owners' needs.

A more specialised working area has been identified in the *Casa della Mazza di Breccia* (Militello 2000). Workshops were located in the group of rooms to the east. Weaving tools were found in Rooms l and n (last phase), b and q (first phase), tools to be used in the manufacture of stone vases were recovered from Room q, and food processing was carried out in spaces s–t. The nature of the production is not clear, since the complex comprising the *Casa della Mazza di Breccia* and *Tomba degli Ori* was perhaps something more than a large private house, and may have been related to the control of religious activities (La Rosa 2000; Cucuzza 2003, 164),

In the *Villaggio* three further groups of spherical weights were found. The first group was recovered from Room 12 of the *Bastione*. This building, with huge walls, has been interpreted as serving as a granary, which contrasts with its use as a working or storage area, unless these finds had fallen from an upper storey. The association of bulk storage perhaps already linked with funerary activities in LM I (Puglisi 2003, 188). If this hypothesis is correct, the textile production in the *Casa della Mazza di Breccia* could bear some analogies with the weaving activities in Building 4 of the necropolis of Archanes (Deleghianne 1995).

The weaving activity carried out in the villa and in the *Casa della Mazza di Breccia* is likely to have been a specialised production, probably based on dependent labourers. The same hypothesis can perhaps be suggested for the other main groups of tools from the *Casa delle Sfere Fittili* and the *Casa del Lebete* due to the official character of these buildings, although a private, domestic activity cannot be excluded (Militello 2012c).

For the Final Palatial period a contrasting picture emerges. Spindle whorls and loom weights are almost totally absent, but the Mesara area is present in the Linear B documents referring to textile production. *Dawo* and *paito*, the best candidates for Ayia Triada, feed large numbers of sheep; spinners of/from the same site are involved in the *tarasija* system (Nosch 2001).

This apparently contrasting phenomenon can be explained by the profound change in the nature of the site and the overwhelming importance of political and ritual aspects compared to industrial and domestic activities. In LM III the official, public character of almost all the buildings from Ayia Triada – a houseless town according to Privitera (2011) – explains the existence of very few items linked with textile production in what should have been, on the other hand, a major centre for the management of textile production. The few textile tools recovered come from secondary contexts or from contexts which could have belonged to the very early phase of LM III reoccupation of the site, before the booming of the official building activity. The women from *paito* or *dawo* did not reside in these towns or work in workshops located there, but were simply administratively attached to these main managing centres (P. M.).

Ninety-five Bronze Age textile tools from Ayia Triada are registered in the CTR database, of which 90 are from dated contexts (Fig. 6.3.2).[1]

The majority of the textile tools (59) were recovered from LM I deposits, and the discussion below will therefore focus on these contexts.

Loom weights and weaving

Fifty-eight loom weights (43 spherical, 10 discoid, two cylindrical, one spool, one torus, one rectangular) are dated to the LM I period (Figs 6.3.2, 6.3.3 and 6.3.4). Two of the loom weights (the torus and the rectangular) are made of stone, the remainder are made of fired clay. Forty-two of the weights had a recordable weight and thickness (Fig. 6.3.5). The loom weights weigh between 50 g and 900 g, and have thicknesses varying from 1.1 cm to 10 cm. An incomplete spherical loom weight, without a preserved thickness, has an estimated complete weight of 1200 g, thus further extending the weight range. The discoid loom weights lie at the lower end of the overall weight range, and are also much thinner than the spherical weights.

The Casa della Mazza di Breccia

Twenty-one of the LM I loom weights were recovered from the *Casa della Mazza di Breccia*: one discoid and eight spherical weights were from Room l, and one torus and five spherical weights were found in Room n, while Room b contained two discoid weights and Rooms i, q, o and s each contained a spherical loom weight. Two spherical weights were additionally recovered from the general area of the building.

Sixteen of the spherical weights had a recordable weight and thickness. They vary in weight from 120 g to 770 g (Fig. 6.3.6), although it should be noted that one of the spherical weights from this building without a preserved thickness has an estimated weight of 1200 g. There is no clear difference in the range of weights of the loom weights recovered from the various rooms. The thicknesses vary from 5.2 cm to 10 cm.

The majority of the spherical loom weights would be optimal for use with medium thread needing *c.* 25–30 g tension (Fig. 6.3.7). Lower numbers would also work well with thread needing *c.* 10–20 g or *c.* 35–55 g tension, whereas only a few would be suitable for use with very thin thread requiring *c.* 5 g tension, or very thick thread needing *c.* 60 g tension. Used in a tabby setup with *c.* 25 g tension thread, the loom weights could be used to produce a fabric with *c.* 3–6 warp threads per centimetre; with *c.* 30 g tension thread, the thread count would be *c.* 3–5 threads per

Fig. 6.3.5 Loom weights from LM I contexts: type and weight/thickness.

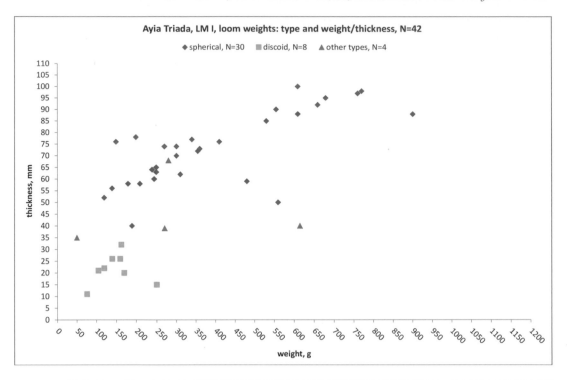

Fig. 6.3.6. LM I, Casa della Mazza di Breccia, spherical loom weights: context and weight/thickness.

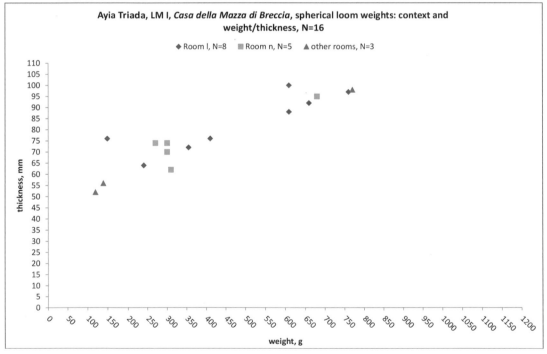

centimetre. In a balanced weave, these would be quite open textiles and it is therefore likely that the fabrics would have been weft faced.

The three discoid loom weights from the building weigh 81–160 g and therefore lie at the lighter end of the weight range of the spherical weights. They are also thinner, and would therefore be suitable for making denser fabrics, with fine thread. The stone torus weight, with a weight of 615 g and a thickness of 4 cm, if used as a loom weight, would be optimal for producing a relatively dense fabric with medium to thick thread. Neither the torus nor the discoid weights could be used in the same loom setups as the spherical loom weights, and it is therefore

Warp thr/cm	5 g, N=3	10 g, N=7	15 g, N=8	20 g, N=7	25 g, N=12	30 g, N=11	35 g, N=8	40 g, N=7	45 g, N=6	50 g, N=5	55 g, N=5	60 g, N=2
3 thr			1		4	4	3	3	5	5	5	2
4 thr		1		4	3	2	4	4	1			
5 thr		2	3	2	2	5	1					
6 thr			1	1	3							
7 thr		1	3									
8 thr	1	2										
9 thr	1	1										
10 thr	1											

Fig. 6.3.7. LM I, Casa della Mazza di Breccia, spherical loom weights: weight tension/number of threads per cm in a tabby. The total number of analysed loom weights is 16.

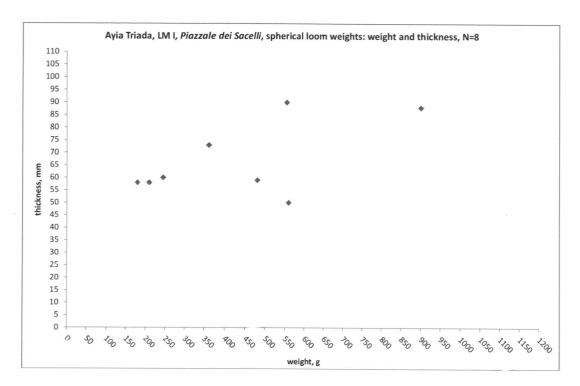

Fig. 6.3.8. LM I, Piazzale dei Sacelli, spherical loom weights: weight and thickness.

Warp thr/cm	10 g, N=3	15 g, N=4	20 g, N=6	25 g, N=5	30 g, N=5	35 g, N=5	40 g, N=4	45 g, N=4	50 g, N=3	55 g, N=2	60 g, N=1	65 g, N=1	70 g, N=1
3 thr					1	1	1	1	1	1		1	1
4 thr		1	2	1	1	1	1	1	2	2			
5 thr		2	1	1	1	1	1		2				
6 thr	1		1	1		2	1						
7 thr	1	1				1							
8 thr	1		1			1							
9 thr					1								
10 thr													
11 thr			1										

likely that the preserved weights represent only a proportion of the original total of weights. The five spinning bowls from LM IB contexts provide additional evidence for textile production within this building.

The Piazzale dei Sacelli
Fifteen spherical loom weights and a discoid weight were recovered from the *Piazzale dei Sacelli*, to the west of the Byzantine period church. Eight of the spherical weights had a recordable weight and thickness: these vary in weight from 180 g to 900 g and have a thickness of 5.0–9.0 cm (Fig. 6.3.8).

Most of the loom weights would be best suited for use with thin to medium thread needing *c.* 20–35 g tension (Fig. 6.3.9). Some could also be used with thread needing

Fig. 6.3.9. LM I, Piazzale dei Sacelli, spherical loom weights: weight tension/number of threads per cm in a tabby. The total number of analysed loom weights is 8.

c. 10–15 g or *c.* 40–55 g tension. The heaviest weight, weighing 900 g, could be used with very thick thread needing up to *c.* 85 g tension. In a balanced tabby weave, the resulting textiles would be quite open, however (for example, *c.* 3–6 warp threads per centimetre with *c.* 35 g tension thread). They are therefore likely to have been weft faced.

Spinning and weaving

Only one spindle whorl from the site dates to the Neopalatial period: a stone discoid whorl weighing 8 g was recovered from an LM IA context in the *Tomba degli Ori* (elsewhere interpreted as a balance weight: Militello 1993). This whorl, according to the CTR experiments, would be optimal for spinning thin thread needing *c.* 18 g tension on the loom. There is a similar lack of spindle whorls at other Neopalatial (and Protopalatial) sites on Crete. It is possible that during this period whorls were made of a perishable material; alternatively, spinning may have been carried out at different locations.

Summary

The LM I loom weights recorded in the database could be used with a variety of thread, varying from very thin to very thick. The presence of different types of loom weights also indicates a varied production, since the lighter, thinner discoid loom weights would be suitable for making denser fabrics with thinner threads, in contrast to the open/weft faced fabrics in a range of thread types that could be produced with the spherical weights. Similarly, the stone torus weight weighing 615 g, if used as a loom weight, would be best suited for producing a denser fabric than the spherical loom weights with a similar weight.

Note

1 A complete catalogue of the material is now in P. Militello, *Festòs e Haghia Triada. Rinvenimenti Minori I. Materiale per la tessitura*, (SAC 11), Padova 2012. A few differences between the CTR Database and the catalogue of the book are due to newly found material, which, however, does not change the picture given here.

Bibliography

Carinci, F. M. (2003) Haghia Triada nel periodo Medio Minoico, *Creta Antica,* 4, 97–144.

Cucuzza, N. (2003) Il volo del grifo: osservazioni sulla Haghia Triada "micenea", *Creta Antica,* 4, 199–272.

D'Agata, A. L. (1999) *Haghia Triada II: statuine minoiche e post-minoiche dai vecchi scavi di Haghia Triada (Creta).* Padova. Bottega d'Erasmo.

Deleghianne, E.-E. (1995) Stoicheia biotechnikon enkatastaseon apo te kterio 4 tou nekrotapheiou Phourni sto Archanon, *Pepragmena tou Z' diethnous kretologikou sinedriou* A1, 187–196.

Halbherr, F., Stefani, B. and Banti, L. (1977) Haghia Triada nel periodo tardo palaziale, *Annuario della Scuola archeologica di Atene e delle Missioni italiane in Oriente,* 55, 13–296.

Hallager, H. (2002) One Linear A tablet and 45 noduli, *Creta Antica,* 3, 105–110.

La Rosa, V. (1997) Hagia Triada à l'époque mycénienne: l'utopie d'une "Ville Capitale", in Driessen, J. and Farnoux, A. (eds), *La Crète Mycénienne,* 249–266. Paris. Ecole française d'Athènes.

La Rosa, V. (2000) Preghiere fatte in casa? Altari mobili da un edificio di Haghia Triada, *Pepragmena tou H' diethnous kretologikou synedriou,* 137–153.

Militello, P. (1988) Riconsiderazioni preliminari sulla documentazione in lineare A da Haghia Triada, *Sileno,* 14, 233–261.

Militello, P. (1993) Un peso (?) con segno inciso da Haghia Triada (Ht Zg 163), *Annuario della Scuola archeologica di Atene e delle Missioni italiane in Oriente,* 66–67 (1988/1989) (50–51), 163–172.

Militello, P. (2000) Organizzazione dello spazio e vita quotidiana nelle case TM I di Haghia Triada, *Pepragmenta tou H' diethnous kretologikou synedriou,* A2, 131–334.

Militello, P. (2006) Attività tessile a Festòs e Haghia Triada dal neolitico al Bronzo Tardo, *Pepragmena Th' Diethnous Kretologikou Synedriou,* 173–187.

Militello, P. (2007) Textile Industry and Minoan Palaces, in Gillis, C. and Nosch, M.-L. (eds), *Ancient Textiles. Production, Craft and Society.* 173–178. Ancient Textiles Series 1. Oxford. Oxbow Books.

Militello, P. (2012a) Textile activity in Neolithic Phaistos, in Nosch, M.-L. and Laffineur, R. (eds), *KOSMOS. Jewellery, Adornment and Textiles in the Aegean Bronze Age,* 199–206. Liège. Peeters.

Militello, P. (2012b) Emerging authority: a functional analysis of the MM II settlement of Festòs, in Driessen, J., Schoep, I. and Tomkins, P. (eds), *Back to the Beginning. Reconsidering Prepalatial and Protopalatial Crete,* 236–272. Oxford. Oxbow Books.

Militello, P. (2012c) New evidence for textile activity in Phaistos and Ayia Triada, *Praktikà tes B Kritiki Synantisi,* 203–216.

Nosch, M.-L. (2001) The geography of the tarasija obligation, *Aegean Archaeology,* 4, 27–44.

Puglisi, D. (2003) Haghia Triada nel periodo Tardo Minoico I, *Creta Antica,* 4, 145–198.

Puglisi, D. (2007) L'organizzazione a terrazze nel "Villaggio" TM I di Haghia Triada, *Creta Antica,* 8, 169–200.

Schoep, I. (2002) *The Administration of Neopalatial Crete. A Critical Assessment of the Linear A Tablets and their Role in the Administrative Process.* Salamanca. Universidad de Salamanca.

Todaro, S. (2003) Haghia Triada nel periodo Antico Minoico, *Creta Antica,* 4, 69–96.

Textile tools from Phaistos, Crete, Greece

Pietro Militello, Eva Andersson Strand, Marie-Louise Nosch and Joanne Cutler

The site of Phaistos (Fig. 6.4.1), situated on a hill system in the Mesara plain, southern Crete, was occupied from the Neolithic to the Hellenistic period. It has been excavated by F. Halbherr and L. Pernier (1900–1909, restorations in the 1930s), D. Levi (1950–1966), and V. La Rosa (1994, 2000–2004).[1]

Six main phases of the settlement can be distinguished during the Neolithic and Bronze Age. In Phase I (Final Neolithic, 3500–3000 BC), at least two groups of houses were built around a central space to be used in ritual ceremonials, located under Room 29 and in front of Room 24 of the later palace (Vagnetti 1972–1973; Todaro and Di Tonto 2008; Militello 2012a). Other communal spaces were perhaps the centre of ritual production focused on pottery and other crafts as well (Todaro 2012).

In Phase 2 (Prepalatial, EM I-MM IA, 3000–1950 BC), growing complexity brought about the erection of some major buildings at the end of the period which suggests on the one hand the presence of communal structures, and on the other hand the continuity of the central part of the lower hill as a ritual centre (Benzi 2001; Todaro 2005, in press; La Rosa 2002a).

Phase 3 (the Protopalatial period, MM IB-MM IIB, *c.* 1950–1700 BC) saw the emergence of the Phaistian 'state', with a three-tiered architectural and social structure. During this period the first palace was constructed at the site, encircled by public areas (the central and western courts), a few private buildings and private houses (Carinci and La Rosa 2009; Militello 2012b). The palace was destroyed by an earthquake in MM IIB (Tortorici and Monaco 2003).

In Phase 4 (early Neopalatial period, MM III-LM IA, *c.* 1700–1500 BC) two large buildings perhaps took over the political and ritual function of the earlier palace: the *Casa a Sud della Rampa* (MM IIIA) and the *Complesso Nord-Est* (MM IIIB) (Carinci 1989, 2001; La Rosa 2002b; Girella 2011).

In Phase 5 (the late Neopalatial, LM IB, *c.* 1500–1450 BC) the process ended with the final erection of the palace, which was destroyed at the end of the same period (La Rosa 1995; Palio 2001; La Rosa 2002b).

The evidence for the nature of occupation in Phase 6 (the Final Palatial period, LM II-IIIA, *c.* 1450–1300 BC) is very scanty, comprising only some structures at Chalara (Palio 2001), and some additional sporadic areas on the hill (Borgna 2003, 40–41). Evidence for occupation in the subsequent phase, Phase 7 (Postpalatial, LM IIIA2-B) is apparently lacking, unless it has been hidden

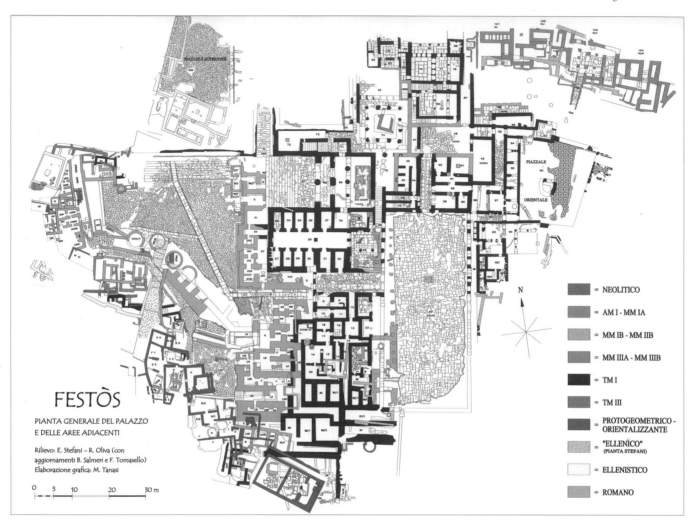

FESTÒS

PIANTA GENERALE DEL PALAZZO
E DELLE AREE ADIACENTI

Rilievo: E. Stefani - R. Oliva (con
aggiornamenti B. Salmeri e F. Tomasello)
Elaborazione grafica: M. Tanasi

0   5   10   20   30 m

= NEOLITICO

= AM I - MM IA

= MM IB - MM IIB

= MM IIIA - MM IIIB

= TM I

= TM III

= PROTOGEOMETRICO -
ORIENTALIZZANTE

= "ELLENICO"
(PIANTA STEFANI)

= ELLENISTICO

= ROMANO

*Fig. 6.4.1. Site plan
(plan: courtesy of
P. Militello).*

by a different organisation of the settlement (Borgna 2003, 39). The nature and the role of the site during this period is difficult to understand, since *paito* is known only from the Linear B texts from Knossos, as part of the wider Knossian polity (Bennet 1985, 1990). Moreover, *paito* could be Ayia Triada (see chapter 6.3, *Ayia Triada*). The date of the Linear B archives and of the final destruction of Knossos (LM IIIA1 or LM IIIB) is still a subject of debate.

In the Final Neolithic and the Protopalatial period the settled area has been calculated as extending up to 2 ha (Whitelaw 2001) or 5 ha (Watrous *et al.* 2004), with an estimated population of *c.* 450 people or *c.* 900 people respectively. After a period of decline in EM III, the town grew again in MM IA. A figure of 25 ha in the Protopalatial and Neopalatial periods (Militello 2012a), is more likely than 40 ha (Branigan 2001) or 60 (Watrous *et al.* 2004),

with an estimated population of *c.* 5000–6000 people (Militello 2012a). In the Final Palatial period the archaeological evidence is too scanty for estimates of area or population to be made. Postpalatial Phaistos seems to be confined to the area west of the palace, with a consistent reduction in both extent and population. Population could be resident, however, in many hamlets scattered in the area around the hill and in the plain.

The fertile Mesara plain offered a rich agricultural background for crop cultivation, a favourable area for stock breeding and good sources of stone and clay. The material evidence additionally suggests that there had already been a major concern for craft production, especially pottery (but also, in some way, textile production), since the Final Neolithic period. Later, the crafts of stone working and seal-cutting were also added. It is also possible that part of these activities happened within a ritual setting, with the hill already being the meeting point of scattered communities in the Mesara in the Final Neolithic, and that this ritual function was formalised during the EM period, ending in the construction of the central building (Todaro 2009, 2012). In the Protopalatial period, the interest of the palace is more on consumption, rather than the breeding of animals and the production of agricultural products and crafts, but a direct interest is attested in the production of some prestige items.

The analysis of sheep bones indicates that sheep were already being slaughtered at an old age in the Final Neolithic period at the site, suggesting that wool is likely to have been the main raw material used in textile production. The use of linen cannot be demonstrated, but cannot be excluded.

In the Final Neolithic period, textile activity is represented almost exclusively by spindle whorls. They show a distinct pattern of distribution, since the largest concentration (groups of 3–6) is located in the trenches along the western part of the central court, with a greater concentration, consisting of eight whorls, in front of Room 25, and a further 17 whorls within the same room. Although these whorls were recovered from two different strata, this pattern of deposition is notable. Due to the absence of a centralised mode of production, the concentration of spindle whorls in a limited area could be the result of ritual depositions or of the discard from ritual activities, following Todaro and Di Tonto's suggestion regarding the presence of ritual areas under Cortile 40 (Todaro and Di Tonto 2008; Di Tonto 2009). The interpretation is in any case linked to the broader interpretation of the nature of the settlement on the hill. Textile activity appears to have been a prestige activity within a household production at this time, until the Early Bronze Age, when the vertical warp-weighted loom was perhaps first introduced at the site.

In the Prepalatial period, textile tools (both spindle whorls and loom weights) are unfortunately scattered in dumps and secondary contexts, so that no specific pattern can be discerned. The decrease of the evidence during this period is striking, when the longer time span is considered (*i.e.* almost a millennium). This decrease may be partly explained by the limited extent of the investigated areas, but might also be the consequence of a more mundane function for spinning or weaving, no longer linked to ritual performances and limited to the realms of domestic activities.

In the Protopalatial period, patterns of production radically change. The emergence of the palace brought about the centralisation of at least some craft production, but there was also a large sector of 'private' production. The picture is very clear in the case of textiles. Sets of tools, sometimes stamped with a seal, were stored in the palace, suggesting a centralised mode of textile production (Militello 2006, 2007). The tools show a distinct concentration within the palace, with a particular preference for some areas: Room IL, LIV, Sottoscala LIII–LIV, Room LXIV. Here spindle whorls (although very rare), loom weights and also needles and *Vasi a corna* and *a gabbietta* (perhaps used as a wool winder), are found in association, giving the impression of a complete set focused on the central phases of textile operations: spinning and weaving. The palace seems to have organised and strictly controlled the finishing of some specialised items, probably to be used for ritual consumption or for exchange. There is no proof that the palace controlled all the textile activity; on the contrary, a large part of the manufacture seems to be outside palatial control. The range of production increased, but the palace was mainly a consumer, and not a producer of goods (Schoep 2001).

In both the Neopalatial and Final Palatial periods there is no evidence of a palatial production, notwithstanding the large corpus of iconography featuring costumes which characterises these periods. A shift from palatial to extra-palatial contexts can be detected in these periods, but the evidence is limited to loom weights recovered from the Chalara mansion, being scarce elsewhere. The total absence of evidence in LM IIIA contrasts with the mention of spinners from *paito* in the Linear B texts of Knossos. This paradox can be explained by setting the evidence against the wider picture. Phaistos was no longer the centre of a state, but a part of a wider system where control of production and delocalisation went hand in hand. The LM IB palace may have been only a ritual and traditional centre, leaving the administrative role to the nearby site of Ayia Triada. The LM I emerging administrative elite may have provided for their own needs,

Pietro Militello, Eva Andersson Strand, Marie-Louise Nosch and Joanne Cutler

Fig. 6.4.2. Textile tools from dated Bronze Age contexts, by type and date.

	Spindle whorl	Kylix stem whorl	Loom weight	Total
Prepalatial/Protopalatial	3			3
EH II	2			2
EH II–III	3			3
EH III–MM IA			1	1
MM IA			1	1
MMIB			1	1
MM I			1	1
MM II	6		4	10
Protopalatial	8		96	104
MM II–III			6	6
MM III			1	1
MM	1		3	4
LM I	3		1	4
LM IB			34	34
Neopalatial			2	2
Palatial			9	9
LM III	2	5		7
LM IIIB		2	3	5
LM IIIB–C	3	13	1	23
Total	31	20	164	221

which explains the complex architecture and organisation of the Chalara mansion, as is the case for the important houses in Ayia Triada. For LM IIIA, the toponym of *paito* could have shifted to indicate a larger district, and perhaps Ayia Triada itself.

The collapse of the palatial system during LM III brought a change in settlement patterns and in the organisation of the Mesara. The hill of Phaistos was inhabited once again in the Postpalatial period. Unfortunately, the picture has been widely destroyed by subsequent Greek building activities. It is not possible, based on the available evidence, to identify specialised storage or working areas devoted to textile production. The loom weights and spindle whorls dating to this period were scattered in the rooms of the houses, without any significant concentration. The Postpalatial settlement was small in extent and demography was low; craft activities were at the *oikos* level, so that few looms were probably in operation. Spools and perhaps also clay torus shaped loom weights appeared for the first time during this period, sometimes poorly baked or unbaked, while there was an increase in the number of stone spindle whorls.[2]

In conclusion, household production seems to have been the rule during the Neolithic and Prepalatial, as well as during the Final Palatial and Postpalatial, periods. Only in the case of the large building at Chalara (LM IB) can the suggestion be made that textile workers were dependent personnel and not the owners themselves. Dependent personnel, in the form of servants or of corvée workers, should also be supposed for the Protopalatial period, when some form of specialised textile production was under the control of the main building. Dependent personnel are also attested in the Linear B documents, but no archaeological evidence of such activity has at present come to light in the excavations (P. M.).

Four hundred and thirty textile tools from Phaistos are recorded in the CTR database, of which 221 are from dated Bronze Age contexts (Fig. 6.4.2).[3] Forty-seven of the registered tools (two probable loom weights and 45 spindle whorls) were recovered from Neolithic contexts, while the majority of the remainder, from later or mixed contexts, are also likely to be dated to the Bronze Age.

Loom weights and weaving

Since significant numbers of loom weights were only recovered from Protopalatial and LM IB deposits, the discussion below will focus on these contexts.

Protopalatial loom weights from the palace

One hundred and one loom weights date to the Protopalatial period: one weight is from an MM IB context, four are from MM II deposits and 96 are more broadly dated to the Protopalatial period (Fig. 6.4.2). All of the Protopalatial loom weights were recovered from palatial contexts. The majority of the weights (83) are cylindrical in shape; 77 are made of fired clay, while four are made of unfired clay and 19 are made of stone (Figs. 6.4.3 and 6.4.4).

Seventy of the Protopalatial loom weights (63 cylindrical, two cuboid, two torus, one spherical, one flat rectangular and one 'other') had a recordable weight and thickness. One of the cylindrical weights, weighing 27 g, is more likely to be a spindle whorl. With the exception of two heavier weights, a stone torus weight weighing 600 g and a stone flat rectangular weight weighing 700 g, all of the remaining loom weights weigh between 51 g and 350 g and have a thickness of 2.8–6.7 cm (Fig. 6.4.5).

The 62 cylindrical loom weights from Protopalatial contexts (excluding the weight weighing 27 g) would be suitable for use with a range of very thin to medium thread types, requiring *c.* 5–35 g tension (Fig. 6.4.6).

The majority of the loom weights would be best suited for use with very thin thread needing *c.* 10 g tension, while a number would work well with thread needing *c.* 5 g or *c.* 15–25 g tension. Only a few would be optimal for use with thread requiring *c.* 30–35 g tension. In a tabby weave, most of the loom weights suitable for use with thread requiring *c.* 5 g tension could be used to produce a fabric with *c.* 5–11 warp threads per centimetre. Used with thread needing *c.* 10 g tension, 47 of the loom weights could produce a textile with *c.* 4–10 warp threads per centimetre, while with *c.* 15 g tension thread the thread count would be *c.* 4–9 threads per centimetre. Using thread requiring *c.* 20 g tension, the thread count would range from *c.* 3 to 7 threads per centimetre.

Fig. 6.4.3. Loom weights from Protopalatial contexts: type and material.

	Fired Clay	Unfired Clay	Stone	Unspecified	Total
Cylindrical	73	3	6	1	83
Spherical	2		8		10
Biconical			1		1
Cuboid	2				2
Flat rectangular			1		1
Torus			2		2
Other		1	1		2
Total	77	4	19	1	101

Fig. 6.4.4. Protopalatial cylindrical loom weights (photo: courtesy of P. Militello).

Fig. 6.4.5. Protopalatial loom weights from palace contexts: type and weight/thickness. Please note that in some cases one cylindrical weight marker represents more than one loom weight.

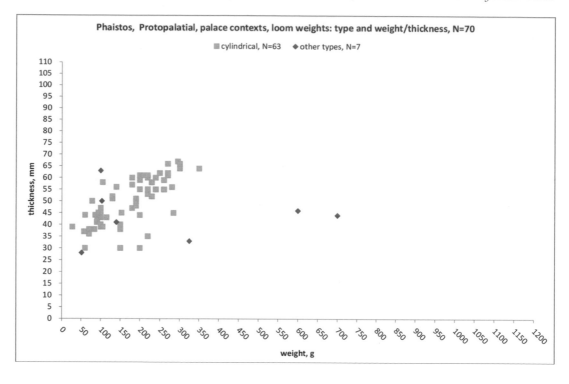

Fig. 6.4.6. Protopalatial cylindrical loom weights from palace contexts: weight tension/number of threads per cm in a tabby (excluding cylindrical weight weighing 27 g). The total number of analysed loom weights is 62.

Warp thr/cm	5 g, N=26	10 g, N=50	15 g, N=40	20 g, N=32	25 g, N=16	30 g, N=4	35 g, N=1
3 thr				2	4	3	1
4 thr		3	5	17	11	1	
5 thr	1	6	15	9	1		
6 thr	2	4	13	3			
7 thr	2	8	4	1			
8 thr	4	11	1				
9 thr	6	12	2				
10 thr	5	3					
11 thr	2						
12 thr		1					
13 thr		2					
14 thr							
15 thr	1						
16 thr	1						
17 thr							
18 thr							
19 thr							
20 thr	2						

In a twill weave, the thread counts would be approximately double. If the finished tabby textiles were balanced, with approximately the same number and type of weft threads as warp threads per centimetre[2], they would be open fabrics, and it is therefore likely that many of the textiles produced would instead have been weft faced. With the exception of the stone weights weighing 600 g and 700 g

(if they were used on the loom), the remaining loom weights of other types fall within the same weight/thickness range as the cylindrical weights and could be used with a similar range of thread types.

Room LXIV

Low numbers of loom weights were found in a number of rooms within the palace. A larger group of 19 cylindrical loom weights was recovered from Room LXIV. Sixteen of these had a recordable weight and thickness; all except one weigh between 180 g and 300 g, with thicknesses varying between 3.5 cm and 6.6 cm (Fig. 6.4.7).

The lightest loom weight, weighing 57 g, would only be optimal for use with thread needing *c.* 5 g tension. All of the remaining loom weights would work well with thread requiring *c.* 10–15 g tension, with 13 of these also being suitable for use with thread needing *c.* 20 g tension (Fig. 6.4.8). A few could also

function with thread requiring *c.* 25 g tension. In a tabby weave, with thread needing *c.* 10 g tension, the loom weights could be used to make a fabric with *c.* 6–13 warp threads per centimetre; this is quite a large thread count range, but all except one could produce a textile with a narrower thread count range of *c.* 6–10 warp threads per centimetre. With thread needing *c.* 15 g tension the thread count would be *c.* 4–9 threads per centimetre. These would be open textiles in balanced weaves and they are therefore likely to have been weft faced fabrics. The 15 weights could be used to make

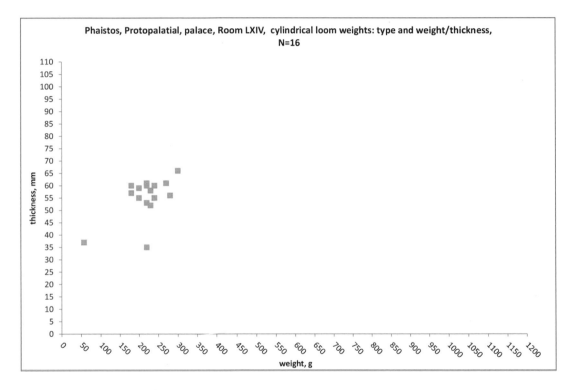

Fig. 6.4.7. Protopalatial loom weights, palace, Room LXIV: type and weight/thickness.

Warp thr/cm	5 g, N=1	10 g, N=15	15 g, N=15	20 g, N=13	25 g, N=5	30 g, N=1
3 thr				1	1	1
4 thr			3	7	4	
5 thr	1		5	4		
6 thr		2	5	1		
7 thr		4	1			
8 thr		3				
9 thr		4	1			
10 thr		1				
11 thr						
12 thr						
13 thr		1				

Fig. 6.4.8. Protopalatial loom weights, palace, Room LXIV: weight tension/number of threads per cm in a tabby. The total number of analysed loom weights is 16.

a tabby fabric *c.* 44 cm wide; allowing for the three fragmentary weights, the fabric would be *c.* 50 cm wide. It is possible that Room LXIV may have been used as a collecting area for tools after a severe earthquake at the end of MM II (Carinci 2001). However, these loom weights would work very well together in the same loom setup. Five of the loom weights are stamped by a seal, perhaps to indicate that they formed a set, or part of a set.

Room IL

Twelve loom weights (11 cylindrical and one stone flat rectangular) were recovered from Room IL. The flat rectangular weight weighs 700 g, while the 10 cylindrical loom weights with a recordable weight and thickness weigh 91–270 g, with a thickness of 4.0–6.2 cm (Fig. 6.4.9).

Nine of the cylindrical weights would work well with very thin thread requiring *c.* 10 g tension, while lower numbers could also be

Fig. 6.4.9. Protopalatial loom weights, palace, Room IL: type and weight/thickness. Please note that one of the cylindrical weight markers represents two loom weights.

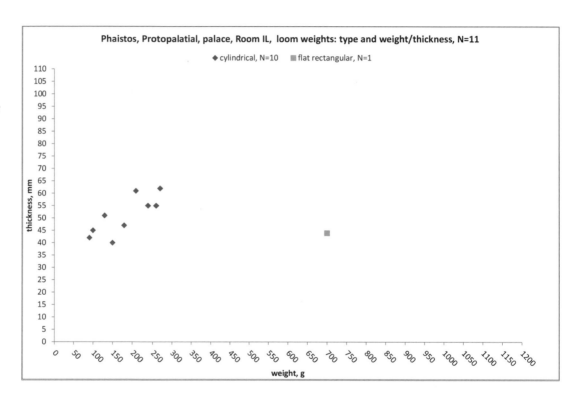

Fig. 6.4.10. Protopalatial loom weights, palace, Room IL: weight tension/number of threads per cm in a tabby. The total number of analysed loom weights is 10.

Warp thr/cm	5 g, N=4	10 g, N=9	15 g, N=6	20 g, N=5	25 g, N=4
3 thr					
4 thr		1		2	4
5 thr		1	2	3	
6 thr			4		
7 thr		1			
8 thr		2			
9 thr	2	4			
10 thr	1				
11 thr					
12 thr					
13 thr					
14 thr					
15 thr	1				

used with thread needing *c.* 5 g tension or *c.* 15–25 g tension (Fig. 6.4.10). Used with thread needing *c.* 10 g tension, they could be used to produce a textile with *c.* 4–9 warp threads per centimetre. This would again be an open textile in a balanced weave and is therefore likely to have been weft faced. The lighter weight, weighing 91 g, could also be used with the other cylindrical weights, if slightly fewer than 10 threads were attached to it, or if 10 threads were provided with a little less than 10 g tension. Like the cylindrical loom weights in Room LXIV, this group of loom weights would be best suited for use with thread requiring *c.* 10 g tension, and could produce a fabric with a very similar thread count range. The weights from the two rooms could therefore work well together in the same loom setup. The heavier, flat rectangular weight from Room IL, if used as a loom weight, would only be optimal for use with medium to very thick thread, needing *c.* 25–70 g tension, so would not function well in the same loom setup with the other weights.

Room LIV

A group of 16 loom weights (seven spherical and nine cylindrical) were stored in Room LIV, along with other items. Only two of these had a recordable weight and thickness, so it is not possible to say whether they could have functioned together in the same loom setup.

LM IB loom weights from Chalara

The 34 loom weights from LM IB contexts were all recovered from the house at Chalara. Twenty-nine loom weights of fired clay were found in Corridor gamma, and are likely to have fallen from an upper floor (Palio 2001, 357): 27 of these are spherical, and two are cylindrical (Fig. 6.4.11). The remaining five weights are made of stone, and are cylindrical with a groove around the middle; they were recovered from a fill under the hellenistic Room W1 (Fig. 6.4.12). Thirty-one of the loom weights had a recordable weight and thickness (24 spherical, two cylindrical and the five stone weights). These weigh 120 g–1 kg, and have thicknesses ranging from 4.6 cm to 8.7 cm (Fig. 6.4.13).

Corridor gamma

The spherical loom weight weighing 1 kg recovered from Corridor gamma would be suitable for use with medium to very thick thread needing *c.* 35–100 g tension. All except the lightest of the remaining loom weights from this group would work well

Fig. 6.4.11. LM IB spherical loom weight (photo: courtesy of P. Militello).

Fig. 6.4.12. LM IB stone weights with a groove around the middle (photo: courtesy of P. Militello).

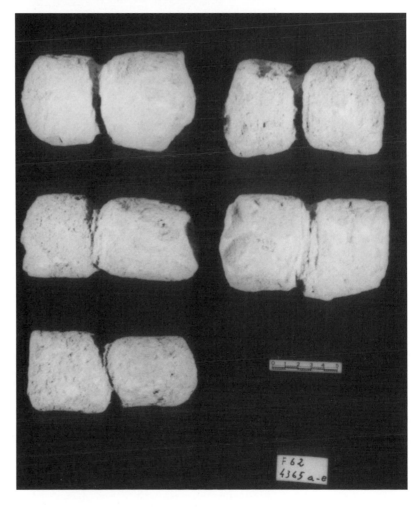

Fig. 6.4.13. LM IB loom weights from Chalara: type and weight/thickness. Please note that one of the spherical weight markers represents two loom weights.

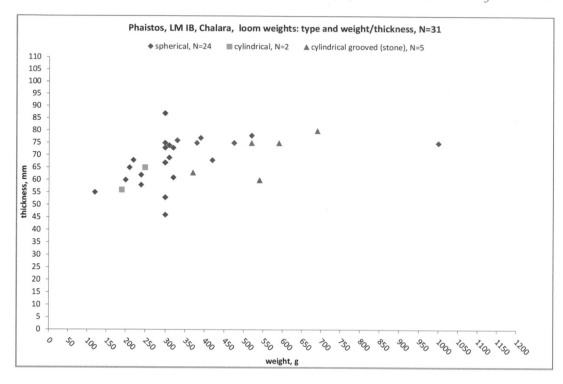

Warp thr/cm	5 g, N=1	10 g, N=15	15 g, N=22	20 g, N=24	25 g, N=20	30 g, N=16	35 g, N=5	40 g, N=5	45 g, N=2	50 g, N=2
3 thr				4	9	10	2	5	2	2
4 thr		1	3	11	6	6	3			
5 thr			6	4	5					
6 thr		2	7	3						
7 thr		3	3	2						
8 thr		5	2							
9 thr	1	2	1							
10 thr										
11 thr		1								
12 thr										
13 thr			1							

Fig. 6.4.14. LM IB loom weights from Chalara, Corridor gamma: weight tension/number of threads per cm in a tabby (excluding spherical weight weighing 1 kg). The total number of analysed loom weights is 25.

with thread requiring *c.* 20 g tension and in a tabby weave could produce a relatively open/weft faced fabric with *c.* 3–7 warp threads per centimetre (Fig. 6.4.14). The narrow thread count range suggests that these loom weights would function well together in the same loom setup with this type of thread; the textile produced would be *c.* 81 cm wide. If the three fragmentary loom weights would also be suitable for use in the same setup, the fabric would be *c.* 1 m wide. A number of the loom weights from Corridor gamma could also be used with thread requiring *c.* 10–15 g or *c.* 25–30 g tension, while only a few would be optimal for use with *c.* 5 g or *c.* 35–50 g tension thread. The fabrics produced would similarly be open/weft faced.

Fill under Room W1

The five stone 'waisted' weights from the fill under the hellenistic Room W1, if used on the loom, would all work well with medium thread needing *c.* 25–35 g tension and could be used to produce a tabby fabric with *c.* 5–7 warp threads per centimetre (*c.* 25 g tension thread), *c.* 4–6 warp threads per centimetre (*c.* 30 g tension thread), or *c.* 3–5 warp threads per centimetre (*c.* 35 g tension thread). They could therefore all function together in the same loom setups with these types of threads; the textiles produced would be relatively open or weft faced. Since a tabby fabric woven with these weights would only be *c.* 20 cm wide, it is likely that more loom weights would have been used in any loom setup.

Spindle whorls and spinning

Of the 48 whorls from dated contexts, 28 are recorded as spindle whorls and 20 are registered as kylix stem whorls (for the discussion of the interpretation of different categories of spindle whorls see chapter 7). Very few whorls were recovered from Protopalatial or Neopalatial contexts. The number of whorls found in Protopalatial or Neopalatial contexts from other Cretan sites is equally low. It is possible that during these periods whorls were made of perishable materials; alternatively, spinning may have been carried out in different locations.

Fourteen spindle whorls (six cylindrical, four biconical, two discoid, one conical, and one spherical) were recovered from Protopalatial contexts: six of these are from MM II deposits, while eight are more broadly dated to the Protopalatial period. Based on their fabric and/or decoration, some of these whorls may be earlier in date, however.

Protopalatial spindle whorls from the palace

With the exception of the conical whorl, all of the Protopalatial spindle whorls had a recordable weight and diameter. They vary in weight from 10–82 g, and have diameters ranging from 2.6–4.9 cm (Figs. 6.4.15 and 6.4.16). All of the whorls were recovered from palace contexts, *i.e.* an underground grotto in the south western part of the court in front of the palace which was used as a cult place.

Six of the whorls (three cylindrical, one biconical and two discoid) weigh between 10 g and 24 g. These whorls would, according to the results of the spinning tests, be suitable for spinning thin to medium thread that would need *c.* 20–30 g tension on the loom. The spherical and the cylindrical spindle whorl weighing 38 g and 42 g respectively would be

Fig. 6.4.15. Spindle whorl from a Protopalatial context (photo: courtesy of P. Militello).

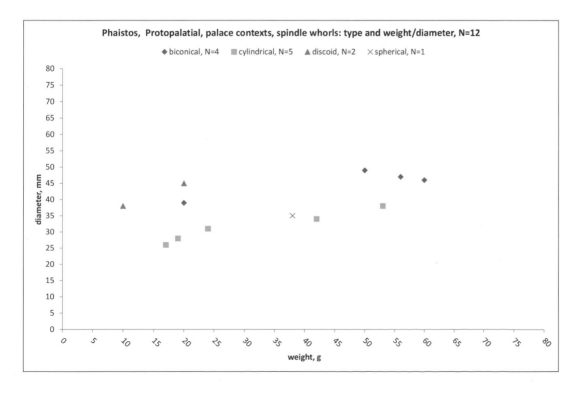

Fig. 6.4.16. Protopalatial spindle whorls from palace contexts: type and weight/diameter (excluding cylindrical whorl weighing 82 g).

best suited for spinning thick thread requiring *c.* 40–50 g tension. Even thicker thread could be spun with the remaining whorls, weighing 50 g or more.

Only one spindle whorl, weighing 9 g, was recovered from a secure Neopalatial context at Chalara.

Summary

The loom weights dating to the Protopalatial period were all recovered from the palace, whereas the Neopalatial loom weights are from a non-palatial context. This suggests that textile production was organised differently in these two periods. Furthermore, the majority of the Protopalatial loom weights are cylindrical in shape, whereas most of the Neopalatial weights are spherical. Additionally, the Neopalatial loom weights are on the whole both heavier and thicker than the Protopalatial weights.

The majority of the Protopalatial loom weights would be best suited for use with very thin thread needing *c.* 10 g tension, and in a tabby weave they could be used to produce an open/weft faced fabric with *c.* 4–10 warp threads per centimetre. A number of the loom weights could also be used to produce open/weft faced fabrics with thread needing *c.* 5 g or *c.* 15–20 g tension. There was therefore an emphasis on the production of textiles made with very thin to thin thread.

The majority of the Neopalatial weights, on the other hand, would be optimal for use with thicker thread requiring *c.* 20 g tension; with this type of thread they could be used to produce a tabby textile with *c.* 3–7 warp threads per centimetre. A number of the loom weights could also be used with thread requiring *c.* 10–15 g or *c.* 25–30 g tension. There was therefore a greater emphasis on the production of textiles made with slightly thicker thread during this period.

Although a few spindle whorls were recovered from Protopalatial contexts, only some of them would be suitable for spinning the types of warp threads suitable to be used with the Protopalatial loom weights. Additionally, it should be borne in mind that the low numbers of whorls recovered would not be sufficient to produce the large amount of yarn likely to have been required.

Notes

1 The first excavations were published in Pernier 1935 (Prepalatial and Protopalatial periods) and Pernier and Banti 1951 (Neopalatial period). The second cycle of excavations has been extensively published as far as the MM period is concerned by Levi 1976 and Levi and Carinci 1988. The data referring to other periods have appeared only in the preliminary reports of the excavations published in *Bullettino d'Arte* and ASAA 1950–1966. The data from Levi's excavations are currently under study. See the overview in La Rosa 2001 and 2010.

2 The clay torus loom weights come from an unclear context, datable to LM IIIC-Geometric period.

3 A complete catalogue of the material is now in P. Militello, *Festòs e Haghia Triada. Rinvenimenti Minori I. Materiale per la tessitura*, (SAC 11), Padova 2012. A few differences between the CTR Database and the catalogue of the book are due to newly found material, which, however, does not change the picture given here.

Bibliography

Bennet, J. (1985) The structure of the Linear B administration at Knossos, *American Journal of Archaeology*, 89 (2), 231–249.

Bennet, J. (1990) Knossos in context: comparative perspectives on the Linear B administration of LM II–III Crete, *American Journal of Archaeology*, 94 (2), 193–211.

Benzi, M. (2001) Il periodo prepalaziale a Festòs, in La Rosa, V. (ed.), *I cento anni dello scavo di Festòs*, 123–155. Rome. Accademia Nazionale dei Lincei.

Borgna, E. (2003) *Il complesso di ceramic tardominoica III dell'Acropoli mediana di Festòs*. Padova. Bottega d'Erasmo.

Branigan, K. (2001) Aspects of Minoan urbanism, in Branigan, K. (ed.), *Urbanism in the Aegean Bronze Age*, 38–50. London. Sheffield Academic Press.

Carinci, F. (1989) The 'III fase protopalaziale' at Phaistos. Some observations, in Laffineur, R. (ed.), *Transition. Le Monde égéen du Bronze moyen au Bronze récent*, 73–80. Liège. Université de Liège.

Carinci, F. (2001) La Casa a Sud della Rampa e il Medio Minoico III a Festòs in La Rosa, V. (ed.), *I cento anni dello scavo di Festòs*, 203–241. Rome. Accademia Nazionale dei Lincei.

Carinci, F. and La Rosa, V. (2009) Revisioni festie II, *Creta Antica*, 10, 147–300.

Di Tonto, S. (2009), Il Neolitico Finale a Festòs: per una riconsiderazione funzionale dei dati dagli scavi Levi, *Creta Antica* 10 (1), 57–95.

Girella, L. (2011), Bridging the gap: the function of houses and residential neighborhoods in Middle Minoan III Phaistos, in Glowacki, K. T. and Vogeikoff-Brogan, N. (eds), ΣΤΕΓΑ: *The Archaeology of Houses and Households in Ancient Crete*, 81–97. Princeton. American School of Classical Studies at Athens.

La Rosa, V. (1995) A hypothesis on earthquakes and political power in Minoan Crete, *Annali di Geofisica*, 38, 881–891.

La Rosa, V. (2001) *I cento anni dello scavo di Festòs*. Rome. Accademia Nazionale dei Lincei.

La Rosa, V. (2002a) Le campagne di scavo 2000–2002 a Festòs, *Annuario della Scuola archeologica di Atene e delle Missioni italiane in Oriente* 80, 635–869.

La Rosa, V. (2002b) Pour une révision préliminaire du second palais de Phaistos, in Driessen, J., Schoep, I., Laffineur, R. and Relaki, M. (eds), *Monuments of Minos. Rethinking the Minoan Palaces*, 1–97. Liège. Université de Liège.

La Rosa, V. (2010) Ayia Triada, in Cline, E. H. (ed.), *Oxford Handbook of the Aegean Bronze Age*, 495–508. New York. Oxford University Press.

Levi, D. (1976) *Festòs e la civiltà minoica, I*. Rome. Ateneo.

Levi, D. and Carinci, F. (1988) *Festòs e la civiltà minoica, II: L'arte festia nell'età protopalaziale*. Rome. Ateneo.

Militello, P. (2006) Attività tessile a Festòs e Haghia Triada dal neolitico al Bronzo Tardo, in Tampakaki, E. and Kaloutsakis, A. (eds), *Pepragmena Th' Diethnous Kretologikou Synedriou, Proïstoriki Periodos, Techni kai Latreia. 9th International Cretological Congress*, 173–187.

Militello, P. (2007) Textile industry and Minoan palaces, in Gillis, C. and Nosch, M.-L. (eds), *Ancient Textiles: Production, Craft and Society*, 36–45. Ancient Textiles Series 1. Oxford. Oxbow Books.

Militello, P. (2012a), Textile activity in Neolithic Phaistos, in Nosch, M.-L. and Laffineur, R. (eds), *KOSMOS. Jewellery, Adornment and Textiles in the Aegean Bronze Age*, 199–206. Liège. Peeters.

Militello, P. (2012b) Emerging authority: a functional analysis of the MM II settlement of Festòs, in Driessen, J., Schoep, I. and Tomkins, P. (eds), *Back to the Beginning. Reconsidering Prepalatial and Protopalatial Crete*, 236–272. Oxford. Oxbow Books.

Palio, O. (2001) La casa TM I di Chalara a Festòs, *Studi di Archeologia Cretese* 2, 239–405.

Pernier, L. (1935) *Il palazzo minoico di Festòs, I*. Rome. Libreria dello stato.

Pernier, L. and Banti, L. (1951) *Il palazzo minoico di Festòs, II*. Rome. Libreria dello stato.

Schoep, I. (2001) Managing the hinterland: the rural concerns of urban administration, in Branigan, K. (ed.), *Urbanism in the Aegean Bronze Age*, 5, 87–102. London. Sheffield Academic Press.

Todaro, S. (2005) EM I-MM IA ceramic groups at Phaistos: towards the definition of a Prepalatial ceramic sequence in south central Crete, *Creta Antica*, 6, 11–46.

Todaro, S. (2009) Pottery production in the Prepalatial Mesara: the Artisans' Quarter to the west of the palace at Phaistos, *Creta Antica* 10 (2), 333–352.

Todaro, S. (2012) Craft production and social practice at Prepalatial Phaistos: the background to the first palace, in Driessen, J., Schoep, I. and Tomkins, P. (eds), *Back to the Beginning. Reconsidering Prepalatial and Protopalatial Crete*, 195–235. Oxford. Oxbow Books.

Todaro, S. and Di Tonto, S. (2008) The Neolithic settlement of Phaistos revisited: evidence for ceremonial activity on the eve of the Bronze Age, in Isaakidou, V. and Tomkins, P. D. (eds), *Escaping the Labyrinth: New Perspectives on the Neolithic of Crete*, 177–190. Oxford. Oxbow Books.

Tortorici, C. and Monaco, L. (2003) Effects of earthquakes on the Minoan "Royal Villa" at Ayia Triada (Crete), *Creta Antica*, 4, 403–417.

Vagnetti, L. (1972–1973) L'insediamento neolitico di Festòs, *Annuario della Scuola archeologica di Atene e delle Missioni italiane in Oriente* 50–51, 7–138.

Watrous, L. V., Hadzi-Vallianou, D., Blitzer, H. and Bennet, J. (2004) *The Plain of Phaistos. Cycles of Social Complexity in the Mesara Region of Crete*. Los Angeles. Institute of Archaeology, UCLA.

Whitelaw, T. (2001) From sites to communities: defining the human dimension of Minoan urbanism, in Branigan, K. (ed.), *Urbanism in the Aegean Bronze Age*, 15–37. London. Sheffield Academic Press.

CHAPTER 6.5

Textile tools from Quartier Mu, Malia, Crete, Greece

Jean-Claude Poursat, Françoise Rougemont, Joanne Cutler,
Eva Andersson Strand and Marie-Louise Nosch

The palatial settlement of Malia is situated on the north coast of Crete. The buildings of Quartier Mu, excavated by the French School at Athens, were constructed in MM II (18th century BC) above earlier MM IB structures and were contemporary with the first palace at Malia (Poursat 1992, 1996).[1] This area of the town contained two large building complexes, Buildings A and B, as well as a series of much smaller units located around the periphery (Fig. 6.5.1). Five of these smaller buildings have been identified as the combined living quarters and workshops of artisans: the Seal workshop, Founder's workshop, Potter's workshop, South workshop and Building C. Building F may also have been a workshop/living unit, while two further units, Buildings D and E, appear to have been used as storage structures, possibly associated with building complexes A and B.

The entire quarter was destroyed by fire *c.* 1700 BC. The period of use of the buildings is therefore limited to MM II.

Spindle whorls and spinning

No objects recorded as spindle whorls are registered in the TTTC database. However, among the MM II textile tools recorded as loom weights there are nine objects that, from their shape (two cylindrical, three spherical and four spherical lenticular), weight (20–40 g) and dimensions, are likely to have functioned as spindle whorls. Very few spindle whorls dating to the Protopalatial or Neopalatial periods have been found on Crete, and when they are present they are only present in very small numbers. While it is possible that during these periods whorls were made out of a perishable material, such as wood, it is also possible that spinning was not being carried out in the same locations as weaving, which is well attested at Quartier Mu.

Loom weights and weaving

More than 600 loom weights have been recovered from Quartier Mu, the majority (527) dating to MM II (Fig. 6.5.2). Many of the loom weights with an unknown date, most of which come from fills or outdoor spaces where the stratigraphy is unclear, are also likely to date to the MM II use of the area. Others, including four spools found on the surface, may be associated with the adjacent LM IIIA-B settlement area (Quartier Nu). Only three loom weights were recovered from MM IB contexts.

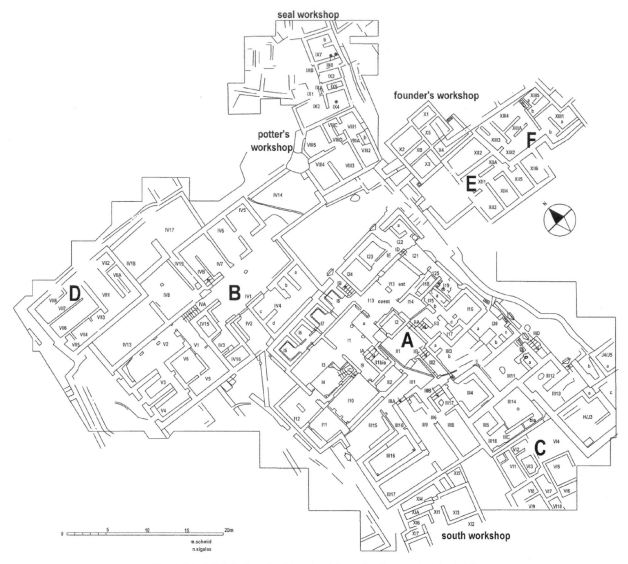

Fig. 6.5.1. MM II Quartier Mu, plan (plan: after Poursat 1996, pl. 81).

	MM IB	MM I–II	MM II	LM III	Unknown	Total
Spherical			267		25	292
Spherical lenticular			15		1	16
Discord	1		106	1	21	129
Pyramidal	1		37		30	68
Biconical			1			1
Conical			1		2	3
Cuboid			5		1	6
Cylindrical		2	38		5	45
Rectangular, flat			6		4	10
Rectangular, thick	1		5		5	11
Torus			17		8	25
Torus (small hole diam)			25		2	27
Spool					4	4
Other			4			4
Total	3	2	527	1	108	641

Fig. 6.5.2. Loom weights, by type and date.

A number of different loom weight types are present; the most common shapes, however, are spherical, discoid and pyramidal (Figs. 6.5.2 and 6.5.3). One of the discoid weights and 21 of the torus weights are made of stone, the rest of the loom weights are made of clay. In addition to the objects that were intentionally manufactured as loom weights, a further 134 naturally pierced pebbles (132 from MM II contexts and two of unknown date) are also likely to have been used on the loom (Poursat 2012).

Of the 527 loom weights from MM II contexts, 472 were found within the individual buildings. All of the buildings contained loom weights. Low numbers of weights were recovered from each of the small workshop units and from Buildings B, E and F; substantially larger numbers were found in Buildings A and D (Fig. 6.5.4). Within each of the individual buildings, more than one type of loom weight was present. The majority of the loom weights were found scattered over the ground floors of the buildings, and are likely to have fallen from rooms above. Unlike the lower storey rooms, the upper floors were almost certainly provided with windows (Schmid 1996, 79–80). Most of the living quarters and work areas were situated on the upper floors, and it is probable that weaving also took place in the upper storey rooms.

Building A
Building A (sectors I–III), the largest complex in Quartier Mu, contained several storage areas and rooms with a ceremonial function as well as an archival deposit (Poursat 1992). Loom weights were recovered from many of the rooms within the building; the majority appear

to have fallen from an upper floor. Of the 162 loom weights found in MM II contexts, 143 had a recordable weight and thickness (Fig. 6.5.5). The weights of these loom weights range between 20 g and 1040 g, with the majority weighing between 50 g and 300 g. Two clusters relating to loom weights with a weight of 75–150 g are visible: one corresponding to discoid loom weights with a thickness of 1.5–2.3 cm and the other representing spherical loom weights with a thickness of 4.0–5.2 cm. Two of the spherical lenticular weights, weighing 20 g and 35 g, would not work well as loom weights and it is more likely that they are spindle whorls.

In most cases, only low numbers of loom weights were recovered from the individual rooms in Building A, but Rooms I 8 and III 1 contained 30 and 25 loom weights respectively. In contrast to the majority of the loom weights found within the building, the group of 30 weights (27 spherical, two torus and one cylindrical) recovered from Room I 8 were

Fig. 6.5.3. Textile tools: a) spherical, discoid and pyramidal loom weights b) spherical, discoid and torus (small hole diameter) loom weights c) pyramidal and rectangular loom weights (photos: EfA/J. C. Poursat).

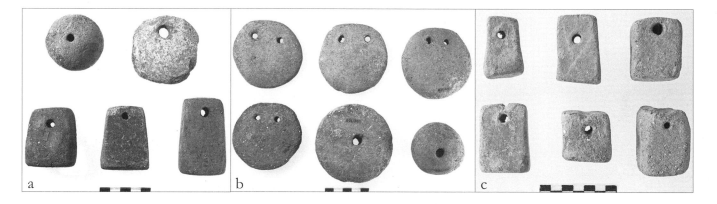

Fig. 6.5.4. Loom weights from individual buildings, MM II, by type.

	Seal workshop	Potter's workshop	Founder's workshop	South workshop	Building A	Building B	Building C	Building D	Building E	Building F	Total
Spherical		13	2	2	75	18	11	126	8		255
Spherical lenticular	1				3	4	1	1			10
Discord		14	2	3	47	4	4	5	4		83
Pyramidal		3	1	1	13	4	7	2		1	32
Biconical					1						1
Conical		1									1
Cuboid			1		2	1					4
Cylindrical		1	1		7	6	1	20			36
Rectangular, flat					4	1					5
Rectangular, thick			1		2					1	4
Torus		1		2	4	3		4		1	15
Torus (small hole diam)				2	2		17			1	22
Other					2			2			4
Total	1	33	8	10	162	40	42	160	12	1	472

in situ, in what appears to have been a storage area. Twenty-eight of these had a recordable weight and thickness (Fig. 6.5.7). Except for the two torus weights (weighing 620 g and 1040 g and made of stone), all of the loom weights weigh between 105 g and 185 g, with a thickness of 4.0–5.5 cm.

Excluding the two, much heavier, torus weights, all the remaining loom weights would function well with very thin thread requiring *c.* 10 g tension, and all except the heaviest spherical weight (weighing 185 g) would also work well with very thin thread needing *c.* 5 g tension. Only five of the 26 spherical/cylindrical loom weights would be optimal for use with thin thread requiring *c.* 15 g tension, and none would function well with thread needing *c.* 20 g tension or more. Used in a tabby weave with thread needing *c.* 5 g tension, the majority of the loom weights would give a warp thread count of *c.* 9–12 threads per centimetre, whereas with thread requiring *c.* 10 g tension, the resulting fabric would have a narrower thread count range of *c.* 5–7 threads per centimetre (Fig. 6.5.7). In a twill weave, the thread counts would be approximately double. Since all the spherical/cylindrical loom weights would function well with thread needing *c.* 10 g tension, with only a small variation in the thread count per centimetre in the finished fabric, the

group would appear to be best suited for use with this type of thread and would work well together in the same loom setup. However, in both a tabby and a twill weave the resulting textile would have been extremely open if the fabric was balanced and it is therefore likely that in either a tabby or a twill the textile would have been weft faced.

The 25 loom weights from Room III 1 (11 spherical, eight discoid, four cylindrical, one pyramidal and one torus) are likely to have fallen from an upper storey. It is therefore not possible to say whether they were originally part of the same group. However, an analysis of the loom weights suggests that they fall into more than one category. All of the loom weights had a recordable weight and thickness (Fig. 6.5.8). The discoid loom weights weigh 90–140 g, with a thickness of 1.7–2.5 g; they would function well with thread needing *c.* 5–10 g tension. Used with thread requiring *c.* 5 g tension they could produce a tabby fabric with *c.* 18–24 warp threads per centimetre; with thread needing *c.* 10 g tension the thread count would be *c.* 10–12 threads per centimetre. The narrower thread count range for *c.* 10 g tension thread suggests that the discoid weights would be optimal for use with this type of thread. With the exception of the stone torus weight and the heaviest

Fig. 6.5.5. Loom weights, MM II, Building A: type and weight/thickness. Please note that some markers represent more than one loom weight.

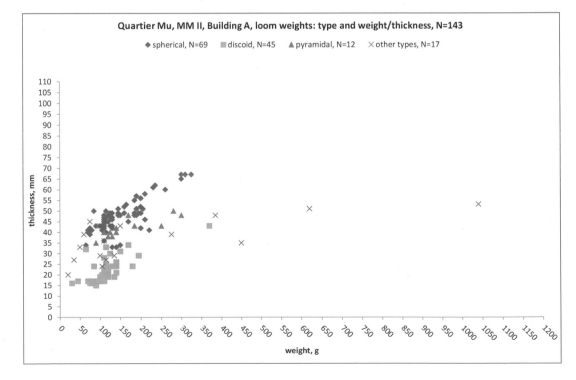

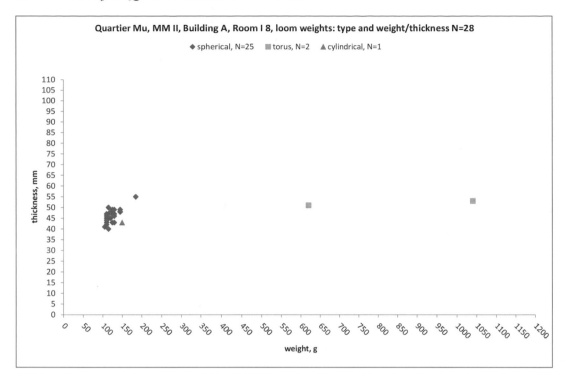

Fig. 6.5.6. Loom weights, MM II, Building A, Room I 8: type and weight/thickness. Please note that some markers represent more than one loom weight.

cylindrical weight, the remaining loom weights (11 spherical and three cylindrical) weigh 100–235 g and would also function well with very thin thread requiring *c.* 10 g tension. The warp thread count would vary between *c.* 6 and 11 threads per centimetre in a tabby, so the fabric produced would have fewer threads per centimetre than a fabric produced with the discoid weights. In a balanced tabby weave, both fabrics would have been very open, however, and are therefore likely to have been weft faced. In a twill weave using four rows of loom weights, the thread count would be approximately double; this would also be likely to be a weft-faced textile, since the fabric would otherwise be very open.

In Room I 11 of Building A, three loom weights were found *in situ* in a closet, along with 65 naturally pierced pebbles. The 62 pebbles with a recordable weight and thickness mostly lie within the same weight/thickness range as the loom weights that were recovered from the building as a whole (Fig. 6.5.9), and it is likely that they were also used on the loom.

Building B

Of the 40 loom weights recovered from MM II contexts in Building B (sectors IV and V), 37 had a recordable weight and thickness (Fig. 6.5.10). Four of these, with a weight of

Warp thr/cm	5 g, N=25	10 g, N=26	15 g, N=5
3 thr			
4 thr			4
5 thr		14	1
6 thr		10	
7 thr		2	
8 thr			
9 thr	2		
10 thr	10		
11 thr	6		
12 thr	6		
13 thr			
14 thr	1		

Fig. 6.5.7. Loom weights, MM II, Building A, Room I 8 (excluding two stone torus weights): weight tension/number of threads per cm in a tabby. The total number of analysed loom weights is 26.

34–40 g, are more likely to be spindle whorls (one spherical, two spherical lenticular and one cylindrical). The weights of the remaining loom weights range between 55 g and 240 g, and their thickness varies between 1.8 cm and 6.6 cm. The weight range of the loom weights is therefore more limited than the weight range of the loom weights from Building A. The majority would be optimal for use with very thin thread, needing *c.* 5-10 g tension.

As in Building A, the majority of the loom weights from Building B appear to have fallen from above. However, nine loom weights of different types (five spherical, two discoid and

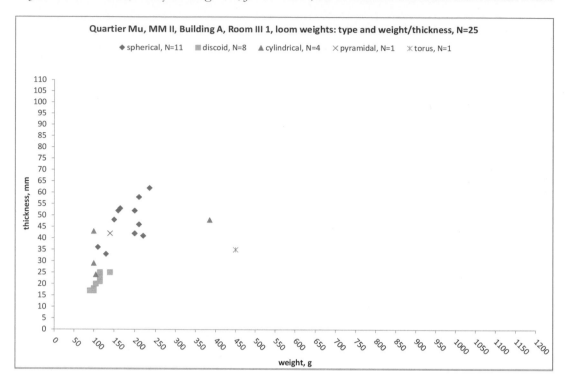

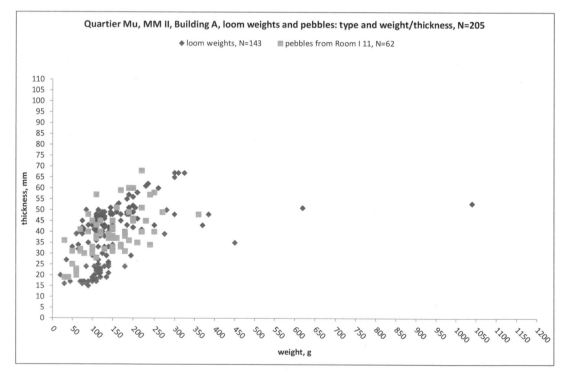

two cylindrical) from Room IV 5 were found *in situ*, together with 25 naturally pierced pebbles. The loom weights and pebbles were found lying in the shape of a square, suggesting that they may originally have been stored in a box or a chest. The room appears to have been used for storage (being one in a row

of storage magazines), but did not contain anything other than the loom weights and pebbles. It is possible that perishable materials such as finished textiles or raw fibre may also have been stored here, but have not survived. In this respect, it is interesting to note that a Cretan Hieroglyphic tablet (HM 1676) with a

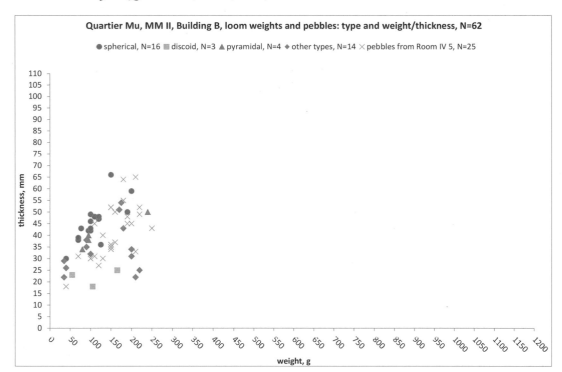

Fig. 6.5.10. Loom weights and pebbles, MM II, Building B: type and weight/thickness. Please note that some markers represent more than one loom weight/pebble.

suspension hole pierced through it was found in the doorway of Room IV 5, possibly having fallen from an upper floor (Poursat 1990, 27; Godart and Olivier 1978, 70). On one side of the tablet, the Cretan hieroglyphic sign P41 occurs twice; this sign takes the same form as the Linear A logogram *54 and the Linear B TELA textile logogram. A sign that has been interpreted as the equivalent of the Linear B wool unit, LANA, is also present (Younger 2005). Younger has proposed that the entry should be read as, 'TA <-PE>+CLOTH LANA = 3 double minas CLOTH', thus possibly recording the assessment of the amount of TA<-PE> cloth made from one unit of wool, with TA<-PE> perhaps representing the Minoan predecessor of the Mycenaean *te-pa* variety of cloth (Younger 2005). Whether or not this interpretation is accepted, the presence of the hieroglyphic sign P41 does suggest the possibility that the tablet may be associated with the recording of textiles.

All of the pebbles had a recordable weight and thickness. Their weight varies between 40 g and 250 g, and their thickness ranges from 1.8 cm to 6.5 cm. (Fig. 6.5.10).

The pebbles found in storage lie within a similar weight/thickness range as the loom weights from Building B, and could have been used in various combinations with the loom weights recovered from the building.

Building D

Building D (sector VII), which appears to have been a storage structure, contained 160 loom weights. These were all found *in situ*, in Rooms VII 3 and VII 4. The majority of the loom weights (126) are spherical in shape.

Room VII 3 contained 119 loom weights (94 spherical, 13 cylindrical, four discoid, four torus, two pyramidal, one spherical lenticular and one 'other'). All except one of these had a recordable weight and a thickness (Fig. 6.5.11).

The four, thinner, discoid loom weights would not work well with the other loom weights in the group, since they would produce a higher number of warp threads per centimetre. Similarly, the six loom weights weighing more than 450 g could not optimally be used with the other weights. Only two of the remaining loom weights would function well with thread requiring *c.* 5 g tension (Fig. 6.5.12). Forty-six of the weights could be used with very thin thread needing *c.* 10 g tension, the majority of which would give a warp thread count of between 7 and 12 threads per centimetre in a tabby. Over 100 of the weights would work well with thin thread requiring *c.* 15 g or 20 g tension. With thread needing

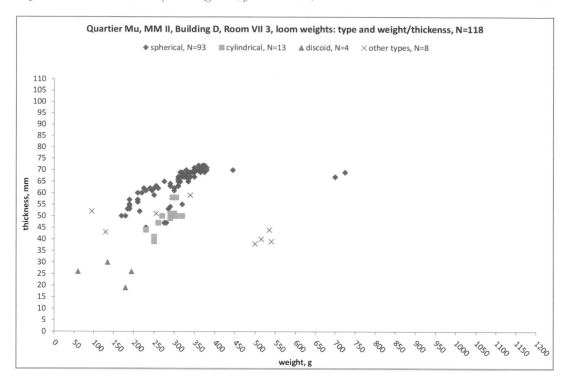

Fig. 6.5.11. Loom weights, MM II, Building D, Room VII 3: type and weight/thickness. Please note that some markers represent more than one loom weight.

Warp thr/cm	5 g, N=2	10 g, N=46	15 g, N=106	20 g, N=103	25 g, N=89	30 g, N=74	35 g, N=38	40 g, N=3	45 g, N=1
3 thr				1	8	58	37	3	1
4 thr		1	1	19	68	16	1		
5 thr			20	66	13				
6 thr		1	23	16					
7 thr	1	12	50	1					
8 thr		10	10						
9 thr		4	2						
10 thr		6							
11 thr		5							
12 thr	1	6							
13 thr		1							

Fig. 6.5.12. Loom weights, MM II, Building D, Room VII 3: weight tension/number of threads per cm in a tabby. The total number of analysed loom weights is 108.

c. 15 g tension the majority could produce a tabby with *c.* 5–8 threads per centimetre, while with thread requiring *c.* 20 g tension, most would be suitable for making a fabric with *c.* 4–6 threads per centimetre. Eighty-nine of the loom weights could be used with thread needing *c.* 25 g tension, to produce a tabby fabric with *c.* 3–5 threads per centimetre. A number of the weights could also be used with thread requiring *c.* 30 g or 35 g tension, to produce a tabby with *c.* 3–4 warp threads per centimetre. Only a few weights could be used with thread needing *c.* 40–45 g tension. In a twill weave, the thread counts would be approximately double.

Twenty-eight pierced pebbles were additionally found in Room VII 3. With the exception of one pebble weighing 1170 g, these have a weight of between 100 g and 380 g and a thickness of 2.7–7.0 cm. They therefore lie within the weight/thickness range of the loom weights recovered from this room and it would be possible to use the pebbles together with the loom weights in various loom setups.

Room VII 4 contained 41 loom weights (32 spherical, seven cylindrical, one discoid and one 'other'), 35 of which had a recordable weight and thickness (31 spherical and four cylindrical). These weigh 175–380 g and their thickness varies from 4.7 cm to 7.2 cm (Fig. 6.5.13).

They therefore fall within the same weight/thickness range as a large number of the loom weights recovered from Room VII 3.

The loom weights from Room VII 4 would have been suitable for use in the manufacture of a very similar range of fabrics to those that could have been made with the loom weights from Room VII 3, with very similar warp thread counts (Fig. 6.5.14). All of them could be used with thread needing *c.* 15 g tension, and the majority would give a thread count of *c.* 5–7 threads per centimetre in a tabby weave; 34 could also be used in a setup with thread requiring *c.* 20 g tension, and could produce a tabby fabric with *c.* 3–6 threads per centimetre.

A number could additionally be used with thread needing *c.* 10 g and *c.* 30–35 g tension. The loom weights stored in Rooms VII 3 and VII 4 could therefore have been used together in various loom setups.

Potter's workshop

Thirty-three loom weights were scattered over the ground floor area of the Potter's workshop, and appear to have fallen from the upper floor. Thirty-one of these had a recordable weight and thickness (12 spherical, 14 discoid, three pyramidal, one conical and one torus). With the exception of the stone torus weight weighing 1400 g, the loom

Fig. 6.5.13. Loom weights, MM II, Building D, Room VII 4: type and weight/thickness. Please note that some markers represent more than one loom weight.

Warp thr/cm	10 g, N=19	15 g, N=35	20 g, N=34	25 g, N=25	30 g, N=21	35 g, N=4
3 thr			1	4	15	4
4 thr		1	12	18	6	
5 thr		13	18	3		
6 thr	1	8	3			
7 thr	6	10				
8 thr	7	2				
9 thr	2	1				
10 thr						
11 thr	1					
12 thr	1					
13 thr	1					

Fig. 6.5.14. Loom weights, MM II, Building D, Room VII 4: weight tension/number of threads per cm in a tabby. The total number of analysed loom weights is 35.

weights weigh 70–230 g, with a thickness of 1.8–6.2 cm (Fig. 6.5.15). The loom weights of all types would be best suited for use with very thin threads requiring *c.* 5–10 g tension. The thicker, spherical weights would produce a more open or weft faced fabric than the discoid weights, however.

Building C

The 42 loom weights from Building C, all with a recordable weight and thickness, were scattered over the ground floor, as if they had fallen from above. They have a weight range of 50–405 g, with a thickness varying from 1.6 cm to 6 cm (Fig. 6.5.16).

Fig. 6.5.15. Loom weights, MM II, the Potter's workshop: type and weight/thickness (excluding 1400 g torus weight). Please note that some markers represent more than one loom weight.

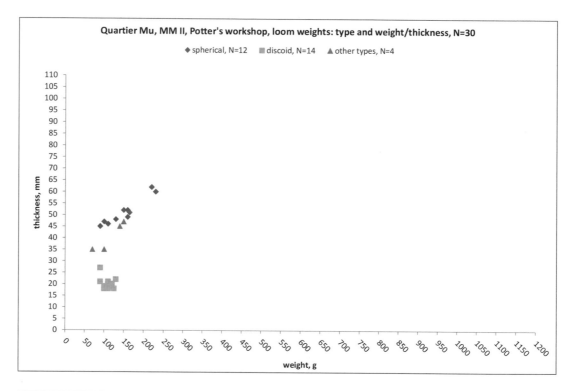

Fig. 6.5.16. Loom weights, MM II, Building C: type and weight/thickness. Please note that some markers represent more than one loom weight.

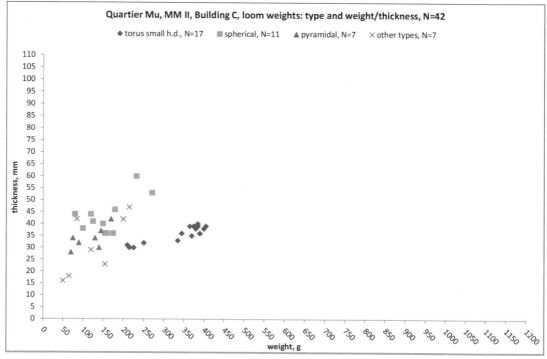

The 17 torus loom weights with a small hole diameter represent the majority of the loom weights of this type from the site as a whole. None of them would work well with thread needing c. 5 g tension; only four would be suitable for use with thread requiring c. 10 g tension (Fig. 6.5.17). All of them would function well with c. 15–20 g tension thread, and 13–14 would also be suitable for use with thread needing c. 25–35 g tension thread. Eight of these could additionally function with thread requiring c. 40 g tension. In a tabby weave with thread needing c. 15 g tension, the loom weights could produce a fabric with c. 9–14 threads per centimetre; with thread needing c. 20 g tension the thread count would be c. 7–11 threads per centimetre. In a twill weave, the thread count would be approximately double. Used with thread needing c. 15–40 g tension, this type of loom weight could be used to produce a denser fabric than it would be possible to make with any of the other main loom weight types found in Quartier Mu.

Other buildings

The 12 loom weights from Building E had also fallen from a floor above. Ten of these (eight spherical and two discoid) had a recordable

Warp thr/cm	10 g, N=4	15 g, N=17	20 g, N=17	25 g, N=14	30 g, N=13	35 g, N=13	40 g, N=8
4 thr							
5 thr						1	6
6 thr				1	1	12	2
7 thr			3		12		
8 thr			1	12			
9 thr		2	2	1			
10 thr		1	7				
11 thr		1	4				
12 thr		1					
13 thr		7					
14 thr	1	5					
15 thr	2						
16 thr	1						

Fig. 6.5.17. Torus loom weights with small hole diameter, MM II, Building C: weight tension/number of threads per cm in a tabby. The total number of analysed loom weights is 17.

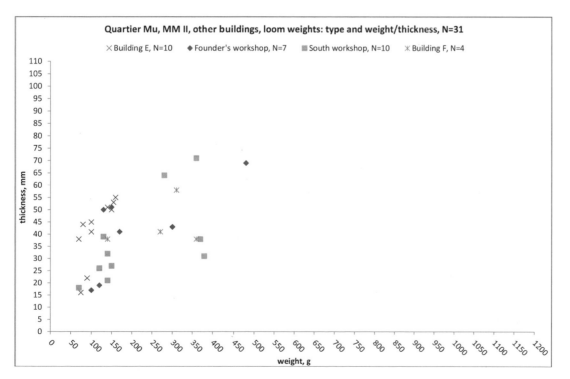

Fig. 6.5.18. Loom weights, MM II, other buildings: type and weight/thickness.

weight and thickness (Fig. 6.5.18). The ground floor of this building consists of a series or rooms which appear to have been storage magazines, but no *in situ* material was recovered from them (Poursat 1992, 48). The upper storey rooms also appear to have been used for storage. The few loom weights from the remaining buildings similarly appear to have fallen from an upper storey (see Fig. 6.5.18 for those with a recordable weight and thickness).

Summary

Although a large number of loom weights were recovered from Quartier Mu, it is not possible to suggest how many looms were actually being used. In most cases, only a few loom weights were found together and even if they could have been used in the same loom setup, it is likely that these sets of weights would have contained more loom weights. It is also likely that the width of the fabric to be woven differed, depending on the type of textile to be produced.

In Building A, the loom weights from Room I 8 and Room III 1 would be best suited for the manufacture of textiles using very thin threads, that could be either dense or open/weft faced, depending on the loom weights used. The loom weights from Room III 1 would not all function optimally in the same loom setup and it is likely that (excluding the two heavier weights) they belong to two different sets.

The range of loom weights from Building B also suggest a varied production, but the majority would be best suited for a production of fabrics with very thin thread needing a tension of *c.* 5–10 g.

In contrast to the two main concentrations of loom weights from Building A, the two groups of loom weights stored in Rooms VII 3 and VII 4 of Building D would have been most suitable for use with thread needing *c.* 15–25 g tension. Various combinations of weights from these two rooms would function very well together in a range of loom setups.

The group of torus loom weights with a small hole diameter from Building C would function best with thread needing *c.* 15–20 g tension and the fabric produced would be relatively dense. It would be possible to

weave balanced tabby fabrics (with the same number and type of warp and weft threads per centimetre[2]) with this type of loom weight. In a twill weave, the fabric could even be warp faced (more warp threads than weft).

In the Potter's workshop, the majority of the loom weights are either spherical or discoid. It would not be optimal to use these two types of loom weight in the same setup, but they would function very well in two different loom setups. It is therefore likely that at least two different types of fabric were being produced in this workshop. Although produced with the same type of thread, the fabrics would visually be very different; for example, in a tabby weave, one would be more open or weft faced and the other would be denser, with a high number of warp threads per centimetre.

Only 12 loom weights were found scattered across the ground floor of Building E (a probable storage magazine), but they give the impression of a varied production. Loom weights were also only recovered in low numbers from the other buildings. However, the loom weights from the Founder's workshop and the South workshop are of different types, which suggest that the weavers may also have produced different types of textiles in these workshops; not only with very thin threads needing *c.* 5–10 g tension, but also with thin to medium threads needing *c.* 15–25 g tension.

Different types of fabric therefore appear to have been produced in different buildings, and even in different rooms within the buildings. In some locations, such as the Potter's workshop and Building A, it is most likely that fabrics with very thin threads were being manufactured. The loom weights stored in Building D, however, would have been more suitable for use with thicker thread.

Of the nine possible spindle whorls, it is important to note that only one, weighing 20 g, would have been optimal for producing the thinner thread types likely to have been used in Quartier Mu. It is clear that much of the warp yarn used in Quartier Mu was thin or very thin. For this, it would also have been necessary to have had access to raw material that was well prepared and of a good quality. Production of this thread would have been time consuming and would have demanded specialist knowledge.

Note

1 A more comprehensive analysis of the textile tools from Quartier Mu can be found in (Cutler *et al.* 2013).

Bibliography

Cutler, J., Andersson Strand, E. and Nosch, M.-L. (2013) Textile production in Quartier Mu, in Poursat, J.-C. (with contributors), *Fouilles exécutées à Malia. Le Quartier Mu V. Vie quotidienne et techniques au Minoen Moyen II,* 95–119. Athens. École française d'Athènes.

Godart, L. and Olivier, J.-P. (1978) Écriture hiéroglyphique crétoise, in Poursat, J.-C., Godart, L. and Olivier, J.-P., *Fouilles exécutées à Malia. Le Quartier Mu I. Introduction générale/Écriture hiéroglyphique crétoise,* 29–217. Athens. École française d'Athènes.

Poursat, J.-C. (1990) Hieroglyphic documents and sealings from Malia, Quartier Mu, in Palaima, T. G. (ed.), *Aegean Seals, Sealings and Administration,* 25–33. Liège. Université de Liège.

Poursat, J.-C. (1992) *Guide de Malia au temps des premiers palais. Le Quartier Mu.* Athens. École française d'Athènes.

Poursat, J.-C. (1996) *Fouilles exécutées à Malia. Le Quartier Mu III. Artisans minoens: les maisons-ateliers du Quartier Mu.* Athens. École française d'Athènes.

Poursat, J.-C. (2012) Of looms and pebbles. Weaving at Minoan coastal sites, in Nosch, M.-L. and Laffineur, R. (eds), *KOSMOS. Jewellery, Adornment and Textiles in the Aegean Bronze Age,* 31–34. Liège. Peeters.

Schmid, M. (1996) Appendice I. L'architecture: éléments de restitution, in Poursat, J.-C. (with contributors), *Fouilles exécutées à Malia. Le Quartier Mu III. Artisans minoens: les maisons-ateliers du Quartier Mu,* 75–98. Athens. École française d'Athènes.

Younger, J. (2005) Cretan Hieroglyphic wool units (LANA, double mina), in Perna, M. (ed.), *Studi in onore di Enrica Fiandra. Contributi di archeologia egea e vicinorientale,* 405–409. Paris. De Boccard.

Textile tools from Akrotiri, Thera, Greece

Iris Tzachili, Stella Spantidaki, Eva Andersson Strand, Marie-Louise Nosch and Joanne Cutler

The Late Bronze Age settlement of Akrotiri, on the island of Thera in the Cyclades, was destroyed in Late Cycladic I (contemporary with LM IA on Crete) by a volcanic eruption. In the excavated area of the town, approximately 35 houses have been located to date; of these, 11 have been either completely or partially excavated (Tzachili 2007, 191). Loom weights have only been recovered from four of the houses, however. Textiles were manufactured not only to meet the inhabitants' own needs, but also for trade and exchange. This interpretation is supported by finds of large numbers of loom weights, as well as a Linear A inscription relating to the distribution of textiles (Del Freo *et al.* 2010), and artistic representations of the finished products on wall-paintings found in the excavated houses. The majority of the loom weights, which are extremely uniform in shape, weight and dimensions, appear to have fallen from the upper storeys of the buildings (Tzachili 2007, 190–191, with further references).

Loom weights and weaving

Complex B

Only 38 loom weights from one of the buildings, Complex B, are included in the TTTC database. These loom weights obviously cannot be taken as representative of the total loom weight assemblage and thereby the textile production at Akrotiri, but it will be possible to integrate the results with future analyses. Furthermore, the study of these loom weights has made it possible to gather a considerable amount of information about what types of textiles could be produced with these specific weights.

All the objects have the same date (LC I). Twenty loom weights were found together in the middle of Room B2, among a large amount of ceramic material. The remaining loom weights were found in other contexts within Complex B. The majority of the loom weights are considered to have been made in a medium production quality.

All the loom weights are made of fired clay and are discoid in shape (Fig. 6.6.1). The clay of four of the weights from Room B2 is non-local. At the macroscopic level, the fabric of three of the weights is considered to possibly originate from Miletos on the southwest coast of Anatolia, while the fourth visually resembles clay from the Cycladic island of Naxos. Twenty-five of the loom weights are complete or only have small fragments missing. There is no difference between the

Fig. 6.6.1a, b and c. LC I discoid loom weights (photos: courtesy of I. Tzachili).

Fig. 6.6.1a, b and c. LC I discoid loom weights (photos: courtesy of I. Tzachili).

weight/thickness range of the loom weights found in the middle of Room B2 and the loom weights from other contexts in Complex B (Fig. 6.2).

Room B2

The 18 complete or nearly complete loom weights found in the middle of Room B2 have a weight range of 130–270 g and a thickness range of 1.8–3.2 cm. They could all have functioned with different types of thread. All of the loom weights could be used with with thread requiring *c.* 10 g tension, but the resulting thread count range, in a tabby weave, of *c.* 11–20 warp threads per centimetre must be considered too large a variation (Fig. 6.3). In a twill weave, the thread count range would be approximately double. Sixteen of the loom weights would work well with thread needing *c.* 15 g tension, giving a narrower thread count range of *c.* 8–13 warp threads per centimetre in a tabby fabric. If threads needing *c.* 12.5–15 g tension were used, however, the range would be more limited; *c.* 10–14 warp threads per centimetre, which would be more likely. This demonstrates that these loom weights could have functioned in the same setup.

In a tabby weave (with nine loom weights in the front row and nine loom weights in the back row), these 18 loom weights could be used to produce a fabric *c.* 22 cm wide; if the thickness of the two partially preserved weights is included, the width would be *c.* 25 cm. Even if there was some space between the weights (see chapter 4.1), the width of the fabric would have been quite narrow. However, it is important to note that this group of loom weights was found among a large amount of pottery, and it is not known whether the weights represent a specific loom setup; it is possible that they could have been used together with other loom weights found elsewhere in Complex B to produce a wider fabric, or that they were used in various combinations with the loom weights found elsewhere in the building to produce different types of fabric.

Summary

The analyses of the loom weights found in Room B2 demonstrate that they could all have been used with thin thread needing *c.* 10–15 g tension. However, some of the individual loom weights from Room B2 and elsewhere

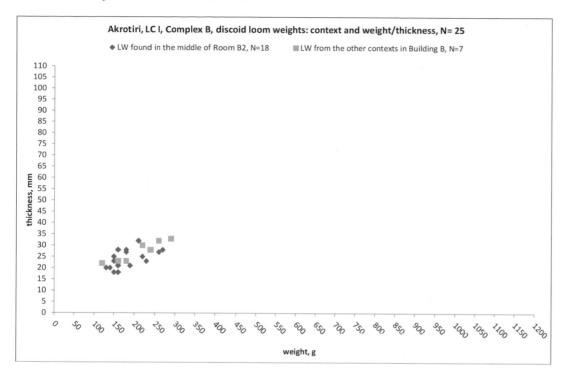

Fig. 6.6.2. LC I, Complex B, discoid loom weights: context and weight/thickness. Please note that some markers represent more than one loom weight.

Warp thr/cm	5 g, N=5	7.5 g, N=14	10 g, N=18	12.5 g N=18	15 g, N=16	20 g, N=8	25 g, N=3
6 thr							
7 thr						1	2
8 thr					2		1
9 thr				1	4	3	
10 thr				5	1	4	
11 thr			1	2	2		
12 thr			1	1	4		
13 thr			5	1	3		
14 thr			1	5			
15 thr		1	1				
16 thr		1			3		
17 thr		3	2				
18 thr		2	4				
19 thr		1	2				
20 thr		1	1				
21 thr							
22 thr		1					
23 thr		3					
24 thr	1	1					
25 thr							
26 thr	2						
27 thr							
28 thr	1						
29 thr							
30 thr							
31 thr							
32 thr							
33 thr	1						

Fig. 6.6.3. LC I, Complex B, Room B2, discoid loom weights: weight tension/number of threads per cm in a tabby. The total number of analysed loom weights is 18.

in Complex B could also have been used with thicker warp threads, needing more tension. Thus it would be possible to produce a range of different fabrics. Further investigation of the rest of the loom weight material from Akrotiri is necessary in order to give any detailed suggestions of the range of textiles that could have been made at the site.

Bibliography

Del Freo, M., Nosch, M.-L. and Rougemont, F. (2010) The terminology of textiles in the Linear B tablets, including some considerations on Linear A logograms and abbreviations, in Michel, C. and Nosch, M.-L. (eds), *Textile Terminologies in the Ancient Near East and Mediterranean from the Third to the First Millennia BC*, 338–73. Ancient Textiles Series 8. Oxford. Oxbow Books.

Tzachili, I. (2007) Weaving at Akrotiri, Thera. Defining cloth-making activities as a social process in a Late Bronze Age Aegean town, in Gillis, C. and Nosch, M-L. (eds), *Ancient Textiles. Production, Craft and Society*, 190–196. Ancient Textiles Series 1. Oxford. Oxbow Books.

CHAPTER 6.7

Textile tools from Midea, mainland Greece

Katie Demakopoulou, Ioannis Fappas, Eva Andersson Strand, Marie-Louise Nosch and Joanne Cutler

The citadel of Midea is an impressive fortified acropolis built on the top of a rocky hill, overlooking the east edge of the Argolid plain. The acropolis, which is surrounded by a huge cyclopean wall, was destroyed by a severe earthquake followed by a great conflagration that happened around the end of the 13th century BC (*c.* 1200 BC). Greek-Swedish excavations at the site have uncovered a number of buildings within the citadel. A significant building complex, consisting of many small rectangular rooms in the West Gate Area, attached to the inner side of the fortification wall, has been excavated by a Greek team of archaeologists, under the direction of Dr K. Demakopoulou, in the area of the West Gate. These rooms may have served as store rooms and workshops, which is indicated by the many pithoi, storage jars, tools and raw materials that have been recovered from them. It is notable that the 14 rooms of the complex have all yielded numerous textile tools, indicating that

textile manufacture was most probably one of the activities conducted there. Rooms VIa–VIb, VII, and VIIIa–VIIIb of the building complex are situated next to each other and form a 'closed context'; they therefore constitute an ideal situation for the study of Midea's textile production.

A total of 191 textile tools from the Greek-Swedish excavations at Midea are recorded in the TTTC database: 49 of these were recovered from the Greek excavations of the building complex at the West Gate, while 142 are from the Swedish excavations at the site (Fig. 6.7.1). The 49 tools from the West Gate complex were recovered from LH IIIB2 Late contexts (Demakopoulou and Divari-Valakou 1997–1998; Demakopoulou and Fappas 2007, unpublished). The majority of the textile tools from the Swedish excavations are from contexts that are more broadly dated to the LH III period and in general they are from trenches that have not been identified

	Spindle whorl	Loom weight	Needle	Pin beater	Spindle	Wool comb tooth	Total
LH III	115		2	4	7	1	**129**
LH IIIB2 Late	48		1				**49**
Unknown	3	1		9			**13**
Total	**166**	**1**	**3**	**13**	**7**	**1**	**191**

Fig. 6.7.1. Textile tools by date and type.

	Clay		Stone	
	LH III	**LH IIIB2 Late**	**LH III**	**LH IIIB2 Late**
Biconical	7		3	1
Concave conical	1		25	5
Conical	6	4	67	38
Convex	2			
Spherical	3		1	
Total	19	4	96	44

Fig. 6.7.2. (top) Stone spindle whorls (photo: courtesy of the Greek-Swedish excavation project).

Fig. 6.7.3. Spindle whorls: date, type and material.

as belonging to a specific room or building (Walberg 1998; Demakopoulou and Fappas 2007, unpublished).

Spindle whorls and spinning

One hundred and sixty-six spindle whorls are recorded in the database. The majority of the spindle whorls from both general LH III and LH IIIB2 Late contexts are made of stone (steatite) and are conical in shape (Figs. 6.7.2 and 6.7.3).

The conical and biconical spindle whorls have a large weight/diameter range and no clear pattern of distribution is discernible (Fig. 6.7.4). The whorls with a concave conical shape, however, tend to be very light, weighing less than 10 g.

There is no difference in the weight/diameter range of the spindle whorls from contexts that are broadly dated to the LH III period and the whorls from LH IIIB2 Late contexts (Fig. 6.7.5). In general, the whorls display a wide variation: the weight varies from 1 g to 86 g and the diameter varies from 1.4 cm to 5.2 cm. This distribution pattern indicates a production of many types of yarn from very thin to very thick. However, the majority of

the spindle whorls have a weight below 15 g, suggesting an emphasis on the production of thin and very thin spun yarn.

Forty-eight spindle whorls were recovered from LH IIIB2 Late contexts in the West Gate complex. Twenty-five of these are from Room VI; 15 whorls were found in Room VII and the remaining eight whorls are from Room VIII (VIIIb). All except one of the whorls had a recordable weight and diameter (Fig. 6.7.6).

Rooms VIa and VIb

Two large walls abutting the fortification wall and a shorter wall, parallel to the fortification wall, form a large space (6 × 4 m) which is divided by a short cross wall into two rooms: Room VIa, which is larger, and Room VIb, which is smaller and built against the fortification wall. The two rooms communicate through a large opening that is 1.20 m wide. Rooms VIa and VIb were basement rooms and were evidently store rooms and workshops, demonstrated by the large number of storage vessels and tools found in them. Both rooms were destroyed by the earthquake that struck Midea *c.* 1200 BC and the great conflagration that was caused by it. Most of the vessels found in both rooms were for storage; these include pithoi, large amphorae, hydriae, pithoid jars, and coarse stirrup jars, some of Cretan origin. Among them is a storage stirrup jar with a painted Linear B inscription that reads *wi-na-jo*. The same inscription also appears on two storage stirrup jars from Crete, one found at Knossos and the other at Armenoi. It seems that all three stirrup jars come from the same workshop and that the Midea stirrup jar was sent to the Argolid from Crete. Another important find from Room VIb is a complete prismatic perforated clay nodule bearing the GRA ideogram (=WHEAT). A large quantity of LH IIIB2 painted pottery was found in Rooms VIa and VIb, along with abundant unpainted domestic pottery. Many coarse ware pots were also found, including household vessels. In addition, Rooms VIa and VIb contained a few stone and lead vessels, which, like the clay vases, were found *in situ*. Among the numerous tools and other small objects of stone, bronze, bone, glass and clay recovered from both rooms were millstones, pounders, pestles, a hammer-axe, whetstones, obsidian and flint blades, two bronze chisels, a mirror, pins and needles also of bronze, a large wheelmade terracotta female statuette, as well

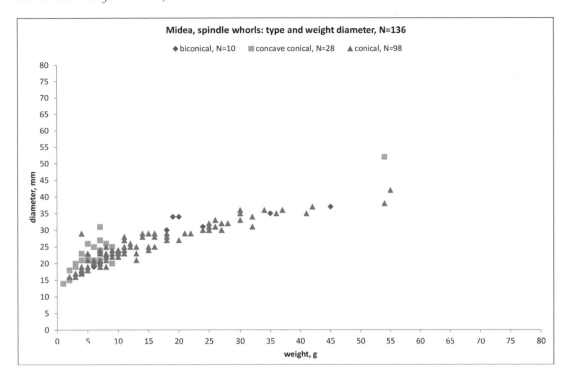

Fig. 6.7.4. Spindle
whorls: type and weight/
diameter (excluding the
whorl, conical in shape,
weighing 86 g). Please
note that types represented
by two or less whorls are
not included in the graph.
Please also note that some
markers represent more
than one spindle whorl.

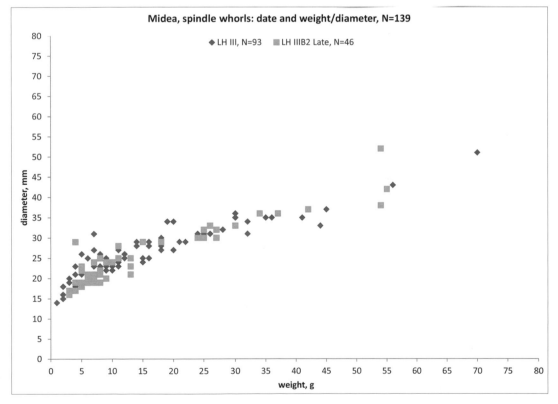

Fig. 6.7.5. Spindle
whorls: date and weight/
diameter (excluding the
LH IIIB2 Late whorl
weighing 86 g). Please
note that some markers
represent more than one
spindle whorl.

as the spindle whorls. Twelve of the spindle whorls, including conical and papyrus-shaped whorls, were found in a tall rounded alabastron in Room VIb (Demakopoulou and Divari-Valakou 1994–1995; Demakopoulou and Divari Valakou 1997–1998; Demakopoulou 1998, 1999).

Seven whorls were recovered from Room VIa, while 13 were found in Room VIb; a further five whorls are from general Room VI

Fig. 6.7.6. Spindle whorls, LH IIIB2 Late: context and weight/ diameter (excluding the whorl from Room VI weighing 86 g). Please note that some markers represent more than one spindle whorl.

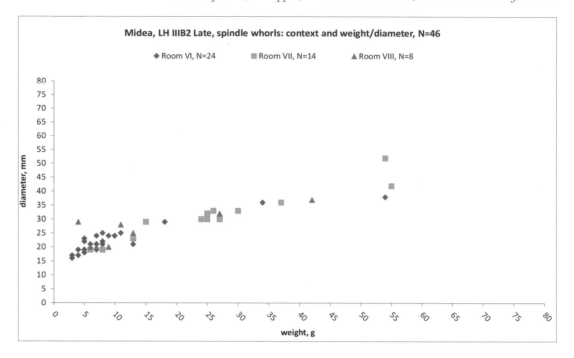

contexts. The whorls display a wide weight/ diameter variation, indicating a production of many types of yarn from very thin to very thick (Fig. 6.7.7). However, the majority of the whorls weigh less than 13 g, indicating a larger production of very fine spun yarn. The spindle whorls found in the same pot in Room VIb are all light, weighing less than 12 g. It should be noted that the light whorls also display a weight/diameter variation, and the CTR experiments have demonstrated that there is a visible difference between a thread spun with a 4 g spindle whorl and a thread spun with an 8 g spindle whorl (see chapter 4.1).

Room VII
Room VII was also a basement room built against the fortification wall, lying next to Rooms VIa and VIb to the west. It constitutes a narrow rectangular space, with an opening in its east wall giving access to Rooms VIa and VIb via two stone steps. The floor of the room was made of trodden earth and covered in places with stone slabs. Room VII was also destroyed by the earthquake and the great conflagration that followed it. Its interior contained numerous finds. Many vessels and tools were found on its floor and large pithoi were placed in its southwest corner. Large coarse stirrup jars as well as abundant LH IIIB2 painted and plain domestic pottery,

including a large number of household vessels, were also present. An almost intact stone spouted tripod mortar was additionally found *in situ* on the floor of the room. Numerous stone tools, including pounders and pestles, were also recovered, as well as a large elliptical millstone. In addition to the spindle whorls found in the room, some clay loom weights were also recovered (Demakopoulou and Divari-Valakou 1997–1998; Demakopoulou 1998).[1]

The 14 spindle whorls from Room VII with a recordable weight and diameter similarly display a wide weight/diameter variation, indicating a production of many types of yarn from very thin to thick (Fig. 6.7.6). However, the majority of the whorls weigh over 20 g, which suggests an emphasis on the production of relatively thick yarn.

Rooms VIIIa and VIIIb
Rooms VIIIa and VIIIb, also basement rooms, lie next to Room VII to the west and were similarly built against the fortification wall. As in the case of Rooms VIa and VIb, a large space, formed by two walls abutting the fortification wall and by one wall parallel to it, is divided into two rooms by a short cross wall. Room VIIIa, which is long and narrow, lies to the north, and the more spacious Room VIIIb lies to the south, adjacent to the fortification

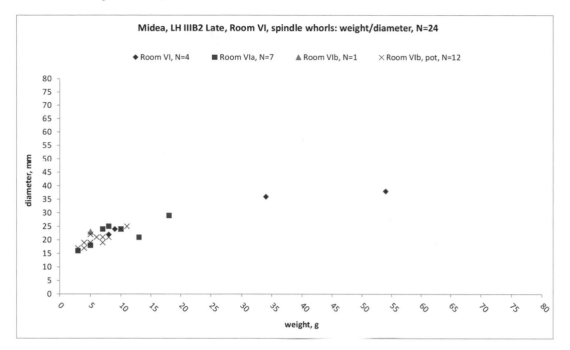

wall. The rooms communicate through a large opening. A large amount of LH IIIB2 painted pottery, along with abundant domestic plain and coarse ware pottery, was recovered from both rooms. In addition to the ceramic vessels, three stone tripod mortars, one together with its pounder, and one lead vessel were found on the floor of Room VIIIb. The very fragmentary status of the pottery found in Room VIIIa indicates that it may have fallen from an upper storey. Numerous tools, such as pounders and whetstones, were also recovered from Rooms VIIIa and VIIIb, as well as a large number of other objects of stone, bronze, ivory, bone, glass and clay that include millstones, bronze arrowheads and an ivory model of a figure-of-eight shield. In addition to the spindle whorls, an intact bronze needle or pin was also recovered (Demakopoulou 1998; Demakopoulou and Divari-Valakou 2000–2001).

The eight spindle whorls were all recovered from Room VIIIb. Like the whorls from Rooms VI and VII, these whorls also display a wide weight/diameter variation (Fig. 6.7.6). However, in contrast to the whorls from Room VII, the majority of the whorls from Room VIII weigh less than 14 g, indicating a focus on the production of thin to very thin thread.

Other textile tools

Only one loom weight, from a general LH III period context, is recorded in the database. Among the LH III/LH IIIB2 Late textile tools are four objects that could have functioned as 'pin beaters'. A pin beater is a multifunctional weaving tool that is thrust up between the warp threads at regular intervals in order to drive the weft home, and it can also be used for pushing up the weft after changing the shed (Hoffmann 1964, 135).

Seven other objects may have functioned as spindles. These objects are all made of bone and are rounded in section. They are all fragmentary or partly preserved. However, when complete they would probably have been *c.* 10–12 cm long, which is a perfect length for a spindle if spinning with a small and light spindle whorl. The maximum diameter varies from 3–6 mm and the minimum diameter varies from 1–5 mm. Since the hole diameter of the spindle whorls varies from 2–9 mm (Fig. 6.7.8) they would function well with these spindles. These objects may also have functioned as pin beaters.

Three needles were also found in LH III/LH IIIB2 Late contexts at Midea. Two of these are dated to general LH III contexts and are made of bone; they have a maximum diameter of 5 mm. Neither of these needles is completely preserved, but it is estimated that they were at least 10 cm in length. These two needles could have functioned well as sewing needles for a range of fabrics. The third needle, made of bronze, is from Room VIII (VIIIa) and is dated to LH IIIB2 Late. It is 19 cm in length and has a maximum diameter of 2 mm. The object is too long to function optimally as a sewing needle, but it may have been used for sewing a specific type of fabric, or when producing a special type of textile. Some fragments of bronze needles were also recovered from the West Gate complex (Demakopoulou and Divari-Valakou 2000–2001).

Fig. 6.7.8. Complete spindle whorls: weight and maximum hole diameter.

Summary

The analysis of the spindle whorls demonstrates a varied production of many different types of yarn. No difference can be seen between the spindle whorls from general LH III contexts and the spindle whorls from contexts that are dated more precisely to LH IIIB2 Late. The majority of the spindle whorls are small and light, indicating an emphasis on the production of very thin or thin spun yarn. The general lack of loom weights indicates that loom types other than the vertical warp-weighted loom also may have been in use at Midea, although the possibility that weaving took place at another location cannot, of course, be excluded. The presence of pin beaters, however, does suggest that people were weaving at the site. The results gained on the basis of the spindle whorls indicate a production of fabrics in many different qualities, from fine fabrics woven with thin threads to very coarse fabrics woven with thick threads. The analyses of the spindle whorls deriving from the LH IIIB2 Late West Gate building complex suggest that slightly different types of yarn may have been produced in the different rooms.

Note

1 These loom weights are not recorded in the tool database.

Bibliography

Demakopoulou, K. (1998) Stone vases from Midea, in Cline, E. H. and Harris-Cline, D. (eds), *The Aegean and the Orient in the Second Millennium*, 221–227. Liège. Université de Liège.

Demakopoulou, K. (1999) A Mycenaean terracotta figure from Midea in the Argolid, in Betancourt, P., Karageorghis, V., Laffineur, R. and Niemeier, W.-D. (eds), *Meletemata: Studies in Aegean Archaeology Presented to Malcolm H. Wiener as he Enters his 65th Year*, 197–207. Liège. Université de Liège.

Demakopoulou, K. and Divari-Valakou, N. (1994–1995) New finds with Linear B inscriptions from Midea (MI Z 2, Wv 3, Z 4), *Minos*, 29–30, 323–328.

Demakopoulou, K. and Divari-Valakou, N. (1997–1998) Excavations in Midea 1995–1996. A. Excavation in the area of the West Gate, *Opuscula Atheniensia*, 22–23, 57–72.

Demakopoulou, K. and Divari-Valakou, N. (2000–2001) Work in Midea 1997–1999. Excavation, conservation, restoration, *Opuscula Atheniensia*, 25–26, 35–45.

Demakopoulou, K. and Fappas, I. (2007, unpublished) 'Midea (Mainland Greece). Lists of contexts, which provided artifacts for the database', (Provided for use in the CTR TTTC database).

Hoffmann, M. (1964) *The Warp-Weighted Loom: Studies in the History and Technology of an Ancient Implement*. Oslo. Universitetsforlaget.

Walberg, G. (1998) *Excavations on the Acropolis of Midea. I. The Excavations on the Lower Terraces, 1985–1991*. Stockholm. Swedish Institute at Athens.

Number of Spindle whorls	Weight	Max. hole diameter
16	1–5 g	2–4 mm
38	6–19 g	5 mm
11	24–37 g	6 mm
3	44–55 g	7 mm
1	86 g	9 mm
Total: 69		

CHAPTER 6.8

Textile production at Mycenae, mainland Greece

Iphiyenia Tournavitou, Eva Andersson Strand, Marie-Louise Nosch and Joanne Cutler

The acropolis of Mycenae, which commands a spectacular view to the southwest, down the plain towards Argos, occupies a naturally defensive hill, dominating the surrounding area and possibly part of the Argive plain. To the east, two mountains, Prophet Elias and Mt. Zarra, form a natural barrier, leaving only a narrow pass that leads to and from the Berbatti-Limnes plain, while on the north and south the citadel is protected by two ravines, the Kokoretsa and the Chavos ravines, respectively (Fig. 6.8.1). The main entrance to the citadel, the Lion Gate, lies on the west, the only naturally accessible side.

The Mycenae acropolis was a fortified citadel, with the palatial complex at the top of the hill. Inside the fortification walls, a considerable number of other buildings served as residential quarters, storage areas, workshop installations and as cult facilities (Fig. 6.8.2).[1] The so-called Lower Town, outside the fortification walls, occupied an area of 32 hectares to the north, west and southwest of the citadel (Fig. 6.8.1), while what has been termed the Greater Mycenae area, *i.e.* a single directly administered district, covered an area of *c.* 350 hectares, including chamber tomb cemeteries and natural resources (clay beds, stone quarries: French and Iakovidis 2003, 22).

The first concrete remains of a fortification circuit and of a palatial complex at the top of the hill, date from the second half of the 14th century BC (LH IIIA2). Individual buildings or groups of buildings, both residential and more specialised, were erected on the slopes to the north and the west of the citadel,[2] forming what we now call the Lower Town of Mycenae. The end of this period is marked by fire destructions both inside and outside the walls.

The vast majority of the extant buildings, including the Cult Centre within the citadel, date from the next century (13th century BC). During the first half, part of the palace bureaucracy spread outside the walls into the Lower Town (the "Ivory" Houses: Tournavitou 1995; 2006, 217–267; Fig. 6.8.1, D4.F), which grows in size (the Panagia Houses: Mylonas-Shear 1987; Fig. 6.8.1, E4.06, the House of the Tripod Tomb: Onasoglou 1995; Fig. 6.8.1, D4.G). The end of this period is marked by a major destruction, again evidenced both inside and outside the walls, which results in the abandonment of some of the establishments in the Lower Town (the "Ivory" Houses: Tournavitou 1995; 2006, 217–267; Fig. 6.8.1, D4.F). The second stage of the fortifications dates to the

*Fig. 6.8.1. Map of the
citadel and surrounding
area (map: French and
Iakovidis 2003).*

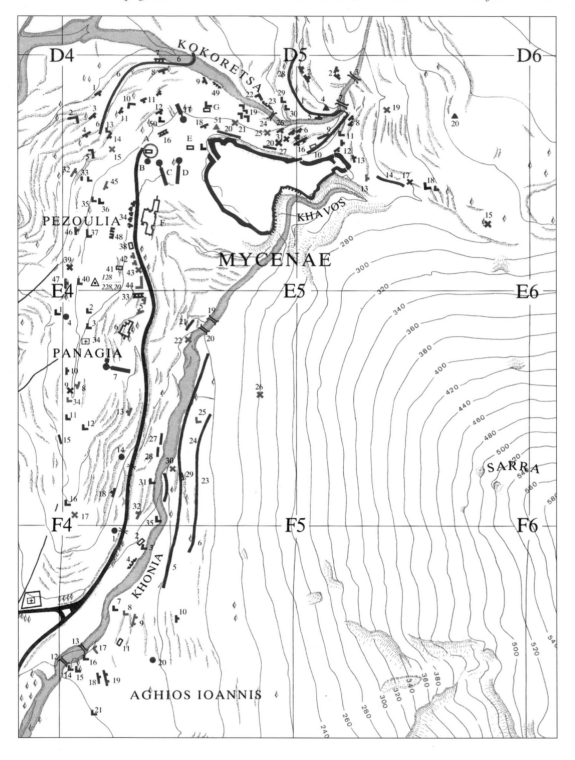

middle of the 13th century BC, following this
extensive destruction horizon. It was part of
the most ambitious building programme ever
attempted at Mycenae. It involved the extension
of the fortified area of the acropolis to enclose

the entire west slope, including the remodelled
Grave Circle A and the Cult Centre to its south,
as well as the erection of the Lion Gate. A
processional way led from the Cult Centre to
the newly rebuilt palace at the top.

Textile production at the site: tools and contexts

The study of the relevant material from the citadel and the Lower Town of Mycenae is fraught with unsolved questions and grey areas. One of the most problematic aspects involves the original function of the extant buildings (residential, private or official, specialised, *etc.*), an issue severely handicapped in this case by a) the unpublished state of the vast majority of the buildings inside the citadel and the Lower Town, a factor unavoidably affecting the availability of information concerning both their original function and details on textile related material and b) the state of preservation of the buildings.

Out of a total of 40 extant buildings, 28 were excavated within the citadel and 12 in the Lower Town, outside the fortification walls. Eleven of these buildings are preserved at ground floor level, three have both ground floors and basements, while the rest survive only at basement level and the existence of upper floors can only be inferred on an architectural and/or stratigraphical basis. In many of these buildings, especially inside the citadel, the stratigraphy is seriously disturbed by later overbuilding activities and cannot afford a clear picture of the original state of affairs.[3] Inside the citadel, only a few of the residential non-specialist buildings are published beyond the preliminary excavation reports (The Northwest Quarter, Iakovidis 2006; The Southwest Quarter, Iakovidis 2013). The same applies to the buildings with a more specialised function, the only exception being the British excavations at the Cult Centre.[4]

Outside the walls, function and status are more clearly indicated.[5] Four of the fully published buildings/clusters of buildings, the Panagia group Houses I, II, III (Mylonas-Shear 1987) the "Ivory" Houses (Tournavitou 1995: West House, House of Shields, House of the Oil Merchant, House of Sphinxes), the House of the Tripod Tomb (Onasoglou 1995) and the "Workshop" (Daniilidou 2008), will comprise the main body of this study and the CTR database,[6] a rather limited sample and perhaps not entirely representative of the site.

The so-called "Ivory" Houses, on the slope facing the west fortification wall (Fig. 6.8.1,

Fig. 6.8.2. The citadel of Mycenae (plan: Albers 1994, taf. 2).

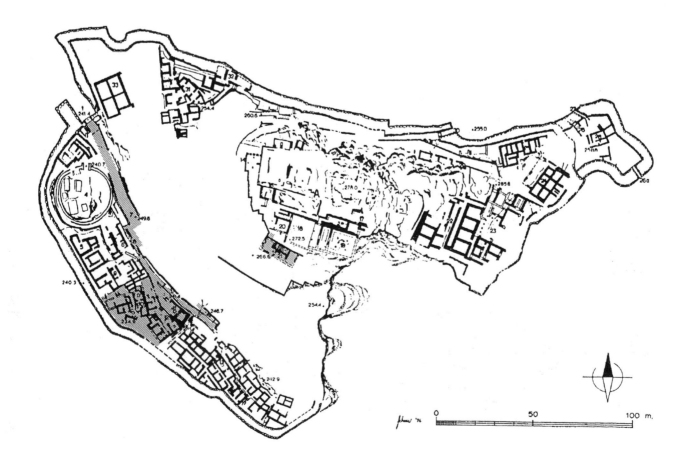

D4.F; 9), stand apart as multifunctional complexes, combining domestic and residential aspects with a range of industrial activities and official administrative interests (Tournavitou 1995, 285–299; 2006). The Panagia House group (Mylonas-Shear 1987, 150–154) to the north of the Treasury of Atreus (Fig. 6.8.1, E4.6; 10) and the House of the Tripod Tomb to the north of the citadel (Fig. 6.8.1, D4.G; 11), were exclusively or chiefly residential, although some kind of workshop activity has been ascertained in the latter.[7]

In addition to the question of the general availability of material for study,[8] the nature of the museum classification systems has resulted in a discrepancy between the published material and the extant specimens, unavoidably affecting the number of items finally studied and entered in the CTR database.[9]

In an attempt to maximise the credibility of the contextual assessment concerning the textile related material from the site, the discussion in this section will include all the extant data, *i.e.* both the relevant entries from the CTR database and the items appearing only in the final publications of individual buildings or clusters of buildings. The material from the British excavations in the Citadel House area, including the Cult Centre, which has not been

incorporated into the CTR database, will be only briefly discussed here.[10]

Four hundred and eighty objects are recorded in the CTR database, of which 331 (68.95%) are dated to the LH III period (Fig. 6.8.3).[11] The vast majority of the recorded items, 383 (79.79%), were associated with funerary or unspecified contexts, which automatically exclude them from the final assessment of the site. Of the remaining 97 items from stratified settlement contexts (20.20%), three (0.62%) were found in closed contexts of a later date and should also be excluded from the final assessment.[12]

The true number of textile tools discovered at the site,[13] including items which were not available for detailed study, or items located in museum storerooms, but not published and thus not included in the CTR database due to lack of context, is a total of 1,585 finds.[14] Only 839 objects (52.93% of the total) were available for study.[15] The textile tools recorded in stratified residential quarters in the Lower Town do not exceed 7.5%–8% of the total (120–127 objects).[16] The remaining material, coming from funerary or unspecified contexts inside the acropolis, *i.e.* 1,465 objects (92.4%), was excluded from the overall contextual assessment of the site.[17] Based on these calculations, the 480 objects recorded in the CTR database constitute only 30.28% of the total number of textile tools recorded at Mycenae.

The vast majority of the objects registered in the database, and of the extant textile related material in general, with the exception of the material from the Citadel House area, are spindle whorls, mostly of stone, in both settlement and funerary contexts (Fig. 6.8.4).[18] Most of the spindle whorls recorded in the CTR database (315 whorls, or 78.55%), and as many as 1,393 of 1,493 spindle whorls discovered at the site (93.3%), were found in funerary or unspecified contexts, which automatically excludes them from this contextual assessment. The remaining spindle whorls, 86 of 401 whorls recorded in the database or 96 of 1,493 spindle whorls in total, which were discovered in domestic/residential contexts, do not amount to more than 22.44% and 6.43% of the total respectively.

The true number of spindle whorls discovered in the three buildings or clusters of buildings in the Lower Town of Mycenae exceeds the total recorded in the CTR database

Fig. 6.8.3. Textile tools recorded in the CTR database, by type.

	Number of objects
Spindle whorls	401
Loom weights	12
Needles	21
Spindles	1
Buttons	45
Total	480

Fig. 6.8.4. Spindle whorls: type and material.

	Clay	Stone	Bone	Glass	Total
Spherical	4				4
Convex	3				3
Discord		1		1	2
Lenticular	2	1			3
Conical	41	138	1	1	181
Biconical	29	4			33
Cylindrical	5				5
Concave conical	3	18			21
Various shapes with hollow tops	3	7			10
Other		139			139
Total	90	308	1	2	401

by 14.[19] With the exception of the 343 conuli recorded in the Citadel House area inside the acropolis, which have also not been incorporated into the CTR database, the vast majority of the extant spindle whorls were attested in the "Ivory" Houses (46 examples)[20] and in the Panagia group of houses (39 examples),[21] while a smaller number (15 examples) were recorded in the House of the Tripod Tomb.

The "Ivory" Houses

House of Sphinxes
In the first cluster of buildings, the greatest concentration of spindle whorls is attested in the basement of the House of Sphinxes (19 whorls),[22] and more specifically in Room 2 (eight whorls), one of the two northernmost rooms of the house (Tournavitou 1995, 47–51, 231–232; spindle whorls: 53–105, 53–107, 53–109, 54–101, 54–106, 54–207, 54–551, 55–315 and a loom weight, 54–552). This room, which at basement level was apparently empty at the time of the destruction, contained the debris from the collapsed ground floor of the house, which, apart from the eight spindle whorls and a single stone spool weighing 52 g, possibly used as a loom weight (Tournavitou 1995, 47–51, 231–232, no. 54–552), included a considerable amount of worked ivory, wood, stone and other workshop type materials. Although none of the finds can be definitely assigned to the basement room, the upper floor was apparently associated with secondary workshop activities related to the working of ivory, wood and possibly stone, as well as with the temporary storage of materials and objects (Tournavitou 1995, 48–49, 291). The same applies to the three whorls recorded in Room 4 (Tournavitou 1995, 51–54, 231–232, nos. 53–56, 53–57, 54–254), to the south of Room 2, which contained a similar range of finds, but fewer in number than the upper floor which could have served as the principal work area of the house (Tournavitou 1995, 51–52, 291). The single glass paste whorl from Room 1 (Tournavitou 1995, 44–47, no. 53–304) had also fallen, with the collapsed workshop debris, from the ground floor. The single terracotta whorl (Tournavitou 1995, 54–56, no. 55–309) was found in the burnt debris that collapsed from the room above Room 6, which was probably used as an archive (Tournavitou

1995, 292). Four of the remaining whorls, two of which are from the south part of the basement corridor (Tournavitou 1995, 58–59, nos. 54–554, 54–558), were also part of the contents of the upper floor, as were the two whorls in Room 3 (Tournavitou 1995, 59–61, nos. 53–610, 54–107), an open air space along the east side of the house, associated with domestic activities requiring the use of water (Tournavitou 1995, 292). Finally, the two spindle whorls recorded outside the main part of the house, in the area south of Room 10 (Tournavitou 1995, 64–65, no. 55–210) and in the so-called "Box" (Tournavitou 1995, 64–65, no. 55–104), representing the remains of a wooden chest to the south of the Vestibule, were also originally part of the contents of the upper floor, but out of context.

Although the two whorls discovered in the area south of the Vestibule as well as the whorls from Room 3 and the corridor, all from the upper floor of the house, cannot be assigned to a specific and meaningful context, the distribution of the majority of the finds from the building, mostly in specialised storerooms and work areas of the upper floor (13 of 19 whorls), which are all unrelated to textile production, suggests a non-functional role for these specimens, *i.e.* that they were not actually used as textile tools.[23]

House of the Oil Merchant
Of the 20 spindle whorls discovered in the House of the Oil Merchant, only 14 were recorded in the CTR database, including one example of Protogeometric date, which should therefore be excluded from the overall assessment of the house, and three examples out of context, in the West Terrace fill (Tournavitou 1995, 39–40, nos. 54–143, 54–238, 59–29). The 16 remaining whorls were all found inside the burnt debris from the collapsed upper floor of the house.[24] The greatest concentrations were attested in Room 5 (four whorls) (Tournavitou 1995, 37–38, nos. 52–216: two whorls, 52–312, 52–313) in the same layer as two bronze tools, a stone axe head and two whetstones (Tournavitou 1995, 37–38), all part of the contents of the upper floor, which possibly served as a general purpose work area and storage area, and in Room 2 further north (four whorls) (Tournavitou 1995, 33–35, nos. 52–66, 52–67, 52–68, 52–163). It is worth pointing out that

the four whorls recorded in the burnt fill of Room 2 were associated with the only set of Linear B tablets (a total of 29 tablets) at Mycenae dealing with wool (Oe) (Bennett 1958; Chadwick 1962; Tournavitou 1995, 259–261; Shelmerdine 1997). All the finds belonged to the upper floor of the house, which apparently served as a local archive, the basement room possibly serving as a storeroom for raw wool.[25] The spindle whorls in the archive room on the upper floor, dealing mostly with wool, could have been associated with occasional spinning activities.

The three spindle whorls in the south half of the basement corridor (Tournavitou 1995, 30–32, no. 50–203: three whorls) were also part of the contents of the upper floor, as were the two examples from Room 8 (Tournavitou 1995, 39, no. 53–55: two whorls), a cupboard under a staircase leading to the ground floor of the house, and the isolated whorls in Rooms 1, 3 and 4 (Tournavitou 1995, 32–33, 35–36, nos. 52–12, 52–61, 52–164). The whorl from Room 4 was found just above the basement floor, along with a lead strip and a winged axe mould, which suggests that the room above was probably used as a general storage or work area (Tournavitou 1995, 35–36). The wide distribution of the extant spindle whorls all over the east wing of the house on the ground floor, as well as the non-specialised function of most of the rooms, with the exception of Room 2, suggests that the surviving specimens were apparently used for casual domestic spinning activities, not restricted to one room or area of the upper floor.

House of Shields

Only five of the seven spindle whorls recorded as coming from the House of Shields were actually found inside the building, the majority (three whorls) in the West Room (Tournavitou 1995, 18–23, nos. 53–170, 53–479, 54–64). They were attested at various levels inside the burnt debris, which included a wide range of finds, and which represented either the remains of the superstructure of the ground floor room or the remains of an upper floor.[26] Of the two whorls in the North Room (Tournavitou 1995, 25–27, nos. 55–12, 55–66), another ground floor room to the north, one was found at the top of the burnt debris and one near the floor of the room (Tournavitou 1995, 25–27). The two remaining whorls were

out of context, outside the southwest corner of the house and west of the west wall of the North Room, respectively, probably part of fill/ house debris thrown outside the house during the Hellenistic period (Tournavitou 1995, 28, nos. 53–167, 55–120). Although all the whorls belonged to the contents of the house, the ground or upper floors, the specialised, non-domestic character of the building as a whole, as suggested both by its layout and by the type of finds recorded therein (Tournavitou 1995, 16–28, 287–289), does not suggest a functional role for these items. This conclusion is reinforced by the small number of extant spindle whorls and the lack of concentrations in their distribution.

The Panagia group of houses

The next big group of spindle whorls (39 whorls) was discovered in the Panagia group of houses (House I, II and III) (Fig. 6.8.1, E4.6; 10). To House I, a ground floor house, can be assigned the smallest number of whorls, three examples, only one of which was discovered inside the building, in the main room with the hearth (Room 5) (Mylonas-Shear 1987, 17, 134, no. 239), indicating casual domestic spinning on a very limited scale. The other two examples were recorded among the pottery deposit inside the drain running along the north face of the house (Mylonas-Shear 1987, 49, 135, nos. 267, 268), along with three fragmentary bronze needles or pins (Mylonas-Shear 1987, 49, 121, nos. 186, 190, 191), not recorded in the database, which could have once been part of the contents of the building. The remaining two whorls in the courtyard are Geometric in date and come from a funerary context (Mylonas-Shear 1987, 16, 134, nos. 249, 250).

In House III, there are no marked concentrations of spindle whorls. Single whorls were recorded in five of the ground floor rooms of the building and more specifically in two storage areas (Rooms 29 and 33) (Mylonas-Shear 1987, 58, 135, nos. 257, 265), in a work area (Room 28) (Mylonas-Shear 1987, 58, 135, no. 260) and in two small compartments (Rooms 34 and 36). The latter originally formed larger areas and were subsequently subdivided after the earthquake, for reasons related to the stability of the building, and the related finds could therefore belong to the earlier phase (Mylonas-Shear 1987, 58–59, 135, nos. 261, 266). None of the extant whorls can be associated with other finds or any textile related tools. In the best case scenario they were used for casual domestic spinning on a limited scale.

The largest number of whorls (16, or 41.02% of the total), were discovered in House II, mostly in the storerooms to the north, *i.e.* Rooms 15–18, 21 (12 whorls). No spindle whorls were discovered in the main room of the house with the hearth (Room 9), and the isolated examples in Room 10, a backroom, serving as sleeping quarters in the first, pre-earthquake phase, and in Room 8, a vestibule to the main room, are rather obscure with regards to context. In the first case, the single example could represent wash from higher up the slope (Mylonas-Shear 1987, 31–32, 135, no. 256) and the single whorl from Room 8 could possibly belong to the first, pre-earthquake phase of the house (Mylonas-Shear 1987, 27–28, 134, no. 251). Nine of the 13 whorls in the storerooms of the house could be excluded for the same contextual reason. The same could be said for an isolated example from a Mycenaean grave inside Room 21 (Mylonas-Shear 1987, 27–47, 134, no. 244). Only three whorls, two in Room 15 and one in Room 17, can be safely assigned to the last phase of the building, all part of the contents of the upper floor (Mylonas-Shear 1987, 37, 40–41, 134, nos. 241, 242, 246).

Six more whorls were recorded to the west of the Panagia group of houses, where remains of other Mycenaean buildings were apparently located. Two whorls in Room 26, an open area between the houses, probably represent wash from higher up. Three whorls derive from Room 23, which is part of a floor deposit of the LH IIIC period, and one whorl is from Room 25, probably from a floor deposit (Mylonas-Shear 1987, 64–66, 133–136, nos. 254, 255, 259, 269, 270, 271). Finally, seven whorls were discovered out of context, in test trenches around the houses (Mylonas-Shear 1987, 64–66, 133–136).

House of the Tripod Tomb

Fifteen whorls were recovered from the House of the Tripod Tomb (Fig. 6.8.1, D4.G; 11), only seven of which were recorded in the final publication of the house (Onasolgou 1995, 16–74, 74–82, 86–93, 98–100, 120–121, 123–124). Of the latter, one was out of context in a mixed Protogeometric-LH IIIB2 deposit lying above the floor deposit of Room 19 (Onasolgou 1995, 123–124), while of the remaining six whorls, one example in Area 10 was found high up in the fill (Onasoglou 1995, 120–121). In addition, one example in Area 11 was lying in the fill below a LH IIIB floor (B) (Onasoglou 1995, 98–100) and four examples were part of distinct floor deposits of different dates (LH IIIB, LH IIIB2/C), in Area 16 (two examples), Area 17 (one example) and Area 5 (one example) (Onasoglou 1995, 16–74, 74–82, 86–93). Only Area 5 has been assigned a specific function, tentatively labelled a workshop area, domestic or otherwise (Onasoglou 1995, 86–89). The remaining eight whorls were not published, but were apparently registered in the Mycenae museum as coming from the building, but without a context. Judging by the available evidence, only casual domestic spinning of a limited scale can be hazarded as a suggestion for this building.

Citadel House area

The material from the Citadel House area, currently under study by S. Diamant, comprises 343 steatite spindle whorls, also known as conuli, of which only 157 are securely stratified.[27] The most notable concentrations were apparently attested in the Shrine with the Frescoes (Room 32) and in Area 36. The latter was an open air area between the South House, the Temple and the Shrine, serving as a repository and/or distribution point for a variety of everyday tools and objects for the manufacture of luxury artefacts and containing what appears to be one of the most extensive closed deposits of conuli in the Mycenaean world (55 examples). The conuli in the inner room of Room 32 were part of a votive deposit and therefore not functional in this context.

Loom weights are represented by a surprisingly small number of items (only 12 possible examples), eight of which come from a Middle Helladic domestic context and are considered too light to be used in a warp-weighed loom (the complete examples weighing 10–12 g). Of the four remaining objects that have been recorded as loom weights, only one comes from a non funerary, contextually meaningful context: a stone spool-shaped weight from the House of Sphinxes (Room 2).[28]

The only other types of textile tool attested at Mycenae are sewing needles and spindles. Unfortunately, all the extant needles recorded in the database are associated with funerary or unspecified contexts inside the acropolis and are therefore automatically excluded from the overall discussion.[29] Even so, six of these were possibly used as awls, spindles or pin-beaters. A further 16 fragmentary examples of needles and/or pins discovered in the Lower Town of Mycenae,[30] and not recorded in the CTR database, do not really alter the emerging picture of low scale domestic activities involving textile and/or garment manufacture. The range of textile tools at Mycenae is completed by a single example of a bone spindle, apparently fully functional, which is nevertheless excluded by virtue of its funerary context (Grave E, in Grave Circle B; Mylonas 1973, 101, E512α).

On the whole, the extant evidence from the Lower Town of Mycenae is limited. Only 64 tools were discovered in meaningful contexts, 56 of which (87.5%) are spindle whorls.[31]

Organisation of the textile production at the site

The only Linear B documents referring to textile manufacture at Mycenae were discovered in the "Ivory" Houses (Bennett 1958; Chadwick 1962; Tournavitou 1995; Shelmerdine 1995, 1997, 1999). Of the 56 Linear B tablets recorded in the buildings, originally part of the contents of the upper or ground floors, only 29 were related to the textile industry.[32] They belong to a specific sector of the industry, the wool series (Oe), and were all recorded in Room 2 of the House of the Oil Merchant (Tournavitou 1995, 33–35, 259). The series includes records of disbursements of wool to named individuals or groups, inventories of wool and payment in wool in return for the manufacture of different kinds of textiles. Similar scribal activities are also attested at Knossos (Od) and Thebes (Of) (Tournavitou 1995, 259; Shelmerdine 1997, 390–394; Nosch 2007). The fact that the other two classes of documents in the building, *i.e.* personnel management and oil disbursement, were represented by only two documents (Au 102, Fo 101), and that the five scribes responsible for the wool series were not employed for any other class of document in any of the other houses, suggests that this house

not only employed its own group of scribes, but that activities involving wool were among the top priorities, if not the top priority, of its occupants (Tournavitou 1995, 259). No other tablet of the Oe series was recorded at Mycenae, inside or outside the citadel.

The total amount of wool recorded in the Oe series, has been estimated as *c.* 457 units, *i.e.* 1,371 kg wool (Shelmerdine 1997, 390; *contra* Tournavitou 1995, 259: 177 units, *i.e.* 561 kg of wool). The largest group of 22 tablets involves disbursements of wool to named individuals, both men and women. Among the women, only two were probably occupied in the textile industry (*i-ti-we-ri-di, a-ke-ti-ri-ja*) (Tournavitou 1995, 259). The male recipients received a slightly smaller amount than the women (126 kg as opposed to 156 kg) (Tournavitou 1995, 259–260). Only two of the five occupational terms recorded were related to the textile industry (*ka-na-pe-we, pe-re-ke-we*), the others being *a-to-po-qo* (bakers), *ka-ke-wi* (bronze smiths) and *ke-ra-me-wi* (potters). A *ka-na-pe-we*, a fuller, receiving 12 kg of wool, is also attested at Pylos and in two of the Citadel House tablets (Oi 701, Oi 704) (Tournavitou 1995, 260; Palaima 1997, 410). Although the occupation *pe-re-ke-we*, translated as weaver, is also attested at Pylos, it should be pointed out that the translation is doubtful, since men were mostly associated with finishing and fulling and seldomly with weaving (Killen 1979, 167–168; Tournavitou 1995, 260). The amounts assigned to the other three specialists were so small that they were probably intended for personal use of house or palace dependents. The term *ta-ra-si-ja* attested in one of the tablets (Oe 110), interpreted as an allocation of raw material by the central authority to fully or semi-dependent workers, also implies an obligation of the worker to deliver a finished product. The implied meaning of the term and the relatively large amounts of wool recorded suggest a possibly industrial use of the wool in this case (Tournavitou 1995, 260; on *ta-ra-si-ja* see: Duhoux 1976, 132; Killen 1985, 273–275; 2001).

Four tablets in the group recorded a payment in wool in return for the manufacture of different types of textiles, which is confirmed by the presence of the word *o-no* in one of the tablets (Tournavitou 1995, 261; on *o-no* and the *ta-ra-si-ja* system see Duhoux 1976, 132; Killen 1985, 273–275; 2001). The word *e-we-pe-se-so-me-na* (boiled or requiring finishing) in another tablet (Oe 127) implies that 60 kg of wool, a substantial amount, was issued for cloth to be boiled or finished, and possibly treated with perfumed oil (Shelmerdine 1995, 103). Finally, a single tablet including the heading: "this year's and last year's *o-u-ka*", followed by large amounts of wool, probably referred to disbursements of wool required for the manufacture of textile (Tournavitou 1995, 261).

The only other document from the houses clearly related to textiles is a single tablet (X 508) in the House of Shields, the only one in this particular building. It is a record of *pu-ka-ta-ri-ja* cloth, a folded garment of double thickness at Knossos (L-series), which was going to be sent or had been sent to Thebes, thus providing a unique example of a transaction involving another Mycenaean kingdom (Killen 1985, 268–269; Tournavitou 1995, 261–262; Rougemont 2009, 206). The personal name on this tablet, *ma-ri-ne-u*, received spices and honey (As, Ga) at Knossos, whilst at Thebes he was a recipient of wool (Tournavitou 1995, 261–262; for Knossos and Thebes see Chadwick and Spyropoulos 1975, 93; Killen 1979, 179).

The single Fo tablet, from Room 1 of the House of the Oil Merchant, records the distribution of plain oil to various individuals, apparently organised in four groups, supervised by overseers, some recorded by name, and some by occupation (Tournavitou 1995, 266–267; for a more in depth analysis see Killen 1981, 40–41; Shelmerdine 1997, 391; Fappas 2010, 119). The recipients or recipient groups include two female occupational terms traditionally associated with the textile industry (*a-ke-ti-ri-jai, e-ro-pa-ke-ja*), who were assigned exceptional quantities of oil, possibly for textile manufacture (Killen 1981, 39; 2001, 180; Tournavitou 1995, 266–267; Shelmerdine 1997, 389–391; 1999, 572; Fappas 2010, 118, 260). The type of oil featuring in this tablet (OIL and WE), is a product of the perfume industry and is attested at other major palatial centres in connection with the treatment of woven textiles (Shelmerdine 1995, 103–104; 1997, 390–391; 1999, 572; Fappas 2010, 118, 260). It has also been suggested that some of the named individuals on this tablet, also attested in Au 102 from Room 2 of the House of the Oil Merchant and V 659 from Room 5 in the West House, might be textile workers working

in the vicinity of the houses and therefore in need of rations and local accommodation (Shelmerdine 1997, 391–392; 1999, 572). The scribe who wrote this tablet was not associated with any other document in the houses, which not only suggests specialisation of personnel, but also the possibility of more tablets dealing with oil that have not survived the destruction of the house (Tournavitou 1995, 267).

Judging by the overall character of this group of buildings, including the House of the Oil Merchant, it seems that they functioned as repositories and clearing houses, amongst other things. The House of the Oil Merchant in particular, was obviously used as a depot and as a clearing house for oil and wool, to be distributed to different groups or individuals, probably for industrial purposes (Tournavitou 1995, 267; Shelmerdine 1997, 394; Varias Garcia 1999, 596).

Conclusion

The evidence from the study of the available textile related material at the palatial centre of Mycenae, although not entirely representative of the site, seems to refute the testimony of the Linear B documents in the House of the Oil Merchant and the single document from the House of Shields. It weighs heavily in favour of occasional spinning activities of domestic scale and does not seem to encourage speculation on the existence of a large, centrally organised textile production at the site.

In spite of the absence or the scarcity of direct evidence of actual weaving activities (a phenomenon that is also attested in other mainland sites during the Bronze Age), and although the textile tools in the CTR database do not constitute a truly representative sample, the spindle whorls from Mycenae indicate that several types of yarn were being spun at the site, ranging from very thin to very thick. These would have been suitable for making many different types and qualities of textiles, although there appears to have been an emphasis on the production of thinner thread types.

There is no difference in weight and diameter between the spindle whorls from funerary and "other", non funerary contexts. Although it is likely that both finer and coarser fabrics were produced at Mycenae, this coarser production is invisible in the data. The existence of looms is suggested only by the existence of the ten possible pin-beaters. It is possible that loom types, other than the warp-weighted loom, were in use, but, if this was indeed the case, it is impossible to reach any definite conclusions on the weaving technology at the site. The possibility that textiles were woven at another location inside or outside Mycenae cannot be excluded.

Considering the extant Linear B documents in the House of the Oil Merchant and the House of Shields, however limited these may be, it appears likely that the central authority was directly involved in transactions concerning the disbursement of raw material, the manufacture of textiles and transactions in textiles with other palatial centres. This suggests that textile production was strictly monitored at Mycenae, as at the other major palatial centres of Knossos, Pylos and Thebes (Shelmerdine 1999, 564). Most of the administration took place in the ground floor rooms of the "Ivory" Houses, which housed only partly linked, but related departments (Shelmerdine 1999, 573).

The apparent discrepancy between the archaeological and the textual evidence, however unwelcome and awkward, may not in fact be a discrepancy, considering that the recorded finds represent only a fraction of the excavated material from the site. The scarcity of loom weights, on the other hand, may have to remain an enigma for many of the Bronze Age sites on the mainland.

Notes

1 Mycenae is the only palatial centre to include an actual cult centre, i.e. a distinct area with various buildings and installations devoted to cult.

2 Petsas House, a commercial, possibly official establishment, involved in the production, distribution and exchange of pottery (Papadimitriou and Petsas 1950, 203–233; 1951, 192–196; Iakovidis 2000, 63–66; 2001, 49–55; 2002, 18–19; 2003, 21–24; 2004, 24–26; 2005, 28–32; 2006b, 26–29; Shelton 2002–2003, 387–396; 2004, 181–182; see Fig. 6.8.1, D4.10), the Cyclopean Terrace Building and the House of the Wine Merchant – residential establishments, the latter with a possibly commercial aspect (Wace 1952, 15–17; 1953, 267–291; 1956, 81–87), buildings in the area of the "Ivory" Houses (Tournavitou 1995, 31, 293; Fig. 6.8.1, D4.F), the House of Lead (Wace 1955, 119–122; Fig. 6.8.1, E4.11).

3 Some, like the House of Columns on the east slope, House M on the north slope, the Granary,

the Ramp House, House of the Warrior Vase and the South House in the vicinity of Grave Circle A on the west slope, Tsoundas House in the Cult Centre and various buildings in the Northwest and Southwest Quarters, have been labelled residential, on the basis of the architectural evidence and their contents. Others, like the House of the Artisans on the east slope, have been assigned a primarily workshop function, while the North Storerooms, and the remaining buildings within the Cult Centre, are labelled storerooms and cult buildings respectively. Many buildings preserved only at basement level, like Houses A, B, Γ, Δ, could possibly be described as residential, but their interpretation is still tentative.

4 See Taylour 1981; Evely and Runnels 1992; Moore and Taylour 1999; French and Taylour 2007 and Krzyszkowska 2007. The recently published sectors inside the citadel including the cluster of buildings in the Northwest and Southwest Quarters of the acropolis, by Professor Spyr. Iakovidis, on behalf of the Archaeological Society at Athens (Iakovidis 2006a); 2013, were unfortunately published too late to be incorporated into the CTR database. Other groups of buildings like Houses Γ, Δ, House M, the Granary, the House of Columns and the House of the Artisans are currently under study, which renders the material from these buildings unavailable for inclusion in this study.

5 The "Ivory" Houses, to the south of Grave Circle B (Fig. 6.8.1, D4.F), the Panagia Houses, to the north of the Treasury of Atreus (Fig. 6.8.1, E4.6), the House of the Tripod Tomb and the so-called Workshop, in the vicinity of the new museum (Fig. 6.8.1, D4.G), to the north of the acropolis, have already been published (Tournavitou 1995, 2006; Mylonas-Shear 1987; Onasoglou 1995; Daniilidou 2008). The Petsas House, originally excavated in the early 1950s was re-excavated by Professor Spyr. Iakovidis and Kim Shelton (see note 2). The House at Plakes (Mylonas 1975, 153–161; Fig. 6.8.1, D4.29), was recently published by Prof. Spyr. Iakovidis (2013b), and the East House has been included in a new research and excavation project, under Professor Spyr. Iakovidis and Iphiyenia Tournavitou.

6 The so-called Workshop was unfortunately published too late to be incorporated in the CTR database (Daniilidou 2008).

7 The House of Lead on the ridge to the southwest of the Atreus tholos (Wace 1955, 119–122; Fig. 6.8.1, E4.11), and the House at Plakes to the northwest of the citadel (Mylonas 1975, 153–161; Fig. 6.8.1, D4.29), were probably residential. Petsas House and the House of the Wine Merchant (Wace 1952, 15–17; 1956, 81–87; Fig. 6.8.1, D4.13), to the northwest of the citadel,

seem to have had commercial and possibly artisanal aspects, the former with close ties to the central authority.

8 Material not recorded in the CTR database includes the textile related tools from the British excavations in the Citadel House area, which are currently under study for publication by S. Diamant, the material from the other British excavations at Mycenae and the textile related tools from the excavations of the Archaeological Society at Athens, which are also currently under study for publication. Three of the complexes excavated under the auspices of the Archaeological Society at Athens, the Northwest and the Southwest Quarters inside the acropolis and the so-called Workshop and the House at Plakes to the north of the citadel, had not been published at the time that the CTR database was created, and are therefore not included in the final study (Iakovidis 2006a; 2013a; 2013b; Daniilidou 2008).

9 A certain number of textile related tools from some locations (House of the Oil Merchant, House of Sphinxes, House II of the Panagia group, House of the Tripod Tomb), as well as a number of examples from funerary contexts, have not been available for detailed study, while the relevant material from the House of the Tripod Tomb, for example, was apparently only selectively published and therefore most of the objects available for study were not included in the final publication of the building and were thus not included in the overall assessment.

10 The contextual information available at this moment is only very general.

11 Eight of the recorded objects (1.66%) are Middle Helladic; two (0.41%) are from LH I contexts; 18 (3.75%) date to LH II; three (0.62%) date to LH II-IIIB; 331 (68.95%) date to LH III; 118 (24.58%) are of unknown date.

12 Protogeometric or Geometric tombs: House of the Oil Merchant, one example, no. 52–53; Panagia House I, two examples (Mylonas-Shear 1987, 134, nos. 249, 250). A spindle whorl from Panagia House II, found in a grave under the floor of Room 21 (Mylonas-Shear 1987, 134, no. 244), should also be excluded from the assessment of textile related activities in the building, alongside a number of other spindle whorls that did not belong to the original contents of the buildings (see section on Panagia Houses).

13 By "true number" is meant the total sum of textile related material recovered from the sample of contexts available for study (House of the Tripod Tomb, the "Ivory" Houses, the Panagia Houses, the MH building near Grave Circle B, the chamber tombs, Grave Circle B and unspecified contexts from Schliemann's

excavations inside the acropolis), and not the total of textile related material excavated at the entire site of Mycenae, which remains unfortunately unknown.

14 This total does not include the 343 stone conuli from the Citadel House area. A further seven objects from the House of the Oil Merchant (Tournavitou 1995, 37, no. 52–215: three examples, no. 52–311, fragmentary bone pins/needles, in Room 5) and the House of Sphinxes (Tournavitou 1995, 44–56, nos. 53–154, 55–316, 54–828, bronze pins/needles, in Rooms 1, 2 and 6), some of which were too fragmentary to be securely identified and therefore not included in the study sample, were probably used as needles and should be perhaps added to the total, which would then amount to 1,592 objects.

15 760 spindle whorls, 12 loom weights, 21 needles, one spindle and 45 objects classified as buttons.

16 100 spindle whorls (97 from Bronze Age contexts), 10 loom weights, nine needles (plus seven additional examples) and one object classified as a button.

17 1,393 spindle whorls, two loom weights, 25 needles, one spindle and 44 objects classified as buttons.

18 401 examples, *i.e.* 83.54% of the 480 objects recorded in the CTR database; 1,493 of 1,585 examples, *i.e.* 94.19%, of the true number of items discovered at the site. The material from the Cult Centre, being studied by Steve Diamant, is not incorporated in the present database and will be discussed separately.

19 According to the new total, the spindle whorls in these buildings amount to *c.* 83% of the textile related material.

20 Seven from the House of Shields, 20 from the House of the Oil Merchant and 19 from the House of Sphinxes.

21 Five from House I, 16 from House II, five from House III and 13 from outlying areas.

22 One terracotta whorl from Room 6 and one glass paste whorl from Room 1 have not been included in the study sample and were therefore not entered into the CTR database corpus.

23 The remaining seven whorls (from Rooms 3, 6, corridor, Area south of Room 10), could have been used for domestic spinning activities, but this would be pure conjecture on our part. The three fragmentary bronze pins from the doorway of Rooms 1, 2 and 6 (Tournavitou 1995, 247–248, nos. 53–154, 55–316, 54–828), have not been positively identified as textile tools (sewing needles) and were mostly found in areas unrelated to textile production.

24 Including a terracotta whorl from Room 1 (nos. 52–12), four stone whorls from Room 2 (nos. 52–66, 52–67, 52–68, 52–163), one stone whorl

from Room 3 (nos. 52–61), one terracotta whorl from Room 4 (nos. 52–164), four stone whorls from Room 5 (nos. 52–216: two examples, 52–312, 52–313), two stone whorls from Room 8 (nos. 53–55: two examples) and three stone whorls from the corridor (nos. 50–302: three examples). The four whorls from Room 2 and the single examples from Rooms 1 and 4 were not included in the study sample and were thus not entered into the CTR database.

25 Tournavitou (1995, 33–34, 289) and Shelmerdine (1997, 390), having calculated the total amount of wool recorded in the tablets, are of the opinion that the quantity of wool involved is more than the room could hold.

26 Including a large number of worked ivory pieces, wood, stone, faience, *etc.* (Tournavitou 1995, 18–23).

27 Since the material from the Citadel House is being published elsewhere, only a summary is given here.

28 (Tournavitou 1995, 47–51, 231–232, nos. 54–552). It was found in a secondary context, inside the debris that had collapsed from the ground floor. Of the other three, one was found in the street between the House of the Oil Merchant and the West House, in a dubious context, one in an unspecified context from Schliemann's excavations in the acropolis, and one in a funerary context (Grave O, in Grave Circle B; Mylonas 1973, 207, 0.526.9).

29 The majority of the sewing needles in the CTR database come from unspecified contexts, from Schliemann's excavations inside the acropolis (15 examples), while the remaining six examples belong to funerary contexts, mostly chamber tombs.

30 House of the Oil Merchant: four bone pins/needles, three of which were in a fragmentary state, were recorded in the burnt fill of Room 5 (Tournavitou 1995, 37–38, nos. 52–215: three examples, 52–311). In the House of Sphinxes: three fragmentary bronze pins were found in Rooms 1, 2 and 6 (Tournavitou 1995, 247–248, nos. 53–154, 54–828, 55–316). From the Panagia Houses, nine bronze pins/needles have not been included in this study (Mylonas-Shear 1987, 121–122, nos. 176, 184–191). All the examples from the "Ivory" Houses are in context (LH IIIB1), but are too fragmentary for precise identification. Of the nine Panagia examples, only one (no. 176) is in a meaningful context (House II, Room 21, floor deposit; Mylonas-Shear 1987, 43, 119, 121). The remaining bronze examples (nos. 184–191), are not *in situ* (Mylonas-Shear 1987, 49, 66, 121).

31 House of Shields: five spindle whorls; House of the Oil Merchant: 16 spindle whorls and four bone pins/needles; House of Sphinxes: 19 spindle whorls, one loom weight and three bronze pins/needles; Panagia House I: one spindle whorl; Panagia House II: three spindle whorls; Panagia House III: three spindle whorls and four spindle whorls from other houses to the west, as well as eight bronze pins/needles and one bone pin/needle, five of which were not in a primary context (see section on needles); House of the Tripod Tomb: five spindle whorls.

32 With the exception of Fo 101 from Room 1 of the House of the Oil Merchant and perhaps of Ui 709 from Room 4 of the House of Sphinxes (Tournavitou 1995, 33–35, 51–53, 266).

Bibliography

Albers, G. (1994) *Spätmykenische Stadtheiligtümer. Systematische Analyse und vergleichende Auswertung der archäologischen Befunde*. Oxford. Archaeopress.

Bennett, E. L. (1958) *The Mycenae Tablets II*. Philadelphia. The American Philosophical Society.

Chadwick, J. (1962) *The Mycenae Tablets III*. Philadelphia. The American Philosophical Society.

Chadwick, J. and Spyropoulos, T. (1975) *The Thebes Tablets II*. Salamanca. University of Salamanca.

Daniilidou, D. (2008) Ανασκαφές Μυκηνών. II. Το "Εργαστήριο" των Μυκηνών. Athens. Archaeological Society at Athens.

Duhoux, Y. (1976) *Aspects du vocabulaire économique mycénien*. Amsterdam. A. M. Hakkert.

Evely, D. and Runnels, C. (1992) *Well Built Mycenae: The Helleno-British Excavations within the Citadel at Mycenae, 1959–1969. Fascicle 27, Ground Stone*. Oxford. Oxbow Books.

Fappas, I. (2010) Ελαιον ευώδες τεθυωμένον. Τα Αρωματικά Έλαια και οι Πρακτικές της Χρήσης τους στη Μυκηναϊκή Ελλάδα και την Αρχαία Εγγύς Ανατολή. Khania. Ιστορική, Λαογραφική και Αρχαιολογική Εταιρεία Κρήτης.

French, E. B. and Iakovidis, S. (2003) *Archaeological Atlas of Mycenae*. Athens. Archaeological Society of Athens.

French, E. B. and Taylour, W. D. (2007) *Well-Built Mycenae: The Helleno-British Excavations within the Citadel at Mycenae, 1959–1969. Fascicle 13, The Service Areas of the Cult Centre*. Oxford. Oxbow Books.

Iakovidis, Spyr. E. (2000) Ανασκαφή Μυκηνών, Πρακτικά της εν Αθήναις Αρχαιολογικής Εταιρείας, 63–66.

Iakovidis, Spyr. E. (2001) Ανασκαφή Μυκηνών, Πρακτικά της εν Αθήναις Αρχαιολογικής Εταιρείας, 49–55.

Iakovidis, Spyr. E. (2002) Ανασκαφή Μυκηνών, Πρακτικά της εν Αθήναις Αρχαιολογικής Εταιρείας, 18–19.

Iakovidis, Spyr. E. (2003) Ανασκαφή Μυκηνών, Πρακτικά της εν Αθήναις Αρχαιολογικής Εταιρείας, 21–24.

Iakovidis, Spyr. E. (2004) Ανασκαφή Μυκηνών, Πρακτικά της εν Αθήναις Αρχαιολογικής Εταιρείας, 24–26.

Iakovidis, Spyr. E. (2005) Ανασκαφή Μυκηνών, Πρακτικά της εν Αθήναις Αρχαιολογικής Εταιρείας, 28–32.

Iakovidis, Spyr. E. (2006a) Ανασκαφές Μυκηνών. I. Η Βορειοδυτική Συνοικία, Βιβλιοθήκη της εν Αθήναις Αρχαιολογικής Εταιρείας 224.

Iakovidis, Spyr. E. (2006b) Ανασκαφή Μυκηνών, Πρακτικά της εν Αθήναις Αρχαιολογικής Εταιρείας, 26–29.

Iakovidis, Spyr. E. (2013a) Ανασκαφές Μυκηνών. III. Η Νοτιοδυτική Συνοικία, Βιβλιοθήκη της εν Αθήναις Αρχαιολογικής Εταιρείας 278.

Iakovidis, Spyr. E. (2013b) Ανασκαφές Μυκηνών. IV. Η Οικία στις Πλάκες, Βιβλιοθήκη της εν Αθήναις Αρχαιολογικής Εταιρείας 288.

Killen, J. T. (1979) The Knossos Ld(1) tablets, in Risch, E. and Muhlestein, H. (eds), *Colloquium Mycenaeaum*, 151–181. Geneva. Librairies Droz and Université de Neuchatel.

Killen, J. T. (1981) Some puzzles in a Mycenae personnel record, *Ziva antika. Antiquité vivante*, 31, 37–45.

Killen, J. T. (1985) The Linear B tablets and the Mycenaean economy, in Morpurgo-Davies, A. and Duhoux, Y. (eds), *Linear B: A 1984 Survey*, 241–305. Louvain-la-Neuve. Peeters.

Killen, J. T. (2001) Some thoughts on *ta-ra-si-ja*, in Voutsaki, S. and Killen, J. T. (eds), *Economy and Politics in the Mycenaean Palace States*, 161–180. Cambridge. Cambridge Philological Society

Krzyszkowska, O. H. (2007) *Well Built Mycenae: The Helleno-British Excavations within the Citadel at Mycenae, 1959–1969. Fascicle 24, The Ivories and Objects of Bone, Antler and Boar's Tusk*. Oxford. Oxbow Books.

Moore, A. D. and Taylour, W. D. (1999) *Well Built Mycenae: The Helleno-British Excavations within the Citadel at Mycenae, 1959–1969. Fascicle 10, The Temple Complex*. Oxford. Oxbow Books.

Mylonas, G. (1973) Ο Ταφικός Κύκλος Β των Μυκηνών. Athens. Archaeological Society at Athens.

Mylonas, G. (1975) Ανασκαφή Μυκηνών. *Πρακτικά της εν Αθήναις Αρχαιολογικής Εταιρείας*, 158–161.

Mylonas-Shear, I. (1987) *The Panagia Houses at Mycenae*. Philadelphia. The University Museum, University of Philadephia.

Nosch, M.-L. (2007) *The Knossos Od Series: An Epigraphical Study*. Wien. Verlag der Österreichischen Akademie der Wissenschaften.

Onasoglou, A. (1995) Η Οικία του Τάφου των Τριπόδων στις Μυκήνες. Athens. Archaeological Society at Athens.

Palaima, T. G. (1997) Potter and fuller: the royal craftsmen, in Laffinneur, R. and Betancourt, P. (eds), *TEXNH. Craftsmen, Craftswomen and Craftsmanship in the Aegean Bronze Age*, 407–412. Liège. Université de Liège.

Papadimitriou, I. and Petsas, P. (1950) Ανασκαφαί εν Μυκήναις, *Πρακτικά της εν Αθήναις Αρχαιολογικής Εταιρείας*, 203–233.

Papadimitriou, I. and Petsas, P. (1951) Ανασκαφαί εν Μυκήναις, *Πρακτικά της εν Αθήναις Αρχαιολογικής Εταιρείας*, 192–196.

Rougemont, F. (2009) *Contrôle économique et administration à l'époque des palais mycéniens (fin du IIème millénaire av. J.-C.)*. Paris. École francaise d'Athènes.

Shelmerdine, C. (1995) Shining and fragrant cloth in Homeric epic, in Carter, J. P. and Morris, S. P. (eds), *The Ages of Homer. A Tribute to Emily Townsend Vermeule*, 99–107. Austin. University of Texas.

Shelmerdine, C. (1997) Workshops and record keeping in the Mycenean world, in Laffineur, R. and Betancourt, P. (eds), *TEXNH. Craftsmen, Craftswomen and Craftsmanship in the Aegean Bronze Age*, 388–396. Liège. Université de Liège.

Shelmerdine, C. (1999) A comparative look at Mycenaean administration(s), in Hiller, S., Deger-Jalkotzy, S. and Panagl, O. (eds), *Floreant Studia Mycenaea*, 555–576. Wien. Österreichische Akademie der Wissenschaften.

Shelton, K. (2002–2003) A new Linear B tablet from Petsas House, Mycenae, *Minos*, 37–38, 387–396.

Shelton, K. (2004) Open and ready for business: the excavations at Petsas House and the LH IIIA2 period at Mycenae, *Bulletin of the Institute of Classical Studies*, 47, 181–182.

Taylour, W. D. (1981) *Well Built Mycenae: The Helleno-British Excavations within the Citadel at Mycenae, 1959–1969. Fascicle 1, The Excavations*. Warminster. Aris and Phillips.

Tournavitou, I. (1995) *The "Ivory Houses" at Mycenae*. London. British School at Athens.

Tournavitou, I. (2006) A Mycenaean building reconsidered: the case of the West House at Mycenae, *Annual of the British School at Athens*, 101, 217–267.

Varias Garcia, C. V. (1999) The palace of Mycenae in LH IIIB2 according to the documents in Linear B: a general description, in Hiller, S., Deger-Jalkotzy, S. and Panagl, O. (eds), *Floreant Studia Mycenaea*, 595–600. Wien. Österreichische Akademie der Wissenschaften.

Wace, A. J. B. (1952) The Cyclopean Terrace Building and the House of the Wine Merchant. *Annual of the British School at Athens*, 48, 15–17.

Wace, A. J. B. (1953) The Cyclopean Terrace Building and the deposit of pottery beneath it, *Annual of the British School at Athens*, 49, 267–291.

Wace, A. J. B. (1955) The House of Lead, *Annual of the British School at Athens*, 51, 119–122.

Wace, A. J. B. (1956) The Cyclopean Terrace Building and the House of the Wine Merchant. *Annual of the British School at Athens*, 52, 81–87.

CHAPTER 6.9

Textile tools from Tiryns, mainland Greece

Lorenz Rahmstorf, Małgorzata Siennicka, Eva Andersson Strand, Marie-Louise Nosch and Joanne Cutler

Tiryns is situated on an elongated hillock rising up to 25 m above the Argive plain. Traces of habitation date from the Late Neolithic to the Archaic/Early Classical period (Fig. 6.9.1).

The site is especially well known for its Mycenaean occupation; however, the Early Bronze Age (EBA) and Early Iron Age (EIA) were also important in its history. Tiryns was situated only 300 m from the shoreline during the EBA, while the LBA citadel was separated from the shore by a 1 km wide coastal plain (Zangger 1994, 196). Nevertheless, Tiryns was always orientated towards the sea and hence to contacts, communication and trade. The Mycenaean palatial citadel was divided into the upper citadel (Oberburg), middle citadel (Mittelburg) and lower citadel (Unterburg). In addition, there are also extensive remains of domestic architecture outside the citadel; this area is known as the town/city (Stadt/Unterstadt) of Tiryns. The remains of the citadel date to Late Helladic (LH) IIIA to LH IIIC (*c.* 1425–1075 BC), *i.e.* the Palatial and Postpalatial phases (Rahmstorf 2008, pl. 100–102). There are also important remains dating to the EBA, especially the Early Helladic (EH) II phase (*c.* 2750–2300/2200 BC). Middle Helladic (MH) remains are very scant. The palace on the upper citadel was excavated by H. Schliemann in the late 19th century and succeeding excavations in Tiryns were carried out by German and Greek archaeologists during the early 20th century, the 1920s, the late 1950s and the 1960s (on the history of the excavation see: Rahmstorf 2008, 6–12). Systematic and careful excavations were undertaken between 1976 and 1983 by K. Kilian, mainly in the lower citadel. These excavations brought to light a neatly stratified sequence from LH IIIA2 until LH IIIC Late, so far unique for a Mycenaean centre. The most recent excavations have been carried out by J. Maran since 1997 (Maran 2000; Maran and Papadimitriou 2006; Maran 2008a, 2008b).

Certainly, during EH II Tiryns was one of the most important sites in southern Greece. The unique monumental circular building (*e.g.* Marzollf 2004) on the highest point of the hill, a densely settled lower citadel and a large lower town at its foot, as well as significant classes of artefacts (*i.e.* clay sealings and weights) give the impression of a prosperous town.[1] Unquestionably, Tiryns was also one of the most important centres of the Mycenaean culture during the Palatial period of the 14th and 13th centuries. However, a reconstruction of demographic and social aspects of the people living in the lower

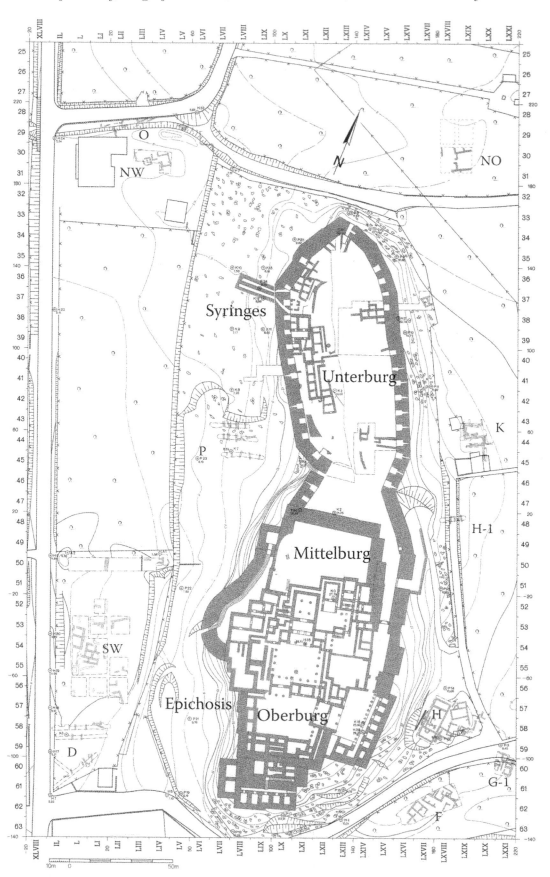

Fig. 6.9.1. Plan of the citadel and of the lower town of Late Bronze Age Tiryns (plan: Rahmstorf 2008, pl. 99).

citadel remains difficult.[2] There is insufficient evidence for storage facilities and workshops (pottery, lapidary, *etc.*) in the LH IIIB lower citadel to indicate the existence of specialised workshops; however, there are indications of metal working.[3] Spindle whorls are more or less evenly distributed over the lower citadel, hinting at spinning as a daily activity.[4] Still, the high quality of the domestic architecture and the luxury items uncovered in the houses suggest that (at least some of) the inhabitants had a higher socio-economic position in the society. During the Postpalatial period, *i.e.* after the collapse of the palace and the palatial culture, the social structure of the people living in the lower citadel was possibly different. A qualitative difference is evident in the amount of labour investment in architecture and objects used during this phase. Luxury objects become very rare, especially during the later LH IIIC. Single household units seem to have worked rather autonomously in this period. With the disappearance of the bureaucratic order every household became responsible for its own needs, including textile production.

The LH small finds from Tiryns, including over 700 (possible) tools for spinning and weaving, have been published (Rahmstorf 2008). Of these, *c.* 660 are from Kilian's excavations in the lower citadel. Of the total number of textile tools, 171 objects are recorded in the TTTC database (Fig. 6.9.2). However, in this chapter, results from Rahmstorf's work (for example Rahmstorf 2008) will be included and discussed together with the results from the TTTC tool analyses.[5] The majority of the tools recorded in the database are dated to LH IIIA-C (147 objects), while 13 spindle whorls and 11 loom weights are dated to EH.[6] The tools recorded in the database are mostly from secure contexts and can be considered as representative for the site/periods.

Spindle whorls, conuli and spinning

Spinning during the Early Helladic period[7]
There are 20 clay spindle whorls from the EH layers and another 16 EH whorls were found in later Mycenaean layers (Rahmstorf 2008, 21, 27–30, 34, 36, figs. 6, 13, pl. 6 (upper part)). The typical EH spindle whorls are convex or slightly stretched hemispherical with rounded transitions to base and top (Fig. 6.9.3).

	Spindle whorls	Conulus	Kylix stem	Loom weight	Total
EH	13			11	24
LH IIIA	2	1			3
LH IIIB	5	22		3	30
LH IIIC	25	20	1	68	114
Total	45	43	1	82	171

Fig. 6.9.2. Textile tools recorded in the TTTC database, by type and date.

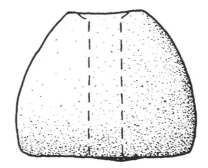

Fig. 6.9.3. Clay spindle whorl, Early Helladic (drawing: Rahmstorf 2008, cat.-no. 2394 (LXI 54/9 2615 I). D: 5.1 cm, H: 4.1 cm, Wt: 116 g).

The uniformity of this type during the EH and especially during EH II in the northeast Peloponnese and central Greece is striking and has been noted previously (Carington Smith 1992, 682). The size of the spindle whorls varies considerably. There are a few large examples (diameter 5–5.4 cm, height 3.6–4.3 cm, weight of completely preserved objects 94–120 g), some are of medium size (diameter 4.1–4.4 cm, height 3.4–3.7 cm, weight of completely or almost completely preserved objects 63–72 g) and there are several smaller spindle whorls (diameter 2.1–3.9 cm, height 1.8–2.9 cm, weight of completely or almost completely preserved objects 9–48 g). The perforations are of average diameter: 0.9 cm in the large examples, 0.7–0.8 cm in the medium, 0.4–0.8 cm in the small whorls. Bone spindle whorls are EH in date[8] and are rather homogenous in size (diameter 4.2–5.3 cm, height 1.7–2.3 cm) due to the bone material used. Their weight varies between 14 and 36 g (Fig. 6.9.4). Their shape is reminiscent of the EH clay spindle whorls. The diameters of the perforations measure 0.4–1.1 cm. The bone spindle whorls were probably made from the heads of the humerus/femur of large ruminants (Bovidae, Cervidae) and/or Equidae. They were nicely shaped, with their curved surfaces usually well polished and the flat bases polished or left unworked and rough.

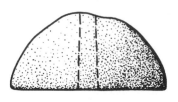

Fig. 6.9.4. Bone spindle whorl, Early Helladic (drawing: Rahmstorf 2008, cat.-no. 1468 (Ti 17228). D: 4.53 cm, H: 2.22 cm, Wt: 25.4 g).

Fig. 6.9.5. Clay spindle whorl, Late Helladic (drawing: Rahmstorf 2008, cat.-no. 790 (LXII 43/42 a1224 XX R215). D: 3.3 cm, H: 2.5 cm, Wt: c. 22 g).

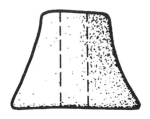

Fig. 6.9.6. Clay spindle whorl, Late Helladic (drawing: Rahmstorf 2008, cat.-no. 816 (LXI 41/97 a1578 Pl. IVa). D: 3 cm, H: 2.7 cm, Wt: 25.4 g).

Fig. 6.9.7. Stone spindle whorl, Late Helladic (drawing: Rahmstorf 2008, cat.-no. 177 (LXII 44/6 a1355 XVI). D: 3.12 cm, H: 2.31 cm, Wt: c. 22 g).

To conclude, the range in the weight and diameter of the spindle whorls suggests a very varied production of different types of spun yarn. If the heaviest whorls were used as spindle whorls this yarn must have been very thick and could only have been used for producing coarse textiles, or for plying.

Spinning during the Late Helladic Period

Clay spindle whorls from LH Tiryns can be assigned either to the Palatial or Postpalatial period. So far 143 spindle whorls are known. A dozen different types can be distinguished according to shape (Rahmstorf 2008, 18–21, fig. 6). In particular, whorls with a straight sharp conical profile and a concave top ("hollow top") seem to be typical for the Palatial period (Fig. 6.9.5). During the Postpalatial period whorls with a conical concave profile were

preferred, also with a concave or convex top (Fig. 6.9.6).

In Tiryns all whorls made of stone (steatite or similar stone) are defined as conuli, despite size. They are likely to have had a function ranging between whorl and bead. Two hundred and eighty-seven objects from Tiryns have been published (Rahmstorf 2008, 126–138, pl. 47–51, 91, 9–11). The most common type (Rahmstorf 2008, 128, fig. 34: type 1: *c.* 80%) is conical (Fig. 6.9.7), others have a concave-conical profile (Rahmstorf 2008, 128, fig. 34: type 2: *c.* 10%) or are 'disc-shaped', 'shanked' or 'button-shaped' (Rahmstorf 2008, 128, fig. 34: type 3: *c.* 10%).

The different shapes are evenly distributed through Palatial and Postpalatial levels. No biconical conuli have been found in Tiryns; evidence from other sites suggests that this type may not have been produced anymore after LH IIIA (Rahmstorf 2008, 132–133). The weight of most conuli from Tiryns falls between 4 and 20 g, the minimum is 1.5 g and the maximum 41 g. On average, the conuli are lighter than clay spindle whorls, but if one excludes the 'button-shaped' type (type 3) – which possibly was not used as a spindle whorl – the difference is not so strong anymore (Rahmstorf 2008, 28, fig. 11). In addition, the stone conuli became less common after the Palatial period and were supplemented more and more by clay spindle whorls and possibly to a certain extent by rounded perforated sherds in Postpalatial times (Rahmstorf 2008, 25 fig. 10). This would imply that during the Palatial period a thinner thread on average was produced.

Rounded, perforated sherds have been considered to be spindle whorls, as the weight distribution of these artefacts is very similar to the normal clay spindle whorls (Rahmstorf 2008, 50 with fig. 12, pl. 7–9). In addition, these 67 artefacts are especially typical (80%) for LH IIIC Late when there is a general deterioration in the quality of artefacts. The rounded perforated pot sherds (Fig. 6.9.8) were easy and quick to produce and it is plausible that some of the rounded pot sherds with a (central) perforation made from finer Mycenaean pottery were used as provisional spindle whorls during LH IIIC Late.

Thirty-three of the LH III spindle whorls, of which one KS whorl and 12 are pierced sherds, are recorded in the TTTC database, as well as 43 conuli. Sixty-nine of these whorls had a recordable weight and diameter. As can be seen in Figure 6.9.9, they vary in weight from 3 g to 50 g and in diameter from 1.7–6.5 cm.

The groups of spindle whorls and the conuli are more homogeneous in weight, diameter and hole shape than the pierced sherds (compare Rahmstorf 2008, fig. 13 and fig. 19). The weight and the diameter vary within these two groups, but there is a more or less standardised relationship between these two parameters. The yarn spun with the lightest conulus would be much thinner than the yarn spun with the heaviest conulus. The thin type of yarn would demand well prepared raw materials. The fabrics produced with these fine threads would have taken a considerable amount of time to make. If using the same type of prepared raw material, the yarn produced with the heaviest conulus would be thicker and the fabric coarser.

However, there is also a difference between, on the one hand, the spindle whorls and conuli, and on the other, the pierced sherds (Fig. 6.9.9). The pierced sherds generally have a larger diameter than the spindle whorls and conuli. According to the recordings in the database, the pierced sherds from Tiryns are also often irregular in shape and not rounded. Another difference is that the hole shape of the pierced sherds is often hourglass shaped (Fig. 6.9.10). It would be difficult to

fix this type of whorl firmly on the spindle, as the spindle would be likely to wobble too much. More tests are therefore needed to see whether these pierced sherds would function well as spindle whorls. During the TTTC spinning tests a slightly irregular spindle whorl was used and both spinners considered that it was not optimal as a spinning tool. The main reason was that the spindle wobbled, and according to their experience, was therefore difficult to spin with and also more time consuming. Another problem was that spinning with this unbalanced spindle gave them pain in their hands and shoulders (chapter 4.1). Nevertheless, other tests (Gibbs 2008) demonstrated that spinning with irregular pierced potsherds with hourglass shaped holes was effective. In the external

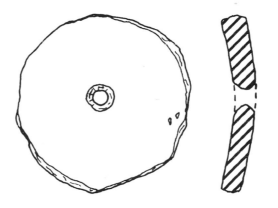

Fig. 6.9.8. Pierced sherd, Late Helladic (drawing: Rahmstorf 2008, cat.-no. 1138 (LXII 36/24 a1382 IIId). D: 4.3–4.6 cm, Wt: 16.7 g).

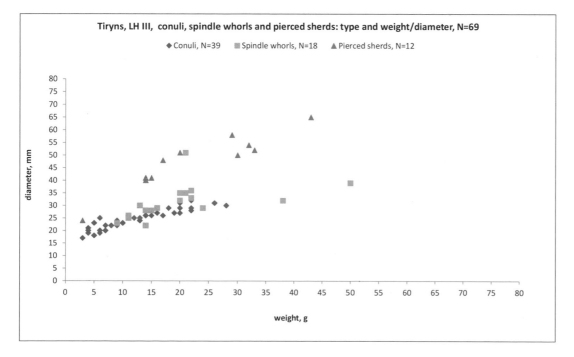

Fig. 6.9.9. LH III spindle whorls recorded in the TTTC database: type and weight/diameter. Please note that some markers represent more than one spindle whorl.

	Plain	Cone	Hourglass	Not available	Total
Spindle whorls	30	4			34
Conuli	39	1		3	43
Pierced sherds			11	1	12
Total	69	5	11	4	89

Fig. 6.9.10. The relationship between whorl type and hole shape.

analyses of the thread spun with an irregular spindle whorl in the TTTC tests, there were no visual differences from the yarn spun with a functional spindle whorl (chapter 4.2).

To conclude, the range in the spindle whorls' weight and diameter suggests a very varied production of different types of spun yarn and it should be noted that the heavier spindle whorls present in EH contexts are missing during this period.

Loom weights and weaving

Weaving during the Early Helladic

The EH material from Tiryns includes five different types of clay objects, which may be interpreted as loom weights (Siennicka 2012, 68–71, pl. XXV d–h). First, there are the cylindrical objects with two or three perforations and without perforations (Figs. 6.9.11, 6.9.12 and 6.9.13), second, large cones with a horizontal perforation, and crescent objects with perforations at both ends. Cylinders with only one lengthwise perforation have not to date been recovered from Tiryns, but occur sporadically at other EBA or MBA sites, e.g. Eutresis (see Goldman 1931, 193, fig. 266, 3, 6).

Large conical weights or cones are so far known only from Tiryns, where they are only present in EH contexts. Only five fragments have been recovered, all in a bad state of preservation. The cones have straight but uneven (slightly concave or convex) sides and flat oval bases rounded at the edges. Only in one case, where approximately 85% of the object is preserved, is a horizontal perforation placed at *c.* 2/3 of its height visible. Because of similar sizes, diameters, side gradient and material, one can assume that the other fragments belonged to the same conical type with perforation. The best preserved example (Fig. 6.9.14) 10.7 cm in height, but originally it must have been larger (its upper end is not preserved). Its diameter measures *c.* 11 cm and the perforation is 1.2–1.3 cm. It has

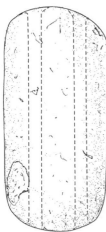

Fig. 6.9.11. Clay cylinder, Early Helladic (drawing: M. Siennicka, unpublished (LXII 39/42 a1472 uNr. 18). D: 5.1 cm, H: 10.7 cm, Wt: c. 335 g).

an estimated original weight of *c.* 800 g. The surface was smoothed, but no traces of paint or wash are visible. Even if badly damaged and only preserved as fragments, the cones give an impression of homogeneity regarding their size, form, material and production. Since all the conical weights come from the same area (although from different excavation layers), it cannot be ruled out that they were all used together.

Crescent shaped weights or 'heavy bananas' (nine examples) are usually thicker in the central part and narrower at the ends. The section is more elliptical than oval. The weights have a horizontal perforation at each end, placed symmetrically. Crescent shaped weights are extremely rare in the EBA Aegean and were possibly inspired by EBA Anatolia.[9] Only two examples from Tiryns have been preserved completely or almost completely, while another seven are fragmentary, *i.e.* only half preserved or less than half preserved (see for example, Müller 1938, 64, fig. 50; Weißhaar 1981, 237, fig. 77, 7; 82, 7). The maximum lengths (measured across the two most distant points) are 16 cm and 16.8 cm; maximum diameters are 4.8 cm and 5.8 cm respectively. A few examples are a little thinner, but they do not differ much in size. The perforations measure 0.9 cm in both of the completely preserved objects and are 2.2 cm and 2.9 cm deep. The distance between the holes at each end of these two objects is 13 cm. The complete crescent weighs 592 g (Fig. 6.9.15), while the reconstructed weight of the second smaller one would be *c.* 480 g. Here again the group is very homogenous and all the objects appear to have been manufactured in a similar way. It is notable that the weaving tests have demonstrated that this type of loom weight is very functional, especially when weaving twill (chapter 4.4; Lassen 2013).

Only four examples of perforated spheres, from the lower citadel, were found. Three have a diameter of 9.5–10 cm, the diameter of the fourth is 6.2 cm. They were described as unbaked and crumbling when dried. Unfortunately, they were not illustrated in the publication (see Siedentopf 1971, 82) and have not been loctaed in the excavation depot.. Siedentopf referred to rather similar objects from Eutresis (Goldman 1931, 192, fig. 265). The archaeological context is dated to EH II.

Only 11 of the Early Helladic loom weights are recorded in the TTTC database, only six of which had an original weight that could be estimated. These loom weights therefore cannot be considered as representative. However, the general impression is that the loom weights during this period, due to their size, are most suitable for use in a production of coarser textiles, or at least textiles produced with warp threads needing a lot of tension (chapters 4.1 and 4.5), which supports the interpretation of the spindle whorls dated to the same period.

Weaving during the Late Helladic Period

From the LH period there are three possible classes of clay loom weights: disc (Fig. 6.9.16), spool (Fig. 6.9.17) and torus shaped objects (Fig. 6.9.18). Of these only the disc-shaped weights are definitely loom weights. The majority (68) of the loom weights recorded in the TTTC database are from LH IIIC contexts.

Forty-nine of the loom weights have a recordable weight and thickness (five loom weights and 44 spools); they vary in weight from 15 g to 464 g and in thickness from 1.8 cm to 5.0 cm (Fig. 6.9.19).

Weaving with spools

Spools are the most common type of loom weight recorded in the database, but the weight and the thickness vary within this group (Fig. 6.9.19). Over 200 (fragmentary or complete examples) have been published or mentioned in the literature (Rahmstorf 2008, 59–73, pl. 23–32; Maran 2008a, 78, fig. 71–73). For various reasons it has been argued before by Rahmstorf (Rahmstorf 2003, 2005) that the spools might have functioned as loom weights in a warp-weighted loom. TTTC weaving tests have demonstrated that it is possible to use spools as loom weights, but it is plausible that the smaller spools (weighing below 50 g) would be more suitable for use as weights in tablet weaving or in other band weaving techniques (chapters 2 and 4.1). However, it is of course also possible that extremely thin warp yarn needing less than 5 g tension was used (see also Siennicka and Ulanowska in press).

Loom weights and spools in contexts, an example

In some cases, several spools are found together. For example, 11 spools recorded in the database, made of fired clay, are from the same context (Ti LXII 42/59 IV G9). Eight of these spools

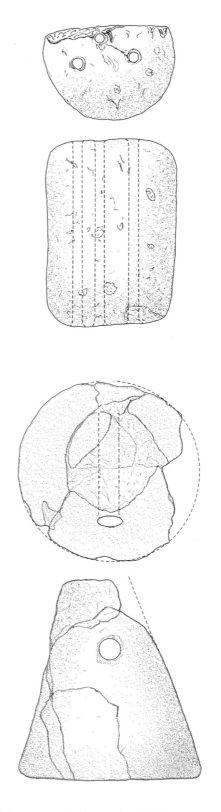

weigh between 23–28 g, with a thickness varying from 2.4 cm to 2.8 cm (Fig. 6.9.20). None of these spools would have functioned optimally as weights on a warp-weighted loom. The weight of the other three spools varies from 104 g to

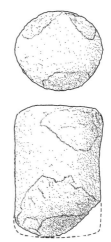

Fig. 6.9.12. (left) Clay cylinder, Early Helladic (drawing: M. Siennicka, unpublished (LXII 39/47 VI a). D: 7.2 cm, H: 10.5 cm, Wt (rec.): c. 607 g).

Fig. 6.9.13. (above) Clay cylinder, Early Helladic (drawing: M. Siennicka, unpublished (LXIV 38/67 a1531 XIb). D: 4.8 cm, H: 7.15 cm, Wt (rec.): c. 187 g).

Fig. 6.9.14. Clay cone loom weight, Early Helladic (drawing: M. Siennicka, unpublished (LXIII 39/18 VI). D: c. 11 cm, H: 10.7 cm, Wt (rec): c. 800 g).

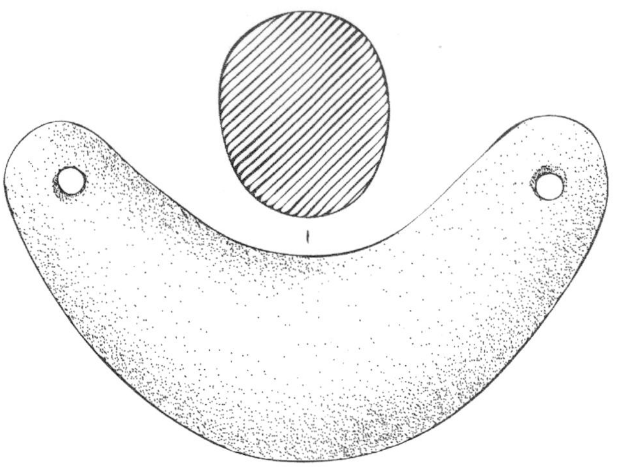

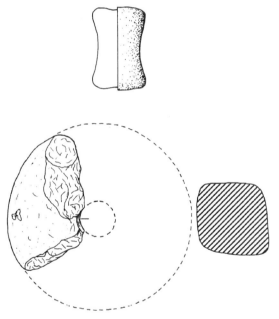

Fig. 6.9.15. (left) Clay crescent loom weight, Early Helladic (drawing: M. Siennicka, unpublished (LXI 38/60 a1461 VI) L: 16.5 cm, D: 5.8 cm, Wt: 592 g).

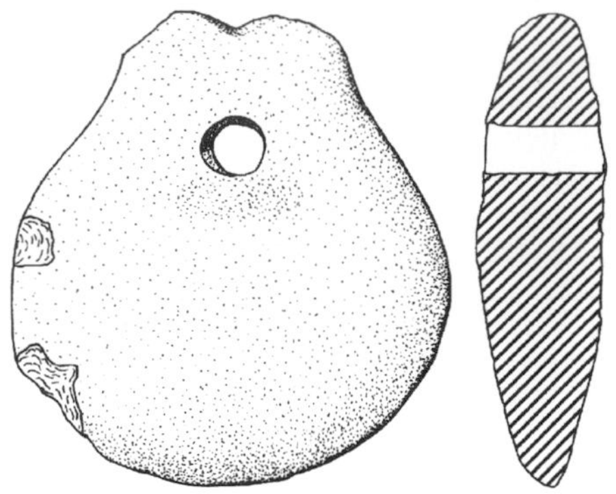

Fig. 6.9.16. (right) Clay disc shaped loom weight, Late Helladic (drawing: Rahmstorf 2008, cat.-no. 1536 (LXI 40/82 XIIIa). W: 9.05 cm, H: 10.6 cm, Th: 2.4 cm, Wt (rec.): c. 211 g)

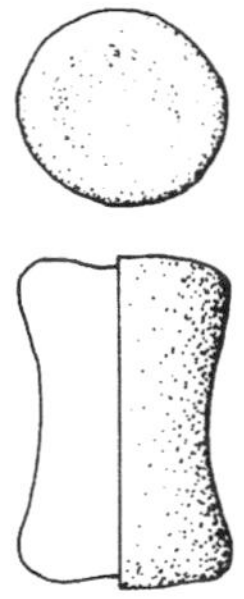

Fig. 6.9.17. Clay spool shaped loom weight, Late Helladic (drawing: Rahmstorf 2008, cat.-no. 1672 (LXII 42/59 IV G9). D: 2.45 cm, H: 3.88 cm, Wt: c. 23 g).

Fig. 6.9.18. Clay torus shaped loom weight, Late Helladic (drawing: Rahmstorf 2008, cat.-no. 2484 (LXI 43/9 XIIIa). D: 10.5 cm, H: 4 cm, Wt (rec.): c. 464 g).

122 g and the thickness varies from 3.7 cm to 4.2 cm; these spools could have been used as loom weights using warp threads needing *c.* 5–10 g tension. The spools were found together, but according to their weight and thickness they are clearly divided into two groups, demonstrating that they would not optimally be functional together in a regular setup on a warp-weighted loom (Rahmstorf 2008, pl. 141). Another nine spools from the same period were found nearby (Ti LXII 42/70 IV G9). The original weight has been

estimated on four of these incomplete spools and varies from 15 g to 33 g. Their thickness varies from 2.0 cm to 2.7 cm. They could therefore have been used with the other eight spools from Ti LXII 42/59 IV G9 (Fig. 6.9.20). However, if these spools were used in a setup it would have been either for a tablet/band weave or in a very special setup on the warp-weighted loom.

Summary

The EH levels from the lower citadel are not published yet[10] and only a few textile tools have some contextual information. Seven fragments of cylinders with three lengthwise perforations were uncovered in Room 143 in the central part of the lower citadel.[11] Room 143, a spacious central chamber, belonged to an only partially excavated large house complex, which Kilian compared to important EH II Late buildings at other sites. Because of the accumulation of the cylinders, Kilian suggested weaving activities in that room (like House B6 and the House of the Tiles at Lerna and the corridor house at Akovitika: Kilian 1981, 189, fig. 45; 1983, 312, fig. 39, a). The relevant layers in Room 143 should rather be dated to the EH II–EH III transitional horizon (for this "Übergangshorizont" see Maran 1998, 12–13, pl. 80–81). In addition, fragments of four large cones and two fragments of crescent shaped weights were uncovered in adjacent squares to the east, and may be contemporary in date.[12] In general, the architecture and the finds of the EH II and the transition to EH III from the lower citadel give the impression of a vibrant town with combined use of houses for living, working, craft, storage and trading activities.[13] The constant activity in spinning and weaving surely belonged to these daily practices.

The number of tools from EH recorded in the TTTC database is small and no detailed conclusions about EH textile production can be drawn from these items. However, it is interesting to note that the results from the analyses of both the spindle whorls and the loom weights suggest a production of slightly coarser fabrics than during the Late Helladic period.

For the Palatial period it is not possible to identify particular concentrations of textile tools in the lower citadel. Sometimes 2–3 clay spindle whorls or 4–5 conuli were found rather close to each other (Rahmstorf 2008, 23, 130 pl. 111; 117; 138, 2; 139), but otherwise they are ubiquitous finds apparently scattered over the lower citadel. Spinning was probably practised in every household. Since only a few disc shaped loom weights were found in the lower citadel it is hard to tell where, if at all, a warp-weighted loom was originally installed. Two different pairs of disc shaped loom weights might imply two looms at different locations (in a building). Nevertheless, the evidence is very weak and poses the question whether weaving on a warp-weighted loom played any important role during LH IIIB in the lower citadel.

A number of spindle whorls, above all conuli, date to LH IIIB, demonstrating a varied production of different yarns from very fine to thicker spun thread. In this period, however, the few loom weights recovered means that it is almost impossible to suggest which types of fabrics were produced. The analysis of the whorls suggests a varied production of different types of fabrics woven with very thin thread to fabrics woven with thicker thread. To spin and weave with the thinnest threads would have been time consuming and demanded specialist knowledge.

There is a distinct increase in the number of recorded regular spindle whorls dating to LH IIIC and it is interesting to note that these spindle whorls are within the same weight/ diameter range as the conuli. On the other hand, if the pierced pot sherds are not included, the analysis of the whorls from LH IIIC does not demonstrate any changes from LH IIIB in the production of different or new types of yarn, despite the typological change in spindle whorls.

In the Postpalatial period there are no more typical loom weights. Clay spools only appeared during LH IIIC Middle and may have taken over the function of loom weights. Concentrations in certain areas in the lower citadel suggest that during the Postpalatial period weaving was practised throughout the

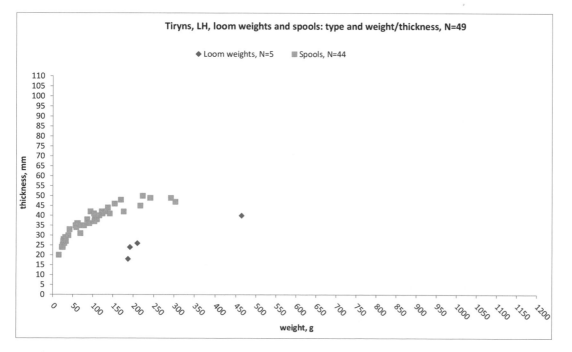

Fig. 6.9.19. LH loom weights and spools: type and weight/thickness. Please note that some markers represent more than one loom weight.

Fig. 6.9.20. Spools from Ti LXII 42/59 IV G9 and Ti LXII 42/70 V G9: weight/thickness. Please note that some markers represent more than one spool.

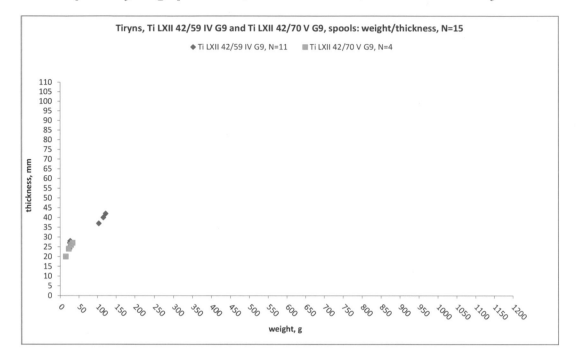

area of the lower citadel (Rahmstorf 2008, 60, pl. 130; 138, 1; 140; 141; 148, 1). It is possible to interpret the spools as deterioration in textile production during later LH IIIC, as they were produced quickly and easily, similarly to the contemporary rounded pierced sherds. It is uncertain whether the smaller spools (under 100 g) replaced other, heavier loom weights, or were used for other types of weaving (band or tablet weaving). However, the large spools would be suitable for use as loom weights. Therefore, it is probable that a new type of fabric was being produced compared to the textiles woven in earlier phases, *i.e.* a fabric with very thin threads.

In conclusion, the textile tools from LH IIIB and LH IIIC demonstrate a production of 'very fine' and 'fine' fabrics. It is plausible that other coarser textiles were also produced in Tiryns, but this production seems to be invisible and was probably performed with other types of spindles and looms, if not at another location. The visible production, however, demonstrates high quality textiles that would have demanded well prepared raw materials, textiles that were time consuming to produce (compared to coarser types) and demanded skilled craftspeople with the knowledge, time and ability to produce these types of fabrics.

Notes

1 For most recent finds of EH II sealings in the lower town see Maran 2008b, 103, fig. 9. For EH II weights see Rahmstorf 2006, 25–27, fig. 4.

2 It is likely that individuals of higher social status lived within the citadel during the Palatial period but it is difficult to systematically compare their situation with the contemporary domestic quarters outside the citadel due to the lack of adequately published remains of the Palatial period.

3 This is indicated by installations and small finds at three to four different places in the lower citadel during LH IIIB Developed and Late: (Rahmstorf 2008, 240–241, 248–249, 252–253, 274, 287, pls. 104, 111, 114, 135, 150–151). For recent results on new excavations in building XI see Maran 2008a.

4 This, however, was probably not restricted to a certain class of people (*e.g.* servants, slaves, craftspeople), as persons with high status were spinning as well. Compare *Odyssey* 4.130–35 where "a princess is given gold and silver spinning gear as a present by a high-born lady-friend"; Barber (1991, 60–64, fig. 2.24–28) also makes references to spindles and whorls made of gold, silver and ivory from Bronze Age contexts in the Eastern Mediterranean.

5 The majority of the textile tools from Tiryns are published in Rahmstorf 2008. Approximately 60 EH textile tools from pure EH contexts are going to be published separately.

6 In this chapter, results on the EH material from Rahmstorf's and Siennicka's works (Rahmstorf 2008; Siennicka 2012) will be included and discussed together with the results from the TTTC tool analyses. The EH material from Tiryns includes 30 clay spindle whorls, seven bone spindle whorls and 30 loom weights.

7 For a detailed discussion on the Early Helladic textile tools from Tiryns see Siennicka 2012.

8 Only one of the bone spindle whorls was recovered from a pure EH layer, but from the comparative material from other sites it is clear that bone spindle whorls were used only during the EBA or Neolithic in southern Greece (see Rahmstorf 2008, 209).

9 Very few similar objects are known: only from Troia (Schmidt 1902, 296, no. 8240) and Thermi on Lesbos (Lamb 1936, pls. 24, 31, 61) and a recent find from Geraki in Laconia (Crouwel *et al.* 2007, 6–9, fig. 4, pl. II). In Anatolia they appeared much more often at EBA sites (*e.g.* Demircihöyük: Korfmann 1981, 33–34, fig. 45; Aphrodisias: Joukowsky 1986, 516, fig. 369, 4) and continued to be typical loom weights during the second millennium BC.

10 Only short comments in preliminary reports are available at the moment: Kilian 1979, 408–409, fig. 32–33; 1981, 186–192, fig. 44–47; 1982, 420–424, fig. 39–47; 1983, 314–326, fig. 39–56; Siedentopf 1971; Grossmann and Schäfer 1975.

11 K. Kilian mentioned the cylinders, but they have not been illustrated as a separate picture or drawing. One can recognise them, however, on a detailed plan of the complex R 142–144 in Room 143 just north of the entrance in the partition wall between Rooms 143 and 144 (Kilian 1981, 189, fig. 45).

12 Without stratigraphical analysis, it is not yet clear if they are contemporary with Room 114. The large cones were discovered in LXII 39/18, LXII 39/29 layer Va, LXII 39/78 layer Va, LXIII 39/18 layer VI. The crescent objects came to light in LXII 39/18, LXII 39/20 layer VI.

13 For example, the thick destruction deposit in Room 196 yielded a rich array of pottery, pithoi, grinding tools, lead objects, obsidian tools, bone points and balance weights. See Kilian 1982, 420–424, fig. 41–46; Rahmstorf 2006, 25–27, fig. 4.

14 For more on the EH textile tools and production see Siennicka 2012

Bibliography

Barber, E. J. W. (1991) *Prehistoric Textiles: The Development of Cloth in the Neolithic and Bronze Ages with Special Reference to the Aegean.* Princeton. Princeton University Press.

Carington Smith, J. (1992) Spinning and weaving equipment, in Macdonald, W. A. and Wilkie, N. C. (eds), *Excavations at Nichoriain in Southwestern Greece. 2. The Bronze Age Occupation*, 674–711. Minneapolis. University of Minnesota Press.

Crouwel, J., Prent, M. and Shipley, D. G. J. (2007) Geraki. An acropolis site in Lakonia. Preliminary report on the thirteenth season, *Pharos*, 15, 1–16.

Gibbs, K. T. (2008) Pierced clay disks and Late Neolithic textile production, in Córdoba, J. M., Molist, M., Pérez, M. C., Rubio, I., and Martínez, S. (eds), *Proceedings of the 5th International Congress on the Archaeology of the Ancient Near East, Madrid, April 3–8 2006*, 89–96. Madrid. UAM Ediciones.

Goldman, H. (1931) *Excavations at Eutresis in Boeotia: Conducted by the Fogg Art Museum of Harvard University in Cooperation with the American School of Classical Studies at Athens, Greece.* Cambridge, Massachusetts. Harvard University Press.

Grossmann, P. and Schäfer, J. (1975) Tiryns: Unterburg 1968. Grabungen im Bereich der Bauten 3 und "4", in Müller, K. (ed.), *Tiryns. Forschungen und Berichte VIII*, 55–96. Mainz. Philipp von Zabern.

Joukowsky, M. S. (1986) *Prehistoric Aphrodisias. An Account of the Excavations and Artefact Studies.* Providence. Brown University.

Kilian, K. (1979) Ausgrabungen in Tiryns 1977, *Archäologischer Anzeiger*, 379–411.

Kilian, K. (1981) Ausgrabungen in Tiryns 1978–1979, *Archäologischer Anzeiger*, 149–194.

Kilian, K. (1982) Ausgrabungen in Tiryns 1980, *Archäologischer Anzeiger*, 393–430.

Kilian, K. (1983) Ausgrabungen in Tiryns 1981, *Archäologischer Anzeiger*, 277–328.

Korfmann, M. O. (1981) *Demircihüyük. Die Ergebnisse der Ausgrabungen 1975–1978. 1. Architektur, Stratigraphie und Befunde.* Mainz. Philipp von Zabern.

Lamb, W. (1936) *Excavations at Thermi in Lesbos.* Cambridge. Cambridge University Press.

Lassen, W. A. (2013) Technology and palace economy in Middle Bronze Age Anatolia: the case of the crescent shaped loom weight, in Nosch, M.-L., Koefoed, H. and Andersson Strand, E. (eds), *Textile Production and Consumption in the Ancient Near East. Archaeology, Epigraphy, Iconography*, 78–92. Ancient Textiles Series 12. Oxford. Oxbow Books.

Maran, J. (1998) *Kulturwandel auf dem griechischen Festland und den Kykladen im späten 3. Jahrtausend v.Chr.: Studien zu den kultuellen Verhältnissen in Südosteuropa und dem zentalen sowie östlichen Mittelmeerraum in der späten Kupfer- und frühen Bronzezeit.* Bonn. Rudolf Habelt.

Maran, J. (2000) Das Megaron im Megaron. Zur Datierung und Funktion des Antenbaus im mykenischen Palast von Tiryns, *Archäologischer Anzeiger*, 2000/1, 1–16.

Maran, J. (2008a) Forschungen in der Unterburg von Tiryns 2000–2003, *Archäologischer Anzeiger*, 2008/1, 35–111.

Maran, J. (2008b) Tiryns, Deutsches Archäologisches Institut, Jahresbericht 2007. *Archäologischer Anzeiger*, 2008/1, Beoheft, 103–105.

Maran, J. and Papadimitriou, A. (2006) Forschungen im Stadtgebiet von Tiryns 1999–2002, mit Beiträgen von R. Pasternak, P. Stockhammer, C. Hübner und S. Giese, *Archäologischer Anzeiger*, 2006/1, 97–169.

Marzollf, P. (2004) Das zweifache Rätsel Tiryns, in Schwandner, E.-L. and Rheidt, K. (eds), *Macht der Architektur – Architektur der Macht*, 79–91. Mainz. Philipp von Zabern.

Müller, K. (1938) *Tiryns IV. Die Urfirniskeramik.* München. F. Bruckmann.

Rahmstorf, L. (2003) Clay spools from Tiryns and other contemporary sites. An indication of foreign influence in LH IIIC?, in Kyparissi-Apostolika, N. and Papakonstantinou, M. (eds), *Η περιφέρεια του μυκηναϊκού κόσμου./The Periphery of the Mycenaean World*, 397–415. Athens. Greek Ministry of Culture.

Rahmstorf, L. (2005) Ethnicity and changes in weaving technology in Cyprus and the eastern Mediterranean in the 12th century BC, in Karageorghis, V. (ed.), *Cyprus: Religion and Society: From the Late Bronze Age to the End of the Archaic Period*, 143–169. Möhnesee-Wamel. Bibliopolis.

Rahmstorf, L. (2006) In search of the earliest balance weights, scales and weighing systems from the Eastern Mediterranean, the Near and Middle East, in Alberti, M. E., Ascalone, E. and Peyronel, L. (eds), *Weights in Context. Bronze Age Weighing Systems of Eastern Mediterranean: Chronology, Typology, Material and Archaeological Contexts*, 9–45. Rome. Istituto Italiano di Numismatica.

Rahmstorf, L. (2008) *Kleinfunde aus Tiryns, Terrakotta, Stein, Bein und Glas/Fayence vornehmlich aus der Spätbronzezeit.* Wiesbaden. Reichert Verlag.

Rahmstorf, L. (2011) Handmade pots and crumbling loom weights: 'Barbarian' elements in the Eastern Mediterranean in the last quarter of the 2nd millennium BC, in Kouka O. and Karageorghis V. (eds), *On Cooking Pots, Drinking Cups, Loomweights and Ethnicity in Bronze Age Cyprus and Neighbouring Regions*, 315–330. Nicosia. A. G. Leventis Foundation.

Schmidt, H. (1902) *Heinrich Schliemann's Sammlung trojanischer Altertümer.* Berlin. Georg Reimer.

Siedentopf, H. B. (1971) Frühhelladische Siedlungsschichten auf der Unterburg von Tiryns, in Jantzen, U. (ed.), *Tiryns. Forschungen und Berichte V*, 77–85. Mainz. Philipp von Zabern.

Siennicka, M. (2012) Textile production in Early Helladic Tiryns, in Nosch, M.-L. and Laffineur, R. (eds), *KOSMOS. Jewellery, Adornment and Textiles in the Aegean Bronze Age*, 65–75. Liège. Peeters.

Siennicka, M. and Ulanowska, A. (in press) So simple yet universal. Experimental approach to clay spools from Bronze Age Greece, in Alfaro, C. *et al.* (eds), *Purpureae vestes VI. Textiles and Dyes in the Mediterranean World, Abbey of Montserrat, 19–23.03.2014.*

Weißhaar, J.-H. (1981) Ausgrabungen in Tiryns 1978–1979. Bericht zur frühhelladischen Keramik, *Archäologischer Anzeiger*, 220–256.

Zangger, E. (1994) Landscape changes around Tiryns during the Bronze Age, *American Journal of Archaeology*, 98 (2), 189–212.

CHAPTER 6.10

Textile tools from Thebes, mainland Greece

Maria Emanuela Alberti, Vassilis Aravantinos, Ioannis Fappas, Athina Papadaki, Françoise Rougemont, Eva Andersson Strand, Marie-Louise Nosch and Joanne Cutler

The site of Thebes is located in Boeotia, central Greece, and has been a centre of primary importance throughout its history, from the Early Bronze Age to the present day. Parts of the Bronze Age settlement, which lies under the modern town, have been brought to light through a series of rescue excavations by the IXth Ephorate of Prehistoric and Classical Antiquities (Archaeological Museum of Thebes). The excavated plots can only provide a partial picture of the nature of the Bronze Age occupation, however. During Mycenaean times, Thebes was a first-order centre, the seat of a palatial administration. The whole upper town was variously involved in storing, craft and recording activities, and its excavated sectors seem to have been linked with the palace to varying degrees. The most well-known and impressive Mycenaean complexes are located roughly in the centre of the town: the so-called "House of Kadmos", the "Treasury" and the "Room of the Pithoi" (Fig. 6.10.1).

An international project was initiated in 2006, with the aim of reconstructing the organisation of the textile production at Thebes, combining both textual and archaeological evidence. Textile tools from various Theban plots were recorded, and their contexts studied in order to provide a chronological framework and some

insights into the function of the excavated buildings.

A total of 236 textile tools from Bronze Age Thebes are included in the TTTC database. Two hundred of these are from securely dated contexts, with 30 objects dating to the Early Bronze Age and 170 dating to the Late Bronze Age, *i.e.* Mycenaean, Thebes (Fig. 6.10.2). All of the Late Bronze Age tools were recovered from LH III contexts, with the majority (95) dating to LH IIIB2 Late. Since there are so few textile tools from Early Bronze Age contexts, the discussion below focuses on the Late Bronze Age material.

Mycenaean Thebes: the included contexts

The evidence presented here comes from the Mycenaean levels of various excavated plots, each plot designated by the name of its owner, followed by the year of excavation. The plots considered here are: Christodoulou and Stamati (1983–1984), Kofini (2005), Loukou (1980), Pavloyiannopoulou (1963–1964 and 1994–1995) and Soteriou-Dougekou (1970–1971). In addition, the evidence from the excavations under Pelopidou Street (1993–1995) is also presented. The excavations are

*Fig. 6.10.1. Thebes
(Boeotia). Excavated
plots in the grid of the
modern town.
1) "House of Kadmos"
2) "Treasury" and
"Room of Pithoi"
3) "Wool workshop"
(Soteriou-Dougekou plot)
4) "Armoury"
(Pavloyiannopoulou plot)
5) Pelopidou street
6) "Ivory Workshop"
(Loukou plot)
7) Christodoulou,
Stamati and Liaga plots
8) Kofini plot
(plan: courtesy of the
Museum of Thebes).*

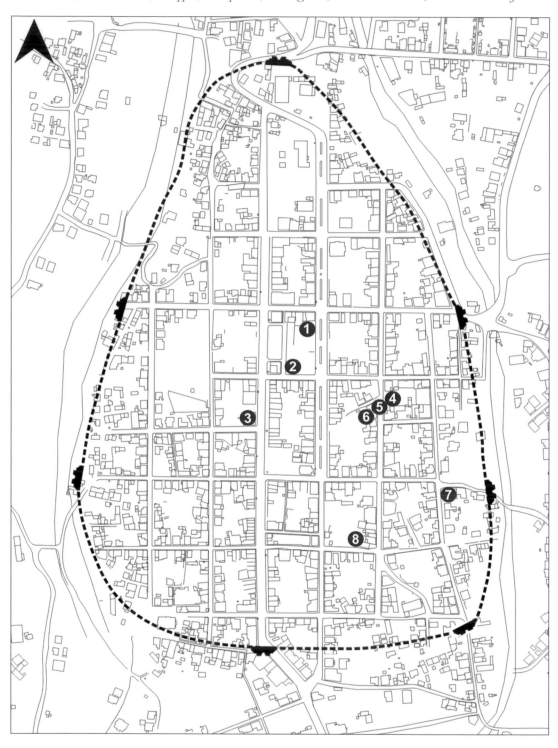

located in various parts of the Mycenaean town, spreading from the centre to the southeast gates, and comprise a series of functionally different contexts (Fig. 6.10.1). Most of them are known through preliminary or partial publications or are still under study.[1]

In these structures, the large majority of the pottery assemblage consists of coarse, medium-coarse and plain fine wares: storage, cooking, pouring and drinking vessels. This pattern of shapes fits very well with other evidence for the apparently utilitarian function of the associated areas. It seems that these architectural units were all dedicated to working (or domestic) activities, with tools of various kinds, including textile tools, and one or more

	Spindle whorl	Conulus	Kylix stem whorl	Pierced sherd	Pierced disc	Loom weight	Spool	Pointed tool	Needle	Total
EH I–III	4					1				5
EH II Late	13	1		2		5		1	3	25
LH IIIA2	1			2			1	3		7
LH IIIA–B	6									6
LH IIIB							1	2		3
LH IIIB2	3	4		1		1	2	1		12
LH IIIB2 Late	47	17	1	11	1	4	6	6	2	95
LH IIIB2–C	2									2
LH IIIC Early	5	7						1	1	14
LH IIIC Middle	11	15					1	3	1	31
Total	92	44	1	16	1	11	11	17	7	200

Fig. 6.10.2. Textile tools from securely dated contexts, by type and date.

bath-tubs positioned on the floor. Some of these units also yielded traces of administrative (Linear B tablets, inscribed and uninscribed nodules, seals and sealings) and/or craft activity, especially ivory working, and were possibly used as storage area for cereals, craft products (bronzes, ivories, pottery) or raw material (wool).

The Christodoulou and Stamati plots (1983–1984) (Fig. 6.10.1, n. 7) are situated in the southeastern part of the Kadmeia (between Oidipodos and Oikonomou streets): they are part of the same archaeological complex as the Liaga plot (1981–1983), where many inscribed and a few uninscribed nodules were found. They are also close to the ancient town border and fortification line, in an area where the Homoloides Gate was traditionally thought to have been located. Two main destruction phases have been reported: the first in LH IIIB1 and the second in LH IIIB2.[2] Only the evidence from Christodoulou and Stamati is considered here (Aravantinos 1988). The buildings seem to have been used as storage and work structures rather than as habitation quarters: there are many large- and medium-sized containers as well as indicators of craft activities, including evidence for textile processing. The Christodoulou plot also yielded a seal and a sealing.[3] Various assemblages of textile tools were found in the buildings, including spindle whorls, spool shaped loom weights, and some bone implements (such as a needle).

The Kofini plot (2005) is situated between Pelopidou and Dirkis Streets, in the southeast part of the Kadmeia, not far from the Elektrai gate (Fig. 6.10.1, n. 8). The bulk of the material is dated to LH IIIB2 and the area appears to

have had a utilitarian function.[4] The textile tools mainly consist of spindle whorls (Figs. 6.10.3 and 6.10.4).

In the central area of the Kadmeia, in its southeastern part, between Pelopidou and Zeggini streets, a large Mycenaean complex has come to light through various excavations of different neighbouring plots (Fig. 6.10.1, n. 4, 5 and 6). The buildings that have been uncovered are very probably parts of the same urban unit, but, because of the physical limits of the rescue excavations, their relationships are still not fully understood. The main excavated areas are: the Pavloyannopoulou plot (or "Armoury", 1963–1964 and 1994–1995), the Loukou plot (or "Ivory Workshop", 1980) and Pelopidou street itself, which divides the two plots, where rich Linear B archives were uncovered (1993–1995). The "Armoury"

Fig. 6.10.3. Kofini plot: stone tools and textile tools (photo: courtesy of the Museum of Thebes).

Fig. 6.10.4. Kofini plot: spindle whorls (drawing: courtesy of the Museum of Thebes).

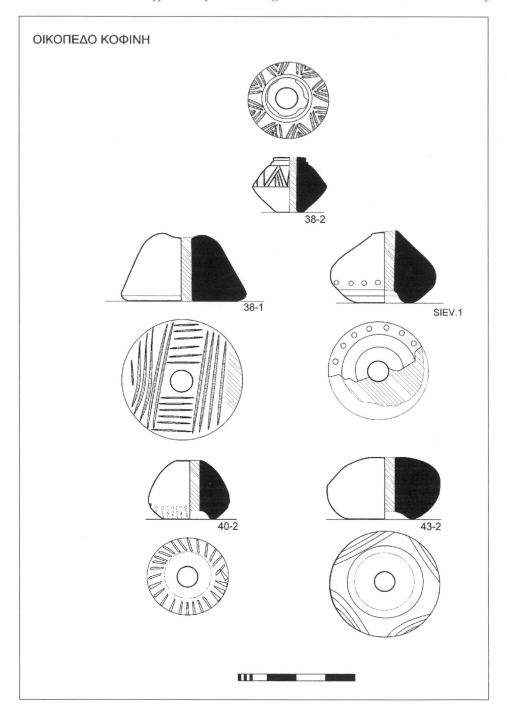

OIKOΠEΔO KOΦINH

38-2

38-1

SIEV.1

40-2

43-2

(LH IIIB1 or IIIB2 according to different scholars) was given its name because horse equipment and parts of bronze cuirasses as well as substantial quantities of bronze weapons were recorded in the course of the excavations, along with a deposit of Linear B tablets (TH Ug) and two lead balance weights. However, many ivory items were also found, thus connecting this context with the evidence from the Loukou plot (LH IIIB1 or LH IIIB2), where evidence of ivory working was securely identified (for spindle whorls from the Loukou plot see Figs. 6.10.5 and 6.10.6).[5] A large number of textile tools were recovered from the Pavloyannopoulou plot, including spindle whorls, loom weights and bone needles (Figs. 6.10.7 to 6.10.17). It should be noted that one of the two balance weights from the plot has a mass roughly similar to the Mycenaean unit for weighing and counting wool: that is, *c.* 3 kg.

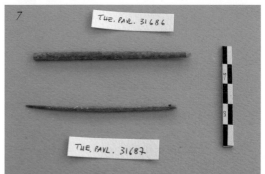

Fig. 6.10.5. (left) Loukou plot: steatite convex-conical spindle whorl, view 1 (photo: courtesy of the Museum of Thebes).

Fig. 6.10.6. (right) Loukou plot: steatite convex-conical spindle whorl, view 2 (photo: courtesy of the Museum of Thebes).

Fig. 6.10.7. (left) Pavloyiannopoulou plot: bone needles (photo: courtesy of the Museum of Thebes).

Fig. 6.10.8. (right) Pavloyiannopoulou plot: incised spindle whorl (photo: courtesy of the Museum of Thebes).

Fig. 6.10.9. (left) Pavloyiannopoulou plot: clay spool shaped loom weight (photo: courtesy of the Museum of Thebes).

Fig. 6.10.10. (right) Pavloyiannopoulou plot: clay spool shaped loom weight (photo: courtesy of the Museum of Thebes).

Fig. 6.10.11. (left) Pavloyiannopoulou plot: steatite biconical spindle whorl, view 1 (photo: courtesy of the Museum of Thebes).

Fig. 6.10.12. (right) Pavloyiannopoulou plot: steatite biconical spindle whorl, view 2 (photo: courtesy of the Museum of Thebes)

Fig. 6.10.13. (left) Pavloyiannopoulou plot: steatite biconical spindle whorl, view 3 (photo: courtesy of the Museum of Thebes).

Fig. 6.10.14. (right) Pavloyiannopoulou plot: stone conical spindle whorl, view 1 (photo: courtesy of the Museum of Thebes).

Fig. 6.10.15. (left) Pavloyiannopoulou plot: stone conical spindle whorl, view 2 (photo: courtesy of the Museum of Thebes).

Fig. 6.10.16. (left) Pavloyiannopoulou plot: stone incised spindle whorl, view 1 (photo: courtesy of the Museum of Thebes).

Fig. 6.10.17. (right) Pavloyiannopoulou plot: stone incised spindle whorl, view 2 (photo: courtesy of the Museum of Thebes).

Fig. 6.10.18. (left) Pelopidou street: steatite conical spindle whorl, view 1 (photo: courtesy of the Museum of Thebes).

Fig. 6.10.20. (right) Pelopidou street: steatite conical spindle whorl, view 3 (photo: courtesy of the Museum of Thebes).

Fig. 6.10.19. (left) Pelopidou street: steatite conical spindle whorl, view 2 (photo: courtesy of the Museum of Thebes).

The buildings excavated under Pelopidou street date to three main phases: LH IIIB2, LH IIIC Early and LH IIIC Middle. Layers dating to LH IIIB2 yielded a substantial deposit of Linear B tablets *etc.*, evidence of large scale storage and some textile tools.[6] The most extensive evidence for textile activity (most notably a quantity of spindle whorls) comes from the LH IIIC Early and Middle layers, which have a more domestic character (Figs. 6.10.18 to 6.10.21).

The Soteriou-Dougekou plot (1970–1971) is situated in the central part of the Kadmeia, adjacent to the central square

Fig. 6.10.21. Pelopidou street: clay spindle whorls (photo: courtesy of the Museum of Thebes).

Fig. 6.10.22. Soteriou-Dougekou plot: stirrup jar (photo: courtesy of the Museum of Thebes).

Fig. 6.10.23. Soteriou-Dougekou plot: stirrup jar (photo: courtesy of the Museum of Thebes).

of the modern city (Fig. 6.10.1, n. 3).[7] The building uncovered (LH IIIB2) yielded possible washing installations, a clay bath-tub, some small stirrup jars still *in situ* on the floor (Figs. 6.10.22 and 6.10.23) and a number of Linear B tablets recording quantities of wool (TH Of, Figs. 6.10.24 and 6.10.25). A multiple sealing was also found (Fig. 6.10.26). The recovered pottery assemblage included plain drinking ware and many storage vases, with heavy traces of burning (which seems to strengthen the hypothesis that oil was stored there). The unit has been interpreted as a location for processing and storing wool or as a clearing house (Chadwick and Spyropoulos 1975; Shelmerdine 1997). The presence of the small stirrup jars *in situ* on the floor, near the possible washing installations, could suggest that the processing of wool included also its treatment with (perfumed?) oil, a practice that is well known from the Linear B tablets of Knossos and from ancient tradition (Foster 1977; Shelmerdine 1995; Fappas 2010, 255–256). Textile tools include many small spindle whorls.

Spindle whorls and spinning

Among the Late Bronze Age textile tools are 75 spindle whorls, 43 conuli, a kylix stem whorl and a pierced bone disc, as well as 14 pierced sherds. Many of the pierced sherds are irregular in shape, and have drilled, hourglass shaped holes; because of this, the spindle would have rotated unevenly if they were used as spindle whorls. They would not, therefore, have been optimal for use as whorls.

Forty-one of the conuli and 51 of the spindle whorls are made of stone, the remainder are made of fired clay (Fig. 6.10.27). A variety of shapes are present among both the conuli and the spindle whorls, but the majority are conical/conical concave in form.

Excluding the pierced sherds, 106 whorls (including the conuli, kylix stem and pierced disc) had a recordable weight and diameter (Fig. 6.10.28). The objects classified as conuli all weigh 10 g or less, but there are a number of spindle whorls that also weigh 10 g or less, so there is a degree of overlap between the two categories.

Fig. 6.10.24. Soteriou-
Dougekou plot: Linear B
tablet TH Of 25 (photo:
courtesy of the Museum
of Thebes).

Fig. 6.10.25. Soteriou-
Dougekou plot: Linear B
tablet TH Of 36 (photo:
courtesy of the Museum
of Thebes).

Fig. 6.10.26. Soteriou-Dougekou plot: multiple sealing (photo: courtesy of the Museum
of Thebes).

Sixty-six of the whorls are from LH IIIB2 Late
contexts: 19 from the Kofini plot; nine from the
Stamati plot; 22 from the Pavloyiannopoulou
plot, 12 from the Soteriou-Dougekou plot and
four from the Loukou plot. Of these, 60 had a
recordable weight and diameter (Fig. 6.10.29).
Excluding the Loukou plot, where only two
of the four whorls had a preserved weight (6 g
and 7 g) and diameter, the weight/diameter
of the whorls from the various plots cover
a range, indicating that a range of different
thread types were being spun in each of
these locations. The whorls from the Kofini,
Stamati and Pavloyiannopoulou plots would
have been suitable for spinning threads varying
from very thin to thick. However, in the case
of the Soteriou-Dougekou excavation, the
weight/diameter range of the whorls is much
narrower (but still covering a range); all of the
whorls from this area weigh 13 g or less and
would have been suitable for spinning very thin

threads. This would suggest that a narrower range of yarn types was being spun in this location, perhaps associated with a more focused production of particular thread types. The building also yielded other indicators of possible textile specialisation, as discussed above.

Thirty-eight whorls, all from the Pelopidou plot, were recovered from LH IIIC contexts (LH IIIC Early and LH IIIC Middle). Thirty-three of these had a recordable weight and diameter (Fig. 6.10.30). The LH IIIC whorls have a weight/diameter range similar to the LH IIIB2 Late whorls and indicate that a range of thread types, from very thin to thick, were being spun in the Pelopidou plot during this period. However, 24 of the whorls weigh 11 g or less, suggesting a greater focus on spinning very thin thread.

Loom weights and weaving

Of the 16 loom weights from securely dated Late Bronze Age contexts, 11 are spool shaped, two are discoid and three are torus shaped (Fig. 6.10.31). Seven of the spools are made of unfired clay, while one of the torus weights is made of stone; the remaining loom weights are made of fired clay.

Four of the spools were recovered from LH IIIB2 Late contexts in the Stamati plot and a further four are from the Pelopidou plot (one in a LH IIIA2 context, two in LH IIIB2 contexts and one in a LH IIIC Middle deposit). Six loom weights were found in LH IIIB2 Late contexts in the Pavloyiannopoulou plot (two spool shaped, one discoid and three torus shaped), while the remaining two weights (one spool and

Fig. 6.10.27. Spindle whorls and conuli, LH III: type and material.

Conuli	Fired Clay	Stone	Total
Biconical		1	1
Concave conical		23	23
Conical	2	16	18
Convex			0
Discord		1	1
Spherical			0
Total	2	41	43
Spindle whorls	**Fired Clay**	**Stone**	**Total**
Biconical	9	10	19
Concave conical	1	9	10
Conical	13	30	43
Convex		1	1
Discord		1	1
Spherical	1		1
Total	24	51	75
Overall total	**26**	**92**	**118**

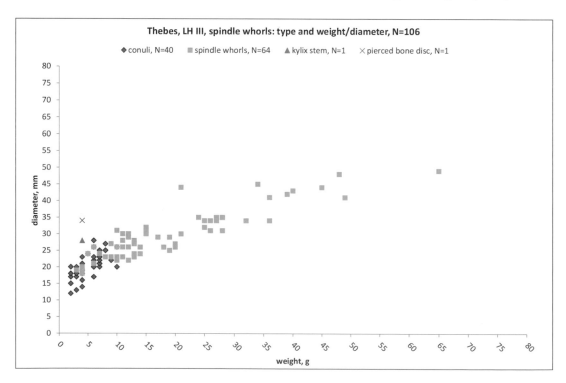

Fig. 6.10.28. Spindle whorls, LH III: type and weight/diameter. Please note that some markers represent more than one spindle whorl.

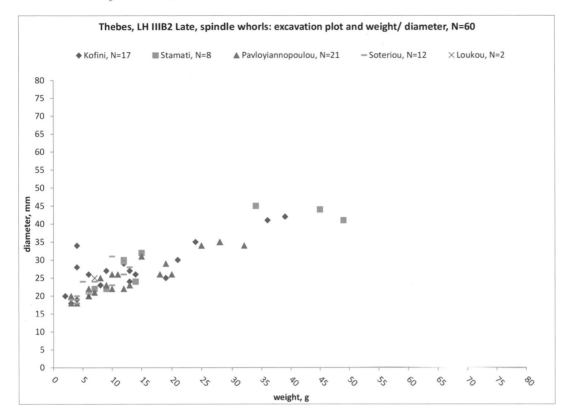

Fig. 6.10.29. Spindle whorls, LH IIIB Late: excavation plot and weight/diameter.

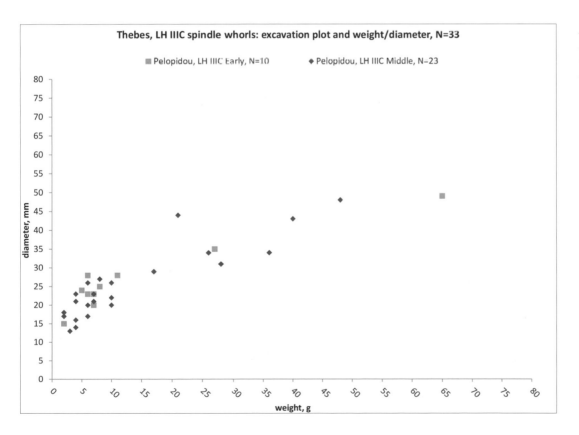

Fig. 6.10.30. Spindle whorls, LH IIIC: excavation plot and weight/diameter.

one discoid) were recovered from an LH IIIB and an LH IIIB2 context respectively in the Christodoulou plot.

Thirteen of the loom weights from securely dated Late Bronze Age contexts had a recordable weight and thickness (nine spools, two discoid and two torus shaped). Although there are only very limited numbers of each type, it can be noted that while the discoid and torus weights lie within the overall weight range of the spool weights, they are thinner than the spools (Fig. 6.10.32). The spools weighing less than 50 g (if they were used as loom weights) would only be suitable for use with extremely fine thread requiring less than *c*. 5 g tension each, or for use with threads requiring *c*. 5 g tension, but with less than 10 threads fastened to the spool. The thinner, discoid weights would be suitable for weaving fabrics with a higher number of warp threads per centimetre. The spools would have been

better suited for producing fabrics with fewer warp threads per centimetre that may have been either open or weft faced.

All of the loom weights with a recordable weight and thickness weigh less than 200 g; therefore, none of them would be ideally suited for use with threads requiring a tension of 20 g or more (although it should be noted that there is one incomplete torus weight weighing 421 g in an LH IIIB2 context from the Pavloyiannopoulou plot, which would have been suitable for use with much thicker thread). Ten of the loom weights weigh 100 g or less and would be best suited for use with very thin thread, requiring up to *c*. 10 g tension.

Summary

The range of whorl weights indicates that a large range of yarn types, from very thin to thick, was being spun at the site in the LH III period, although the large number of whorls weighing less than 15 g suggests that there was a greater focus on spinning thinner thread. This is true both for LH IIIB2 contexts, *i.e.* during the last phase of the Palatial period (see especially the evidence from the specialised Soteriou-Dougekou plot), and LH IIIC phases, *i.e.* during the Postpalatial period (see especially the Pelopidou domestic contexts).

Fig. 6.10.31. Loom weights from securely dated Late Bronze Age contexts, by type and date.

	Discoid	Spool	Torus	Total
LH IIIA2		1		1
LH IIIB		1		1
LH IIIB2	1	2		3
LH IIIB2 Late	1	6	3	10
LH IIIC Middle		1		1
Total	2	11	3	16

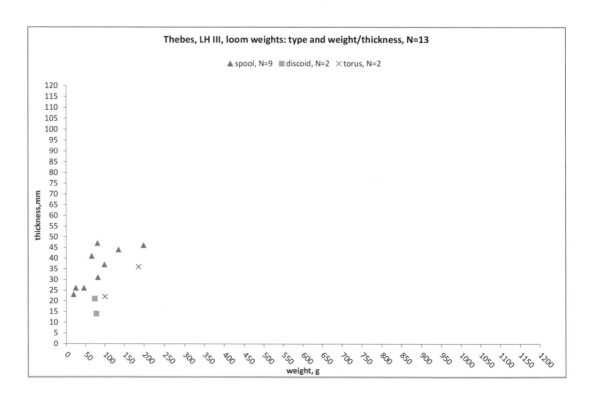

Fig. 6.10.32. Loom weights, LH III: type and weight/thickness.

Nearly all of the loom weights from LH III Thebes are best suited for use with thin thread types, with most of them being optimal for use with thread requiring up to *c.* 10 g tension; a few would be more suitable for use with thread requiring *c.* 15–20 g tension. The number of whorls weighing *c.* 15 g or less would correspond well with the production of this range of thread types. However, it is interesting to note that there are a number of heavier spindle whorls that would be more suitable for spinning thicker threads, which would need correspondingly higher tension. This is true both in the case of the general weight ranges, and in the case of loom weights and spindle whorls dating to the same period from the individual excavation areas. Loom weights suitable for weaving a fabric with these thicker threads are not present among the textile tools from the site (although the incomplete torus weight weighing 421 g in an LH IIIB2 context in the Pavloyiannopoulou area should be noted). It is possible that this is the result of recovery factors, or that another type of loom was being used to weave the heavier fabrics.

Notes

1 For a further discussion of the evidence and on the organisation of textile and other craft activity and administration in Late Mycenaean Thebes, and full bibliography, see Alberti *et al.* 2012.
2 See Aravantinos 1983 (Christodoulou and Stamati plots) and Piteros *et al.* 1990 (Liaga plot) with references. The material from the Christodoulou (1983) and Stamati (1983–1984) plots is presently under study by Françoise Rougemont and Maria Emanuela Alberti respectively.
3 Seal: *CMS* V I B, n° 352, n° inv. 12933; sealing: *CMS* V suppl. 1B, n°353, n° inv. 12933. On sealing practices in Thebes see Aravantinos 1987, 1990 and Piteros *et al.* 1990.
4 See Aravantinos 2005. The material is presently under study by Maria Emanuela Alberti.
5 For the archaeological contexts from Pavloyiannopoulou, Loukou and Pelopidou see Sampson 1985; Aravantinos 1993, 1994, 1995 and 2000 with references. TH Ug: see Aravantinos *et al.* 2002 and Aravantinos 2006. Balance weights: Aravantinos and Alberti 2006.
6 The archives have been published in Aravantinos *et al.* 2001, the pottery in Aravantinos *et al.* 2006 and Andrikou 2006. The Pelopidou textile tools were examined by M. E. Alberti and A. Papadaki.

7 The excavation and the Linear B tablets were published respectively by Th. Spyropoulos and John Chadwick (Chadwick and Spyropoulos 1975). More recently, on the TH Of texts, see Del Freo and Rougemont 2012. Textile tools and archaeological context were reviewed by I. Fappas.

Bibliography

Alberti, M. E., Aravantinos, V. L., Del Freo, M., Fappas, I., Papadaki, A., and Rougemont, F. (2012), Textile production in Mycenaean Thebes. A first overview, in Nosch, M.-L., and Laffineur, R. (eds), *KOSMOS. Jewellery, Adornment and Textiles in the Aegean Bronze Age*, 87–105. Liège. Peeters.

Andrikou, E. (2006) The Late Helladic III pottery, in Aravantinos, V., Godart, L., Sacconi, A. and Vroom, J., *Fouilles de la Cadmée*, 11–180. Pisa. Istituti editoriali e poligrafici internazionali.

Aravantinos, V. (1983) Θήβα. Οδός Οιδίποδος καί πάροδος Π. Οικονόμου (οικόπεδο Ε. καί Μ. Χριστοδούλου), *Αρχαιολογικόν Δελτίον* 38 (1983), B 1, 129–131.

Aravantinos, V. (1987) The Mycenaean inscribed sealings from Thebes: preliminary notes, in Ilievski, P. H. and Crepajac, L. (eds), *Tractata Mycenaea*, 13–27. Skopje. Macedonian Academy of Sciences and Arts.

Aravantinos, V. (1988), Η μυκηναϊκή οχύρωση της Καδμείας. Προκαταρκτική ανακοίνωση, in *Α' Συνέδριο Βοιωτικών Μελετών, Α'*, 113-136. Αθήνα. Επετηρίς της Εταιρείας Βοιωτικών Μελετών.

Aravantinos, V. (1990) The Mycenaean inscribed sealings from Thebes: problems of content and function, in Palaima, T. G. (ed.), *Aegean Seals, Sealings and Administration*, 149–176. Liège. Université de Liège.

Aravantinos, V. (1993) Οδός Πελοπίδου 28 (αρχείο πινακίδων Γραμμικής Β), *Αρχαιολογικόν Δελτίον* 48, B 1, 170–173.

Aravantinos, V. (1994) Οδός Πελοπίδου 28 (αρχείο πινακίδων Γραμμικής Β) καί "Οπλοθήκη" (οικόπεδο Παυλογιαννόπουλου. Οδός Πελοπίδου 28), *Αρχαιολογικόν Δελτίον* 49, B 1, 271–276.

Aravantinos, V. (1995) Οδός Πελοπίδου καί Οδός Πελοπίδου 28, *Αρχαιολογικόν Δελτίον* 50, B 1, 275–281.

Aravantinos, V. (2000) Νέα μυκηναϊκά ελεφαντουργήματα από τη Καδμεία (Θήβα), in *Γ' Συνέδριο Βοιωτικών Μελετών, Θήβα, 4–8 Σεπτεμβρίου 1996 (Επετηρίς της Εταιρείας Βοιωτικών Μελετών)*, Αθήνα 2000, Γ', α', 31–120.

Aravantinos, V. (2005), Οδός Δίρκης 10 (Ο.Τ. 314, οικόπεδο Κ. Κοφίνη – Γ. Σκουρτανιώτη – Δ. Γερμακόπουλου), *Αρχαιολογικόν Δελτίον* 60, 400–401.

Aravantinos, V. (2006) La tavoletta frammentaria TH Ug 43. Un interessante caso di conflitto tra dati di scavo e dati epigrafici, in B. Adembri (ed.), *ΑΕΙΜΝΗΣΤΟΣ. Miscellanea di Studi per Mauro Cristofani*, 25–31. Florence. Centro Di.

Aravantinos, V. and Alberti, M. E. (2006) The balance weights from the Kadmeia, Thebes, in Alberti, M. E., Ascalone, E. and Peyronel, L. (eds), *Weights in Context. Bronze Age Weighing Systems of Eastern Mediterranean. Chronology, Typology, Material and Archaeological Context*, 293–314. Rome. Istituto Italiano di Numismatica.

Aravantinos, V., Godart, L. and Sacconi, A. (2001) *Thèbes. Fouilles de la Cadmée I. Les tablettes en Linéaire B de la odos Pelopidou: édition et commentaire*. Pisa/Rome. Istituti editoriali e poligrafici internazionali.

Aravantinos, V., Godart, L. and Sacconi, A. (2002) *Thèbes. Fouilles de la Cadmée III. Corpus des documents d'archives en Linéaire B de Thèbes* (1–433). Pisa/Rome. Istituti editoriali e poligrafici internazionali.

Aravantinos, V., Godart, L., Sacconi, A. and Vroom, J. (2006) *Thèbes. Fouilles de la Cadmée II.2. Les tablettes en Linéaire B de la Odos Pelopidou: Le contexte archéologique; La céramique de la Odos Pelopidou et la chronologie du Linéaire B*. Pisa/Rome. Istituti editoriali e poligrafici internazionali.

Chadwick, J. and Spyropoulos, T. (1975) *The Thebes Tablets II*. Salamanca. Universidad de Salamanca.

Del Freo, M. and Rougemont, F. (2012) Observations sur la série Of de Thèbes, *Studi Micenei ed Egeo-Anatolici*, 54, 263–280.

Fappas, I. (2010), Έλαιον ευώδες, τεθυωμένον: Τα αρωματικά έλαια και οι πρακτικές χρήσης τους στη Μυκηναϊκή Ελλάδα και την αρχαία Εγγύς Ανατολή (14ος–13ος αι. π.Χ.) (*Well-scented, perfume oil: Perfumed oils and practices of use in Mycenaean Greece and the ancient Near East (14th–13th cent. BC)*. Chania. Ιστορική, Λαογραφική και Αρχαιολογική Εταιρεία Κρήτης.

Foster, E. (1977) An administrative department at Knossos concerned with perfumery and offerings, *Minos* XVI.1–2, 19–51.

Piteros, C., Olivier, J. P. and Melena, J. L. (1990) Les inscriptions en Linéaire B des nodules de Thèbes (1982): la fouille, les documents, les possibilités d'interprétation, *Bulletin de correspondance hellénique*, 114, 103–184.

Sampson, A. (1985) La destruction d'un atelier palatial mycénien à Thebes, *Bulletin de correspondance hellénique*, 109, 21–29.

Shelmerdine, C. (1995) Shining and fragrant cloth in Homeric epic, in Carter, J. P. and Morris, S. P. (eds), *The Ages of Homer. A Tribute to Emily Townsend Vermeule*, 99–107. Austin. University of Texas Press.

Shelmerdine, C. (1997) Workshops and record keeping in the Mycenean world, in Laffineur, R. and Betancourt, P. (eds), *TEXNH. Craftsmen, Craftswomen and Craftsmanship in the Aegean Bronze Age*, 388–396. Liège. Université de Liège.

CHAPTER 6.11

Textile tools from Archontiko, northern Greece

Evi Papadopoulou, Eva Andersson Strand, Marie-Louise Nosch and Joanne Cutler

Evi Papadopoulou, Eva Andersson Strand, Marie-Louise Nosch and Joanne Cutler

Fig. 6.11.1. House A (from west). Detail of its interior. A group of clay storage bins and some thermal structures characterise its fixed equipment (photo: Papanthimou and Pilali 2003, 26–27).

Archontiko is a tell settlement, situated in northern Greece. Systematic excavation at the site has brought to light three successive building horizons that belong to the Early Bronze Age period. The earliest one, Phase IV, is dated to 2135–2020 BC and has yielded seven oblong post-framed houses that were destroyed by a fire incident which produced rich archaeological deposits often containing contexts of closed finds (Papaefthymiou-Papanthimou *et al.* 2003; Papadopoulou *et al.* 2010; Papanthimou and Papadopoulou in press). House interiors were equipped with various types of clay features, namely storage bins and thermal structures, that were preserved in good condition (Papaefthymiou *et al.* 2007). Phase IV strata were uncovered over an area of 220 m^2 and yielded 160 artifacts related to textile production. Spindle whorls, loom weights and rounded sherds constitute the basic textile tool categories.

The tools recorded in the TTTC database originate from a Phase IV building, House A, and constitute a closed assemblage representative of domestic textile production at EBA Archontiko (Fig. 6.11.1)

Although only partially excavated, House A yielded a total of 33 textile tools, namely 27 loom weights and six spindle whorls that were collected from a surface area of *c.* 23 m^2 (Fig. 6.11.2).

Spindle whorls and spinning

The six recorded spindle whorls from House A (four conical, one flattened biconical and one cylindrical) vary in weight from 25 g to 68 g, indicating that the Archontiko spinners could have spun different types of yarn by choosing different whorls (Figs. 6.11.3 and 6.11.4). The yarn, according to the results of the spinning tests, would generally be quite thick, however (see chapters 2 and 4.1).

Loom weights and weaving

Fig. 6.11.2. Textile tools from House A, EBA, Phase IV, by type and context.

Twenty-six of the recorded loom weights from House A are pyramidal truncated in shape and are made of clay (17 are made of fired clay, five of unfired clay and four are unspecified) (Fig.

6.11.5). There is, however, one example that is a naturally perforated irregular pebble. Twenty-three of the loom weights had a recordable weight and thickness; their weight varies from 154 g to 1179 g and their thickness varies from 4.1 cm to 8.8 cm (Fig. 6.11.6).

Twelve loom weights (11 clay weights and the naturally perforated pebble) were found near a clay storage bin at the eastern end of the house (Trench ID-Y). The weight of the clay loom weights varies from 220 g to 337 g and the thickness from 4.1 cm to 5.8 cm (Fig. 6.11.4) These loom weights could all be used in the same setup, with thread needing *c.* 15–20 g tension. Used in a tabby weave with thread requiring *c.* 15 g tension, the resulting fabric would have *c.* 6–9 warp threads per centimetre; with thread needing *c.* 20 g tension, the thread count would be *c.* 4–7 threads per centimetre (Fig. 6.11.7). However, in a balanced weave the finished textile would have been open, and it is therefore likely that the textile would have been weft faced. These loom weights could also have been used for producing different types of twills, with a resulting denser fabric (approximately double the thread count of a tabby weave). Even this fabric would have been quite open if balanced, and it is likely that the textile would have been slightly weft faced. If this group of loom weights was used in the same tabby setup, with six loom weights in the front row and six loom weights in the back row, the width of the

	Spindle whorl	Loom weight	Total
Trench IG, House A	4	8	12
Trench IG-ID, House A		1	1
Trench IG-P, House A	2	2	4
Trench ID, House A		4	4
Trench ID-Y, House A		12	12
Total	6	27	33

Fig. 6.11.3. Spindle whorls, EBA, Phase IV, House A (photo: courtesy of E. Papadopoulou).

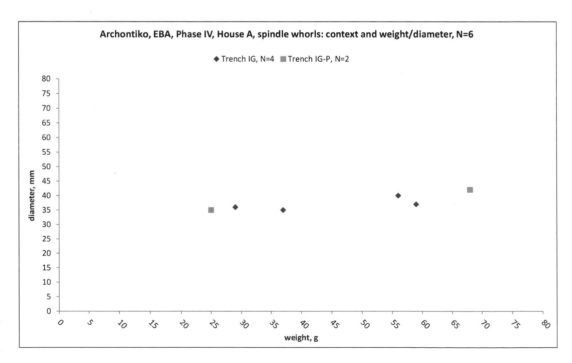

Fig. 6.11.4. Spindle whorls, EBA, Phase IV, House A: context and weight/diameter.

fabric would have been *c*. 26.5 cm, which has to be considered as a narrow fabric. If producing a twill fabric with four rows of loom weights, the width would be only *c*. 13.2 cm.

A group of eight loom weights was recovered near the centre of the house (Trench IG). They have a heavier weight and larger thickness than the loom weights from Trench ID-Y (Fig. 6.11.6). Seven of the loom weights vary in weight from 468 g to 600 g and have a thickness of 5.5–6.3 cm. The eighth loom weight weighs 1134 g and is 8.3 cm thick, and would not have functioned optimally with the other weights in the same loom setup. The seven loom weights would all function with thread needing *c*. 20 g to 50 g tension (Fig. 6.11.8). In a tabby weave with thread requiring *c*. 20 g tension, the warp thread count would be *c*. 8–11 threads per centimetre, whereas with thread needing *c*. 50 g tension the thread count would be *c*. 3–4 threads per centimetre (in a twill the thread count would be approximately double). In both a tabby and a twill weave, the fabrics could have been quite balanced. The total thickness of the loom weights is 41.3 cm. In a tabby setup with eight loom weights with a similar weight and thickness (four in the front row and four in the back row), the width of the fabric would be a minimum of 23.6 cm, which has to be considered as a narrow fabric. The heavier loom weight weighing 1134 g could only function with yarn needing *c*. 40 g tension

or more; the four loom weights from Trench ID, located at the east part of the house would also only work well with thread requiring *c*. 40 g tension or more.

Summary

The number of tools from Archontiko presented in this chapter is small, but the 33 objects recorded reveal a considerable diversity in the textile production. The same picture also emerges from the study of the textile toolkits

Fig. 6.11.5. Pyramidal loom weights, EBA, Phase IV, House A (Trench ID-Y) (photo: courtesy of E. Papadopoulou).

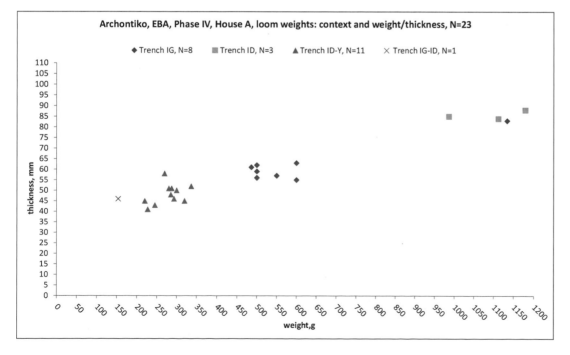

Fig. 6.11.6. Loom weights, EBA, Phase IV, House A: context and weight/thickness.

Warp thr/cm	10 g N=9	15 g, N=11	20 g, N=11	25 g, N=9	30 g, N=6	35 g, N=1
3 thr						
4 thr				1	3	5	1
5 thr				4	5	1	
6 thr			1	3	1		
7 thr			5	3			
8 thr			3				
9 thr	1	2					
10 thr	1						
11 thr	3						
12 thr	3						
13 thr	1						

Warp thr/cm	20 g, N=7	25 g, N=7	30 g, N=7	35 g, N=7	40 g, N=7	45 g, N=7	50 g, N=7	55 g, N=2	60 g, N=2
3 thr							3		1
4 thr				3	6	4	2	1	
5 thr			2	5	4	1			
6 thr		2	4	2					
7 thr		2	1						
8 thr	3	2							
9 thr	1	1							
10 thr	2								
11 thr	1								

recovered from other contemporaneous houses belonging to Phase IV as well as from the two successive EBA Phases II and III (Papadopoulou 2012; 2002, unpublished). The yarns produced with the spindle whorls would have been suitable for several types of fabrics, as suggested by the analyses of the loom weights.

For example, the thread spun with the whorls weighing 55 g or more would have probably functioned very well in the weaves with the heavy loom weights weighing more than 900 g. The result would have been a coarse textile with few but thick threads per centimetre. The spindle whorls weighing between 25–40 g would have been optimal for producing yarn that needed *c.* 20 g tension or more on the loom.

The majority of the tools are considered to have been made in a good production quality. The majority of the loom weights (except for the stone weight) are of the same type regarding shape. As far as the material and the surface treatment there is some diversity, since the light group consists of fired and polished weights, whereas the other two categories are mainly made of unfired clay and are burnished. Four of the six spindle whorls were of the same type and shape. This fact does not seem coincidental, and suggests considerable knowledge of how to produce textiles in an optimal way.

The textile production in Archontiko appears to have been well developed. The spinners and weavers knew how different types of tools affected the final products and also the tools themselves were well made. The analysis of the spindle whorls demonstrates that the spinners spun different types of yarn; the variation within the loom weights and the variation within the spindle whorls indicate that the people of Archontiko produced many different types of textiles with both thin and thick threads and in balanced, open and/or weft faced weaves.

Bibliography

Papadopoulou, E. (2002, unpublished) *Clay Small Finds from Archontiko Giannitson*. Master thesis, Aristotle University of Thessaloniki.

Papadopoulou, E. (2012) Textile technology in northern Greece: evidence for a domestic craft industry from Early Bronze Age Archontiko, in Nosch, M.-L. and Laffineur, R. (eds), *KOSMOS. Jewellery, Adornment and Textiles in the Aegean Bronze Age*, 57–63. Liège. Université de Liège.

Papadopoulou, E., Papanthimou, A. and Maniatis, Y. (2010) Issues of spatial organization at the end of the Early Bronze Age: the new evidence from Archontiko Giannitson, *Το Αρχαιολογικό Έργο στη Μακεδονία και Θράκη, 21 (2007)*, 77–82.

Papaefthymiou-Papanthimou, A., Pilali-Papasteriou, A., Giagoulis, T., Basogianni, D., Papadopoulou, E., Tsagaraki, E. and Fappas, I. (2003) Early Bronze Age houses and 'households' at Archontiko Giannitson, *Το Αρχαιολογικό Έργο στη Μακεδονία και Θράκη, 15 (2001)*, 461–470.

Papaefthymiou, A., Pilali, A. and Papadopoulou, E. (2007) Les installations culinaires dans un village du Bronze Ancien en Grèce du nord: Archontiko Giannitsa, in Mee, C. and Renard, J. (eds), *Cooking Up the Past: Food and Culinary Practices in the Neolithic and Bronze Age Aegean*, 136–147. Oxford. Oxbow Books.

Papanthimou, A. and Papadopoulou, E. (in press) The Early Bronze Age in Macedonia: the evidence from Archontiko Giannitson, in Doumas, C. G., Giannikouri, A. and Kouka, O. (eds), *The Aegean Early Bronze Age: New Evidence*. Athens. Ministry of Culture and Archaeological Institute of Aegean Studies.

Papanthimou, K. and Pilali, A. (2003) *The Prehistoric Settlement at Archontiko Giannitson*. Giannitsa. Prefecture of Giannitsa.

CHAPTER 6.12

Textile tools from Sitagroi, northern Greece

Ernestine S. Elster, Eva Andersson Strand, Marie-Louise Nosch and Joanne Cutler

Sitagroi is a prehistoric settlement mound located on the Drama plain 25 km inland from the north Aegean Sea. Its 10.5 m of occupational debris appears as a gentle rise above the level of the plain (Renfrew *et al.* 1986, map 1.3). The mound (Fig. 6.12.1) was excavated from 1969 to 1970 under the joint direction of Colin Renfrew and the late Marija Gimbutas (UCLA) with the goal of exploring an Aegean region midway between Europe and the Near East, virtually *terra incognita* at that time. It is no longer unknown (Renfrew and Hardy 2003, 471, fig. 13.1; Treuil *et al.* 1992). The excavations yielded whorls, weights, anchors, hooks, spools, bone tools, and mat and cloth impressions (Renfrew *et al.* 1986; Elster 2003, 229–282; Elster and Renfrew 2003).

Twenty-nine calibrated radiocarbon dates from the site (Renfrew 1986b, 173, table 7.3) provided a framework for *c.* three millennia of occupation and also allowed for a re-evaluation of the then accepted Early Bronze Age chronology and archaeological cultures *vis-à-vis* the Aegean and the Balkans (Renfrew 1986a, 3–6). The millennia at Sitagroi were divided into five phases based on the calibrated radiocarbon determinations and a statistical analysis of changes in pottery from a sounding (5.0 × 5.0 m) in excavation Square "ZA" (see

Fig. 6.12.1) which reached sterile earth at a depth of 10.5 m (Renfrew 1986b, 158, fig. 7.9; 165, 166, fig. 7.16).

Pottery comparanda (Keighley 1986, 363–369) for Sitagroi Phase I (5500–5200 BC) and Phase II (5200–4600 BC) refer to the shapes and many styles of the prehistoric Vinča culture of the former Republic of Yugoslavia, and from the Middle Neolithic Greek Thessalian painted wares, as well as prehistoric Bulgarian sites such as Slatino (Chohadziev 2007) and Kovaçevo (Demoule and Lichardus-Itten 1994). A fair degree of weaving skill is illustrated by a tabby weave textile impression on a clay sherd recovered in a clear Phase I context (Elster 2003, 246, fig. 6.31a). There is no hiatus in occupation between Phases I and II; both time periods are referred to as Middle Neolithic.

The Chalcolithic Phase III (4600–3500 BC), considered a flourishing period, is defined by flamboyantly shaped and decorated pottery painted in silvery graphite and/or in red paint on a black burnished surface, surely a prestigious commodity. This pottery is easily comparable to graphite painted pottery of the Gumelnitsa culture of Romania (Evans 1986, 406–410). Furthermore, Phase III yielded considerable evidence for specialised

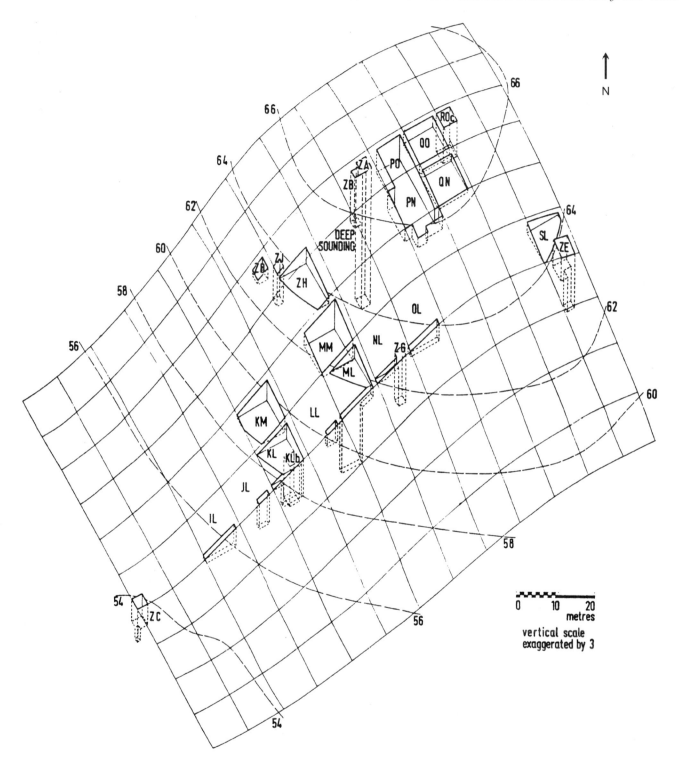

Fig. 6.12.1. An axonometric view of the excavation with squares delineated (drawing: Renfrew et al. 1986a, 18, fig. 2.2).

crafters – potters, spinners, weavers – and their likely interaction with traders, middlemen, and travellers who introduced the various exotic raw materials utilized at Sitagroi (Elster 2007, 193–201). A particular Phase III stylistic innovation was the intentional addition of decorative incisions on the shallow faces of rather flat/discoid whorls (Fig. 6.12.2, d–g), discussed further below.

Three phases divide the millennia of the Early Bronze Age: Phase IV, 3500–3100 BC; Phase Va, 3100–2700 BC; and Phase

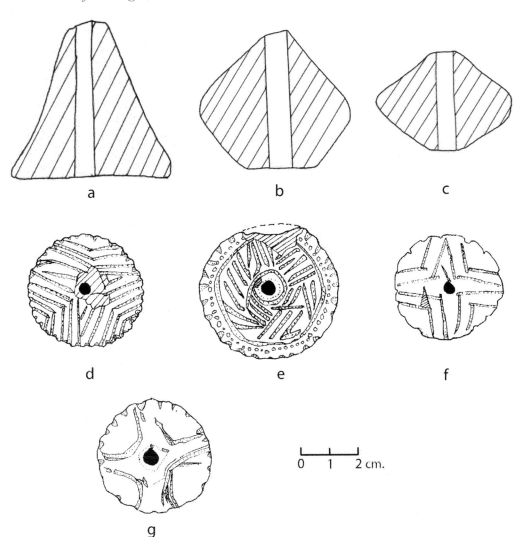

Fig. 6.12.2. Whorl forms: conical, a (Elster 2003, 232, fig. 6.3:a); biconical, b (Elster 2003, 232, fig. 6.2:a), c (Elster 2003, 232, fig. 6.1:a); Phase III incised whorls: shallow/conical, d (Elster 2003, 235, fig. 6.6:d), e (Elster 2003, 237, fig. 6.11:a), f (Elster 2003, 235, fig. 6.6:a); flattened/discoidal, g (Elster 2003, 235, fig. 6.7:b).

Vb, 2700–2200 BC. They reflect a variety of changes from the Chalcolithic in terms of subsistence base and material culture: pottery shapes and decoration, craft, elite, prestigious and/or imported goods including raw materials, and artefacts suggesting symbolic roles (Sherratt 1986).

A total of 579 textile tools from Sitagroi are recorded in the database, of which 542 are from secure Phase III–V contexts (Fig. 6.12.3).

Spindle whorls and spinning

The majority of the textile tools (363) are spindle whorls. Of these, 265 are Early Bronze Age in date. A further 98 whorls are from Chalcolithic Phase III contexts. Although the Bronze Age is the focus of this volume, the Chalcolithic whorls are included in the following discussion, since they provide a valuable comparison with the Phase IV and V whorls.

Conical whorls are the dominant type in Phases III and IV, whereas in Phase V biconical whorls are the most frequent shape (Fig. 6.12.4).

One hundred and sixty-one of the whorls had a recorded weight and thickness (Fig. 6.12.5). The weight of the spindle whorls varies from 8 g to 135 g and the diameter varies from 2.4 cm to 6.1 cm. This indicates that several types of yarn, from very thin to very thick, were produced at Sitagroi. There is no clear relation between spindle whorl type and weight; however, the conical whorls and "other types" display greater variation in diameter than the biconical spindle whorls.

The variation in whorl weight is considerably wider during Phase V, indicating the production of a greater range of different types of thread, with an emphasis on thicker thread. However, it should be noted that spindle whorls with a recorded weight and thickness are less numerous during Phases III and IV (34 and 15 objects respectively) compared to Phase V (112 objects). Additionally, the diameter of the whorl in relation to the whorl's weight is in general larger in Phases III and IV than in Phase V (Fig. 6.12.6). This could of course be due to the change in shape of the whorls, but this change could also affect the outcome with regard to the spun yarn. The conical whorls are very suitable for spinning hard spun threads while the thread spun with the biconical spindle whorls with the same weight would be more loosely spun. The Sitagroi spinners were therefore producing a harder spun yarn in Phases III and IV than in Phase V. The change to more loosely spun thread could be due to a change in the type of fibres being spun. There is evidence for wool (or at least sheep) during all three phases (Bökönyi 1986, 69). The indications of flax and other plant fibres are rare, but are present (Elster 2003, 230). This indicates that the whorls from Sitagroi could have been used for spinning both wool and plant fibres. The analysis of the whorls demonstrates that the spinners at Sitagroi were already spinning different types of thread, from very thin to very thick, in the Chalcolithic period. The yarn spun with the heaviest whorls would have been very thick and would therefore have been used for coarser textiles (the heavier whorls could also have been used for plying).

The incised whorls

Incised whorls are especially associated with Chalcolithic Phase III (Elster 2003, 240, table 6.3). A total of 50 are recorded and 41 of these were recovered from Phase III contexts. These whorls were either flat/discoid or shallow conical (Elster 2003, 237, 238), shapes which provide a "face" for the incisions, more so than the biconical form (Fig. 6.12.2, d–g). An incised whorl reflects the investment of extra thought, effort and time, but is no more effective as a tool than an unadorned but burnished example. The incised and undecorated whorls were both produced and used concurrently along with a few pottery sherds recycled into whorls; some of the latter had painted designs of woven patterns (Elster 2003, 238, fig. 16.b). The incisions on the whorl face are not only decorative, but perhaps may convey a self-conscious and symbolic message of pride; pride in the tool which a skillful spinner employs to practise his/her craft. This suggests the importance of the craft in Phase III when trade/exchange was at its height, with textile production as one element in this system, based on the following evidence (Elster 2004, 81–91):

- The pattern of sheep husbandry changes from 50/50 young and adult to a majority of adult animals, which produce more wool (Bökönyi 1986, 80).
- Patterns depicting woven goods are painted in graphite on highly burnished, large vessels (Evans 1986, 417, figs. 12.4, 12.6:2) which require pyrotechnical skill in firing (Gardner 1979, 18–23) thus connecting two crafters: potters and weavers.
- Imported raw materials: (a) stone for polished edge tools – axes, adzes, chisels from sources 30–100 km away (Dixon 2003, 133); (b) *spondylus gaederopus* from the Aegean (25 km away) for bracelets and pendants (Nikolaidou 2003, 331); (c) honey-brown flint from northeast Bulgaria (*c.* 300 km away) for chipped stone tools.
- Copper objects, few in number (sources of copper are not yet clearly identified; Renfrew and Slater 2003, 301), also a small gold ring: exotica perhaps traded as ores and/or small artefacts.

The crafts of spinning and weaving are likely to have become an important link in the trading or exchange pattern of this village during Chalcolithic Phase III. Based on the artefacts, the data indicate that the spinners were able to skillfully produce different types of yarn and thus to vary the types of textiles produced. By the Early Bronze Age, new societal forces

Fig. 6.12.3. Textile tools from securely dated Phase III–V contexts, by type and date.

	Spindle whorl	Loom weight	Spool	Pointed bone tool	Hook	Anchor	Total
Phase III, Chalcolithic	98	4					102
Phase IV, EH I	67	17	2	30			116
Phase V, EH II	198	28	31	20	26	21	324
Total	363	49	33	50	26	21	542

	Phase III, Chalcolithic	Phase IV, EH I	Phase V, EH II	Total
Biconical	6	13	118	137
Concave conical	1	1		2
Conical	49	40	27	116
Convex		9		9
Convex?			6	6
Cylindrical			1	1
Discord	33		2	35
Other	8	4	34	46
Spherical	1		9	10
Not available			1	1
Total	98	67	198	363

Fig. 6.12.4. Spindle whorls, Phases III–V, by type and date.

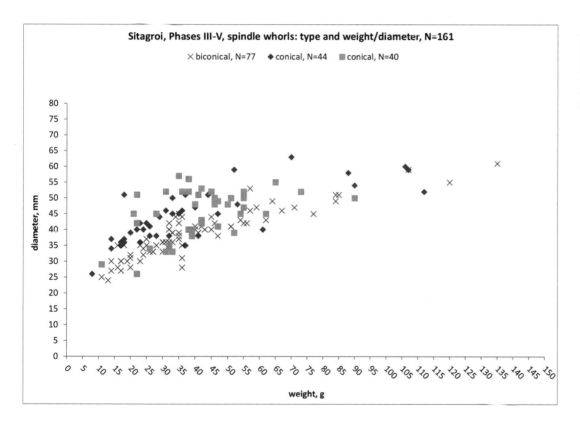

Fig. 6.12.5. Spindle whorls, Phases III–V: type and weight/diameter. Please note that some markers represent more than one spindle whorl.

were at play; the grape had been domesticated, drinking cups appear in the various Early Bronze Age levels and prestige goods changed (for example *spondylus* recovery diminished greatly). Spinning and weaving continued to be very important and necessary, but perhaps the emphasis on the products of these crafters was not the same as during the Chalcolithic when spinning tools were purposely decorated, suggesting significance beyond the simple utilitarian level.

Undecorated spindle whorls have been recovered from Neolithic to Early Bronze Age sites all over Greece and beyond and widely published: for example, from northern Greece (Hochstetter 1987; Aslanis 1985; Carington Smith 1977, 2000), Thessaly (Weisshaar 1989; Gimbutas *et al.* 1989), Bulgaria (Hiller and Nikolov 1997), and the former Republic of Yugoslavia (McPherron and Srejovic 1988; Tringham and Krstic 1990). But incised whorls are a particular find from sites in the Drama

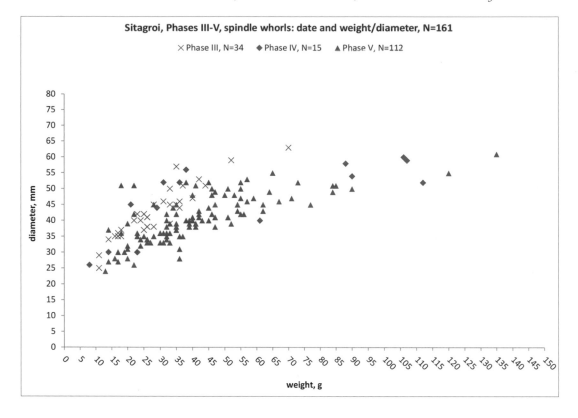

Plain such as Dikili Tash (Treuil *et al.* 1992, 124–130, plates 201 b–d, f; 202 a–f), Dhimitra (Grammenos 1997, 36:4) and Paradeisos (Hellström 1987, 88, fig. 48:21),[1] and also in southwest Bulgaria (*e.g.* Chohadzhiev 2006, 141, fig. 60:2; Chohadziev 2007). A study of the incisions suggests a coherent vocabulary or "symbolary" of radiating lines, forming sets of angles dividing the face into zones (Fig. 6.12.2, d, f), curving lines nested or dividing the face into registers (Fig. 6.12.2, g), circling frames around the yarn hole or the whorl edge (Fig. 6.12.2, e). However, whether decorated or not, the hundreds of Sitagroi whorls underscore a real investment of human energy in spinning different types of yarn and thread and producing woven products of utility and value. Along with other unidentified goods, the textiles were likely exchanged, traded, or gifted for some of the imports outlined above.

Loom weights and weaving

Of the 82 loom weights recorded in the database (49 loom weights and 33 spools), only four date to Chalcolithic Phase III (not discussed here). The Early Bronze Age Phase IV and V loom weights include a range of types (Fig. 6.12.7).

Weight and thickness measurements were only available for 28 of the loom weights. It is therefore not possible to provide a comprehensive interpretation of the overall textile production at Sitagroi during Phases IV and V, but it is possible to give an indication of what types of fabric may have been produced with the preserved tools.

Six of the Phase IV loom weights, all of them long cylinders in shape, had a recorded weight and thickness. They vary in weight from 600 g to 1170 g, with a thickness varying from 6.2–9.8 cm. All of these loom weights would be suitable for producing coarser fabrics with thick to very thick thread needing *c.* 40–60 g tension. With thick thread requiring *c.* 40 g tension, a tabby textile would have *c.* 5–6 warp threads per cm. With very thick, *c.* 60 g tension thread, the resulting textile would have *c.* 3–4 warp threads per cm. These fabrics could be balanced textiles, with approximately the same number of warp and weft threads per cm.

Nineteen of the Phase V loom weights, all of them spools, had a recorded weight and thickness. They vary in weight from 21 g to 68 g and in thickness from 2.1 cm to 3.9 cm (Fig. 6.12.8).

Such light spools cannot be considered functional as loom weights on a warp-weighted loom. The spools weighing less than 50 g could only be used with thread needing less than *c.* 5 g tension, or with *c.* 5 g tension thread with fewer than 10 threads attached to them. Therefore, the spools are not particularly suitable as loom weights (see chapter 4.1). However, the analysis of the spools supports an earlier suggestion (Elster 2003, 239) that they would be very useful as weights for tablet weaving, where one adds two to four threads per tablet, or for other types of band weaving and braiding (Gleba 2008). They would also be very useful when setting up a warp on a loom (see chapter 4.1)

The pyramidal loom weights from Phase V vary considerably in size (Elster 2003, 241, fig. 6.18 and plates 6.11 and 6.12), suggesting that they could have been used to produce a variety of fabrics. The two examples recovered from the Bin Complex, with incomplete weights of 1510 g and 1285 g, would be suitable for the production of coarser textiles with very thick threads.

Anchors and hooks

It has previously been suggested (Elster 2003, 242–245) that the anchors and hooks recovered from the site may have functioned as loom weights. No weights for these objects are recorded in the database, but their thickness (hooks 0.8–2.1 cm and anchors 1.4–2.1 cm) indicates that, if they are not too light, it is possible that they may have functioned as loom weights. Their thickness also suggests that any fabrics woven with them are likely to have been quite dense.

Other textile tools

Thirty pointed bone tools from Phase IV and 20 from Phase V are recorded in the database. These could have been used as pin beaters – a multifunctional weaving tool, used to distribute the weft thread in the weave, for example. Some of these tools, made from rib bones, could have been used as weft beaters for band weaving. These types of tools are suitable for use in association with different types of looms, both the warp-weighted loom and the two-beam vertical loom.

The following discussion of textile tools in context (Elster 2003, 229–282) will focus on Square ROc, and tools from three building episodes of the Early Bronze Age (Renfrew 1986c, 184–203).

Contexts

Square ROc

The excavation of Square ROc provided a long EBA stratigraphy with the exposure of numerous contiguous Phase IV (ROc 73–49), Phase Va (ROc 49–33), early Phase Vb (ROc 30–13), and later Phase Vb (ROc 12–2) layers. Phase IV yielded several loom weights in a context which is described as "…part of a destruction deposit from a burned house…" (Renfrew 1986c, 205). It seems that these weights were part of a warp-weighted loom and were found in the context in which they fell as the house burned (Fig. 6.12.9). Although ROc yielded some discontinuous evidence of house walls (Renfrew 1986c, 203–204), its importance was in the continuous sequence of Early Bronze Age Phase IV through Vb living floors upon which almost two dozen textile tools were recovered (though not on every floor). Among other finds, hook and anchor fragments first appear in ROc during Phase Va.

The Early Bronze Age Building Episodes

The deep sounding "ZA" indicated that the mound (Fig. 6.12.1) was built up as a proverbial "layer cake" and the final Early Bronze Age structures were indeed exposed at the summit of the mound. Over the three seasons of excavation, a large exposure (20 × 20 m) was opened in Squares PO, PN, QO, and QN which revealed three successive building episodes in stratigraphic sequence: late Phase Vb: "Bin Complex", early Phase Vb "Long House", and Phase Va "Burnt House"; their orientations were similar and much of the Long House was directly under the Bin Complex. The Burnt House was on levels lower than the Long House, but not directly underneath.

Phase IV, EH I	Conical	1
	Cylindrical long	11
	Discord	3
	Other	2
	Spool	2
	Total	**19**
Phase V, EH II	Cylindrical long	1
	Discord	2
	Other	2
	Pyramidal	21
	Spool	31
	Torus	2
	Total	**59**

Fig. 6.12.7. Loom weights, Phases IV and V, by type.

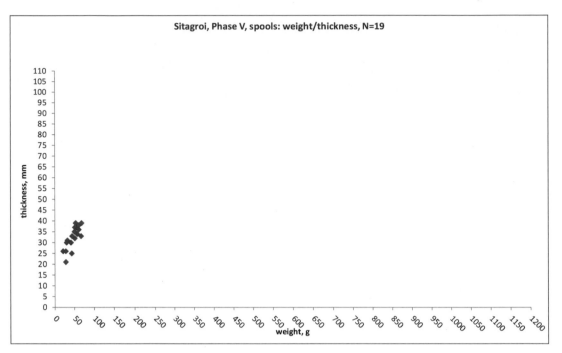

The Burnt House

Excavation of the Burnt House revealed the complete plan and remaining contents of a house 5.0 × 3.5 m (Renfrew 1970, 131–134; 1986c, 190–203; Elster 1997, 19–35, pl. II–VIII) including seven spindle whorls (Elster 2003, 249, fig. 6.1.c and pl. 6.6.a). These are all biconical and weigh between 57 g and 84 g; they would therefore be optimal for spinning thick to very thick thread. Two whorls were broken and one of these (SF 4430) exhibited incisions angled across the shoulder which provided no extra utility and thus must be considered a purely decorative addition.

The Long House

Above the Burnt House, a series of postholes outlined an early Phase Vb structure *c*. 15 × 5 m. Textile tools recovered included 22 whorls, two fragmentary pyramidal weights, five spools, three anchor fragments, and five worked bone tools. The whorl shapes vary: 13 are biconical, four are flat/discoid, two are conical and three are spherical. One conical form weighs 74 g. The three spherical forms weigh 22 g, 32 g and 47 g. Eight other whorls with a complete/estimated weight weigh 31–41 g. The whorls would therefore be suitable for spinning a variety of thread types, ranging from medium to thick, but none of them would be optimal for producing thin

thread. The weights of four of the five spools range between 12 g and 68 g; the fifth was not weighed.

No cloth or mat impressions were found, and there was a paucity of pottery. However, one remarkable shaft-holed stone axe was recovered: a "sceptre", its butt carved in the shape of and incised with the features of a lion or feline (Elster 2003, 191, pl. 5.42; Renfrew 1986c, 189, pl. XXV), perhaps representing the power held by the household or its chief (Gimbutas 1986, 264).

The Bin Complex

Above the Long House, excavators uncovered an area close to the surface of the mound outlined by post holes, with numerous large bins or pits sunk into the ground. It has been interpreted as a courtyard (Renfrew 1986c, 185, 187–188), exceedingly rich in all types of artefacts, including 70 spindle whorls, nine loom weights (of which two pyramidal shapes weigh 1285 g and 1510 g), nine spools (one fragmentary, the rest weighing 30–61 g) and 16 hook and anchor fragments. The weights of the whorls range widely: 14 g to 90 g, but the main cluster consists of whorls weighing between 25 and 45 g, with one-third of these being biconical in shape. The whorls would be suitable for the production of a range of thread types, varying from thin to very thick.

Fig. 6.12.9. Exposure of loom weights and a bowl from Square ROc, level 73, EBA IV (photo: Renfrew 1986c, 205, pl. XXXIV: 1).

Summary

The analysis of the spindle whorls suggests a production of many different types of yarn, from thin to very thick. During Phase V the results indicate a larger range of different types of thread, with an emphasis on thicker threads. It has also been noted that the majority of the Phase IV spindle whorls in general have a larger diameter in relation to the weight than the whorls from Phase V. This could indicate a change in fibre material, or just a change from the use of a hard spun to a more loosely spun yarn.

Only a limited analysis of the loom weights and weaving has been possible, and the results cannot therefore be considered as representative. The cylindrical weights from Phase IV indicate the production of coarser textiles, with thick thread needing c. 40–60 g tension. The size range of the pyramidal weights from Phase V suggests that a variety of textiles were being made, with a range of thread types. If the anchors and hooks present in Phase V were used as loom weights, their thickness additionally suggests the production of some relatively dense fabrics.

Mat and textile impressions from the site (Elster 2003, 246–247) suggest a well developed textile production at Sitagroi and the recorded tools support this. Unfortunately, there are no cloth impressions from Phase IV or V, but the elaborate mat techniques clearly indicate that the textile producers at Sitagroi had a good knowledge of fibres and textile techniques. The textile impression dated to Phase I (Elster 2003, 246, fig. 6.31a) demonstrates a long textile tradition at the site.

Note

1 But see also the large assemblage from Early Bronze Age Troy (Balfanz 1995, 117–144).

Bibliography

Aslanis, I. (1985) *Kastanas. Die Frühbronzezeitlichen Funde und Befunde*. Berlin. Wissenschaftsverlag Volker Spiess.

Balfanz, K. (1995) Bronzezeitliche Spinnwirtel aus Troja, *Studia Troica*, 5, 117–144.

Bökönyi, S. (1986) Faunal remains, in Renfrew, C., Gimbutas, M. and Elster, E. S. (eds), *Excavations at Sitagroi: A Prehistoric Village in Northeast Greece*. 1, 61–132. Los Angeles. Institute of Archaeology, UCLA.

Carington Smith, J. (1977) Cloth and mat impressions, in Coleman, J. E. (ed.), *Keos I. Kephala, a Late Neolithic Settlement and Cemetery*, 114–125. Princeton. American School of Classical Studies.

Carington Smith, J. (2000) The spinning and weaving implements, in Ridley, C., Wardle, K. A. and Mould, C. A. (eds), *Servia I. Anglo-Hellenic Rescue Excavations 1971–73*. 207–263. London. British School at Athens.

Chohadzhiev, S. (2006) *Slatino Prehistoric Settlements*. 2nd edition. Veliko Tarnovo. Faber.

Chohadzhiev, S. (2007) *Neolithic and Chalcolithic Cultures in the Struma River Basin*. Veliko Tarnovo. Faber.

Demoule, J.-P. and Lichardus-Itten, M. (1994) Rapport préliminaire (campagnes 1986–1993), *Bulletin de correspondance hellénique*, 118 (2), 561–618.

Dixon, J. (2003) Lithic petrology, in Elster, E. S. and Renfrew, C. (eds), *Prehistoric Sitagroi: Excavations in Northeast Greece, 1968–1970. 2. The Final Report*, 133–147. Los Angeles. Institute of Archaeology, UCLA.

Elster, E. S. (1997) Construction and use of the Early Bronze Age Burnt House at Sitagroi: craft and technology, in Laffineur, R. and Betancourt, P. (eds), *TEXNH. Craftsmen, Craftswomen and Craftsmanship in the Aegean Bronze Age*, 19–35. Liège. Université de Liège.

Elster, E. S. (2003) Tools and the spinner, weaver and mat maker, in Elster, E. S. and Renfrew, C. (eds), *Prehistoric Sitagroi: Excavations in Northeast Greece, 1968–1970. 2. The Final Report*, 229–251, 258–282. Los Angeles. Institute of Archaeology, UCLA.

Elster, E. S. (2004) Figuring out social archaeology in Sitagroi, in Cherry, J. F., Scarre, C. and Shennan, S. (eds), *Explaining Social Change: Studies in Honour of Colin Renfrew*, 81–91. Cambridge. McDonald Institute for Archaeological Research, University of Cambridge.

Elster, E. S. (2007) Odysseus before Homer: trade, travel and adventure in Prehistoric Greece, in Morris, S. P. and Laffineur, R. (eds), *EPOS: Reconsidering Greek Epic and Aegean Bronze Age Archaeology*, 193–201. Liège. Université de Liège.

Elster, E. S. and Renfrew, C. (eds) (2003) *Prehistoric Sitagroi: Excavations in Northeast Greece, 1968–1970. 2. The Final Report*. Los Angeles. Institute of Archaeology, UCLA.

Evans, R. (1986) The pottery of Phase III, in Renfrew, C., Gimbutas, M. and Elster, E. S. (eds), *Excavations at Sitagroi: A Prehistoric Village in Northeast Greece*. 1, 393–428. Los Angeles. Institute of Archaeology, UCLA.

Gardner, E. J. (1979) Graphic painted pottery, *Archaeology*, 32 (4), 18–23.

Gimbutas, M. (1986) Mythical imagery of the Sitagroi society, in Renfrew, C., Gimbutas, M. and Elster, E. S. (eds), *Excavations at Sitagroi: A Prehistoric Village in Northeast Greece*. 1, 225–301. Los Angeles. Institute of Archaeology, UCLA.

Gimbutas, M., Shimabuku, D. M. and Winn, S. M. M. (1989) *Achilleion: a Neolithic Settlement in Thessaly, Greece, 6400–5600 BC*. Los Angeles. Institute of Archaeology, UCLA.

Gleba, M. (2008) *Textile Production in Pre-Roman Italy*. Ancient Textiles Series 4. Oxford. Oxbow Books.

Grammenos, D. V. (1997) *Neolithiki Makedonia*. Athens. Ekdosi tou Tameio Archaiologikon Poron kai Apallotrioseon.

Hellström, P. (1987) Small finds, in Hellström, P. (ed.), *Paradeisos. A Late Neolithic Settlement in Aegean Thrace*, 83–88. Stockholm. Medelhausmuseet.

Hiller, S. and Nikolov, V. (1997) *Karanovo. Die Ausgrabungen im Südsektor 1984–1992*. Horn/Wien. Berger.

Hochstetter, A. (1987) *Kastanas. Die Kleinfunde*. Berlin. Volker Spiess.

Keighley, J. M. (1986) The pottery of Phases I and II, in Renfrew, C., Gimbutas, M. and Elster, E. S. (eds), *Excavations at Sitagroi: A Prehistoric Village in Northeast Greece*. 1, 345–390. Los Angeles. Institute of Archaeology, UCLA.

McPherron, A. and Srejovic, D. (1988) *Divostin and the Neolithic of Central Serbia*. Pittsburgh. Department of Anthropology, University of Pittsburgh.

Nikolaidou, M. (2003) Items of adornment, in Elster, E. and Renfrew, C. (eds), *Prehistoric Sitagroi: Excavations in Northeast Greece, 1968–1970. 2. The Final Report*, 331–360. Los Angeles. Institute of Archaeology, UCLA.

Renfrew, C. (1970) The Burnt House at Sitagroi, *Antiquity*, 44, 131–134.

Renfrew, C. (1986a) Northeast Greece: The archaeological problem, in Renfrew, C., Gimbutas, M. and Elster, E. S. (eds), *Excavations at Sitagroi: A Prehistoric Settlement in Northeast Greece*. 1, 3–13. Los Angeles. Institute of Archaeology, UCLA.

Renfrew, C. (1986b) The Sitagroi sequence, in Renfrew, C., Gimbutas, M. and Elster, E. S. (eds), *Excavations at Sitagroi: A Prehistoric Village in Northeast Greece*. 1, 147–174. Los Angeles. Institute of Archaeology, UCLA.

Renfrew, C. (1986c) The excavated areas, in Renfrew, C., Gimbutas, M. and Elster, E. S. (eds), *Excavations at Sitagroi: A Prehistoric Settlement in Northeast Greece*. 1, 175–222. Los Angeles. Institute of Archaeology, UCLA.

Renfrew, C. and Hardy, D. (2003) Prehistoric sites in the Plain of Drama, in Elster, E. S. and Renfrew, C. (eds), *Prehistoric Sitagroi: Excavations in Northeast Greece, 1968–1970. 2. The Final Report*, 469–474. Los Angeles. Institute of Archaeology, UCLA.

Renfrew, C. and Slater, E. A. (2003) Metal artifacts and metallurgy, in Elster, E. S. and Renfrew, C. (eds), *Prehistoric Sitagroi: Excavations in Northeasr Greece, 1968–1970. 2. The Final Report*, 301–319. Los Angeles. Institute of Archaeology, UCLA.

Renfrew, C., Gimbutas, M. and Elster, E. S. (eds) (1986) *Excavations at Sitagroi: A Prehistoric Village in Northeast Greece*. 1. Los Angeles. Institute of Archaeology, UCLA.

Sherratt, A. (1986) The pottery of Phases IV and V: the Early Bronze Age, in Renfrew, C., Gimbutas, M. and Elster, E. S. (eds), *Excavations at Sitagroi: A Prehistoric Village in Northeast Greece*. 1, 429–476. Los Angeles. Institute of Archaeology, UCLA.

Treuil, R., Deshayes, J. and Blécon, J. (1992) *Dikili Tash: village préhistorique de Macédoine orientale, Fouilles de Jean Deshayes (1961–1975). 1*. Athens. École française d'Athènes.

Tringham, R. and Krstic, D. (1990) *Selevac: a Neolithic Village in Yugoslavia*. Los Angeles. Institute of Archaeology, UCLA.

Weisshaar, H.-J. (1989) *Die deutschen Ausgrabungen auf der Pevkakia Magula in Thessalien. I. Das späte Neolithikum und das Chalcolithikum*. Bonn. Rudolf Habelt.

CHAPTER 6.13

Textile tools from Troia, western Anatolia

Marta Guzowska, Ralf Becks, Eva Andersson Strand, Joanne Cutler and Marie-Louise Nosch

The settlement of Troia is located on the low mound of Hisarlık in northwest Anatolia. Its position in relation to the sea has been changing over millennia, as the estuary bay of the rivers Karamenderes (ancient Skamander) and Dümrek (Simoeis) has gradually silted up (Kayan 1995). The mound has revealed archaeological material from over 3000 years of almost uninterrupted occupation, from the Early Bronze Age to the Late Roman and Byzantine periods.

Ten subsequent occupation phases have been distinguished at Troia, from Troia I in the Early Bronze Age to the Byzantine Troia X. The Bronze Age is represented by occupation phases I to VII (Fig. 6.13.1).

Troia was already a citadel surrounded by a fortification in the Early Bronze Age. In Troia II the walled area reached the size of *c.* 11,000 sq m and was surrounded by a Lower Town (Jablonka 2001; 2006). To this period belongs a spectacular hoard of gold finds ascribed by Schliemann to Troia VI, which revealed strong cultural affinity to the northeast Aegean (Tolstikov and Treister 1996; Treister 2002; Sazcı and Treister 2006; for the characteristics of the period see also Ünlüsoy 2006; Çalış–Sazcı 2006).

During Troia IV and V Aegean influence diminished, while Anatolian influence increased (Blum 2006). The beginning of Troia VI in

c. 1780/50 (Pavúk in press) is connected with a noticeable transition in all aspects of material culture, including architecture, pottery and economic production (Becks 2006; Pavúk 2007; Çakırlar and Becks 2009). The Lower Town reached *c.* 300,000 sq m (Easton *et al.* 2002; Jablonka 2006). Towards the end of Troia VI and in the following phase Troia VIIa the settlement was part of the Hittite-related political system in western Anatolia and was also involved in contacts with the Minoan/Mycenaean world (Korfmann 1997, 33–38; Becks and Guzowska 2004; Guzowska and Becks 2005; Becks 2006; Guzowska 2009; Mountjoy 1997; 2006). A small cemetery of cinerary urns excavated by Blegen at the southern edge of the settlement (Blegen *et al.* 1953, 370–391; Becks 2002) and a cemetery at Beşik Bay, *c.* 8 km southwest of Troia, date

Troia I	*c.* 2920–2550
Troia II	*c.* 2550–2250
Troia III	*c.* 2250–2200
Troia IV	*c.* 2200–1950
Troia V	*c.* 1950–1780/1750
Troia VI	*c.* 1780/1750–*c.* 1300
Troia VIIa	*c.* 1300–*c.* 1190/1180
Troia VIIb1	*c.* 1190/1180–1150
Troia VIIb2 and VIIb3	*c.* 1150–950

Fig. 6.13.1. Absolute chronology of Troia I–VII (Korfmann 2006; Pavúk in press).

to this period (Basedow 2000). No major cemetery for Troia has as yet been discovered.

After the earthquake destruction marking the end of the VIth settlement Troia was settled within the same limits and likely by the same population during the VIIa phase; it was destroyed again after *c.* 100 years, possibly as the result of warfare (Becks and Thumm 2001). The new settlement phases of VIIb1 and VIIb2 reveal new cultural traits: the so-called Barbarian ware and Buckelkeramik, handmade pottery with strong Balkan tradition, appearing at the site alongside local wheelmade ceramics (Guzowska *et al.* 2003; Becks *et al.* 2006b).

The occupation phase VIIb3 was followed by a partial break in occupation, with limited activities continuing in the area of the Sanctuary (Chabot Aslan 2002). The post Bronze Age occupation at Troia/Ilion started in the 8th century BC (Rose 1997, 82; 1999, 37).

The mound of Hisarlık has been excavated for almost 140 years. Schliemann, using the preparatory work by Frank Calvert, started digging in 1871 and continued until 1890 (Allen 1999; Schliemann 1881; Schmidt 1902; Easton 2002, 2006). After Schliemann's death, Dörpfeld, who had worked with Schliemann as an architect, conducted two further campaigns on his own in 1893 and 1894 (Dörpfeld 1902). In the years 1932–1938, a team of archaeologists from the University of Cincinnati, directed by Carl W. Blegen, continued to excavate the mound. Their publication still serves as an up-to-date guide to the architectural phases and ceramics of Troia (Blegen *et al.* 1950; 1951; 1953; 1958; Thumm-Doğrayan 2006). Since 1988 the excavations have been continued jointly by the universities of Tuebingen and Cincinnati, directed by Manfred O. Korfmann, Ch. Brian Rose and, after Korfmann's death in 2005, Ernst Pernicka (Cf. excavation reports in *Studia Troica* since 1991).

A total number of 1,975 textile tools are recorded in the CTR database.[1] Of these, 1,833 tools can be assigned to specific settlement phases (Fig. 6.13.2).[2] The majority of the tools in all phases are spindle whorls.

The largest number of tools (528) are from Troia VI, while only 97 tools are from Troia V contexts. The majority of the tools (1,381) are from the Citadel area. These disparities can be attributed to a number of factors, one of the most important being that different excavation teams focused on different areas and periods of the site. Blegen mainly excavated within the Citadel (Blegen *et al.* 1950, 34, 203–3; 1951, 4–5, 101–102, 222; 1953, 4; 1958, 4–6, 140–141), Korfmann within both the Citadel and the Lower Town (excavation reports in *Studia Troica* 1991–2006). Larger areas of the Citadel of Troia II and Troia VI are preserved and have been excavated, whereas only a small percentage of the Lower Town of Troia II and VI have been excavated so far. Deposits of Troia V have rarely been exposed at all (Blegen excavated more than Korfmann), so, although the layers dated to this period revealed large concentrations of spindle whorls, the data are incomplete. Additionally, it should be noted that not all of the textile tools recovered from Troia are recorded in the database, so any analyses can only provide a partial picture of the site's textile tool assemblage.

In the following, only the textile tools from V, VI and VII will be discussed: the textile production tools from other settlement phases will be the subject of a future study.

Troia V

Of the 97 textile tools from Troia V contexts, 71 objects (70 spindle whorls and one loom weight) can be assigned to specific sub-phases within this period (Fig. 6.13.3). All of the recorded tools are from household contexts

Fig. 6.13.2. Textile tools from Troia I–VII, by type and phase. The type of brush included among the textile tools could have been used to remove the last woody parts of the flax stems from the flax fibres (see chapter 2).

	Spindle whorl	Conulus	Pierced sherd	Loom weight	Spool	Small spool	Brush handle	Spindle	Needle	Total
Troia I	104		7	3					1	115
Troia II	249		4	12			6		1	272
Troia III	203		3	14	1		1		1	223
Troia IV	171		12	45			5		2	235
Troia V	91		3	3						97
Troia VI	431	3	43	27	1	13			10	528
Troia VII	244	7	18	85	3			1	5	363
Total	1493	10	90	189	5	13	12	1	20	1833

within the Citadel. The majority date to sub-phases Vc and Vd, while lower numbers are from sub-phases Va and Vb.

Spindle whorls and spinning

All of the spindle whorls from Troia V contexts are made of clay. A variety of types are present, although the majority of the whorls are of the 'various shapes with hollow top' type (Fig. 6.13.4).

Sixty-seven of the Troia V whorls had a recordable weight and diameter (38 'various shapes with hollow top', 14 lenticular, eight biconical and seven spherical). No difference in the weight/diameter ranges of the different types of whorls can be observed (Fig. 6.13.5).

The spindle whorls from all the Troia V sub-phases similarly vary in weight/diameter, indicating a varied production of thin to thick yarn during Troia V (Fig. 6.13.6).

In most cases, only low numbers of whorls were recovered from individual contexts. However, 30 whorls were recovered from House 501. Of these, eight are from Troia Va contexts, while four date to Troia Vb and 18 date to Troia Vc (Blegen *et al.* 1951, 252–255, 272–276). All of the whorls from this building had a recordable weight and diameter (Fig. 6.13.7). As in the case of the Troia V whorls as a whole, the whorls from

Fig. 6.13.3. Textile tools from Troia V, by type and phase.

	Area	Type of context	Spindle whorl	Loom weight	Total
Troia Va	Citadel	Household	11		**11**
Troia Vb	Citadel	Household	5	1	**6**
Troia Vc	Citadel	Household	32		**32**
Troia Vd	Citadel	Household	22		**22**
Total			**70**	**1**	**71**

Fig. 6.13.4. Spindle whorls from Troia V, by type and phase.

	Material	Biconical	Conical	Cylindrical	Lenticular	Spherical	Various shapes with hollow top	Total
Troia Va	clay		1		4	1	5	**11**
Troia Vb	clay	1				1	3	**5**
Troia Vc	clay	4	1		8	4	15	**32**
Troia Vd	clay	3		1	2	1	15	**22**
Total		**8**	**2**	**1**	**14**	**7**	**38**	**70**

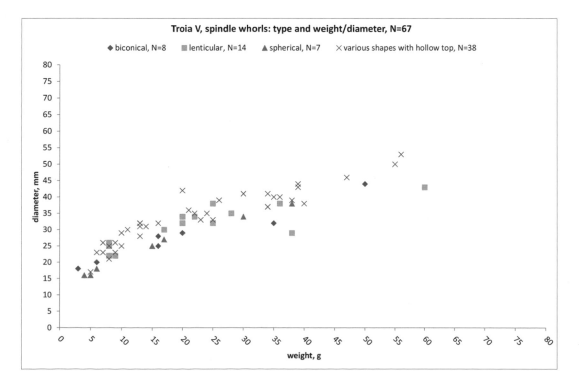

Troia V, spindle whorls: type and weight/diameter, N=67

◆ biconical, N=8　■ lenticular, N=14　▲ spherical, N=7　✕ various shapes with hollow top, N=38

Fig. 6.13.5. Spindle whorls, Troia V: type and weight/diameter. Types represented by ≤2 whorls are not included in the graph. Please note that some markers represent more than one spindle whorl.

Fig. 6.13.6 Spindle whorls, Troia Va–d: weight/diameter. Please note that some markers represent more than one spindle whorl.

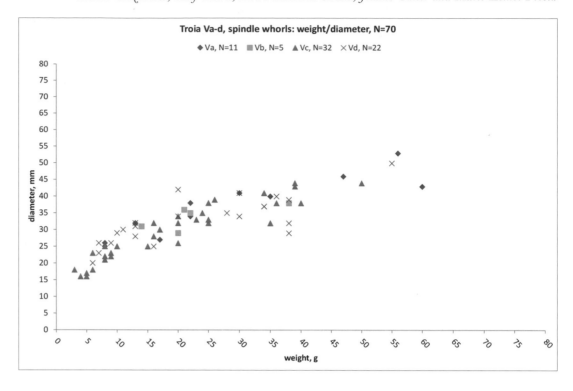

Fig. 6.13.7. Spindle whorls, Troia Va–c, House 501: weight/diameter. Please note that some markers represent more than one spindle whorl.

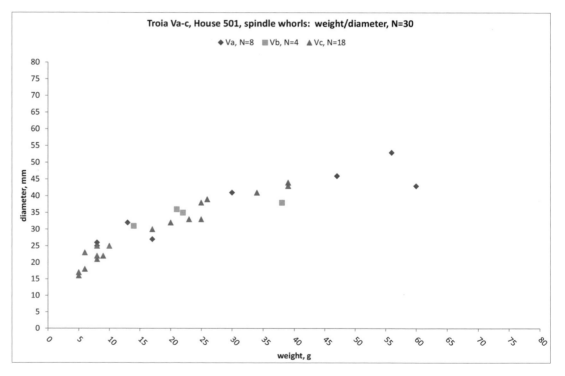

different sub-phase contexts within House 501 vary in weight/diameter. There is therefore no indication of specialised production of one type of yarn within this building, or in other areas, during Troia V.

Troia VI

Two hundred and ninety-seven of the textile tools from Troia VI contexts can be assigned to a specific sub-phase (Fig. 6.13.8a; see Fig. 6.13.8b for a plan of the Troia VI Late

	Area	Type of context	Spindle whorl	Conulus	Loom weight	Spool	Small spool	Needle	Total
Troia VIa	Citadel	Household	9						9
Troia VIb	Citadel	Household	1						1
	Citadel	Other	1						1
Troia VIc	Lower Town	Other	2						2
Troia VId	Citadel	Other	7						7
	Lower Town	Other	1						1
Troia VIe	Citadel	Other	11						11
	Lower Town	Other	1						1
Troia VIf	Citadel	Household	13						13
	Citadel	Other	7		2				9
Troia VIg	Citadel	Household	32						32
	Citadel	Other	11		5				16
Troia VIh	Lower Town	Household	4						4
	Lower Town	Other	11						11
	Citadel	Household	117	1	9			1	128
	Citadel	Other	8		1	1	13		23
	Tomb		28						28
Total			264	1	17	1	13	1	297

Fig. 6.13.8a. Textile tools from Troia VI, by type and phase.

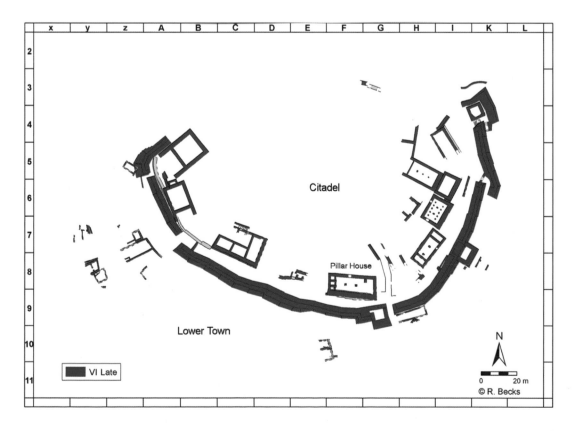

Fig. 6.13.8b. Plan of Troia VI Late (plan: courtesy of Ralf Becks).

	Material	Biconical	Conical	Cylindrical	Convex	Lenticular	Other	Spherical	Various shapes with hollow top	Total
Troia VIa	clay	5	2						2	9
Troia VIb	clay	1	1							2
Troia VIc	clay	2								2
Troia VId	clay	7							1	8
Troia VIe	clay	9							3	12
Troia VIf	clay	16					2	1	1	20
Troia VIg	clay	38			1	1	2		1	43
Troia VIh	clay	136	1	3	10	2		11	4	167
	stone		1							1
Total		214	5	3	11	3	4	12	12	264

Fig. 6.13.9a. Spindle whorls from Troia VI: type and material, by phase.

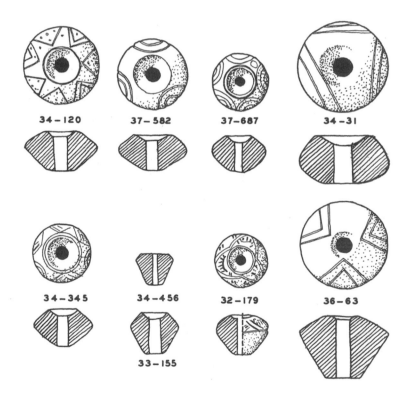

Fig. 6.13.9b. Examples of spindle whorl types from Troia VI (drawing: Blegen et al. 1953, Fig. 296).

settlement). Of these, 194 items date to Troia VIh, while only nine tools date to Troia VIa. Most of the tools were recovered from household contexts in the Citadel; 28 spindle whorls are from tombs (Blegen *et al.* 1953, 370–391).[3]

Spindle whorls and spinning

The majority of the spindle whorls from all sub-phases of Troia VI are biconical in shape; other types of spindle whorls are present in small numbers (Fig. 6.13.9a–b). All of the whorls are made of clay, with the exception of one stone whorl from a Troia VIh context.

Two hundred and twenty-four of these spindle whorls had a recordable weight and diameter (Fig. 6.13.10).

As in Troia V, no difference in the weight/ diameter range between the types of spindle whorls can be observed (Fig. 6.13.11).

The spindle whorls from the different sub-phases all vary in weight/diameter, indicating a varied production of different types of thread throughout the Troia VI period (Fig. 6.13.10).

The spindle whorls from the Citadel and the Lower Town also vary in weight/diameter, demonstrating a varied production of thin to thick yarn in all areas of the site during this period (Fig. 6.13.12). A similar variation in size is additionally observable among the whorls from tomb contexts (Fig. 6.13.12).

Two hundred and four of the Troia VI whorls were recovered from Troia VIf–h contexts in the Pillar House (see Blegen *et al.* 1953, 233–237). Of these, 141 had a recordable weight and diameter (Fig. 6.13.13). The whorls from the different sub-phases vary in weight and diameter, demonstrating a varied production of different types of yarn, from thin to thick, especially in Troia VIh, to which sub-phase the majority of the whorls from the Pillar House date.

The analyses of the Troia VI spindle whorls demonstrate a varied production of yarn ranging from thin to thick, as in the earlier Troia V period. There is no indication of the existence of workshop areas where only one type of yarn was spun. The appearance of conuli for the first time in Troia VI may indicate the beginning of a need for very fine thread.[4]

Whereas the majority of the spindle whorls from Troia V were of the 'various shapes with

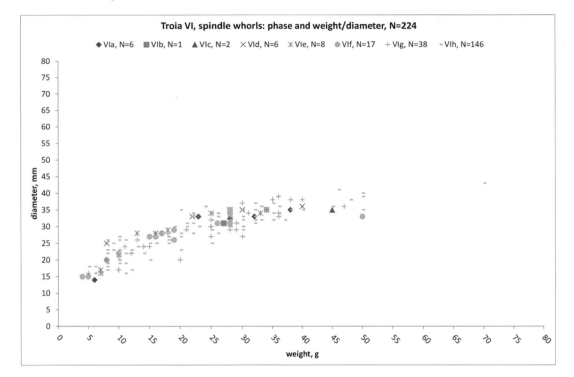

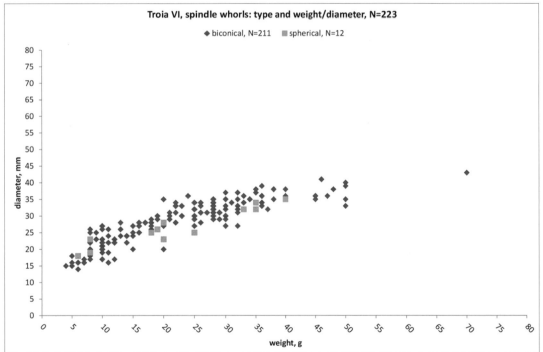

Fig. 6.13.11. Spindle whorls, Troia VI: type and weight diameter. Please note that some markers represent more than one spindle whorl and that a single conical whorl, weighing 28 g, is not included in the graph.

hollow top' type, the most common whorl shape during Troia VI was biconical. This typological change may reflect a general shift in material culture during the transition from Troia V to Troia VI (Blegen *et al.* 1953, 5–11, 39; Pavúk 2007). It has to be stressed, however, that there is no notable difference in the range of spindle whorl weight and/or diameter to indicate that a difference in textile production accompanied the typological change in textile tools.

Loom weights and weaving
Of the 27 loom weights from Troia VI contexts, 19 weights, all made of clay, can be assigned to specific sub-phases (Fig. 6.13.14).

Fig. 6.13.12. Spindle whorls, Troia VI: context and weight/diameter. Please note that some markers represent more than one spindle whorl.

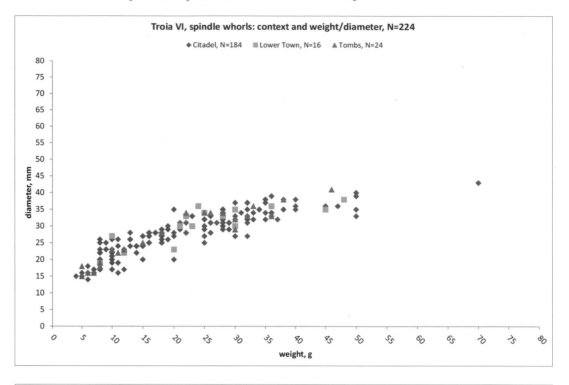

Fig. 6.13.13. Spindle whorls, Troia VI, Pillar House: phase and weight/diameter. Please note that some markers represent more than one spindle whorl.

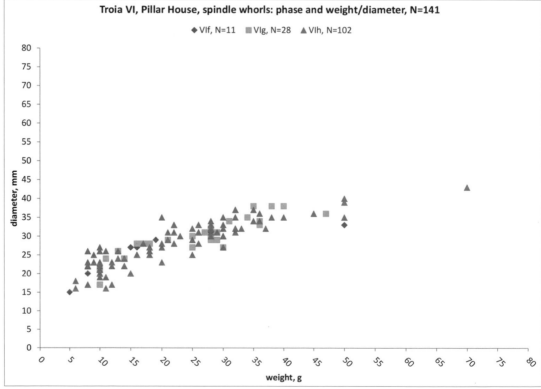

Nine loom weights were recovered from the Pillar House, and date to phase VIh. Seven of these have a recordable weight and thickness; they vary in weight from 105 g to 425 g and in thickness between 2.0 cm and 4.2 cm (Fig. 6.13.15).

The lighter, thinner loom weights from the Pillar House would not have functioned optimally in a weave together with the heavier, thicker weights from the building. The lightest of the weights would only be optimal for use with very thin threads needing *c.* 5–10 g tension, while the heaviest weight would be best suited for use with thread requiring between *c.* 15 g and *c.* 40 g tension. In a tabby setup with thread needing *c.* 5 g tension, the lightest weight could produce a fabric with *c.* 21 warp threads per centimetre (in a twill the thread count would be approximately double). The heaviest weight could produce a tabby with between *c.* 6–14 warp threads per centimetre with thread needing between *c.* 15 g and *c.* 40 g tension.

A number of small, vertically pierced spools have been noted in Troia VI early and middle phases. Thirteen such objects have been found during the most recent excavations (Pavúk in press, chapter 6, Type T1; 2012).[5] Blegen did not mention small, vertically pierced spools in his publication but Schliemann registered 15 of them, dating from his Settlement VI (Schmidt 1902, 299–300, cat. nos. 8439–8445, 8446 and seven fragments without ascribed catalogue numbers). The recently found small spools in Troia come from the layers of Troia VIa,

b/c, d–e and f. No two of them were found together and they always appear as single finds in different contexts. The exact function of small spools is not clear. It is possible that they were used for preparing the warp for horizontal looms. Their presence is widely noted on the Greek mainland in the same period.

Summary Troia VI
The spindle whorls from Troia VI demonstrate a varied production of different types of yarn, from thin to thick. No predominance in production of one type or quality of fabric was possible with the available tools. The analyses of the loom weights also suggest a varied production, but the weights preserved from this period are too few for further conclusions to be drawn. It is possible that, at least in certain sub-phases of Troia VI, the horizontal loom was used alongside the vertical loom, although no direct evidence for the existence of the horizontal loom has

	Discoid	Flat rectangular	Flat trapezoidal	Other	Pyramidal	Spool	Torus	Total
Troia VIf					2			2
Troia VIg	2				3			5
Troia VIh	7	1	1	1		1	1	12
Total	9	1	1	1	5	1	1	19

Fig. 6.13.14. Loom weights from Troia VI, by type and phase.

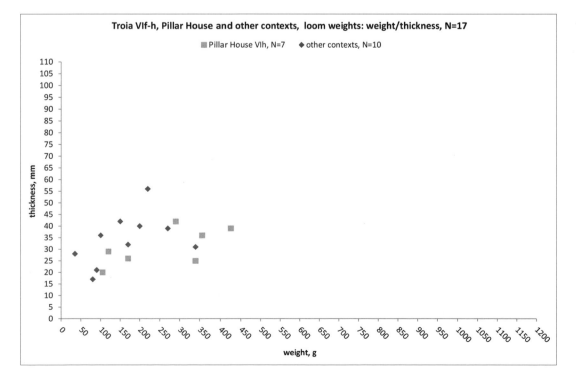

Fig. 6.13.15. Troia VIf–h, loom weights: context and weight/ thickness.

been found. The Pillar House represents an important textile production context, with unchanged production during three subsequent chronological phases. Future studies are planned to reconstruct the possible textile production areas within the house.

Troia VII

Three hundred and thirty-one of the textile tools from Troia VII can be assigned to specific sub-phases (Fig. 6.13.16a; see Fig. 6.13.16b–c for plans of the Troia VIIa and VIIb2 settlements). The majority (182) of these are from Troia VIIa contexts, while only five tools date to phase VIIb3.[6] Most of the tools come from the Citadel and were found in various household contexts.

Spindle whorls and spinning

As in the preceding Troia VI period, the majority of the spindle whorls from all the Troia VII sub-phases are biconical in shape (Fig. 6.13.17a–c.). Most of the whorls are made of clay; one is made of stone and one whorl is made of metal. In spite of a discontinuity in material culture observable at the beginning of Troia VIIb2, the spindle whorl types from Troia VIIb1 and VIIb2 contexts are similar to those from Troia VIIa (Blegen *et al.* 1958, 141–148; Guzowska *et al.* 2003, especially 249–239; Becks and Thumm 2001; Becks *et al.* 2006b).

One hundred and ninety-four of the whorls had a recordable weight and diameter (Fig. 6.13.18). No difference in the weight/diameter range between different whorl types can be observed (Fig. 6.13.19).

Fig. 6.13.16a. Textile tools from Troia VII, by type and phase.

The range of whorl sizes present in the various Troia VII sub-phases demonstrates a varied production of yarn, from thin to thick threads (Fig. 6.13.18). The spindle whorls from the Citadel and the Lower Town also vary in weight/diameter, demonstrating a varied production of thin to thick yarn in all areas of the site during this period.

In cases where five or more whorls were recovered from Troia VIIa and VIIb2 contexts within the same building, a similar variation in weight/diameter is also observable (Figs. 6.13.20a and 6.13.20b). Only Troia VIIa House 731 contained a group of whorls similar in size (Fig. 6.13.20a), which suggests that a more concentrated production of one type of yarn may have taken place in this building (Blegen *et al.* 1958, 94–101).

Loom weights and weaving

Eighty-three loom weights can be dated to specific Troia VII sub-phases (Fig. 6.13.21). The largest number of the loom weights are conical in shape; all of the conical weights were recovered from Troia VIIa contexts.

Thirty-seven loom weights from Troia VIIa and 19 weights from Troia VIIb1–2 contexts had a recordable weight and thickness (Fig. 6.13.22). Their weight varies from 36 g to 1150 g and their thickness varies from 1.5 cm to 11 cm.

The Citadel: E9, Room B

Thirty-three loom weights (20 conical, six pyramidal, three spools, two flat trapezoidal, one flat rectangular and one discoid) were recovered from a floor deposit dating to the final VIIa destruction, in the southwest

	Area	Type of context	Spindle whorl	Conulus	Pierced sherd	Loom weight	Spool	Spindle	Needle	Total
Troia VIIa	Citadel	Household	47	4	3	41				**95**
	Citadel	Other	36	2	2	5				**45**
	Lower Town	Household	15		4	10		1	1	**31**
	Lower Town	Other	6		3	1			1	**11**
Troia VIIb1	Citadel	Household	17	1		8	1			**27**
	Citadel	Other	5							**5**
	Lower Town	Household	3		1					**4**
	Lower Town	Other	4			2			3	**9**
Troia VIIb2	Citadel	Household	60		2	6	2			**70**
	Citadel	Other	12	1		6				**19**
	Lower Town	Household	8			2				**10**
Troia VIIb3	Citadel	Other	5							**5**
Total			**218**	**7**	**16**	**81**	**3**	**1**	**5**	**331**

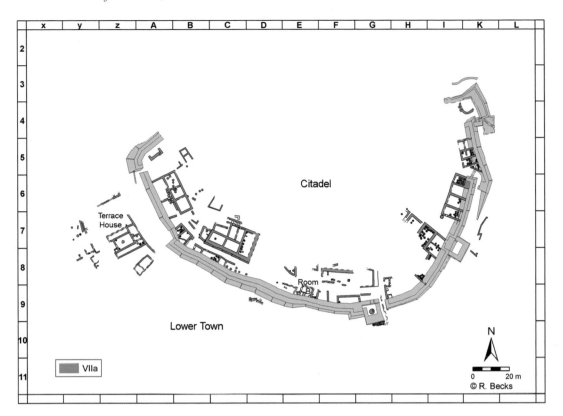

Fig. 6.13.16b. Plan of Troia VIIa (plan: courtesy of Ralf Becks).

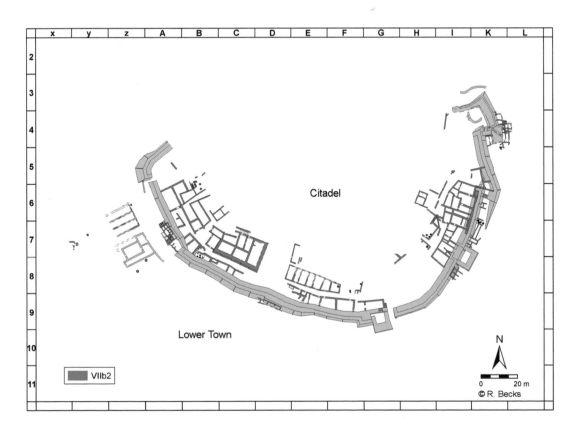

Fig. 6.13.16c. Plan of Troia VIIb2 (plan: courtesy of Ralf Becks).

	Material	Biconical	Concave conical	Conical	Cylindrical	Convex	Discoid	Lenticular	Other	Spherical	Various Shapes with Hollow Top	Total
Troia VIIa	clay	81	2	4			2	1	2	10	2	104
	stone		1	4		1						6
Troia VIIb1	clay	22	1	2			1			2	1	29
	stone			1								1
Troia VIIb2	clay	51	2	10	1		1	1		7	4	77
	stone	1					1					2
	metal			1								1
Troia VIIb3	clay	3		1						1		5
Total		158	6	23	1	1	5	2	2	20	7	225

Fig. 6.13.17a. Spindle whorls from Troia VII: type and material, by phase.

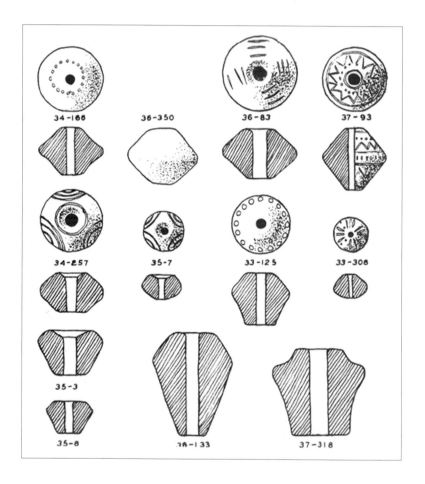

Fig. 6.13.17b.
Examples of spindle
whorl types from Troia
VIIa (drawing: Blegen
et al. 1958, fig. 221).

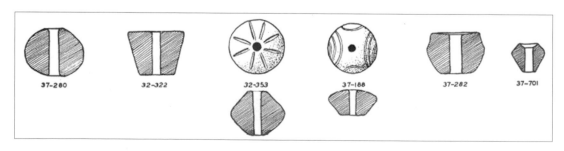

Fig. 6.13.17c.
Examples of spindle
whorl types from Troia
VIIb (drawing: Blegen
et al. 1958, fig. 257).

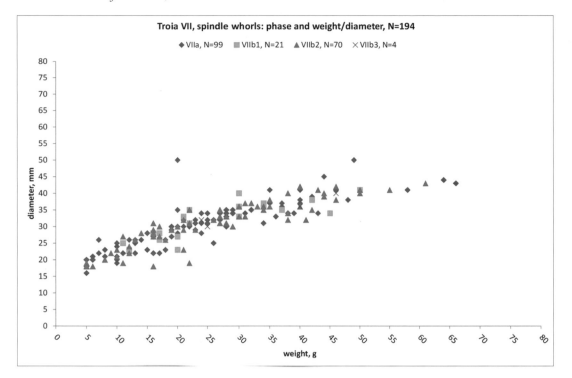

Fig. 6.13.18 Spindle whorls, Troia VII: phase and weight/diameter. Please note that some markers represent more than one spindle whorl.

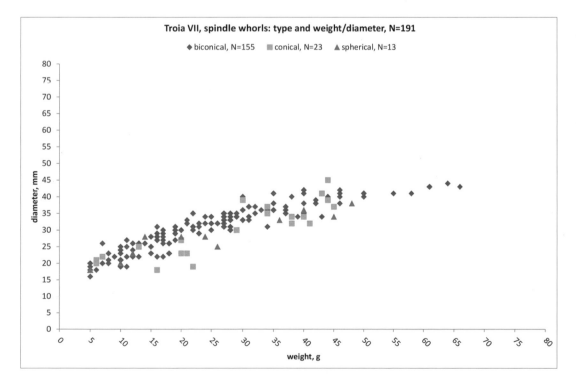

Fig. 6.13.19. Spindle whorls, Troia VII: type and weight/diameter. Types represented by < 3 whorls are not included in the graph. Please note that some markers represent more than one spindle whorl.

corner of E9, Room B (Korfmann 1997, 27–32; Guzowska *et al.* 2012). Twenty-eight of the weights were found in two clusters: the first cluster consisted of eight weights (five conical, two pyramidal and one spool) lying close to each other in two rows, while the second cluster, approximately 1 m further to the east, contained 20 weights (15 conical, four pyramidal and one spool) lying partly in a double row. It is possible that the two clusters of loom weights represent a single loom (see Korfmann 1997, 27–32; Guzowska *et al.* 2012),

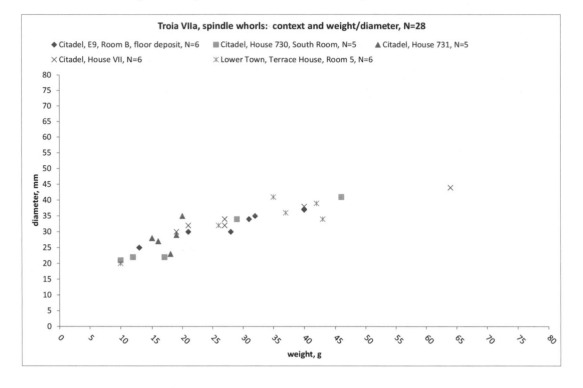

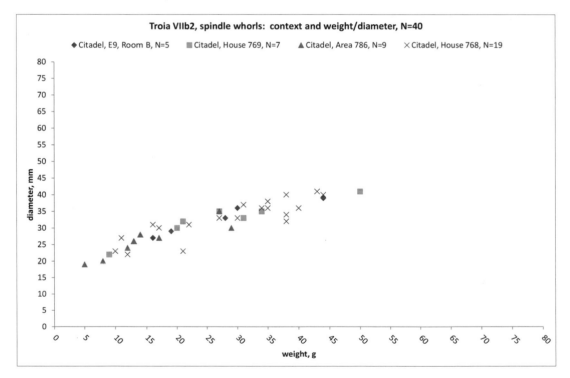

or each cluster may alternatively represent a separate loom.

Fourteen of the loom weights from the two clusters had a recordable weight and thickness (Fig. 6.13.23a–b.).

All of the loom weights in the two clusters would work well with thread requiring

c. 40 g tension, suggesting that the woven fabric would have been quite coarse (Figs. 6.13.24a–b) (Guzowska *et al.* 2012). In a tabby weave, the resulting fabric would have *c.* 3–6 warp threads per centimetre.

The seven spindle whorls recovered from Room B indicate a varied production of different types of yarn, from thin to thick (Fig. 6.13.20b). The thread needed for the suggested loom setups could have been produced with some of the heavier spindle whorls from this room. Two pierced sherds were also recovered from the same context. However, in both cases the hole is hourglass shaped, which would make fastening the spindle rod difficult and would affect the spinning process; these objects would therefore not be optimal for use as whorls.

Lower Town: Terrace House
In the Lower Town, five loom weights were recovered from a Troia VIIa context in the Central Room of the Terrace House (Guzowska *et al.* 2012).[7] Four of the weights have a shallow groove on the top: more than 30 grooved loom weights of two basic types have been found in the levels dating from the end of Troia VI middle to Troia VIIa, revealing a strong Aegean influence (Becks and Guzowska 2004).

The loom weights vary in weight between 87 g and 150 g and their thickness ranges from 2.0 cm to 3.0 cm (Fig. 6.13.23a).

The weights were not found together and cannot be considered as a group, but they would be optimal for use with thread needing *c.* 5–12.5 g tension (Fig. 6.13.25). All of the weights could be used with thread needing 5–7.5 g tension, and in a tabby setup the resulting fabric would have *c.* 17–20 warp threads per centimetre and *c.* 12–13 threads per cm respectively; four of the weights would work well with thread needing *c.* 10 g tension the thread count would be *c.* 9–10 warp threads per centimetre (in a 2/2 twill the thread counts would be approximately double).

Fig. 6.13.21. Loom weights from Troia VII: type and material, by phase.

	Material	Conical	Discoid	Flat rectangular	Flat trapezoidal	Other	Pyramidal	Spool	Torus	Total
Troia VIIa	clay	21	7	1	9	1	10	5		**54**
	stone			1			1			**2**
Troia VIIb1	clay		1		1	1	2	2	1	**8**
	stone		1		1	1				**3**
Troia VIIb2	clay		3	1	3			8		**15**
	stone			1						**1**
Total		**21**	**12**	**4**	**14**	**3**	**13**	**15**	**1**	**83**

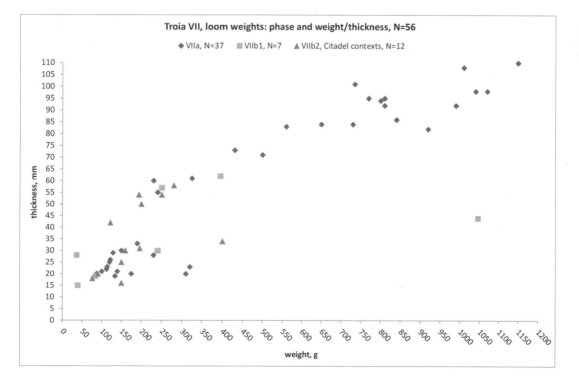

Fig. 6.13.22. Loom weights, Troia VII: phase and weight/thickness.

Fig. 6.13.23a. Loom weights, Troia VIIa: context and weight/thickness.

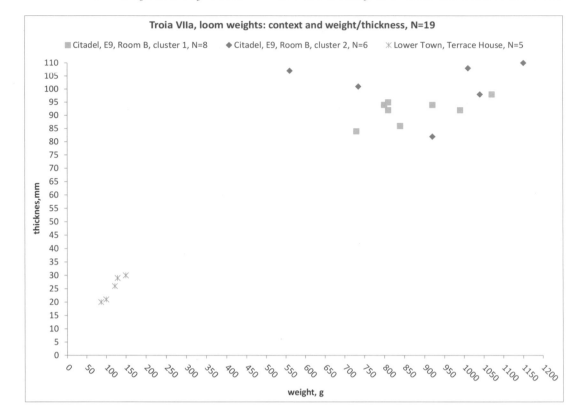

Fig. 6.13.23b. Some of the loom weights from the Citadel, E9, Room B (photo: courtesy of Troia Project, Troia Dia 26583).

Warp thr/cm	25 g, N=1	30 g, N=5	35 g, N=7	40 g, N=8	45 g, N=8	50 g, N=8	55 g, N=8	60 g, N=8	65 g, N=8	70 g, N=6
3 thr						3	5	6	8	6
4 thr				4	6	5	3	2		
5 thr			4	3	2					
6 thr		4	3	1						
7 thr	1	1								

Fig. 6.13.24a. Troia VIIa, Citadel, E9, Room B, cluster 1: weight tension/number of threads per cm in a tabby. The total number of analysed loom weights is eight.

Warp thr/cm	20 g, N=1	25 g, N=2	30 g, N=2	35 g, N=5	40 g, N=6	45 g, N=5	50 g, N=5	55 g, N=5	60 g, N=4	65 g, N=4	70 g, N=4
3 thr				1	1	1	1	2	3	4	4
4 thr		1	1	1	1	1	4	3	1		
5 thr	1		1	1	3	3					
6 thr		1		2	1						

Fig. 6.13.24b. Troia VIIa, Citadel, E9, Room B, cluster 2: weight tension/number of threads per cm in a tabby. The total number of analysed loom weights is six.

The fabrics that could be produced using the loom weights from the Central Room of the Terrace House would be considerably different to the fabrics that could be produced using the loom weights from the two clusters in E9, Room B on the Citadel (Figs. 6.13.24a–b). The loom weights from the Terrace House would be best suited for use with very fine thread needing *c.* 5–12.5 g tension. In contrast, the loom weights from E9, Room B would be optimal for use with thick thread needing *c.* 40–50 g tension.

No spindle whorls were recovered from the Central Room, but 13 whorls were found elsewhere in the building, together with a spindle. The whorls indicate a varied production of many different types of spun yarn (see Fig. 6.13.26 for the nine whorls with a recordable weight and thickness). The lightest of the spindle whorls could have been used to produce the thread for the suggested loom setup. However, the other spindle whorls would have been suitable for spinning thicker types of thread.

The other loom weights from phases VIIa, VIIb1, and VIIb2–3 are, in general, from different contexts, and could have been used for producing many different types of fabrics. The analyses therefore suggest that a variety of textiles were being woven during all the sub-phases of Troia VII.

Warp thr/cm	5 g, N=5	7.5 g, N=5	10 g, N=4	12.5 g N=3	15 g, N=1
6 thr					
7 thr				1	1
8 thr				2	
9 thr			2		
10 thr			2		
11 thr					
12 thr		4			
13 thr		1			
14 thr					
15 thr					
16 thr					
17 thr	1				
18 thr	2				
19 thr	1				
20 thr	1				
21 thr					

Fig. 6.13.25. Loom weights, Troia VIIa, Terrace House: weight tension/number of threads per cm in a tabby. The total number of analysed loom weights is five.

Summary

The analyses clearly demonstrate a varied textile production in Troia V, VI and VII. There is no evidence for specialisation, suggesting, for example, a concentration on the production of very thin spun or thick spun yarn. All qualities of yarn and textiles seem to have been produced in all of these phases.

Textile production in the Citadel area and in the Lower Town also appears to have been similar in nature.

Fig. 6.13.26. Spindle whorls, Troia VIIa, Terrace House: context and weight/diameter.

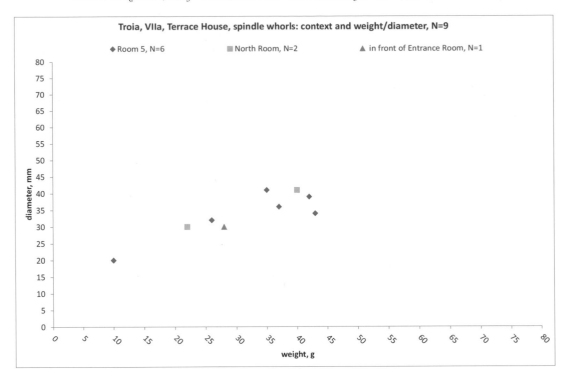

Acknowledgements

The authors would like to thank the Director of the Troia excavations Prof. Ernst Pernicka for allowing us to include the unpublished Troian material in this research. Special thanks goes also to Dr. Peter Pavúk for allowing us to use in this paper the latest version of the Troian absolute chronology, still awaiting publication, and for extensive discussions of the material, and to Dr. Stephan Blum for discussing with us the problems of strata deposition in Troia. Diane Thumm-Doğrayan helped us in organizing the finds at Troia.

Notes

1 The objects included in the database come from the excavations conducted by Blegen (Blegen *et al.* 1950; Blegen *et al.* 1951, 1953; Blegen *et al.* 1958) and unearthed during the most recent course of excavation directed by Manfred O. Korfmann and Ernst Pernicka since 1988. Only part of the recently excavated material has been published (Balfanz 1995a, 1995b; Korfmann 1997, 30; Becks and Guzowska 2004), a large part still awaits publication.

2 For Troia I (Blegen *et al.* 1950, 36–41); Troia II (Blegen *et al.* 1950, 204–213); Troia III (Blegen *et al.* 1951, 6–10); Troia IV (Blegen *et al.* 1951, 104–107); Troia V (Blegen *et al.* 1951, 224–226); Troia VI (Blegen *et al.* 1953, 11–20); Troia VIIa (Blegen *et al.* 1958, 8–10); Troia VIIb (Blegen *et al.* 1958, 142–148).

3 The cemetery of cinerary urns excavated by Blegen at the southern border of the plateau dated to the final phase of Troia VI and included only 19 burials; according to Blegen the burials represented poorer social strata. The regular cemetery of Troia still remains undiscovered.

4 Although it has been argued by Carington Smith that the whorls weighting less than 10 g were unsuitable for spinning and their function must have therefore been different (Carington Smith 1992), it has been demonstrated during the experiments carried out at the CTR that a fine thread can be spun with 4 g and 8 g whorls (Mårtensson *et al.* 2006). It can therefore be safely assumed that the conuli found in Troia may have been used for spinning fine thread.

5 The authors are grateful to Dr. Peter Pavúk for allowing them to use the unpublished material from his dissertation and for discussing the chronological and functional aspects of the small spools.

6 The occurrence of VIIb3 phases has only been noted in limited areas in the square D9, after the destruction of the VIIb2 settlement only limited activities took place at the mound of Hisarlık (Korfmann 2000, 30–32; 2001, 22–27; Chabot Aslan 2002, esp. 80–89).

7 For the description and chronological evaluation of the Terrace House, see Becks *et al.* 2006a.

Bibliography

Allen, S. H. (1999) *Finding the Walls of Troy: Frank Calvert and Heinrich Schliemann at Hisarlik*. Berkeley and London. University of California Press.

Balfanz, K. (1995a) Eine spätbronzezeitliche Elfenbeinspindel aus Troja VIIA, *Studia Troica*, 5, 107–116.

Balfanz, K. (1995b) Bronzezeitliche Spinnwirtel aus Troja, *Studia Troica*, 5, 117–144.

Basedow, M. A. (2000) *Beşik Tepe. Das spätbronzezeitliche Gräberfeld*. Mainz. Philipp von Zabern.

Becks, R. and Thumm, D. (2001) Untergang der Stadt in der Frühen Eisenzeit. Das Ende aus archäologischer Sicht, in Archäologisches Landesmuseum Baden-Württemberg (ed.), *Troia. Traum und Wirklichkeit*, 419–424. Stuttgart. K. Theiss.

Becks, R. (2002) Bemerkungen zu den Bestattungsplätzen von Troia VI, in Aslan, R., Blum, S. W. E., Kastl, G., Schweizer, F. and Thumm, D. (eds), *Mauerschau. Festschrift für Manfred Korfmann*, 295–306. Remshalden-Grunbach, Greiner.

Becks, R. (2006) Troia in der späten Bronzezeit – Troia VI und Troia VIIa, in Korfmann, M. O. (ed.), *Troia. Archäologie eines Siedlungshügels und seiner Landschaft*, 155–166. Mainz, Philipp von Zabern.

Becks, R. and Guzowska, M. (2004) The evidence for Minoan style weaving at Troia, *Studia Troica*, 14, 101–116.

Becks, R., Rigter, W. and Hnila, P. (2006a) Das Terrassenhaus im westlichen Unterstadtviertel von Troia, *Studia Troica*, 16, 27–88.

Becks, R., Hnila, P. and Pieniążek-Sikora, M. (2006b) Troia in der fruhen Eisenzeit – Troia VIIb1–VIIb3, in Korfmann, M. O. (ed.), *Troia. Archäologie eines Siedlungshügels und seiner Landschaft*, 181–188. Mainz. Philipp von Zabern.

Blegen, C. W., Caskey, J. L., Rawson, M. and Sperling, J. (1950) *Troy I: General Introduction: The First and Second Settlements*. Princeton. Princeton University Press.

Blegen, C. W., Caskey, J. L. and Rawson, M. (1951) *Troy II. The Third, Fourth, and Fifth Settlements*. Princeton. Princeton University Press.

Blegen, C. W., Caskey, J. L. and Rawson, M. (1953) *Troy III. The Sixth Settlement*. Princeton. Princeton University Press.

Blegen, C. W., Boulter, C. G., Caskey, J. L. and Rawson, M. (1958) *Troy IV. Settlements VIIa, VIIb and VIII*. Princeton. Princeton University Press.

Blum, S. W. E. (2006) Troia an der Wende von der frühen zur mittleren Bronzezeit – Troia IV und Troia V, in Korfmann, M. O. (ed.), *Troia. Archäologie eines Siedlungshügels und seiner Landschaft*, 145–154. Mainz. Philipp von Zabern.

Çakırlar, C. and Becks, R. (2009) 'Murex' dye production at Troia: an assessment of archaeomalacological data from old and new excavations, *Studia Troica*, 18, 87–103.

Çalış–Sazcı, D. (2006) Die Troianer und das Meer – Keramik und Handelsbeziehungen der sog. "Maritimen Troia-Kultur", in Korfmann, M. O. (ed.), *Troia. Archäologie eines Siedlungshügels und seiner Landschaft*, 201–208. Mainz. Philipp von Zabern.

Carington Smith, J. (1992) Spinning and weaving equipment, in Macdonald, W. A. and Wilkie, N. C. (eds), *Excavations at Nichoria*, 2, 674–711. Minneapolis. University of Minnesota Press.

Chabot Aslan, C. (2002) Ilion before Alexander: Protogometric, Geometric and Archaic pottery from D9, *Studia Troica*, 12, 81–129.

Dörpfeld, W. (1902) *Troja und Ilion. Ergebnisse der Ausgrabungen in den vorhistorischen und historischen Schichten von Ilion 1870–1894*. Athen. Beck and Barth.

Easton, D. F. (2002) *Schliemann's Excavations at Troia 1870–1873*. Mainz. Philipp von Zabern.

Easton, D. F. (2006) Mit der Ilias im Gepacck – Die Erforschung der Troas bis 1890, in Korfmann, M. O. (ed.), *Troia. Archäologie eines Siedlungshügels und seiner Landschaft*, 107–116. Mainz. Philipp von Zabern.

Easton, D. F., Hawkins, D. J., Sherratt, A. G. and Sherratt, E. S. (2002) Troy in recent perspective, *Anatolian Studies*, 52, 75–109.

Guzowska, M. (2009) En vogue Minoenne… On the social use of Minoan and Minoanizing objects in Troia, in Macdonald, C. F., Hallager, E. and Niemeier, W.-D. (eds), *The Minoans in the Central, Eastern and Northern Aegean – New Evidence*, 183–189. Aarhus. Aarhus University Press.

Guzowska, M. and Becks, R. (2005) Who was weaving at Troia? in Laffineur, R. and Greco, E. (eds), *EMPORIA. Aegeans in the Central and Eastern Mediterranean*, 279–286. Liège. Université de Liège.

Guzowska, M., Kuleff, I., Pernicka, E. and Satir, M. (2003) On the origin of coarse wares of Troia VII, in Wagner, G. A., Pernicka, E. and Uerpmann, H.-P. (eds), *Troia and the Troad. Scientific Approaches*, 233–249. Berlin and Heidelberg. Springer.

Guzowska, M., Becks, R. and Andersson Strand, E. (2012) "She was weaving a great Web". Textiles in Troia, in Nosch, M.-L. and Laffineur, R. (eds) *KOSMOS. Jewellery, Adornment and Textiles in the Aegean Bronze Age*, 107–111. Leuven and Liège. Peeters.

Jablonka, P. (2001) Eine Stadtmauer aus Holz. Das Bauwerk der Unterstadt von Troia II, in Archäologisches Landesmuseum Baden-Württemberg (ed.), *Troia. Traum und Wirklichkeit*, 391–394. Stuttgart. K. Theiss.

Jablonka, P. (2006) Leben außerhalb der Burg – Die Unterstadt von Troia, in Korfmann, M. O. (ed.), *Troia. Archäologie eines Siedlungshügels und seiner Landschaft*, 117–180. Mainz. Philipp von Zabern.

Kayan, I. (1995) The Troia Bay and supposed harbour sites in the Bronze Age, *Studia Troica*, 5, 211–235.

Korfmann, M. O. (1997) Troia – Ausgrabungen 1996, *Studia Troica*, 7, 1–71.

Korfmann, M. O. (2000) Troia – Ausgrabungen 1999, *Studia Troica*, 10, 1–52.

Korfmann, M. O. (2001) Troia/Wilusa – Ausgrabungen 2000, *Studia Troica*, 11, 1–50.

Korfmann, M. O. (2006) Troia – Archäologie eines Siedlungshügels und seiner Landschaft, in Korfmann, M. O. (ed.), *Troia. Archäologie eines Siedlungshügels und seiner Landschaft*, 1–12. Mainz. Philipp von Zabern.

Mountjoy, P. A. (1997) Local Mycenaean pottery at Troia, *Studia Troica*, 7, 259–267.

Mountjoy, P. A. (2006) Mykenische Keramik in Troia – Ein Überblick, in Korfmann, M. O. (ed.), *Troia. Archäologie eines Siedlungshügels und seiner Landschaft*, 241–252. Mainz. Philipp von Zabern.

Mårtensson, L., Andersson, E., Nosch, M.-L. and Batzer, A. (2006) *Technical Report, Experimental Archaeology, Part 2:2. Whorl or Bead? Tools and Textiles – Texts and*

Contexts Research Program. http://ctr.hum.ku.dk/
research/tools/Technical_report_2-2__experimental
_arcaheology.PDF/.

Pavúk, P. (2007) What can Troia tell us about the
MH period in the southern Aegean? in Felten, F.,
Gauß, W. and Smetana, R. (eds), *Middle Helladic
Pottery and Synchronisms*, 293–306. Wien. Verlag der
Österreichischen Akademie der Wissenschaften.

Pavúk, P. (2012) Of spools and discoid loomweights:
Aegean type weaving at Troy revisited, in Nosch,
M.-L. and Laffineur, R. (eds), *KOSMOS. Jewellery,
Adornment and Textiles in the Aegean Bronze Age*,
121–130. Leuven and Liège. Peeters.

Pavúk, P. (in press) Troia VI Früh und Mitte. Keramik,
Stratigraphie und Chronologie, *Studia Troica
Monographs* 3.

Rose, C. B. (1997) The 1996 Post-Bronze Age excavations
at Troia, *Studia Troica*, 7, 73–110.

Rose, C. B. (1999) The 1998 Post-Bronze Age excavations
at Troia, *Studia Troica*, 9, 35–71.

Sazcı, G. and Treister, M. (2006) Troias Gold – Die
Schätze des dritten Jahrtausends vor Christus,
in Korfmann, M. O. (ed.), *Troia. Archäologie eines*

Siedlungshügels und seiner Landschaft, 209–218. Mainz.
Philipp von Zabern.

Schliemann, H. (1881) *Ilios. Stadt und Land der Trojaner.*
Leipzig. Brockhaus.

Schmidt, H. (1902) *Heinrich Schliemann's Sammlung
Trojanischer Altertümer.* Berlin. Reimer.

Thumm-Doğrayan, D. (2006) Und doch war alles
anders… William Dörpfeld und Carl William Blegen,
in Korfmann, M. O. (ed.), *Troia. Archäologie eines
Siedlungshügels und seiner Landschaft*, 117–122. Mainz.
Philipp von Zabern.

Tolstikov, W. P. and Treister, M. (1996) *Der Schatz aus Troja.
Schliemann und der Mythos des Priamos-Goldes. Katalogbuch
zur Ausstellung in Moskau.* Stuttgart. Belser.

Treister, M. (2002) The relative and absolute chronology
of the Trojan treasures, in Aslan, R., Blum, S. W.
E., Kastl, G., Schweizer, F. and Thumm, D. (eds),
Mauerschau. Festschrift für Manfred Korfmann, 245–258.
Remshalden-Grunbach. Greiner.

Ünlüsoy, S. (2006) Vom Reihenhaus zum Megaron –
Troia I bis Troia III, in Korfmann, M. O. (ed.), *Troia.
Archäologie eines Siedlungshügels und seiner Landschaft*,
133–144. Mainz. Philipp von Zabern.

CHAPTER 6.14

Textile tools from Apliki, Cyprus

*Joanna S. Smith, Joanne Cutler, Eva Andersson Strand
and Marie-Louise Nosch*

The Late Bronze Age mining settlement of Apliki *Karamallos* (Taylor 1952; Kling and Muhly 2007; see Fig. 6.14.1 for a plan of the site) is situated on the north coast of Cyprus. Sixty-one Bronze Age textile tools from Joan du Plat Taylor's excavations at the site are recorded in the TTTC database; of these, 49 are loom weights, and 12 are spindle whorls. All of the textile tools are dated to Late Cypriot (LC) IIC/IIIA (1300–1200/1156 BC) (for the absolute dating, see Manning and Kuniholm 2007). Sixty of the tools come from House A. This building, which has extensive evidence for metal working activities, has a central courtyard and contains a large storage room; it may represent either one or two households, depending on whether the building is interpreted as a single complex or as two residences. Most of the textile tools were recovered from Rooms 2, 3 and 5; these rooms are only a few metres wide, and appear to have been multi-purpose spaces, used for the storage of food and tools as well as for food preparation (Smith 2007, 229).

Only one pyramidal weight comes from a Late Bronze Age context in Area B, which consists of three smaller buildings.

Spindle whorls and spinning

Of the 12 textile tools from House A that are classified as spindle whorls, six are biconical, four are lenticular, one is cylindrical and one is spherical. All of these objects are manufactured from clay; four are made of fired clay, seven (four lenticular, three biconical) are of burnt clay (not intentionally baked) and one biconical whorl is low fired.

Eight of the spindle whorls were found in Room 2, while two were recovered from Room 5. The remaining two whorls were from Rooms 1 and 3 respectively.

House A, Room 2
Only one of the whorls recovered from Room 2 was complete, with a weight of 45 g and a diameter of 4.1 cm; this whorl, found among the floor debris, is spherical in shape and is made of fired clay. The remaining seven whorls (three biconical and four lenticular) are of burnt clay and were found in a group, together with three loom weights, under a layer of burnt ash with carbonised wood immediately above (Smith 2007, 236). Two of these whorls are approximately half preserved, and weigh 20 g and 25 g,

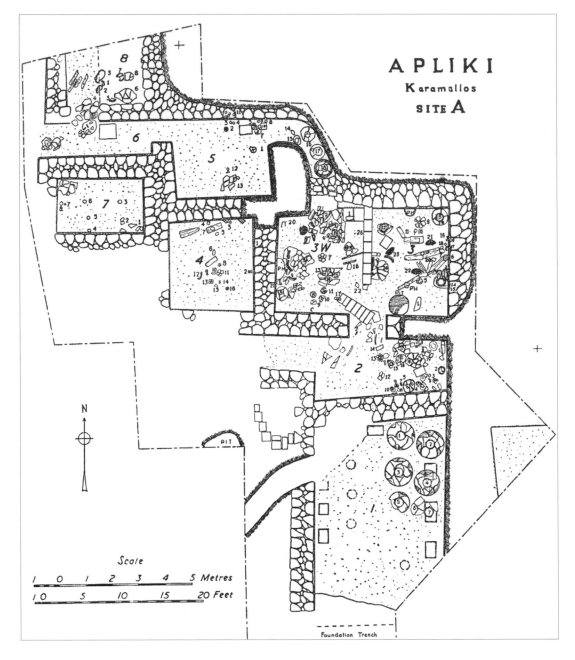

suggesting original weights of *c.* 40 g and 50 g. The rest are more than half preserved, with weights ranging from 35 g to 105 g. It is estimated (Smith 2007, 230) that the partially preserved spindle whorls are each missing less than 20 g of their original weights, thus suggesting a range of original weights varying from >35–<55 g to >105 g–<125 g. The lightest of these whorls, at *c.* 40 g, would be suitable for spinning thick thread. It is possible that the heaviest tools may have been used for spinning twine (cf. Smith 2007, 230). However, it should be noted that the whorls are made of unbaked clay. Whorls of unbaked clay are

rare, although ethnographic examples are not unknown (McCafferty and McCafferty 2000, 42). The use of unbaked clay would be far from optimal (although may have been expedient), given the wear caused by fitting the whorl on a spindle ready for use, the constant rotation during spinning, and the friction of the secured yarn against the whorl. The shape and weight of the unbaked clay whorls (as well as that of the fired clay whorl), would not rule out the possibility that some or all of them were used as loom weights, rather than as spindle whorls. If they were used as whorls, they are likely to have had a short use life.

House A, Rooms 1, 3 and 5

The single, fired clay, cylindrical whorl from Room 1 is almost complete, and weighs 145 g. The whorl from Room 3 (biconical in shape and made of low fired clay), was found in a basket in black ash with burnt timbers, along with 27 loom weights (Fig. 6.14.2; for the loom weights, see below). It is more than half preserved, with a weight of 90 g.

The two whorls from Room 5, both made of fired clay, are biconical in shape. One of the whorls is complete, with a weight of 40 g and a diameter of 4.3 cm; the other is more than half preserved, and weighs 45 g. They appear to have fallen from a niche, along with 11 loom weights.

Like the whorls from Room 2, the whorls from other contexts in House A may have been used to spin thick thread or twine, but it is also possible that some or all of them were used as loom weights rather than as spindle whorls.

Loom weights and weaving

Thirty-one of the 48 loom weights from House A are torus shaped, 13 are pyramidal, three are cylindrical and one is conical. The torus loom weights include two pierced sherds and a pierced stone. Thirty-two of the loom weights are complete or only have small fragments missing (17 torus, 12 pyramidal, two cylindrical and one conical); they vary in weight from 20 g to 270 g, with the majority weighing less than 150 g (Fig. 6.14.3). The presence of a few heavier, incomplete weights should also be noted (a torus weight weighing 200 g and a cylindrical weight weighing 280 g).

The two main types of weight, pyramidal and torus, fall within very similar weight ranges. The torus weights are generally thinner, however, and would therefore have been suitable for producing denser fabrics, with more warp threads per centimetre. With the exception of the two cylindrical weights,

Fig. 6.14.2. Five loom weights and a spindle whorl from House A, Room 3, LC IIC/IIIA (photo: after Smith 2007, 248, plate 65.A3:22.4-9).

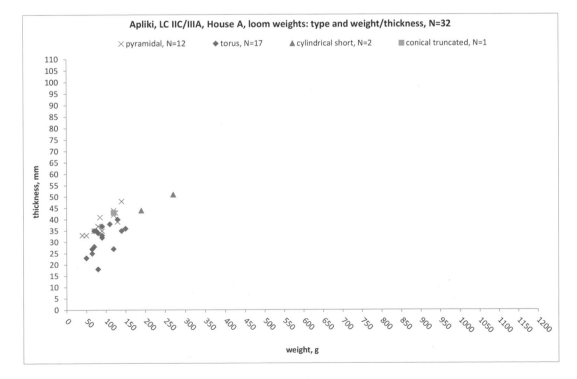

Fig. 6.14.3. Loom weights, LCIIC/IIIA, House A: type and weight/thickness. Please note that some markers represent more than one loom weight.

Apliki, LC IIC/IIIA, House A, loom weights: type and weight/thickness, N=32

✕ pyramidal, N=12   ◆ torus, N=17   ▲ cylindrical short, N=2   ■ conical truncated, N=1

thickness, mm

weight, g

none of the loom weights would be suitable for use with thread needing *c.* 15 g tension or more.

Most of the loom weights were recovered from Room 3 (27 weights) and Room 5 (11 weights), with low numbers of weights deriving from other rooms in the building (four from Room 1, four from Room 2, one from Room 4 and one from Room 7).

House A, Room 3

The 27 loom weights (26 torus and one cylindrical) recovered from Room 3 are all of burnt clay (not intentionally baked) (Fig. 6.14.2). They were found in a basket, in black ash, together with one spindle whorl and three further shapeless fragments of unbaked clay, which may also represent between one and three further loom weights. Fourteen of the torus loom weights are complete or only have small fragments missing; their weight varies from 50 g to 140 g, and their thickness ranges from 2.3 cm to 4.0 cm. (Fig. 6.14.4).

All of these loom weights would work well with very thin thread requiring *c.* 5 g tension, but the resulting thread count range of *c.* 8–16 warp threads per centimetre is too large a variation to be optimal (Fig. 6.14.5). In a twill weave, the thread count would be approximately double. All of the loom weights would also work well with thread

needing *c.* 7.5 g tension, but the thread count range of *c.* 5–10 warp threads per centimetre is still quite large. However, if thread needing *c.* 5–7.5 g tension were used, the thread count range would be a much narrower *c.* 8–11 warp threads per centimetre. This demonstrates that these loom weights would function very well together in the same loom setup. The fabrics made with them would be open in a balanced weave, and they may therefore have been weft faced.

The preserved weights and thicknesses of the remaining 13 loom weights suggests that all except one of them would have fallen within the same weight/thickness range as the complete loom weights. The exception is the cylindrical loom weight, with a preserved weight of 280 g, which would not be suitable for use with thread requiring less than *c.* 10 g tension, and would not be optimal for use with the other loom weights in the group.

The object recorded as a biconical spindle whorl, made of low-fired clay and with a preserved weight of 90 g and thickness of 4.1 cm, would also fit well within the overall weight/thickness range of the loom weights, and this suggests that it may have been used as a loom weight rather than as a spindle whorl. If used as a spindle whorl, it could not have been used to spin the very thin thread suitable for use with the associated loom weight group.

Fig. 6.14.4. Torus loom weights, LC IIC/IIIA, House A, Room 3: weight/thickness. Please note that some markers represent more than one loom weight.

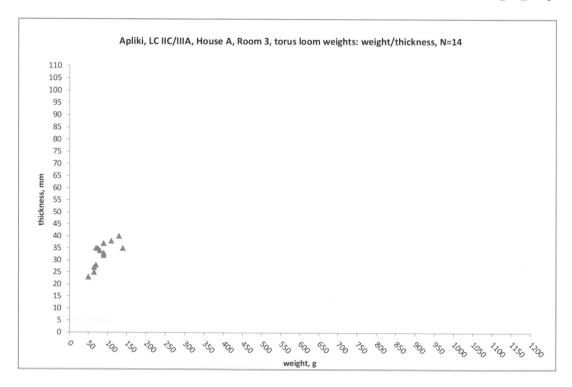

The loom weights in Room 3 were in storage at the time of the destruction of the building. The combined thickness of the 14 complete or almost complete weights is *c.* 46 cm. Adding in the thickness of the partially preserved torus loom weights and the object registered as a probable spindle whorl gives a total width of *c.* 85 cm. In a tabby weave (with 14 loom weights in the front row and 14 loom weights in the back row), the weights could be used to produce a fabric *c.* 43 cm wide. If the three additional fragments represent one to three further loom weights, the fabric woven could have been up to *c.* 50 cm wide. It is additionally possible that the loom weights stored in Room 3 may have been used in different combinations with the preserved and fragmentary weights found in Room 2.

Warp thr/cm	5 g, N=14	7.5 g, N=14	10 g, N=3
4 thr			
5 thr		1	
6 thr		4	1
7 thr		3	1
8 thr	1	4	1
9 thr	3	1	
10 thr	5	1	
11 thr	2		
12 thr	1		
13 thr	1		
14 thr			
15 thr			
16 thr	1		

Fig. 6.14.5. Torus loom weights, LC IIC/IIIA, House A, Room 3: weight tension/number of threads per cm in a tabby. The total number of analysed loom weights is 14.

House A, Room 2

Three of the loom weights from Room 2 (two torus and one cylindrical), were found together, under burnt ash and carbonised wood; they are made of burnt clay (not intentionally baked). Only one of these loom weights (cylindrical) is complete, with a weight of 190 g and a thickness of 4.4 cm. The remaining two weights are more than half preserved, with extant weights of 200 g and 105 g and thicknesses of 4.7 cm and 3.3 cm respectively.

The seven spindle whorls found in the same deposit are also made of burnt clay. If, as discussed above, the objects classified as spindle whorls are also considered as possible loom weights, the weights of the overall group would therefore range from >35 g to >200 g, and the thickness range is 1.6–4.7 cm. Twenty-one other fragments were also recovered, possibly representing the remains of additional loom weights/spindle whorls (Smith 2007, 232).

If used as loom weights, the tools registered as whorls would be suitable for use with very thin thread, requiring *c.* 5 g tension (with, in a few cases, a few less than 10 threads fastened to them). The complete loom weight and the heavier of the incomplete weights, on the other hand, would be optimal for use with slightly heavier thread tensions, with the complete weight being best suited for use with *c.* 10–20 g thread tension. If used for spinning, the tools registered as whorls would not be suitable for producing thread appropriate for use with the associated loom weights.

a

b

Fig. 6.14.6(a) and (b) Pyramidal loom weights from House A, Room 5, LC IIC/IIIA (photos: (a) after Smith 2007, 250, plate 67.A5:28; (b) after Smith 2007, 249, plate 66.A5:26).

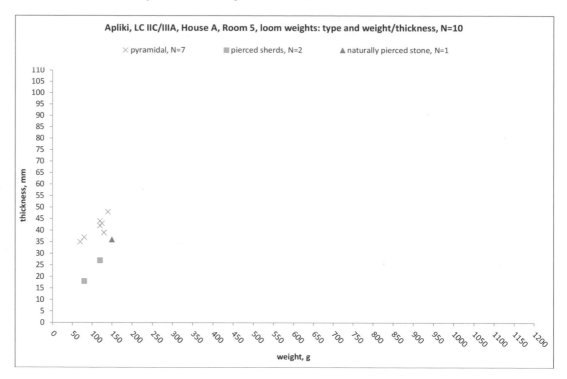

House A, Room 5

The 11 loom weights recovered from Room 5 were found in or near (as if they had fallen from) a niche in the north wall; 10 polishers and rubbers, a whetstone, a pottery disk and two bronze gravers were also found in the niche (Smith 2007, 232–233). Eight of the loom weights are pyramidal (Fig. 6.14.6) and three are torus; two of the torus weights are re-used pottery sherds and one is a pierced stone. All except one of the loom weights are complete or only have small fragments missing (Fig. 6.14.7). They vary in weight from 80 g to 150 g and their thickness ranges from 1.8 cm to 4.8 cm. The preserved weight of the remaining incomplete loom weight, at 150 g, suggests that it would have been heavier than the other weights.

All of the loom weights would function well with very thin thread requiring *c.* 5 g tension. Five would additionally work well with very thin thread needing *c.* 10 g tension, but only one would be optimal for use with slightly thicker *c.* 15 g tension thread. In a tabby weave with thread needing *c.* 5 g tension, the resulting fabric would have *c.* 9–18 warp threads per centimetre. If the two pierced sherds and the pierced stone were excluded, the thread count range would be much narrower (9–13 per

centimetre for thread requiring *c.* 5 g tension). This suggests that it would not be optimal to use the pierced sherds and the pierced stone in the same setup as the other loom weights. In balanced weaves, with approximately the same number and type of warp and weft threads per centimetre[2], the textiles produced would have been open, and the fabrics may therefore have been weft faced. The two fired clay whorls from this deposit, weighing 40 g and >45 g, would not be suitable for spinning the very thin thread appropriate for use with the associated loom weights.

Summary

The majority of the loom weights from Apliki would be suitable for use with thread requiring less than 10 g tension, suggesting an emphasis on the production of textiles made with very thin thread. If used to weave balanced tabby fabrics, many of the resulting textiles would be open, and they therefore may have been weft faced textiles. In general, the torus loom weights could be used to produce a textile with a slightly higher number of warp threads per centimetre than the pyramidal weights. None of the objects registered as spindle whorls would have been suitable for spinning the types of thread that could have been used with the loom weights. From their weight, shape and dimensions, it is possible that some or all of these tools may have been used as loom weights.

Bibliography

Kling, B. and Muhly, J. D. (2007) *Joan du Plat Taylor's Excavations at the Late Bronze Age Mining Settlement at Apliki* Karamallos, *Cyprus*. Sävedalen. Paul Aaström.

Manning, S. W. and Kuniholm, P. I. (2007) Absolute dating at Apliki *Karamallos*, in Kling, B. and Muhly, J. D. (eds), *Joan du Plat Taylor's Excavations at the Late Bronze Age Mining Settlement at Apliki* Karamallos, *Cyprus*, 325–335. Sävedalen. Paul Åström.

McCafferty, S. D. and McCafferty, G. G. (2000) Textile production in Postclassic Cholula, Mexico, *Ancient Mesoamerica*, 11, 39–54.

Smith, J. S. (2007) Loom weights and spindle whorls from Apliki *Karamallos*, in Kling, B. and Muhly, J. D. (eds), *Joan du Plat Taylor's Excavations at the Late Bronze Age Mining Settlement at Apliki* Karamallos, *Cyprus*, 229–251. Sävedalen. Paul Åström.

Taylor, J. du Plat (1952) A Late Bronze Age settlement at Apliki, Cyprus, *The Antiquaries Journal*, 32 (3–4), 133–67.

CHAPTER 6.15

Textile tools from Kition, Cyprus

*Joanna S. Smith, Joanne Cutler, Eva Andersson Strand
and Marie-Louise Nosch*

The Late Bronze Age settlement of Kition (Fig. 6.15.1) is situated on the south coast of Cyprus. Areas I and II, excavated by the Department of Antiquities of Cyprus (Karageorghis 1985; Karageorghis and Demas 1985), were first occupied in the 13th century BC, towards the end of the Late Cypriot IIC (LC IIC) period. The sequence of occupation down to the eleventh century BC is recorded in a series of 'Floors'. In Area I, the buildings contain relatively small rooms, while Area II contains five monumental structures that have been interpreted as temples and administrative areas (Smith 2009, 31–70), as well as two workshop areas. One of these workshop areas, the 'northern' workshop, has significant evidence for metal working, whereas the other, the 'western' workshop, was associated with textile production; 80% of the textile tools from Area II were recovered from rooms or outdoor spaces associated with the area of the western workshop (Smith 2002, 299).

A total of 323 textile tools from Kition are recorded in the TTTC database; 275 of these date to the Late Bronze Age (Figs. 6.15.2 and 6.15.3). Forty-seven objects date to the Cypro-Geometric I period (not discussed here).

Spindle whorls and spinning

Of the 13 spindle whorls (four spherical, four biconical, three conical and two convex) dating to the Late Bronze Age, nine are from LC IIIA contexts, while four were recovered from LC IIIA-B deposits (Fig. 6.15.4). A number of small conical yet very flattened steatite and ivory objects (not recorded in the database), sometimes thought to be buttons rather than whorls, were additionally recovered from the site.

The two convex whorls, one of the spherical and one of the conical whorls are made of stone (all dated to LC IIIA). One of the LC IIIA conical whorls is made of unfired clay, another is made of low baked clay; the remaining nine whorls are made of fired clay.

One of the LC IIIA-B biconical whorls has an hourglass hole. This would have caused the spindle to rotate unevenly if used as a spindle whorl, and it therefore would not have functioned well if used for this purpose. Similarly, the use of unbaked clay for a whorl would not be optimal (see comments on unbaked whorls from Apliki in chapter 6.14).

Five of the 13 Late Bronze Age whorls were recovered from Area I (one dated to

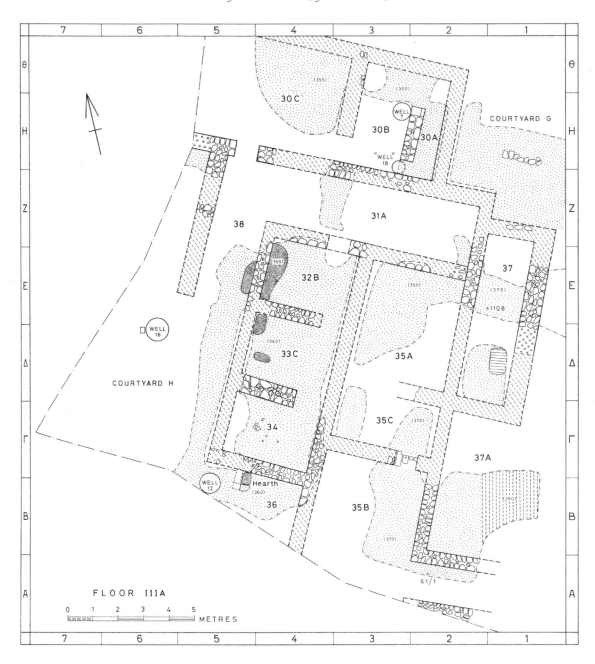

Fig. 6.15.1.a. Site plan: Area I, Floor IIIA (LCIIIA) (plan: reproduced with the permission of the Department of Antiquities, Cyprus, after Karageorghis and Demas 1985c, Plan 9, as reproduced in Smith 2009, fig. II.17b).

LC IIIA and four dated to LC IIIA-B). The remaining nine whorls (all dating to LC IIIA) were recovered from Area II.

Nine of the Late Bronze Age whorls are complete or only have small fragments missing; they range in weight from 14 g to 82 g (Fig. 6.15.5). The stone convex whorls are heavier than the other whorls, weighing 45 g and 82 g.

The lighter spindle whorls, weighing 14–19 g, would be suitable for spinning a thin to medium thread that would require a tension of *c.* 20–30 g in a loom setup. The heavier, 40–47 g whorls could be used to spin thick thread, while the 82 g whorl could produce a very thick thread. The complete or nearly complete whorls from Area I weigh 18–45 g and those from Area II weigh 14–82 g. One incomplete, LC IIIA conical whorl from Area II, made of low fired clay and with a partial weight of 120 g, should also be noted. It is possible that this may have been used for spinning twine (cf. Smith 2007, 230), but it is also possible that it may have functioned as a loom weight.

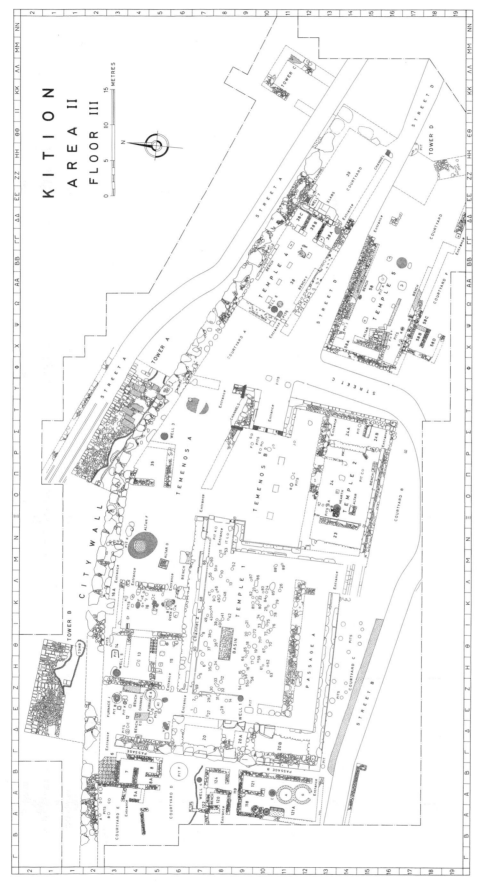

Fig. 6.15.1.b. Site plan: Area II, Floor III (LCIIIA) (plan: reproduced with the permission of the Department of Antiquities, Cyprus, as adapted from Karageorghis and Demas 1985c, Plan V, with channels, basin, and other cuttings in courtyard of Temple 1 included. After Smith 2009, fig. II.3).

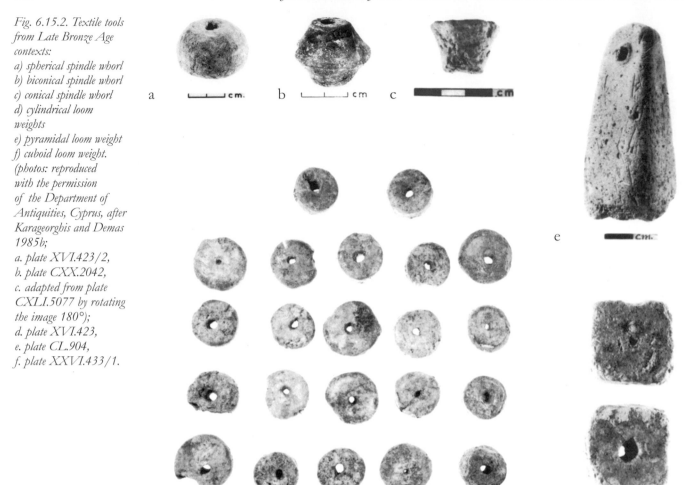

Fig. 6.15.2. Textile tools from Late Bronze Age contexts:
a) spherical spindle whorl
b) biconical spindle whorl
c) conical spindle whorl
d) cylindrical loom weights
e) pyramidal loom weight
f) cuboid loom weight.
(photos: reproduced with the permission of the Department of Antiquities, Cyprus, after Karageorghis and Demas 1985b;
a. plate XVI.423/2,
b. plate CXX.2042,
c. adapted from plate CXLI.5077 by rotating the image 180°);
d. plate XVI.423,
e. plate CL.904,
f. plate XXVI.433/1.

	Spindle whorl	Loom weight	Spool	Pointed tool	Total
LC IIC–IIIA		14		2	**16**
LC IIIA	9	124	32	14	**179**
LC IIIA-B	4	70	3	1	**78**
LC IIIB				1	**1**
LC		1			**1**
CGI	1	36	9	1	**47**
Unstratified	1				**1**
Total	**15**	**245**	**44**	**19**	**323**

Fig. 6.15.3. Textile tools, by type and date.

	Biconical	Conical	Convex	Spherical	Total
LC IIIA	2	3	2	2	**9**
LC IIIA–B	2			2	**4**
Total	**4**	**3**	**2**	**4**	**13**

Fig. 6.15.4. Spindle whorls, by type and date.

Loom weights and weaving

Of the 244 loom weights (including spools) dating to the Late Bronze Age, 117 were recovered from Area I, while 127 come from Area II (Fig. 6.15.6). The majority of the loom weights from both areas are from LC IIIA contexts (62 from Area I and 94 from Area II). A variety of loom weight types are represented, but the cylindrical and pyramidal types are the most frequent (Fig. 6.15.6). A higher number of spools were recovered from Area II than from Area I.

The majority of the loom weights (232) are made from fired clay; 11 are made from unfired clay (six cylindrical, four pyramidal and one spool) and one flat trapezoidal weight is made of stone.

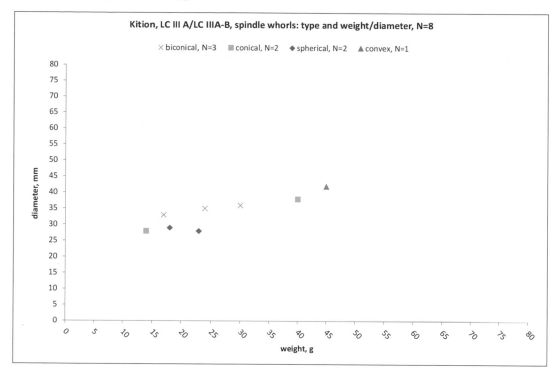

Fig. 6.15.5. Spindle whorls, LC IIIA/ LC IIIA-B: type and weight/diameter (excluding a convex whorl weighing 82 g).

Area 1	Conical	Cuboid	Cylindrical	Flat trapezoidal	Pyramidal	Spherical	Spool	Total
LC IIC-IIIA			2	2	5			**9**
LC IIIA	1		32		26		3	**62**
LC IIIA-B		2	25		15	1	2	**45**
LC						1		**1**
Total	1	2	59	2	47	1	5	**117**
Area II	**Conical**	**Cuboid**	**Cylindrical**	**Flat trapezoidal**	**Pyramidal**	**Spherical**	**Spool**	**Total**
LC IIC-IIIA					5			**5**
LC IIIA	1		34	1	29		29	**94**
LC IIIA-B		1	8		18		1	**28**
LC								**0**
Total	1	1	42	1	52	0	30	**127**
Overall Total	**2**	**3**	**101**	**3**	**99**	**1**	**35**	**244**

Fig. 6.15.6. Loom weights by area, type and date.

One hundred and thirty-one of the loom weights from LC IIC-IIIB contexts were complete, or only have small fragments missing (Fig. 6.15.7). The majority of the loom weights weigh less than 200 g, and would have been suitable for use with very thin to thin thread requiring less than 20 g tension. A smaller number weigh 200–355 g; the heaviest weight (355 g) would be suitable for use with thin to medium thread requiring *c.* 15–35 g tension. The pyramidal loom weights and the spools lie within a similar weight/thickness group, although the pyramidal weights lie at the lower end of the weight/thickness range, while the majority of the spools are at the upper end. Most of the spools weigh more than 50 g and would work well as loom weights. The lightest spools would also be suitable for use in tablet weaving or other band weaving techniques (see chapter 4.1).

The cylindrical weights, on the other hand, are generally thinner, and would be suitable for producing denser textiles than the other types. This category of loom weight also contains a number of heavier weights, weighing more than 275 g.

Fig. 6.15.7. Loom weights, LC IIC-IIIB: type and weight/thickness. Please note that some markers represent more than one loom weight.

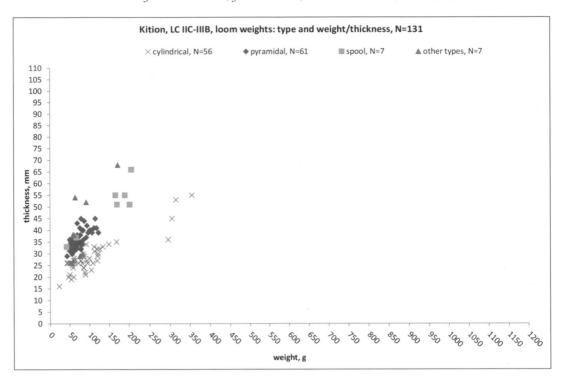

Fig. 6.15.8. Loom weights, LC IIC-IIIB, Area I and Area II: weight/thickness. Please note that some markers represent more than one loom weight.

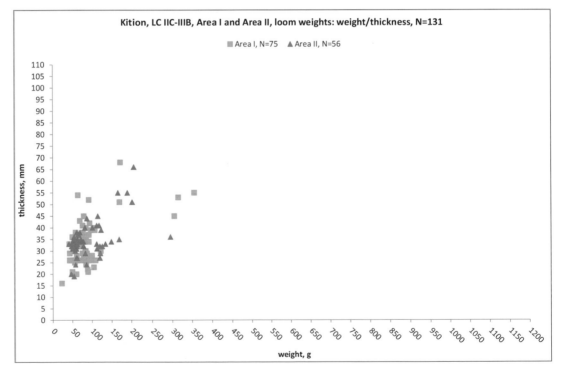

Seventy-five of the complete or almost complete loom weights come from Area I, while the remaining 56 are from Area II. The loom weights from the two areas fall within very similar weight/thickness ranges (Fig. 6.15.8).

Area I, Floor IIIA, Courtyard H

In Area I, 33 loom weights (25 cylindrical, seven pyramidal and one conical) were recovered from Floor IIIA, Courtyard H (LC IIIA). Twenty-two of the cylindrical weights were found in a group, while a further five pyramidal

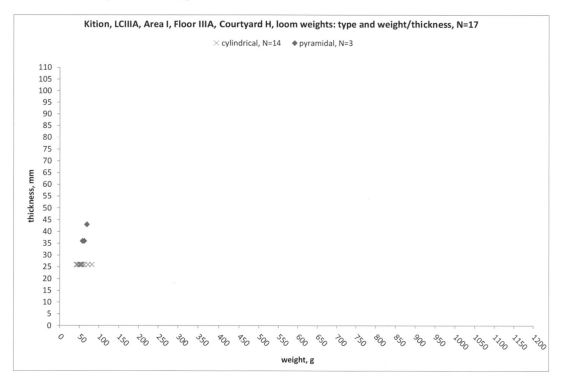

Kition, LCIIIA, Area I, Floor IIIA, Courtyard H, loom weights: type and weight/thickness, N=17

✕ cylindrical, N=14   ◆ pyramidal, N=3

Fig. 6.15.9. Loom weights, LCIIIA, Area I, Floor IIIA, Courtyard H: type and weight/thickness. Please note that some markers represent more than one loom weight.

weights associated with them were possibly lying in a row; 17 of the weights are complete or only have small fragments missing. Their weights range between 43 g and 82 g (Fig. 6.15.9). Most of the incomplete weights are also likely to have fallen within a similar weight range, although a few are slightly heavier (with partial weights of 106 g and 109 g).

All 17 of the complete or nearly complete loom weights would function well with very thin thread needing *c.* 5 g tension. In a tabby weave, the pyramidal weights could produce a fabric with *c.* 7 warp threads per centimetre; based on their average thickness, the cylindrical loom weights could produce a fabric with *c.* 7–12 threads per centimetre. If the fabrics were balanced, they would be open, and they are therefore likely to have been weft faced. In a twill weave the thread count would be approximately double, but this would still be an open fabric and would also be likely to be weft faced. The loom weights weighing less than 50 g would provide a slightly lower tension, unless fewer than 10 threads were fastened to each one. None of the loom weights would be suitable for use with thread requiring 10 g tension. It is interesting to note that the two types of loom weights – cylindrical and pyramidal – in this deposit could function well

together. The stone (white chalk) spindle whorl, possibly from this deposit (or from between Floors IIIA and III), weighing 45 g, would not be suitable for spinning such fine thread, but with a height (thickness) of 2.6 cm, it would function well with the other weights if it was used as a loom weight.

Area I, Floor II, Courtyard D

Seventeen loom weights were recovered from Area I, Floor II, Courtyard D (LC IIIA-B). Eleven of these (eight cylindrical, two cuboid and one pyramidal) were found in a group. Only four of the loom weights found together are complete or only have small fragments missing (two cylindrical and two cuboid). These range in weight from 76–122 g, suggesting that, like the loom weights from Courtyard H, they would be optimal for use with thinner threads. However, five of the incomplete weights have partial weights of 220–295 g, and these would not be suitable for use with thread requiring less than *c.* 10 g tension. The spherical spindle whorl also recovered from this deposit with a partial weight of 41 g would be optimal for spinning much thicker thread than would be suitable for use with the loom weights (although it is possible that this object may have been used as a loom weight).

Area II, Floor III, Room 118

In Area II, 18 weights (13 cylindrical and five spools) were found on Floor III, Room 118 (LC IIIA) of the western workshop; eight of the cylindrical weights were found in a group. Only three of these have a complete weight; their weight range, 48–126 g, indicates that they would be suitable for use with very thin threads. The weights of the incomplete weights (70–132 g) suggests that the weight range of the group would have extended further, however. The object classified as a spindle whorl found with this group, with a partial weight of 120 g, would not be suitable for spinning the thread that could be used with the loom weights, but if it was used as a loom weight it would fit well with the other loom weights in the deposit.

Area II, Floor II, Room 8

Ten loom weights (five pyramidal, four cylindrical and one spool) were recovered from Area II, Floor II, Room 8 (LC IIIA-B). Seven of these (four cylindrical and three pyramidal) were possibly in a row. Three of the cylindrical and three of the pyramidal weights are complete or only have small fragments missing and weigh 47–86 g. Although the group contains two types of weights, they could function together if used in a tabby setup with thread requiring *c.* 5 g tension, but the variation in the thread count, *c.* 6–14 warp threads per centimetre, is high, largely as a result of the cylindrical weight weighing 86 g, which would be suitable for producing a denser weave than the other weights in the group (Fig. 6.15.10).

Fig. 6.15.10. Loom weights, LC IIIA-B, Area II, Floor II, Room 8: weight tension/number of threads per cm in a tabby. The total number of analysed loom weights is six.

Warp thr/cm	5 g, N=6
5 thr	
6 thr	1
7 thr	2
8 thr	1
9 thr	1
10 thr	
11 thr	
12 thr	
13 thr	
14 thr	1

Summary

None of the spindle whorls recovered from Areas I and II would be optimal for spinning very thin thread requiring *c.* 5–10 g tension. The lightest whorls (14–19 g) could be suitable for spinning thread needing *c.* 20–30 g tension. It is possible that the heaviest spindle whorls were used for spinning twine (cf. Smith 2007, 230), but it is also possible that they were used as loom weights rather than as spindle whorls.

Most of the loom weights weigh less than 200 g, with the majority weighing less than 150 g. This indicates that they would have been most suited for use with thread requiring less than 20 g tension, with a concentration of loom weights being optimal for use with very thin thread needing less than 15 g tension. Many of the resulting textiles would be open, however, unless they were weft faced. Fewer loom weights could be used with thicker thread needing 20 g tension or more and none would be suitable for use with thread requiring more than 35 g tension. On the whole, the cylindrical loom weights, being generally thinner than the pyramidal loom weights with the same weight, would produce a denser weave. However, there is some overlap between the two groups, as can be seen in the case of the group of loom weights from Area I, Floor IIIA, Courtyard H and Area II, Floor II, Room 8.

A number of pointed bone tools were recovered from the same contexts as the textile tools; these bone tools would also be well-suited for use in weaving. Prior to the TTTC study Smith proposed that they were for beating in the weft in tapestry production (see Smith 2001, 2002, 2012, 2013; Smith and Tzachili 2012).

Although the loom weights from Area I were recovered from household contexts, while the majority of those from Area II come from the western workshop, the tools suggest that there was no significant difference in the range of textiles produced in the two areas. A series of pits and vats, together with materials such as bone ash, lime and copper fragments present in each floor of Area II, possibly associated with the washing and dyeing of textiles, suggests that fulling and dyeing activities on a larger scale may have taken place in this area, however (Smith 2002, 303). The finds of *in situ* loom weights in courtyard contexts in both Area I and Area II suggest that some weaving took place outside.

Bibliography

Karageorghis, V. (1985) *Excavations at Kition V. The Pre-Phoenician Levels Part II.* Nicosia. Department of Antiquities, Cyprus.

Karageorghis, V. and Demas, M. (1985a) *Excavations at Kition V. The Pre-Phoenician Levels Areas I and II Part I.* Nicosia. Department of Antiquities, Cyprus.

Karageorghis, V. and Demas, M. (1985b) *Excavations at Kition V. The Pre-Phoenician Levels. Plates.* Nicosia. Department of Antiquities, Cyprus.

Karageorghis, V. and Demas, M. (1985c) *Excavations at Kition V. The Pre-Phoenician Levels. Plans and Sections Areas I and II.* Nicosia. Department of Antiquities, Cyprus.

Smith, J. S. (2001) Bone Weaving Tools of the Late Bronze Age, in P. M. Fischer (ed.), *Contributions to the Archaeology and History of the Bronze and Iron Ages in the Eastern Mediterranean. Studies in Honour of Paul Åström*, 83–90. Vienna. Austrian Archaeological Institute.

Smith, J. S. (2002) Changes in the workplace: women and textile production on Late Bronze Age Cyprus, in Bolger, D. and Sewint, N. (eds), *Engendering Aphrodite. Women and Society in Ancient Cyprus*, 281–312. Boston, MA. American School of Oriental Research.

Smith, J. S. (2007) Loom weights and spindle whorls from Apliki *Karamallos*, in Kling, B. and Muhly, J. D. (eds), *Joan du Plat Taylor's Excavations at the Late Bronze Age Mining Settlement at Apliki* Karamallos, *Cyprus*, 229–251. Sävedalen. Paul Åström.

Smith, J. S. (2009) *Art and Society in Cyprus from the Bronze Age into the Iron Age*. Cambridge. Cambridge University Press.

Smith, J. S. (2012) Tapestries in the Mediterranean Late Bronze Age, in Nosch, M.-L. and R. Laffineur (eds), *KOSMOS: Jewellery, Adornment and Textiles in the Aegean Bronze Age*, 241–250. Liège. Peeters.

Smith, J. S. (2013) Tapestries in the Bronze and Early Iron Ages of the ancient Near East, in Nosch, M.-L. and Koefoed, H. (eds), *Textile Production and Consumption in the Ancient Near East: Archaeology, Epigraphy, Iconography*, 159–186. Ancient Textiles Series 12. Oxford. Oxbow Books.

Smith, J. S. and Tzachili, I. (2012) Cloth in Crete and Cyprus, in Cadogan, G., Iacovou, M., Whitley, J. and Kopaka, K. (eds), *Parallel Lives: Ancient Island Societies in Crete and Cyprus*, 141–155. London. British School at Athens.

CHAPTER 6.16

Textile tools from Tel Kabri, Israel

Assaf Yasur-Landau, Nurith Goshen, Eva Andersson Strand, Marie-Louise Nosch and Joanne Cutler

Tel Kabri is located in the western Galilee region of modern Israel. Excavations were initially conducted by Aharon Kempinski and Wolf-Dietrich Niemeier from 1986–1993 and renewed by Eric Cline and Assaf Yasur-Landau in 2005 (Kempinski 2002; Cline and Yasur-Landau 2007; Yasur-Landau *et al.* 2008). During the Middle Bronze Age, Kabri was the centre of a Canaanite polity, ruling the northern part of the Acco plain. At the time, Kabri had economic and cultural connections with Egypt, Cyprus, and the Aegean. It is one of only four sites in the Eastern Mediterranean to have Bronze Age Aegean paintings adorning a palatial structure (Niemeier and Niemeier 2000).

A total of 90 textile tools from Tel Kabri are recorded in the TTTC database. They represent available textile tools from the Kempinski and Niemeier excavations published by Oren (2002). Unfortunately, not all the textile tools from the old excavations were located in the Israel Antiquities authority storerooms and so this chapter will refer only to objects available at the time of the data entry. Of the 90 textile tools, 67 tools are dated to the MB II period, and mostly belong to the latest phase of the palace (Kempinski Phase 3c, our Phase DWIII). These include four spindle whorls, 62 loom weights and one needle, while the remaining 23 tools have a wide range of dates, from the Late Neolithic through to the Ottoman period. This analysis will focus on the MB II tools from the palace area. Additional tools found in the renewed excavations, directed by Eric H. Cline and Assaf Yasur-Landau are discussed in Goshen, Yasur-Landau and Cline (2013).

Spindle whorls and spinning

From the old excavations, 38 spindle whorls are recorded, of which only 13 are dated to the MBA and only eight of them securely (Oren 2002: table 10.3). When creating the database, only six spindle whorls dated to the MBA period were found and out of them only four derive from secure MBA contexts in Area D. Therefore, the information currently available to us is limited, yet still illuminating.

Of the four spindle whorls, one spherical and one lenticular whorl are made of clay, while two convex shaped whorls are made of bone and stone respectively (Fig. 6.16.1). Only one of the whorls was found in a room context, on the floor of Room 740, another was found in the east wall of the room, wall 692. The two other spindle whorls were found in a second storey collapse layer. The weight range of the spindle whorls is 8–21 g, which indicates a production of very thin to medium spun yarn.

Loom weights and weaving

With the exception of one stone loom weight, all of the MB II weights are made of fired clay. Forty-three of the clay loom weights have a conical shape; the remaining 18 are either fragmentary or do not have an assigned type. The loom weights were found in a variety of contexts; however, 13 were recovered from the eastern part of Room 690 in the palace, and 13 from the centre of the same room.

Nine of the loom weights from the eastern part of Room 690, nine of the weights from the the centre of Room 690 and a further 21 loom weights from other contexts had a recordable weight and thickness. The weight of these 39 loom weights varies from 235 g to 600 g and their thickness varies from 5.4 cm to 7.2 cm (Fig. 6.16.2).

None of the loom weights would have been suitable for use with thread needing less than *c.* 10 g tension. The smallest loom weight would function with very thin to thin thread needing *c.* 10–20 g; the heaviest weight would be suitable for use with thread requiring *c.* 20–60 g tension.

The nine loom weights from the eastern part of Room 690 would all be suitable for use with thin to medium thread needing

Fig. 6.16.1. MB II spindle whorls: material, type, weight and diameter.

Type	Material	Weight (g)	Diameter (mm)
Spherical	clay	8	28
Convex	stone	14	30
Convex	bone	not known	26
Lenticular	clay	21	42

Fig. 6.16.2. Loom weights, MB II: context and weight/thickness. Please note, some markers represent more than one loom weight.

Tel Kabri, MB II, loom weights: weight/thickness, N=39

✕ palace, eastern part of Room 690, N=9   ■ palace, centre of Room 690, N=9   ◆ other contexts, N=21

Fig. 6.16.3. Loom weights, MB II, palace, eastern part of Room 690: weight tension/ number of threads per cm in a tabby. The total number of analysed loom weights is nine.

Warp thr/cm	15 g, N=6	20 g, N=9	25 g, N=9	30 g, N=9	35 g, N=7	40 g, N=5	45 g, N=3	50 g, N=3	55 g, N=2
3 thr				1	2	2		2	2
4 thr			3	5	2	2	3	1	
5 thr		2	3	2	3	1			
6 thr	1	4	1	1					
7 thr	2		2						
8 thr	2	2							
9 thr	1	1							

c. 20–30 g tension (Fig. 6.16.3). In a tabby weave with thread needing *c.* 20 g tension the fabric produced would have *c.* 5–9 warp threads per centimetre; with thread needing *c.* 25 g or *c.* 30 g tension, the thread count would be *c.* 4–7 and *c.* 3–6 threads per centimetre respectively (in a twill weave the thread count would be approximately double). The loom weights could therefore work well together in the same loom setup.

The nine loom weights from the centre of Room 690 would also function well with thread needing *c.* 20–30 g tension and could produce fabrics within the same thread count ranges as the loom weights from the eastern part of the room.

Summary

The analyses of the textile tools from late MB IIB contexts at Tel Kabri indicate a varied production of different types of textiles: textiles woven with thin threads and textiles woven with thicker thread. However, the analyses of the four spindle whorls demonstrate that only the thinner thread types would have been spun with these whorls.

The loom weights from the the centre of Room 690 in the palace and the loom weights from the eastern part of the same room could function together in setups using thread needing *c.* 20–30 g tension.

Acknowledgement

We are very grateful to the Israel Antiquities Authority for facilitating this study.

Bibliography

Cline, E. H. and Yasur-Landau, A. (2007) Poetry in motion: Canaanite rulership and Aegean narrative at Kabri, in Morris, S. P. and Laffineur, R. (eds), *EPOS: Reconsidering Greek Epic and Aegean Bronze Age Archaeology*, 157–165. Liège. Université de Liège.

Goshen, N., Yasur-Landau, A. and Cline, E. H. (2013) Textile production in palatial and non-palatial contexts: the case of Tel Kabri, in Nosch, M.-L., Koefoed, H. and Andersson Strand, E. (eds), *Textile Production and Consumption in the Ancient Near East. Archaeology, Epigraphy, Iconography*, 45–53. Ancient Textiles Series 12. Oxford. Oxbow Books.

Kempinski, A. (2002) *Tel Kabri. The 1986–1993 Excavations*. Tel Aviv. Emery and Claire Yass Publications in Archaeology, Institute of Archaeology, Tel Aviv University.

Niemeier, B. and Niemeier, W.-D. (2000) Aegean frescoes in Syria-Palestine: Alalakh and Tel Kabri, in Sherratt, S. (ed.), *The Wall Paintings of Thera*, 763–802. Athens. Thera Foundation.

Oren, R. (2002) Loom weights and spindle whorls, in Kempinski, A. (ed.), *Tel Kabri. The 1986–1993 Excavations*, 363–372. Tel Aviv. Emery and Claire Yass Publications in Archaeology, Institute of Archaeology, Tel Aviv University.

Yasur-Landau, A., Cline, E. H. and Pierce, G. A. (2008) Middle Bronze Age settlement patterns in the western Galilee, Israel, *Journal of Field Archaeology*, 33 (1), 59–83.

CHAPTER 7

Summary of results and conclusions

Eva Andersson Strand and Marie-Louise Nosch

In this final chapter, it is our pleasure to summarise the most important findings of this volume. We will present our analysis of spindle whorls and loom weights, respectively, and highlight the results and conclusions, but also discuss potential pitfalls in textile tool analysis and interpretation. This also includes our assessments of the more challenging categories of textile tools, beads, kylix stems, pierced sherds and conuli for spinning, and pebbles for weaving.

The analysis of these textile tool categories is then compared to the results we gained from the experimental testing and from the external analysis of the spinning and weaving tests.

In the second part of this chapter, we open up the discussion of how textile tools can bring about new information concerning Bronze Age textiles and textile workers. The analysis of textile tools can inform us about time consumption, workshops and the mobility of textile workers, about various craft traditions, the usage of tools and how they are made. When the functional analysis is combined with the study of archaeological textiles and iconography, we gain new knowledge of potential techniques, colours and patterns, and on available fibres. Written records name the textile workers and their textile tools, provide detailed information

about those textile industries of interest to palaces and administrations, and also afford a glimpse of the non-functional parameters of textiles and textile tools.

Spinning

Spindle whorls
More than 4000 items were recorded as potential spinning tools in the TTTC database; these include not only spindle whorls, but also conuli, beads, kylix stems and pierced sherds. As discussed in the introduction to the textile tools database (chapter 5.1), the tools recorded cannot be considered as representative for the entire Bronze Age, or for the Eastern Mediterranean region as a whole. It is, therefore, difficult to compare and contrast the production of spun yarn in different sites, regions and periods.

However, the TTTC database includes a large number of spindle whorls from Troia (1,493, and an additional 10 conuli), spanning the entire Bronze Age and representing more than 35% of the total number of whorls recorded. In the following, the spindle whorl types from Troia are discussed from a technological perspective, in order to shed light on the development of spinning at the

Fig. 7.1. Troia I–VII, number of spindle whorls with a recordable weight and diameter, by period and weight group.

Period	I	II	III	IV	V	VI	VII
No. of spindle whorls with recordable weight and diameter	100	231	194	159	90	367	219
spindle whorls 1–10 g	17	39	18	14	21	68	29
spindle whorls 11–20 g	22	50	58	31	22	97	59
spindle whorls 21–30 g	36	64	52	41	20	114	63
spindle whorls 31–40 g	13	50	46	50	17	62	38
spindle whorls 41–50 g	6	17	14	17	6	17	24
spindle whorls 51–60 g	5	7	5	2	4	3	3
spindle whorls 61–70 g	1	4	1	4		4	3
spindle whorls 71–80 g						2	

Fig. 7.2. Troia I–VII, percentage of spindle whorls with a recordable weight and diameter, by period and weight group. Percentages of 15% and above are highlighted in grey.

Period	I	II	III	IV	V	VI	VII
No. of spindle whorls with recordable weight and diameter	100	231	194	159	90	367	219
spindle whorls 1–10 g	17%	17%	9%	9%	23%	19%	13%
spindle whorls 11–20 g	22%	22%	30%	19%	24%	26%	27%
spindle whorls 21–30 g	36%	28%	27%	26%	22%	31%	29%
spindle whorls 31–40 g	13%	22%	24%	31%	19%	17%	17%
spindle whorls 41–50 g	6%	7%	7%	11%	7%	5%	11%
spindle whorls 51–60 g	5%	3%	2.50%	1%	4%	1%	1%
spindle whorls 61–70 g	1%	2%	0.50%	3%		1%	1%
spindle whorls 71–80 g					0.50%		

specific site of Troia itself, and, possibly, in the Bronze Age Eastern Mediterranean as well (see also chapter 6.13 for Troia). Various whorl categories are then compared and contrasted in terms of their suitability for spinning.

2000 years of spinning in Troia

The spindle whorls from Troia are dated to all periods of the site (Troia I–VII, *c.* 3000–950 BC) and are generally from household contexts. The majority of the whorls are made of clay and have a biconical shape. Of the total number of whorls recorded, 1,360 have a recordable weight and diameter. In order to compare the types of thread that the whorls within and between the different periods would be suitable for spinning, the various weight groups of these whorls were analysed (Figs. 7.1 and 7.2).

It is significant that the distribution of the whorls in different weight groups does not change dramatically during a period of over 2000 years. Throughout the period, the largest group is spindle whorls weighing between 11–40 g. This distribution of spindle whorls into different weight groups is evidence of a consistently varied production of very thin to thick threads.

It is also worth noting that, in period I, the spindle whorls weighing 10 g or less already constituted 17% of the total number of spindle whorls (Fig. 7.2), a percentage that continues more or less unchanged throughout the Bronze Age. The spinning experiments (chapters 1 and 4.2) clearly demonstrate that it is possible to spin suitable thread on a very light whorl of only 4 g. Furthermore, ethnographic sources show that whorls as light as 1 g and only 0.8 cm in diameter have been used for spinning (chapter 2). The analysis of the spindle whorls from Troia thus indicates that spinning with very light spindle whorls was already taking place at the beginning of the Bronze Age.

When studying the spindle whorls from the same context and period, it is evident that even if several spindle whorls are from the same room and/or house, they are often of

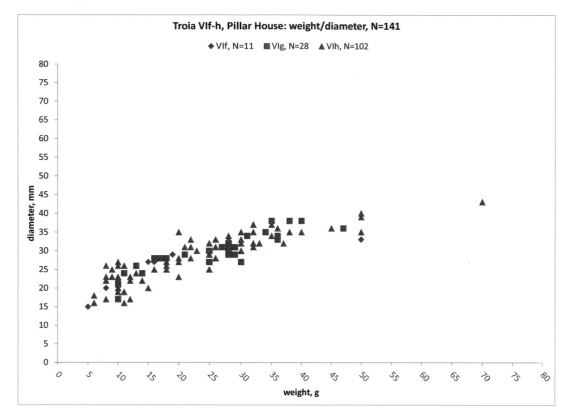

Troia VIf-h, Pillar House: weight/diameter, N=141

◆ VIf, N=11   ■ VIg, N=28   ▲ VIh, N=102

Fig. 7.3. Troia VIf–h spindle whorls: weight/ diameter. Please note that some markers represent more than one spindle whorl.

different sizes and weight groups, suggesting that, in all contexts and periods, different types of yarn were being spun. The spindle whorls primarily derive from household contexts. If yarn was solely produced for household consumption, the presence of the different whorls clearly shows that different spindle whorls were needed, *i.e.* that different types of yarn were required on a household basis. If the households also produced yarn for others, again, the spinning tools suggest a varied yarn production. If we hypothesise that spinning workshops existed in Troia, we must conclude that in these workshops, different types of yarn were produced, and not merely a single standard type.

A salient example from one of the later periods (Troia VI phases f–h) is the 141 spindle whorls from the Pillar House. Even if the majority of the whorls are dated to phase h, the whorls in all phases vary in weight and diameter, signifying a continued varied production of different types of yarn from thin to thick (Fig. 7.3).

The results of the analyses demonstrate that the inhabitants of Troia, throughout the Bronze Age, required and produced yarn in different qualities, indicating that they were making textiles of very different types and qualities. This suggests that spinners in Troia could select the type of yarn they wished to produce; they possessed adequate spinning tools and, in all probability, the skills and knowledge of how to use them.

Summary of the analyses of other types of spinning tools

In this section, some object types that are sometimes included in the textile tool repertoire – conuli, beads, kylix stem whorls and pierced sherds – are discussed from a functional perspective, and the suitability of these items as spinning tools and their place and distribution within spindle whorl assemblages and contexts are considered.

Conuli

Conulus is a technical term applied by some Aegean archaeologists to small objects mostly defined as:

1. Weighing less than 10 g
2. Conical in shape
3. Made of stone.

In the TTTC database, conuli were recorded at six different sites (Asine, Thebes, Tiryns, Troia, Phaistos, Nichoria) and are all dated to the Late Bronze Age. This type of object is also well known from other Late Bronze Age sites, such as Mycenae. The possible function of the conuli as spindle whorls has been questioned and discussed, and similar objects are sometimes termed 'buttons' (Iacovidis 1977; Dickinson 2006, 158; Andersson *et al.* 2008; Rahmstorf 2009). The significant question here is whether conuli are a distinct object type, with their own properties and functionality, or whether they are part of the spindle whorl repertoire; whether the conulus classification mirrors functionality, or is a stylistic description; and ultimately whether conuli should be considered as spinning tools.

In some sites conuli are found with other textiles tools, but they are also found in burials, and sometimes a large number of conuli are found together (Iakovidis 1977). This could indeed be an argument for the conuli having been used for something other than spinning, for example, dress adornments. However, the

relatively standardised shape and weight of the conuli may suggest standardised Late Bronze Age spinning tools for achieving a standardised, thin yarn.

Spinning experiments (*e.g.* Andersson 2003; chapter 4.1) have clearly demonstrated that it is possible to spin on a whorl weighing less than 10 g and produce a thin but tenable thread. It is important to consider, therefore, the technical, functional and morphological differences that lie between a conulus and a spindle whorl. In order to explore this further, assemblages of conuli and spindle whorls from securely dated contexts (LH IIIA–C) at Midea, Tiryns and Thebes on mainland Greece are here compared (Fig. 7.4).

Conuli material and shape compared to spindle whorls

The objects classified as conuli from Tiryns and Thebes are, in general, made of stone, while only a few are made of clay (Fig. 7.5a). The most common conulus type is conical, as the name indicates. However, the objects recorded as spindle whorls from Tiryns, Thebes and Midea are generally also made of stone, with 60% having a conical shape (Fig. 7.5b). There is no universal definition of what constitutes a conulus; this is partly due to factors such as academic conventions and traditions, and the classification requirements integral to archaeology.

When comparing the weight/diameter of the spindle whorls with the weight/diameter

Fig. 7.4. Midea, Tiryns and Thebes: number of spindle whorls and conuli from securely dated contexts (LH IIIA–C) recorded in the TTTC database.

	Spindle whorls	Conuli
Midea	48	
Tiryns	32	43
Thebes	63	40
Total	142	82

Fig. 7.5a. Tiryns and Thebes, LH III, conuli, by type and material.

Conuli		Biconical	Concave conical	Conical	Convex	Discoid	Various shapes with hollow top
Tiryns	stone		3	34	1		5
Thebes	clay			2			
	stone	1	20	16		1	

Spindle whorls		Biconical	Concave conical	Conical	Convex	Cylindrical	Discoid	Other	Spherical	Various shapes with hollow top
Tiryns	clay	4	3	7		1	12	1	1	3
Thebes	clay	9	1	10					1	
	stone	10	9	22	1		1			
Midea	clay			4						
	stone	1	5	38						

Fig. 7.5b. Tiryns, Thebes and Midea, LH III, spindle whorls, by type and material.

of the conuli, it is evident that the latter are mostly smaller than the former. However, in Tiryns several of the spindle whorls and conuli are of the same size (Fig. 7.6). When including the spindle whorls from Midea (Fig. 7.7), it is clear that some of these spindle whorls are of precisely the same type and are similar in size and weight to the smallest conuli from Thebes and Tiryns.

Thus, we can conclude that the weight and diameter of the objects classified as conuli lie within the overall spindle whorl weight/diameter range. They may have been utilised for several purposes, and possibly had specific significance; however, from a functional perspective, there is no reason to assume that they could not have been used as spindle whorls.

Beads

It can be very difficult to differentiate between a small spindle whorl/conulus and a bead. Moreover, ethnographic sources demonstrate that spindle whorls have sometimes been used as beads and beads as spindle whorls (Liu 1978), indicating that both object categories can have more than one function. Thus, some objects classified as beads may also have functioned as

spindle whorls, as an example from the TTTC database of 16 beads from LM III contexts at Khania, Crete, demonstrates: 10 of these beads are made of stone, nine have a conical shape (the remaining whorl is concave conical), and they have the typological characteristics of conuli (Fig. 7.8).

The beads from Khania are of the same size as many of the whorls recorded as conuli elsewhere (Fig. 7.9). However, all beads cannot be interpreted as spindle whorls; if the hole measures merely a few millimetres it will be too small for a spindle rod. It is important to consider their find context, as well as their morphology, and to verify whether they were found with other textile tools.

Kylix stem whorls

Kylix stem whorls, here termed KS whorls, constitute another category of whorls. Fifty KS whorls from Khania with a secure LM III date were recorded in the TTTC database. Eighteen of these were excluded as spinning tools on the basis that the hole is not centered and/or that the stem is unevenly cut. The analyses demonstrate that the KS whorls form a more homogenous group than the spindle whorls, not only in shape, but also in weight

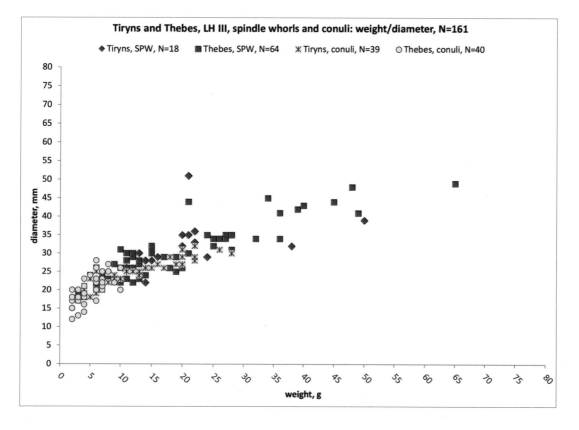

Fig. 7.6. Tiryns and Thebes, LH III, spindle whorls and conuli: weight/diameter. Please note that some markers represent more than one spindle whorl or conulus.

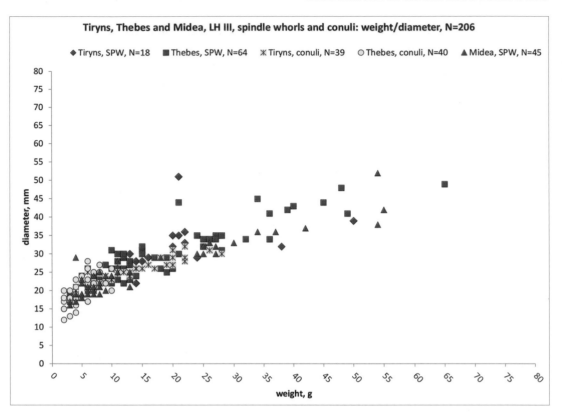

Beads		Biconical	Concave conical	Conical	Convex
Khania	bone				1
	clay	2		2	1
	stone			1	9

Fig. 7.8. Khania, LM III, objects classified as beads.

and diameter. This is not surprising; the KS whorls are naturally more homogenous since they are all cut from kylix stems, thus deriving from a quite standardised form. It is plausible that in a large-scale production, and if aiming to produce a standardised yarn and textile, standardised textile tools would also have been made and used. By cutting the spindle whorls from kylix stems, it would have been quite easy to produce many similar spindle whorls that could be utilised to spin similar yarns. It should also be noted that only a very few spindle whorls from the same period and site fall within this cluster of KS whorls: in general, the spindle whorls of the same period and place are either smaller or larger than these KS whorls. This suggests that KS whorls indeed form a separate spinning tool category, an integral part of the spinning tool kit, but with its own characteristics in terms of tool shape and output, indicating that

regular spindle whorls were utilised for a variety of yarns, while KS whorls were chosen for a specific yarn quality.

This stands in contrast to the conuli, which to a large degree overlap the shape and weight distribution of regular spindle whorls, and therefore appear to represent a specific supplement to the spindle whorls, rather than a separate category.

Pierced sherds
Pierced sherds (ceramic sherds with a drilled hole) have also been recorded as possible spinning tools. They are present during the entire Bronze Age period at several sites, for example, Arslantepe, Turkey and Tiryns, mainland Greece. Most of these objects are rounded, but the shape is in general irregular. If a spinning tool does not have a regular shape, it will not rotate in an optimal way: it will be hard to spin with and the yarn is likely to be unevenly spun. Furthermore, the hole is often not centred and/or is hourglass in shape, and this would not be convenient for spinning. Therefore, it is difficult to confirm a general interpretation of these objects as spinning tools, since many would not have functioned in an optimal way when spinning

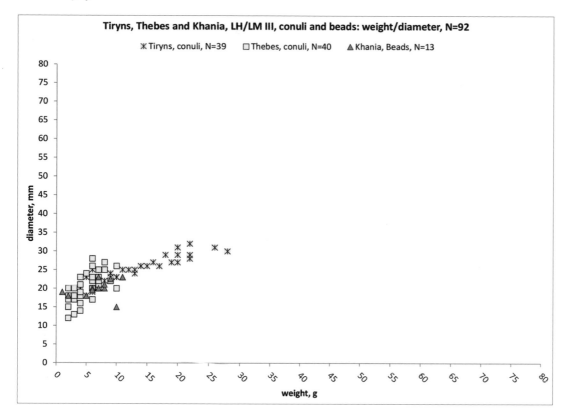

Fig. 7.9. Tiryns, Thebes and Khania, LH/LM III, conuli and beads: weight/diameter. Please note that some markers represent more than one conulus or bead.

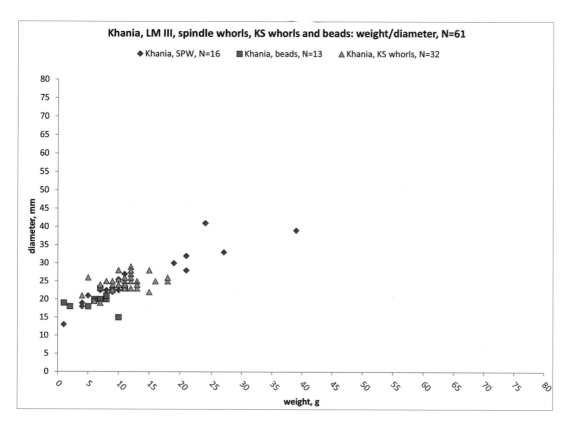

Fig. 7.10. Khania, LM III, three types of spinning tools. Please note that some markers represent more than one spindle whorl, bead or KS whorl.

with a suspended spindle. However, pierced sherds are often found with textile tools, and it is likely that some, which are evenly shaped, with a centred hole, could have functioned as spindle whorls, while others could have been used for other purposes.

The majority of the pierced sherds that could function as spindle whorls have a larger diameter than regular spindle whorls. This is evident, for example, when comparing spindle whorls and conuli with pierced sherds from LH III Tiryns (Fig. 7.11). Previous experiments have demonstrated that a large diameter, in relation to the weight, results in a thread that is harder spun (Andersson 1996).

Bronze Age spinning tools: summary and conclusions

The spinning tools in the TTTC database are scattered in time and across regions; however, it is striking that when several spindle whorls are found in the same context at any given site, they vary in size.

The spinning technique was already fully developed at the beginning of the Bronze Age. The very light spindle whorls dated to the Early Bronze Age at Troia are not unique; for

example, whorls weighing less than 9 g dated to 3000–2750 BC are found in Arslantepe, Turkey. From the same site and period, textiles with very thin threads (0.1 mm) have been found (see chapters 3 and 6.1). Another example is an Early Bronze Age spindle whorl from Sitagroi that weighs only 8 g.

Heavy spindle whorls are also recorded from Late Bronze Age sites. The results of the various analyses suggest that not only the spinners in Troia, but also Bronze Age spinners in general, could produce different types of yarn and thereby different types of textiles, ranging from very fine to very coarse.

The spindle whorl data do not indicate the types of fibres that were spun. It has been suggested that very light spindle whorls are more suitable for spinning short fibres; for example, short staple wool, cotton and silk (Tiedman and Jakes 2006). However, experiments have clearly demonstrated that it is possible to spin a thin linen thread with a spindle whorl as light as 5 g (Andersson 2003, see also chapter 4.1) and the experiments in this research programme have also demonstrated that it is possible to spin flax fibres with an 8 g spindle whorl. We therefore conclude that spinning long fibres with light spindles cannot be excluded. Furthermore,

Fig. 7.11. LH III Tiryns, spindle whorls, conuli and pierced sherds: weight/diameter. Please note that some markers represent more than one spindle whorl, conulus or pierced sherd.

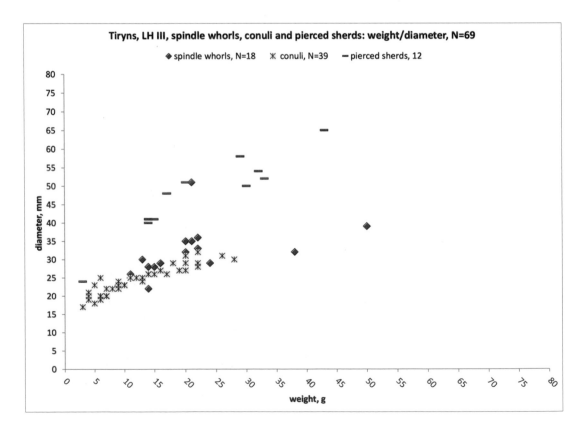

cotton and silk were not used in the Bronze Age Eastern Mediterranean, as far as is known today (chapter 3). Independently of fibre material, the spinning experiments demonstrate that when spinning with a light spindle, the raw material has to be very well prepared in order to be able to spin a thread strong enough to function as a warp thread on a loom. The spinning experiments have also demonstrated that it takes a longer time to spin a thinner thread than a thicker thread (chapter 4.1).

It is also necessary to take into account that the amount of yarn required would be considerably larger if using a thinner thread rather than a thicker thread. If producing 1 m² of textile with 20 threads per centimetre in a balanced tabby, one would need to spin at least 4,080 m of thin yarn. If producing the same type of fabric with thicker threads, and weaving it less densely with 5 threads per centimetre, the amount of yarn needed would be 1,010 m. Not only would it take longer to prepare the fibres and spin a thin thread, the fabrics produced with these threads would have taken considerably longer to weave. Thus, the choice of spindle whorl not only reflects the choice of yarn and fabric quality, it also defines the length of time required for production. Yet, the survey of Bronze Age archaeological textiles (chapter 3) demonstrates that Bronze Age people often chose to spend the time on achieving very fine and elaborate textiles.

Spinning technology stands on a tradition of plying threads. The survey of archaeological threads demonstrates that Neolithic thread is often z- or s-spun and subsequently Z- or S-plied. Perhaps different spinning tools were used for spinning and for plying. In the Bronze Age plying is still widely used, but some areas such as Syria also have many attestations of delicate textiles woven from single spun yarn only.

When analysing and comparing the whorls from the TTTC database it is evident that in some regions, and during some periods, the number of whorls recovered is surprisingly low. This is especially the case in the Cretan sites of the Protopalatial and Neopalatial periods. The absence of spindle whorls is particularly intriguing in places with records of loom weights, as it suggests a weaving activity, but very little or no direct trace of spinning tools. This could be due to various factors, such as the selection of whorls recorded in the database, the use of whorls made of perishable material, such as wood and bone, or spinning taking place elsewhere. It is also possible that spinners used alternative spinning tools and spinning techniques, such as spinning on a wooden spinning hook (chapter 2), which would leave no archaeological trace. We can conclude that it is likely that different spinning tools and techniques were utilised simultaneously in the same site, region and period. However, only the drop spindle with a stone or clay spindle whorl is archaeologically traceable.

When comparing the objects classified as conuli, KS stems and beads in terms of type, material, weight and diameter, it is not possible from a functional perspective to distinguish any clear-cut differences. The categories mirror academic typologies rather than functional differences. In terms of methodology, it is not the chosen find category that defines whether or not an object is functional as a spindle whorl. The objects in the different categories could have been used as spindle whorls, although this does not exclude the possibility that they could be utilised for other purposes as well.

The analyses in this volume conclude that it is likely that many of the smaller whorls, conuli, KS whorls and beads were used for spinning. This suggests the use of well-prepared fibre material (and indicates that the Bronze Age spinners had the necessary knowledge, skills and time); otherwise, the spun thread would be thin but fragile and not suitable to use in a fabric. The resulting textiles would be of fine quality, and a large amount of yarn – and a great deal of time – would have been required if a dense fabric in this quality was desired.

With regard to the functionality and use of pierced sherds as spinning tools, it does seem likely that these were sometimes used as part of the Bronze Age textile tool kit, but their function(s) require further contextual and experimental investigation.

Summary of the spinning experiments and the external analyses of spinning test samples

All the spindle whorl analyses are based on the study of the objects, their contexts and the assemblages of textile tools they are part of, and are informed by the TTTC spinning tests (chapter 4). A total of 64 spinning tests (1 test being one full spindle) were conducted

Fig. 7.12. Calculation of metres of yarn per 100 g wool, 4 g, 8 g and 18 g whorls, comparing the metres of yarn spun by the two spinners.

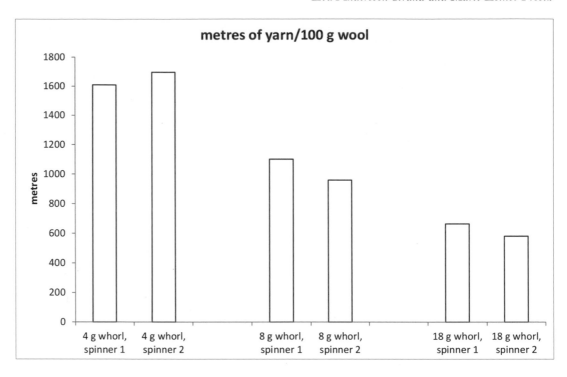

Fig. 7.13. Calculation of metres of yarn per 100 g flax fibres and wool fibres, 8 g whorl, comparing the metres of yarn spun by the two spinners.

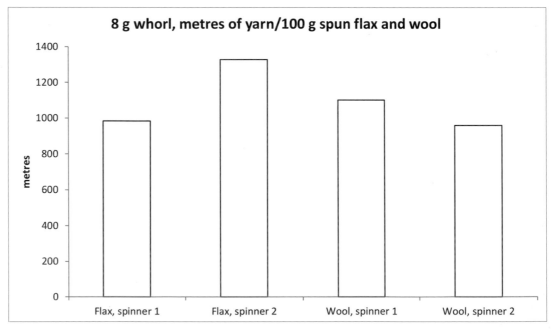

by two experienced craftspeople using spindles with whorls of different weights. Our choices, strategies and procedure in carrying out these tests were fully documented, enabling other researchers to verify our work and results, and also making it possible for further tests to be conducted using the same guidelines, in the future.

The two spinners reported a qualitative and quantitative difference in output when using the different tools. On the basis of numerous spinning tests, we were able calculate the yarn output per 100 g for both wool (4 g, 8 g and 18 g whorls) and flax (8 g whorl), and compare the results (Figs. 7.12, 7.13).

In order to counter any subjective bias on the part of the two spinners, since they had handled the spindle whorls of different sizes themselves and were therefore aware of the difference between them, we submitted the reported results for further evaluation and testing by an external expert, thereby rendering the interpretation more objective and less dependent on the spinners' impressions. Was the perceived difference in the yarn spun by the different spindle whorls real, and visible in the yarn? Is there a direct and visible relationship between spindle whorl weight and yarn quality? It was possible to ascertain, by measuring, that a longer length of yarn was produced using the lighter spindle whorls than when spinning the same amount of raw material using the heavier spindle whorls, but was yarn spun on an 18 g spindle whorl thicker, containing more fibre, than the yarn spun on an 8 g spindle whorl? And could this be verified without prior knowledge of who had spun it, using which tools? Firmer answers to these vital questions would both inform our analyses of archaeological textile tools, and be valuable for the analysis of archaeological textile remains.

The spinners also reported that the 4 g spindle whorl needed a harder twist in order to achieve smooth spinning, and this observation needed verification, in order to be able to indicate whether the spin angle is related to personal practice or to the spinning tool.

From the spinning tests, 12 samples (four samples of the yarn spun with each of the three different spindles used in the test) were sent for external analysis and 20 measurements per sample were made. The yarn samples were 'anonymised' in order not to reveal the identity of the spinner or the type of spindle whorl used. Even in this anonymised form, without any knowledge of the spinners and tools, the external analysis confirmed that there was indeed a difference in the yarn output when using an 8 g and an 18 g spindle whorl, respectively. However, the difference is 0.086 mm in mean diameter, and thus not easy to measure, or to see with the naked eye. Nevertheless, when these yarns are woven, two quite different fabric qualities are produced.

The external analyses also demonstrated that it is not always straightforward to state that a difference in a spindle whorl's weight would automatically be reflected in the yarn diameter. For Spinner 2's yarn production, this equation was always evident, but not for Spinner 1. Nevertheless, the overall mean diameter of yarns for both spinners was 0.3667–0.3759 mm for an 8 g spindle whorl, and 0.4421–0.4734 for an 18 g spindle whorl, therefore two clearly distinguishable yarn types.

The spinning experiments also revealed that the different tools may yield yarns with different spin angles: when the two spinners used the 8 g spindle whorl, their yarns had spin angles of 31.03°–37.27°, while when spinning with an 18 g spindle whorl, they would tend to spin harder and achieve spin angles of 36.83°–40.5°. However, it should be noted that individual spinning techniques and preferences are also at play here, since Spinner 2 was generally observed to spin a little harder than Spinner 1.

Finally, the external analysis confirmed that yarns spun on an 18 g spindle whorl are heavier per metre than those spun on an 8 g spindle whorl: the difference is quite clear: 0.0976 g/m (8 g spindle whorl) and 0.1606 g/m (18 g spindle whorl). We can extrapolate that 1 km yarn spun on an 8 g spindle whorl would weigh 97.6 g while 1 km yarn spun on an 18 g spindle whorl would weigh 160.6 g. These results enable us to confirm that even if the visible difference between the yarns is small and hard to perceive with the naked eye, the fabrics made with these two types of yarn would be significantly different, especially in terms of weight: a 1 m² balanced tabby with 10 threads per centimetre would require *c.* 2 km yarn, with the piece of fabric then weighing 195.2 g if the yarn came from the 8 g spindle whorl, or 321.2 g if it came from the heavier 18 g spindle whorl. Therefore, even though the difference in weight appears small when measured on single yarn samples, this difference is amplified and scaled up when the yarns are utilised in fabrics comprising many kilometres of yarn.

The external analysis of wool yarns spun on the light 4 g spindle whorl highlighted the uniformity in yarn quality that the two spinners were able to achieve with this small tool, despite the fact that spinning with it was not an easy task. Approximately one third of the thread measurements yielded a diameter of 0.3 mm. The tests with the 8 g whorl also clearly demonstrate that, even if there was a difference between the linen yarn that was spun by the two spinners, very fine linen yarn can be spun with light spindle whorls. The TTTC tests also indicated that one can spin a thinner linen thread than wool yarn using the same tool; however, this requires further testing with different qualities of fibres.

The analysis of the weaving samples further showed that both the wool and the linen thread opened up in the woven fabric, so the nature of the thread changes, with the diameter increasing slightly. This is again valuable information for future analyses of archaeological textiles.

Weaving

Loom weights demonstrate the use of the warp-weighted loom in the Bronze Age. Where no loom weights come to light, we can conclude that either weaving did not take place, or was conducted with tools which did not survive in the archaeological record. In Middle and Late Bronze Age mainland Greece, or in the Early Bronze Age Levant, numerous spindle whorls and even archaeological textiles testify to an extensive textile production but loom weights are mostly absent. Therefore, we can conclude that several loom types were used in the Eastern Mediterranean; in some places the warp-weighted loom dominated, in others it

was absent, and in others again more than one loom type was probably used simultaneously. We know from Egyptian iconographical sources that the vertical two-beam loom was used for tapestry weaving in the Late Bronze Age; Joanna Smith (2001; 2012; 2013) has surveyed the epigraphical, technical and iconographical evidence for tapestry and suggested that tapestry was a widespread technique. This would not be surprising, given the advanced textile technology in the Bronze Age. The simultaneous use of the horizontal two-beam loom and another type of loom is possibly illustrated on a bowl from mid-4th millennium Badari, Egypt (Fig. 7.14). It has been suggested that the upper part of the image showing two figures standing either side of a structure with threads of double-length hanging over a rope or pole, may depict the preparation of the weft for the horizontal ground loom below (see for example, Cortes 2011; 'Textile production and clothing: technology and tools in ancient Egypt' n.d.). An alternative interpretation is that this image may show another type of loom, such as a loom used for twining (Andersson Strand forthcoming).

Loom weights

Approximately 4,000 objects from 27 sites were recorded as loom weights in the TTTC database. However, while the number of weights from some sites is high, for example, Malia on Crete (775), the number from other sites is very low, for example, Ebla in Syria (2).

Often, when several loom weights are found at a site, they are of different types. A vital question we wished to answer, therefore, was why loom weights appear in so many variations, not only regarding type and numbers, but also regarding sizes.

If all loom weights were suitable for producing all types of fabrics, why do these variations appear? What is the functionality of these many types and shapes? Based on loom weight tests/weaving tests, we can now conclude that the weight of a loom weight governs the number of warp threads of a particular tension that would be optimal to attach to it (chapter 4). Furthermore, the thickness of a loom weight regulates the number of warp threads per centimetre in the finished fabric.

All the loom weights in the TTTC programme were analysed according to the results from the experimental testing; we also

Fig. 7.14. a–b Bowl (UC9547), possibly depicting two types of loom. From Badari, Egypt, dated to Naqada II (c. 3500–3200 BC) (photos: published with kind permission from The Petrie Museum of Egyptian Archaeology UCL).

UC9547

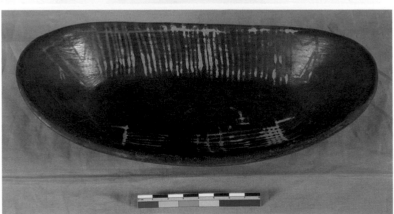

made preliminary decisions concerning the design of the tests, for example the estimate that 10–30 warp threads per loom weight is considered an optimal range. Naturally, these decisions have affected the interpretation of the loom weight data; they could be discussed further at a later stage.

Based on the analyses of the loom weights in the TTTC programme, we can also conclude that, independently of loom weight type and shape, the same loom weight can be used in different setups with different types of yarn requiring different tensions. Thus, with one specific type of loom weight a variety of fabrics can be woven (see chapter 6). In fact, we have established that certain loom weights are more or less multifunctional and by simply changing the type of thread, new types of fabrics could be produced with them. For example, a loom weight weighing 350 g and with a thickness of 3.5 cm could function with warp threads requiring tensions between *c.* 12.5–35 g and would therefore be suitable for producing fabrics with very different yarn types, both thin and thick. Moreover, this particular loom weight could have been used for producing both tabbies and twills, and fabrics with a warp thread count varying greatly between 6–32 threads per centimetre (chapter 4.5). Indeed, a flexible and multifunctional tool.

Yet, certain other loom weights will necessarily produce a much narrower range of fabrics, and are much less multifunctional. Only a limited range of yarns are suitable to be used with them, and they can produce a smaller variety of cloth types based on the loom weight and the warp tensions. For these fabrics, and for these kinds of loom weights, the weaver's flexibility does not consist in changing the yarn types; instead new fabric qualities are made by keeping a quite specific warp setup and instead changing the fabric types by adding more and/or thicker weft. As an example, a loom weight weighing 150 g and with a thickness of 3.5 cm would function best with warp threads requiring lower tensions, between *c.* 5–15 g, and would therefore mostly be suitable for producing fabrics with thinner warp yarns. This lighter loom weight could be used to weave balanced tabbies with *c.* 4–12 threads per centimetre, but could also be used for weft faced tabbies or twills (chapter 4.5).

Any loom weight typology is obviously related to the shape of the loom weight: a spherical weight is rounded; a discoid weight is rounded and flattened, *etc.* However, it is interesting that from a functional perspective, with regard to a loom weight's suitability for use in a loom setup, a spherical loom weight can have the same weight as a discoid weight, and a cylindrical loom weight the same thickness as a pyramidal weight. The question to be answered is, therefore, how does the choice of loom weight type affect the finished fabric?

Different types of loom weights, different types of fabrics? A discussion based on loom weights from Quartier Mu, Malia

In Quartier Mu at Malia, Crete, 532 loom weights were recovered from MM I–II contexts (chapter 6.5; Cutler *et al.* 2013). This number includes several different loom weight types; the most common shapes are spherical, discoid and pyramidal truncated, but biconical, conical, cube, cylindrical, rectangular and torus-shaped types are also recorded (Fig. 7.15).

The majority of the loom weights weigh between 50 g and 400 g, and have a thickness of 1.5–7.2 cm (Fig. 7.16; 498 of the weights had a recordable weight and thickness).[1] Although the weight and thickness of the Malia loom weights cover a wide range, there are clusters around certain weight/thickness combinations. One cluster consists of loom weights weighing 300–380 g, with a thickness of 6.5 to 7.2 cm. Two other clusters are visible among the loom weights weighing 75–150 g;

Fig. 7.15. Malia, Quartier Mu, MM I–II, loom weights, by type.

	MM IB	MM I–II	MM II	Total
Spherical			267	**267**
Spherical lenticular			15	**15**
Discoid	1		106	**107**
Pyramidal truncated	1		37	**38**
Biconical			1	**1**
Conical			1	**1**
Cuboid			5	**5**
Cylindrical		2	38	**40**
Rectangular, flat			6	**6**
Rectangular, thick	1		5	**6**
Torus			17	**17**
Torus (small hole diam)			25	**25**
Other			4	**4**
Total	**3**	**2**	**527**	**532**

these represent loom weights with a thickness of 1.5–2.3 cm, and 3–5.2 cm respectively. These two latter clusters of loom weights, have similar weight distribution, but one cluster is composed of thin loom weights which enable a dense weave, while the other cluster is composed of thicker loom weights which will yield either an open or a weft faced weave. Both clusters, however, are designed to weave with thin threads.

The weight/thickness variation is also related to the loom weight type (Fig. 7.17). The spherical weights form one group, while the discoid weights and torus weights (torus and torus with small hole diameter) form separate groups. The cylindrical and pyramidal types form intermediary groups. The difference particularly with regard to the spherical and discoid types, is indeed largely a result of the loom weights' morphology.

A further 132 naturally pierced pebbles were also recovered from MM I–II contexts in Quartier Mu. The majority of the 129 pebbles with a recordable weight and thickness weigh 100–250 g, with a thickness of 3–6 cm. When comparing the pebbles to the loom weights, we can conclude that these may also have functioned as loom weights. Furthermore, for the most part, the pebbles have properties that are intermediate between the spherical and discoid loom weights (Fig. 7.18).

The weight of the loom weights naturally influences the range of textiles that can be manufactured with them. Figure 7.19 shows that, based solely on their weight, some of the Quartier Mu loom weight types are more suitable than others for use with warp threads that require a particular tension. For example, the discoid loom weights are associated with the production of textiles made with very thin threads corresponding to warp tensions of 5–15 g. In contrast, the spherical loom weights could have been used to produce textiles made with a wider range of thread types.

Fig. 7.16. Malia, Quartier Mu, MM I–II, loom weights: weight/ thickness, three clusters.

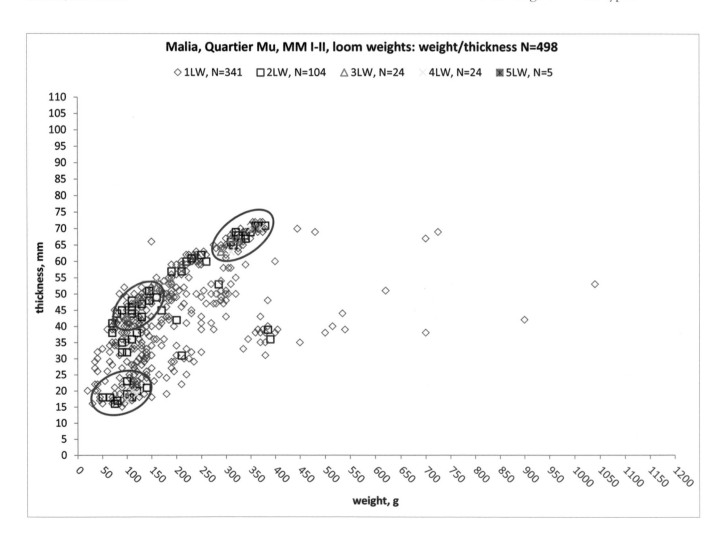

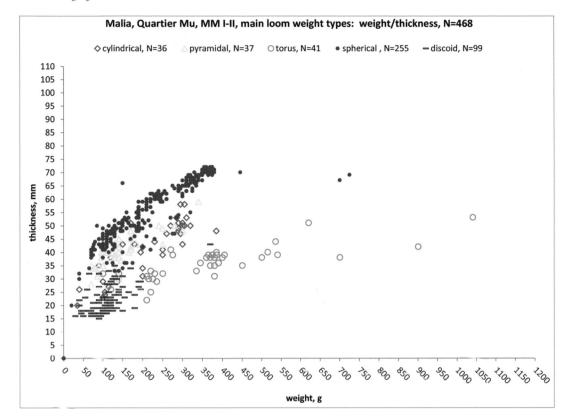

Fig. 7.17. Malia,
Quartier Mu,
MM I–II, main loom
weight types: weight/
thickness. Cylindrical;
pyramidal; torus (torus
and torus with small
hole diameter); spherical;
discoid. Please note that
types with less than 20
weights are not included,
and a weight weighing >
1200 g is also excluded
from the graph.

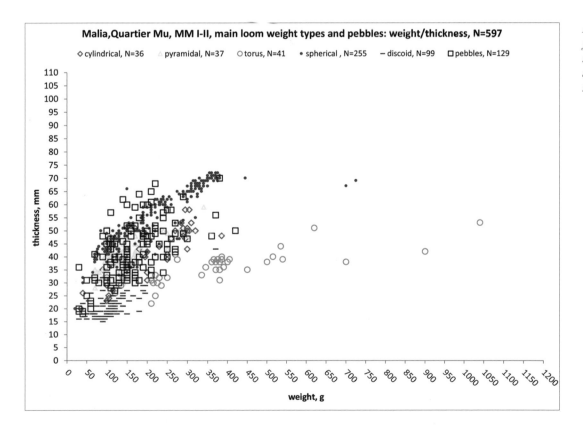

Fig. 7.18. Malia,
Quartier Mu, MM I–II,
main loom weight types
and pebbles: weight/
thickness.

Fig. 7.19. Malia, Quartier Mu, MM I–II, loom weight types and their suitability for use with different warp tensions (based on the loom weights recovered from the excavated buildings).

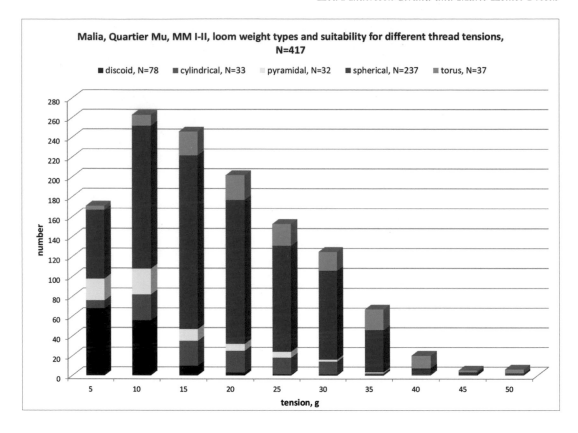

Through an analysis of the warp thread count per centimetre that could have been obtained in different types of weave when using a loom weight of a given weight and thickness with thread requiring a particular tension, it became evident that the main loom weight types could be used for both tabby and twill techniques (chapter 4.5).

Since the discoid and the spherical weights constitute the two largest categories of loom weights from Quartier Mu, it is especially interesting to compare the differences between these two types. The analysis includes 237 spherical and 78 discoid loom weights (representing the loom weights found in secure MM I–II contexts within the excavated buildings).

As demonstrated in Figures 7.20 and 7.21, we can conclude that the fabrics produced with the discoid loom weights would be denser than the fabrics produced with the spherical loom weights. The discoid loom weights are better suited for use with thinner warp threads that need less tension, while the spherical loom weights are more suitable for thicker warp threads that require more tension. Although it would be possible to use the discoid loom

weights with warp threads needing between 5 g and 35 g tension, the distribution demonstrates that the majority are best suited for use with very thin thread needing 5–10 g tension (Fig. 7.20). This suggests to us that the discoid loom weights would have been suitable for making a range of fabrics with very thin threads. The analysis also shows that the majority of the discoid loom weights could have been used for producing tabbies with *c.* 21–24 warp threads per centimetre using thread requiring 5 g tension, or *c.* 10–13 warp threads per centimetre with thread needing 10 g tension (Fig. 7.20). If weavers in Quartier Mu wished instead to produce a 2/2 twill with four rows of discoid loom weights, the majority of the loom weights could have produced a fabric with *c.* 42–47 warp threads per centimetre if using warp thread requiring 5 g tension, or *c.* 22–24 warp threads per centimetre if using warp thread needing 10 g tension. It would also be possible to use the spherical loom weights with threads requiring a tension of between 5 g and 35 g, but the largest number are best suited for use with thread needing 10–20 g tension (Fig. 7.21). With 10 g tension thread, the majority of the spherical weights could produce a fabric with *c.* 5–9 warp threads per centimetre.

Warp thr/cm	5 g, N=68	10 g, N=56	15 g, N=10	20 g, N=3	25 g, N=1	30 g, N=1	35 g, N=1
5 thr							1
6 thr			2			1	
7 thr		1	1	1	1		
8 thr	1	3		1			
9 thr	1	1	3	1			
10 thr	1	8	2				
11 thr	1	16					
12 thr		13	1				
13 thr	3	6	1				
14 thr	3	4					
15 thr	1	3					
16 thr	3						
17 thr	3						
18 thr	2						
19 thr	5	1					
20 thr	2						
21 thr	7						
22 thr	12						
23 thr	5						
24 thr	10						
25 thr	3						
26 thr	1						
27 thr	2						
28 thr	2						

Fig. 7.20. Malia, Quartier Mu, MM I–II, discoid loom weights: weight tension/number of threads per cm in a tabby. N= the number of loom weights from the specific group (in this case 78 loom weights) that could be used with thread needing the given tension.

Fig. 7.21. Malia, Quartier Mu, MM I–II, spherical loom weights: weight tension/number of threads per cm in a tabby. N= the number of loom weights from the specific group (in this case 237 loom weights) that could be used with thread needing the given tension.

Warp thr/cm	5 g, N=69	10 g, N=144	15 g, N=175	20 g, N=145	25 g, N=107	30 g, N=90	35 g, N=42	40 g, N=6	45 g, N=3	50 g, N=2	55 g, N=2	60 g, N=2	65 g, N=2	70 g, N=2
3 thr			1	3	14	76	39	4	1			1	2	2
4 thr		3	19	48	87	12	1			2	2	1		
5 thr		29	51	88	4			2	2					
6 thr		23	42	6			2							
7 thr	9	28	58			2								
8 thr	7	33	3		2									
9 thr	10	16	1											
10 thr	16	6												
11 thr	10	4												
12 thr	11	2												
13 thr	1													
14 thr	1													
15 thr	1													
16 thr	1													
17 thr	1													
18 thr	1													

The difference in thickness between the spherical and discoid loom weights also has a direct effect on the corresponding loom setups, since for loom weights of the same weight, used with warp threads requiring the same tension, the number of loom weights in each row of loom weights would be considerably lower for spherical weights than for discoid loom weights. Twice as many loom weights would have been required if weaving twill with four rows of weights.

To conclude, it is evident that the various types of loom weights in Quartier Mu were used to produce various types of fabrics. When analysing the loom weights from the same contexts, this becomes even more evident (see chapter 6.5). A further finding is that the discoid weights are preferable if a denser fabric (both tabby and twill) is desired; it was also ascertained that the discoid weights are not optimal for use with as many types of yarn as the spherical weights. Moreover, it is clear that the suggested minimum of 10 threads per loom weight works well with the spherical weights, since with less than 10 threads per loom weight, the fabric would become extremely open.

Weaving in Phaistos during the Protopalatial and LM IB periods

In Phaistos, Crete, loom weights have been recorded from both the Protopalatial (1950–1700 BC) and LM IB (1500–1450 BC) periods (chapter 6.4, Cutler *et al.* 2015).

As can be seen in Figure 7.22, most of the loom weights from both the Protopalatial and LM IB periods are made of fired clay; the majority of the Protopalatial weights are cylindrical, whereas those from LM IB are mostly spherical.

It is not only the loom weight type that differs between these two periods, but also the weight and thickness range: the LM IB loom weights are generally larger and thicker than the earlier loom weights from the Protopalatial period (Fig. 7.23). Moreover, the loom weights from the Protopalatial period are from contexts within the palace whereas the LM IB weights are from a household context.

In the following, the production during the two periods is compared. However, very few loom weights are from exactly the same context (room, *etc.*); therefore, the comparison can only be made on a general basis.

The analysis of the cylindrical loom weights from the Protopalatial period demonstrates that they are suitable for the production of fabrics woven with threads requiring 5–35 g tension (Fig. 7.24; chapter 6.4). In certain cases, only one or two loom weights would function with a given thread tension, for example 30–35 g, while as many as 50 loom weights would function with thread needing 10 g tension. The number of warp threads per centimetre with 10 g tension thread would in general vary between 5 and 9 threads per centimetre (41 of the loom weights), while fabrics woven with yarn requiring 15 g tension would have 5–6 warp threads per centimetre. If the weavers were weaving twill, the thread counts would be approximately double.

We can therefore conclude that there was an emphasis on the production of textiles woven with quite thin and/or light threads, but a smaller amount of fabrics with thicker and/or heavier threads could also have been woven. The fabrics would generally have been

Fig.7.22. Phaistos, loom weights from Protopalatial and LM IB contexts: type and material.

		Fired clay	Unfired clay	Stone	Unspecified	Total
Protopalatial	**Cylindrical**	73	3	6	1	83
	Spherical	2		8		10
	Biconical			1		1
	Cuboid	2				2
	Flat rectangular			1		1
	Torus			2		2
	Other		1	1		2
LM IB	**Cylindrical**	2		5		7
	Spherical	27				27
	Total	106	4	24	1	135

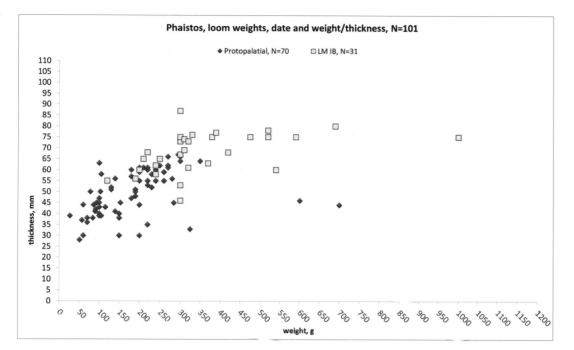

Fig. 7.23. Phaistos, Protopalatial and LM IB loom weights: weight/thickness.

Warp thr/cm	5 g, N=26	10 g, N=50	15 g, N=40	20 g, N=32	25 g, N=16	30 g, N=4	35 g, N=1
3 thr				2	4	3	1
4 thr		3	5	17	11	1	
5 thr	1	6	15	9	1		
6 thr	2	4	13	3			
7 thr	2	8	4	1			
8 thr	4	11	1				
9 thr	6	12	2				
10 thr	5	3					
11 thr	2						
12 thr		1					
13 thr		2					
14 thr							
15 thr	1						
16 thr	1						
17 thr							
18 thr							
19 thr							
20 thr	2						

Fig. 7.24. Phaistos, Protopalatial cylindrical loom weights from palace contexts: weight tension/ number of threads per cm in a tabby (excluding a cylindrical weight weighing 27 g). N= the number of loom weights from the specific group (in this case 62 loom weights) that could be used with thread needing the given tension.

quite open, especially when weaving with the thinner yarn. This suggests that many of the fabrics would have been weft faced, *i.e.*, with more and/or thicker weft threads than warp threads per centimetre.

The analysis of the LM IB loom weights from the house at Chalara demonstrates that they would have been suitable for use with a wider range of thread tensions (chapter 6.4). Most of the loom weights (27 spherical and two cylindrical) are from Corridor Gamma. The thickest of these, a spherical weight weighing 1 kg, would work well with thread needing 35–100 g tension. The rest of the weights from

Warp thr/cm	5 g, N=1	10 g, N=15	15 g, N=22	20 g, N=24	25 g, N=20	30 g, N=16	35 g, N=5	40 g, N=5	45 g, N=2	50 g, N=2
3 thr				4	9	10	2	5	2	2
4 thr		1	3	11	6	6	3			
5 thr			6	4	5					
6 thr		2	7	3						
7 thr		3	3	2						
8 thr		5	2							
9 thr	1	2	1							
10 thr										
11 thr		1								
12 thr										
13 thr		1								

Fig. 7.25. Phaistos, Chalara, Corridor Gamma, LM IB loom weights: weight tension/number of threads per cm in a tabby (excluding a spherical weight weighing 1 kg). N= the number of loom weights from the specific group (in this case 25 loom weights) that could be used with thread needing the given tension.

this group could be used with thread requiring 5–50 g tension (Fig. 7.25). In some cases, only one or two loom weights would function with thread needing a specific tension, for example 5 g and 45–50 g, while as many as 24 of the 25 loom weights with a recordable weight and thickness would function with thread needing 20 g tension. Based on this analysis, we can state that textile production in this LM IB household was more varied, with an emphasis on slightly coarser textiles, than the Protopalatial palatial production. Another significant difference is the number of warp threads per centimetre: only a few of the LM IB loom weights would be suitable for producing a fabric with more than 9 warp threads per centimetre and it is noteworthy that most fabrics would have only *c.* 3–5 warp threads per centimetre, indicating either very open or weft faced fabrics.

To conclude, at Phaistos a small but significant difference is observed in the production between the two periods and the two contexts. The analysis of the loom weights from Protopalatial palace contexts gives an impression of fabrics primarily produced with very thin to thin threads and in several qualities, depending on 1) the type of yarn, 2) if it was a balanced tabby or a weft faced tabby, and finally 3) the weight and thickness of the loom weight. The analysis of the LM IB weights from the house at Chalara instead suggests a more varied production with thicker/heavier threads. Even if LM IB fabrics could have been produced with the same thin/light thread used during the Protopalatial period, the LM IB fabrics would be different: either more open, or more weft-faced.

Spools as loom weights

Approximately 340 weights in the database are recorded as spools. A spool, according to the TTTC typology, has a cylindrical shape.[2] The majority are un-pierced, but some pierced objects are also registered in the database. Spools have been recorded at 14 sites. It is important to note that the number of spools recorded from some sites is high, for example from Sitagroi and Tiryns in mainland Greece (34 and 64, respectively), while the number from other sites is low, for example Arslantepe in Turkey (8). The majority of the spools are dated to the Late Bronze Age, but spools are found in Early Bronze Age contexts too, for example at Sitagroi. Most spools are made of fired or unfired clay, while a small number are made of stone. In general, the spools are small and weigh less than 100 g, while only 19 spools have a weight of more than 100 g. These heavier spools are dated to the Late Bronze Age.

The suitability of the spools as loom weights has been debated, and spools have also been interpreted as having other functions, such as spacers in pottery kilns or game markers. However, we observe that spools are often from the same contexts as textile tools, which suggests that the spools had a function in textile production (see *e.g.* Gleba 2008, 140). Lorenz Rahmstorf has thus far identified spools at 57 sites, all dating to the last two centuries of the 2nd millennium BC (Rahmstorf 2011, 320) and they continued in use in the Early Iron Age, also in Cyprus, Italy and central Europe. This sudden popularity of a new weight type reveals that the warp-weighted loom continued in use, but that new loom weight forms were introduced. This change has thus far not been fully understood or explained, but may be related to mobility at the end of the Bronze Age (Rahmstorf 2003; 2005; 2011; Cutler forthcoming b; Nosch forthcoming c).

The TTTC weaving experiments with spools, reconstructed on the basis of spools from Khania, have clearly demonstrated that especially the heavier spools would function very well as loom weights for different types of fabrics (see chapter 4.1). However, the calculations also demonstrate that very light spools are unlikely to be functional as loom weights in a warp-weighted loom. Such a light weight would only provide sufficient warp tension for very few warps, and, because of the thickness of the spools, the fabric would become very open. The lighter spools could, instead, have been utilised as weights for tablet weaving, braiding or warping.

Bronze Age weaving tools: summary and conclusions

Loom weights of many different types and sizes were present in the Bronze Age Eastern Mediterranean and it is evident that their sizes, *i.e.* the weight and thickness, affect the final product, the fabric, more than the specific type does.[3] Furthermore, analyses of textiles from the same region and period demonstrate a very varied production of textiles; for example, tabby fabrics with more than 40 warp threads per centimetre, but also very coarse textiles with merely a few threads per centimetre (chapter 3). We can conclude that it is not the loom weight type itself that determines what fabric could be produced, but rather the relationship between its weight and thickness (Mårtensson *et al.* 2009). However, as demonstrated, some loom weight types are more suitable than others for use in the production of a specific textile.

It is often difficult to interpret groups of loom weights, because loom weights being found together does not necessarily suggest that they were used together in the same loom setup. They could also have been stored together, and the weaver would have known which loom weights to select and combine in a specific setup.

Another challenge is that even if it can be suggested that loom weights had fallen from a loom and been found *in situ*, some loom weights could still be missing. An example of this is the loom weights from Building 1 in Khania: it is likely that they had fallen from a loom, but they were spread out on the floor, indicating that some weights are likely to be missing. It is very rare that all the original weights survive. However, on the basis of the remaining loom weights, we are able to calculate the range of fabrics that could have been made using these loom weights together on the loom. The analyses of the loom weights provide an estimate of the range of textiles manufactured, even if it is not always possible to be specific about precisely what fabrics were woven.

The question of twill is still intriguing. We have certain evidence for the existence of twills in the Bronze Age, in textiles from Alishar (chapter 3). In this volume we have furthermore demonstrated how the existing textile technology is perfectly suitable for weaving twills as well as tabbies, both with the 'conventional' Bronze Age loom weights and with the crescent shaped loom weights.

In the loom weight typology (Fig. 5.1.4) we included at least 18 types. Yet, the functional analysis demonstrates how they overlap. Functionally, the three main categories are spherical, pyramidal and discoid. These three categories mark the most distinct functional features of loom weights and contain a number of loom weight types of different shapes. The choice of shapes within these categories probably relates to cultural and personal choices, and less to function. We hope that these personal choices and cultural conventions in textile tools will be further explored in the future.

Bronze Age textiles: discussion and research outlook

In this final discussion, we summarise the most significant results, and also discuss the remaining open issues and unanswered questions. We present our assessment of the extent to which the textile tools enable us to make definite conclusions, and we highlight the questions textile tools cannot help us answer. This section also intertwines the other major element of the *Tools and Textiles, Texts and Contexts* research programme, the examination of Bronze Age textile terminologies (Michel and Nosch 2010), considered also in the context of Aegean images of textiles (for Aegean representations of textiles see Chapin and Shaw 2015).

In recent years, new research projects on textile tools have carried our research forward and complemented our results. With regard to the early periods of textile production in the Aegean, for example, current research being conducted at the time of writing that will enhance our understanding of this area include the following: Joanne Cutler (Cutler *et al.* 2015; Cutler forthcoming b) and Malgorzata Siennicka (2012; forthcoming) are investigating Neolithic and Early Bronze Age textile tools in terms of technology, craft knowledge and potential changes in the fibres used, as well as the wider social context of textile production during these periods. Sophia Vakirtzi is currently examining spinning technologies in the Early Bronze Age (Vakirzti *et al.* 2014; Vakirtzi 2015) and Kalliopi Sarri (forthcoming) is exploring Neolithic textile techniques and clothing.

Comparing different sources of evidence

As researchers, we separate textile tools into distinct categories, such as spindle whorls, loom weights and needles; but from a craft perspective they all belong together and depend on each other. A spinning tool must produce a thread that can hold in a weave, or that can be used for sewing; the choice of loom weights depends on the fabric the weaver aims to weave, but also on the qualities of the yarns available. Therefore, an optimal analysis of the potential textile production at a site will merge the data and analytical results from the spinning, weaving and sewing tools, enabling a discussion of how they could be used together. This is not always possible, however, since, as we have seen above, certain tool categories are systematically absent in certain regions and periods (*e.g.* the very few spindle whorls in Crete in the Protopalatial and Neopalatial periods); secondly, and equally importantly, even when tools are found together, they would not necessarily have been used together.

A place where the tools could have functioned well together to make a range of textiles is in Early Bronze Age Archontiko Phase IV (2135–2020 BC) House A, where spindle whorls of 25–68 g came to light together with pyramidal truncated loom weights (covering a wide range of 154–1179 g and 4.1–8.8 cm thick) (chapter 6.11). The inhabitants of Archontiko could have used the tools together to produce fabrics with threads ranging from thin to thick.

In Sitagroi, textile tools can be compared with textile imprints (chapter 6.12). However, the imprints do not necessarily derive from locally produced fabrics, and the Neolithic textile impression at Sitagroi is dated to Phase I (5500–5200 BC), while loom weights only appear from the Chalcolithic Phase III (4600–3500 BC). This raises the question of the date and reasons for the introduction of the warp-weighted loom. Again, it emphasises the crucial issue of the invisible aspects of textile production – within the textiles themselves, the textile tools, and in the technology (Andersson Strand forthcoming).

In Arslantepe (Frangipane *et al.* 2009) and in Quartier Mu, Malia (Cutler *et al.* 2013) it is possible to compare the recorded textile tools with remains of archaeological textiles: an extremely fine goat hair textile at Arslantepe and a fine tabby at Malia. At both places, the functional parameters of some of the tools correspond well to the preserved textiles, *i.e.*, the textiles could have been made with the recorded tools.

At Thebes another valuable comparison is possible, between the textile tools and the Linear B inscriptions recording textiles (chapter 6.10). The type of yarn produced with the LH IIIB2 spindle whorls, which was very probably used to make some of the Mycenaean textile types recorded in the tablets, seems to continue uninterrupted into the LH IIIC strata, therefore after the fall of the Mycenaean palaces. This makes us wonder what impact the fall of the many Bronze Age palace cultures in the Aegean, Egypt and the ancient Near East, as well as the shift from the Bronze Age to the Early Iron Age, had on the local textile production (Rahmstorf 2003; 2005; 2011; Sauvage 2013; Nosch forthcoming c).

Comparing tools from different periods and contexts

With the mass of information gathered in the present volume, it is tempting to arrange the material into schemes and to search for patterns of development over time. Although we do indeed do this in the texts, we also proceed with the utmost degree of caution. Overall, in the TTTC database we observe a trend towards heavier and larger spindle whorls in the earlier phases, and smaller and lighter spindle whorls at the end of the Bronze Age. This statement, however, needs to be treated with caution, since the Late Bronze Age conuli take up much of the space in the statistics, and because Troia represents such a large part of the spindle whorl data. There are also significant exceptions, for example Arslantepe and Troia, where all types and sizes of spindle whorls are attested already in the beginning of the Bronze Age. Moreover, other recent research has demonstrated that a range of spindle whorl weights were present in Neolithic and Early Bronze Age Crete (Cutler *et al.* 2015; Cutler forthcoming b) and Early Bronze Age mainland Greece (Siennicka 2012; forthcoming), including some lighter whorls, although these were not present in large numbers.

Likewise for the loom weights, caution is crucial when comparing tools from different periods and contexts: in the palace context at Phaistos, Crete, Protopalatial (MM IB to MM IIB, *c.* 1950–1700 BC) loom weights are cylindrical and the majority of them are best suited for use with thread needing a warp tension of *c.* 10 g, while in the subsequent Neopalatial period (MM III–LM IB, *c.* 1700–1450 BC) loom weights become heavier and thicker and the majority are optimal for use with thread needing a warp tension closer to 20 g. However, the Neopalatial loom weights are not from a palace context. Thus, what reality do we see here? An evolution towards coarser fabrics? Or, a qualitative difference between palatial and non-palatial textile production? Continuing in Crete, in LM I Agia Triada, the tools testify to an even larger variety of fabric types and qualities in the range of spherical and discoid loom weights.

Naming textile tools

We are rarely as lucky as Sauvage and Hawley (2013) to find a spindle whorl inscribed 'spindle', so terms for textile tools must be identified in different contexts, such as work assignments or ritual descriptions. In Linear B, female textile workers are designated as *a-ra-ka-te-ja*, spindle/distaff women=spinners, and this could suggest that **i-te-ja* (weavers), *ra-pte-ri-ja* (seamstresses) and *pe-ki-ti-ja* (combers) would also contain the root for the occupational designation and for the name of their textile tools, the loom, the needle and the comb. The Hittite texts refer to textile tools, such as the spindle ($^{(GIŠ)}$*ḫue/iša-*), distaff ($^{(GIŠ)}$*ḫulāli-*), and spindle whorl (*panzakitti-*) (Ofitsch 2001; Baccelli *et al.* 2014, 110–111).

Workshops

Even in cases when a room suitable for use as a textile workshop is identified, it is not possible to conclusively identify it as such a workshop (Tournavitou 1988; Alberti 2008). This raises the question: how do we indeed define a textile workshop? What would it look like? It is likely that the answer depends on the organisation of textile manufacturing. If the production is organised on a household level, even in a household industry or putting-out mode, the work would have taken place in the domestic settlement area. Such domestic workplaces are crucial for the Old Assyrian trade based on workshops in private homes in Assur (Michel 2006; Michel and Veenhof 2010).

The fibre preparation tools, the spindles and spindle whorls, the looms and the loom weights and baskets filled with different yarns dyed in a range of colours might have been stored in the same room, but this room could also have had several other functions. However, the plant fibre preparation most likely occurred outside the buildings, and spinning could be done everywhere. Washing and dyeing could have taken place in the cooking area, where the dyes could also have been stored. Even if a room was used solely for textile work, it is likely that other materials, for example pottery (artisans do need to drink!), or bone (and eat!), or other objects would be present in the same archaeological context. A general methodological challenge is also that textile tools are generally used to identify a domestic area, in contrast to bronze casting moulds, for example, which are considered to be evidence for a (non-domestic) bronze casting workshop. The loom could also have been set up outside, as is evidenced in ethnographical studies (Breniquet 2008).

In Late Bronze Age palace texts, women (and children) in the textile industries are often recorded in groups. Ur III texts record that 2–3 women work side by side to warp and weave (Waetzoldt 1972; Firth and Nosch 2012). Textile production also occurred in palaces, sanctuaries or other official buildings. There could have been separate rooms for spinning and weaving, but this work could also have been done together. If spinning on a spindle with a whorl, this can easily be done when walking around, but if using a spinning bowl, one needs to stay in one place while spinning. Similarly, when working on a spinning hook (chapter 2), it is preferable to work seated. Moreover, when spinning very thin threads with few fibres, warping the loom and weaving elaborate fabrics, such as textiles with many threads per centimetre, or tapestries, artisans need a lot of light. The colour of the wall against which the loom leans, too, is of importance. If the wall is white, it is very difficult to see thin white threads, yet a white plaster does provide a good light. There could also have been special installations for dyeing and wool washing (Alberti 2007; Mazow 2013), but here again, it is difficult to identify these contexts. The rooms and the spaces for producing textiles must have been numerous and diverse, yet to identify them requires a more detailed discussion on how to identify a textile workshop.

Who were the textile workers?

Over the course of this project, a frequently asked question at lectures and conferences was about gender and textiles: did only women make textiles, or did men also participate in the production? As this volume demonstrates, textile tools are key to the understanding of textile production, but textile tool analyses can provide no individual information on who the textile workers were: their age, gender or ethnicity. Through experimental archaeology, we may be able to assess the level of skill the textile workers possessed and thus evaluate the necessary training level. Yet, textile tools cannot reveal who held them in their hands.

The texts are instead an informative source. Generally, there are many indications of a gendered division of tasks in the Bronze Age texts, but it is notable that the assignment of these tasks is not consistently linked to a gender or an age group, neither in the archives nor in a given cultural sphere (Garcia-Ventura

2014). In Ur III texts of the 21st century BC, women are recorded as textile workers with children, even babies, but men are also recorded as performing textile tasks (Waetzoldt 1972). In Assur women produced textiles (Michel 2014), but men provided the wool and sold these textiles in far off Anatolia in the early centuries of the 2nd millennium BC (Veenhof 1972; Michel 2001; 2014). The Late Bronze Age Linear B texts primarily record female textile workers with children (boys and girls, divided into age groups), but there are also male weavers, and textile finishing is done by both men and women (Nosch 2001; 2003b). If there are some general trends, it is that spinning is mainly associated with women; sheep herding and fulling are tasks connected to men; weaving and finishing/decoration are activities shared by both sexes, and children are often involved in textile work.

Mobility

As this volume demonstrates, textile tools are key to the understanding of textile production. However, textile tool analyses and experimental archaeology can provide less information on mobility; they can rarely enlighten us as to how textiles travelled, were traded, and how textile workers, too, may have travelled. Nevertheless, texts and images inform us about how textiles and fibres moved, as gifts, commercial objects, investments, or along with textile workers. The 6th book of Homer's *Iliad* mentions Sidonian women, most probably textile workers, who were taken to Troia by prince Paris; Linear B records of female textile workers at Pylos suggest that some of them could originate from Anatolia, as migrant workers or captives (Nosch 2003a).

At the end of the 3rd and beginning of the second millennium BC in Mesopotamia, wool was exchanged over short and long distances for copper and silver (Sallaberger 2014). In cases of shortage, wool could be sent all the way from Anatolia to Assur (Michel 2014), and textiles, too, were sent from Assur to Anatolia on a regular basis as the Kaniš documentation demonstrates (Veenhof 1972; Michel 2001; Michel and Veenhof 2010).

Did textile tools, too, travel? Joanne Cutler has observed that a number of textile tools from various Bronze Age southern Aegean settlements are not made of local clay, suggesting that they arrived with the craftspeople who used them, from elsewhere (Cutler 2011; 2012; forthcoming a; Cutler *et al.* 2013; see also chapter 6.6 for Akrotiri, Thera). Moreover, recent isotopic tracing of wool in northern Europe, both from the Bronze Age and the Iron Age, has identified surprisingly large amounts of non-local fibres, suggesting that both wool and textiles were traded as a commodity (Frei *et al.* 2009; 2015; Andersson *et al.* 2010; Nosch *et al.* 2013).

Textile fibres – wool or flax?

Much attention is focused on wool as the new fibre in the Bronze Age. This is an obvious and attractive choice since wool engenders innovations, changes in animal husbandry and a series of new professions and new technologies (McCorriston 1997; Breniquet 2008; Nosch forthcoming a; see also all contributions in Breniquet and Michel 2014). Wool is also used as a payment for workers in Bronze Age palace administrations, and it is used as an investment and currency for obtaining copper and silver in late third millennium BC Mesopotamia (Sallaberger 2014). In the written records we perceive a clear interest – and bias – towards wool textiles, and the Bronze Age scribes had a keen interest in wool products (Breniquet and Michel 2014). Already in the fourth millennium BC at Jemdet Nasr (Charvát 2014), we encounter two similar round signs for wool and textile, respectively (Fig. 7.26).

The amounts of wool textiles recorded in the Bronze Age accounting texts are highly impressive: "in Mesopotamia, around 2050 BC, the annual production of textiles was huge, certainly significantly more than 60,000 pieces", writes Waetzoldt (2010, 201). In 23rd to 22nd centuries BC Akkadian and Sargonic texts, wool is a vital commodity for the palaces, and it is given as rations to workers (Foster 2014). For Late Bronze Age Crete there are records of some 100,000 sheep recorded by palace officials, and this would give yields of 75,000 kilos of raw wool.

Wool represents a Bronze Age innovation, even a revolution (McCorriston 1997), and a new name for the Bronze Age could be the *Wool Age*. Flax, however, continued to be a major textile crop and an important textile fibre (Helbæk 1959; Van Zeits and Bakker-Heeres 1974; Nosch forthcoming b), and perhaps held

Fig. 7.26: SIG$_2$ 'wool' and TUG$_2$ 'textile'.

a special significance for the cult (Bacchelli *et al.* 2014; Quillien 2014). It is also important to bear in mind that wool and flax are two different types of fibres and partly used for different types of textiles (chapter 2).

A methodological bias in trying to assess the relative importance of wool and plant fibres in the Bronze Age Eastern Mediterranean is that sheep, and also goats, leave much more abundant archaeological traces (Ryder 1983; Vila 1998; 2002) than do plant fibres, such as flax (Karg 2011). In contrast, chapter 3 of this volume clearly shows that from a textile archaeological perspective, the vast majority of recovered textiles are linen, a situation that may also be at least partly due to preservation factors.

In the experiments of the present volume, we primarily chose to test wool: preparation, time, spinning and weaving. More experimental tests of flax would substantiate the discussions on fibres and enable a more precise comparison of tools, techniques, and time consumption for animal fibres and plant fibres. Exploring flax species diversification and agriculture, and the technologies related to flax fibres, constitute other key areas for future research. Iconography is rarely of much help in the exploration of flax outside Egypt, but texts testify to the ranking of many linen fabric qualities and to extensive flax cultivation, both for linseed oil and for linen fibres (Herslund 2010; Jones 2010). It only adds to the complexity of the fibre question that some of the archaeological textiles that have been analysed are made of goat hair and possibly nettle fibre (Frangipane *et al.* 2009; Moulhérat and Spantidaki 2009).

It would be marvellous if the textile tools could be used as markers for the introduction of wool in textile production in the Neolithic and Early Bronze Age, but thus far, we are still unable to determine whether changes in spindle whorls or loom weights can be related to the choice of fibres; it is our hope that future scholars are able to develop a methodology for answering this crucial question about prehistoric and early historic resources.

Time and time consumption

The experiments conducted in the TTTC project clearly demonstrate how time consuming it is to produce even the coarsest textiles (chapter 4.1). It is, certainly, difficult to judge how much time was needed in ancient times, for example, how skilled and fast the craftspeople were. Another challenge is to understand the concept of time in the past. Today, there is a general assumption that the longer it takes to produce an object, the higher its value, but it is questionable if this assumption is valid in the Bronze Age. However, what we can conclude, based on both experimental archaeology and on written sources, is that textile production during this period, too, took up a great deal of time. Spinning, in particular, is very time consuming. These are the average spinning speed results of our tests:

- 18 g spindle whorl: 50 m/h.
- 8 g spindle whorl : 40 m/h.
- 4 g spindle whorl : 35 m/h.

Two Bronze Age texts enable us to compare the time allocated to textile tasks with our experimental results (chapter 4). The two textile types concerned are *guz-za* and *bar-dul₅* fabrics.

In one Ur III text (*ITT* V 9996 iii 4-r. I 4=T.32 III 4-Rev. I 4 in Waetzoldt 1972) we read about the production of a *guz-za* fabric made from fourth-class wool, here cited in Waetzoldt's (2010, 205) translation:

1 guz-za-fabric from fourth-class wool, the mixed wool for it (weighs) 4 kg
1 woman cleans and combs 125 g in a day (and)
1 woman 'mingles' (HI.HI.) 1 kg in a day (possibly production of roving/slubbing) the warp threads for it (weigh) 333 g (and)
1 woman spins 8.3 g strongly twisted threads (for the warp);
the weft threads for it (weigh) 1.66 kg (and)
1 woman produces 61 g (of them) in a day (for the weft);
(the) length (of the guz-za-fabric is) 3.5 m (and)
(the) width (is) 3.5 m;
3 women warp in 3 days (and)
2 women weave 50 cm in a day.

Another Ur III text (T.32 Rs. I 6–14) describes the production of a type of textile called *tⁱᵍbar-dul₅* or *bar-dul₅* (Waetzoldt 1972; 2010, 207):

1 bar-dul₅-U₂-fabric from fifth-class (wool), the mixed wool for it (weighs) 2 kg;
1 woman cleans and combs 125 g in a day (and)
1 woman 'mingles' (HI.HI.) 1.5 kg in a day (possibly production of roving/slubbing);
the warp yarns for it (weigh) 666 g (and)
1 woman spins 16.6 g strongly twisted threads (for the warp);
the weft yarns for it (weigh) 833.3 g (and)
1 woman produces (of them) 41.6?? g in a day (for the weft)

For the *guz-za* fabric, an amount of 4 kg of wool is allocated, and for the *bar-dul₅* fabric 2 kg. For the *guz-za* fabric, the warp weighs 333 g and the weft 1.66 kg, which suggests a highly weft faced textile; moreover, the warp and weft yarn must be of very different quality since the output is given per day and there is a clear difference in spun thread output between the 8.3 g warp/per day and the 61 g weft/per day; this would suggest thin, strong and tightly twisted warps interwoven with thicker wefts (Firth and Nosch 2012; Andersson Strand and Cybulska 2013).

For the *bar-dul₅* fabric, the warp weighs 666 g and the weft 833.3 g, suggesting a more balanced weave. However, for the *bar-dul₅* fabric, a woman spins 16.6 g warp per day and 41.6 g weft per day which suggests that it was much faster to spin the weft. It seems plausible that the spinners used different spinning tools for the warp and the weft, respectively. Both types of textile, balanced and weft faced, are well attested in the archaeological record, as we demonstrate in chapter 3.

In both Ur III texts, a woman was able to clean 125 g wool per day. This corresponds quite well to the TTTC experiments in which the textile technicians cleaned 133 g in 12 hours, as we discuss in chapter 4.2.

The time measurements from the CTR tests are within the same time frame as the time given in the Ur III texts. The TTTC textile technicians were both skilled, and had long experience of spinning and weaving, which we also assume to be the case of the Bronze Age artisans of Ur. Even if time was not held to be as valuable as it is today, this is still clear evidence of the high value placed on textiles.

Similar methods are now employed on other source materials. For example, experimental data combined with Old Assyrian texts have been used to estimate how many textiles a household was able to produce per year, and this hypothesis was then confirmed by including textual data related to the transport of these textiles (Michel forthcoming).

In the Linear B texts, information is given about various types of textiles and the amount of wool required to make them (Killen 1964; 1966), which can be compared to the TTTC experimental tests. The following example concerns the Mycenaean textile called *pa-wo* or *pa-we-a* in the plural form. It requires *c.* 1.67 units of wool per piece of *pa-wo*, which is equivalent to *c.* 5 kg of raw wool. According to the TTTC experimental testing, the 5 kg of raw wool would be reduced in the cleaning and sorting process to 40% of its original weight, thus 2 kg of prepared clean wool. The combing would reduce this further by 22% to 1.56 kg of wool. In the TTTC spinning tests, the following spinning outputs per 100 g of prepared wool were achieved: 623.5 m on an 18 g spindle whorl, and 1,031 m on an 8 g spindle whorl. When these results are applied to Mycenaean *pa-we-a*, it implies that 1.56 kg of prepared wool would yield *c.* 10 km when spun on an 18 g spindle whorl, or *c.* 16 km when spun on an 8 g spindle whorl. It would take a spinner *c.* 200 hours to spin the *c.* 10 km on an 18 g spindle whorl (50 m/h), and *c.* 400 hours to spin 16 km on an 8 g spindle whorl (40 m/h) (Nosch 2012 with revised numbers).

These figures raise a series of questions that we did not anticipate previously when studying Linear B: first of all, the *ta-ra-si-ja* obligation to receive wool and turn it into specific textiles is highly time consuming; secondly, a *pa-wo* is generally considered the Mycenaean ancestor of the Homeric *pharos*, a mantle, and thus a piece of wearable clothing. The TTTC experiments suggest that this piece of clothing would weigh *c.* 1–2.5 kg and contain between 10–16 km of thread, and these figures point towards a very large and densely woven cloth, larger than a regular mantle. Thus, it is legitimate to consider alternative interpretations to the equation of raw wool allocated to textile workers equalling a piece of cloth. Perhaps a part of the wool was kept by the textile workers as remuneration?

Texts, the textile tools and the archaeological textiles from the Bronze Age clearly demonstrate the use of various fabrics, which would have taken different lengths of time to produce, and required different textile tools. As discussed earlier, textiles produced with very thin threads and woven in complicated techniques take much longer to produce than coarser textiles in simpler techniques.

Temporality and seasonal textile activities

In the written records of Mycenaean Greece as well as in various account systems of Mesopotamia, wool yields are counted annually, and so is the predicted number of new-born lambs (Michel 2014; Nosch 2014). In Mesopotamia, wool was plucked in spring, before the harvest, and we can assume that in the Aegean plucking also took place at the end of spring when the climate and animal hormones change and provoke moulting, *i.e.*, the natural shedding of the fibres. Experimental archaeology and research in ancient breeds have shown that the timing of plucking is crucial and can neither be started too early nor delayed. If too early, the fibres cannot be detached easily; if too late, the new wool will start growing out from under the old dead wool and this will damage the quality of both. The plucking period was a major operation in Bronze Age palace and temple economies and very large numbers of primarily men were mobilised for this labour-intensive task (Michel 2014). The rapidity of plucking varies according to the sources (Andersson Strand 2014 estimates a rate of 10–12 sheep plucked per man, per day, while at Ur III, Waetzoldt (1972, 14–17) has documentation for 38 sheep being plucked by one man a day). Choosing the right moment for plucking was essential and it is thus not surprising that at Mari a sample of the first plucked wool had to be sent to the king to assess its quality and determine if the time was right (Michel 2014).

A sheep can only be plucked once a year, when it is moulting. Early sheep breeds moult during the late spring/early summer, but the timing of the moulting naturally varies according to climate and regions, *i.e.*, between lowlands and highlands (Barber 1991; Andersson Strand 2012; 2014). A significant change in the temporal organisation of textile production occurred when shearing became common, probably in the Early Iron Age, because by then sheep could be sheared twice a year (Andersson Strand 2014).

Textile production follows a linear sequence of essential processes carried out in a certain order. At the same time, tasks related to agriculture and animal husbandry are cyclical in nature, defined by the year and the seasons.

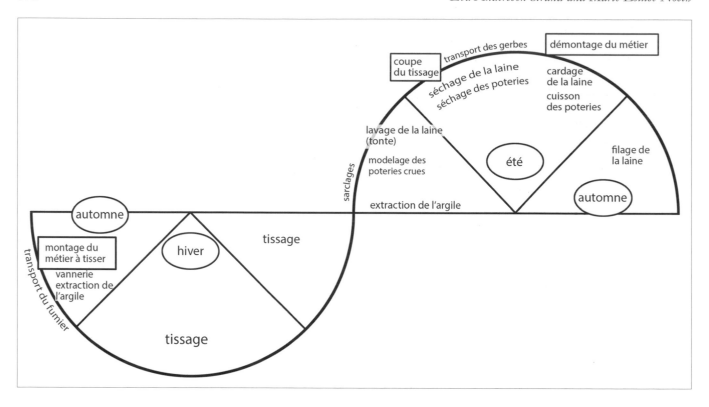

Figure 7.27: Le cycle des travaux féminins. (The cycle of female labour). After Bourdieu 1980, 409.

The textile tools cannot inform us when textile related processes took place, but a potentially useful model in approaching this question is Pierre Bourdieu's visualisation of two work seasons, summer and winter, which was based on his fieldwork in Kabylian villages in northern Algeria (1980) (Fig. 7.27). Here, the female textile activities are fixed at certain periods and intervals; some of these activities are based on practicalities, such as flax harvest and shearing time, while other tasks such as textile fibre processing, spinning and weaving are instead much more flexible processes which can be undertaken, interrupted, and restarted when time and place allow, and fitted in with other fixed agricultural tasks such as the harvesting of other crops, threshing, *etc.* Beyond the practicalities, Bourdieu also emphasised the many other symbolic, religious and gendered aspects of life that govern the daily activities in a village, including the activities related to textile production. Weaving was conducted primarily in winter. This seasonal model of Bourdieu's may be more suitable to visualise the extended temporarily of textile production, and Catherine Breniquet (2008) introduced this line of thought into her analysis of Mesopotamian textile production.

Patterns and images

As has often been observed, a large visual and conceptual gap exists between the standardised textile logograms noted in Linear A and B, and the Minoan and Mycenaean textiles and costumes depicted in contemporary frescoes. The iconography demonstrates that Bronze Age clothing combined textiles and animal skins, and men and women, ages, classes, status, even ethnicity, are clearly distinguished (Chapin and Shaw 2015). That the frescoes do not only illustrate the elite is seen, for instance in the West House frescoes, which depict people wearing simple clothing devoid of decoration. Social hierarchies are expressed in the richly decorated garments of the 'priestess' depicted in the same building, but textiles with elaborate patterns are also often found on furnishing textiles, curtains and wall hangings. The taste for patterned textiles is highly visible among the Minoan elites, but it may have become more confined to a ceremonial and ritual context in the Mycenaean societies (Chapin and Shaw 2015).

From a functional perspective, this volume demonstrates how Bronze Age communities possessed an adequate tool kit for producing both coarse and fine textiles, plain or patterned, and the texts enable us to quantify the textiles and name them, but only the images can inform us how they looked, who wore them, and on what occasions.

The non-functional qualities of textile tools

We focus in this volume on the functional properties of textile tools in order to assess production and yields. Thus, only tools from contexts where they may have been in use were selected for analysis (houses, palaces, courtyards), and textile tools from graves were, therefore, omitted. The latter may, however, weave another story of the spiritual and symbolic properties of textile tools. They accompanied the deceased, mostly woman but also men, into the next world, ensuring them useful tools and textiles in the hereafter. Yet, beyond this pragmatic purpose lie the rich spiritual and symbolic Indo-European connotations of spinning as denoting life, death and destiny (Andrés-Toledo 2010), and weaving as the metaphorical action of connecting and joining, creating unities and cohesion (Fanfani, Harlow and Nosch 2016). We have no direct evidence of this from the Aegean Bronze Age, but in the underworld, the Hattian goddesses of Fate (*Gulšeš*) spin the lives of the Hittite kings and queens with spindles and distaffs (Haas 1994, 372–373; Baccelli *et al.* 2014, 114). In the Homeric epics these symbolic concepts of weaving also abound. Penelope, the faithful and resourceful wife of Odysseus and queen of Ithaca, kept her many suitors at bay by promising to remarry only when she had finished a shroud which she wove by day and unravelled at night. It took them years to discover her plot. Her lawful husband Odysseus weaves plans and plots, too, and Greek uses the same verb for weaving and plotting. Circe and Calypso, enchantresses encountered by Odysseus on his long journey, were weavers, as are all women, elite or poor, in the Homeric epics (Pantelia 1993, with references). It seems that for the Greeks of the first millennium BC, textiles were closely associated with myths of the Bronze Age: Ariadne, the daughter of King Minos of Knossos, gave Theseus a ball of thread so that the young Athenian prince would not get lost in the labyrinth on his quest to slay the monstrous Minotaur. Theseus travelled between Athens and Crete in a ship with two sets of sails, one white to announce the victory over the monster, and a black set to announce defeat.

Final remarks

Our approach to textiles is that they are not simply binary systems of spun, twisted, or spliced fibres, but, first and foremost, the result of a complex interaction between resources, technology and society. The catalyst for this interaction is driven by the needs, desires, and choices of any society, which in turn influence the exploitation of resources and development of technology. Conversely, the availability of resources and the state of technology conditions the choices of individuals and society.

In the *Tools and Textiles, Texts and Contexts* research programme, textile tools, textile terminologies, archaeological textiles, textile contexts, and images of textiles have been interwoven. Each has been explored extensively in the last decade. We hope that our readers will take up the thread here and continue the exploration into new areas, asking new questions. With this book, we have laid the methodological foundations for this enterprise.

Notes

1 In measuring the thickness of the loom weights, it is assumed that the spherical and cylindrical loom weights would have hung with the hole positioned horizontally (as indicated by string wear). It is further assumed that the discoid weights would have hung at right angles to the shed bar; if they had hung parallel to the shed bar, with the thickness therefore being equal to the maximum diameter, the loom weights would have moved out of alignment during shed changes, and they would furthermore produce an extremely open fabric.

2 These objects are sometimes called bobbins or reels in archaeological publications (Gleba 2008, 140; Siennicka and Ulanowska forthcoming).

3 This result can be compared with, for example loom weights recorded from Viking Age Scandinavia (AD 800–1050). The Viking loom weights vary in weight from *c.* 100 g to over 2000 g and in thickness from *c.* 15 mm to over 120 mm. However, the Vikings only had one type of loom weight, which was donut shaped (Andersson 2003).

Bibliography

Alberti, M. A. (2007) Washing and dyeing installations of the ancient Mediterranean: towards a definition from Roman times back to Minoan Crete, in Gillis, C. and Nosch, M.-L. (eds), *Ancient Textiles: Production, Craft and Society*, 59–63. Ancient Textiles Series 1. Oxford. Oxbow Books.

Alberti, M. A. (2008) Textile industry indicators in Minoan work areas: problems of typology and interpretation, in Alfaro, C. and Karali, L. (eds), *Vestidos, Textiles Y Tintes. Estudios sobre la producción de bienes de consumo en la Antigüedad*, 25–36. Valencia. University of Valencia.

Andersson, E. (2003) *Tools for Textile Production from Birka and Hedeby: Excavations in the Black Earth 1990–1995*. Stockholm. Birka Project, Riksantikvarieämbetet.

Andersson, E. and Nosch, M.-L. (2003) With a little help from my friends: investigating Mycenaean textiles with help from Scandinavian experimental archaeology, in Foster, K. P. and Laffineur, R. (eds), *METRON: Measuring the Aegean Bronze Age*, 197–205. Liège. Université de Liège.

Andersson, E., Mårtensson, L., Nosch, M.-L. and Rahmstorf, L. (2008) New research on Bronze Age textile production, *Bulletin of the Institute of Classical Studies* 51, 171–174.

Andersson, E., Frei, K., Gleba, M., Mannering, U., Nosch, M.-L. and Skals, I. (2010) Old textiles – new possibilities, *European Journal of Archaeology* 13 (2), 1–25.

Andersson Strand, E. (2012) The textile chaîne opératoire: using a multidisciplinary approach to textile archaeology with a focus on the Ancient Near East, *Paléorient* 38 (1–2), 21–40.

Andersson Strand, E. (2014) Sheep wool and textile production. An interdisciplinary approach to the complexity of wool working, in Breniquet, C. and Michel, C. (eds), *Wool Economy in the Ancient Near East and the Aegean*, 41–51. Ancient Textiles Series 17. Oxford. Oxbow Books.

Andersson Strand, E. (forthcoming) First looms: loom types in ancient societies, in Siennicka, M. and Rahmstorf L. (eds), *First textiles. The beginnings of textile manufacture in Europe and the Mediterranean*. Ancient Textiles Series. Oxford. Oxbow Books.

Andersson Strand, E. and Cybulska, M. (2013) Visualising ancient textiles – how to make a textile visible on the basis of an interpretation of an Ur III text, in Nosch, M.-L., Koefoed, H. and Andersson Strand, E. (eds), *Textile Production and Consumption in the Ancient Near East: Archaeology, Epigraphy, Iconography*, 113–127. Ancient Textiles Series 12. Oxford. Oxbow Books.

Andrés-Toledo, M. Á. (2010) *El hilo de la vida y el lazo de la muerte en la tradición indoirania*. Valencia. Institucio Alfons el Magnanim.

Baccelli, G., Bellucci, B. and Vigo, M. (2014) Elements for a comparative study of textile production and use in Hittite Anatolia and in neighbouring areas, in Harlow, M., Michel, C. and Nosch, M.-L. (eds), *Prehistoric, Ancient Near Eastern and Aegean Textiles and Dress: an Interdisciplinary Anthology*, 96–142. Ancient Textiles Series 18. Oxford. Oxbow Books.

Barber, E. J. W. (1991) *Prehistoric Textiles: The Development of Cloth in the Neolithic and Bronze Ages with Special Reference to the Aegean*. Princeton. Princeton University Press.

Bourdieu, P. (1980) *Le sens pratique*. Paris. Les éditions de minuit.

Breniquet, C. (2008) *Essai sur le tissage en Mésopotamie, des premières communautés sédentaires au milieu du 3e millénaire avant J.-C.* Paris. De Boccard.

Breniquet, C. and Michel, C. eds (2014) *Wool Economy in the Ancient Near East and the Aegean: From the Beginnings of Sheep Husbandry to Institutional Textile Industry*. Ancient Textiles Series 17. Oxford. Oxbow Books.

Chapin, A. and Shaw, M. eds (2015) *Woven Threads. Patterned Textiles of the Aegean Bronze Age*. Ancient Textiles Series. Oxford. Oxbow Books.

Charvát, P. (2014) Lambs of the gods. The beginnings of the wool economy in Proto-Cuneiform texts, in C. Breniquet and C. Michel (eds), *Wool Economy in the Ancient Near East and the Aegean*, 79–93. Ancient Textiles Series 17. Oxford. Oxbow Books.

Cortes, E. 2011. An early weaving scene, in Craig Patch, D., with contributors, *Dawn of Egyptian Art*, 94–95. New York. Metropolitan Museum of Art.

Cutler, J. (2011) *Crafting Minoanisation: Textiles, Crafts Production and Social Dynamics in the Bronze Age Southern Aegean*. PhD thesis, University College London, UK.

Cutler, J. (2012) Ariadne's thread: the adoption of Cretan weaving technology in the wider southern Aegean in the mid-second millennium BC, in Nosch, M.-L. and Laffineur, R. (eds), *KOSMOS. Jewellery, Adornment and Textiles in the Aegean Bronze Age*, 145–154. Liège. Peeters.

Cutler, J. (forthcoming a) Fashioning identity: weaving technology, dress and cultural change in the Middle and Late Bronze Age southern Aegean, in Gorogianni, E, Pavúk, P. and Girella, L. (eds), *Beyond Thalassocracies. Understanding the Processes of Minoanisation and Mycenaeanisation in the Aegean*. Oxford. Oxbow Books.

Cutler, J. (forthcoming b) First threads: textile production in Neolithic and Early Bronze Age Crete, in Siennicka, M. and Rahmstorf L. (eds), *First textiles. The beginnings of textile manufacture in Europe and the Mediterranean*. Ancient Textiles Series. Oxford. Oxbow Books.

Cutler, J., Andersson Strand, E. and Nosch, M.-L. (2013) Textile production in Quartier Mu, in Poursat, J.-C. (with contributors), *Fouilles exécutées à Malia. Le Quartier Mu V. Vie quotidienne et techniques au minoen Moyen II*, 95–118. Athens. École française d'Athènes.

Cutler, J., Andersson Strand, E. and Nosch, M.-L. (2015) Textile tools from Phaistos, in Militello, P., *Festòs e Haghia Triada. Rinvenimenti Minori I: Materiale per la tessitura*. (Revised edition). Padova. Bottega D'Erasmo.

Fanfani, G., Harlow, M. and Nosch, M.-L. eds (2016) *Spinning Fates and the Song of the Loom: The Use of Textiles, Clothing and Cloth Production as Metaphor, Symbol and Narrative Device in Greek and Latin Literature*. Ancient Textiles Series 24. Oxford. Oxbow Books.

Firth, R. and Nosch, M.-L. (2012) Spinning and weaving wool in Ur III administrative texts, *Journal of Cuneiform Studies*, 64, 67–84.

Foster, B. (2014) Wool in the economy of Sargonic Mesopotamia, in Breniquet, C. and Michel, C. (eds), *Wool Economy in the Ancient Near East and the Aegean*, 115–123. Ancient Textile Series 17. Oxford. Oxbow Books.

Frangipane, M., Andersson, E., Nosch, M.-L., Laurito, R., Rast-Eicher, A., Möller-Wiering, S. and Wisti

Lassen, A. (2009) Arslantepe (Turkey): Textiles, tools and imprints of fabrics from the 4th to the 2nd millennium BC, *Paléorient* 35 (1), 5–29.

Frei, K., Frei, R., Mannering, U., Gleba, M., Nosch, M.-L. and Lyngstrøm, H. (2009) Provenance of textiles – a pilot study evaluating the Sr isotope system in wool, *Archaeometry* 51 (2), 252–276.

Frei, K., Mannering, U., Kristiansen, K., Allentoft, M., Wilson, A., Skals, I., Tridico, S., Nosch, M.-L., Willerslev, E., Clarke, L. and Frei, R. (2015) Tracing the dynamic life story of a Bronze Age female, *Scientific Reports*, 21 May 2015, 5:10431 | DOI: 10.1038/srep10431 (2015).

Garcia-Ventura, A. (2014) Constructing masculinities through textile production in the ancient Near East, in Harlow, M., Michel, C. and Nosch, M.-L. (eds), *Prehistoric, Ancient Near Eastern and Aegean Textiles and Dress: An Interdisciplinary Anthology*, 167–183. Ancient Textiles Series 18. Oxford. Oxbow Books.

Gleba, M. (2008) *Textile Production in Pre-Roman Italy*. Ancient Textiles Series 4. Oxford. Oxbow Books.

Haas, V. (1994) *Geschichte der hethitischen Religion*. Leiden. Brill.

Herslund, O. (2010) Cloths – garments – and keeping secrets. Textile classification and cognitive chaining in the ancient Egyptian writing system, in Michel, C. and Nosch, M.-L. (eds), *Textile Terminologies in the Ancient Near East and Mediterranean from the Third to the First Millennia BC*, 68–80. Ancient Textiles Series 8. Oxford. Oxbow Books.

Helbæk, H. (1959) Note on the evolution and History of *Linum*. *Kuml*, 103–129.

Iacovidis, S. (1977) On the use of Mycenaean buttons, *Annual of the British School at Athens* 72, 113–119.

Jones, J. (2010) The 'linen lists' in Early Dynastic and Old Kingdom Egypt: text and textile reconciled, in Michel, C. and Nosch, M.-L. (eds), *Textile Terminologies in the Ancient Near East and Mediterranean from the Third to the First Millennia BC*, 81–109. Ancient Textiles 8. Oxford. Oxbow Books.

Karg, S. ed. (2011) New research on the cultural history of the useful plant *Linum usitatissimum L.* (flax), a resource for food and textiles for 8,000 years, *Vegetation History and Archaeobotany* 20(6), 507–584.

Killen, J. T. (1964) The Wool Industry of Crete in the Late Bronze Age, *Annual of the British School at Athens* 59, 1–15.

Killen, J. T. (1966) The Knossos Lc (Cloth) tablets, *Bulletin of the Institute of Classical Studies* 13, 105–111.

Liu, R. (1978) Spindle whorls. Part I: some comments and speculations, *The Bead Journal* 3, 87–103.

Mårtensson, L., Nosch, M.-L. and Andersson Strand, E. (2009) Shape of things: understanding a loom weight, *Oxford Journal of Archaeology* 28(4), 373–398.

Mazare, P. (2014) Investigating Neolithic and Copper Age textile production in Transylvania (Romania). Applied methods and results, in Harlow, M., Michel, C. and Nosch, M.-L. (eds), *Prehistoric, Ancient Near Eastern and Aegean Textiles and Dress: An Interdisciplinary Anthology*, 1–42. Ancient Textiles Series 18. Oxford. Oxbow Books.

Mazow, L., (2013) Throwing the baby out with the bathwater: innovations in Mediterranean textile production at the end of the 2nd/beginning of the 1st millennium BCE, in Nosch, M.-L., Koefoed, H. and Andersson Strand, E. (eds), *Textile Production and Consumptions in the Ancient Near East*, 215–223. Ancient Textiles Series 12. Oxford. Oxbow Books.

McCorriston, J. (1997) The fiber revolution. Textile extensification, alienation and social stratification in ancient Mesopotamia, *Current Anthropology* 38 (4), 517–549.

Michel, C. (2006) Femmes et production textile à Assur au début du IIe millénaire avant J.-C., *Techniques et culture* 46, 281–297.

Michel, C. (2001) *Correspondance des marchands de Kaniš au début du IIe millénaire avant J.-C.* Paris. Libraire du Cerf.

Michel, C. (2014) Wool trade in Upper Mesopotamia and Syria according to Old Babylonian and Old Assyrian texts, in Breniquet, C. and Michel, C. (eds), *Wool Economy in the Ancient Near East and the Aegean: From the Beginnings of Sheep Husbandry to Institutional Textile Industry*, 232–254. Ancient Textiles Series 17. Oxford. Oxbow Books.

Michel, C. (forthcoming) Estimating an Old Assyrian household textile production with the help of experimental archaeology: feasibility and limitations, in Andersson Strand, E. and Harlow, M. (eds), *Traditional Textile Craft – an Intangible Cultural Heritage* (ebook).

Michel, C. and Nosch, M.-L. eds (2010) *Textile Terminologies in the Ancient Near East and Mediterranean from the Third to the First Millennia BC*, Ancient Textiles Series 8. Oxford. Oxbow Books.

Michel, C. and Veenhof, K. R. (2010) Textiles traded by the Assyrians in Anatolia (19th–18th Centuries BC), in Michel, C. and Nosch, M-L. (eds), *Textile Terminologies in the Ancient Near East and Mediterranean from the Third to the First Millennia BC*, 209–269. Ancient Textiles Series 8. Oxford. Oxbow Books.

Militello, P. (2007) Textile industry and Minoan palaces, in Gillis, C. and Nosch M.-L. (eds), *Ancient Textiles. Production, Craft and Society*, 35–43. Ancient Textiles Series 1. Oxford. Oxbow Books.

Moulhérat, C. and Spantidaki, Y. (2009) Cloth from Kastelli, Chania, *Arachne* 3, 8–15.

Nosch, M.-L. (2001) Kinderarbeit in den mykenischen Palästen, in Blakholmer, F. and Szemethy, H. (eds), *8. Österreichischer Archäologentag*, 37–43. Vienna. Phoibes.

Nosch, M.-L. (2003a) Centre and periphery in the Linear B archives, in Kyparissi-Apostolika, N. and Papakonstantinou, M. (eds), Η περιφέρεια του μυκηναϊκού κόσμου/*The Periphery of the Mycenaean World*, 397–415. Athens. Ministry of Culture.

Nosch, M.-L. (2003b) The women at work in the Linear B tablets, in Strömberg, A. and Larsson Lovén, L. (eds), *Gender, Culture and Religion in Antiquity*, 12–26. Jonsered. Paul Åström.

Nosch, M.-L. (2012) From texts to textiles in the Aegean Bronze Age, in Nosch, M.-L. and Laffineur, R. (eds), *KOSMOS. Jewellery, Adornment and Textiles in the Aegean Bronze Age*, 43–56. Liège. Peeters.

Nosch, M.-L. (2014) The Wool economy in Greece in the end of the II millennium BCE, in Michel, C. and Breniquet, C. (eds), *Wool Economy in the Ancient Near East and the Aegean: From the Beginnings of Sheep Husbandry to Institutional Textile Industry*, 371–400. Ancient Textiles Series 17. Oxford. Oxbow Books.

Nosch, M.-L. (forthcoming a) The Wool Age: textile traditions and textile innovations, in Ruppenstein, F. and Weilhartner, J. (eds), *Tradition and Innovation in the Mycenaean Palatial Polities*. Vienna. Österreichische Akademie der Wissenschaften.

Nosch, M.-L. (forthcoming b) Textile crops and textile labour in Mycenaean Greece, in Oller, M., Pàmias, J. and Varias Garcia, C. (ed.), *Land, Territory and Population in the Ancient Greece: Institutional and Mythical Aspects*. Barcelona.

Nosch, M.-L. (forthcoming c) Textiles, in Kotsonas, A. and Lemos, I. (eds), *Blackwell's Companion to the Archaeology of Early Greece and the Mediterranean*. Oxford. Wiley-Blackwell.

Nosch, M.-L., Mannering, U., Andersson Strand, E. and Frei, K. (2013) Travels, Transmissions, and Transformations – and Textiles, in Sabatini, S. and Bergerbrant, S. (eds), *Counterpoint: Essays in Archaeology and Heritage Studies in Honour of Professor Kristian Kristiansen,* 469–476. Oxford. Archaeopress.

Ofitsch, M. (2001) Zu heth. *ḫueša-*: Semantik, Etymologie, kulturgeschichtliche Aspekte, in Wilhelm, G. (ed.), *Akten des IV. Internationalen Kongresses für Hethitologie,* 478–498. Wiesbaden. Harrassowitz.

Pantelia, M. C. (1993) Spinning and weaving: ideas of domestic order in Homer, *American Journal of Philology* 114, 493–501.

Quillien, L. (2014) Flax and linen in the first millennium Babylonia BC: the origins, craft industry and uses of a remarkable textile, in Harlow, M., Michel, C. and Nosch, M.-L. (eds), *Prehistoric, Ancient Near Eastern and Aegean Textiles and Dress: An Interdisciplinary Anthology,* 271–296. Ancient Textiles Series 18. Oxford. Oxbow Books.

Rougemont, F. (2007) Flax and linen textiles in the Mycenaean palatial economy, in Gillis, C. and Nosch, M.-L. (eds), *Ancient Textiles. Production, Craft and Society,* 46–49. Ancient Textiles Series 1. Oxford. Oxbow Books.

Rahmstorf, L. (2003) Clay spools from Tiryns and elsewhere. An indication of foreign influence in LH III C?, in Kyparissi-Apostolika, N. and Papakonstantinou, M (eds), Η Περιφέρεια του Μυκηναϊκού Κόσμου/*The Periphery of the Mycenaean World,* 397–415. Athens. Ministry of Culture.

Rahmstorf, L. (2005) Ethnicity and changes in weaving technology in Cyprus and the Eastern Mediterranean in the 12th century BC, in Karageorghis, V., Matthaus, H. and Rogge, S. (eds), *Cyprus: Religion and Society from the Late Bronze Age to the End of the Archaic Period,* 143–169. Möhnesee. Bibliopolis.

Rahmstorf, L. (2009) *Kleinfunde aus Tiryns, Terrakotta, Stein, Bein und Glas/Fayence vornehmlich aus der Spätbronzezeit.* Tiryns Forschungen und Berichte Band XVI, Deutsches Archäolgisches Institut. Reichert Verlag Wiesbaden.

Rahmstorf, L. (2011) Handmade pots and crumbling loomweights: 'Barbarian' elements in the eastern Mediterranean in the last quarter of the 2nd millennium BC, in Kouka, O. and Karageorghis, V. (eds), *On cooking Pots, Drinking Cups, Loomweights and Ethnicity in Bronze Age Cyprus and Neighbouring Regions,* 315–330. Nicosia. A. G. Leventis Foundation.

Rast-Eicher, A. and Bender Jørgensen, L. (2013) Sheep wool in Bronze Age and Iron Age Europe, *Journal of Archaeological* Science 40, 1224–1241.

Ryder, M. (1983) *Sheep and Man.* London. Duckworth.

Sallaberger, W. (2014) The value of wool in Early Bronze Age Mesopotamia. On the control of sheep and the handling of wool in the Presargonic to the Ur III Periods (*c.* 2400 to 2000 BC), in Breniquet, C. and Michel, C. (eds), *Wool Economy in the Ancient Near East and the Aegean,* 94–114. Ancient Textiles Series 17. Oxford. Oxbow Books.

Sarri, K. (forthcoming) Looking for a lost thread: Aegean Later Neolithic textiles through pictorial evidence, in Siennicka, M. and Rahmstorf L. (eds), *First textiles. The beginnings of textile manufacture in Europe and the Mediterranean.* Ancient Textiles Series. Oxford. Oxbow Books.

Sauvage, C. (2013) Spinning from Old Threads: the Whorls from Ugarit at the Musée d'Archéologie Nationale (Saint-Germain-en-Laye) and at the Louvre, in Koefoed, H., Nosch, M.-L. and Andersson Strand, E. (eds), *Textile Production and Consumption in the Ancient Near East,* 189–214. Ancient Textiles Series 12. Oxford. Oxbow Books.

Sauvage, C. and Hawley, R. (2013) Une fusaïole inscrite au MAN, in Matoïan, V. and Al-Maqdissi, M. (eds), *Études Ougaritiques* III, 365–394. Leuven. Peeters.

Siennicka, M. (2012) Textile production in Early Helladic Tiryns, in Nosch, M.-L. and Laffineur, R. (eds), *KOSMOS. Jewellery, Adornment and Textiles in the Aegean Bronze Age,* 65–75. Liège. Peeters.

Siennicka, M. (forthcoming) Textile production in the Early Bronze Age Argolid – continuity or change?, in Siennicka, M. and Rahmstorf L. (eds), *First textiles. The beginnings of textile manufacture in Europe and the Mediterranean.* Ancient Textiles Series. Oxford. Oxbow Books.

Siennicka, M. and Ulanowska A. (forthcoming) So simple yet universal. Experimental approach to clay spools from Bronze Age Greece, in Alfaro C. (ed.), *Vth Purpureae Vestes. Textiles and Dyes in the Mediterranean World: International symposium, Barcelona-Montserrat, 19–22 March 2014.*

Smith, J. (2001) Bone weaving tools of the Late Bronze Age, in P. M. Fischer (ed.), *Contributions to the Archaeology and History of the Bronze and Iron Ages in the Eastern Mediterranean. Studies in Honour of Paul Åström,* 83–90. Vienna. Austrian Archaeological Institute.

Smith, J. (2012) Tapestries in the Mediterranean Late Bronze Age, in Nosch, M.-L. and Laffineur, R. (eds), *KOSMOS. Jewellery, Adornment and Textiles in the Aegean Bronze Age,* 241–250. Liège. Peeters.

Smith, J. (2013) Tapestries in the Bronze and Early Iron Ages of the Ancient Near East, in Nosch, M.-L., Koefoed, H., Andersson Strand, E. (eds), *Textile Production and Consumption in the Ancient Near East,* 159–186. Ancient Textiles Series 12. Oxford. Oxbow Books.

Textile production and clothing: technology and tools in ancient Egypt (n.d.) http://www.ucl.ac.uk/museums-static/digitalegypt/textil/tools.html.

Thureau-Dangin, F., Genouillac, H. de, L. Delaporte (1910–1921) *Inventaire des Tablettes de Tello conservées au Musée Impérial Ottoman I–IV.* Paris. Leroux.

Tiedemann, E. and Jakes K. A. (2006) An exploration of prehistoric spinning technology: spinning efficiency and technology transition, *Archaeometry* 48 (2), 293–307.

Tournavitou, I. (1988) Towards the Identification of a Workshop Space, in French, E. B. and Wardle, K. A. (eds), *Problems in Greek Prehistory.* Bristol, British School at Athens, 447–467.

Tzachili, I. (2012) The myth of Arachne and weaving in Lydia, in Tzachili, I. and Zimi, E. (eds), *Textiles and Dress in Greece and the Roman East: A Technological and Social Approach,* 131–142. Athens. Ta Pragmata.

Vakirtzi, S. (2015) *Yarn Production in the Aegean Islands During the Bronze Age, as Attested through the Presence of Spindle Whorls at Archaeological Sites: A Study of Typology, Functionality and Distribution of Whorls at Settlements and Cemeteries*. PhD thesis, in Greek, University of Crete.

Vakirtzi, S., Koukouli-Chryssanthaki, C. and Papadopoulos, S. (2014) Spindle whorls from two prehistoric settlements on Thassos, North Aegean, in Harlow, M., Michel, C. Nosch, M.-L. (eds), *Prehistoric, Bronze Age and Ancient Near Eastern Textiles and Dress: An Interdisciplinary Anthology*, 43–56. Ancient Textiles Series 18. Oxford. Oxbow Books.

Van Zeist, W. and Bakker-Heeres, J. (1974) Evidence for linseed cultivation before 6000 BC. *Journal of Science* 2, 215–219.

Veenhof, K. R. (1972) *Aspects of Old Assyrian Trade and its Terminology*. Leiden. Brill.

Vila, E. (1998) *L'exploitation des animaux en Mésopotamie aux IVe et IIIe millénaires avant J.-C.* Paris. CNRS.

Vila, E. (2002) L´évolution de la taille du mouton dans le nord de la Mésopotamie : les faits et leurs causes, in Bodson, L. (ed.), *D'os, d'image et de mots. Contribution à la réflexion sur les sources de l'histoire des connaissances zoologiques. Colloques d'histoire des connaissances zoologiques* 13, 47–79. Liège. University of Liège.

Waetzoldt, H. (1972) *Untersuchungen zur Neusumerische Textilindustrie*. Rome. Instituto per l'Oriente.

Waetzoldt, H. (1980) Leinen, *Reallexikon der Assyriologie und vorderasiatischen Archäologie*, 583–594. Berlin. W. de Gruyter.

Waetzoldt, H. (2010) The colours and variety of fabrics from Mesopotamia during the Ur III period (2050 BC), in Michel, C. and Nosch, M.-L. (eds), *Textile Terminologies in the Ancient Near East and Mediterranean from the Third to the First Millennia BC*, 201–209. Ancient Textiles Series 8. Oxford. Oxbow Books.

APPENDICES

Appendix A: Textile remains in the Eastern Mediterranean area: Neolithic and Chalcolithic.

Neolithic and Chalcolithic

Site	Date BCE	Type of find	Technique	Warp/weft twist	Warp/weft thread diameter in mm	Thr/cm	Fibre	Additional information	Reference
Iran									
Ali Kosh	7000–6000	fragments of matting and textile preserved in bitumen (1 impression in clay)	basketry; tabby weave					possibly remains of caulking	Hole & von Flannery 1962, 220–223; Barber 1991, 131; Rothenhäusler forthcoming a
Tepe Yāhyā	5th millennium	evidence of weaving							Adovasio 1975–77, 228; Barber 1991, 132
Deb Luran	4100–3700	impression	tabby; in one area the weaving looks like rep or possibly basket weave	s					Hole et al. 1969, 222; Völling 2008, 202
Susa	4th–3rd millennium	2 fragments attached to copper axe from burial context	tabby	S2z	0.3; 0.23–0.26; 0.6	9–15 × 7–13	plant; probably flax	1 striped textile; stripes created by thicker threads (possibly 2 different textiles?)	Lecaisne 1912, 163–164; Barber 1991, 132–133; Völling 2008, 202; Breniquet 2008, 56
	4th–3rd millennium	impression on jar from context of settlement	tabby						Amiet 1986, 20; Breniquet 2008, 56
	3000	mineralised fragment on silver figurine of bull	tabby, faced	S2z		22–30 × 10	animal fiber like wool	From Nippur and Lagash similar remains of cloths on figurines are preserved	Hansen 1970, 7; Barber 1991, 164
Tepe Lungar	4000	impression; grave find	tabby			40 × 40	probably flax		Adovasio & Lamberg-Kalovsky 1986, 206; Völling 2008, 202
Iraq									
Jarmo	7000	impressions in clay and bitumen from settlement	tabby; basket; basketry						Adovasio 1975–77, 223–230; 1983, 425; Rothenhäusler forthcoming a; Barber 1991, 126; Völling 2008, 206; Breniquet 2008, 56
Sawwan	6000	impression in bitumen from burial context	tabby, faced					unpublished find	Breniquet 2008, 56
Telul eth Thalathat	7th millennium	impression on ceramic	tabby	hard spinning			wool according to archaeologist; not verified, and questioned by Völling		Egami 1970, 77; Völling 2008, 206
Eridu	4th millennium	several fragments from garment	undefined weaving				unknown (possibly flax)		Giller 1981, 318; Völling 2008, 206; Breniquet 2008, 56
Oueili	4th millennium	2 impressions in bitumen	tabby, balanced						Breniquet 1987, 141–157; Völling 2008, 206; Breniquet 2008, 56

Israel and Palestinian authority									
Netiv Hagdud	7700	13 mm charred fragment of string, and loose fibres		Z2s			fibre of string identified as plant	loose fibres un-identifiable	Schick 1997, 197–200; Völling 2008, 221
Nahal Hemar	7000	2000–3000 fragments of yarn of different thicknesses, some with knots, some in bundles, some preserved in bitumen. A few fragments of weavings	looping, knotted netting, interlinking, weft-wrapping/weft-twining		0.2/4–0.6/7 (?)		flax	one piece identified as a head covering; decorations with tassels, shells, beads; traces of red and blue dyes	Schick; 1986c; 1988a; 1988b; 1989, 41,52; Bar-Yosef 1985; Shimony & Rivka 1988; Barber 1991, 130–132; 2007, 173–178; Völling 2008, 222; Breniquet 2008, 55; Shamir 2014; Shamir forthcoming
Beth-Shean	3800–3500	impressions in 2 pithoi	tabby		thick threads		unknown		Tsori 1967, 101–103; Völling 2008, 226
Teleilat Ghassul	Chalcolithic	poorly preserved fabrics	tabby			12 × 13–14			Crowfoot 1954:432; Crowfoot 1960, 519–526; Barber 1991, 165; Shamir forthcoming
Tel Lachish	4th millennium	impressions in pot sherds	tabby; balanced				probably flax	similar to Jericho	Tufnell & Lankester 1958, 72; Barber 1991, 165; Völling 2008, 227; Breniquet 2008, 57; Rothenhäusler forthcoming a
Nahal Ze'elim	Chalcolithic	16 textiles	tabby, fine threads				flax	small handbag of leather, beads and linen thread	Aharoni 1961; Bar-Yosaf Mayer & Porat 2010; Shamir 2014; Shamir forthcoming
Nahal 'Arugot	Chalcolithic	11 textiles					flax		Shamir forthcoming
Nahal Yishai	Chalcolithic	2 textiles					flax		Shamir forthcoming
Cave of the Horror	Chalcolithic	1 textile					flax		Shamir forthcoming
Christmas Cave	Chalcolithic	71 textiles		s; S2s			flax	most are not worn and in a good state of preservation	Shamir & Sukenik 2010; 2011; Shamir forthcoming
Pool Cave	Chalcolithic	5 textiles				11–14 × 8–11	flax		Shamir forthcoming
Cave VIII/28 Cave of the Sandal	Chalcolithic	1 textile	tabby				flax		Shamir 2014; Shamir forthcoming
Northern Judean Desert Cave III/3	Chalcolithic	5 fragments of woven textiles	tabby; balanced/warp-faced	s		10–20 × 10–14	flax	open weave	Schick 2002; Shamir 2005; Völling 2008, 225–226; Shamir 2014; Shamir forthcoming
Northern Judean Desert Cave III/7	Chalcolithic	4 fragments of woven textiles	tabby; balanced/warp-faced	s		9–28 × 9–20	flax	open weave; part of selvedge preserved	Schick 2002; Shamir 2005; Völling 2008, 225–226; Shamir forthcoming
Judean Desert Cave V/49	Chalcolithic	7 fragments of woven textiles; 2 fragments of yarn and 1 fragment of a cord	tabby	s; S2z			flax	open weave	Schick 2002; Shamir 2005; Völling 2008, 225–226

Site	Date/Period	Description	Weave	Spin	Thread count	Fibre	Notes	References
Northern Judean Desert Cave VI/46 Qarantal Cliff	Chalcolithic	46 fragments of different weavings; mostly similar to fragments from other caves; one differs in density	tabby	s	11–46 × 9–26	flax	part of selvedge preserved in the denser fragment; part of finishing border with fringes preserved	Schick 2002; Shamir 2005; Völling 2008, 225–226; Shamir forthcoming
Northern Judean Desert Cave VIII/9	Chalcolithic	9 fragments of open weave	tabby	s	11–32 × 10–22	flax	open weave; part of finishing border as from Cave VI/46 preserved; part of selvedge with thicker warp threads preserved	Schick 2002; Shamir 2005; Völling 2008, 225–226; Shamir 2014; Shamir forthcoming
Northern Judean Desert Cave X/31	Chalcolithic	3 fragments of woven textiles	tabby; warp-faced		14–16 × 7–8	flax	open weave	Schick 2002; Shamir 2005; Völling 2008, 225–226; Shamir forthcoming
Judean Desert Cave XIV/6	Chalcolithic	fragments of braided textiles				flax		Schick 2002, Shamir 2005; Schick 1986, 8; Völling 2008, 225–226
Nahal Lehat	Chalcolithic	5 fragments of textiles. The largest measuring 27 × 8 cm; remains of a mat, cordage and skin	tabby	s; S2z		flax	selvedges preserved in 2 textiles	Schick 1986b; 2002; Shamir 2014; Shamir forthcoming
Nahal Mishmar Cave of the Treasure	Chalcolithic	67 fragments of textiles	tabby, balanced/faced	S2z	9–45 × 7–30. One piece is 44–45 × 30	87 linen textiles	parts of loom, shuttles, rope, bastetry	Cindorf et al. 1980; Barber 1991, 165; Völling 2008, 226; Breniquet 2008, 57; Shamir 2014; Shamir forthcoming
Lower Wadi el-Makkukh. Cave of the Warrior	Chalcolithic	3 intact textiles (A: 7 × 2 m; B: 1.4 × 0.9m; C: 2 × 0.2 m; D: 1.4 × 0.07 m)	A: tabby; basket weave; B: warp faced tabby, and C: tabby; D: tabby	A:S2z; B:S2s; C:S2s; D: S2s	A:15 × 2 0–11 × 13; B:12–20 × 10–12; C: 13 × 13–21 × 16; D:19 × 15	flax	decorated with black bands – paint or smeared asphalt. warp fringes; weft fringes; corded selvedge, counter-weft twining decoration warp fringes; weft fringes; decorative effects of basket weave, weft twining and darker coloured threads; corded selvedge	Schick 1998, 127, Schick 1999; Schick 2000, 15–21; Breniquet 2008, 57; Levy J. and Isaac G. 2013, 35–37; Shamir 2014; Shamir forthcoming; Shamir personal information July 2014
Lower Wadi el-Makkukh (3 caves)	textiles				7–28 × 7–22	flax		Schick 1998; Shamir forthcoming; Shamir & schick forthcoming
Wadi Murabba'at	Chalcolithic	threads on wooden comb dated 8000 BCE; fragment of textile	twining; tabby	S2z (threads on comb)		flax	Also textiles from Roman period	Crowfoot 1961; Tuohy 1990; 1992; Ryder 1991; Schick 1992; 1995; Völling 2008, 218–21; Shamir 2014; Shamir forthcoming; Shamir personal information July 2014
Jordan								
Shimshara	6500–5500	impression from settlement	tabby, balanced		13 × 14			Mortensen 1970, 123–124; Barber 1991, 132; Breniquet 2008, 56

Site	Date	Description	Weave	Twist	Diameter	Count	Fibre	Notes	References
Abu Hamid	4th millennium	impression from burial context	tabby						Martin 1993, 22; Dolfus 2001, 74–75; Breniquet 2008, 56
Dhuweila	Chalcolithic	impressions	tabby, diagonal structure	z; S2z			cotton?	tablet weaving?	Betts et al. 1994; Breniquet 2008, 57; Rothenhäusler forthcoming a
Ghassul	Chalcolithic	fragment	weaving	S2z		13 × 12		knots	Crowfoot 1960, 519; Breniquet 2008, 57
Syria									
Jerf el-Ahmar	PPNA	impression in terracotta					flax?		Stordeur & Jammous 1997, 41; Breniquet 2008, 55
Aswad	PPNB?	impression					flax?	embroidered?	Stordeur 2002; Breniquet 2008, 55
El Kowm 2	7100–6000	impression	tabby, balanced		1	8 × 8	probably flax		Maréchal 1989, 53-68; Stordeur 2000; Völling 2008, 215–216; Breniquet 2008, 55
Tell Halula	PPNB	fragment	weft-wrapping/ weft-twining, warp-twining	S2z	0.7–1.6; 0.3–0.5		flax		Molist Montana 2001; Breniquet 2008, 55; Alfaro 2012, 41–54
Hama	6th millennium	impression in clay brick	tabby			17 × 10-12			Bender Jorgensen L. 1988; Völling 2008, 216
Kashashok	6000	impression in clay	tabby			12–13 × 13–14			Matsutani 1991, 35; Breniquet 2008, 56
Egypt									
Fayum	5000	woven textile and basketry	tabby	S2z	0.75–0.9	10 × 12	flax	(loosely woven)	Midgley 1928; Caton Thompson & Gardner 1934, 46; Crowfoot 1955, 418; Wendrich 2000, 256; Jones & Oldfield 2006; Barber 1991, 145; Jones 2002b, 2–8
Badari	5500–3050	basketry; textiles made by weft-wrapping / -twining also mentioned							Midgley 1928; 1937; Brunton & Caton Thompson 1928, 19; Crowfoot 1955, 20–40; Wendrich 2000, 256; Jones 2002b, 2–8
Gersheh	5500–3050	textile							Midgley 1912, 6; 1915, 50; Jones 2002 b, 2–8
Qau	5500–3050	textile							Midgley 1912, 6; 1915, 50; Jones 2002 b, 2–8
Mostagedda	4500–3800	traces of cloth from early levels are not studied; from later levels fragments have been analysed	tabby of various degrees of fineness					possible fringe described but not preserved	Brunton 1937, 27, 34, 47–47; Midgley 1937, 61–62; Barber 1991, 145
Gebelein (Naga-el-Gherira)	4000–3500	painted textile found folded beside mummified body	tabby					fragments of possible warp fringe preserved	Scamuzzi 1965, foreword; Barber 1991, 145–146
Naga-ed-Dêr	3500	woven textiles from excavation of 634 graves		s; S2s visible on photos of some textiles			flax, no technical analyses exist		Lythgoe and Dunham 1965, 68; Jones 2002 b, 2–8

Site	Date	Description	Technique	Spin	Thickness	Count	Fibre	Notes	References
Abydos	3600	textile wrapped around malachite	tabby – balanced	S2z	0.25–0.5	18 × 18	flax	comparable to textile from Fayum but finer	Jones 2002a; Jones 2002b, 2–8
	3250	intricately woven textile (K747-Tomb U-j chamber 8) with diamond shaped patterns of 3 different colours	floating wefts form diamond pattern	warp: 3 s-spun, 2 S-plied threads cabled together; weft: cabled threads	0.9–1.0 / 0.5–0.65; red weft 0.75	6 × 14	flax	found in multi-chambered, elite tomb U-j; the description of the cabled threads are unclear	Jones 2002a, 327–329; Jones 2002b, 2–8
	3050	9 fragments from the same textile (Tomb U–w)	tabby, open weave	s; some plied	0.3	26 × 13	flax		Jones 2002a, 329–330; Jones 2002b, 2–8
Hierakonpolis		Finds from three different locations. 1:textile fragments from cemetery HK43 excavated 2001; 2:resin-impregnated textiles of different qualities from 'working class' burials – finer textiles close to body, coarser textiles in outer layers – remains of weft frings found in one burial; 3:spindle whorls and fragments of spun yarn found in outbuildings of large farm (HK11)							
	3600–3500		tabby	1:s; a few S2s; 2:s / S2s; S2s / S2z; 3:S2z; S2s	0.15–0.3	18 × 25–21 × 25 (fine gauze-like type and slightly coarser type)	flax	Jones 2002b for discussion regarding s and z spinning in Egypt; from 3500 BC only s-spun yarns are used	Wattrall 2000; Jones 2001, 13-14, 18; Jones 2002a, 327 n.22; Jones 2002b, 2–8
Turkey									
Çatal Hüyük	PPNB	several 100 charred fragments from different locations	tabby, balanced/faced, of different quality; weft-wrapping and weft-twining with paired weft in net-like structure	Z2s; z	0.8	warp: 10–12 × weft: 12–15	flax	textiles of wool was earlier believed to have been preserved, but has recently been identified as flax	Mellart 1962; 1963; 1964; 1967; 1989; Helbaek 1963; Burnham 1965, 170–172; Ryder 1965; Vogelsang-Eastwood 1987a; Hirsch 1989a; Balpinar 1989; Barber 1991, 127–130; Breniquet 2008, 55; Völling 2008, 235–238
		fragment of woven textile and finely twisted cord from a child's burial		cord has S-ply (visible on photograph)				excavation in 2008	Çatal Hüyük Archive Report 2008, 146–147
Cayönü	8th–6th millennium	8 × 4 cm traces of mineralised textile on bone sickle	twining technique with paired threads in one system	S2z		7 × 5	bast, possibly flax		Özdoğan 1999; Vogelsang-Eastwood 1993; Breniquet 2008, 55
Mersin	Neolithic	impression of textile from burial context	basket 3/3			strands arranged by 3 with total of nine strands		the impression is not preserved	Garstang 1953, 33; Barber 1991, 132; Breniquet 2008, 55
Gülpinar	5th millennium	20 impressions	possibly 2/1 twill				probably plant	technical analysis not verified; possibly basketry	Takaoğlu 2006, 307–308; Völling 2008, 238

Site	Period	Description	Weave	Twist	Fibre	Textures	References
Alişar Höyük	Chalkolithic	few fragments from burial	twill (?)				Fogelberg & Kendall 1937; Barber 1991, 167; Völling 2008, 238–239; Breniquet 2008, 57
Zeytinli Bahce	3600–3400	several finds described. 1: burnt mat 62/2002; 2: interwoven fibres 110/2002; 3: interwowen fibres 111/2002; 4: mat covered with bitumen 122/2002			probably plant / 62/2002: no id possible; 110/2002: Esparto-grass; 111/2002: plant, possibly Cyperis papyrus; 122/2002: rusè, possibly Juncaceae-type		Laurito 2007b; Rast-Eicher 2009 technical report
Greece							
Sitagroi	5500–5200	impression on potsherd	tabby				Renfrew 1972, 351; Barber 1991, 174; Elster 2003
Keos	late Neolithic	impression on potsherd	tabby				Carington Smith 1977, 116; Barber 1991, 174
Kephalonia. Drakaina Cave	late Neolithic	mineralised fragment of fibre, possible thread		z			Nosch et al. 2011
Georgia							
Ochamchira	4th–3rd millennium	impressions on pot sherds	tabby			various textures	Kuftin 1950, pl 74–77; Barber 1991, 168

Appendix B: Textile remains in the Eastern Mediterranean area: Bronze Age.

Bronze Age textiles

Site	Date BC	Type of find	Technique	Warp/weft twist	Warp/weft thread diameter in mm	Thr/cm	Fibre	Additional information	Reference
Iran									
Shahr-i Sokhta	3rd mill.	textile and basketry impressions in plaster and ceramic; woven textiles, cordage and nets recovered from several different contexts	tabby, weft-faced; slit tapestry, warp-faced strap bands	wide variety in spin, gauge, density of weave			sheeps wool, camel wool, goat hair; flax in plied threads; sunn hemp fibres in loose fibre samples;	Constantini et al. list 50 fragments. Völling additionally 80 fragments. Ropes and nets; jute	Tosi 1983, 164; Good 2007, 179–184; Völling 2008, 203; Constantini et al. 2012
Tepe Hissar	3rd mill.	one large, several small coloured fragments;	loose weave	s, z; different spin direction in warp and weft		8–10 × 8–10	animal (probably sheep wool)	trace of dye in larger fragment	Ellis 1989; Völling 2008, 203
Tepe Sialk	3200–3000	mineralised fragments on copper mirror							Girshman 1938; 1939; Völling 2008, 203–204
Iraq									
Tell Abu Salabikh	EB III?	impression	tabby, balanced			12 × 10			Biggs 1974, 23–26; Breniquet 2008, 58
Hafagi	2800–2600	few remains of thread, some strings/cords					plant fibre		Delougaz 1940, 54–58; Völling 2008, 208–209
Tello	3rd mill.	one fragment of basketry	tabby				possibly reed		De Genouillac 1934; Völling 2008, 208–209
Karrana 3	late Uruk (2700)	small mineralised fragment from a child's burial	knotless netting	s (S2z?)	0.2		plant		Hägg 1993; Völling 2008, 207; Breniquet 2008, 57
Ur	3rd mill.	fragments of 6 different textiles from the Royal Tombs	tabbby; twill; band with pearls				flax, wool?	diagonal weaving red	Wolley 1934, 238–240; Barber 1991, 164; Völling 2008, 208; Breniquet 2008, 58
	2000	strings, ropes, mats etc					sheep wool, goat hair, reeds etc.		Waetzoldt 2007
Nippur	2100–2000	textile remains and imprints on figurines	tabby, open weave	possibly S-plied				similar find in Susa	Haines 1956, 266; Hansen 1970, 14; Garcia-Ventura 2009
Marlik Tepe	2nd part of 2nd mill.	fragments with knotted strings	tabby, faced or possibly twill					fringes as finishing border preserved	Negahban 1996, 987–988; Völling 2008, 204
Nuzi	16th–15th cent.	charred fragment attached to spindle							Starr 1939, 413; Völling 2008, 209
United Emirates									
Hili	2200–2000	thread from inside cornelian beads		s	0.1		5 strips of tree bark fibres plied together	collective burial; tomb N	Reade & Potts 1993; Médard et al. 2004

Site	Date	Description	Weave	Spin	Warp/weft	Thread count	Material	Remarks	References
Umm an-Nar	middle 3rd mill.	fragments of yarn inside beads		?			flax	beads	Frifelt 1991; Médard et al. 2004
Israel and Palestinian authority									
Arad	EBA	impressions of textiles on pottery; threads wound on metal (copper) tools, threads	tabby	s			flax threads	s-spun threads on metal tools; no information on the threads of the weave	Amiran 1978; Schick 1986a
Bareqet	EBA	mineralised textile on copper-alloy dagger	tabby	s ; S2s	warp threads thinner than weft threads	15 × 8	flax		Shamir 2005
Hurvat Gilan	EBA	threads					flax		Shamir 2005
Ramon I	EBA c. 3000	3 textiles	tabby; some weaving faults	s; S2S. Medium spun	warp threads thinner than weft threads	A: 17-12 × 14-12, B: 12 × 10, C: 12-12	flax	pergaps from garments	Shamir and Rosen forthcoming
Jericho	early BA	cloth, garment?	tabby	S2z; Z2s			flax	5 different textiles	Crowfoot 1982, 546–548; Breniquet 2008, 59
	MBA	poorly preserved fabrics	tabby				wool		Crowfoot 1960, 519–526; Barber 1991, 165; Shamir 2014; Shamir forthcoming
	2200–1550	fragments of weavings and strings from several burials	tabby				bast, raffia, rush, wool	selvedge in half-basket; some sewing and possibly embroidery	Crowfoot 1960, 519–524; 1965, 662–663; 1982, 546–548 ;Barber 1991, 165; Shamir 2005, 20; Breniquet 2008, 57; Völling 2008, 228
Tel Masos	late 2nd mill.	impressions in pots	tabby, faced				wool(?)	traces of double-knotted fringe preserved	Sheffer 1976, 84–86; Barber 1991, 166; Rothenhäusler forthcoming a
Timna	13th cent.	heavy cloth (tent?); impressions					wool	Undyed, the colours stemms from the groupd, Shamir, personal information July 2014	Sheffer 1986, 8; Shamir & Baginski 1993, 9–10; Sheffer & Tidhar 1988.
	14th–12th cent.	76 textiles; 30 impressions; 89 threads and cords; 2- fragments of basketry	tabby, faced; half-basket; basket						Sheffer & Tidhar 1988, 224–231; Shamir and Baginski 1993, 9–10
		63 textiles	tabby, weft-faced/1 balanced	Z3s, s/s		2–12 × 11-4	wool	5 fragments dyed or decorated; remains of sewing threads	
		9 textiles	tabby, weft-faced	Z2s/z		3–5 × 8–20	goat hair		
		4 textiles	tabby, balanced: 1 warp–faced	Z2s		9–12 × 9–18	flax		

Site	Date	Description	Weave	Spin	Thickness	Thread count	unidentified fibres of different colours	Notes	References
Tell Qasileh	12 cent, early IA	traces of fabric on a plaster wall surface	tabby, balanced					the blue colour identified as minerals used in wall painting; the red colour unidentified	Sheffer 1976, 85; Barber 1991, 166; Shamir 1992; 1992a
Beth Shean	12 cent, early IA	fragment wrapped around silver scrap	tabby	s medium/s loose	varying thickness	16–20 × 10–12	flax	textile not of Egyptian origin, rather locally produced	Shamir 1992, 4
Der el-Balah	12th cent, early IA	fragments, fibre remains	tabby				flax	Egyptian style (according to Barber)	Dothan 1979, 46; Barber 1991, 166; Völling 2008, 230
Jordan									
Bāb edh-Dhrā	EBA-MBA I–III	9 fragments and 2 imprints of possible clothes and shrouds and basketry and cordage from 1965–1967 excavation	tabby, balanced;	z/S2z; S2z/ S2z	subtype 1: z: 0.15; 0.3; subtype 8: 0.37	13 × 14; 9 × 9;	flax	found in burials	Luffman-Yedlowski & Adovasio 1989, 521–543
		1 fragment	half basket	Z2s/Z2s	0.26	11 × 30			
		fragments from shaft tombs A-110NE and A-114N	tabby, balanced/ warp- and weft-faced; 2/1 twill	mostly S2z, some s		11–12 × 16–18; 9 × 22; 16 × 39			Fröhlich & Ortner 1982; Ballard & Skals 1996
	3100–2000	9 fragments and 2 impressions;17 fragments of yarn/string	tabby, balanced/ warp-faced				flax; som possible palm fibres		Adovasio & Andrews 1981, 181–185; Adovasio & Yedlowski 1989, 523–528; Völling 2008, 227–228
	EBA	cloth on tool	tabby, balanced	Z2s			flax		Adovasio & Andrews 1982; Breniquet 2008, 58
Tell Abu al-Kharaz	3100–2900	impression	tabby	z/z		25 × 13			Möller-Wiering 2008
Tell es-Sa'idyeh	13th cent.	fragment:impression; mineralised weave	tabby	s	0.3–0.4	24 × 14			Pritchard 1980, 15–16; 1985; Völling 2008, 229
Lebanon									
Kamid el-Loz	12th–11th cent.	Impression and charred fragment	tabby			24 × 14	probably flax		Hachmann & Kuschke 1966, 48–49; Völling 2008, 235
Syria									
Tell Mardikh, Ebla	EBA	mineralised fibres on human bones from two levels of an excavation					fibres with similarity to papyrus; grass or bast fibres	basketry or matting	Andersson et al. 2010
Tell Beydar	EBA	impressions	tabby; twill?						Teissier 1997; Breniquet 2008, 58
Terqa	17th–16th cent.	fragments of cloth from burial	all tabby						Barber 1991, 166; Völling 2008, 217

Site	Date	Description	Weave/binding	Twist	Thickness	Thread count	Fibre	Notes	Reference
Tomb of Qatna/Tell Mishrife	1350	mineralised fragments. 12 different fabric types	mostly tabby; multi-coloured tapestry weave		0.07–1	16 × 70–80	wool?	purple dye detected; details of threads and weavings concern tapestry weave	James et al. 2009; Reifarth 2010
Tall Bderi	2850–2100	plaster imprints of 64 different textiles	balanced tabbies	s/s, s/z	0.75/1.3; 0.8/1.6	8 × 6; 5 × 4			Rothenhäusler forthcoming b
			faced tabbies	s/s, s/z	0.5–1.1	6 × 19			Rothenhäusler forthcoming b
			twined weave	s/s, s/z, z/z	0.7/0.5	5 × 12			Rothenhäusler forthcoming b
Tall Mozan	2700/2600–2250	Imprints of basketry and textiles on sealings, ceramic and bitumen	5 different bindings and 9 different types of textile	most s-spun			flax; wool identified in 2 cases: Abdruck 21 and Abdruck 86	various borders and selvedges preserved	Rothenhäusler forthcoming a
		10 medium-fine weavings	tabby	s/s	0.9/1.25	5–11 × 2–18	flax		Rothenhäusler forthcoming a
		4 medium-fine weavings	tabby	s/s; s/z	0.7/0.85	4–12 × 4–10	flax		Rothenhäusler forthcoming a
		16 coarse-medium-fine weavings	tabby	s/s; s/z; s/?	0.8/1.5	4–17 × 3–5	flax		Rothenhäusler forthcoming a
		17 weavings	tabby, faced	s/s; s/?; ?/?	0.3/0.8	26–96 × 3–17	flax		Rothenhäusler forthcoming a
		20 weavings	tabby, faced	ss; s/?; ?/?	0.8–1.3	7–18 × 4–56	flax		Rothenhäusler forthcoming a
		3 weavings	half-basket weave	s/s	0.6/1.6	16–26 × 4–6	flax		Rothenhäusler forthcoming a; Sheffer & Tidhar 1988, 224–231
		6 weavings	basket weave	no twist; s/s;	0.6/1.6	10–72 × 4–56	flax		Rothenhäusler forthcoming a
	2500/24–2100	1 textile Abdruck 21	tabby	s/s	0.2/0.7	42 × 7	wool		Rothenhäusler forthcoming a
	2700/2600–2500/2400	1 textile Abdruck 86	tabby		0.3	7 × 7	wool		Rothenhäusler forthcoming a
Egypt									
Umm el-Qaab Royal Tomb complexes	3100–2890	85 textiles, from different contexts, resin soaked, burnt, extremely fine to medium fine qualities	tabby	s spliced yarn, a few S2s	0.1–0.3		flax		Jones 2002a, 329–340
		1 extremely fine dense tabby, C46b			0.12	64 × 35	flax		Jones 2002a, 339
		1 extremely fine dense tabby, C17					flax		Jones 2002a, 339

		1 coarser tabby S8		plied, spun	0.25 × 0.38 and 0.34–0.5	30 × 10, 16 × 12	flax		Jones 2002a, 339
		1 coarser tabby C16			0.3	14 × 9	flax		Jones 2002a, 339
	2970–2930	1 coarser tabby C1 T-NO, K1000		S2s	0.5		flax		Jones 2002a, 340
Tomb of Djer	3073–3036	tabby				64 × 48	flax		Petrie 1910, 147
		tabby UC 35716B			0.14–0.16	97 × 28	flax		Jones 2002a, 339 n. 64
Tarkhan	2965–2705	17 textiles and a dress with pleats and fringes from mastaba 2050. Mastaba 1060 contained a textile with an open weave with sparsely laid weft yarns, giving the impression of a lace-like fabric	tabby, faced (the textile with lacy texture)	double warp or weft threads, sometimes twisted together		28 × 24	flax	tunic is woven from a slubbed, darker yarn that forms an irregular grey stripe in the warp. Only bodice and sleeves are pleated.	Petrie 1914; Landi & Hall 1979, 141, 143; Hall 1981b; Barber 1991, 145; Jones 2014
Meydum	2705–2180	2 mummy cloths		double warp or weft threads, sometimes twisted together			flax		Midgley 1911, 37; Barber 1991, 148
Saqqara	2705–2180	textiles from the pyramid of king Unas				40 × 20–25; 45–50 × 10	flax	stripes along selvedges	Riefstahl 1944, 49; Barber 1991, 149
	2125–1985 (11th dynasty)	pleated 'half dress'					flax		Munro 1984; Jones 2014
Qau	2705–2180	bead net/dress					flax	beads strung with flax thread	Hall 1981b; Barber 1991, 154
Deshasheh	2494–2345 (5th dynasty)	9 long-sleeved garments					flax	One dress has alternating groups pf thinner and thicker yarn to create pleats	Petrie 1898; 1982; Jones 2014. 2 of the dresses are examined by Hall 1981b
Gebelein	2494–2345 (5th dynasty)	sleeved garment used as shroud in female frave	lengh 140 cm						Brunton 1940; Hall & Pedrini 1984, 138
	2345–2181 (6th dynasty)	1 pleated linen sleeved dress	122 × 59 cm and 135 × 42 cm				flax	3 pieces stitched together. Leather sandals	Hall & Pedrini 1984
Naga ed-Dêr	2345–2181 (6th dynasty)	tomb 94, female burial with 14 dresses						4 pleated dresses in Boston	Reisner 1932; Riefstahl 1944, 8 fig 7; Riefstahl 1970; Landi & Hall 1979; Hall & Pedrini 1984; Illustrated in Stevenson Smith 1935, 139 fig. 1. Jones 2014

Site	Date	Description	Technique	Thread/spin	Material	Notes	References
El-Hawawish	2345–2181 (6th dynasty)	2 dresses					McFarlane 1991; Jones 2014
Asyût	12th dynasty?	several identical garments				1 garment preserved in louvre	Chassinat & Palanque 1911
Meir		2 dresses					Kamal 1914; Jones 2014
Kahum	1880–1650	unspun and spun flax			flax	unspun and spun wool on the site was radiocarbonated to Roman period	Allgrove McDowell 1986; Jana Jones, personal communication July 2014
Deir el-Bahari	1987–1640	textile with border of blue stripes; 2 so-called 'towels' from mass grave of 60 soldiers of King Mentuhotep II	tabby, pattern of weft-looping (2 towels)				Naville *et al.* 1907, 44; Winlock 1945, 32; Barber 1991, 149; Jones 2014
		textile from burial	tabby, pattern of weft-looping		flax		Winlock 1942, 206; 1945, 32; Riefstahl 1944, 16,17; Barber 1991, 149
		textiles with patches of gauze weave from tomb of Wah			flax	textiles with fringes made of inlaid threads	Barber 1991, 151
		among textiles from burial of Senmut a warp-faced band sewn to horse cloth, from a horse mummy	tabby, warp-faced, patterned		flax	pattern created by different coloured warp threads	Lansing & Hayes, 1937, 10; Riefstahl 1944, 20; Barber 1991, 156
The tomb of Thutmoses IV	1479–1426	earliest evidence of tapestry	tabby		flax, wool		Carter & Newberry 1904; Barber 1991, 157
Deir el-Medina; Tomb of Kha	1550–1070	piles of household textiles among which, two large furniture coverings in tapestry weave and with pattern of weft-looping and a tunic with polychrome warp-faced edgings are described	tabby, pattern of weft-looping, resembling pile				Schiaparelli 1927, 93, 114–116, 129–130; Riefstahl 1944, 21–22; Barber 1991, 159; Jana Jones, personal communication July 2014
Valley of the Kings: Tomb of Tutankhamun	1332–1322	many textiles preserved; warp-faced bands; tapestry; tunic with embroidered panels	various techniques		flax	embroidered tunic possibly of Syrian origin	Pfister 1937; Crowfoot & de Garis Davies 1941, 117–125; Barber 1991, 156; Vogelsang-Eastwood 1999
Tell el-Armana	1348–1332	c. 5000 textiles	tabby; half-basket; basket	s; S2s;S2z; z; Z2s (also Z3 and 4s; S6z; S3s and more)	most flax, some sheep wool and goat hair	some textiles bear traces of dye; sewing threads Z2s or Z3s	Kemp & Vogelsang-Eastwood 2001; Barber 1991, 88–89; Vogelsang-Eastwood 1985, 8; 1987 b, 4; Shamir and Baginski 1993

Site	Date	Description	Weave	Twist	Thickness	Thread count	Fibre	Notes	References
Ramses III	1187–1156	tapering girdle	double-faced warp-faced weave				flax	tablet weaving? length: 5.2 m; width tapers from 12.7 to 4.8 cm	Staudigel 1975; Barber 1991, 156
Turkey									
Aphrodisias	early BA	impression of textile on floor	tabby						Kadish 1969, 56; Barber 1991, 167
Arslantepe	c. 3000	funerary sheet (309/1996)	tabby, faced	s/s, low	0.08/0.11	38 × 18	probably plant	textiles from royal tomb	Frangipane 2001; Frangipane et al. 2009, 18; Breniquet 2008, 58
		mineralised fragment in metal bowl	tabby, balanced	s/s	0.3	16–17 × 16–17	unidentifiable	fragment has greyish-brown colour	Frangipane et al. 2009, 19
		mineralised textiles on metal bowl (086/2002)	tabby	s/s	0.1		wool, probably goat		Frangipane et al. 2009, 19
		remains of woven mat					grass		Frangipane et al. 2009, 19
		impression of weavings on more than 160 cretulae	tabby	s		11–12 × 8–9			Laurito 2007, 380–394
		ribbons	tightly woven fabric					width of ribbons 8–18 mm	
		woven textile coverings	tabby	s; S2z		11–12 × 8–9			
Tekeköy	EBA	remains of textile on surface of bronze blade	tabby						Kökten et al. 1945, 373–374; Barber 1991, 167
Troia	EBA	impression; mineralised spun yarn and textile fragment from objects no Sch 5871 and 5873	tabby						Born 1997; Völling 2008, 239
		spindle with thread attached						remains of textile and small beads	Schliemann 1880, 361; Dörpfeld 1902, 340; Barber 1991, 54, 172
		gold beads scattered in room with loom							Blegen et al. 1950, 350; Barber 1991, 171; Völling 2008, 241
Acemhüyük	19th–18th cent.	3 fragments of same material						thick, compact weaving. Embroidered with blue pearls (faïence) and gold thread	Özgüç 1966, 47; Istanbul Catalogue 1983; Barber 1991, 171; Völling 2008, 241
Kaman-Kalehöyük	19th–18th century	charred fragments of loose threads; one patterned weaving	tapestry				probably plant		Kipling 2004; Fairbairn 2004; Völling 2008, 240
Kültepe-Kanish	19th–18th cent.	impression of 3 weavings	tabby, faced					Kt.87/k328; Dt.87/k329; unknown	Özgüç & Tunca 2001, pl. 92, pl. 93, description 3; Völling 2008, 240
Greece									
Agia Kyriaki	3000–1000	textile remains among burial goods	tabby, balanced	ZZs	0.4	14 × 14	flax	technique characteristic for Aegean BA	Spantidaki & Moulherat 2012

Site	Period	Description	Technique	Twist	Thread diameter	Thread count	Fibre	Notes	References
Amorgos	EBA	fragment on dagger blade from tomb	tabby, weft-faced with additional floating wefts						Zisis 1955, 587; Carington Smith 1977, 116; Barber 1991, 174
Khania	2700–1450	20 carbonised fragments of a narrow ribbon; width 6mm			0.8/0.8–1.2	4–5 × 10	warp: flax; weft: goat hair and nettle (supplementary weft)		Barber 1991; Möller-Wiering 2006; Moulherat & Spantidaki 2009, Spantidaki & Moulherat 2012
Kommos	MBA to LBA	impression of coiled basket on surface of clay vases							Betancourt et al. 1990; Möller-Wiering 2006
Zafer Papoura, near Knossos	LBA	traces of fibres on sword	tabby?				flax		Evans 1935, 866; Åström 1964, 111; Möller-Wiering 2006; Barber 1991, 174
Knossos		impression on clay	tabby					Unexplored Mansion	Popham 1984, pl. 222.5; Barber 1991, 174
Mochlos	MBA	textiles preserved on surface of bronze objects and a textile described as a possible bag	tabby	s/s	0.2–0.3	9 × 18	flax (not verified)		Möller-Wiering 2006
Akrotiri, Santorini	MBA	wrapping of a handle of a jar	braiding				plant		Whitley 2005, 96, Moulherat and Spantidaki 2007
		fragment of a fishing net	knotting	S2z					Whitley 2005, 96
		25 carbonised fragments, measuring 0.5–3 cm, belonging to the same textile (pillar pit 52 excavated 1999)	tabby, balanced	S2z	0.25 – 0.4	20–22 × 20–22	flax	decorative elements preserved (hems, embroidery, fringes, knots)	Moulhérat et al. 2004, 15–19; Moulherat and Spantidaki 2007, 49–52; Spantidaki and Moulherat 2012
		fragment 8 × 13 cm: (pit 68a excavated 2000)	tabby, weft-faced	warp: S2z; weft: z	0.7 / 1.2	4–5 × 10 –12	warp: flax; weft: unidentified plant	two layers; remains of an edge with thicker threads is possibly a fragment of different textile	Spantidaki & Moulherat 2012
		remains of an edge attached to fragment measuring 8 × 13 cm			1 / 1	low thread count		probably a fragment of a simple utilitarian textile as indicated by the thread diameter and low thread count	Spantidaki & Moulherat 2012
		assemblage of textiles associated with barley	tabby	warp: S2z; weft: no twist	0.3–0.4 /0.6–1.2	5–6 × 7	warp: plan; weft: unspun strips	in one area a weaving is visible	Spantidaki & Moulherat 2012
		assemblage of textiles associated with grains of barley	net					two areas show traces of net	Spantidaki and Moulherat 2012
		50 fragments (pillar 65N)					wool		Moulherat and Spantidaki 2008, 37–42; Spantidaki and Moulherat 2012
		impressions of coarse cloth on straw mats; baskets; strings; one ribbon.						in 2003 a piece of coarse cloth and pieces of nets were found	Tzachili, 2007

Location	Date	Description	Weave	Twist	Diameter	Thread count	Fibre	Notes	References
Thebes	LBA	charred fragments of 2 textiles	tabby					one is coarser than the other	Personal communication from Christina Margariti
Mycenae	16th cent.	textile remains on surface of bronze daggers and spearhead	tabby, balanced	S2z	0.3	20 × 22	flax	fragments of same textile	Mylonas 1973 ; Barber 1991, 174; Spantidaki and Moulherat 2012
	LBA	small piece of carbonised textile	tabby					described as canvas	Wace 1921–1923, 55; Barber 1991, 174
Agora Athens	14th cent.	weave pattern preserved in soil covering mouth of pot. Trace of pattern interpreted as holes for draw string						Mycenean chamber tomb, excavated 2001	Unruh 2007
	14th cent.	mineralised fibre structure preserved in soil						pattern of holes possibly from draw string	Unruh 2007
Pylona, Rhodes	14th cent.	calcified textiles in pitcher 16496	tabby, balanced	s/s possibly plied S	0.3–0.6/0.4–0.9	14 × 16–18	probably flax		de Wild 2001; Spantidaki and Moulherat 2012
		calcified textiles in jar 16494	tabby, balanced	s/s possibly plied S	0.3–0.5/0.3–0.7	16–18 × 16–18	probably flax		de Wild 2001; Spantidaki and Moulherat 2012
Kazarma	LBA	undescribed fragments							Protonotariou-Deilaki 1969, 4–5; Barber 1991, 174
Dendra	LBA	Differently coloured faïance beeds in pattern						remains of decorated textile	Persson 1931, 106 no. 51; Barber 1991, 172
		large textile from inside bowl of a lamp in chamber tomb 2	tabby						Persson 1931, 77, 94; Barber 1991, 174
Lefkandi	1200–1100	mineralised fragment on iron pin, tomb S.38.12	tabby, weft-faced	z/z		28 × 9; 22 × 10; 18 × 6	possibly wool	Predominance of single Z-twisted threads	Spantidaki & Moulherat 2012
		mineralised fragment on iron pin, tomb S.38.11	tabby, weft-faced	z/z (low)		10 × 22			Spantidaki & Moulherat 2012
		mineralised fragment on iron pin, tomb S.38.11	tabby, balanced	z/z (low)		22 × 22	possibly wool		Spantidaki & Moulherat 2012
		mineralised fragment on iron fragment, tomb S.38.13	tabby, weft-faced	z/z (low)		10 × 19	possibly wool		Spantidaki & Moulherat 2012
Azoria, Crete	LBA or IA	thread found in decorative top of helmet		z	3		probably bast	possibly sewing thread	Hoffman 1972, table 3; Möller-Wiering 2006
Cyprus									
Idalion	LBA	unspecified fragments							Barber 1991, 174
The southwest of Cyprus (?)	EBA to MBA	thread attached to spindle whorl							Webb 2002
Paleoskoutella	MBA	unspecified fragments	tabby						Åström 1964, 112; Barber 1991, 174
Russia and vicinity									
Tri Brata, Republic of Kalmykia	3rd mill.	impression of patterned rug							Barber 1991, 169–170

Republic of Kalmykia	late 3rd mill.	possibly a belt	tabby	z/z	14 × 7	wool		Orfinskaya et al. 1999
Shakhaevskaya, Manych River	2500–2000	headdress	tabby	z	10	wool		Fedorova-Davidova & Forbenko 1974, 93–137; Orfinskaya et al. 1999, 58–184; Shishlina et al. 2005
Tsarskaja, Black Sea area	mid/late 3rd mill.	two garments from burial					undergarment of linen-like fabric, brightly decorated with purple colour and covered with red threads like tassels, an overgarment of fluffy yellow cloth ornamented with narrow black stripes forming a … plaid	Veselovskij 1898, 37; Barber 1991, 168–169

Acknowledgements

We are grateful to the Danish National Research Foundation for its generous funding of the Centre for Textile Research 2005–2015 and for funding this ten-year research programme, *Tools and Textiles, Texts and Contexts*.

Our special gratitude to Joanne Cutler for generously sharing her knowledge with us and helping us in so many ways, sharing her knowledge and ensuring that the language in the publication is of a high standard throughout. While working on her own PhD project, she has since 2009 continually contributed to this research programme and been a source of inspiration to us.

During these ten years, we were also fortunate to have eminent Aegean Bronze Age scholars on our team at CTR in Copenhagen for shorter or longer periods of time: Marta Guzowska, Brendan Burke, Margarita Gleba, Lorenz Rahmstorf, Lena Klintberg, Françoise Rougemont, Richard Firth and Joanne Cutler.

We thank our textile technicians Linda Olofsson (née Mårtensson) and Anne Batzer for their fine work and assessments; Birgitta Piltz Williams for the database design; and Annika Jeppsson and Tina Borstam[†] for the drawings.

All along the way we have received inspiration and support from numerous colleagues, and here we particularly thank: Costas Paschalidis, Marianne Rasmussen, Peter Fischer, Rainer Feldbacher, Carole Gillis, Youlie Spantidaki[†], Elizabeth Barber, Oliver Dickinson, Erik Hallager, Orit Shamir, Jana Jones, Ulrike Rothenhäusler, Ann-Louise Schallin, Maria Vlasaki, Caroline Sauvage, Cécile Michel, Catherine Breniquet, Phil Betancourt, Ulla Lund Hansen, André Verhecken, Anna Fahlén and Henriette Lyngstrøm.

At Oxbow Books, we kindly thank Samantha McLeod and Clare Litt and their publication team for their unwavering support and commitment.

At CTR we warmly thank our student helpers past and present: Vibe Maria Martens, Line Lerke, Sidsel Frisch, Ziff Jonker, Laura Mazzaglia and Gabriella Longhitano and our editorial assistant Cherine Munkholt for assisting with publication tasks.

Finally, this book is a valuable and fruitful collaboration with our cherished colleagues and co-authors, around the world. We thank our collaborators for brilliant contributions, for sharing their knowledge about their sites, contexts and textile tools, and for their patience. Preliminary results of this volume were discussed and published with our collaborators Romina Laurito, Marcella Frangipani, Antionette Rast-Eicher, Agnete Wisti Lassen, Luca Peyronel, Elena Felucca, Ulla Mannering, Karin Margarita Frei, Joanne Cutler and Margarita Gleba. In the present volume you will find the results of our collaborations with Lorenz Rahmstorf, Linda Olofsson, Susan Möller-Wiering, Irene Skals, Agnete Wisti Lassen, Richard Firth, Joanne Cutler, Maria Bruun-Lundgren, Birgitta P. Hallager, Yannis Tzedakis, Pietro Militello, Jean-Claude Poursat, Françoise Rougemont, Iris Tzachili, Stella Spantidaki, Katie Demakopoulou, Iphiyenia Tournavitou, Gerasimoula Nikolovieni, Małgorzata Siennicka, Maria Emanuela Alberti, Vassilis Aravantinos, Ioannis Fappas, Athina Papadaki, Françoise Rougemont, Evi Papadopoulou, Ernestine S. Elster, Marta Guzowska, Ralf Becks, Joanna Smith, Assaf Yasur-Landau, and Nurith Goshen, all of whom we thank most profoundly.

Copenhagen, August 2015

Eva Andersson Strand
and Marie-Louise Nosch